ISBN 978-1-5285-0054-8
PIBN 10927647

Thirty-Sixth Annual Report

of the

Chief Inspector of Mi

Compliments of

Geo. Harrison

Chief Inspector of Mines

Year Ending December 31, 1910

COLUMBUS, O.:
THE F. J. HEER PRINTING CO.
1911.

TABLE OF CONTENTS.

PERSONNEL OF STATE MINING DEPARTMENT.

CHIEF INSPECTOR OF MINES.

GEO. HARRISON...Wellston, O.

FIRST DISTRICT.

John Burke...Wellston, O.

SECOND DISTRICT.

Edward Kennedy...Carbon Hill, O.

THIRD DISTRICT.

John L. McDonald...Glouster, O.

FOURTH DISTRICT.

Isaac Hill...Zanesville, O.

FIFTH DISTRICT.

W. H. Turner (Resigned June 30, 1910).........................Cambridge, O.
(Succeeded by Abel Ellwood, Cambridge, O., July 1, 1910.)

SIXTH DISTRICT.

Alex. Smith...New Philadelphia, O.

SEVENTH DISTRICT.

W. H. Miller...Massillon, O.

EIGHTH DISTRICT.

Lot Jenkins...Bellaire, O.

NINTH DISTRICT.

Thomas Morrison...Sherodsville, O.

TENTH DISTRICT.

L. D. DeVore...Bellaire, O.

ELEVENTH DISTRICT.

James Hennessy...Barton, O.

TWELFTH DISTRICT.

Robert S. Wheatley...Salineville, O.

Chief Clerk.................................Mary Kincaid, Columbus, O.
Stenographer.................................Sue Senff, Columbus, O.
Statistical Clerk.................................Hazel Sims, Columbus, O.
Recording Clerk.................................Zella P. Harrison, Columbus, O.

LETTER OF TRANSMITTAL.

HON. JUDSON HARMON, *Governor of Ohio.*

SIR:— As provided for in Section 908 of the General Code, relating to mines and mining, I have the honor of submitting to you the Thirty-sixth Annual Report of this department.

Very truly yours,

GEORGE HARRISON,
Chief Inspector of Mines.

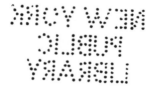

May 1, 1911.

REPORT OF THE CHIEF INSPECTOR OF MINES.

HON. JUDSON HARMON, *Governor of Ohio.*

SIR:— In compliance with Section 908 of the General Code, I herewith submit to you the Thirty-sixth Annual Report of this Department.

It is indeed a great pleasure to us to report that the year 1910 was the most prosperous year ever recorded in the mining industry of the State, at least in point of coal production, the total production being 34,424,951 tons, and the total number of persons employed in producing that amount of coal was 48,830, as compared with a total production of coal in 1909 of 27,755,032 tons and the total number of employes 47,019. The increase of coal production in 1910 over that of 1909 was 6,669,919 tons, or over 24%, while the increase of employes in 1910 over 1909 was only 1,811, or less than 4%, showing that the aggregate average earnings were substantially increased in 1910 over that of 1909. The increased rate in wages of 5.55 per cent., which took effect April 1st., together with the increased production of coal per man, made the year one of the most prosperous in point of actual earnings the miners in Ohio ever enjoyed.

When we look back and consider the steady growth and increase of the coal production in the United States, from year to year, especially for the past forty years, its growth is indeed phenomenal. In the year 1870 the coal production of the country was given in round numbers at 20,000,000 tons; in 1890 at 104,000,000 tons, and in the year 1910 it is estimated to be 400,000,000 tons, and it may possibly reach the unprecedented figures of 500,000,000 tons, or half billion mark.

In Ohio in the year 1872, the tonnage was recorded as 5,315,294 tons; in the year 1890, 11,788,859 tons; in the year 1900, 19,426,649 tons, and in the year 1910 the tonnage reached the high mark of 34,424,951 tons, a gain of 6,669,919 tons as compared with the year 1909, and so we see in the large growth of this wonderful industry that Ohio has played no small part, as only ten years out of a total of thirty-eight show a decrease in production, compared with the preceding year, caused, in some instances, by strikes and financial depressions which have periodically visited the country.

The abnormal increase in tonnage in Ohio during 1910 was due to three causes: 1st., the general prosperity of the coal trade; 2nd., to the increased demand for Lake coal and, 3rd., to the strike of miners for *seven* months in Illinois, which gave Ohio the opportunity of additional markets west and northwest which producers could not have reached if the mines in Illinois had been in operation.

We are reliably informed that the prices of coal on board cars at the mines, in few instances, advanced in proportion to the increase paid to the miners. On the other hand the cost of production was increased during the last half of the year, incident to the operation of the new mining laws. Yet the mine operators in most instances seemed content to make contracts at figures which were based on conditions when the cost of production was not so high as it was during the last nine months of 1910. Taking all in all, however, the year 1910 will be recorded as a very satisfactory one to those connected with the mining industry of Ohio.

There are a number of districts in the State known as thin vein districts, where the natural disadvantages are such that coal cannot be produced only at an extra cost compared with cost where more natural favorable conditions prevail; unfortunately where this is so the natural disadvantage causing extra cost in producing the coal is not overbalanced by realizing higher prices for a superior quality of coal, as was the case in years gone by when the celebrated Jackson and Massillon high grade domestic fuel coals were produced in such large quantities in Jackson and Stark counties, both of which are nearing exhaustion.

During the year the mines in the Crooksville, Perry County, district were closed down for seven months and in the Tuscarawas district a strike was declared on the 11th day of June, because of a disagreement between operators and miners regarding mining prices, the operators claiming inability to compete with the prices at which coal was produced in other districts, and preferring to quietly close down their mines in preference to operating at a loss by paying higher relative prices than the other districts referred to, while the miners contended that on account of the thin coal and other natural disadvantages which required more labor to produce they could not suffer any curtailment in their earnings. This was still unsettled at the close of the year.

UNIFORM BUSINESS POLICY.

It is evident that the time has come, owing to the many intricate phases which enter into an industry which, at best, is more or less fluctuating and uncertain, and also on account of keen competition, that miners and operators will begin to recognize the fact that there will have to be established some sound uniform business policy, and that the actual cost of production will have to enter more largely into these business transactions, placing all thin coal districts, where conditions are similar, on the same plane of equality and making the basis of operation the two broad and vital principles of ability to earn living wages and fair returns for investment of capital.

INSPECTIONS.

Two thousand, eight hundred inspections and investigations of fatal accidents were made during the year, an increase of 329.

Two additional Inspectors were appointed and served a period of six months, making twelve Inspectors in all on the present force.

LEGISLATION.

The new Mining Code went into operation June 11, 1910, and its effect on the industry at large, and the results anticipated by its inauguration, is commented on elsewhere in this report.

FATALITIES.

The greatest calamity which ever befell the Department occurred at the Amsterdam Mine, April 21st., in which fifteen lives were lost by an explosion of gas, which occurred about 9:30 P. M. when there were about twenty-three men in the mine and was the result of a mule driver propping open a door and misdirecting the air current, allowing the gas to accumulate and cause a local explosion in a remote part of the mine where two miners were working; the two men referred to and the mule driver, who was in the direct course of the current of the force from the explosion, were the only men that were killed from the actual explosion and resultant force, the other twelve victims being overcome by the deadly after-damp in trying to make their way out of the mine. Many newspaper writers, and others, seemed to think it was fortunate that the explosion occurred at night instead of during the day when three hundred men might have been victims, overlooking the fact that during the day turn a constant attendant would have been at the door and no accumulation of gas to cause an explosion. A full account of this accident will be found on pages 20-27 in this report, one report being submitted to this Department by Thomas Morrison, District Inspector, in whose district this accident occurred, and the other one made to you by this office. The legislature appropriated the sum of $10,000.00 for the relief of those left dependent on account of this accident. See pages 28-29.

One hundred and sixty-one (161) fatal accidents were reported during the year, eight more than were reported during the preceding year. This number includes the fifteen persons who lost their lives at the Amsterdam Mine by an explosion of gas. This is the greatest number ever recorded in the history of the Department, the number in 1907 reaching 153. The number of persons killed by high speed haulage motors, mining machinery and mine cars, is increasing annually.

The desire to increase the tonnage of mines to their greatest capacity, and the willful recklessness and disregard for law and orders for their own safety by employes is clearly accountable for much of the increase in the number of fatalities during the year.

ADVANCEMENT OF KNOWLEDGE.

Never was there a time when there was such an awakening of the public conscience in matters pertaining to the prevention of mine calamities, with which this country, of late years, has been so direly dealt with. The best intellects of the country have been active in advancing theories which would tend to eliminate causes and conditions which have led to these terrible catastrophes, and we feel confident that from out of it all there will come some sound, uniform, basis of mine operations which will bear fruit in the number of lives saved for humanity.

There is one very fruitful cause of accidents in mines which can not be reached and effectively dealt with by any legislation, or by any action of the state or federal jurisdiction, unless they have the willing co-operation and earnest assistance of mine operators and miners generally, viz., the individual accidents resulting from want of due diligence on the part of the management of mines, and from carelessness or recklessness on part of employes. Mining records in this office show that a large majority of all accidents are traceable to these causes. The mine foreman, in many instances, instead of spending his time looking after the working places in the interior of the mine and seeing that those under his jurisdiction are doing their duty, is usually found looking after the getting out of coal, while his most important duties are either neglected or left to some careless or irresponsible subordinate, and the most important matters are overlooked or neglected. On the other hand a great many employes disregard laws calculated to safeguard themselves and others, by their mad recklessness in jumping on trips of cars, neglecting to prop their working places, or take down dangerous roof at the proper time or until it falls down and they sustain fatal injuries. A number of fatalities are caused by miners leaving their working places to visit others and coming in contact with unseen dangers from various causes in traveling hastily from place to place in the mines where their duty does not call them. When reasoned with about such practices they assert their right to individual liberty in such matters and most of those having charge of mines seem more interested in "hustling to get out coal" than they are in establishing proper discipline in their mines and seeing that those under their charge comply with the laws, as the laws require them to do. The secret of the low per cent. of fatalities in Great Britain, and other foreign countries, in mines is the rigid discipline maintained by the coal companies, having men continually traveling the mines and promptly prosecuting persons indulging in dangerous practices of violation of mine discipline and law.

Our own Federal Government has awakened to the situation and has inaugurated, what has long been advocated, a Government Bureau of Mines, and much good has resulted and will continue to result from its co-operation and suggestions to state mining departments.

APPOINTMENTS.

Three new District Mine Inspectors were appointed during the year 1910 and one re-appointed. Abel Ellwood, of the Fifth Mining District, succeeded W. H. Turner, as district mine inspector, having been appointed for a term beginning July 1, 1910, and ending June 30, 1913. Thomas Morrison, of the Ninth Mining District, was re-appointed for a term beginning July 1, 1910, and ending June 30, 1913. James Hennessy, of the Eleventh Mining District, was appointed for a term beginning June 11, 1910, and ending June 10, 1913. Robert S. Wheatley, of the Twelfth Mining District, was appointed for a term beginning July 1, 1910, and ending June 30, 1913. These two last appointments were in accordance with the provisions of the new Mining Code, which increased the number of inspectors to twelve in all.

FINES.

There has been collected and turned into the State Treasury, since the enactment of the new mining law, which went into effect June 11, 1910, fines for violations of its provisions, amounting to $600.00.

For your co-operation in matters pertaining to the welfare of the Department, we are deeply indebted. The policy which we have endeavored to pursue in selecting for appointment Inspectors of wide, practical, knowledge, sanctioned by your approval, has, we believe, been justified by the present excellent personnel of Inspectors, and the splendid work which they have accomplished during the year is exemplified by the improved conditions of the mines of the state today. They have ever been eager to judiciously enforce the laws for the protection of life, limb, and mine properties, without fear or favor, irrespective of who the individual might be if guilty of willfully and persistently violating the law. However, taking into consideration the number of mines in the state and the number of persons employed, the number of prosecutions has not been exceedingly large. The new mining laws also went into effect, which were much more rigid in requirements, provisions, penalties, etc., than the old law, and some violations may have been due to ignorance of the law rather than a disposition to willfully and flagrantly violate it.

We also desire to thank the Inspectors for their conscientious devotion to their duties, and for the hearty co-operation of the office force.

The year 1911 seems to have opened up auspiciously for a successful and prosperous one, and with conditions normal ought to be one of interest and profit to all.

Very truly yours,

GEO. HARRISON,

May 1, 1911. *Chief Inspector of Mines.*

SUMMARY AND COMPARISON OF THE COAL TRADE OF OHIO FOR THE YEARS 1909 AND 1910.

	1909	1910
Number of pick miners	7,741	7,214
Number of drillers, shooters and loaders	23,803	25,176
Number of hands operating machines	3,159	3,293
Number of day hands employed in both pick and machine mines	12,316	13,147
Total number of persons employed	47,019	48,830
Gain in number employed as compared with '09	....	1,811
Average number of days worked by pick miners	182	168
Average number of days worked by D. S. & L.	172	209
Average number of days worked by machine runners	171	201
Number tons coal produced by pick	4,608,402	4,341,483
Number tons coal produced by machinery	23,146,630	30,083,468
Total number tons of coal produced	27,755,032	34,424,951
Gain in output as compared with the year '09	....	6,669,919
Per cent. of machine-mined coal	83.4	87.4
Per cent. of pick-mined coal	16.6	12.6
Number of coal-producing counties	29	28
Average number tons lump coal mined by each pick miner per year	395	408
Average number tons lump coal mined by each pick miner per day	2.2	2.4
Average number tons lump coal mined by each driller, shooter and loader per year	658	823
Average number tons lump coal mined by each driller, shooter and loader per day	3.8	3.9
Average number tons lump coal mined by each machine runner per year	4,956	6,291
Average number tons lump coal mined by each machine runner per day	29.0	31.3
Average number tons run-of-mine produced by each pick miner per year	595	602
Average number tons run-of-mine produced by each pick miner per day	3.3	3.6
Average tons run-of-mine produced by driller, shooter and loader per year	972	1,195
Average tons run-of-mine produced by driller, shooter and loader per day	5.7	5.7
Average tons run-of-mine produced by each machine runner per year	7,327	9,136
Average tons run-of-mine produced by each machine runner per day	42.8	45.5
Number of fatal accidents	115	161
Number of serious accidents	467	471
Number of minor accidents	226	201
Total number of accidents	808	833
Number of deaths per thousand employed	2.4	3.3
Number serious accidents per thousand employed	9.9	9.6
Number minor accidents per thousand employed	4.8	4.1
Number tons of coal mined to the life lost	241,348	213,819
Number persons employed for each life lost	409	303
Number kegs of powder used as reported	248,426	273,406
Total number of new mines opened up	38	55
Number large mines suspended	59	47
Number large mines abandoned	34	41
Total number mines in operation	1,034	983
Number mining machines in use	1,395	1,473
Number motors in use	405	451
Total number of inspections made	2,471	2,800

SUMMARY AND COMPARISON OF THE COAL TRADE OF OHIO FOR THE YEARS 1909 AND 1910 — Concluded.

	1909	1910
Number sets scales tested	82	75
Number permanent improvements	232	279
Number maps filed	417	425
Number tons fire clay produced	2,289,088	2,028,852
Number fire clay producing counties	20	19
Number persons employed in clay-producing counties	1,319	1,242
Average number days worked in fire clay mines	266	259
Number counties producing limestone	34	34
Number persons employed in limestone quarries	4,705	4,361
Average number days worked in limestone quarries.	285	287
Number tons gypsum mined	228,804	213,325
Number persons employed in gypsum mines	200	405
Average number days worked in gypsum mines	265	297
Number tons iron ore produced	12,392	9,719

SPECIAL ARTICLES, RULINGS, ETC.

ORDER RELATING TO UNDERGROUND STABLES.

On November 13, 1909, the country was shocked at the appalling loss of life which occurred at the Cherry Mine, Illinois, the cause of which was attributed, in a large degree, to the inflammable material of which many under-ground stables are constructed.

There being no specific law regulating the construction of underground stables in this state, and the Mining Commission being at that time engaged in framing the new mining code, the Department issued the following order requiring all under-ground stables to be made as nearly fire-proof as possible, although the District Mine Inspectors had been active in securing at all times as many interior openings for escape as they reasonably could in the absence of any special statute to enforce them, and much credit is due many of the operators who willingly complied with these requests, realizing their importance in case of any grave calamity which might at any time take place.

STATE MINING DEPARTMENT
COLUMBUS, OHIO.

TO MINE OPERATORS AND MINE MANAGERS.

NOTICE

Wherever there are stables in mines for the housing of stock, such stables must be made to conform to the following Order, which has been approved by the members of the Mining Commission, and recommended to be enacted into law:

RELATING TO UNDERGROUND STABLES

I. The stable or stalls shall be separated from the main inlet and main outlet air courses by not less than twenty feet of solid strata or a solid wall of brick or masonry not less than twelve inches in thickness, except at two doors not more than four feet wide, which shall be made of steel plate not less than one-quarter inch in thickness and hinged to the solid strata or masonry without the use of wood.

II. The ventilation for the stable shall be taken from main inlet air course by a by-pass or separate split and returned to the main outlet air-course so that the air passing the stables will not enter the inward working places of the mine, and arranged so that the by-pass or split can readily be closed at both inlet and outlet sides of the stable by steel doors hinged to the solid strata or masonry without the use of wood.

III. The construction of the stable inside shall be free from pine or light lumber; shall be of brick or masonry as much as practicable, and any timber used shall be of hardwood of a cross section not less than three by six inches.

IV. No hay or straw shall be taken into the mine or stable unless same be compressed into compact bales, and then only from time to time in such quantities as will be required for two days' use; no greater quantity of hay or straw shall be stored in the mine or stable, and when such is taken into the mine it shall be taken inside the stable at once.

V. The lights used in the stable shall be incandescent electric lamps placed so that same will not be injured by the stock or by persons required to enter the stable, or lanterns of railroad type suitable for using lard or signal oil, and only such oil shall be used therein.

VI. All refuse and waste shall be promptly removed from the stable and the mine, and shall not be allowed to accumulate.

VII. Hereafter, stables constructed underground shall be located not nearer than one hundred and fifty feet of any opening to the mine used as a means of ingress or egress.

GEO. HARRISON,
Chief Inspector of Mines.

COLUMBUS, OHIO, February 2, 1910.

The following report of the investigation of the explosion which took place at the Delmore Mine, Columbiana County, O., January 24, 1910, is herewith re-printed as a matter of the 1910 records, but all the facts and circumstances connected with this and other similar explosions which took place in connection with the system of Blasting Coal off the Solid, will be found in the report for the year 1909.

REPORT OF THE DELMORE MINE EXPLOSION MADE BY INSPECTORS SMITH, MORRISON AND MILLER.

NEW PHILADELPHIA, O., FEB. 18, 1910.

HON. GEO. HARRISON, *Chief Inspector of Mines, Columbus, O.*

DEAR SIR: — We herewith submit to you the facts in connection with the explosion which took place on January 24, at the Delmore mine, Leetonia, Columbiana county, O., and which resulted in the death of Mr. Jas. Blaemire, who was employed as shot firer to fire the shots in the mine after the miners had left the mine.

District Inspector W. H. Miller being in the neighborhood, and learning of the explosion, immediately went to the mine, at the same time notifying District Inspector Alex Smith, in whose district the mine is located, and who arrived on the scene the following day. With the assistance of mine foreman and miners, Mr. Miller and Mr. Smith succeeded in recovering the body of the victim about 2 p. m., the day following the explosion. This body was found on the right entry, just beyond the No. 9 room.

On the 26th ult., in company with yourself, we again visited the mine, but as the ventilating system was entirely disarranged, were unable to enter the mine. Instructions were given to the company to reconstruct the stoppings and build the fan house reversible; then notify the Department when they were ready for inspection.

On being notified that the mine was ready for inspection, we again returned, and in company with yourself, Mr. Percy Tetlow, president of the United Mine Workers in that district, and Mr. Daniel McGrath, the mine foreman, made a thorough inspection of the mine on the 17th inst., the result being our firm conviction that the explosion which resulted in the death of Mr. Blaemire occurred from shots fired in the No. 5 room on the third right entry, being the same place where the blown-out shots caused the explosion on December 16. In this room, two shots had been fired; one on the right hand rib, and another near the center of the room. Both of these were drilled and fired in violation of the orders given by the Mining Department, which specified that no hole should be drilled beyond the depth of the mining or cutting, and that if shot firers were employed they should not fire any shot drilled contrary to that order.

. The hole next to the rib was drilled 18 inches, and the center hole 23 inches deeper than the cutting, and in consequence could not possibly do the work intended to be done, the result being a portion of the hole only being blown out.

In the No. 2 entry, all the shots were fired, with no evidence that the explosion had exerted any force in this part of the mine, but two shots were fired without any mining being done.

In the fourth right entry, some of the shots were fired and the coal blown out so that we were unable to tell whether any mining had been done or not.

In the No. 4 room of No. 4 entry, two shots were tamped. There was some mining done on one of these shots, but the other was not mined in any part, and was a very heavy shot.

At the head of the entry, a place turning off to the left, another hole was tamped, but not fired. We do not know how deep this hole was, but the shearing was not over 18 inches deep, with no mining whatever. On this entry, there had been considerable force. The track was torn up for some distance on the outer end of the entry, and there had been some fire, as we found some burned paper and dust burned on the posts. The shots had also been fired in the main entry, but no damage done. In the fourth left entry, the shots were fired. In these the coal was blown out. We could not tell much about whether they had been mined or not, but some were found standing; no mining had been done on these.

It is a conclusive fact that the order of this Department in regard to firing shots was violated, as well as the law in regard to the kind of tamping to be used, as we found holes tamped with dummy cartridges, filled with drill dust, and shots fired without any mining being done whatever.

The shot firers and the miners were aware of the fact that orders had been given that no shots were to be fired unless at least one-half of the coal was undercut, and no person to fire any shot unless he tamped it himself, or had seen the charge tamped. As these orders have been violated, we consider that those who have violated them are the parties responsible for these accidents.

By careful examination of all the places in advance of the air, and in abandoned places where fire-damp would be most likely to be found, we were unable to find a single trace of explosive gas and we are thoroughly convinced that gas played no part in this explosion.

After our investigation of this mine, we are more than satisfied that the reckless system of mining practiced in this and other mines in the same district, and previously condemned by the Mining Department, is not only a continual menace to life, but is also an unwarrantable waste of coal, as great quantities are pulverized and blown back in the rooms and working places, where it remains; in fact, it is almost impossible to load it out.

The Department has time and again advised both miners and operators to stop this dangerous and destructive method of producing coal, and advised them to adopt a safer method; and not wishing to impose any unreasonable burden on any one, we recommend that "permissible explosives" be used, and gave orders that at least one-half of the coal be undercut before being blasted.

The Department is loath to give arbitrary or stringent orders when it can be avoided, but as its duty is to protect life, limb and property, and we find that those who need and should try to protect themselves ignore orders given solely for their protection, we feel that it is time to give such orders that will not only protect them while at work, but will protect them from endangering lives of their fellow workmen unnecessarily.

We again recommend that all coal be undercut before being blasted. If this mine resumes operation, the orders previously given must be thoroughly complied with; that is, that at least one-half of the coal be undercut, and no hole drilled beyond the mining, and if the coal must be mined in this manner, the use of black powder must be prohibited, and nothing but "permissible explosives" used. The necessary precautions must be exercised in keeping the mine free from dust and it must be clearly understood that if those orders are again violated, steps will immediately be taken to enjoin the company from operating under the present system of mining.

Respectfully submitted,

ALEX SMITH,
Inspector Sixth District.
THOS. MORRISON,
Inspector Ninth District.
W. H. MILLER,
Inspector Seventh District.

Approved:
GEO. HARRISON,
Chief Inspector of Mines.

NOTE:—Following the investigation and report of the above explosion, the company operating this property suspended all operations at this mine, and commenced the installation of mining machinery to cut the coal, which has been attended with much success, and no serious accidents such as took place during the year 1909, and 1910, in which the lives of three shot firers lost their lives, have occurred.

The following circular was issued in order to familarize all persons connected in any way with the mining of coal in the state with the provisions of the new mining laws which went into effect June 11, 1910, in order that there might be as little delay and inconvenience in complying with its requirements as possible.

STATE MINING DEPARTMENT,
COLUMBUS, OHIO.

TO MINE OPERATORS, MINERS, OIL WELL DRILLERS, MANUFACTURERS OF ILLUMINATING OILS FOR USE IN MINES, AND ALL OTHERS INTERESTED IN THE OPERATION OF MINES:

NOTICE.

The new mining code passed March 23rd by both Houses of the Ohio Legislature, and approved by the signature of Governor Harmon on April 11, 1910, will take effect and be in full force on and after June 11, 1910.

Many important changes have been made in the old law, and many new provisions, which were necessary to cover new conditions and new dangers.

. The duties and obligations of owner, lessee or agent, and all employes in the mines, have been carefully and impartially considered and clearly defined.

The dangers liable to result to life and property in the operation of mines from the hitherto "wild-cat" system of drilling oil and gas wells through workable veins of coal and abandoning them without leaving any record, have been fully provided against. Any person, firm or corporation desiring to commence the drilling of an oil or gas well that will penetrate a vein of coal must first secure permission in writing from the Mining Department, and comply with all the provisions of law pertaining to that work.

The manufacture, sale and use of impure oil for illuminating purposes in the mines is prohibited, and an effective means of detecting it provided.

The size of miners lamps has been regulated, and open torches as stationary lights in mines have been prohibited.

The volume of air has been increased so that better and more powerful artificial ventilation equipments will be necessary in many instances.

Penalties in all cases of violation, and a quick and ready means of prosecution is also provided. A person cannot longer ignore or violate any provision of the mining law with impunity, and when brought before the lower court waive examination and give bond to appear before the Grand Jury of the county, taking unscrupulous and undue advantage of the interval to prevent the forthcoming of evidence against him. For first offense his case must be put on record by trial before a Justice of the Peace, while it is new and the evidence obtainable. State and county lines are sometimes convenient land-marks to those who disregard law, and are sometimes used by criminals, as well as witnesses, to defeat the ends of justice.

The new code was the work and recommendations of a Commission composed of three operators, recommended by the operators, and three representative miners, recommended by the miners, and appointed by Governor Harris, and the writer, who was selected by the other six members and also appointed by Governor Harris as the seventh member.

We fully realize that objections may be taken to some of the provisions of the bill, but it could not be expected that an entire code of laws could be drafted covering so many new and varied conditions in mines, that would not have some defects. From time to time, necessary changes can easily be made.

In the consideration of almost every question, the cost of the production of coal, the liberties of the employes, or the increased responsibility of some person, was necessarily affected, necessitating in most instances keen argument, in which the interests of all were zealously guarded and logically protected by their respective representatives. To secure a unanimous and harmonious agreement, and insure a good code of laws, it required reasonable concessions from both sides, which was commendable to both parties, and the fact that Governor Harmon sent the recommendations of the Commission to the Senate and House of Representatives, accompanied by special message of approval, and that both Houses of the Legislature enacted them into law without a single change, or a dissenting voice or vote against them, is the highest compliment that could be paid to the Ohio mine operators and miners.

Sixty days after the passage and approval of the bill has been allowed, to give time to prepare to meet its requirements. This provision was made so that there could be no misunderstanding on that point, and no room for any excuse of ignorance of the law. All must be prepared to meet with a reasonable compliance of the new law, or the inspectors will be compelled to seek an application of the penalties. This must not be understood to mean, however, that there will be any change of policy on part of the Department, or that the inspectors will pursue any harsh, radical, unreasonable or unfriendly course. It means that the law will be reasonably and judiciously enforced alike to all, and we trust they will have the friendly coöperation of all to that end.

Copies of the entire code can be had by writing the Secretary of State, or the Mining Department, Columbus, Ohio.

Very respectfully yours,

GEO. HARRISON,
Chief Inspector of Mines.

April 12, 1910.

"AMSTERDAM EXPLOSION."

(Report of Thos. Morrison, district mine inspector, Sherodsville, Ohio, on the Amsterdam mine explosion, which occurred April 21st, 1910.)

STATE MINING DEPARTMENT,
COLUMBUS, O.

SHERODSVILLE, OHIO, May 9, 1910.

HON. GEO. HARRISON, *Chief Inspector of Mines, of Columbus, Ohio.*

DEAR SIR:— I herewith submit the following report on the Amsterdam mine explosion, which took place about 9:30 P. M., on April 21st last.

I was informed over the telephone by the Superintendent of the Youghiogheny & Ohio Coal Co.'s mine at Amsterdam, that an explosion had occurred at that mine. Being at the Hotel at Amsterdam at the time, I reached the mine inside of an hour thereafter. Learning that the explosion was of a serious nature, I notified you by wire, with a request for assistance. We then entered the mine by means of the hoist in the air shaft, the main shaft being wrecked so that we were unable to use the cages in it.

The ventilating fan, which is a Robinson make, 14' x 6', operated by steam power, was found on examination to be much damaged. The bearings were so damaged that the end of the fan shaft dropped down, throwing the fan out of line, causing it to run against the casing and heating the bearings. This was a serious draw-back, as we had every hope of rescuing some of the men in the mine alive. After a hurried consultation, Mr. Jones, the Superintendent of the mine, concluded that by putting men at the fan to keep continually pouring lubricating oil on the boxings, he could keep it running for a few hours at least, and succeeded in doing so until 4 o'clock the following morning.

During this time, an exploring party staid in the mine, and we tried to reach the places where men were known to have been working. We succeeded in reaching the head of the 1st and 2nd West on the South Side of the mine, entering the No. 2 Room on 2nd West Entry, where two men had been working, and found their dinner buckets, but could see no trace of the men, who had evidently left this place after the explosion and tried to reach the shaft, as we found them later lying side by side on the 3rd Southwest Entry, where they had evidently been overcome with after-damp and lay down and died. The after-damp was so strong, our party was nearly overcome, and we were forced to retreat; some of the party having difficulty in reaching fresh air.

We reached the surface at 2:30 A. M., on the morning following the explosion. A few minutes after we had reached the surface, we heard a signal from the bottom of the main shaft, and immediately returned and found that one man had made his way to the bottom alive, carrying with him an open light. After bringing him out, we again started to explore the mine, and this time entered the old 1st Southwest Entry, where three other men had been working, taking out track rails. We explored this section, and found the tools, but the men were gone. We then concluded to make our way through a short pair of face entries to the 3rd Southwest, where we supposed the men had gone in their efforts to reach the shaft. On reaching this entry, we found the three men lying dead on the passway, where the after-damp had evidently done its deadly work. We put one of them on the stretcher, and started towards the bottom, but had not gone over 100 ft. along the 3rd Southwest Entry until we found the two men who had left the No. 2 Room on 2nd Southwest Entry, also dead from the effects of the after-damp.

As our party was again almost overcome, and believing that all the others were dead, we decided to return to the surface, which we did at 4 o'clock in the morning, and on learning that the fan was in such a condition that it could not be run much longer, we decided to stop and repair it, as we could not get along without an air current.

At 7 A. M., the fan was again put in operation, and the cage in the main shaft cut loose. We then proceeded to take in material to build temporary stoppings and carry the air current with us. With the officials of the mine, and the assistance of the miners of this and the surrounding mines, who willingly volunteered their assistance, this work progressed as rapidly as it was possible for it to be done.

On coming out of the mine about noon, we found that you and other members of the department had arrived at the mine and were ready to go in with the party which was going down. This party worked its way along the South Main Entry, and about 3 P. M., located seven bodies near the entrance of the 4th East Entry; these, and three other men were working in No. 18 Room, 4th East, when the explosion occurred.

From information received from three men who were afterwards rescued, those ten men tried to reach the shaft bottom; the last three men finding the after-damp too strong, retreated to the interior of the mine where they were found about 11 o'clock on the night of the 22nd.

Mr. Jas. W. Paul and Mr. J. R. Cavanaugh, from the United States Geological Survey Rescue Station at Pittsburg, arrived at 5 o'clock on the evening of the day after the explosion, bringing with them, helmets and other equipment necessary for the rescue and resuscitation of men that might be rescued. They, with another rescue party, entered the mine, all the men who were in the mine at the time of the explosion having been accounted for except five.

The efforts of the Geological men, with the use of the helmets, were directed to where it was supposed the explosion had occurred. After reaching within about 1400 or 1500 feet of the point referred to, they were compelled to retreat, on account of the exhaustion in their efforts against falls and other obstructions, and because of the high temperature in the mine. It was then decided that a force of men should remove some of the obstructions and conduct the ventilation by temporary means, nearer to the point desired to reach, and the exploring party returned to the surface.

Another exploring party, composed of Mr. John Rees, the General Manager of the Company, the officials of the mine, mine inspectors, and a number of others, commenced to explore the Southeast side of the mine, and after being compelled to retreat a time or two, finally succeeded in reaching the face of No. 3 and No. 4 S. E. Butt Entries, finding three of the missing men alive at No. 35 Room on 3rd S. E. Entry, but, though conscious, in a very exhausted condition.

The party at once communicated with the outside, and a force of men with blankets and stretchers was sent in to carry them to the surface, a distance of over 2,000 feet. After being carried to a point reached by the pure air, they were met in the mine by Mr. Paul and Mr. Cavanaugh, of the U. S. Geological Survey; Dr. Atwell of Amsterdam, and others, and the work of resuscitation and reviving was done before taking the men to the surface. They were taken on top about 1:00 A. M., on the second morning after the explosion, and soon began to show signs of recovery. There were twenty-three men in the mine at the time of the explosion; five of them, including the night-foreman, were on the North side of the mine, which was not affected by the force of the explosion. These men made their way to the bottom of the shaft and were hoisted. With the eight men already rescued, and the thirteen bodies which had been recovered, the two machine men who were working at or near the supposed location of the explosion were all that were not accounted for, and the work of conducting the ventilation in the direction of that point was prosecuted as vigorously as the obstacles met with would permit. By this means, we were able to get within about 500 feet of the face of the workings, and form good judgment as to where the explosion had taken place, but owing to the presence of after-damp, and the obstructions from falls of roof, our progress became very slow, and we decided to go out and report.

Another force of explorers then entered the mine, accompanied by Mr. Paul and Mr. Cavanaugh, with their helmets, and proceeded to the point where the other party had succeeded in reaching. Resuming the use of the helmets at this point, Mr. Paul and Mr. Cavanaugh proceeded cautiously to the seat of the explosion, finding the bodies of the two unfortunate men, and with great difficulty carrying one of them to the rescue party, who removed it to the bottom of the shaft. Knowing that the other man was dead, and there was great danger of losing life in trying to rescue the body without conducting a volume of air to the point where the body was lying, a consultation was held and it was considered that it would take at least twelve hours to erect the necessary brattices and recover the body without the use of the helmets.

Mr. Paul, Mr. Cavanaugh, and mine inspector Jno. L. McDonald, each with the use of a helmet, proceeded to the face of the entries where the explosion occurred, placing the body on a stretcher, and it was drawn 400 feet by use of a rope through the deadly after-damp by the exploring party with whom they were accompanied, and thus the last body was brought to the surface about 1:30 P. M., on Saturday, April 23rd, forty hours after the explosion.

You instructed inspectors McDonald, Kennedy and Burke, to remain in the district with me and assist in the restoring of the airways in the mine, and to advise you when the mine was in readiness for inspection; this, we did, and later advised you that the mine would be in readiness on May 3rd for investigation, to ascertain if possible the cause of the explosion, and under your direction, the inspection was made on that date.

To you, and through you, I desire to express my sincere thanks to the officials of the Youghiogheny & Ohio Coal Co., and other neighboring Coal Companies; to the miners and community at Amsterdam for their loyal aid and heroic efforts in assisting in the work immediately after the explosion, and also to yourself and members of the mining department, and the Geological rescue men for ready response to my appeal for help and for the valuable counsel and active assistance in the hazardous work of rescue and recovery of the bodies of the unfortunate victims of the explosion.

Very respectfully yours,

THOMAS MORRISON,
Inspector 9th District.

STATE MINING DEPARTMENT,
COLUMBUS, O.

MAY 7, 1910.

Y. & Q. COAL CO., *Cleveland, Ohio.*

DEAR SIRS: — Before resuming operations at the Amsterdam mine, the following orders must be complied with:

(1) The permanent stoppings must be replaced, and would prefer that they be made of brick and cement, or concrete.

(2) All obstructions, such as falls, must be removed from the air-courses, and doors repaired; would recommend that they be replaced with automatic doors.

(3) The dust in the airways, haulways, gobs, and on the timbers, sprinkled and removed from the mine.

(4) No open lights to be used unless on the passway at the bottom of

the shaft, and no one allowed to go beyond that point, or in any manner enter the return airway, without a locked safety lamp.

(5) The cages should be given a thorough overhauling, the ropes examined, and the guides in the shaft lined up. We would recommend that automatic doors be used at all important points in the mine, where it is necessary to use doors to direct the air current.

(6) After the above orders have been complied with, and the mine restored to its normal condition, the mining department must be notified, so that an inspection of the mine can be made before resuming operations.

Very respectfully yours,

THOS. MORRISON,
Inspector 9th District.
JOHN BURKE,
Inspector 1st District.

Approved:
GEO. HARRISON,
Chief Inspector of Mines.

AMSTERDAM EXPLOSION.

(Report of Geo. Harrison, Chief Inspector of Mines, Columbus, Ohio, on Amsterdam mine explosion, which occurred April 21st, 1910.)

HON. JUDSON HARMON, *Governor of Ohio.*

DEAR SIR:— About midnight on April 21st, I received the following telegram:

"BERGHOLZ, OHIO, April 21, 1910.

GEO. HARRISON, *Chief Inspector of Mines, Phone* 5124, *Columbus, Ohio.*

Explosion Y. & O. mine, Amsterdam, Ohio. Bad. Send for helmet men at once.
THOS. MORRISON."

At 12:14 A. M., a message was on the Western Union wire to Jas. W. Paul, United States Rescue Station, Pittsburg, Pa., asking for helmets and helmet men, and from that time until 7 o'clock in the morning, when I left the city for the scene of the explosion, the time was spent in securing communication with all the district inspectors, requiring them to report at Amsterdam as quickly as they could get transportation to that point, which they did.

On arriving at the mine about 1:30 P. M., with district inspector W. H. Turner, who had also arrived, we at once examined the ventilating machinery, and went into the mine with an exploring party.

Mr. Morrison, in his report to this department, a copy of which is herewith attached, has covered the work of rescue so fully that it is not necessary to repeat it.

THE EXPLORING PARTY

And rescue work was entirely under the charge of Mr. Richard Jones, Superintendent of the Youghiogheny & Ohio Coal Co., and his subordinate officials at the mine, and Mr. Thos. Morrison, district inspector, who evidently had plenty of good, willing volunteers to assist in the hazardous work.

Mr. Morrison was on the ground within less than an hour after the explosion, and from the time of the explosion until the last body was recovered, there was not a single hitch in the work, everything being done with cool deliberation, good judgment and foresight, and what was most remarkable, not a single person in any of the rescue parties received any injury, only from the effects of the after-damp, and nothing serious in that particular.

INSPECTION.

On the 3rd inst., in company with inspectors Thos. Morrison and John Burke, we made an inspection of the mine, to ascertain, if possible, the cause of the explosion. Mr. Jas. W. Paul, who is in charge of the United States Geological Rescue Station at Pittsburg, Pa., and the various persons composing the management of the mine, were also present.

There was little difficulty in locating the seat of the explosion, which all agreed was in the Left or East Entry of three parallel entries known as the Sub-South Main Entries, being driven in a Southwesterly direction, advancing into solid coal in the extreme Southwest section of the mine. These entries are each driven about 16 ft. wide, with a pillar of coal about 20 feet thick between the center entry and the one on each side. Breakthroughs are made between all the entries, as the law requires, namely: Sixty feet apart, and, in addition, canvas cloth is used to conduct the ventilating current from the last breakthrough to the face of the working place, so as to dilute and carry away the carbureted hydrogen gas (fire-damp), generated as the places advance.

A mining machine was found at the face of the center entry, mining the second cut in a breakthrough to the left entry, having made three runs when the explosion occurred. One of the bodies of the machine runners was in the center entry, nearly 200 feet from the face, somewhat burned. The other body was found near the last breakthrough in the left entry, considerably burned. The clothing on those bodies was not burned to any extent, but considerable charred dust was found in the left entry near where the body was found, and a little in the right corner at the face of the center entry.

CAUSE OF EXPLOSION.

All indications show that one of the machine runners went into the left entry, for some purpose which can only be surmised, and that he came in contact with, and ignited, a body of gas which had accumulated from defective ventilation.

MINE REPORTED "ALL RIGHT" AT SEVEN O'CLOCK.

E. O. Jones, the night-foreman, stated that Charles Howarth, one of the victims, whose duty it was to travel the South Side of the mine every night to see if any fire existed from firing of shots, or any irregularity, reported to him at 7 o'clock that everything was "all right", and those places were ready to cut.

The explosion was entirely local in character, and judging from the number of stoppings blown down, and falls of roof and destruction in other ways, the force from the concussion and expansion of flame was in as direct a line as could be made to the bottom of the hoisting shaft, which was the intake of air, the distance from the seat of the explosion to the shaft being about 2,600 feet. There are no old workings on that side of the mine, and nothing but entries being driven. There was no destruction in any other part of the mine, and no indication of explosion, only in the line of the force on the South Main Entry, towards the shaft and near it, charred dust was found, and a number of the mules and ponies in the stable a distance from the shaft was dead and the hair on them somewhat singed, while others close to were alive and showed no signs of injury.

Joe Sampietro, a driver, was found at the bottom of the shaft, immediately after the explosion, in a dying condition and never recovered. This man's duty was to move the mining machines from place to place, and go between the working places and the shaft to secure sharp bits, machine oil, or anything needed by machine men. His team of ponies was standing on the South side of the shaft in the passway, the harness and tail chain hanging hooked to the outer end of an empty car, showing that he had started to the shaft after moving the mining machine into the center entry where the explosion occurred. This machine had been moved about 800 feet, evidently from the work done about an hour or an hour and a half before the explosion.

THE FIRST EXPLORING PARTY

That entered the mine, in exploring the Main South Entry, found a main door standing wide open and fastened back to a post in such a way that it must have been intentionally done by some human being. The only conclusion reached is that the driver in coming out fastened it back to save climbing out of the car to open it as he returned into the mine again.

There was another door about 500 feet from the face of the entries where the explosion took place, through which this driver had to pass. The inference is that he was just as liable to prop that door open as he was to fasten the main door open. If this was done, the entire current of air would be cut off from that part of the mine. There was another door at another point on the South Main Entry, which, if kept open at the same time as the first door named, the result would have been precisely the same. Inspector Morrison and Superintendent Jones were both with the first party that reached the open door. The other two doors mentioned, when reached, were both found buried under a big fall of roof, resulting from the force of the explosion, obliterating any possibility of evidence as to what position they were in at the time of the explosion.

The report of the fire boss shows that on the morning of the 21st, a slight trace of generating gas was found in those entries.

The ventilating fan was equipped with an automatic self-recording pressure gauge, showing the pressure, and that the fan was continually running up to the moment of the explosion.

THE INSPECTOR'S REPORTS,

(Copies of which are herewith submitted), show for the last four inspections that the mine has been well taken care of, and the law in some important instances, more than complied with, but like many other mines in the state, the elements of danger are there, and they cannot be tampered with, without serious risks to life and property.

In this case, the evidences are, that at 7 o'clock in the evening, everything was reported "all right" in that part of the mine, but between that and the time of the explosion, two and a half hours later, indisputably some person inadvertently or carelessly committed some act which cut off the regular air current, allowing the gas generated in the left entry of the three Sub-South Main Entries to accumulate, which was ignited by one of the machine runners, going for some purpose from the center place to the left entry. The two machine runners and the driver were all the men that were killed by the force of the explosion, the other twelve men found dead having succumbed to the effects of the after-damp in their efforts to reach the shaft after the explosion.

Until the time arrives when we can all realize that the lurking dangers in mines require the most rigid discipline of every person in the mine, and each, from the General Manager to the trapper boy, knows and diligently performs his duty, calamities of this kind must and will occur.

Respectfully submitted,

GEO. HARRISON,
Chief Inspector of Mines.
THOMAS MORRISON,
Inspector 9th District.
JOHN BURKE,
Inspector 1st District.

Columbus, Ohio, May 12, 1910.

[House Bill No. 577.]

AN ACT

To make appropriation for the relief of those left dependent on account of the accident at the Youghiogheny & Ohio Coal Company's mine near Amsterdam, Ohio, on the night of April 21, 1910, in which fifteen men lost their lives.

Be it enacted by the General Assembly of the State of Ohio:

Amsterdam mine disaster appropriation.

SECTION 1. That for purposes hereinafter stated there is hereby appropriated out of any money to the credit of the general relief fund, not otherwise appropriated, the sum of ten thousand dollars ($10,000.)

SECTION 2. That the speaker of the house and the president of the senate shall forthwith appoint a committee consisting of three members on the part of the house and three members on the part of the senate, which committee shall have power to distribute this money as they deem proper and right.

Duties of committee.

SECTION 3. The committee appointed under this act shall meet with the local union No. 2581 U. M. W. A., at Amsterdam within fifteen days and determine the amount and to whom such relief shall be given, and shall issue the orders of the committee in accordance therewith.

SECTION 4. The auditor of state shall issue his warrant on the treasurer of state upon the order of this committee, signed by all the members of the committee.

SECTION 5. The committee is vested with power to turn any or all of this money over to a trustee or trustees to be paid to the one for whom it is intended, in installments. The amount of which installments is to be determined by the committee.

GRANVILLE W. MOONEY,
Speaker of the House of Representatives.

FRANCIS W. TREADWAY,
President of the Senate.

Passed April 30, 1910.
Approved April 30, 1910.

JUDSON HARMON,
Governor.

REPORT OF SPECIAL COMMITTEE APPOINTED TO DISTRIBUTE RELIEF FUND, MADE TO THE SENATE.

Mr. Duval submitted the following report:

The joint committee appointed under the provisions of H. B. No. 577 — Mr. Gilson. To make appropriation for the relief of those left dependent on account of the accident at the Youghiogheny and Ohio Coal Company's mine near Amsterdam, Ohio, on the night of April 21, 1910, in which fifteen men lost their lives, submits the following report, accompanied by the minutes of the proceedings of the committee, the latter of which, we recommend be filed with the Clerk of the Senate and that the report proper be spread upon the Journals of the two houses.

The committee organized by the election of Senator Duval as chairman, and Representative Tidrick as secretary, and, after carefully considering all the facts presented, made the following distribution of the funds under its control:

Katrina Roskiewicz, widow of Angelo Roskiewicz, two hundred and fifty dollars;

Maria Reva, widow of Italico Reva, three hundred dollars;

Mrs. Maria Howarth, widow of Charles Howarth, twenty-one hundred dollars;

Isabelle Smith, widow of John Smith, four hundred dollars;

Jean McMaster, mother of Robert McMaster, six hundred and fifty dollars;

Annie Lockhart, widow of James Lockhart, six hundred dollars;

Elizabeth Hay, widow of Herbert Hay, five hundred dollars;

Giavonni Sonavere, injured, fifty dollars;

Luigi Beneditti, injured, fifty dollars;

Erominio Benefitto, injured, fifty dollars;

Ermilio Percello, injured, fifty dollars;

The committee appointed Messrs. Duval and Tidrick to carry out the instructions of the general committee.

It is the opinion of the committee that five thousand dollars will be an equitable relief for those whom the committee has first knowledge of being in distress, and the committee will therefore return to the state treasury the unexpended balance of five thousand dollars.

The People's Banking Company, at Amsterdam, which is made trustee herein will disburse this money according to the instructions of the committee and will take receipts for each payment so made. The bond required herein of said bank will be deposited with the auditor of state with a copy of this report, and, when the bank has deposited with the auditor of state receipts, showing that the amount of money deposited herein has been paid out, and, if the auditor has no reason to believe that the bank has not complied with its part of the agreement, he shall release said bond. The signature on the bond and the signature of this contract and report by the officials of the bank will be deemed a sufficient contract.

Katrina Roskiewicz,—furnish her ticket to her destination in Austria, give her fifty dollars in cash and bill of exchange for balance of two hundred and fifty dollars.

Marie Reva,—fifty dollars now and fifty dollars when her baby is born, ticket to her destination in Italy and balance in cash.

Mrs. Howarth,—thirty-five dollars per month, but the sub-committee, consisting of Messrs. Duval and Tidrick, may expend five hundred dollars of said twenty-one hundred for a home, to be in her name and to be occupied by her so long as any minor children remain and are taken care of by her, provided she survives them, and, in case of her death, the property shall be in trust for any minor children until they become of age, at which time it shall belong to all surviving children equally, and, in case the sub-committee does purchase home for her, the amount allowed per month may be adjusted as the sub-committee deems proper.

Isabelle Smith, twenty dollars per month.

Jean McMasters, twenty-five dollars per month.

Mrs. Lockhart, twenty-five dollars per month.

Elizabeth Hay, twenty dollars per month.

Giavonni Sonavere, cash.

Luigi Beneditti, cash.

Erminio Beneditti, cash.

Ermellio Percello, cash.

MARSHALL N. DUVAL,
Chairman Relief Committee.

R. S. TIDRICK,
Sec'y Relief Committee.

DAVID TOD,
J. P. MAHAFFEY,

EDGAR ERVIN,
A. F. TURNER.

The recommendations of the joint committee were agreed to.

U. G. DENMAN,
Attorney General.

STATE OF OHIO,
OFFICE OF THE ATTORNEY GENERAL.

COLUMBUS, OHIO, June 23, 1910.

HON. GEORGE HARRISON, *Chief Inspector of Mines, Columbus, Ohio.*

DEAR SIR: — You have asked me to submit to you a form to guide manufacturers of illuminating oil for mines which this department considers a compliance with section 974 of the General Code. Part of section 974 is as follows:

> "Each person, firm or corporation compounding oil for illuminating purposes in a coal mine, or mines, shall, before shipment thereof is made, securely brand, stencil or paste upon the head of each barrel or package, a label which shall have plainly printed, marked or written thereon, the name and address of the person, firm or corporation compounding the oil therein contained, the name and address of the person, firm or corporation having purchased same, the date of shipment, the percentage and the gravity in degrees Baume scale, at a temperature of sixty degrees Fahrenheit, of each of the component parts of animal, vegetable and mineral oil contained in the mixture, and the gravity in degrees Baume scale at a temperature of sixty degrees Fahrenheit of the mixture.
>
> Each label shall have printed thereon, over the fac-simile signature of the person, firm or corporation having compounded the oil, the following: 'This package contains oil for illuminating purposes in coal mines in the state of Ohio, and the composition thereof as shown hereon is correct.' "

From the above section I consider the attached form a compliance with the same. I would suggest that this brand or label be placed upon the head of each barrel in some permanent form. I note the law provides that if a label is securely pasted upon the head of a barrel it will be a compliance with this act. I suggest that you warn manufacturers of oil to be careful in this particular for the reason if the label is merely pasted upon a barrel it may be either torn off or on account of dampness come off of its own accord, and would therefore cause trouble to the manufacturers, and for this reason I offer the suggestion that manufacturers brand the head of the barrels or packages in which the oil is contained in some secure form, thereby avoiding any possible trouble. I may add that there are probably other forms of a label that would comply with the section which I have above quoted, but you may inform the manufacturers that all who use this form of label which I have attached to this letter will be safe and free from any possible prosecution for not having their label according to law.

It has come to my notice that some manufacturers in their label use the words "cotton seed oil" in place of "vegetable oil." I understand that "cotton seed oil" is "vegetable oil," but I suggest the manufacturers use the words "vegetable oil" as the law requires, and not "cotton seed oil." Perhaps the use of the words "cotton seed oil" would be a compliance with the law, but by using the words "vegetable oil" the manufacturers do away with all possible chance.

I also understand that a number of manufacturers place the name and address of the person, firm or corporation who purchases the oil on the barrel at a place other than the head. After carefully considering this section, I am of the opinion that the name and address of the person, firm or corporation purchasing the oil must be placed on the head with the label, and that placing such name and address at another place on the barrel is not a technical compliance with the law.

In conclusion, I desire to add that manufacturers who use the attached label will avoid all possible technicalities in regard to the label.

Yours very truly,

F. H. KIRTLEY.

(a) ....

(b) ....

(c) ....

Result of Test of Contents by Baume Scale at 60 deg. Fahr.

(d)	Animal Oil	........................Gravity
	Vegetable Oil (e)	........................Gravity
	Mineral Oil	........................Gravity
	Mixture	........................Gravity

This package contains oil for illuminating purposes in coal mines in the State of Ohio, and the composition thereof as shown hereon is correct.

(f) ....

(g) ....

Legend.

(a) Name of purchaser.
(b) Address of purchaser.
(c) Date of shipment.
(d) Only necessary to have component parts of contents.
(e) Place result of test.
(f) Fac-simile signature of the person, firm or corporation having compounded the oil.
(g) Address of person mentioned in (f).

Caution: BE SURE AND PLACE LABEL ON HEAD OF BARREL OR PACKAGE.

STATE OF OHIO,

OFFICE OF THE ATTORNEY GENERAL.

U. G. DENMAN,
Attorney General.

OPINION.

COLUMBUS, OHIO, September 22nd, 1910.

HON. GEORGE HARRISON, *Chief Inspector of Mines, Columbus, Ohio.*

DEAR SIR: — I am in receipt of your letter of September 16th, in which you ask my opinion upon the following questions:

"Would it be contrary to the provisions of Section 925 of the General Code, which provides for the removal of standing gas in all available parts of old abandoned workings in mines, to permit the sealing up of such old abandoned workings and prevent gases generating therein from flowing out into the air current passing through other parts of the mine where miners are working?"

"In the event that it will not conflict with the provisions of Section 925, will this department be justified in advising or requiring, through its inspectors, the sealing up of the abandoned parts of mines; provided, however, that the sealing up of such abandoned parts will, in the judgment of the inspectors, increase protection to the lives of persons working in other parts of the mine?"

The part of Section 925 of the General Code material to your inquiry is as follows:

"Each mine generating fire-damp so as to be detected by a safety lamp, shall be kept free from standing gas. All traveling ways, entrances to old workings, and places not in the actual course of working, shall be carefully examined with a safety lamp by the fire boss not more than three hours before the appointed time for persons employed therein to enter. Parts of the mine not in the actual course of working and available, shall be examined not less than once each three days, and shall be so fenced as to prevent persons from inadvertently entering therein."

You will note that Section 925 of the General Code deals exclusively with mines which are in some degree being worked and does not apply to abandoned mines. If the abandoned workings of a mine are so sealed up as to cease to be a part of the mine, I am of the opinion that the above section will not have any application in such a case. However, the sealing up of old workings should be done in a manner satisfactory to the mining department and in a manner which would prevent the standing gas of such old workings, which have been sealed up, passing through other parts of the mine where miners are working or are likely to be stationed. The sealing of the abandoned parts of a mine must also not in any way affect the air passages of the mine.

I particularly call your attention to the fact that after such abandoned workings of a mine are sealed up, that part shall in effect be an abandoned mine and be governed by the provisions of Section 938 of the General Code relating to abandoned mines.

Yours very truly,

U. G. Denman,
Attorney General

Owing to the danger of blasting coal off the solid, and to the excessive amount of smoke generated by such shooting, the following notice was posted at the Hazelwood Mine.

NOTICE TO BE POSTED AT THE HAZELWOOD MINE,
Dellroy, Ohio.

To Govern the Blasting of Coal.

First. No shot shall be fired in this mine, unless at least one-half of the coal is undercut, and no hole shall be drilled beyond the undercutting.

Second. In narrow work no hole shall be drilled beyond the shearing, and all holes must be tamped with fire clay, or other uncombustible material.

Third. Shooting shall be restricted so that no shots will be fired, until quitting time, and shooting shall commence at the last working place on the return air current and continue on in turn toward the intake.

Fourth. The mine foreman, or superintendent, shall see that these rules are enforced.

Thomas Morrison,
Inspector 9th District.

Approved, October 18, 1910.
By Geo. Harrison,
Chief Mine Inspector.

REPORT ON THE LONG WALL SYSTEM OF COAL MINING BY DISTRICT MINE INSPECTOR, THOS. MORRISON, OF THE NINTH MINING DISTRICT.

SHERODSVILLE, OHIO, Oct. 22, 1910.

MR. GEORGE HARRISON, *Chief Inspector of Mines, Columbus, Ohio.*

DEAR SIR:— Realizing the necessity of a better and safer method of mining, especially in our deep and gassy mines, we have been advocating for some time that the system in the Amsterdam District be changed from the room and pillar to the Long-wall system of mining.

The operators of this district were equally anxious to adopt a safer system, providing it was practical to work it under existing conditions, and as none of them were familiar with the Long-wall method of mining, no Long-wall mining being practiced in Ohio, was anxious to see the method in operation. After first being advised by you that we had the approval of Governor Harmon to leave the State for the purpose of securing information on methods of mining that would further safe-guard the lives of those employed in the mines, we commenced to make arrangements to visit the Long-wall mines of Illinois and calculated to start on May 21st, but as nearly all the mines in that state had suspended operations, owing to labor troubles, it had to be postponed until a settlement was reached and the mines again in operation.

About the middle of September the labor troubles were adjusted and the mines resumed operations; on the 16th of October, the writer met Mr. Reese and Mr. Jones, representing the Y. & O. Coal Co., Mr. McKeever, representative of the Bergholz Coal Co., and Mr. Marson of the Wolf Run Coal Co., at the Forest City House, Cleveland, Ohio, and proceeded to Chicago where we had arranged to meet Mr. Warner of the Wolf Run Coal Co. On arriving at Chicago, we wired State Mine Inspector, John Dunlop, that we would start for LaSalle, arangements having been previously made with him to meet us there and take us through the mines.

We arrived at LaSalle about noon of the 17th, over the Rock Island Railroad and proceeded to the Cherry Mine, which is located at Cherry, Bureau County, and owned by the St. Paul Coal Co., of Chicago, Ill. This is a shaft mine, 485 feet deep to what is known as the No. 2 seam, the coal being about 3½ feet thick and worked on the Long-wall system. As the mine was not fully opened out along the face after the long suspension, our party could not see the mine under normal conditions, therefore decided to visit another mine in that part of the district that was operated to its full capacity.

While at the Cherry Mine, the writer took a few notes regarding the management and equipment. James Steel is the superintendent and

Walter Waite, one of the men who was entombed for eight days during the recent catastrophe, when so many lives were lost as the result of a mine fire, is the mine manager. The equipment is modern, the tipple being of steel and the engine and boiler room of brick, making the equipment on top fire-proof. Owing to the nature of the roof, great quantities of timber are used to support it, and the bottom of the shaft, for a distance of three or four hundred feet, pine timbers 10" x 14" are put up four feet apart and lagged over with other timber. The fan is of the Clifford Cappell make, 8' x 16', the main shaft 16' x 14', air-shaft 9' x 12'; power furnished by six 150 H. P. boilers.

The party was also taken to the upper seam where the fire originated. This is sealed off with massive concrete walls, but we were able to see the effects of the fire on some of the timbers around the shaft.

On the 18th, we visited the St. Paul Coal Co.'s No. 1 Mine at Granville, and saw this in full operation. The coal is about the same thickness as that of the Cherry Mine, the shaft being 475 feet deep, the equipment being something similar, it is unnecessary to describe it. Our party were very favorably impressed with this mine and all agreed that the Long-wall method was the ideal method of mining coal, both as regards to safety and efficiency, but as the strata over and under the coal was different from theirs, they were desirous of seeing a mine where conditions were nearly similar to theirs, so Mr. Dunlop decided to take them to Bloomington the following day.

On the 19th, we arrived at Bloomington and proceeded to the mine of the McLain County Coal Co. We found a shaft 530 feet deep and two veins being worked; the upper vein being 390 feet deep. Both veins are worked on the Long-wall system, ventilated by a 6 foot Sirocca Fan. The coal from the upper vein is lowered through a 140 ft. shaft in the interior of the mine to the lower vein, and hauled by a tail rope to the main shaft where it is hoisted to the surface. This impressed our party as being similar in a great many respects, as far as the stratas over and under the coal are concerned, and they felt that mining machines could successfully be used under similar conditions, which in their opinion was very important, as they had to compete with machine mined coal.

After leaving this mine our party started for home and I am of the opinion that they were all convinced that the Long-wall method is by far the safer method for removing coal from the vein of coal now being operated in the Amsterdam field, where gas is generated, and the only thing that stands in the way of adopting it, is the question of the cost of production.

It is to be hoped that the parties representing the different companies will make a favorable report, and urge the adoption of this method of working at their mines, as the writer is of the opinion that it is a step in the right direction as far as the protection of life and the conservation of our natural resources are concerned, besides I still believe that the difference in the cost of production will be very little.

Very respectfully,

THOMAS MORRISON,
Inspector 9th District.

IMPORTANT DECISION ON DRILLING GAS WELLS THROUGH COAL MINES.

For years the problem of safeguarding the lives of miners against the dangers of gas wells has perplexed coal operators. In a case decided in Fayette county, Pa., on December 27, 1910, by Judge J. Q. Van Swearingen, in an injunction case brought by the Monongahela River Consolidated Coal & Coke Company against the Greensboro Gas Company, the facts, circumstances and testimony adduced in hearing which are summarized by the court, the following opinion and decree was rendered. This decision so fully covers all the questions involved that it is published in full, and is as follows:

"A preliminary injunction was granted in this case restraining the defendant from proceeding further with the drilling of a gas well through certain coal mines of the plaintiff, and it was agreed by counsel when the testimony was taken that the hearing then should be considered as final, and that we should dispose of the matter accordingly. The plaintiff owns and is operating certain coal mines known as Little Redstone, Washington, Alice, Snow Hill, Chamouni and Albany mines. The operation of these mines consists in mining and removing the nine-foot vein of coal. The mines adjoin each other and are connected together through old workings; and there is claimed to be a general circulation of air through all the mines, in which between 1,200 and 1,300 men are employed. It is estimated that it will take 12 years to exhaust the coal in these mines. In the operation of the Snow Hill mine the coal underlying the Joseph S. Elliott farm in Jefferson township has been mined and removed, the part of the mine formerly occupied by that coal has been abandoned, and the overlying land has subsided to such an extent that this part of the mine is now inaccessible, although, it is alleged, the air therefrom circulates through all the other mines. The defendant is engaged in drilling a well for gas on the Elliott farm, which must pass through, and in fact already has passed through, the abandoned portion of the Snow Hill mine in order to reach the gas-producing sand lying below the coal, and it is asked to restrain.

"In its answer the defendant alleges that by reason of the subsidence and dropping down of the overlying strata the drilling of said well is practically the same as if it were being drilled through land under which there had been no mining operations; that the air cannot circulate through that section of the mine, and cannot escape into the mine, and cannot escape into the mines adjoining the Snow Hill mine; that there are no operations, and that there is no coal to be removed, within a considerable distance from said well; that the defendant is drilling said well in accordance with the approved methods adopted in the drilling of oil and gas wells, with five separate and distinct holes, and four strings of casing and tubing firmly imbedded upon the bottom or sides, all below the coal stratification, which will prevent the escape of gas therefrom and confine any gas obtained within the several strings of casing and tubing, and that no gas could escape [illegible] which [illegible] gauze [illegible] dangerous [illegible] possibility [illegible]

[illegible] outcome [illegible]

[illegible] within the [illegible] where [illegible]

[illegible] through the [illegible]

[illegible] pressure [illegible] which [illegible] electr[illegible]

[illegible] with the [illegible] it is [illegible] effective [illegible] through the [illegible] larger than the [illegible] thus allow the [illegible]

[illegible] water [illegible] shown in [illegible] the [illegible] water alone. [illegible] where [illegible] covered, the [illegible] percautions [illegible] fresh [illegible] water, [illegible] exposed surfaces of sulphur minerals, are not conducive to strong acid sulphur-water, and an exhaustion will gradually take place and the water become harmless. The oxygen of fresh air is necessary. Confined air is soon exhausted of its oxygen. Water dripping through the roof-coal or running down the outside of the casings of the well, having come in contact with air, may become impregnated with a sufficient quantity of sulphuric acid to eat through an iron or steel pipe, although the water, having come through the limestone above, and thereby having become more or less alkaline, has a tendency to neutralize the sulphuric acid as fast as it is formed; but acid sulphate and free sulphuric acid will be produced if sufficient sulphur mineral and water and air be present. There is nearly always a quantity of sulphur in the gob or refuse left in the mine, and water itself at the surface carries oxygen, which, although it may be lost as it works down through the rock, may be carried into the mines. Even though the acid sulphur water be weak, it may eat through the pipes or casings eventually. So if there be water and air and sulphur mineral at the point where this well passes through the abandoned mine there is danger of the pipes being destroyed by sulphuric acid unless this be guarded against in some way. Hydrochloric or muriatic acid also may be formed from sulphur-water and the salt-water coming from the overlying strata, and that acid has as destructive an effect upon the iron pipes as sulphuric acid. If the subsidence of the overlying strata at the well be not yet complete the cavities there are likely to be filled with carbonic acid gas, or black-damp, and if natural gas should escape from the well into this abandoned mine it would drive the carbonic acid gas into the live workings of the mines, and this carbonic acid gas is just as dangerous as the natural gas, because, while the one burns the other suffocates or smothers.

"The coal at the exact point where this well passes through the Snow Hill mine was worked out prior to 1899, although certain chain pillars between butt entries within 50 feet of the well were taken out just prior to 1908. The nearest solid coal yet to be worked is 1,300 feet from the well, and the nearest approach in the mines that now can be had to the well is about the same distance away. It is impossible to tell whether the subsidence of the overlying strata is so complete as to prevent the passage of air from the vicinity of the well to other portions of the mines. There is some evidence that complete subsidence at this point has not yet taken place, and that the pipes might be sheared off or broken by a lateral movement of the strata, caused by a creep or squeeze or swag. We are of opinion, from other evidence in the case, that, though the subsidence may not be complete, there is no danger to be anticipated from a lateral movement of the strata; but if the subsidence be not sufficient to prevent the passage of air from about the well and gas should escape it would be carried all through the live workings of the mines. There is evidence of a loss of ventilation from the force fans in other mines, indicating a leakage of air toward the Snow Hill mine and in the general direction of the gas well. Experience shows that an almost complete subsidence does not always close all openings. Crevices are sometimes left in or above the location of the coal seam. In this case it is impossible to tell whether the crevices have been so completely filled as to prevent the passage of air or gas from the vicinity of the well to the live coal workings. It is insisted by all the mine inspectors who were called as witnesses that the well be encased in cement to a depth below the coal stratum to prevent any possibility of the pipes being eaten through by sulphur water. If it were certain that subsidence had taken place so completely as to prevent the presence of air at the well there might be no danger, but this is not certain, and we cannot permit any chances to be taken when the lives of 1,200 men are at stake.

"The testimony shows that there will be no difficulty in filling such of the spaces surrounding the pipes as may be deemed necessary with liquid cement of the consistency of cream, and that when pure cement is mixed to that consistency with sufficient water-proofing it will resist the entrance of water of any kind so long as it remains solid, and will be impervious to sulphur. The defendant is the owner and holder of an oil and gas lease from the owner of the farm upon which this gas well is being drilled. It has a legal right to sink its wells through the coal stratum owned by the plaintiff, but this right must be exercised with due regard to the rights of the plaintiff and to the safety of the mines and the men employed therein. (Chartiers Block Coal Company vs. Mellon, 152 Pa. 286.)

ORDER OF THE COURT.

"And now, December 27, 1910, after argument by counsel, and upon due consideration and for the reasons set forth in the opinion herewith filed, it is ordered, adjudged and decreed:

"(1)—That the injunction heretofore granted be, and the same is now, dissolved.

"(2)—That as to the well now being drilled upon the Elliott farm, it appearing to the court that the methods to be pursued hereafter cannot be adopted as to this particular well, therefore, as to this well alone, the defendant shall fill the space between the 10-inch casing and the wall of the well, and the space between the 8-inch and the 10-inch casings, with liquid cement of proper consistency, from the bottom of each of said holes to the top of said well.

"(3)—As to all future wells to be drilled by the defendant through the mines of the plaintiff, where like conditions exist as have been shown to exist by the testimony in this case, the defendant shall drill, in the first instance, a 16-inch hole to a point not less than 40 feet below the bottom of the coal seam from which the coal has been removed, and at which point a good and substantial shoulder or seat can be obtained, which hole shall be filled up with liquid cement to the floor of the coal seam, and a 14-inch pipe shall be inserted therein, and the cement from the interior of said pipe shall be removed, and between the pipe and the wall of said hole liquid cement of the proper consistency shall be poured until the space shall be filled to the surface. Within the diameter of said 14-inch pipe the hole shall be drilled to an additional depth of not less than 10 feet, and to a point where a solid shoulder or seat can be obtained on which to rest the pipe to be inserted therein, and the hole shall be filled with liquid cement to a point not less than 60 feet above the floor of said coal seam. A 10-inch pipe shall then be driven to the bottom of the hole and the cement from the interior of said pipe shall be removed, and the space between said 10-inch pipe and said 14-inch pipe shall be filled by pouring in liquid cement of such consistency that said intervening space shall be completely filled.

"(4)—Holes of the proper dimensions shall be drilled for the insertion of strings of 8-inch casing, 6⅝-inch casing and 4-inch tubing, and the intervening spaces between the walls of said holes and said strings of casing and tubing shall be left open so as to permit the escape of gas, if there be any, from the stratifications below the coal to the top of the well, the 4-inch tubing alone to be capped or closed in at the top; and each of said strings of casing and tubing shall extend from the seat on which it is placed to the surface, or top of the well. A suitable packer shall be placed in said well, so as to prevent the gas from escaping except through the 4-inch tubing.

"(5)—All wells shall be inspected daily by the employes of the defendant, and in case of the discovery of any accidents to the tubing, casings, well or appliances, whereby the gas may escape, notice thereof shall be given immediately to one of the mine foremen or mine superintendents of the plaintiff in the vicinity of said well.

"(6)—Upon the abandonment of any of said wells they shall be securely plugged above each oil and gas-bearing sand, and the intervening spaces shall be filled with cement.

"(7)—The defendant shall give bond in the sum of $10,000, with surety to be approved by the court, conditioned to pay all damages that may be recoverable legally by the plaintiff from the defendant by reason of the existence and operation of the gas well now being drilled, or of the wells hereafter to be drilled, through said coal stratum, and also that the defendant shall comply faithfully with all the terms and conditions of this decree.

"(8)—The defendant shall pay the costs of this proceeding."

NOTE:—Published through the courtesy of the Coal & Coke Operator, Pittsburg, Pa.

BARRIER PILLARS DECLARED TO BE NECESSARY IN MINES

(NOTE.—Two weeks ago we printed a paragraph referring to a decision by Judge George S. Ferris, in Luzerne county, Pa., interpreting the law relating to barrier pillars in mines in a case instituted by Mine Inspector Davis versus the Plymouth Coal Company, whose acreage adjoins that of the Lackawanna & Wilkes-Barre Coal Company. This decision is important from the fact that it is the first judicial interpretion of the act, and has aroused a great deal of interest among owners of bituminous as well as of anthracite producing mines; for which reason we publish the decision of Judge Ferris in full.—Editor C & C. O.)

The Anthracite Mining Act of June 2, 1891, P. L. 176, is entitled, "An Act—To provide for the health and safety of persons employed in and about the anthracite coal mines of Pennsylvania, and for the protection and preservation of property connected therewith."

Section 10 of Article III of this Act reads as follows:

"That it shall be obligatory on the owners of adjoining coal properties to leave, or cause to be left, a pillar of coal in each seam or vein of coal worked by them along the line of adjoining property of such width that, taken in connection with the pillar to be left by the adjoining property owner, will be a sufficient barrier for the safety of the employes of either mine in case the other should be abandoned and allowed to fill with water; such width of pillar to be determined by the engineers of the adjoining property owners, together with the inspector of the district in which the mine is situated, and the surveys of the face of the workings along such pillar shall be made in duplicate, and must practically agree. A copy of such duplicate surveys, certified to, must be filed with the owners of the adjoining properties and with the inspector of the district in which the mine or property is situated."

The bill avers that the plaintiff, being the mine inspector for the proper district, gave notice to the defendant company of a meeting to be held at which the said company was notified to instruct its engineer to be present and meet the engineer of the Lehigh & Wilkes-Barre Coal Company, the owner of an adjoining mine, for the purpose of determining the width of a barrier pillar to be left by the said two coal companies between their properties, as required by the mining act; but that the defendant company refused to permit its engineer to attend such meeting, and, generally, refused to leave any barrier pillar between its workings and those of the Lehigh & Wilkes-Barre Coal Company.

The prayers are: (1) for an injunction enjoining the defendant from working its mines or coal property adjoining the mines or coal property of the Lehigh & Wilkes-Barre Coal Company without leaving a barrier pillar of coal of the thickness or width of at least 70 feet in each vein; and (2), requiring the defendant to file with the mine inspector a certified copy of a survey, as required by law, and (3), for general relief.

To this bill the defendant has filed an answer, admitting the plaintiff's averments of fact to be true, but (1), denying the necessity for such a barrier pillar, and (2) averring that section 10 of Article III of the mining act is unconstitutional.

If constitutionality of this provision be conceded for the purpose of discussion, and if the question of the necessity for any barrier pillar at all between these properties may be regarded as an open one, the decision of that question would seem to be committed by the statute to the tribunal of experts thereby constituted, viz., the mine Inspector and the engineers of the owners of the adjoining coal properties. The purpose of the enactment is to secure the safety of the workmen in the mines. The law declares that "it shall be obligatory" on the mine owners to leave such a barrier pillar as the tribunal of mine experts referred to shall determine to be sufficient for that purpose. It is for them to fix its width. Until they say that none at all is needed for the safety of the men the obligation imposed by the statute remains.

It might, perhaps, be well argued that the legislature did not intend to impose upon the owners the burden of leaving a boundary pillar of unmined coal where it clearly appears to be unnecessary for the safety of employes. If none at all were needed it would seem idle for the inspector and engineers to fix a width of, say, one foot, for the sake, merely, of literal compliance with the statutory obligation of leaving a pillar of some width. If, therefore, we may apply the maxim that the law does not require a vain thing there is room for the construction that, in vesting in the inspector and engineers the power to determine how wide the barrier pillar should be to secure safety, the intent of the law-making power was to also empower them to say, if such be the fact, that the safety of the men does not require a barrier pillar of any width at all. Be that as it may, it is evident that the act does not warrant a mine owner in refusing to permit his engineer to participate in determining the question of the width of, or the need for, a barrier pillar simply because he, the mine owner, does not consider one necessary. In our opinion, the law requires such a pillar to be left, unless the inspector and engineers, after due examination of the premises and consideration of the subject, determine that none is needed to secure the safety of the men employed in either mine in case the other should be abandoned and allowed to fill with water.

The constitutionality of the boundary pillar provision of act is attacked npon two grounds: (1) because it is said to violate Section 10 of Article I of the Pennsylvania constitution, which provides that private property shall not be taken or applied to public use without authority of law and without just compensation being first made or secured; and (2) because it is claimed to be in conflict with the fourteenth amendment to the Federal constitution, which provides that no State shall deprive any person of life, liberty or property without due process of law.

The defendant contends that by requiring adjoining mine owners to leave a barrier pillar of coal between their workings the act deprives it of a property right, (viz: the right to mine such coal) without compensation therefore, and without due process of law.

Both the right of eminent domain and the police power of the State are attributes of sovereignty. They are inherent rights of the supreme power founded upon the social compact, and essential to any form of government.

In our jurisprudence the right of eminent domain is defined to be "the power of the State to apply private property to public purposes on payment of just compensation to the owner," (10 Am. & Eng. Encyl. Law 1047). The provision for payment of compensation, however, is no part of the power itself, but a limitation upon its use imposed by the constitution. (U. S. vs. Jones, 109 U. S. 513.)

"The police power of the State," says Judge Orlady, in Commonwealth vs. Beatty, 15 Pa. Super. 5, 15, "is difficult of definition; but it has been held by the courts to be the right to prescribe regulations for the good order, peace, health, protection, comfort, convenience and morals of the community, which does not encroach on a like power vested in Congress or State legislatures by the Federal constitution nor does it violate the provisions of the organic law; and it has been expressly held that the fourteenth amendment to the Federal constitution was not designed to interfere with the exercise of that power by the State (citing Powell vs. Pa., 127 U. S. 678; Powell vs. Com. 114 Pa. 265.) Its essential quality as a governmental agency is that it imposes upon persons and property burdens designed to promote the safety and welfare of the public at large. The principle that no person shall be deprived of life or property without due process of law was embodied, in substance, in the constitutions of nearly all, if not all, of the States at the time of the adoption of the fourteenth amendment, and it has never been regarded as incompatible with the principle, equally vital, because equally essential to the peace and safety of society, that all property in this country is held under the implied obligation that the owners use of it shall not be injurious to the community (citing Boston Beer Co. vs. Mass. 97 U. S. 25) The State still retains an interest in his (the wage earner's) welfare, however reckless he may be. The whole is no greater than the sum of all its parts, and when the individual health, safety and welfare are sacrificed the State must suffer. This declaration was adopted by the United States Supreme Court in Holden vs. Hardy, 169 U. S. 366 42 L. Ed. 780, invalidating a State statute, which limited the employment of men in underground mines, smelting works, etc., to eight hours a day."

By the decision from which we have just quoted it was held that the Act of April 29, 1897, P. L. 30, forbidding the employment of adult women for more than 12 hours a day, etc., which was not in conflict with the constitution of Pennsylvania, nor with the Federal constitution, but was a valid exercise of the police power in the interest of the public health, even though it referred to a particular class of the public, viz.: adult women engaged in the kind of employment mentioned in the act, and even though it did indirectly restrain the employe's freedom of contract.

See also in Commonwealth vs. Brown, 8 Pa. Super, 339. It was said by Judge Rice (p. 351-2) that "In the exercise of the police power of the State it (the legislature) may enact laws in the interest of public morals, and to protect the lives, health and safety of persons following specified callings, and thus indirectly interfere with freedom of contract; i. e. with individual liberty and the right to acquire and use property; but, of course, such classification with reference to occupation must be reasonable and dictated by the necessity springing from manifest peculiarities clearly distinguishing those of one class from each of other classes, and imperatively demanding legislation for each class separately that would be useless and detrimental to the others. Laws enacted in pursuance of such classification and for such purposes are, properly speaking, neither local nor special. They are general laws, because they apply alike to all that are similarly situated as to their peculiar necessities." (Ayres' Appeal, 122 Pa.

266, 281; Com. vs. Gilligan, 195 Pa. 504, 510.) The point we desire to emphasize here is, that, to be a valid exercise of the police power in the interest of the public safety, a statute need not necessarily be applicable to the whole body of the general public, but may affect a specified class only.

Thus, in Holden vs. Hardy, 169 U. S. 366, it was said by our highest court, Mr. Justice Brown speaking (page 393) that, "While the business of mining coal and manufacturing iron began in Pennsylvania as early as 1716, and in Virginia, North Carolina and Massachusetts even earlier than this, both mining and manufacturing were carried on in such a limited way, and by such primitive methods, that no special laws were considered necessary prior to the adoption of the constitution for the protection of the operatives, but in the vast proportions which these industries have since assumed it has been found that they can no longer be carried on with due regard to the safety and health of those engaged in them without special protection against the dangers necessarily incident to these employments. In consequence of this, laws have been enacted in most of the States designed to meet these exigencies, and to secure the safety of persons peculiarly exposed to these dangers. * * * In States where mining is the principal industry special provision is made for the shoring-up of dangerous walls, for ventilation shafts, means of signaling the surface, for the supply of fresh air and the elimination of dangerous gases, (etc., etc.) * * * These statutes have been repeatedly enforced by the courts of the several States, their validity assumed, and, so far as we are informed, they have been uniformly held to be constitutional." Mr. Justice Brown then refers to certain cases where such laws were held to be constitutional under the police power, among them, to Com. vs. Williams (8 Phila. 534) in which the late Judge Harding, of this Court, held the mine ventilation act of March 3, 1870, (P. L. 3,) to be a constitutional exercise of the police power.

So also, in Chicago W. & V. Coal Co. vs. People, (181 Ill. 270, 54 N. E. Repr. 96), a provision in the mining act of that State requiring the mine owner to pay the fees for the inspection of mines by a State inspector was held to be valid and constitutional under the police power, though its effect was to deprive the owner of property, to-wit, the money required to be paid as fees. It was there said, as it might equally well be said in the case at bar: "The mining of coal is recognized as a dangerous and hazardous business, and is a productive industry of the greatest importance. For many years in this State many thousands of men have been engaged in that character of work, and a proper safeguard of their lives and health is a matter of so great interest and necessity that no subject can be mentioned where there is a more positive necessity for the exercise of the police power than in seeking to subserve their safety." * * * (Speaking of the payment of the inspector's fees.) "The expense thus incurred is imposed because of the peculiar dangers of the surrounding situation, and subserves not only the interest of the miners, but alike protects the mine owner; and hence the payment of the fee (in this case, the leaving of coal for a barrier pillar) can be properly imposed upon the mine owner without violating any provision of the constitution." That case was followed by Consolidated Coal Co. vs. People, (186 Ill. 134; 57 N. E. Repr. 880), where it was held that the same mining act (which, in essentials, is similar to our own) did not deny to mine operators the equal protection of the laws, nor take their property without due process of law in violation of the fourteenth amendment of the Federal constitution.

Still closer in its facts to the case now before us is Maple vs. John, (42 W. Va. 30; 32 L. R. A. 800.) There the mining act in question provided, inter-alia, that "No owner or tenant of any land containing coal shall open, or sink, or dig, excavate or work in any coal mine or shaft on such land within five feet of the line dividing said land from that of another person or persons without the consent, in writing, of every person interested in or having title to such adjoining lands, etc." This provision was claimed to be unconstitutional as being an infringement of the rights of private property. It was held to be a proper exercise of the police power and not unconstitutional in the respect claimed, the court saying: "This is no undue assumption of the right to apply the police power to a subject which does not fall within it; for regulations (on this and other subjects mentioned) have long been recognized as wholesome and reasonable and as fit subjects for the exercise of the police power, as tending to preserve the rights of the citizen and promote the welfare of the commonwealth. The mining of coal is one of the largest industries carried on in the State. In mining, proper support and ventilation are necessary * * * for the health and safety of the miner engaged in a dangerous employment, and for that reason the public welfare requires it. * * * This rib of solid coal not to be mined into by either of the adjoining owners was to be contributed by each in equal parts for the mutual benefit of each, for the protection of the surface, to secure independent systems of ventilation, drainage and workings, and in aid of an industry so great and widely diffused that the State as a whole is interested therein. * * * This regulation works no hardship on one for the benefit of another, but is impartial, just and reasonable, imposing a common burden for the benefit of all such owners."

The police power is distinguished from the right of eminent domain in that the State, by exercising the latter right, takes private property for public use, thereby entitling the owner to compensation under the constitution; while the police power, founded, as it is, on the maxim "sic utere tuo ut alieum non laedas," is exerted to make that maxim effective by regulating the use and enjoyment of property by the owner; or if he is deprived of his property altogether, it is not taken for public use, but rather destroyed in order to conserve the safety, morals, health or general welfare of the public; and in neither case is the owner entitled to compensation, for the law either regards his loss as damnum absque injuria, or considers him sufficiently compensated by sharing in the general (and, in this case, also the specific) benefits resulting from the exercise of the police power. (22 Am. & Eng. Encycl. Law 16, and cases there cited). For example, in the case at bar, the State does not take the coal in the barrier pillar and convert it to a public use, but leaves it in the ownership and possession of the adjoining mine owners; the coal itself is not taken. The property right affected by the statute is not ownership, but use, of the material thing—the right to mine it out. Nor does the State take that right for public use. The act does not transfer the right to mine out the coal from the owner to some one else for the public benefit; but prohibits that right from being exercised by anyone—that is, destroys it to prevent a possible calamity, to-wit, the flooding of mines, and to protect the lives of that class of the general public whose safety would be thereby endangered, and, incidentally, to conserve the mine property of the owners themselves. In this latter aspect of the case the destruction of the right to mine the coal bears some analogy to the destruction of buildings to prevent another sort of calamity—a conflagration. True, in the latter case the disaster is imminent, while here it is uncertain; so that perhaps a closer analogy in that respect would be the statute law requiring fire escapes to be placed on certain structures in order to avert a possible remote catastrophe. Such laws were held to be a valid exercise of the police power of the State in Fidelity Insurance, etc., Co. vs. Fridenberg, (175 Pa. 500, 507-8).

The enactment here in question does not authorize a taking of property for public use, is not an exercise of the right of eminent domain, and, therefore, is not unconstitutional because of failure to provide for compensation; but it regulates the use of tangible property — the coal in the pillar — by requiring the owner to so use it (negatively by leaving it unmined) as not to injure the rights of others; or, in another aspect of the case, does not affect tangible property at all, but destroys an intangible property right (that of mining out the pillar coal) in the interest of the public safety. In either case it is, in our opinion, an exercise of the police power, justified by the circumstances, and not violative of either the State or the Federal constitution.

By agreement of counsel this case is to be determined as upon final hearing, the depositions taken for use, on motion, to constitute the preliminary injunction to be considered as evidence produced in open court on such hearing. In pursuance of this agreement of counsel, and upon admissions contained in the answer and from the testimony, we make the following findings of fact:

1 — The plaintiff is the mine inspector of the ninth sub-district of the first anthracite coal inspection district of Pennsylvania; and the Plymouth Coal Company, defendant, and the Lehigh & Wilkes-Barre Coal Company are mining corporations of this Commonwealth, each employing more than 10 persons.

2 — The said two coal companies are owners, proprietors, lessees and occupiers of adjoining coal properties in the borough of Plymouth, Luzerne county, Pennsylvania, and within the limits of the said sub-district of the first anthracite coal inspection district.

3 — The plaintiff, as said mine inspector, gave to the president of the defendant company a written notice, dated August 31, 1909, stating that a meeting would be held at the former's office on September 2, 1909, for the purpose of deciding upon the width of a boundary pillar of coal to be left between the coal properties of the said two companies, pursuant to the provisions of Section 10 of Article III of the Anthracite Mining Act of 1891, a copy of said section being embodied in the notice and requested that the defendant's engineer be instructed to attend such meeting to consult with the engineer of the Lehigh & Wilkes-Barre Coal Company for the purpose aforesaid.

4 — The defendant company declined to permit its engineer to attend such meeting, and refuses to leave any unmined coal as part of a boundary pillar between its coal property and that of the Lehigh & Wilkes-Barre Coal Company, claiming a legal right to mine to the boundary line of its property, and denying the constitutionality of Section 10, Article III of the said Mining Act.

5 — No determination of the width of, or necessity for, such boundary pillar has been made, as required by the act, up to the time of filing the bill in this case, nor has it been made since, so far as the court is advised.

Conclusions of law:

1 — Section 10 of Article III of the Anthracite Mining Act of June 2, 1891, (P. L. 176), is a valid exercise of the police power of the State, and is not in conflict with the constitution of Pennsylvania.

2 — That enactment requires a boundary pillar of coal to be left unmined between the mine working of the defendant company and the Lehigh & Wilkes-Barre Coal Company of such width as the proper mine inspector and the engineers of the said two companies shall deem necessary to the safety of the men employed in either mine in case the other should be abandoned and allowed to fill with water, unless, after due investigation and consultation, they shall decide that no such barrier pillar is required to insure the safety of such employes upon the happening of the contingency stated in the act. The same act requires the making by said engineers and inspector of duplicate surveys of the fact of the workings along such pillar, and the filing of a copy of the same with the owners of the adjoining properties and with the mine inspector.

3 — The preliminary injunction heretofore granted should be continued until

the width of such a boundary pillar, or the absence of necessity for one, shall have been determined by said inspector and engineers, and surveys made and filed as required by the act, or until they shall duly decide that no such pillar is needed for the safety of the employes of either mine.

4 — The costs of this proceeding should be paid by the defendant.

And now, April 18, 1910, the prothonotary is directed to file of record in this case the foregoing findings, both of fact and law, and thereupon to enter the following decree nisi, and give notice to the parties or their counsel, in accordance with Rule 63 of Equity Practice.

DECREE.

Now, April 18, 1910, this cause having come on to be heard, and having been argued by counsel, upon consideration thereof it is ordered, adjudged and decreed,

1 — That the injunction heretofore granted be, and the same is hereby, continued until further order of the court, without prejudice, however, to the right of the defendant to apply to the court for dissolution or modification thereof, upon showing to the satisfaction of the court that the proper mine inspector and the engineers of the defendant company and the Lehigh & Wilkes-Barre Coal Company have, upon due investigation and consultation, determined that a barrier pillar of less width than that stated in the injunction (that is, less than 70 feet on defendant's property) is sufficient for the protection of the men employed in the mines of either company in case the mine of the other should be abandoned and allowed to fill with water, and have made duplicate surveys and filed copies of the same, as required by law, or, upon such investigation and consultation, shall have decided that no such barrier pillar is necessary to the safety of the employes of either company in the event aforesaid.

2 — That the costs of this proceeding be paid by the defendant.

By the Court,

FERRIS, J.

NOTE:— Published through the courtesy of the Coal & Coke Operator, Pittsburg, Pa., issue of May 10, 1910.

(Published in the Coal Trade Bulletin, Pittsburgh, Pa.)

IMPORTANT RULING ON MINING QUESTION.

In an opinion handed down by Judge J. A. McIlvaine at Washington, Pa., it is held that the owner of a vein of coal, in the proper use of it for mining or any lawful purpose, may cut off or divert subterranean streams of water flowing through it, without any responsibility either to the surface owner or to a neighbor whom that flow of water might, undisturbed, have reached. The case in which this decision is given is that of B. C. Winnett against the Monongahela River Consolidated Coal & Coke Co.

Winnett is the owner of a farm of 70 acres in East Pike Run township. The land is crossed by a natural water course which heretofore had furnished an abundance of water for stock and other needed purposes. Further up the stream and adjoining the Winnett farm is the tract known as the "Jefferson Duvall" farm. The Monongahela River Consolidated Coal & Coke Co., several years ago, became the owner of the Pittsburg vein of coal under the Duvall farm. In the mining of the coal under this farm it is claimed that the work was done in such a manner as to cause the surface to crack, and to such an extent that the water flowing along the natural water-course emptied into the mine of the defendant company, leaving the surface watercourse dry where it traverses the plaintiff's land.

The plaintiff alleging that on account of this wrongful act his land had become barren and unproductive, entered suit against the defendant, claiming, $5,000 damages. The case came on for trial at the May term and the plaintiff submitted his testimony, whereupon the defendant moved the court for a compulsory non-suit. The motion was sustained and a non-suit entered.

The court in overruling the motion to lift the non-suit holds that the surface owner, having conveyed the vein of coal with the right to mine it without supplying artificial supports for the surface and released all damage arising therefrom, the defendant company in mining the coal was making a proper use of its own property and the damage that was done to the springs, so far as the evidence shows, was unavoidable and in no way could be attributed to its negligence; that in the absence of any proof of negligence or malice which resulted in the injury complained of, the principle of injury without wrong applies.

B. C. Winnett,
vs.
The Monongahela River Consolidated Coal & Coke Company.

In the Court of Common Pleas of Washington County, Pa.
No. 53 February Term, 1910.

ACTION IN TRESPASS.—MOTION TO LIFT COMPULSORY NON-SUIT.

OPINION.

McIlvaine, P. J.

The plaintiff's statement in this case reads as follows:

"The plaintiff, B. C. Winnett, claims of the defendant company (The Monongahela River Consolidated Coal & Coke Company), the sum of Five Thousand ($5000.00) Dollars, which is justly due and payable to the plaintiff by the defendant company, upon the cause of action whereof the following is a statement:

"The plaintiff, B. C. Winnett, is and has been for some years the owner of a farm situate in East Pike Run township, Washington County, Pa., which farm contains seventy acres, more or less, and until recently was valuable for the purposes of farming and grazing. Said land is crossed by a creek, a stream or natural water-course, which heretofore furnished an abundance of water for the stock kept on said farm, and for other needed purposes.

"Farther up said stream and adjoining the Winnett farm, is the tract known as the 'Jefferson Duvall Farm.' Several years ago the defendant company, by purchase, became the owner of the Pittsburg or River Vein of Coal underlying the said Duvall Farm. Within the past five years, while B. C. Winnett, the plaintiff, was in possession of his said land, the said defendant company mined at least a portion of the coal underlying the 'Duvall Farm' aforesaid. This mining was done in such a manner as to cause the surface of the Duvall land to crack in various places and to such an extent that all the water flowing along the creek or natural water-course hereinbefore mentioned, was diverted from its course and emptied into the mine of said defendant company, leaving the said water-course dry as it passes through plaintiff's land.

"On account of this wrongful act done by the said defendant company and by its workmen and employes, the plaintiff herein has been greatly damaged by having the flow of the water along said natural water-course cut off, thus depriving him of the water supply to which by law and justice he is entitled. Plaintiff alleges that because of this unlawful act of the defendant company, his land has become barren and unproductive, his cattle have suffered from drought, his tenants have refused to remain on the farm, and the value of his said property has greatly depreciated.

"On this account, the plaintiff has been damaged to the extent of $5,000.00 for which sum he brings this suit."

To this statement the defendant pleaded not guilty, and upon the issue thus joined the cause came on for trial and the plaintiff submitted his testimony, whereupon the defendant moved the Court for a compulsory non-suit, which motion was sustained and a non-suit entered. The plaintiff now moves the Court to lift that non-suit and allow the case to be again submitted to a jury for its determination.

The evidence offered by the plaintiff showed that he became the owner of the property which he now complains was injured in October, 1900, and that the defendant became the owner of the coal underlying the Duvall farm in the year 1899. When the plaintiff purchased his farm, the grantor reserved the Pittsburg or River Vein of coal under it, "together with the free and uninterrupted right of way into, upon and under said land, at such places and in such manner as may be proper and necessary for the purpose of digging, mining and taking away said coal, hereby waiving all damages arising therefrom; also the privilege of removing through and under said premises adjoining coal belonging to said parties of the first part or their assigns."

Jefferson Duvall when he sold the coal under his farm also conveyed to the purchaser full mining rights and waived any claim for damages that might be done to the surface by reason of the mining of the coal, and the title to this coal with all these rights vested in the defendant company in 1899.

The testimony further showed that the Winnett farm was situated on either side of this small water-course and that the Duvall farm which contained about 400 acres was above the Winnett farm, and that the head of the stream or water-course was about one mile from the Winnett farm and that the watershed which fed this one mile of water course with surface water was composed of this Duvall farm and one or two other farms. Besides the rainfall which fed this stream, a number of springs from the Duvall farm flowed into this natural water-course. Between four and five years ago the stream in dry weather became dry and has continued so up to the present time; but in times of heavy rains water still flowed during that time along the water-course. Between the time that the owners of the surface of the Duvall farm severed their coal from the surface and the present time, a large amount of the coal underlying both these farms has been mined and carried away. The consequence was that the springs of water which flowed out of the Duvall farm and also the springs of water which flowed out of the Winnett farm ceased to run and were no longer available as a source of supply of water to course along this water-way, and the only water that did flow along it was that which was supplied from the surface at the time of heavy rains. The evidence of the plaintiff showed that there was a number of cracks in the surface of the Duvall farm and it could be fairly inferred that there had been a subsidence of the surface caused by the removal of the coal and the failure to substitute artificial supports therefor It showed that one of these cracks at least was across the bed of this natural water-way. The plaintiff's claim was that the defendant's mining operations under the Duvall farm had depleted the supply of water that came from the springs on the Duvall farm and that this crack across the water-way to some extent allowed any surface water or other water that might flow down the stream from above to disappear down the opening. The evidence clearly established that the springs on the Jefferson Duvall farm did cease to flow and the water supply from that source was not available for the last four or five years. It did not show, however, that the crack across the natural water-way prevented the surface water from flowing down the stream at the time of freshets, because it was testified to by a number of witnesses that water did appear and was present in the water-course on the Winnett farm after heavy rains, and on the day the jury visited the premises under the direction of the Court, water was visible in the stream on the Winnett farm which had been supplied by the flow from above by reason of a rain that had recently fallen. The evidence further showed that this crack that was across the water-way was so diminutive in size that it could have been very easily and without any great expense stopped up, so that the flow of water down the natural water-way would in no way whatever be interfered with. It therefore followed that the only real cause of complaint on the part of the plaintiff was the destruction of the springs on the Duvall farm which constantly flowed down the stream and supplied water for the stock of the Duvall farm. This then raises the question whether there was any evidence in the plaintiff's case to show that the defendant company had committed a wrong when it destroyed those springs. In considering this question, it will be observed that the defendant purchased and had a right under its title to remove all the coal under the Duvall farm without substituting any artificial support, and that the surface owner had specifically waived all right to damages on account of any injury that might result from a subsidence of the surface. It is clear therefore that there was no evidence in the case to show or from which it could be fairly inferred, that the defendant company had done any wrong whatever to the surface owner of the Duvall farm. Another thing that the testimony of the plaintiff failed to show, and that was when the coal was mined out under the Duvall farm which caused the subsidence of the surface which made the cracks that were visible thereon. It also failed to show whether or not the loss of the springs could be fairly attributed to the subsidence of the surface rather than to the striking of subterranean streams of water that fed the springs in the mining of the coal. Indeed, the testimony of the plaintiff as to the defendant mining coal under the Duvall farm is to be found in that of a single witness whose testimony amounted substantially to the fact that he had helped to mine coal under the Duvall farm within the last three or four years while in the employ of the defendant company; but his testimony was so meager and so indefinite as to throw no light upon the question whether or not the evidence of subsidence that appeared on the surface was directly attributable to any work done by the defendant company within the last six years, and it was admitted that there had been mining of coal under the Duvall farm prior to that period. This in our opinion left the plaintiff's claim without any substantial evidence to support it, for it is clearly the law that the owner of a vein of coal, in the proper use of it for mining or any other lawful purpose, may cut off or divert subterranean streams of water flowing through it, without any responsibility either to the surface owner or to a neighbor whom that flow of water might undisturbed have reached.

It will be observed that the plaintiff does not claim in his statement that there was any negligence on the part of the defendant in conducting its mining operations, nor was there a scintilla of proof that such negligence existed, and the fair inference from the testimony is that the defendant company in mining the coal from under the Duvall farm, in the absence of any proof to the contrary, mined it in a proper and workmanlike manner and entirely within their rights. And such being the fact, we are unable to see any evidence in this case of any wrong done by the defendant that could be made the basis of the plaintiff's action.

"Every man has the right to the natural, proper and profitable use of his own land, and if in the course of such use, without negligence or malice, unavoidable loss is brought upon his neighbor, it is *damnum absque injuria*. This is a universal rule of the common law, and nowhere is it more strictly enforced than in Pennsylvania. After elaborate and repeated argument and the most mature consideration, it was applied to a case admittedly of great hardship, difficulty and doubt, involving a serious choice of evils in the Pennsylvania Coal Company vs. Sanderson, 133 Pa. 136. No ordinary case could be sufficient to raise a further doubt on its application where the use is proper and the damage unavoidable."

The coal under the Duvall farm was only about 65 feet under the surface. The surface owner had conveyed this vein of coal with the right to mine it all without supplying artificial supports for the surface and released all damage that might be done to the surface by reason of the mining of the coal or the removal of the support to the surface; and this being the case, the defendant company in mining the coal was making a proper use of its own property and the damage that was done to the springs, so far as the evidence shows, was unavoidable and in no way could be attributed to its negligence; and this being the case, we think the principle laid down in the case referred to is applicable: that is, that in the absence of any proof of negligence or malice in the mining of the coal which resulted in the injury complained of, the principle of *damnum absque injuria* applies.

A reason why we think it is equitable under the facts of this case to apply this principle is found in the fact that the plaintiff himself was the owner of surface that had been severed from the same vein of coal and the owner of that vein of coal in his purchase of it had obtained the same rights to mine the coal without supplying artificial supports and with a release of damages to the surface; and in the further fact that the springs on his farm which supplied the flow of water in this natural water-course had been destroyed by mining operations under his farm, and his grantor's vendee had lessened the flow of water that would reach his neighbor below and also had lessened the water for the stock on his own farm. This being the case, it is plain that such a rule should be adopted in the interests of mining developments as would not result in holding the owner of an adjoining farm liable for destroying the supply of water that would run to the farm immediately below, but would allow the owner of that farm, or the vendee of his grantor, to do the same thing to the landowner below him which he now complains was a wrong on the part of the owner of the land above him.

And now, August 10, 1910, this motion came on to be heard and was argued by counsel, whereupon, upon due consideration, it is ordered, adjudged and decreed that the same be overruled and that judgment be entered for the defendant and against the plaintiff for costs.

BY THE COURT.

The following decisions were rendered by the Athens County, Ohio, Circuit Court at the October term 1909 and the January term of 1910, and will, no doubt, be of interest to Lessors and Lessees of Mining Properties.

ATHENS COUNTY, OHIO, CIRCUIT COURT.

(October Term, 1909)

CHERRINGTON, JONES, WALTERS, JJ.

WILLIAM H. ALLISON, et al., *Plaintiffs,*

vs.

THE LUHRIG COAL COMPANY, *Defendant.*

DECISION OF THE COURT.

JONES, J.

This case comes into this court on appeal from the Common Pleas Court.

William H. Allison, and the other plaintiffs in this case, are the owners and successors to one Dorcas Allison, as lessor, of about twelve hundred acres of land described in the petition in this case.

In the second amended petition the plaintiffs, among other things, say that the lands described are chiefly valuable as coal and mining lands, that there is situated upon said lands a shaft and coal mine and entries from and through which the coal underlying said lands can be removed, and that the value of said lands to the plaintiffs' depends largely upon the maintenance of the same in such condition that the coal underlying the whole of said lands may be easily and readily removed through and by means of the mine situated upon said lands.

On the 27th day of December, 1892, Dorcas Allison, the original lessor of these premises leased them to the Athens Coal Company for a period of thirty years. So much of said original lease as is applicable to the questions raised here, I will briefly refer to. Under the terms of that lease it seems that Dorcas Allison leased this property to the Athens Coal Company for the period mentioned for the purpose of mining, excavating, removing and selling coal therefrom and manufacturing and selling coke, and, together with that, gave the lessee company all of the necessary rights for the purpose of removing coal therefrom, upon condition that The Athens Coal Company, the original lessee, its successors and assigns, should not commit any waste upon the premises. It was covenanted in the original lease referred to, among other things, that the lessee would sink a working shaft, or shafts, for the purpose of mining coal upon said premises and operating upon said premises for the production and shipment of coal therefrom at the earliest practicable period; that it would operate a mine or mines thereon in a workmanlike manner and to the best interest of both parties to said lease. The lease provided for a royalty of seven cents per ton upon all the lump tonnage mined, provided there should be at least seventy-five tons of lump coal mined in a working day, or in lieu thereof it provided for a dead royalty of seven cents per ton in the event the coal was not mined. Among other things, the original lessee covenanted that the mining tools, implements and machinery on said premises when this original lease was made should be utilized for the purpose of operating said mines, and upon the abandonment or termination thereof should revert to the lessor, her heirs and assigns.

The original lessee, The Athens Coal Company of Ohio, subsequently transferred its rights under the lease as lessee to The Athens Coal Company of

West Virginia. Later, that company transferred and assigned its rights under the original lease to the defendant in this case, The Luhrig Coal Company. Subsequent to the execution of the original lease, Dorcas Allison and The Luhrig Coal Company entered into a supplemental lease, by the provisions of which the lessor of these lands, Dorcas Allison, covenanted to allow the defendant lessee the privilege of cutting the barriers between the property of the lessor and the adjoining property and gave the lessee the right to remove and transport coal from the adjoining property through the underground entries and subways on the lands of Dorcas Allison, which lands I shall hereafter call the Allison tract, up through and out of the shaft located on the Allison property. For this privilege the lessee in the supplemental lease agreed to pay the sum of one cent per ton for the transportation of that coal, and it was further stipulated that it should mine one hundred and fifty tons every working day, instead of seventy-five tons as was provided for in the original lease, and pay sevent cents per ton for all the coal mined, and in lieu thereof a dead royalty of seven cents per ton upon an equivalent of one hundred and fifty tons of coal per working day. This supplemental lease contained a provision that the covenants and stipulations provided for in the supplemental lease should be an enlargement of the rights, privileges and easements granted by the original lease. Those were the salient covenants, so far as the disposition of this case is concerned, contained in the original and supplemental leases, and under which the rights of the plaintiffs and the defendant in this case must be worked out.

The petition of the plaintiffs in this case, after reciting the history of the execution and transfers of these leases, and giving the terms therein contained, alleges that the defendant company has ceased to operate the mine upon the premises granted to its predecessor by Mrs. Allison in 1892, and that it owns adjoining lands, adjoining the Allison tract, and that it threatens to and is about to, and has, in fact, extended its entries from the adjoining tract, which The Luhrig Coal Company is now operating, into the leased property covered by the original lease, belonging to Mrs. Dorcas Allison. It further alleges that the action of the defendant company in this behalf will cause irreparable injury to the plaintiffs in this case, who are now the owners and stand in the shoes of the original lessor, in this, to-wit: That the plaintiffs in order to mine and remove the minerals from under their lands would have to drive the entries upon the Allison tract through the entries made by the defendant upon the Allison tract, leading from the shaft of The Luhrig Coal Company upon the adjoining territory; that the driving of the entries from the Allison tract to reach the coal upon their premises through entries so made by The Luhrig Coal Company would be extremely dangerous to life and property, and that it would increase the dangers from gases, from explosion and from fire upon the premises of the plaintiffs. They allege that the plaintiffs' land has been made less valuable as a mining property by reason of the action of the defendant inasmuch as the mining system, which belongs to the Allison tract, and is an integral part thereof, would be damaged by allowing it to be disturbed by the entries made by the defendant company in the maintenance of a system upon its own tract and adjoining. Those are the allegations of the petition.

The answer in the case denies every vital point that is alleged in the petition with the exception of the ownership of these various properties and the execution of these leases.

Some testimony was offered upon the trial of this case, and it was admitted in open court by counsel, that the original tract granted by Dorcas Allison, the lessor, to the lessee contained about twelve hundred acres of mineral stone coal, and that about the time this suit was brought about one hundred acres of that property had been mined over by the defendant and its predecessors. Other testimony was proffered by the plaintiff in this case tending to show that the property of the plaintiffs would be damaged and an irreparable injury would accrue to this property should the actions of the defendant company be permitted. In a series of questions asked by counsel for the plaintiffs, testimony was proffered to prove that by means of the connection of the plaintiffs' property with the mines on the defendant's property on adjoining territory that the mining system laid out upon the property of the Allison's would be disturbed and, in effect, destroyed, and especially would be affected injuriously to the plaintiffs, and that if such entries were permitted to be driven upon the property of the Allisons' that gases would accumulate upon the property to such an extent that it might prove dangerous to life as well as property. That class of testimony was objected to and this court, upon the hearing of the case, sustained the objection to that testimony, and it was not permitted to be given. So that the questions contended for by counsel upon both sides, both for the plaintiffs and the defendant in this case, arise primarily upon the construction of the original lease and the supplemental lease, executed after the original lease.

The question in this case is whether or not a defendant lessee, who owns adjoining property to another, of which he is also the lessee, will be permitted, in the absence of express and positive stipulations to that effect, to use entries upon the second property for the purpose of mining and removing coal out of the adjacent property. As in this case, assuming that The Luhrig Coal Company is the owner of both leases, namely, the Allison lease together with that of the adjoining property, the question is whether or not The Luhrig Coal Company is permitted, under the construction of these two leases, to enter upon the property of the Allisons and remove the coal underlying the Allison property through entries upon the Allison property out into the Luhrig property and through the Luhrig shafts. The counsel for the defendant claims as a proposition of law that in the absence of positive restrictions to the contrary in the lease that an adjoining lessee, owning both leases, may mine not only upon the Allison territory but upon the adjoining territory as well, that he has that right by implication of law; and it is further contended that if he has not that right by implication that the construction of these two leases would give him the right, inasmuch as by the provisions of the supplemental lease Dorcas Allison, the original lessor, did give the right to cut the barriers between the two properties for the purpose of removing coal from the adjoining property through her property, and therefore an implication would arise that the coal could be carried the other way, from the Allison property, out through the barriers through the Luhrig property. The plaintiffs' counsel deny this contention. They claim as a proposition of law that no implication arises by which the owner of the adjoining property can mine over into another. Second, they claim that a proper construction of the covenant of these two leases would necessitate a holding to the effect that by the original lease The Luhrig Coal Company, and its predecessors, were bound to take out the coal from the Allison property through shafts placed upon that property.

That is the question which we are called upon to decide. There are no positive stipulations, no restrictions regulating the right of mining and transporting from adjoining property through the Allison property found in either the original or supplemental lease. If The Luhrig Coal Company has this right, we must find it has such by implication or by the construction of the two leases in question. As I say, there are no restrictions found in either of these leases, nor are there any positive or direct covenants in any wise referring to that fact.

In our judgment, and we have paid some considerable attention to the legal side of this question, The Luhrig Coal Company, under the allegations, at least, made in this petition, together with the evidence proffered upon the trial, have no right to use adjoining property for the purpose of entering the Allison lands to remove this coal. The reasons for this will be stated briefly. The original lease of Dorcas Allison to The Athens Coal Company, which is now held by the defendant in this case, covered an acreage of some twelve hundred acres of coal. That lease provided, among other things, that it should hold this tract of land for a period of thirty years; that the lessee should erect a shaft, or shafts, upon that territory within a practicable period, and that it should continue mining operations thereon. In other words, it provided, to use the language of the lease, that it should operate to the best interests of both parties the twelve hundred acre tract in question, not any particular tract but the twelve hundred acres, or all that is mentioned and described in the original lease. That lease provided, among other things, also, that the mining tools, implements and machinery upon the property at the time that the original lease was executed should be used in the operation of this property and should be returned or revert to the lessor upon the abandonment or forfeiture of this lease.

Now, we have a number of authorities on the converse of this proposition, namely, that where a lessee owns two leases that he has the right to use the underground passages or the chambers left after taking out the coal in an entry, for the purpose of entering other territory and removing it out through shafts of the lessee. In other words, it was decided in the case of Lillibridge et al., v. Lackawanna Coal Company, 143 Pa., p. 293, that the lessee, without any express stipulation, had the right, under a lease, in effect, to use the vacant chamber made by the excavation of the coal in an entry and so much of the overlying strata to remove coal from adjoining territory; but neither in that case, and in no other case, has the court gone farther than to lay down the doctrine within that strict limitation, and it is stipulated by the learned judge in that case that even in that event if any damage or injury is done to the surface owner that such can not be done; that the only right the lessee has is merely to use the vacant chamber, and he has that right by reason of the fact that he is supposed to have the title to the coal and, having the title to the coal, he has, as well, the title to the vacant chamber, which constituted the entry. The Supreme Court of Ohio adopted that rule in this state in the case of Moore v. The Indian Camp Coal Company, and in the syllabus of that case it is found, (and I say this is the converse of the proposition which we have in hand here), that while the lessee has a right to use the vacant chamber for the purpose of reaching adjoining property, it can not do so if in doing so it would result in injury to the owners of the surface. Now, stating the same doctrine conversely and the right of the lessee upon adjoining property to pass through barriers on that property into the lands of another, of which it is also the lessee, shall we apply as strict a rule? It seems to me that the rule ought to be at least as strict for the reason that in the second case, as in the case we have here, under the original or parent lease is a provision for the working of the mines, erection of the shafts and maintenance of the structures upon the property. Conceding for a moment that an implication would arise that in the event no substantial injury should be done by The Luhrig Coal Company to the Allison tract that they might have the right to enter upon the property in taking out this coal, we are quite confident that there can be no case found, or at least we have not been able to find any, which would permit that to be done to the substantial injury to the first leased, contiguous property. When Dorcas Allison executed this original lease it was contemplated by the parties that the entire property should be mined as a whole mining system. Its entries and rooms and side entries were all constructed, no doubt, with relation to the shaft placed upon that property, or which might be placed upon the property. Now, then, when a second lease should have been obtained upon an adjoining property by the owner of the first lease, his interest must necessarily clash with that of the first property leased, for the reason that in extending his entries from the second property into the first he would deem it convenient, looking to the profitable mining of the coal throughout the second shaft, to use it to the interest of the second shaft, which might be injurious to the owner of the first property, as in this case. Suppose that The Luhrig Coal Company in extending its entries into the Allison property has abandoned the Allison property for mining purposes, as it is conceded in this case, abandoned not the lease, but having abandoned that portion of the mining shaft which is located on the Allison land, suppose under those conditions, as they are conceded to be in this case, that The Luhrig Coal Company should extend its entries upon the Allison tract for the purpose of mining the coal from the Allison tract through the second leased tract, there would be a clash of interest between the lessor of the first and lessee of the second. Having abandoned the mining property on the first, it would be, and it should be, the duty of the lessee of the second tract to take the coal out of the first most conveniently and most profitably to the lessee, it would be but natural, and for that reason we think that it comes within the doctrine laid down in these various cases whereby the interest of all parties must be protected. It was not provided in the original lease by Dorcas Allison that any other property should be mined, but that they should mine the coal from under her own land. There is no express provision of that kind so that question would arise, conceding now, as I do for the purposes of this case, that ordinarily they have the right by implication to enter upon the adjoining property, they would have no right where it would do some substantial injury to the property of the first lessor. Testimony was proffered in this case to show substantial injury. The view that the Court had at that time foreclosed the plaintiffs from offering that testimony, and we are satisfied now that this court was in error. Having examined the law of the case, we are satisfied that if the plaintiffs could show substantial injury to the owner of the first leased mine, namely, the Allison tract, in support of the allegations of this petition this court should have allowed them to do it in support of the injunction to restrain The Luhrig Coal Company from operating upon that property. There was something said that the supplemental lease contained a provision of this kind, namely, that an implication might arise by which the owners of this second leased property could enter the first property because of the fact in the supplemental lease is found a provision by which Dorcas Allison consented that the barriers should be broken and the coal transported from adjoining property through her own, and that a consideration was paid for that. That is true, but that provision of the lease has become, admittedly in this case, inoperative for the reason that it is not transported through the shaft on the Allison property, and the shaft itself, as I understand, has been abandoned.

The question that we decide in this case is this. Dorcas Allison, the original lessor, and her successors in title, the plaintiffs in this case, at this time have such an interest in this property that it must be protected against rival interests, as held by The Luhrig Coal Company; that she did not grant the right to have her coal taken out by any other methods or means than by a shaft upon her own premises and under the construction of the covenants in the original lease.

I have gone a little more fully than I intended into these questions because we are not going to decide this case finally at this time, but have undertaken to give our views of the law of this case, and if we should find that the testimony proffered by the plaintiffs below was of such a character that it would do some appreciable injury to the rights of this lessor of this Allison tract we think that an injunction should issue restraining the defendant from further mining operations upon this property through lands of The Luhrig Coal Company, but inasmuch as we foreclosed any testimony upon this question, either upon the part of the plaintiffs or the defendant, and in view of the fact that the answer in this case contains sweeping allegations upon the question of damage and the vital questions in the petition, the only thing we can see that we can do, in justice to all parties, and allow them to make a record in this case, is to hold this case for further hearing. I want to state further that the reason we made the holding upon the evidence before was upon the assumption that upon the final argument of this case the defendant would show that it was not a trespasser, but had the right to enter upon the premises. Of course, if that were true, our holding would have been proper that they would have been relegated for their damages to a court of law. But now upon the consideration of that question we think if the facts should sustain the pleadings in this case, then the facts become vital and the parties should be heard.

The only thing probably that we can do at this time, unless counsel could themselves agree upon an amicable arrangement, is to allow the order to stand practically as made by the Common Pleas Court until the further hearing of this case. It may be that this case can be closed and counsel can prepare a short agreed statement of facts upon the question of damage, etc., from which the case can be taken directly and at once to the Supreme Court, and in that event they can do it. The only thing we can do is to leave the case open.

The case possibly had better be continued.

CIRCUIT COURT, ATHENS COUNTY, OHIO.

January Term, 1910.

Cherrington, Walters, Jones, JJ.

William H. Allison, et al.,
Plaintiffs,

vs.

The Luhrig Coal Company,
Defendant.

DECISION OF THE COURT.

Jones, J.

This same case was before us at a former term of this court, at which term it was partially disposed of. The question came up at that time upon the proffering of certain testimony on the part of the plaintiffs in the case seeking to establish the fact that The Luhrig Coal Company by driving its entries upon the Allison tracts would accomplish some substantial injury to the Allison property. Upon that question this court construed the two leases, and really passed upon what we concede to be the law of the case. The case was continued to this term for the purpose of hearing this testimony, and what I shall have to say will be merely supplemental to the opinion rendered at the former term and will be rather brief.

The real engagement in this action was the skirmish that took place upon the law at the former term and, in our judgment, disposes of the whole case.

The plaintiffs sought to introduce this testimony as to substantial injury, and I might say that were we driven to the question, which we are not, we would very probably hold that no substantial or appreciable injury would have to be shown in a case of this kind, and for this reason: That in neither the original or supplemental lease was there any covenant whatever allowing The Luhrig Coal Company the privilege of making this instroke upon the Allison property. There was a covenant permitting them to go from the Allison property through barriers upon the Luhrig property, but that is quite a different proposition from the case here. The Allison people could very well provide for the integrity of their property by permitting the haulage merely to be made through their barriers from the adjoining property, but this question is of more moment than the former for this reason, that it can not be said that by reason of the coveant that allows the defendant to go from the Allison property to the Luhrig property, then by implication arises this covenant that allows them to go from the Luhrig to the Allison property because the damage may be more substantial and far more appreciable than in the first instance, for having permitted them to cross barriers into the Allison property would permit them to enter upon any mining system the Luhrig people might see fit, and we construe these leases then principally upon that question, that there was no positive covenant permitting this last act on the part of the Luhrig Company, and inasmuch as the original and supplemental leases of the Allison tract were based upon not merely property as leased property, but upon property as a mining property. The original lease contemplated not only the mere leasing of the property, but the leasing of the property as a mining property and a going concern, and that being the case we construe it as the lower court did, that this property ought to be held intact so far as possible and that its own mining system should be located on it in the construction of this lease.

The testimony of George Harrison is offered in this case by way of deposition. A great many exceptions were taken in that deposition, and I will say we overruled all of them with the exception of two. Question 110, on cross-examination, the exception to that question by the plaintiff will be sustained. Question 254, on re-direct examination, the exception of the defendant to that question and answer will be sustained.

Now, the facts in this case are rather brief, as we heard them, and revolve around the question whether any injury was done to this property. The testimony shows that The Luhrig Coal Company through shafts upon the Luhrig property was in the process of driving entries from the Luhrig property on the southeast into the Allison property; and, also, there was another entry being driven into what is known as the 50-acre tract lying east and northeast of the Allison property. We find the facts to be in this case that as a matter of fact the system of mining adopted and pursued by The Luhrig Coal Company does constitute an appreciable and substantial injury to this property, and that if the mining system as proposed should be pursued that there would be irreparable injury. We think this injury and the damage to the property falls probably in three classes: First, we think the testimony shows that some increased damage would occur and accrue to the property if this system should be driven into the Allison property and afterwards should be attempted to be connected up in any way with the Allison system. We think, also, that the system of ventilation that the Allison property might hereafter adopt would be affected materially and injuriously by coming in contact with the old system that has been driven, and possibly might be abandoned, by the Luhrig people. We think, too, there would be an increased burden placed upon the Allison tract by reason of this fact, and it would require the Allison people to so connect and carry on their operations with regard to any excavations that might have been made thereto-fore by the Luhrig people, and in this way, we think there would be not only more burden imposed upon the Allison property, but it would materially affect its value.

The great trouble in this case is that the theory upon which the defendant's counsel are proceeding is based upon a wrong basis entirely. It is possibly true if the Luhrig people pursued their system of mining in a workmanlike manner until the Allison property were exhausted, and if there should be no abandonment by the Luhrig people any time hereafter of this property, and if the system of mining that is now adopted by the Luhrig people and pursued by them in their excavations upon the Allison property should always be done and carried on to the very end, that there possibly might be no damage, but under this original lease there can be no question but that a possibility might arise that The Luhrig Coal Company might at any time abandon the entire property. That being the case, the Allison people would have to conduct their mining operations with regard to the mining system employed by the Luhrig people, and, I say, it is upon the theory that the integrity of the Allison property would never be disturbed that this case has been tried by the defense in this court.

Now, other facts were required to be passed upon probably. There is the 106-acre tract belonging to the Allison people that is connected in a slight degree with the main body of the property. We find from the testimony of the plaintiffs' witnesses as well as of the civil engineer of the defendant company that that 106 acres can be mined practically from entries driven from the Allison shaft.

Now, as to the other tract. The 50-acre tract is disconnected and detached entirely from the main body of the Allison coal. We find as a matter of fact that a shaft driven upon this fifty acres could not be driven so as to mine the coal underlying the fifty acres both practically and profitably. We think that the fair weight of the testimony goes to show that if you consider merely the coal underlying the fifty acres that that coal can not be mined profitably, but in our view of the law of the case that would not be an item that would affect the final issue in this case. In the first place, as I have indicated, we would probably hold there would be no covenants permitting them to enter it in this manner, that they had no right to, but we find as a special finding of fact that this fifty acres has an additional value by reason of its contiguous surroundings. There is evidence going to show a shaft has been begun on this property, and we have the testimony of one witness that this shaft should be sunk on this fifty acres for the purpose of mining this fifty acres of coal and that under the terms of the supplemental lease that shaft should be utilized for the purpose, as Mr. Rowland has stated, of hauling coal from outlying territory. Then there would be a special value there, which would include not only the royalty for the coal taken out of the fifty acres but the additional haulage royalty provided for by the supplemental lease. They would be permitted to get that if the shaft should be sunk on the fifty acres, but would not be permitted to get it if the mining operations should be carried on as the Luhrig people are now doing.

I believe those are all of the facts that this court is required to pass upon, and it follows as a matter of course that the judgment will have to be as indicated by us in our opinion at the former term, and that is that the Luhrig people by means of these entries upon its own property should not be permitted to drive its mining system, or these entries, into any tracts of the Allison property, and the decree may be prepared accordingly.

ADDRESS OF GEO. HARRISON, President.

TO THE MEMBERS OF THE MINE INSPECTORS' INSTITUTE OF THE UNITED STATES OF AMERICA, AT THEIR SECOND ANNUAL MEETING, CHICAGO, ILL., JUNE 14th, 1910.

Fellow Members: —

Again time has made its annual records, and we are enabled to review the important events which have transpired during the year in line with the work in which we are engaged, and note the progress we are making in the promulgation of the principles and objects which prompted the organization of our institute two years ago.

I regret that we cannot congratulate ourselves on any material decrease in the number of mine catastrophes, or console ourselves that the number of individual fatalities has likewise decreased.

It is pleasing, however, to note that the long and persistent agitation in favor of the establishment of a Federal Bureau of Mines has at last borne fruit, and that the bill for its establishment has become a law. With such a bureau conducted along proper lines, and an earnest and faithful co-operation between the persons connected with the bureau and the state mining departments, a great and beneficial work can, no doubt, be accomplished.

While I am heartily in favor of the establishment of rescue training stations for training a number of the most active mine inspectors, and others, in every mining state, in the work of rescue and use of helmets, and being fully prepared for any emergency that may require such service, I wish to impress upon you that it is still a nobler work to bend our energies and exercise our influences in the direction that will eliminate, as far as possible, the necessity for rescue work.

The only way, in my opinion, to accomplish this desirable end, is to seek uniformity of mining laws in every mining state where conditions are similar; removing, as far as possible and practicable, all seen and known dangers, and adopting such safe-guards as are best calculated to reduce ordinary accidents, explosions, and other calamities, to a minimum.

Care, however, should always be fully exercised in order that no false feeling of safety be created, or the idea fostered that no responsibility should be assumed by the ordinary workmen. On the contrary, every man who enters a mine should be taught to understand, and should fully realize that there is no such thing as safety, and that the lurking and unseen dangers in a coal mine are greater than the ordinary dangers in any other vocation in life. He should also be taught the necessity of restraint on his own individual liberties, and that on his conduct and acts depend his own safety, and the safety of all others in the mine.

It is a well-known, but deplorable fact, that a large majority of the lives lost in mines is the result of sheer carelessness, or utter want of ordinary discipline among employes, which is one of the greatest sources of danger we have to fear and with which we have to contend.

OHIO MINING COMMISSION.

My colleagues from Ohio, and myself, are pleased to advise you that the mines in our state commenced operation last Saturday morning under a complete new code of laws. These laws were drafted by a Commission of thorough, practical miners and mine managers, every member of which knew just what was needed, and how to apply it without consulting an army of political lobbyists, or hearing arguments from a group of paid attorneys representing either the plaintiff or the defendant in the case.

This is not any argument, however, that our new mining laws are perfect or faultless, nor is it an indication that they are as complete as the members of the Commission desired them to be. While safety to life and limb should always receive first consideration, the increase in the cost of coal, the earning powers of employes, the increased responsibility and curtailment of the liberties of individuals, as well as competition from other mining states, are all potent factors that are zealously guarded against by one side or the other, and have to be reckoned for in the drafting of state mining laws, a fact which is the strongest evidence of the necessity of federal assistance and influence in securing uniform measures of law to govern mining in every state.

Our Commission, after careful consideration, and trying to cover every conceivable condition of present-day mining by specific law, and giving increased discretionary powers to the state mining department, made a unanimous report, — the first time in mining history where three direct representative miners and three representative operators, and a contrary mine inspector, ever recommended an entire new mining code.

THE RECOMMENDATIONS WERE SUBMITTED TO THE GOVERNOR

And in turn to both Houses of the state legislature, with a special message of recommendation from him in their favor. Committees representing the mine operators and miners of the state were appointed and met a conference committee of mines and mining of the House and Senate, urging the enactment of those recommendations into law. This bill was favorably reported by the Mines and Mining Committees of the House and Senate, passed both Houses without a single change and without a dissenting voice or vote; was signed by Governor Harmon on April 11th last, and went into effect as stated, on the 11th inst., allowing sixty days after the approval of the Governor to prepare for its application and enforcement.

As stated above, in our recommendations we endeavored to cover every important matter, and to clearly define the duties, not only of coal-operating companies, but of every person employed in the mine, creating an easy means of prosecution, and providing penalties for violation, making the mine-foreman responsible to see that every feature of the law is complied with.

I confess that it is a herculean task for seven men to assume the responsibility to settle so many questions of such vast and vital importance, and as the seventh member, and chairman of the Commission, take this opportunity of expressing my high regard for the ability, and spirit of fairness, as well as for the logical fighting qualities of the representatives of both miners and operators on the Commission, but above all, my admiration for their persistent determination to overcome every obstacle and submit a unanimous report.

If you want to leave your measure for a new suit of clothes, you do not leave it with a blacksmith or a bricklayer; if you collide with a flying express and smash your automobile, you do not take it to an apothecary to have it repaired; if your watch fails to keep correct time, you do not call in a veterinary surgeon; if your wife requires a new dress made, or wants a new hat or bonnet, she does not go to a dentist or a druggist, and so on and so forth. If you want good, sane, sensible, practical mining laws, you must have them drafted, not by lawyers; not by doctors; not by dentists or politicians, nor by men who probably never saw a coal mine, but by good, reasonable, broad-minded, practical men who understand and are familiar with all the conditions, difficulties and dangers met with in the operation of mines.

For many years, and against much opposition for a time, particularly from Miners' Leaders, we have been advocating this method of securing legislation to govern the mines in Ohio, and the results so far are so gratifying that we highly recommend it to every mining state anticipating legislation of that nature. No legislation will prevent accidents or calamities where the management of mines are indifferent about the performance of their duties, or the safety of the men under their charge, or where careless employes consider their individual liberties paramount to the safety of others. Willful carelessness and criminal negligence should be vigorously prosecuted, and for repeated offenses such violators of law should be driven out of the mine, in the interest of and protection to those who are careful and law-abiding.

CHERRY MINE CALAMITY.

At Scranton, Pa., a year ago, when we accepted the kind invitation of our brother members from Illinois, to hold our second annual meeting in this city, we little expected to come here to express our sympathy with and share the regrets of these fellow-members of our institute as a result in their home state of one of the most peculiar, unlooked-for, and heart-rending catastrophes that mining history has ever recorded.

Every mine inspector who has knowledge of the careless practice of some mine-foreman in neglecting the ventilating system of their mines where carburetted hydrogen gas is generated, or is familiar with the general indifference of many employes in mines in regard to their own safety and the safety of others, expects, and is not surprised when explosions occur; but who ever would have conceived such a circumstance as a hard-pressed and tightly-wired bale of hay catching fire and developing into a conflagration sufficient to cut off the egress at two mine openings about 500 feet apart, and causing the loss of 265 human lives, particularly where a number of men were working close to and had a full knowledge of the origin and progress of the fire, but seemingly made little effort either to report or extinguish it until too late.

In mine catastrophes, there has been no parallel to the Cherry mine fire. The nearest to it was the Hartley Colliery accident in England on Jan. 16th, 1862, where a cast-iron engine pump beam, weighing about 44 tons, broke in two at the center and one-half of it fell down the shaft, stripping out the partition and timbers, closing the shaft, and two hundred and four persons slowly succumbed to the effects of carbonic oxide gas, generated by the combustion of fuel at the furnace after the shaft was closed; and Avondale, in Pennsylvania, on September 6th, 1869, where fire from the ventilating furnace ignited the partition in the shaft, and carried the flames to the breakers and outside buildings, practically closing the shaft, and about 200 lives were lost.

Unlike the Cherry calamity, however, in both instances, there was only one deep shaft opening, with wooden partition for ventilation, and a ventilating furnace in the mine.

In the case of the Hartley calamity, the sympathies of the people of the entire nation for the entombed miners and their families was such, and popular indignation of such a strong and wide-spread character, that the English government at once enacted a law providing for two separate and distinct means of ingress and egress to mines, with not less than 100 feet of natural strata between. Similar provisions were made by legislative enactment in Pennsylvania, Ohio, and other mining states in this country, forced by the sacrifice of a similar number of lives at Avondale.

At Cherry, however, there were two means of egress, nearly 500 feet apart; no such a thing as a furnace in the mine; no ordinary possibility for fire; two hoisting shafts where men could have readily been brought to the surface, yet we have the worst calamity that has ever occurred from any similar cause, and is proof-positive that with all the safe-guards human mind can conceive and provide, there is no such thing as safety in a mine. A moment of forgetfulness, or a failure to diligently and constantly perform an important duty, may doom the entire force in a mine to death, in the twinkling of an eye. The hasty and cruel criticism indulged in against mine inspectors and others when mine calamities occur, by people totally ignorant of the circumstances, and unfit to pass judgment, makes it necessary that the slogan of this institute, and the watchword of every member, should be a strict performance of duty and a judicial, but rigid enforcement of law.

It is evident, judging from the number and important nature of the subjects on our program, that we are going to have an opportunity to spend a very interesting and profitable week. I am sure that it is not necessary to remind you that we are here from long distances, at considerable cost to the people of our respective states; here, most of us, at the desire, and with the hearty approval of the Governors of our states, for a free and friendly interchange of views, and a full and careful discussion of all important subjects, with a view of reducing the number of fatalities and more securely safe-guarding the lives and limbs of those who labor in our mines, and I trust we will each and all endeavor to utilize the time at our disposal for that purpose, and to that end.

opinion that it was unfair to ask them to return to the old-fashioned method of mining with the picks.

The question of blasting coal off the solid, and the excessive use of powder, or rather the question of eliminating solid-shooting and the excessive use of powder, is just as important as the question of keeping the abandoned workings free from standing gas, as I believe that a very large number of our accidents is due to the reckless and excessive use of powder, and these will continue as long as this reckless and unwarranted system of producing coal prevails.

In the state of Ohio, the mining department has repeatedly warned both miners and operators to refrain from this dangerous method of producing coal. On these occasions, the operators take the stand that their miners would leave and go elsewhere if they were not allowed to shoot the coal to suit themselves, but the fact of the matter is that less fine coal would be produced, and the profit from the sale of powder would be reduced, conditions which would have a tendency to encourage, rather than discourage, this system of mining. With the operator encouraging this dangerous and reckless method of mining, and the miners claiming that we have no right to impose conditions on them that would cause them to perform more labor, even to protect their own lives, the inspector is "between the Devil and the deep Sea", and the public never stops to consider that his only object is to protect the lives of those who work in the mines.

I believe that we should have good laws to protect those who work in the mines; there is, however, danger of going to extremes, and the possibility of creating a feeling of false security in the minds of the workers by leaving the impression that they are surrounded with such safeguards that there is no necessity for them to exert themselves, or use due precaution to protect themselves.

After a careful investigation by the State Mining Department, it should have the power to order the mines worked on a method best adapted to that particular vein, and miners and operators alike should respect the judgment and orders of the department; never losing sight of the fact that any order issued is in the best interests of mining, and the protection of life and property.

Gentlemen, we have met here for the purpose of taking up the questions of protecting or conserving the lives of those who work in the mines. We should also consider the question of conserving our coal veins, as they go hand in hand, especially so in deep and gassy mines, where it is very important that all the coal be taken out, and the roof and floor allowed to come together, so as not to provide space for large quantities of gas to accumulate.

There is another question that should be taken up at this meeting: That is, the question of whether our mines are surrounded with the same elements of danger that are encountered in the mines of foreign countries.

very much whether they generate more gas than some of our mines do; on the other hand, most of our coal is cut with chain machines. These grind up a certain per cent. of the coal as fine as flour; this is carried away by the air current, and deposited along the roadways, also on the timbers and in the old workings, and as this dust is highly explosive when thrown into the atmosphere by a concussion, all that is necessary to cause an explosion is to have a flame come in contact with it.

This dust is unavoidably being stored in the mine day after day, and is one of the most dangerous elements with which we have to contend under our present system of mining.

Take, for instance, our bituminous mines, a great many of which generate large quantities of gas; the majority of these are worked on the room and pillar method. In order to avoid squeezes, about 50% of the coal is left in the mines; as the face of the workings advance, the worked-out places fall in around the pillars, and this coal is lost forever. Not only that, but sufficient open space remains in these old workings to allow great quantities of gas to accumulate. While our law requires them to be kept free from standing gas, the question is, "How is it to be done?" They may be kept ventilated for a time, but as the workings extend, it becomes an utter impossibility, and the result is that we have a magazine stored in our mines between the face of the workings and the shaft.

The fact is, our system of mining is at fault, and it should be changed to suit present conditions. In foreign countries, the method of mining is adopted to suit the conditions, and this dangerous and wasteful method is eliminated. The coal is all, or nearly all, taken out, and most all of the deep-shaft mines are worked on what is known as the "long-wall" system. This system is worked in some parts of the United States, and we seldom, if ever, hear of an explosion in these mines. Why? Because the ventilation travels along the face of the workings, and as all the coal has been removed, the top and bottom come together, leaving nothing open behind but the roadways, consequently there is no place for standing gas to accumulate, and as the weight breaks the coal off at the back of the cut, there is practically no danger from explosives. This is another great element of danger connected with the mining of coal, the excessive use of which is not restricted by law.

We can all recall the time in the history of mining in this country when the miner undercut his coal with picks, as is the custom in foreign countries at the present time, and the man who attempted to shoot coal off the solid was considered a "coal-butcher", or a "Company coal-digger." Today, there are very few miners who care to undercut the coal before blasting it down; in fact, one who was considered an experienced miner expressed himself in my presence before a meeting of miners, operators, and inspectors, in favor of solid shooting, remarking that the miners had reduced mining to a science and he was of the opinion that it was unfair to ask them to return to the old-fashioned method of mining with the picks.

The question of blasting coal off the solid, and the excessive use of powder, or rather the question of eliminating solid-shooting and the excessive use of powder, is just as important as the question of keeping the abandoned workings free from standing gas, as I believe that a very large number of our accidents is due to the reckless and excessive use of powder, and these will continue as long as this reckless and unwarranted system of producing coal prevails.

In the state of Ohio, the mining department has repeatedly warned both miners and operators to refrain from this dangerous method of producing coal. On these occasions, the operators take the stand that their miners would leave and go elsewhere if they were not allowed to shoot the coal to suit themselves, but the fact of the matter is that less fine coal would be produced, and the profit from the sale of powder would be reduced, conditions which would have a tendency to encourage, rather than discourage, this system of mining. With the operator encouraging this dangerous and reckless method of mining, and the miners claiming that we have no right to impose conditions on them that would cause them to perform more labor, even to protect their own lives, the inspector is "between the Devil and the deep Sea", and the public never stops to consider that his only object is to protect the lives of those who work in the mines.

I believe that we should have good laws to protect those who work in the mines; there is, however, danger of going to extremes, and the possibility of creating a feeling of false security in the minds of the workers by leaving the impression that they are surrounded with such safeguards that there is no necessity for them to exert themselves, or use due precaution to protect themselves.

After a careful investigation by the State Mining Department, it should have the power to order the mines worked on a method best adapted to that particular vein, and miners and operators alike should respect the judgment and orders of the department; never losing sight of the fact that any order issued is in the best interests of mining, and the protection of life and property.

Gentlemen, we have met here for the purpose of taking up the questions of protecting or conserving the lives of those who work in the mines. We should also consider the question of conserving our coal veins, as they go hand in hand, especially so in deep and gassy mines, where it is very important that all the coal be taken out, and the roof and floor allowed to come together, so as not to provide space for large quantities of gas to accumulate.

There is another question that should be taken up at this meeting: That is, the question of whether our mines are surrounded with the same elements of danger that are encountered in the mines of foreign countries.

This is important, as the impression has gone forth to the public year after year through the public press, purported to be from authorities who have studied mining conditions in all important mining countries of the world, that our mines are not surrounded with the same elements of danger as other mining countries. If these statements go unchallenged, and the impression is allowed to go to the public that our mines have not the elements of danger found in other mining countries, in the face of all the explosions and other fatalities which have occurred in recent years, it will certainly cast a reflection on the inspectors of the United States; it also has the tendency to create the impression among operators and miners that there is practically no danger, and they become over-confident. This leads to negligence. As there is no surer way to endanger a man's life than to make him feel that there is no danger, it is our duty not only to have the danger removed as much as possible, but to remind both miners and operators that the danger is there, and they must always be on the alert to avoid accidents.

Take, for instance, our most dangerous mines: Those in charge know that they have to be continually on the alert to avoid a calamity, and at the least sign of danger, withdraw the men. Supposing they were being continually told that there was very little danger, they would become over-confident, and like an army without night sentinels to watch the treacherous foe, who would approach and destroy them before they were aware of it.

We know that we have all the elements of danger that are encountered in coal mining, and we should sound the warning to all and entreat them to be ever-careful. Let the miner and operator alike respect the law, and orders of the inspector, and when orders from a mining department are issued, let them never lose sight of the fact that the only object in view is the protection of life, limb, and property.

MINERS LAMP OIL.

The Members of the Mining Commission made provision for what they considered the most healthy and safe illuminant in mines, and advised a compound of 84% animal or vegetable oil with 16% of miners neutral or mineral oil, and required that all oil containers be labeled as per the quality of the oil contained, and provided penalties for all violations both by miners, manufacturers, and for adulteration by manufacturers and storekeepers.

While we have had very little trouble with manufacturers and storekeepers, the number of arrests where miners were found to have adulterated their oil, shows the disposition of miners to adulterate it after making purchases in small quantities.

OIL & GAS WELLS.

The Department has for several years been impressed with the dangers arising from the drilling of oil and gas wells through workable seams of coal, and the Mining Commission drafted a section of the new mining code which they believed would remedy many of the dangers which had come to the attention of the Department in the inspections made at the mines where wells had been carelessly drilled and, in many cases, abandoned without proper precautions being provided against breaking into them in the operation and extension of mining properties. It also required maps to be made and filed with the Department, showing the number and location of wells, and there has been filed with this office during the year one hundred and ten oil and gas well maps. Seventy-seven applications were also filed for the privilege of drilling for oil or gas in the following counties: Belmont, Carroll, Columbiana, Harrison, Jefferson, Meigs, Monroe, Noble, and Tuscarawas.

We herewith publish a schedule, showing what an oil or gas well map should exhibit in order to comply with the law.

STATE OF OHIO,

STATE MINING DEPARTMENT.

Schedule Prepared to Serve as a Guide for Surveyors and Mining Engineers Employed to Survey and Map Oil and Gas Wells which Penetrate the Coal Measures.

In the future all maps filed with this department must conform to the requirements of this schedule as near as possible, and in so far as it relates to the property for which the survey has been made.

SCHEDULE FOR GUIDE TO SURVEYORS AND MINING ENGINEERS IN SURVEYING AND MAPPING OIL AND GAS WELLS.

State ....
County in which located..
Township ....
SECTION OR SECTIONS IN WHICH SAID WELLS ARE LOCATED......
....
Name and P. O. Address of the Operating Company..........................
....
Name and P. O. Address of the Property Owners on whose property the wells are located ....
Name and P. O. Address of the Mining Engineer.............................
Sworn Certificate of the Mining Engineer that it is a true and accurate map, and sworn to before a Notary or J. of P.
Location of each Oil or Gas Well...
Number of each Oil or Gas Well numbered consecutively.......................
Producing Wells marked...
Abandoned Wells marked..
Map must show surface on which wells are located for a distance of 500 feet contiguous thereto ....
Location of all buildings (if any)...
Location of mine opening (if any)..
Location of railroads (if any)...
Location of county roads (if any)...
Location of creeks (if any)...
Location of village (if located near one).......................................
Location of corner stone..
Center of section shown..
Scale on which map has been made...
Date of survey..
North Point ....

EACH WELL MUST BE PLAINLY DESIGNATED BY A NUMBER AND NUMBERED CONSECUTIVELY.

LEGISLATION.

The new Mining Code which was submitted by the Mining Commission, composed of three miners, three operators and a seventh member chosen by the six other members, to the General Assembly in January, 1910, passed both branches of the Legislature without a dissenting vote, and by virtue of its provisions went into effect June 11, 1910.

The vast amount of work entailed in an undertaking of this kind can scarcely be appreciated by the individual, but when we take into consideration the fact that no great changes had been made in the old law since its first enactment in 1874, and that up until the year 1908 no mention of the term "electricity" was to be found in it, the urgent need for such a revision was plain to all interested in the industry.

This work consumed portions of two years time, and cost the state approximately $16,000.00, but the unanimous conclusions reached by the Commission, approved and passed by the State Legislature, and the lasting benefits hoped to be derived from this new law, will more than compensate the appropriations made for it. We believe the members of this Commission are to be congratulated for the work done, and the personal sacrifice made both in the amount of time spent during its deliberations and hearings, as well as the sacrifices made in a financial way, as many of the provisions of this law called for improvements and changes, which could only be made at additional cost to the production of coal by persons engaged in the mining of this product.

This new law is now being put into operation, and, in so far as we are able to judge at this time, is being found practicable, and when all its provisions are known, and its requirements fulfilled, its success will undoubtedly be greater and it will be more appreciated as time goes on.

The most essential features of this new law are those providing increased ventilation, both for persons employed and for the number of animals in use; fire proof stables in shaft mines; the number of escapementways, protection from electric wires and electricity as applied and in use in the operation of mines. Penalties have also been provided for all persons employed in and around the mines who violate the law. These are only a few of the more essential features of this code. Fines have already been imposed, amounting to $600.00. The greatest number were for machine runners operating a mining machine without a shield, ten in all; for persons employed in the mines burning oil mixed with carbon, seven; two for loitering about the premises of coal companies; four for entering a mine before being examined by a fire boss; two for crossing a danger signal; two for failure to provide suitable timber; one for propping open a mine door; and one fire boss for failure to report the condition of old workings after examining them. Several oil companies and retail dealers were also convicted and fined for selling impure oil, and for not having barrels properly labeled. These are the most important, and no doubt the moral influence of these arrests and convictions will result in fewer offenses in the future.

PROSECUTIONS FOR VIOLATIONS OF THE MINING LAW DURING THE YEAR, 1910.

There were in all fifty-two (52) cases for violation of the Mining Laws during the year, forty-seven (47) of which were reported since the enactment of the new Mining Code which took effect June 11, 1910. Of this number forty-one (41) were instituted by members of the Department and eleven (11) by Coal Companies.

The greatest number of violations were for the operation of mining machines without being properly shielded, ten in all; for the violation of the fire boss law, eight; for selling impure oil, four; for violation of the breakthrough law, three; for loitering around coal properties, two; for burning oil mixed with carbon, seven; for entering a mine intoxicated, three; selling oil not properly branded, two; selling oil below the standard, one; pulling casing of oil well, one; riding and jumping on mine cars, two, and propping mine door open, one. These constitute the most important prosecutions made during the year, the offenders representing twenty-nine (29) Miners, eighteen (18) Mine Officials, and Oil Companies, five (5).

COUNTIES.

The greatest number of prosecutions were brought in Belmont County, twenty-seven in all; Jackson County, five; Jefferson County, eight; Harrison County, two; Tuscarawas County, two; Guernsey, three; Athens, Gallia, Lawrence and Noble, one each.

INSPECTORS.

L. D. Devore, Inspector of the Tenth District, is credited with the greatest number of convictions, thirteen in all. James Hennessy, of the Tenth District, eight; Lot Jenkins and Thomas Morrison, four each; John Burke and Geo. Harrison (Chief Inspector of Mines), three, each; Abel Ellwood and Alex Smith, two each; John L. McDonald and Edward Kennedy, one each.

COAL COMPANIES.

The following Coal Companies, through their mine officials, were responsible for twelve prosecutions, as follows: Barton Coal Co., Belmont County, two, one for placing refuse in a breakthrough, and one for entering the mine intoxicated; Morris Coal Co., Guernsey County, prosecuted two persons for crossing a danger signal in the Cleveland Mine; The Roby Coal Co., Harrison County, prosecuted two persons for loitering around their coal property; The Youghiogheny & Ohio Coal Co., Belmont County, prosecuted five persons; for riding on a loaded car, two; for placing powder on an uninsulated car, one; jumping on a moving car, one; for entering a mine intoxicated, one.

The most serious violations which were prosecuted during the year were those in connection with the examination of mines by fire bosses, and reporting false findings; for crossing danger signals made by fire bosses; the employment of minors, propping a mine door open, and pulling the casing of an oil well. The operation of mining machines without being properly shielded was violated by ten machine operators, and resulted in their being held responsible for the penalty. This law was enacted for the purpose of protecting life and limb and should be rigidly enforced by any and all persons under whose notice these violations occur. The practice of jumping on moving mining cars was also enforced by one of the coal companies of the state, and should be by all other companies where such practices exist, as it is accompanied with grave danger both to life and limb. On the whole the Department is highly gratified with the results of the enforcement of the new mining law, and its superiority over the old law in many ways has more than justified its promoters, and if thoroughly enforced cannot help but reduce the number of fatalities in the state.

DETAILED SYNOPSIS OF THE NUMBER OF PROSECUTIONS FOR VIOLATION OF THE MINING LAWS DURING THE YEAR, AND CAUSES TO WHICH THEY WERE ATTRIBUTED.

ATHENS COUNTY.

Date of arrest.	Name of person or firm prosecuted.	City.	Cause.	Action begun.	Verdict	Fine.	Remarks and name of prosecuting witness.
Dec. 29	D. L. Nutter, (Mine Foreman)	Nelsonville, O.	Charged with entering mine intoxicated	December 29.	Guilty	$10.00 and costs.	Jno. L. McDonald, Dist. Insp.

BELMONT COUNTY.

Date of arrest.	Name of person or firm prosecuted.	City.	Cause.	Action begun.	Verdict	Fine.	Remarks and name of prosecuting witness.
May 3	Jas. Giffin, Miner	Bellaire, O.	Operating mining machine not properly shielded	May 3			L. D. Devore, Dist. Insp. Defendant crossed over into W. Va.
April 2	Walter Sykes, Miner	Bellaire, O.	Operating mining machine not properly shielded	April 1	Guilty	$5.00 and costs.	L. D. Devore, Insp.
April 2	Richard Kane, Miner	Bellaire, O.	Operating mining machine not properly shielded	April 1	Guilty	5.00 and costs.	L. D. Devore, Insp.
May 3	Thos. Hughes, Miner	Bellaire, O.	Operating mining machine not properly shielded	May 3			L. D. Devore, Insp. Dismissed, partner crossed over into W. Va.
Aug. 20	Frank Royeski, Miner	Barton, O.	Placing refuse in a break-through	August 18	Guilty	5.00 and costs.	Geo. D. Green, Supt.
Aug. 26	Thos. Bennett, Miner	Bellaire, O.	Operating mining machine not properly shielded	August 25	Guilty	5.00 and costs.	L. D. Devore, Insp.
Aug. 26	Mike Duskey, Miner	Bellaire, O.	Operating mining machine not properly shielded	August 25	Guilty	5.00 and costs.	L. D. Devore, Insp.
Aug. 26	Stanley Kaspen, Miner	Bellaire, O.	Operating mining machine not properly shielded	August 25	Guilty	5.00 and costs.	L. D. Devore, Insp.
Aug. 26	Frank Marimbo, Miner	Bellaire, O.	Operating mining machine not properly shielded	August 25	Guilty	5.00 and costs.	L. D. Devore, Insp.
Aug. 26	Jno. Camek, Miner	Bellaire, O.	Operating mining machine not properly shielded	August 25	Guilty	5.00 and costs.	L. D. Devore, Insp.
Oct. 13	Steve Silas, Miner	Barton, O.	Burning oil mixed with carbon.	October 14	Guilty	5.00 and costs.	Jas. Hennessy, Insp.
Oct. 14	Joe Krul, Miner	Barton, O.	Burning oil mixed with carbon.	October 14	Guilty	5.00 and costs.	Jas. Hennessy, Insp.
Oct. 15	Jno. Engstrom, Miner	Barton, O.	Burning oil mixed with carbon.	October 14	Guilty	5.00 and costs.	Jas. Hennessy, Insp.
Oct. 15	Jno. Suski, Miner	Barton, O.	Burning oil mixed with carbon.	October 14	Guilty	5.00 and costs.	Jas. Hennessy, Insp.
Oct. 15	Frank Yarnes, Miner	Barton, O.	Burning oil mixed with carbon.	October 14	Guilty	5.00 and costs.	Jas. Hennessy, Insp.
Oct. 18	L. Blou, Retail Dealer	Bellaire, O.	Selling impure oil	October 17	Guilty	5.00 and costs.	L. D. Devore, Insp.
Oct. 29	Jos. Subacke, Miner	Barton, O.	Propping [illegible] door open	October 25	Guilty	5.00 and costs.	Jas. Hennessy, Insp.
Oct. 29	Albert Mader, Miner	Barton, O.	Burning oil mixed with carbon.	October 25	Guilty	5.00 and costs.	Jas. Hennessy, Insp.
Oct. 31	Tomey Krisho, Miner	Barton, O.	Burning oil mixed with carbon.	October 27	Guilty	5.00 and costs.	Jas. Hennessy, Insp.

Oct. 14	Martin Yanivich, Miner....	Barton, O............	Entering mine intoxicated......	October 18...	Guilty	5.00	J. D. Goulding, Mine Foreman.
Nov. 28	Jno. Crawford, Mine Boss.	Bellaire, O...........	Violating law governing employment of minors..........	November 28.	Guilty	10.00 and costs.	L. D. Devore, Insp.
Dec. 7	Alex Zulop, Miner..........	Barton, O............	Riding on a loaded car........	December 6..	Guilty	5.00	Y. & O. Coal Co.
Dec. 7	Paul Kato, Miner..........	Barton, O............	Jumping on a moving car......	December 6..	Guilty	5.00	Y. & O. Coal Co.
Dec. 9	Jno. Bendick, Miner.......	Barton, O............	Entering mine intoxicated......	December 8..	Guilty	5.00	Y. & O. Coal Co.
Dec. 14	Joe Bolash, Miner..........	Barton, O............	Riding on a loaded car.........	December 10.	Guilty	5.00	Y. & O. Coal Co.
Dec. 15	G. W. Arbaugh, Retail Dealer	Barton, O............	Selling inferior oil............	December 15.	Guilty	25.00 and costs.	Case carried up—Lot Jenkins, Insp.
Dec. 19	Jos. Barnisky, Miner.......	Barton, O............	Placing powder on an uninsulated car........................	December 19.	Guilty	5.00	Y. & O. Coal Co.

COLUMBIANA COUNTY.

Nov. 28	H. T. Johnson, Oil Well Co.	Wellsville, O........	Pulling casing of oil well......	November 28.	Guilty	$100.00 and costs.	Thos. Morrison, Insp.

GALLIA COUNTY.

Nov. 18	J. H. Summers, Mine Boss.	Gallipolis, O.........	Violating Sec. 968, governing supply of timber..............	November 17.	Guilty	$10.00	Edw. Kennedy, Insp.

GUERNSEY COUNTY.

Aug. 16	Chas. Unclesbee, Miner....	Senecaville, O.......	Crossing danger signal of fire boss	August 16....	Guilty	$25.00 and costs.	Morris Coal Co.
Aug. 17	Jno. Kish, Miner...........	Senecaville, O.......	Crossing danger signal of fire boss	August 16....	Guilty	$25.00 and costs.	Morris Coal Co.
Oct. 8	Geo. Walkinshaw, Supt....	Cambridge, O.......	Running cars ahead of motor without signal light.........	....	....	....	Case withdrawn—Abel Ellwood, Insp.

HARRISON COUNTY.

July 6	Angelis Amberti...........	Adena, O............	Loitering around Coal Co.'s property	July 6........	Guilty	$10.00	Roby Coal Co.
July 7	Edmond Szentgyngyi.......	Adena, O............	Loitering around Coal Co.'s property	July 7........	Guilty	10.00	Roby Coal Co.

DETAILED SYNOPSIS OF THE NUMBER OF PROSECUTIONS FOR VIOLATION OF THE MINING LAWS DURING THE YEAR, AND CAUSES TO WHICH THEY WERE ATTRIBUTED — Concluded.

JACKSON COUNTY.

Date of arrest.	Name of person or firm prosecuted.	City.	Cause.	Action begun.	Verdict	Fine.	Remarks and name of prosecuting witness.
Oct. 28	Lem Ervin, Fire Boss	Wellston, O.	Violating fire boss law	October 27	Guilty	25.00 and costs.	Jno. Burke, Insp.
Oct. 28	Frank Craggs, Mine Boss	Wellston, O.	Violating law in regard to ventilation	October 27	Guilty	25.00 and costs.	Jno. Burke, Insp.
Oct. 28	Sam'l Wilson, Ass't Supt.	Wellston, O.	Entering mine before being examined by a fire boss	October 27	Guilty	25.00 and costs.	Geo. Harrison, Chief Insp.
Oct. 28	Jno. E. Baumgartner, Supt.	Wellston, O.	Entering mine before being examined by a fire boss	October 27	Guilty	25.00 and costs.	Geo. Harrison, Chief Insp.
Nov. 11	Jno. E. Baumgartner, Agent Coal Company	Wellston, O.	Violating Sec. 925, failure of fire boss to inspect gaseous mine	November 11.	Guilty	25.00 and costs. Fines susp.	Geo. Harrison, Chief. Insp.

JEFFERSON COUNTY.

Date of arrest.	Name of person or firm prosecuted.	City.	Cause.	Action begun.	Verdict	Fine.	Remarks and name of prosecuting witness.
May 31	W. L. Pilkington, Mine Boss	Brilliant, O.	Violating law governing breakthrough	May 31	Guilty	$50.00 and costs.	L. D. Devore, Insp.
July 5	S. W. Ruckman, Mine Boss.	Connor, O.	Violating law governing breakthrough	July 5	Guilty	25.00 and costs.	Lot Jenkins, Insp.
Aug. 3	Jas. Briggs, Mine Boss	Plum Run, O.	Violating law governing supply of timber	August 1	....	....	Case was compromised—L. L. D. Devore, Insp.
Sept. 26	Edw. Lee, Mine Boss	Amsterdam, O.	Entering mine before being examined by a fire boss	September 26.	Guilty	10.00 and costs	Thos. Morrison, Insp.
Sept. 26	Jno. Lees, Mine Boss	Amsterdam. O.	Violation of breakthrough law.	September 26.	Guilty	10.00 and costs	Thos. Morrison, Insp.
Sept. 27	Geo. Lucas, Fire Boss	Amsterdam, O.	Wilfully refusing to report condition of old workings	September 26.	Guilty	25.00 and costs	Fines remitted—Thos. Morrison, Insp.
Sept. 27	J. B. Walker, Machine Runner	Yorkville, O.	Operating machines not properly shielded	September 27.	....	....	Escaped to W. Va.—Lot Jenkins, Insp.
Oct. 19	J. B. Neeley, Retail Dealer.	Rush Run, O.	Selling impure oil	October 19	Guilty	25.00 and costs.	Lot Jenkins, Insp.

LAWRENCE COUNTY.

Date of arrest.	Name of person or firm prosecuted.	City.	Cause.	Action begun.	Verdict	Fine.	Remarks and name of prosecuting witness.
Nov. 17	Indian Refining Co., Oil Company	....	Selling oil below the standard.	November 17.	Guilty	$50.00 and costs.	Jno. Burke, Insp.

NOBLE COUNTY.

Aug. 25	M. B. Larrick, Retail Dealer	Ava, O.............	Selling impure oil.............	August 25....	Guilty	$25.00 and costs.	Abel Ellwood, Insp.

TUSCARAWAS COUNTY.

Oct. 7	Geo. Adams, Mine Boss....	Newcomerstown, O..	Selling oil from barrel not labelled	October 7....	Guilty	$25.00 and costs.	Alex Smith, Insp.
Oct. 20	C. R. Sheafe, Operator and Supt.................	Newcomerstown, O..	Selling oil from barrels not labelled	October 20...	Guilty	25.00 and costs.	Alex Smith, Insp.

SALE OF TEST WEIGHTS.

The new law providing that owners, lessees or agents of mines provide test weights at mines for the purpose of testing the accuracy of weigh scales, made it unnecessary for the District Inspectors to keep on hand any number of test weights, and a number of them were disposed of during the year to coal companies of which the following is a list.

The funds derived from the sale of these test weights were deposited with the Treasurer of State, and became a part of the General Revenue Fund.

December 29, 1910.	Carroll Storm Coal Co., Cleveland, O.	$4 00
December 5, 1910.	C. F. Smith, Massillon, O.	2 00
December 6, 1910.	Peacock Mining Co., Mineral City, O.	4 25
December 17, 1910.	Buckeye Fire Clay Co., Uhrichsville, O.	4 50
December 17, 1910.	Powers & Co., Coshocton, O.	4 50
December 17, 1910.	Massillon Elm Run Coal Co., Massillon, O.	4 00
December 19, 1910.	David Davis, Conesville, O.	6 50
December 20, 1910.	Jno. D. Jones, Hametown, O.	2 00
	Total Sales	$31 75

NOTE:— The sale of test weights for the year 1911, will appear in the report for that year.

THE PREVENTION OF MINE ACCIDENTS.

While the safety of life and limb was ever held above any and all considerations in drafting the new mining code, both by the miners and operators of the Commission, it is evident that much remains yet to be accomplished before we reach that ever sought-for-result,— where accidents are reduced to a minimum. While the new mining code has only been effective about six months, and it may be a little premature to pass judgment on its possible effect in lessening the number of accidents, we can not but be impressed when we scan the list of fatalities for the year that has just passed, with the fact, however, we may be loath to acknowledge it, that there is something lacking that no legislation can and will reach, and while there are various theories advocated as to how best to attain this result, the one paramount fact which is daily being forcibly brought to our attention, is the one that the MINER, HIMSELF, must be the one to solve, to a great degree, this most serious and oft-perplexing question. Ninety-seven (97) falls of roof caused the untimely death of this number of victims, the greater portion of which could have been avoided had the proper precautions been taken; fifteen (15) lives were snuffed out during the year at one mine by the carelessness of a driver in leaving a door open, producing a short circuit of air, causing an accumulation of firedamp and an explosion. Had this explosion occurred in the day time instead of the night time, many more persons would have been added to the death list. Our new mining code has made provision for increased ventilation, and safe-guards for mines generating fire damp, besides many other provisions for safety, but if we have not the co-operation of the work-man, himself, in securing the safety of work under-ground, legislation will be of no avail, and there can be but one result,— the continued increase in the number of fatalities.

In connection with this matter, we do not wish to in any way excuse, or hold lightly, the responsibility resting upon mine managements, and the laxity in not surroundnig employes with every known safe-guard, and in maintaining strict discipline such as is in effect in all foreign countries; the prosecutions and fines assessed during the six months of the operation of the new law is ample proof of the fact that there has been negligence upon both the part of the miner and the mine management, but with a co-operation of both these factors which enter so vitally into the production of coal, we can, and will, reduce this uncalled for loss of life.

COAL PRODUCTION.

COAL TRADE IN THE STATE OF OHIO FOR THE YEAR 1910.

The coal trade in the state for the year 1910, was indeed gratifying to all persons connected with the Coal Industry. As reports from coal districts from all over the country are becoming available this unprecedented production and prosperity in connection with the Coal Trade seems to have been general, and to have been participated in by the various activities which enter into the Industry in general.

The trade increased in tonnage in this state 24%, as well as in time worked and in wages paid to the miners.

Those interested in the Coal Industry seem to have fared better than those engaged in other industrial pursuits as financial affairs were in more or less unsettled conditions throughout the year. However, coal, as a commodity, is indispensable, and enters largely into all our large industrial activities, and it continues its increase in production regardless of the outcome of business in general.

DISTRICTS.

The Hocking Valley and Eastern Ohio Districts both report large increases in their production. The Tuscarawas District was idle almost the entire year owing to the failure of securing an amicable settlement between the miners and operators brought about by the new wage-scale agreement entered into by the miners and operators at the expiration of their two year agreement April 1, 1910, and matters were still in an unsettled condition at the close of the year. The Crooksville District was also idle from April 1st. to November 8th., from the same cause.

LABOR.

There was no evident shortage of labor during the year, and the time worked by the miners was about two-thirds. The cessation of work in the districts affected by the new wage-scale agreement caused miners to migrate to other coal districts, and, in some instances, to other states. In the Tuscarawas District, where there was a complete cessation of work, April 1st., which was still unsettled at the close of the year; about 2,500 men were affected, and in the Crooksville District about 2,000 men were effected for about seven months.

Aside from these two districts where there was difficulty in settling the working conditions there were no strikes of any importance. The miners on account of the large consumption of coal enjoyed a year of unusual prosperity, as well as substantial increase in wages.

PRICES.

The year 1910, notwithstanding the large volume of business transacted, and the large increase in tonnage, was not as prosperous a one, especially in large increased profits to those engaged in the industry. Strikes and cessations of work necessarily increase the cost of production, and the increase in wages paid to the miners also added to this cost, and producers seem disposed to accept contracts based on prices which were inaugurated when lower cost of operating expenses prevailed.

LAKE TRADE.

The Lake Trade for the year was the largest ever recorded, and is estimated at over 22,500,000 tons, of which about 4,000,000 tons are shipped from the Ohio Mines.

The general outlook for the year 1911 is fairly good, especially if some satisfactory adjustment of railroad rates can be made in connection with the large shipments which are annually made to the lakes.

COAL TONNAGE IN THE STATE OF OHIO FOR THE YEAR 1910.

The Coal Industry of Ohio for the year that has just closed was one of unusual activity; indeed it will be recorded as the banner year in point of production; never has it been surpassed. The increased activity will also result in increased earnings in wages to the miners.

PRODUCTION.

From reports received from the various mining districts of the state, show the production to have been 34,424,951 tons, an increase of 6,669,919 tons over 1909. Only one other year in any marked degree approached the tonnage for the year 1910, which was the year 1907, when the tonnage amounted to 32,365,949 tons, the year 1910 representing an increase of 2,059,002 tons over that production.

PICK AND MACHINE TONNAGE.

Of the amount of coal produced during the year, 4,341,483 tons, or 12.6% of the entire production of the state, were produced by the use of pick. The number of tons mined by the use of machinery being 30,083,468 tons, or 87.4% of the entire amount.

The pick tonnage decreased 266,919 tons and the amount produced by the use of machinery increased 6,936,838 tons.

COUNTIES SHOWING THE LARGEST PRODUCTIONS.

Belmont County reported a tonnage of 8,336,428 tons, a gain of 2,343,010 tons; Athens County mines 5,943,638 tons, a gain of 1,589,564 tons; Jefferson County mined 5,111,563 tons, a gain of 1,055,415 tons; Guernsey County reported 4,473,022 tons, a gain of 1,364,336 tons.

GAINS AND LOSSES.

The gains amounted to 7,696,074 tons; the losses to 1,026,155 tons. The greatest loss was reported from Tuscarawas County (702,118 tons), due to a protracted cessation of work in that locality.

TIME WORKED.

With the exception of time lost in Districts where there was difficulty in making settlements based on the new wage-scale agreement, the mines of the state were operated about two-thirds time.

DISTRICTS.

The Hocking Valley and Eastern Ohio Districts contributed more largely to the increased tonnage than any others in the state. The Hocking Valley tonnage amounting to 9,789,740 tons, a gain of 2,322,522 tons; the Eastern Ohio production was 14,047,732 tons, an increase of 3,422,004 tons. The protracted idleness in the Crooksville District decreased the tonnage in that locality, where work was suspended from April 1st until November 8th, when work was resumed, pending an investigation and report of a reference committee in regard to differences arising between the miners and operators over the wage-scale agreement as applied to this particular district.

The Tuscarawas District also experienced the same difficulty and the mines there were still closed at the end of the year, pending settlement of local differences. The loss in tonnage from this cause in Tuscarawas County amounted to 702,118 tons.

PERSONS EMPLOYED.

The total number of men employed in the state during the year was reported to be 48,830, of which 7,214 were pick miners, 1,440 inside day pick men and 953 outside pick day hands. In the machine mines 3,293 machine runners were employed; 25,176 drillers, loaders and shooters were employed, 6,960 inside day men and 3,794 outside day men. The number of men increased 1,811 men.

TABLE SHOWING THE COAL PRODUCTION BY COUNTIES DURING THE YEAR 1910.

Name of County.		Tonnage for 1910.			
	Lump.	Nut.	Pea and Slack.	Total.	Rank in Production.
Athens	4,268,846	699,721	975,071	5,943,638	2
Belmont	5,543,745	986,298	1,806,385	8,336,428	1
Carroll	222,973	38,326	48,029	309,328	15
Columbiana	514,835	78,774	146,736	740,345	9
Coshocton	267,360	64,996	103,547	435,903	14
Gallia	10,063	2,035	1,825	13,923	25
Guernsey	2,970,925	512,727	989,370	4,473,022	4
Harrison	382,566	51,145	166,030	599,741	11
Hocking	1,037,417	170,821	242,909	1,451,147	6
Holmes	7,610	2,815	2,778	13,203	26
Jackson	640,014	94,283	198,941	933,238	7
Jefferson	3,498,519	506,046	1,106,998	5,111,563	3
Lawrence	135,540	22,114	32,811	190,465	17
Mahoning	44,098	6,857	15,357	66,312	23
Medina	20,154	2,093	5,357	27,604	24
Meigs	478,795	31,263	138,091	648,149	10
Morgan	86,311	12,723	27,510	126,544	20
Muskingum	184,081	33,863	52,472	270,416	16
Noble	319,415	27,368	95,040	441,823	13
Perry	1,732,758	272,263	389,940	2,394,961	5
Portage	76,484	11,218	17,453	105,155	21
Scioto	7,317	1,063	1,454	9,834	27
Stark	387,649	54,330	105,656	547,635	12
Summit	56,466	15,419	22,461	94,346	22
Trumbull	3,823	719	174	4,716	28
Tuscarawas	519,301	101,472	191,009	811,782	8
Vinton	117,215	12,502	29,289	159,006	19
Wayne	127,490	14,474	22,760	164,724	18
Total	23,661,770	3,827,728	6,935,453	34,424,951	

Increase of tonnage of the year 1910 over 1909 was 6,669,919 tons.

TABLE SHOWING TOTAL PRODUCTION OF PICK AND MACHINE MINED COAL BY COUNTIES DURING THE YEAR 1910.

Counties.	Pick Coal.	Machine Coal.	Total.
Athens	211,984	5,731,654	5,943,638
Belmont	184,284	8,152,144	8,336,428
Carroll	59,837	249,491	309,328
Columbiana	294,566	445,779	740,345
Coshocton	258,014	177,889	435,903
Gallia	13,923	....	13,923
Guernsey	16,890	4,456,132	4,473,022
Harrison	43,502	556,239	599,741
Hocking	200,805	1,250,342	1,451,147
Holmes	13,203	....	13,203
Jackson	616,921	316,317	933,238
Jefferson	291,032	4,820,531	5,111,563
Lawrence	172,534	17,931	190,465
Mahoning	38,528	27,784	66,312
Medina	27,604	....	27,604
Meigs	83,322	564,827	648,149
Morgan	2,258	124,286	126,544
Muskingum	204,080	66,336	270,416
Noble	18,249	423,574	441,823
Perry	243,806	2,151,155	2,394,961
Portage	65,889	39,266	105,155
Scioto	9,834	....	9,834
Stark	486,608	61,027	547,635
Summit	61,617	32,729	94,346
Trumbull	4,716	....	4,716
Tuscarawas	525,155	286,627	811,782
Vinton	58,330	100,676	159,006
Wayne	133,992	30,732	164,724
Totals	4,341,483	30,083,468	34,424,951

Pick mined coal for the year decreased 266,919 tons.
Machine mined coal for the year increased 6,936,838 tons.
Per cent. of machine mined coal 87.4.
Per cent. of pick mined coal 12.6.

TABLE SHOWING THE COAL TONNAGE OF THE STATE OF OHIO FOR THE YEAR 1910 AS COMPARED WITH THE YEAR 1909.

Counties.	1909.	1910.	Gain.	Loss.
Athens	4,354,074	5,943,638	1,589,564	....
Belmont	5,993,418	8,336,428	2,343,010	....
Carroll	398,085	309,328	....	88,757
Columbiana	714,325	740,345	26,020	....
Coshocton	390,302	435,903	45,601	....
Gallia	9,920	13,923	4,003	....
Guernsey	3,108,686	4,473,022	1,364,336	....
Harrison	576,162	599,741	23,579	....
Hocking	1,036,743	1,451,147	414,404	....
Holmes	15,844	13,203	....	2,641
Jackson	823,034	933,238	110,204	....
Jefferson	4,056,148	5,111,563	1,055,415	....
Lawrence	214,685	190,465	....	24,220
Mahoning	63,974	66,312	2,338	....
Medina	12,465	27,604	15,139	....
Meigs	543,595	648,149	104,554	....
Morgan	187,241	126,544	....	60,697
Muskingum	416,217	270,416	....	145,801
Noble	379,055	441,823	62,768	....
Perry	2,076,407	2,394,961	318,554	....
Portage	102,624	105,155	2,531	....
Scioto	8,916	9,834	918	....
Stark	458,392	547,635	89,243	....
Summit	78,268	94,346	16,078	....
Trumbull	5,405	4,716	....	689
Tuscarawas	1,513,900	811,782	....	702,118
Vinton	128,928	159,006	30,078	....
Washington	1,232	....	....	1,232
Wayne	86,987	164,724	77,737	....
Totals	27,755,032	34,424,951	7,696,074	1,026,155

Total Tonnage for the Year 1910	34,424,951
Total Tonnage for the Year 1909	27,755,032
Showing Net Gain	6,669,919
Total Increase	7,696,074
Total Decrease	1,026,155
Showing Net Gain of	6,669,919

TABLE SHOWING PRODUCTION OF PICK-MINED COAL BY COUNTIES AND PERCENTAGE OF LUMP COAL DURING THE YEAR 1910.

Name of County.	Lump.	Nut.	Pea and Slack.	Total.	Per Cent. Lump Coal.
Athens	148,149	24,940	38,895	211,984	69.9
Belmont	120,851	23,198	40,235	184,284	65.6
Carroll	43,336	7,487	9,014	59,837	72.4
Columbiana	224,690	20,784	49,092	294,566	76.3
Coshocton	153,138	39,871	65,005	258,014	59.4
Gallia	10,063	2,035	1,825	13,923	72.3
Guernsey	12,813	1,327	2,750	16,890	75.9
Harrison	28,319	5,879	9,304	43,502	65.1
Hocking	142,263	24,982	33,560	200,805	70.8
Holmes	7,610	2,815	2,778	13,203	57.6
Jackson	394,435	75,280	147,206	616,921	63.9
Jefferson	193,270	36,969	60,793	291,032	66.4
Lawrence	122,505	20,230	29,799	172,534	71.0
Mahoning	23,213	6,680	8,635	38,528	60.2
Medina	20,154	2,093	5,357	27,604	73.0
Meigs	57,112	4,865	21,345	83,322	68.5
Morgan	1,654	98	506	2,258	73.3
Muskingum	138,739	25,545	39,796	204,080	68.0
Noble	14,158	2,181	1,910	18,249	77.6
Perry	176,684	27,651	39,471	243,806	72.5
Portage	49,546	6,072	10,271	65,889	75.2
Scioto	7,317	1,063	1,454	9,834	74.4
Stark	333,257	51,244	102,107	486,608	68.5
Summit	37,888	9,074	14,655	61,617	61.5
Trumbull	3,823	719	174	4,716	81.1
Tuscarawas	333,294	62,678	129,183	525,155	63.5
Vinton	42,764	4,929	10,637	58,330	73.3
Wayne	104,037	11,050	18,905	133,992	77.6
Total	2,945,082	501,739	894,662	4,341,483	*67.8

*Average per cent. of lump coal in pick mines of the state..	67.8	
Per cent. pick mined coal	12.6	
Loss in tonnage pick mined coal as compared with year 1909.	266,919	tons.
Average tons lump coal mined by each pick miner for year 1910	408	
Average tons lump coal mined by each pick miner per day, 1910	2.4	
Average tons "run-of-mine" coal mined by each pick miner for year 1910	602	
Average tons "run-of-mine" coal mined by each pick miner per day in 1910	3.6	

TABLE SHOWING TONS OF LUMP COAL MINED IN 1910, THE NUMBER OF PICK MINERS, AVERAGE DAYS WORKED, AND AVERAGE TONS PRODUCED BY EACH MAN PER DAY AND PER YEAR.

Name of County.	Number of Pick Miners Employed.	Average Days Pick Miners Worked.	Tons Lump Coal Pick Miners Produced.	Average Tons Mined by Each Pick Miner for the Year 1910.	Average Tons Mined by Each Miner Per Day.
Athens	258	154	148,149	574	3.7
Belmont	274	185	120,851	441	2.4
Carroll	124	213	43,336	349	1.6
Columbiana	386	245	224,690	582	2.4
Coshocton	309	222	153,138	496	2.2
Gallia	63	74	10,063	160	2.2
Guernsey	42	205	12,813	305	1.5
Harrison	96	157	28,319	295	1.9
Hocking	222	196	142,263	641	3.3
Holmes	32	181	7,610	238	1.3
Jackson	1,128	151	394,435	350	2.3
Jefferson	349	213	193,270	554	2.6
Lawrence	399	163	122,505	307	1.9
Mahoning	81	228	23,213	287	1.3
Medina	37	170	20,154	545	3.2
Meigs	130	147	57,112	439	3.0
Morgan	7	94	1,654	236	2.5
Muskingum	350	152	138,739	396	2.6
Noble	58	115	14,158	244	2.1
Perry	260	180	176,684	680	3.8
Portage	135	212	49,546	367	1.7
Scioto	17	209	7,317	430	2.1
Stark	784	165	333,257	425	2.6
Summit	98	198	37,888	387	2.0
Trumbull	20	180	3,823	191	1.1
Tuscarawas	1,144	126	333,294	291	2.3
Vinton	174	118	42,764	246	2.1
Wayne	237	173	104,037	439	2.5
Total	7,214	*168	2,945,082	*408	*2.4

* NOTE: —

Average days worked by pick miners 168

Average number tons lump coal mined by each man for year was 408

Average number tons lump coal mined by each man per day... 2.4

TABLE SHOWING PRODUCTION OF MACHINE-MINED COAL BY COUNTIES, AND PERCENTAGE OF LUMP COAL DURING THE YEAR 1910.

Name of County.	Lump.	Nut.	Pea and Slack.	Total.	Per Cent. of Lump Coal.
Athens	4,120,697	674,781	936,176	5,731,654	71.9
Belmont	5,422,894	963,100	1,766,150	8,152,144	66.5
Carroll	179,637	30,839	39,015	249,491	72.0
Columbiana	290,145	57,990	97,644	445,779	65.1
Coshocton	114,222	25,125	38,542	177,889	64.2
Gallia	*	*	*	*	*
Guernsey	2,958,112	511,400	986,620	4,456,132	66.4
Harrison	354,247	45,266	156,726	556,239	63.7
Hocking	895,154	145,839	209,349	1,250,342	71.6
Holmes	*	*	*	*	*
Jackson	245,579	19,003	51,735	316,317	77.6
Jefferson	3,305,249	469,077	1,046,205	4,820,531	68.6
Lawrence	13,035	1,884	3,012	17,931	72.7
Mahoning	20,885	177	6,722	27,784	75.2
Medina	*	*	*	*	*
Meigs	421,683	26,398	116,746	564,827	74.7
Morgan	84,657	12,625	27,004	124,286	68.1
Muskingum	45,342	8,318	12,676	66,336	68.4
Noble	305,257	25,187	93,130	423,574	72.1
Perry	1,556,074	244,612	350,469	2,151,155	72.3
Portage	26,938	5,146	7,182	39,266	68.6
Scioto	*	*	*	*	*
Stark	54,392	3,086	3,549	61,027	89.1
Summit	18,578	6,345	7,806	32,729	56.8
Trumbull	*	*	*	*	*
Tuscarawas	186,007	38,794	61,826	286,627	64.9
Vinton	74,451	7,573	18,652	100,676	74.0
Wayne	23,453	3,424	3,855	30,732	76.3
Total	20,716,688	3,325,989	6,040,791	30,083,468	†68.9

* No machine coal.
† Average per cent. lump coal in machine mines of state.
Per cent. machine-mined coal, 87.4%.
Gain in tonnage machine-mined coal as compared with 1909, 6,936,838 tons.

TABLE SHOWING THE NUMBER OF RUNNERS AND LOADERS EMPLOYED DURING 1910; AVERAGE DAYS WORKED BY EACH; TOTAL TONS LUMP COAL PRODUCED BY EACH AND AVERAGE TONS CUT AND LOADED BY EACH, PER YEAR AND PER DAY.

Name of County.	Number Drillers, Shooters and Loaders Employed.	Number Machine Runners Including Helpers Employed.	Average Days Worked by Each Driller, Shooter and Loader.	Average Days Worked by Each Machine Runner.	Number Tons Lump Coal Produced in Machine Mines.	Average Tons Loaded by Each Driller, Shooter and Loader for Year.	Average Tons Loaded by Each Driller, Shooter and Loader Per Day.	Average Tons Cut by Each Machine Runner for Year.	Average Tons Cut by Each Machine Runner Per Day.
Athens	5,152	529	190	191	4,120,697	800	4.2	7.790	40.8
Belmont	6,0[illegible]8	781	236	231	5,422,894	891	3.8	6,944	30.1
Carroll	300	54	171	149	179,637	599	3.5	3,327	22.3
Columbiana ..	351	66	214	219	290,145	827	3.9	4,396	20.1
Coshocton ..	150	44	234	230	114,222	761	3.3	2,596	11.3
Gallia	......	......	......	......	......	......	......	......	......
Guernsey ...	3,279	355	235	233	2,958,112	902	3.8	8,333	35.8
Harrison ...	331	70	222	216	354,247	1,070	4.8	5,061	23.4
Hocking	1,234	133	194	188	895,154	725	3.7	6,730	35.8
Holmes	......	......	......	......	......	......	......	......	......
Jackson	334	60	179	170	245,579	735	4.1	4,093	24.1
Jefferson	3,494	477	231	225	3,305,249	946	4.1	6,929	30.8
Lawrence ...	85	14	66	92	13,035	153	2.3	931	10.1
Mahoning ...	32	6	223	230	20,885	653	2.9	3,481	15.1
Medina	......	......	......	......	......	......	......	......	......
Meigs	537	92	204	193	421,683	785	3.8	4,627	24.0
Morgan	294	44	73	78	84,657	288	3.9	1,924	24.7
Muskingum .	178	32	89	94	45,342	255	2.9	1,417	15.1
Noble	287	39	254	331	305,257	1,064	4.2	7,827	23.6
Perry	2,267	262	180	153	1,556,074	686	3.8	5,939	38.8
Portage	41	18	189	178	26,938	657	3.5	1,497	8.4
Scioto	......	......	......	......	......	......	......	......	......
Stark	85	26	158	165	54,392	640	4.1	2,092	12.7
Summit	33	6	180	180	18,578	563	3.1	3,096	17.2
Trumbull	......	......	......	......	......	......	......	......	......
Tuscarawas .	470	161	91	90	186,007	396	4.4	1,155	12.8
Vinton	122	16	233	170	74,451	610	2.6	4,653	27.4
Wayne	32	8	143	143	23,453	733	5.1	2,932	20.5
Total ...	25,176	3,293	†209	*201	20,716,688	823	3.9	6,291	31.3

NOTE.

Average tons lump coal cut by each runner for year........ 6,291
Average tons lump coal cut by each machine runner for each day 31.3
Average tons lump coal loaded by each loader for year...... 823
Average tons lump coal loaded by each loader for each day.. 3.9
*Average days worked by machine runners................. 201
†Average days worked by drillers, loaders and shooters..... 209

TABLE SHOWING THE COAL OUTPUT SINCE 1872 IN PICK AND MACHINE MINES, AND THE TOTAL TONNAGE FOR EACH YEAR.

Year.	Total Tonnage Pick Coal Produced Each Year Since 1872.	Total Tonnage Machine Coal Produced Since 1889 When Machinery Was Used to Undercut Coal.	Total Number Tons Produced for Each Year Since 1872.	Gain.	Loss.
1872	5,315,294		5,315,294		
1873	4,550,028		4,550,028		765,266
1874	3,267,585		3,267,585		1,282,443
1875	4,864,259		4,864,259	1,596,674	
1876	3,500,000		3,500,000		1,364,259
1877	5,250,000		5,250,000	1,750,000	
1878	5,500,000		5,500,000	250,000	
1879	6,000,000		6,000,000	500,000	
1880	7,000,000		7,000,000	1,000,000	
1881	8,225,000		8,225,000	1,225,000	
1882	9,450,000		9,450,000	1,225,000	
1883	8,229,429		8,229,429		1,220,571
1884	7,650,062		7,650,062		579,367
1885	7,816,179		7,816,179	166,117	
1886	8,435,211		8,435,211	619,032	
1887	10,301,708		10,301,708	1,866,479	
1888	10,910,946		10,910,946	613,338	
1889	10,007,385	900,000	10,907,385		3,561
1890	10,640,360	1,148,499	11,788,859	881,474	
1891	11,396,106	1,654,081	13,050,187	1,261,328	
1892	12,360,828	2,239,080	14,599,908	1,549,721	
1893	12,275,023	2,553,074	14,828,097	228,189	
1894	9,354,753	2,555,466	11,910,219		2,917,878
1895	10,563,423	3,120,456	13,683,879	1,773,660	
1896	9,544,259	3,368,349	12,912,608		771,271
1897	8,342,698	4,106,124	12,448,822		463,786
1898	8,805,557	5,252,598	14,058,155	1,609,333	
1899	9,167,874	6,741,060	15,908,934	1,850,799	
1900	9,966,872	9,457,777	19,426,649	3,517,715	
1901	9,831,476	10,489,814	20,321,290	894,641	
1902	10,489,619	13,439,648	23,929,267	3,607,977	
1903	10,012,335	14,560,931	24,573,266	643,979	
1904	8,037,360	16,546,455	24,583,815	10,549	
1905	6,825,125	19,009,532	25,834,657	1,250,842	
1906	6,500,263	20,713,232	27,213,495	1,378,838	
1907	6,511,773	25,854,176	32,365,949	5,152,454	
1908	4,676,869	21,610,931	26,287,800		6,078,149
1909	4,608,402	23,146,630	27,755,032	1,467,232	
1910	4,341,483	30,083,468	34,424,951	6,669,919	

TABLE SHOWING ANNUAL PRODUCTION OF PICK AND MACHINE-MINED COAL, AND THE GAIN AND LOSS SINCE THE YEAR 1889 OR THE INTRODUCTION OF MINING MACHINERY.

Year.	Total Tons Pick Coal Produced Since 1889.	Gain.	Loss.	Total Tons Machine Coal Produced Since 1889.	Gain.	Loss.
1889	10,007,385	....	....	900,000	....	....
1890	10.640,360	632,975	....	1,148,499	248,499	....
1891	11,396.106	755,746	....	1,654,081	505,632	....
1892	12,360,828	964,722	....	2,239,080	584,999	....
1893	12,275,023	....	85,805	2,553,074	313,994	....
1894	9,354,753	....	2,920,270	2,555,466	2,392	....
1895	10,563,423	1,208,670	....	3,120,456	564,990	....
1896	9,544,259	....	1,019,164	3,368,349	247,893	....
1897	8,342,698	....	1,201,561	4,106,124	737,775	....
1898	8,805,557	462,859	....	5,252,598	1,146,474	....
1899	9,167,874	362,317	....	6,741,060	1,488,462	....
1900	9,966,872	798,998	....	9,457,777	2,716,717	....
1901	9.831,476	....	135,396	10,489,814	1,032,037	....
1902	10,489,619	658,143	....	13,439,648	2,949,834	....
1903	10,012,335	....	477,284	14,560,931	1,121,283	....
1904	8,037,360	....	1,974,975	16,546,455	1,985,524	....
1905	6,825,125	....	1,212,235	19,009,532	2,463,077	....
1906	6,500,263	....	324,862	20,713,232	1,703,700	....
1907	6,511,773	11,510	....	25,854,176	5,140,944	....
1908	4,676,869	....	1,834,904	21,610,931	....	4,243,245
1909	4,608,402	....	68,467	23,146,630	1,535,699	....
1910	4.341,463	....	266,919	30,083,468	6,936,838	....

TABLE SHOWING THE NUMBER OF COMPANIES WHO REPORTED AS HANDLING POWDER, AND THE NUMBER NOT REPORTED; IN PICK AND MACHINE MINES IN THE COUNTIES OF THE STATE FOR THE YEAR 1910.

Name of County.	Companies Who Reported Powder.	Companies Failing to Report Powder.	Number of Kegs of Powder Reported by Pick Mines.	Number of Kegs of Powder Reported by Machine Mines.	Total Number of Kegs of Powder Reported.
Athens	27	9	3,344	35,432	38,776
Belmont	41	32	1,470	29,373	30,843
Carroll	16	6	2,485	950	3,435
Columbiana	26	12	6,338	2,562	8,900
Coshocton	14	13	5,930	1,817	7,747
Gallia	4	3	301	....	301
Guernsey	20	10	59	33,151	33,210
Harrison	14	27	180	2,160	2,340
Hocking	21	5	3,242	9,672	12,914
Holmes	5	4	47	....	47
Jackson	71	9	25,259	4,116	29,375
Jefferson	24	26	638	12,019	12,657
Lawrence	34	12	4,863	245	5,108
Mahoning	6	9	1,189	80	1,269
Medina	5	1	778	....	778
Meigs	26	14	1,096	4,166	5,262
Morgan	3	2	175	517	692
Muskingum	22	28	8,120	412	8,532
Noble	20	7	89	2,810	2,899
Perry	40	10	4,560	18,822	23,382
Portage	4	1	3,860	540	4,400
Scioto	2	....	379	....	379
Stark	36	14	15,178	848	16,026
Summit	7	1	2,927	758	3,685
Trumbull	4	5	95	....	95
Tuscarawas	50	20	9,519	1,524	11,043
Vinton	17	8	2,882	468	3,350
Wayne	9	2	5,529	432	5,961
Total	568	290	110,532	162,874	273,406

N. B. — This table does not show all the powder used in the production of coal; many miners buy powder independent of the companies, and it is not reported.

TABLE SHOWING THE NUMBER OF MACHINE RUNNERS, DRILLERS, SHOOTERS AND LOADERS; INSIDE AND OUTSIDE DAY HANDS AND NUMBER OF KEGS OF POWDER USED AND TOTAL TONNAGE OF MACHINE MINES OF THE YEAR 1910.

Name of County.	Number Runners.	Number Loaders.	Number Inside Day Hands.	Number Outside Day Hands.	Total No. Men Employed.	Kegs of Powder used in Machine Mines.	Total No. Tons Machine Mined Coal.	Per Cent. of Machine Mined Coal as compared with total Output in County.	Average No. Days worked by Runners.	Average Number Days worked by Drillers, Loaders and Shooters.
Athens	529	5,152	1,385	887	7,958	35,432	5,731,654	96.4	191	190
Belmont	781	6,068	1,478	743	9,090	29,373	8,152,144	97.8	231	236
Carroll	54	301	103	30	487	850	259,491	80.7	149	171
Columbiana	68	351	120	58	795	2,562	445,779	60.2	219	214
Coshocton	44	150	43	37	294	1,817	177,899	40.8	230	234
Gallia	......	......	......	......	......	......	......	......	......	......
Guernsey	325	3,279	1,192	323	5,119	33,151	4,476,132	99.6	233	235
Harrison	70	331	112	72	785	2,160	776,239	92.7	216	222
Hocking	133	1,234	297	233	1,897	9,672	1,250,342	96.2	188	194
Holmes	......	......	......	......	......	......	......	......	......	......
Jackson	60	331	186	129	709	4,116	316,317	33.9	170	179
Jefferson	477	3,494	935	615	5,521	12,019	4,820,531	94.8	225	231
Lawrence	14	85	24	8	131	245	17,931	9.4	92	66
Mahoning	6	32	8	5	51	80	27,784	41.9	230	223
Medina	......	......	......	......	......	......	......	......	......	......
Meigs	92	537	144	82	835	4,166	564,827	87.1	163	204
Morgan	44	294	58	38	434	517	124,296	98.2	78	73
Muskingum	32	178	32	32	274	412	66,336	24.5	94	89
Noble	39	287	112	32	470	2,810	423,574	95.9	331	254
Perry	262	2,267	516	358	3,396	18,822	2,151,155	89.9	153	180
Portage	18	41	20	10	89	540	39,366	37.3	178	189
Scioto	......	......	......	......	......	......	......	......	......	......
Stark	26	85	2	......	113	848	61,027	11.1	165	158
Summit	6	33	12	11	62	758	32,729	34.7	180	180
Trumbull	......	......	......	......	......	......	......	......	......	......
Tuscarawas	161	470	144	98	873	1,524	266,627	35.3	90	91
Vinton	16	122	15	8	161	468	100,676	63.3	170	233
Wayne	8	32	14	10	61	432	30,732	18.7	143	143
Total	3,293	25,176	6,960	3,794	39,223	162,874	30,063,468	†87.4	*201	*209

*Average days worked for the year.
NOTE — †Per cent. of machine-mined coal for the State.

TABLE SHOWING COMPARISON FOR YEARS 1909 AND 1910 PERTAINING TO THE NUMBER OF MINING MACHINES IN OPERATION; AVERAGE NUMBER TONS OF "RUN-OF-MINE" CUT BY EACH RUNNER FOR THE YEAR AND FOR EACH DAY; ALSO NUMBER OF TONS CUT BY EACH MACHINE FOR EACH YEAR AND FOR EACH DAY.

Name of County.	Number Mining Machines in Use in 1909.	Number Mining Machines in use in 1910.	Gain.	Loss.	Average tons "Run-of-Mine" cut by each Runner in 1909.	Average tons "Run-of-Mine" cut by each Runner in 1910.	Average tons "Run-of-Mine" cut by each Runner per day in 1909.	Average tons "Run-of-Mine" cut by each Runner per day 1910.	Average tons cut by each Machine in 1909.	Average tons cut by each Machine in 1910.	Average tons cut by each Machine per day in 1909.	Average tons cut by each Machine per day in 1910.
Athens	169	206	37	....	8,464	10,834	53.6	56.7	24,841	27,824	157.2	145.7
Belmont	283	295	12	....	8,101	10,438	45.8	45.2	20,381	27,634	115.1	119.6
Carroll	33	27	......	6	5,554	4,620	27.0	31.0	10,098	9,240	49.0	62.0
Columbiana	35	32	......	3	5,827	6,754	25.2	30.8	12,154	13,931	52.6	63.6
Coshocton	25	22	......	3	3,961	4,043	26.6	17.6	6,496	8,086	43.6	35.2
Gallia	......	......	......	....	......	......	......	......	......	......	......	......
Guernsey	127	128	1	....	9,395	12,552	54.3	58.9	24,264	34,514	140.3	149.4
Harrison	24	32	8	....	10,121	7,946	50.1	36.8	22,351	17,382	110.6	80.5
Hocking	47	59	12	....	6,780	9,401	49.5	50.0	17,600	21,192	128.5	112.7
Holmes	......	......	......	....	......	......	......	......	......	......	......	......
Jackson	41	53	12	....	3,779	5,272	25.7	31.0	5,714	5,968	38.9	35.1
Jefferson	238	235	......	3	8,152	10,106	45.3	44.9	15,551	20,513	86.4	91.2
Lawrence	6	7	1	....	2,910	1,281	22.4	13.9	5,820	2,562	44.8	27.8
Mahoning	......	4	4	....	......	4,631	......	20.1	......	6,946	......	30.2
Medina	......	......	......	....	......	......	......	......	......	......	......	......
Meigs	38	54	16	....	6,405	6,139	30.4	31.8	12,813	10,460	60.7	54.2
Morgan	14	14	......	....	4,458	2,825	39.1	36.2	13,374	8,878	117.3	113.8
Muskingum	20	20	......	....	4,594	2,073	27.5	22.1	9,188	3,317	55.0	35.3
Noble	13	13	......	....	8,839	10,861	52.6	32.8	27,198	32,583	161.9	98.5
Perry	126	122	......	4	6,200	8,211	41.3	53.7	15,007	17,632	100.0	115.2
Portage	12	11	......	1	2,388	2,181	19.6	12.3	1,592	3,570	13.0	20.1
Scioto	......	......	......	....	......	......	......	......	......	......	......	......
Stark	30	26	......	4	2,127	2,347	12.2	14.2	2,127	2,317	12.2	14.2
Summit	3	3	......	....	2,331	5,455	19.3	30.3	7,771	10,910	64.2	60.6
Trumbull	......	......	......	....	......	......	......	......	......	......	......	......
Tuscarawas	102	96	......	6	3,257	1,780	17.5	19.8	5,428	2,986	29.2	33.2
Vinton	7	9	2	....	3,622	6,292	22.4	37.0	11,383	11,186	70.3	65.8
Wayne	2	5	3	....	812	3,812	8.0	26.9	1,219	6,146	12.0	43.0
Total	1,395	1,473	108	30	7,327	9,136	42.8	45.5	16,593	20,423	97.0	101.6

NOTE.

Number Mining Machines in operation in 1910	1,473
Number Mining Machines in operation in 1909	1,395
Increase as compared with 1909	78
Average number tons "Run-of-Mine" cut by each Runner for year 1910	9,136
Average number tons "Run-of-Mine" cut by each Runner for year 1909	7,327
Increase as compared with 1909	1,809
Average number tons "Run-of-Mine" cut by each Runner per day, 1910	45.5
Average number tons "Run-of-Mine" cut by each Runner per day in 1909	42.8
Increase as compared with 1909	2.7
Average number tons "Run-of-Mine" cut by each Machine for year 1910	20,423
Average number tons "Run-of-Mine" cut by each Machine for year 1909	16,593
Increase as compared with 1909	3,830
Average number tons "Run-of-Mine" cut by each Machine per day in 1910	101.6
Average number tons "Run-of-Mine" cut by each Machine per day in 1909	97.0
Increase as compared with 1909	4.6

TABLE SHOWING NUMBER OF DAYS WORKED BY PICK MINERS, DRILLERS, SHOOTERS AND LOADERS, AND MACHINE RUNNERS; TONS OF LUMP COAL PRODUCED BY EACH PER YEAR AND PER DAY IN 1910 AS COMPARED WITH THE YEAR 1909.

Name of County.	Average Days Pick Miners Worked in 1909.	Average Days Pick Miners Worked in 1910.	Average Days Drillers, Shooters and Loaders Worked in 1909.	Average Days Drillers, Shooters and Loaders Worked in 1910.	Average Days Machine Runners Worked in 1909.	Average Days Machine Runners Worked in 1910.	Average Number Tons Lump Coal Produced by Each Pick Miner in 1909.	Average Number Tons Lump Coal Produced by Each Pick Miner in 1910.	Average Number Tons Lump Coal Produced by Each Pick Miner Per Day in 1909.	Average Number Tons Lump Coal Produced by Each Pick Miner Per Day in 1910.	Avg. No. Tons Lump Coal Produced by Each Driller, Shooter and Loader for Year 1909	Avg. No. Tons Lump Coal Produced by Each Driller, Shooter and Loader for Year 1910.	Avg. No. Tons Lump Coal Produced by Each Driller, Shooter and Loader Per Day in 1909.	Avg. No. Tons Lump Coal Produced by Each Driller, Shooter and Loader Per Day in 1910.	Average Number Tons Lump Coal Cut by Each Machine Runner in 1909.	Average Number Tons Lump Coal Cut by Each Machine Runner for Year 1910.	Average Number Tons Lump Coal Cut by Each Machine Runner Per Day in 1909.	Average Number Tons Lump Coal Cut by Each Machine Runner Per Day in 1910.
Athens	150	154	158	190	158	191	503	574	3.4	3.7	614	800	3.9	4.2	5,960	7,790	37.7	40.8
Belmont	172	185	180	236	177	231	409	441	2.4	2.4	696	891	3.9	3.8	5,346	6,944	30.2	30.1
Carroll	215	213	203	171	206	149	367	349	1.7	1.6	659	599	3.2	3.5	3,798	3,327	18.4	22.3
Columbiana.	219	245	234	214	231	219	367	582	1.7	2.4	623	827	2.7	3.9	3,807	4,396	16.5	20.1
Coshocton ..	196	222	136	234	149	230	431	496	2.2	2.2	427	761	3.1	3.3	2,497	2,596	16.8	11.3
Gallia	135	74	......	......	......	......	228	160	1.7	2.2	......	......	......	......	......	......	......	......
Guernsey ...	189	205	169	235	173	233	310	305	1.6	1.5	712	902	4.2	3.8	6,416	8,333	37.1	35.8
Harrison ...	211	157	195	222	202	216	297	295	1.4	1.9	859	1,070	4.4	4.8	5,998	5,061	20.7	23.4
Hocking	191	196	142	194	137	188	504	641	2.6	3.3	511	725	3.6	3.7	4,661	6,730	34.0	35.8
Holmes	190	181	......	......	......	......	254	238	1.3	1.3	......	......	......	......	......	......	......	......
Jackson	153	151	149	179	147	170	327	350	2.1	2.3	571	735	3.8	4.1	2,890	4,093	19.7	24.1
Jefferson ...	189	213	182	231	180	225	506	554	2.7	2.6	732	946	4.0	4.1	5,368	6,929	29.8	30.8
Lawrence ...	185	163	130	66	130	92	321	307	1.7	1.9	373	153	2.9	2.3	2,022	931	15.6	10.1
Mahoning ..	157	228	......	223	......	230	235	287	1.5	1.3	......	653	......	2.9	......	3,481	......	15.1
Medina	125	170	......	......	......	......	209	545	1.7	3.2	......	......	......	......	......	......	......	......
Meigs	157	147	205	204	211	193	278	439	1.8	3.0	693	785	3.4	3.8	4,294	4,627	20.4	24.0

TABLE SHOWING NUMBER OF DAYS WORKED BY PICK MINERS, ETC.— Concluded.

Name of County.	Average Days Pick Miners Worked in 1909.	Average Days Pick Miners Worked in 1910.	Average Days Drillers, Shooters and Loaders Worked in 1909.	Average Days Drillers, Shooters and Loaders Worked in 1910.	Average Days Machine Runners Worked in 1909.	Average Days Machine Runners Worked in 1910.	Average Number Tons Lump Coal Produced by Each Pick Miner in 1909.	Average Number Tons Lump Coal Produced by Each Pick Miner in 1910.	Average Number Tons Lump Coal Produced by Each Pick Miner Per Day in 1909.	Average Number Tons Lump Coal Produced by Each Pick Miner Per Day in 1910.	Avg. No. Tons Lump Coal Produced by Each Driller, Shooter and Loader for Year 1909	Avg. No. Tons Lump Coal Produced by Each Driller, Shooter and Loader for Year 1910.	Avg. No. Tons Lump Coal Produced by Each Driller, Shooter and Loader Per Day in 1909.	Avg. No. Tons Lump Coal Produced by Each Driller, Shooter and Loader Per Day in 1910.	Average Number Tons Lump Coal Cut by Each Machine Runner in 1909.	Average Number Tons Lump Coal Cut by Each Machine Runner for Year 1910.	Average Number Tons Lump Coal Cut by Each Machine Runner Per Day in 1909.	Average Number Tons Lump Coal Cut by Each Machine Runner Per Day in 1910.
Morgan	....	94	113	73	114	78	....	236	....	2.5	564	288	5.0	3.9	3,479	1,924	30.5	24.7
Muskingum	189	152	154	89	167	94	462	396	2.4	2.6	577	255	3.7	2.9	3,362	1,417	20.1	15.1
Noble	148	115	170	254	168	331	261	244	1.8	2.1	824	1,064	4.8	4.2	5,499	7,827	32.7	23.6
Perry	174	180	172	180	150	153	564	680	3.2	3.8	571	686	3.3	3.8	4,324	5,939	28.8	38.8
Portage	208	212	122	189	122	178	371	367	1.8	1.7	508	657	4.2	3.5	1,588	1,497	13.0	8.4
Scioto	125	209	....	....	....	....	260	430	2.1	2.1	....	....	....	....	....	....	....	....
Stark	193	165	168	158	175	165	340	425	1.8	2.6	408	640	2.4	4.1	1,578	2,092	9.0	12.7
Summit	132	198	121	180	121	180	294	387	2.2	2.0	246	563	2.0	3.1	1,204	3,096	10.0	17.2
Trumbull	135	180	....	....	....	....	204	191	1.5	1.1	....	....	....	....	....	....	....	....
Tuscarawas	215	126	195	91	186	90	505	291	2.3	2.3	770	396	3.9	4.4	2,186	1,155	11.8	12.8
Vinton	98	118	161	233	162	170	181	246	1.8	2.1	521	610	3.2	2.6	2,773	4,653	17.1	27.4
Washington	260	....	....	....	....	....	838	....	3.2	....	....	....	....	....	....	....	....	....
Wayne	145	173	102	143	102	143	446	439	3.1	2.5	217	733	2.1	5.1	650	2,932	6.4	20.5

Average number days worked by Pick Miners in 1909 182
Average number days worked by Pick Miners in 1910 168
Average number days worked by Drillers, Shooters and Loaders in 1909 172

Average number days worked by Drillers, Shooters and Loaders in 1910	209
Average number days worked by Machine Runners in 1909	171
Average number days worked by Machine Runners in 1910	201
Average tons lump coal mined by each Pick Miner in 1909	395
Average tons lump coal mined by each Pick Miner in 1910	408
Average tons lump coal mined by each Pick Miner per day in 1909	2.2
Average tons lump coal mined by each Pick Miner per day in 1910	2.4
Average tons lump coal loaded by each Driller, Shooter and Loader in 1909	658
Average tons lump coal loaded by each Driller, Shooter and Loader in 1910	823
Average tons lump coal loaded by each Driller, Shooter and Loader per day in 1909	3.8
Average tons lump coal loaded by each Driller, Shooter and Loader per day in 1910	3.9
Average tons lump coal cut by each Machine Runner for year 1909	4,956
Average tons lump coal cut by each Machine Runner for year 1910	6,291
Average tons lump coal cut by each Machine Runner for the day in 1909	29.0
Average tons lump coal cut by each Machine Runner for the day in 1910	31.3

TABLE SHOWING TOTAL TONS RUN-OF-MINE COAL PRODUCED; AVERAGE TONS PRODUCED IN BOTH PICK AND MACHINE MINES FOR EACH MINER, RUNNER AND LOADER FOR THE YEAR 1910, FOR YEAR AND DAY.

Name of County.	Number of Tons Mined With Pick.	Number of Tons Mined With Machine.	Average Number of Tons Run-of-Mine Mined by Each Pick Miner Per Year in Pick Mines.	Average Number of Tons Run-of-Mine Mined by Each Pick Miner Per Day in Pick Mines.	Average Number of Tons Run-of-Mine Cut by Each Runner Per Year in Machine Mines.	Average Number of Tons Run-of-Mine Cut by Each Runner Per Day in Machine Mines.	Average Number of Tons Loaded by Each Loader Per Year in Machine Mines.	Average Number of Tons Loaded by Each Loader Per Day in Machine Mines.
Athens	211,984	5,731,654	822	5.3	10,834	56.7	1,113	5.9
Belmont	184,284	8,152,144	673	3.6	10,438	45.2	1,339	5.7
Carroll	59,837	249,491	483	2.3	4,620	31.0	832	4.9
Columbiana	294,566	445,779	763	3.1	6,754	30.8	1,270	5.9
Coshocton	258,014	177,889	835	3.8	4,043	17.6	1,186	5.1
Gallia	13,923	....	221	3.0	....	.....	....	.....
Guernsey	16,890	4,456,132	402	2.0	12,552	53.9	1,359	5.8
Harrison	43,502	556,239	453	2.9	7,946	36.8	1,680	7.6
Hocking	200,805	1,250,342	905	4.6	9,401	50.0	1,013	5.2
Holmes	13,203	....	413	2.3	....	.....	....	.....
Jackson	616,921	316,317	547	3.6	5,272	31.0	947	5.3
Jefferson	291,032	4,820,531	834	3.9	10,106	44.9	1,380	6.0
Lawrence	172,534	17,931	432	2.7	1,281	13.9	211	3.2
Mahoning	38,528	27,784	476	2.1	4,631	20.1	868	3.9
Medina	27,604	....	746	4.4	....	.....	....	.....
Meigs	83,322	564,827	641	4.4	6,139	31.8	1,052	5.2
Morgan	2,258	124,286	323	3.4	2,825	36.2	423	5.8
Muskingum	204,080	66,336	583	3.8	2,073	22.1	373	4.2
Noble	18,249	423,574	315	2.7	10,861	32.8	1,476	5.8
Perry	243,806	2,151,155	938	5.2	8,211	53.7	949	5.3
Portage	65,889	39,266	488	2.3	2,181	12.3	958	5.1
Scioto	9,834	....	578	2.8	....	.....	....	.....
Stark	486,608	61,027	621	3.8	2,347	14.2	718	4.5
Summit	61,617	32,729	629	3.2	5,455	30.3	992	5.5
Trumbull	4,716	....	236	1.3	....	.....	....	.....
Tuscarawas	525,155	286,627	459	3.6	1,780	19.8	610	6.7
Vinton	58,330	100,676	335	2.8	6,292	37.0	825	3.5
Wayne	133,992	30,732	565	3.3	3,842	26.9	960	6.7
Total	4,341,483	30,083,468	*602	*3.6	*9,136	*45.5	*1,195	*5.7

NOTE — *Average for state.

TABLE SHOWING THE NUMBER OF TONS OF PICK AND MACHINE COAL, ALSO TOTAL NUMBER TONS PRODUCED; THE PER CENT. OF MACHINE COAL IN EACH COUNTY, AS COMPARED WITH THE TOTAL TONNAGE; THE NUMBER OF PICK MINERS, MACHINE RUNNERS, DRILLERS, SHOOTERS AND LOADERS; THE AVERAGE NUMBER OF TONS OF LUMP COAL PRODUCED BY EACH PICK MINER, MACHINE RUNNER AND LOADER FOR THE YEAR 1910, NUMBER OF DAY HANDS EMPLOYED; AVERAGE NUMBER OF TONS RUN-OF-MINE PRODUCED BY EACH DAY HAND.

County	Total No. Tons Pick Mined Coal in 1910	Total No. Tons Machine Mined Coal in 1910	Total No. Tons Produced in 1910	Per cent. of Machine Mined Coal, 1910	Total No. Pick Miners	Total No. Machine Runners	Total No. Drillers, Shooters and Loaders	Average No. Days worked by Pick Miners	Average No. Days worked by Machine Miners, 1910	Average No. Tons Lump Coal Mined for each Pick Miner	Average No. Tons of Lump Coal cut by each Machine Runner, 1910	Average No. Tons Lump Coal loaded by each Driller, Shooter, Loader in 1910	Total No. Day Hands Inside and Outside in both Pick and Machine Mines in 1910	Average No. Tons of Run-of-Mine Produced for each day Hand in and out in Pick and Machine in 1910
[illegible]	[illegible]	[illegible]	[illegible]	[illegible]	[illegible]	[illegible]	[illegible]	[illegible]	[illegible]	[illegible]	7,700	800	2,344	2,536
[illegible]	[illegible]	[illegible]	[illegible]	[illegible]	[illegible]	[illegible]	[illegible]	[illegible]	[illegible]	441	[illegible]	891	2,287	3,645
[illegible]	[illegible]	[illegible]	[illegible]	[illegible]	[illegible]	[illegible]	[illegible]	[illegible]	[illegible]	[illegible]	[illegible]	[illegible]	170	1,819
[illegible]	[illegible]	[illegible]	[illegible]	[illegible]	[illegible]	[illegible]	[illegible]	[illegible]	[illegible]	[illegible]	[illegible]	[illegible]	[illegible]	2,484
[illegible]	[illegible]	[illegible]	[illegible]	[illegible]	[illegible]	[illegible]	[illegible]	[illegible]	[illegible]	[illegible]	[illegible]	761	[illegible]	2,158
[illegible]	[illegible]		[illegible]		[illegible]			[illegible]		[illegible]	....	....	24	580
[illegible]	[illegible]	[illegible]	[illegible]	[illegible]	[illegible]	[illegible]	[illegible]	[illegible]	[illegible]	[illegible]	[illegible]	[illegible]	[illegible]	3,006
[illegible]	[illegible]	[illegible]	[illegible]	[illegible]	[illegible]	[illegible]	[illegible]	[illegible]	[illegible]	[illegible]	[illegible]	1,070	198	3,029
[illegible]	[illegible]	[illegible]	[illegible]	[illegible]	[illegible]	[illegible]	[illegible]	[illegible]	[illegible]	[illegible]	[illegible]	725	565	2,481
[illegible]	[illegible]		[illegible]		[illegible]			[illegible]		[illegible]	....	....	5	2,641
[illegible]	[illegible]	[illegible]	[illegible]	[illegible]	[illegible]	[illegible]	[illegible]	[illegible]	[illegible]	[illegible]	[illegible]	[illegible]	[illegible]	1,044
[illegible]	[illegible]	[illegible]	[illegible]	[illegible]	[illegible]	[illegible]	[illegible]	[illegible]	[illegible]	[illegible]	[illegible]	[illegible]	[illegible]	3,119
[illegible]	[illegible]	[illegible]	[illegible]	[illegible]	[illegible]	[illegible]	[illegible]	[illegible]	[illegible]	[illegible]	[illegible]	153	141	1,351
[illegible]	[illegible]	[illegible]	[illegible]	[illegible]	[illegible]	[illegible]	[illegible]	[illegible]	[illegible]	[illegible]	[illegible]	[illegible]	[illegible]	1,745
[illegible]	[illegible]		[illegible]		[illegible]			[illegible]		[illegible]			12	[illegible]
[illegible]	[illegible]	[illegible]	[illegible]	[illegible]	[illegible]	[illegible]	[illegible]	[illegible]	[illegible]	[illegible]	[illegible]	[illegible]	255	[illegible]
[illegible]	[illegible]	[illegible]	[illegible]	[illegible]	[illegible]	[illegible]	[illegible]	[illegible]	[illegible]	[illegible]	[illegible]	[illegible]	97	[illegible]
[illegible]	[illegible]	[illegible]	[illegible]	[illegible]	[illegible]	[illegible]	[illegible]	[illegible]	[illegible]	[illegible]	[illegible]	[illegible]	157	[illegible]
[illegible]	[illegible]	[illegible]	[illegible]	[illegible]	[illegible]	[illegible]	[illegible]	[illegible]	[illegible]	[illegible]	[illegible]	[illegible]	153	[illegible]
[illegible]	[illegible]	[illegible]	[illegible]	[illegible]	[illegible]	[illegible]	[illegible]	[illegible]	[illegible]	[illegible]	[illegible]	[illegible]	919	[illegible]
[illegible]	[illegible]	[illegible]	[illegible]	[illegible]	[illegible]	[illegible]	[illegible]	[illegible]	[illegible]	[illegible]	[illegible]	[illegible]	[illegible]	[illegible]
[illegible]	[illegible]		[illegible]		[illegible]			[illegible]		[illegible]			9	1,065
[illegible]	[illegible]	[illegible]	[illegible]	[illegible]	[illegible]	[illegible]	[illegible]	[illegible]	[illegible]	[illegible]	[illegible]	[illegible]	223	[illegible]
[illegible]	[illegible]	[illegible]	[illegible]	[illegible]	[illegible]	[illegible]	[illegible]	[illegible]	[illegible]	[illegible]	[illegible]	[illegible]	[illegible]	1,470
[illegible]	[illegible]		[illegible]		[illegible]			[illegible]		[illegible]			[illegible]	[illegible]
[illegible]	[illegible]	[illegible]	[illegible]	[illegible]	[illegible]	[illegible]	[illegible]	[illegible]	[illegible]	[illegible]	[illegible]	[illegible]	276	[illegible]
[illegible]	[illegible]	[illegible]	[illegible]	[illegible]	[illegible]	[illegible]	[illegible]	[illegible]	[illegible]	[illegible]	[illegible]	[illegible]	[illegible]	[illegible]
[illegible]	[illegible]	[illegible]	[illegible]	[illegible]	[illegible]	[illegible]	[illegible]	[illegible]	[illegible]	[illegible]	[illegible]	[illegible]	116	1,420
[illegible]	[illegible]	[illegible]	[illegible]	[illegible]	[illegible]	[illegible]	[illegible]	[illegible]	[illegible]	[illegible]	[illegible]	[illegible]	[illegible]	[illegible]

PERSONS EMPLOYED.

TABLE SHOWING NUMBER OF PICK MINERS, INSIDE AND OUTSIDE DAY HANDS, TOTAL PICK TONNAGE, THE PER CENT. AS COMPARED WITH TOTAL OUTPUT OF EACH COUNTY, AND NUMBER OF DAYS MINERS WORKED IN EACH COUNTY IN 1910.

Name of County.	Number of Pick Miners Employed.	Number Inside Day Hands Employed.	Number Outside Day Hands Employed.	Total Number Persons Engaged in Pick Mining.	Kegs Powder Used in Pick Mining.	Total Tons Coal Produced by Pick Miners.	Per Cent. of Pick Mined Coal as Compared with Output in County.	Average Number Days Worked by Each Pick Miner During Year 1910.
Athens	258	43	29	330	3,344	211,984	3.6	154
Belmont	274	36	30	340	1,470	184,284	2.2	185
Carroll	124	25	12	161	2,485	59,837	19.3	213
Columbiana ..	386	67	53	506	6,338	294,566	39.8	245
Coshocton ...	309	68	34	411	5,930	258,014	59.2	222
Gallia	63	14	10	87	301	13,923	100.0	74
Guernsey	42	2	1	45	59	16,890	.4	205
Harrison	96	9	5	110	180	43,502	7.3	157
Hocking	222	26	29	277	3,242	200,805	13.8	196
Holmes	32	2	3	37	47	13,203	100.0	181
Jackson	1,128	389	190	1,707	25,259	616,921	66.1	151
Jefferson	349	52	37	438	638	291,032	5.7	213
Lawrence	399	70	39	508	4,863	172,534	90.6	163
Mahoning	81	11	14	106	1,189	38,528	58.1	228
Medina	37	6	6	49	778	27,604	100.0	170
Meigs	130	15	14	159	1,096	83,322	12.9	147
Morgan	7	1	......	8	175	2,258	1.8	94
Muskingum ..	350	60	33	443	8,120	204,080	75.5	152
Noble	58	4	5	67	89	18,249	4.1	115
Perry	260	30	22	312	4,560	243,806	10.1	180
Portage	135	30	26	191	3,860	65,889	62.7	212
Scioto	17	5	4	26	379	9,834	100.0	209
Stark	784	167	154	1,105	15,178	486,608	88.9	165
Summit	98	21	20	139	2,927	61,617	65.3	198
Trumbull	20	3	4	27	95	4,716	....	180
Tuscarawas ..	1,144	217	117	1,478	9,519	525,155	64.7	126
Vinton	174	22	15	211	2,882	58,330	36.7	118
Wayne	237	45	47	329	5,529	133,992	81.8	173
Total ..	7,214	1,440	953	9,607	110,532	4,341,483	*12.6	†168

NOTE: —

† Average number days worked by each pick miner during year. 168

* Per cent. of pick-mined coal as compared with total output of state 12.6

TABLE SHOWING THE TOTAL NUMBER OF MEN EMPLOYED IN PICK MINING DURING YEAR 1910.

Counties.	Total Number Pick Miners Employed.	Total Number Day Hands Inside.	Total Number Day Hands Outside.	Total Number Employes in Pick Mines.
Athens	258	43	29	330
Belmont	274	36	30	340
Carroll	124	25	12	161
Columbiana	386	67	53	506
Coshocton	309	68	34	411
Gallia	63	14	10	87
Guernsey	42	2	1	45
Harrison	96	9	5	110
Hocking	222	26	29	277
Holmes	32	2	3	37
Jackson	1,128	389	190	1,707
Jefferson	349	52	37	438
Lawrence	399	70	39	508
Mahoning	81	11	14	106
Medina	37	6	6	49
Meigs	130	15	14	159
Morgan	7	1	....	8
Muskingum	350	60	33	443
Noble	58	4	5	67
Perry	260	30	22	312
Portage	135	30	26	191
Scioto	17	5	4	26
Stark	784	167	154	1,105
Summit	98	21	20	139
Trumbull	20	3	4	27
Tuscarawas	1,144	217	117	1,478
Vinton	174	22	15	211
Wayne	237	45	47	329
Total	7,214	1,440	953	9,607

TABLE SHOWING THE TOTAL NUMBER MEN EMPLOYED IN MACHINE MINING DURING THE YEAR 1910.

Counties.	Total Number Machine Runners Employed.	Total Number Drillers, Shooters and Loaders Employed.	Total Number Inside Day Hands Employed.	Total Number Outside Day Hands Employed.	Total Number Men Employed in Machine Mines.
Athens	529	5,152	1,385	887	7,953
Belmont	781	6,088	1,478	743	9,090
Carroll	54	300	103	30	487
Columbiana	66	351	120	58	595
Coshocton	44	150	63	37	294
Gallia	......	......	......	......	......
Guernsey	355	3,279	1,182	303	5,119
Harrison	70	331	112	72	585
Hocking	133	1,234	297	233	1,897
Holmes	......	......	......	......	......
Jackson	60	334	186	129	709
Jefferson	477	3,494	935	615	5,521
Lawrence	14	85	24	8	131
Mahoning	6	32	8	5	51
Medina	......	......	......	......	......
Meigs	92	537	144	82	855
Morgan	44	294	58	38	434
Muskingum	32	178	32	32	274
Noble	39	287	112	32	470
Perry	262	2,267	514	353	3,396
Portage	18	41	20	10	89
Scioto	......	......	......	......	......
Stark	26	85	2	......	113
Summit	6	33	12	11	62
Trumbull	......	......	......	......	......
Tuscarawas	161	470	144	98	873
Vinton	16	122	15	8	161
Wayne	8	32	14	10	64
Total	3,293	25,176	6,960	3,794	39,223

TABLE SHOWING THE TOTAL NUMBER OF PICK MINERS AND SHOOTERS AND LOADERS; RUNNERS; INSIDE AND OUTSIDE DAY HANDS AND THE TOTAL NUMBER OF PERSONS EMPLOYED AROUND THE MINES; ALSO THE TONS PRODUCED FOR EACH PERSON EMPLOYED IN 1910.

Name of County.	Total Number Pick Miners, Shooters and Loaders, 1910.	Total Number Inside Day Hands in Pick and Machine Mines.	Total Number Outside Day Hands in Pick and Machine Mines.	Total Number Machine Runners.	Total Number of all Persons Engaged in the Production of Coal.	Total Number Kegs of Powder Used in Each County.	Total Number Tons of Coal Produced in Both Pick and Machine Mines.	Number Tons Produced for Each Person in and Around the Mines for 1910.
Athens	5,410	1,428	916	529	8,283	38,776	5,943,638	718
Belmont	6,362	1,514	773	781	9,430	30,843	8,336,428	884
Carroll	424	128	42	54	648	3,435	309,328	477
Columbiana	737	187	111	66	1,101	8,900	740,345	672
Coshocton	459	131	71	44	705	7,747	435,903	618
Gallia	63	14	10	......	87	301	13,923	160
Guernsey	3,321	1,184	304	355	5,164	33,210	4,473,022	866
Harrison	427	121	77	70	695	2,340	599,741	863
Hocking	1,456	323	262	133	2,174	12,914	1,451,147	667
Holmes	32	2	3	......	37	47	13,203	357
Jackson	1,462	575	319	60	2,416	29,375	933,238	386
Jefferson	3,843	987	652	477	5,959	12,657	5,111,563	858
Lawrence	484	94	47	14	639	5,108	190,465	298
Mahoning	113	19	19	6	157	1,269	66,312	422
Medina	37	6	6	......	49	778	27,604	563
Meigs	667	159	96	92	1,014	5,262	648,149	639
Morgan	301	59	38	44	442	692	126,544	286
Muskingum	528	92	65	32	717	8,532	270,416	377
Noble	345	116	37	39	537	2,899	441,823	823
Perry	2,527	544	375	262	3,708	23,382	2,394,961	646
Portage	176	50	36	18	280	4,400	105,155	376
Scioto	17	5	4	......	26	379	9,834	378
Stark	869	169	154	26	1,218	16,026	547,635	450
Summit	131	33	31	6	201	3,685	94,346	469
Trumbull	20	3	4	......	27	95	4,716	175
Tuscarawas	1,614	361	215	161	2,351	11,043	811,782	345
Vinton	296	37	23	16	372	3,350	159,006	427
Wayne	269	59	57	8	393	5,961	164,724	419
Total ...	32,390	8,400	4,747	3,293	48,830	273,406	34,424,951	*705

* Average.

NOTE: — Average number tons produced by each person engaged in production of coal was 705.

TABLE SHOWING THE NUMBER OF PERSONS ENGAGED IN THE PRODUCTION OF COAL IN THE SEVERAL COUNTIES DURING THE YEAR 1910, AS COMPARED WITH THE YEAR 1909 AND GAINS AND LOSSES IN EACH COUNTY

Name of County.	Number of Pick Miners, Shooters, Drillers and Loaders, 1909.	Number of Pick Miners, Shooters and Loaders employed, 1910.	Number Runners employed in 1909.	Number Runners employed in 1910.	Inside Day Hands, 1909.	Inside Day Hands, 1910.	Outside Day Hands, 1909.	Outside Day Hands, 1910.	Total Number Employed, 1909.	Total Number Employed, 1910.	Gain.	Loss.
Athens	5,030	5,420	[illegible]	[illegible]	[illegible]	[illegible]	[illegible]	[illegible]	[illegible]	[illegible]	[illegible]	
Belmont	5,830	6,382	[illegible]	[illegible]	[illegible]	[illegible]	[illegible]	[illegible]	[illegible]	[illegible]	[illegible]	
Carroll	461	[illegible]	[illegible]	[illegible]	[illegible]	[illegible]	[illegible]	[illegible]	[illegible]	[illegible]		[illegible]
Columbiana	905	[illegible]	[illegible]	[illegible]	[illegible]	[illegible]	[illegible]	[illegible]	[illegible]	[illegible]		[illegible]
Coshocton	553	450	61	64	[illegible]	[illegible]	[illegible]	[illegible]	[illegible]	[illegible]		[illegible]
Gallia	35	48	....	.	[illegible]	[illegible]	[illegible]	11	[illegible]	[illegible]	[illegible]	
Guernsey	3,026	3,[illegible]	[illegible]	[illegible]	1,[illegible]	2,[illegible]	[illegible]	[illegible]	[illegible]	[illegible]	[illegible]	
Harrison	461	[illegible]	[illegible]	71	[illegible]	[illegible]	[illegible]	[illegible]	[illegible]	[illegible]		14
Hocking	1,402	1,456	[illegible]	[illegible]	[illegible]	[illegible]	[illegible]	[illegible]	[illegible]	[illegible]	[illegible]	
Holmes	[illegible]	[illegible]	......		[illegible]	[illegible]	[illegible]	[illegible]	[illegible]	[illegible]		[illegible]
Jackson	1,[illegible]	1,[illegible]	[illegible]	[illegible]	[illegible]	[illegible]	[illegible]	[illegible]	[illegible]	[illegible]	[illegible]	
Jefferson	3,800	3,682	[illegible]	[illegible]	[illegible]	[illegible]	[illegible]	[illegible]	[illegible]	[illegible]	[illegible]	
Lawrence	462	484	12	14	71	[illegible]	[illegible]	[illegible]	[illegible]	[illegible]	[illegible]	
Mahoning	267	112	...	4	[illegible]	[illegible]	[illegible]	[illegible]	[illegible]	[illegible]		[illegible]
Medina	48	[illegible]	....	.	[illegible]	[illegible]	[illegible]	[illegible]	[illegible]	[illegible]		[illegible]
Meigs	615	667	71	82	140	150	106	[illegible]	[illegible]	[illegible]	[illegible]	
Morgan	320	301	42	44	[illegible]	[illegible]	[illegible]	[illegible]	[illegible]	[illegible]	[illegible]	
Muskingum	590	525	40	[illegible]	[illegible]	[illegible]	[illegible]	[illegible]	[illegible]	[illegible]		[illegible]
Noble	212	245	40	[illegible]	85	110	[illegible]	[illegible]	[illegible]	[illegible]	[illegible]	
Perry	2,540	2,557	305	[illegible]	[illegible]	[illegible]	410	875	[illegible]	[illegible]		130
Portage	164	176	6	[illegible]	[illegible]	[illegible]	47	[illegible]	[illegible]	[illegible]		12
Scioto	[illegible]	17	....	....	[illegible]	[illegible]	[illegible]	[illegible]	[illegible]	[illegible]		[illegible]
Stark	[illegible]	[illegible]	[illegible]	[illegible]	[illegible]	[illegible]	[illegible]	[illegible]	[illegible]	[illegible]		[illegible]
Summit	[illegible]	131	10	6	[illegible]	[illegible]	[illegible]	3	[illegible]	[illegible]		[illegible]
Trumbull	20	20	......	......	[illegible]	[illegible]	[illegible]	[illegible]	[illegible]	[illegible]		
Tuscarawas	1,665	1,614	170	161	[illegible]	[illegible]	[illegible]	[illegible]	[illegible]	[illegible]		[illegible]
Vinton	292	296	[illegible]	[illegible]	[illegible]	[illegible]	[illegible]	[illegible]	[illegible]	[illegible]		21
Washington	1	......	......	......	......	......	......	......	1			1
Wayne	156	[illegible]	[illegible]	6	[illegible]	[illegible]	[illegible]	[illegible]	[illegible]	[illegible]	[illegible]	
Total	31,544	32,800	3,154	3,283	[illegible]	[illegible]	[illegible]	[illegible]	[illegible]	[illegible]	[illegible]	1,[illegible]

NOTE — Gain in 1910 as compared with 1909 [illegible]

TABLE SHOWING NUMBER OF DAY HANDS EMPLOYED IN BOTH PICK AND MACHINE MINES; ALSO TOTAL NUMBER IN ALL THE MINES AND NUMBER TONS OF COAL PRODUCED FOR EACH, PER YEAR AND PER DAY.

Name of County.	Average Number Days Worked in Pick Mines for Year 1910.	Number Day Hands Employed in Pick Mines.	Average **Number** Tons Produced for **Each Day** Hand for Year in Pick Mines.	Average **Number** Tons Produced for **Each Day** Hand Per Day in **Pick Mines.**	Average Number Days Worked in Machine Mines.	Number Day Hands Employed in Machine Mines.	Average **Number** Tons Produced for Each Day Hand for Year in Machine Mines.	Average Number Tons Produced for Each **Day Hand** Per Day **in Machine Mines.**	Total Number Day Men Employed for Year 1910.	Total Number Tons Produced, All Grades.	Average Tons Mined for Each Day Hand in Both Pick and Machine Mines for Year 1910.
Athens	154	72	2,944	19.1	191	2,272	2,523	13.2	2,344	5,943,638	2,536
Belmont	185	66	2,792	15.1	231	2,221	3,670	15.9	2,287	8,336,428	3,645
Carroll	213	37	1,617	7.6	149	133	1,876	12.6	170	309,328	1,819
Columbiana	245	120	2,455	10.0	219	178	2,504	11.4	298	740,345	2,484
Coshocton	222	102	2,530	11.4	230	100	1,779	7.7	202	435,903	2,158
Gallia	74	24	580	7.8	.....	.....	.....	.....	24	13,923	580
Guernsey	205	3	5,630	27.5	233	1,485	3,001	12.9	1,488	4,473,022	3,006
Harrison	157	14	3,107	19.8	216	184	3,023	14.0	198	599,741	3,029
Hocking	196	55	3,651	18.6	188	530	2,359	12.5	585	1,451,147	2,481
Holmes	181	5	2,641	14.6	.....	.....	.....	.....	5	13,203	2,641
Jackson	151	579	1,065	7.1	170	315	1,004	5.9	894	933,238	1,044
Jefferson	213	89	3,270	15.4	225	1,550	3,110	13.8	1,639	5,111,563	3,119
Lawrence	163	109	1,583	9.7	92	32	560	16.1	141	190,465	1,351
Mahoning	228	25	1,541	6.8	230	13	2,137	9.3	38	66,312	1,745
Medina	170	12	2,300	13.5	.....	.....	.....	.....	12	27,604	2,300
Meigs	147	29	2,873	19.5	193	226	2,499	12.9	255	648,149	2,542

Morgan	94	1	2,258	24.0	78	96	1,205	10.0	97	120,514	,305
Muskingum	152	93	2,191	14.4	94	64	1,030	11.0	157	270,410	,782
Noble	115	9	2,027	17.0	331	144	2,041	8.9	158	141,823	2,888
Perry	180	52	4,080	26.1	153	867	2,481	10.2	919	2,391,06[illegible]	2,000
Portage	212	56	1,177	5.6	178	30	1,300	7.3	80	105,155	1,221
Scioto	209	9	1,093	5.2	....	....	....	....	9	9,834	1,093
Stark	165	321	1,516	9.2	165	2	30,514	181.9	323	517,635	1,605
Summit	198	41	1,503	7.6	180	23	1,423	7.9	64	94,310	1,471
Trumbull	180	7	671	3.7	....	....	....	....	7	1,710	674
Tuscarawas	126	334	1,572	12.5	90	242	1,184	13.2	570	811,782	1,409
Vinton	118	37	1,570	13.3	170	23	1,377	25.7	60	150,000	2,050
Wayne	173	92	1,450	8.1	113	24	1,281	9.0	110	161,721	1,420
Total	168	2,393	1,815	10.8	201	10,754	2,797	13.9	13,147	34,424,951	2,019

†Total.
*Average for State.

NOTE:

Average tons produced for each day hand for the year in Pick Mines......... 1,815
Average tons produced for each day hand per day in Pick Mines............. 10.8
Average tons produced for each day hand for the year in Machine Mines... 2,797
Average tons produced for each day hand per day in Machine Mines......... 13.9
Average tons produced for each day hand in the State for the year.... 2,019
Average tons produced for each day hand in the State for day....... 18.6

ELECTRIC MINING MACHINERY.

JEFFREY ELECTRIC MINE LOCOMOTIVES

Cut 4638—M. Jeffrey low vein gathering locomotive. The motor driven or mechanical reel is mounted on the forward end of the locomotive and does not extend above the locomotive covers.

JEFFREY ELECTRIC LOCOMOTIVES are designed and built to withstand the most severe service encountered in underground and surface haulage.

All finished parts are rigidly inspected and tested before and after assembling; every known economy in shop practice is employed in our effort to produce at minimum cost, the most highly perfected and dependable Locomotive in present day use.

Additional information and literature may be obtained by addressing The Jeffrey Manufacturing Company, Columbus, Ohio.

Cut 4673—M. Standard Jeffrey haulage locomotive with armor plate frame.

Jeffrey Armorplate Type Electric Locomotives for Mine Haulage are practically indestructible.

The sides and ends of these Locomotives are built of special, solid steel plates securely bolted together, forming tremendous rigidity in the frames as well as providing absolute security for the mechanical equipment.

Write for Locomotive Bulletin No. 17, Jeffrey Manufacturing Company, Columbus, Ohio.

Cut 4742-M Jeffrey mining machine for continuous and long wall cutting.

The Jeffrey 24-A Electric Coal Cutter was developed after a careful investigation of the various systems of longwall mining in the coal producing countries throughout the world. The design embodies a number of very desirable features not found on any other type of coal cutting machines, such as noiseless running, compactness, power turned cutter arm and the absence of a complicated train of gearing to the cutting chain drive.

This type of Coal Cutter is suitable for the most severe conditions where the disc type is now used, and on account of the use of a chain with a narrow cutter arm, there is no tendency for the coal to squeeze down, such as often occurs with the use of the disc machine.

The overall dimensions are 8 feet 8 inches by 31 inches by 17 inches high, which are exceptionally small for a heavy duty machine, allow the use of one type of motor for all conditions, entirely eliminating the necessity for the large, bulky machines which have heretofore been required for the exceptionally hard places.

The motors are ample in capacity for continuous service, even when cutting in shale, slate and other materials harder than coal.

For compressed air power the machine is similar in design except that a three-cylinder double acting engine is substituted in place of the electric motor.

Coal Cutter Bulletin No. 18, illustrating various types of Jeffrey Machines may be secured by addressing The Jeffrey Manufacturing Company, Columbus, Ohio.

JEFFREY GRAVITY RETURN CAR DUMP.

In coal mining operations the Cross Over and Kick Back Dumps have been used almost universally. In many operations nothing can be offered which will do the work any better, although there are many locations in which this gravity dump is especially applicable. It possesses the quick action of the Cross Over Dump, with the added feature of the under car return.

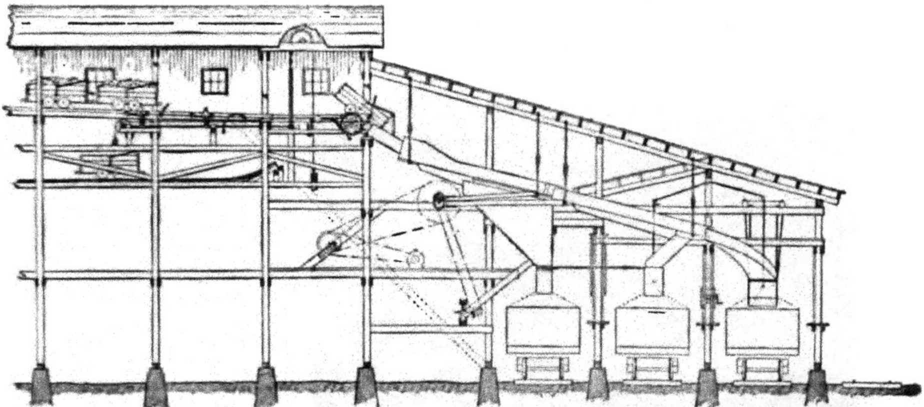

Briefly described, it is made up of a substantially hinged track, at one end of which is located the dumping mechanism. This dumping mechanism is a combination of a friction brake wheel controlled by lever, with steel horns suitably counter balanced by heavy weighted extension. The car in dumping passes over the curved end of this hinged track, and by means of the horns is lowered automatically into its dumping position.

The main feature in this dump is the hinged track interlocking with the main approach track, with its substantial block system of spring cushioned steel dogs as shown in outline drawing "A". The hinged track is supported in a steel frame hung by means of wire rope and counter-weights operating over adjustable eccentric sheave wheels.

This dump is manufactured exclusively by The Jeffrey Manufacturing Company, Columbus, Ohio, who will gladly furnish full particulars upon request.

JEFFREY GRIFFITH CROSS-OVER DUMP.

THIS IS THE ONLY DUMP where the car maintains continuously its natural position throughout the operation and is continuous in its movement over the dump, there being no break or hinge in the track to cause derailment and blocking of Coal.

The Jeffrey Manufacturing Company, Columbus, Ohio, designers and builders of Complete Coal Mine and Tipple Equipments, including: Coal Washeries, Car Haul, Revolving and Shaking Screens, Crushers, Pulverizers, Picking Tables, Chutes, Drop Rail Mine Cages, Elevators, Conveyors, Mine Fans, Coal Drills, Mining Machines, Electric Locomotives, etc. Write for catalog and information on any of these subjects.

JEFFREY ELECTRIC COAL CUTTERS.

are of the very latest and most improved types, and each, in the work for which i designed, represents the highest standard of efficiency thus far attained in the const tion of Coal Mining Machines.

Jeffrey 17-A Electric Coal Cı ter in No. 5 Mine of The Penn Gas Coal Co.

This machine has gre strength in comparison wi its weight.

Jeffrey 21-A Electric Coal Cutter equipped with flame and gas proof motor and starting box.

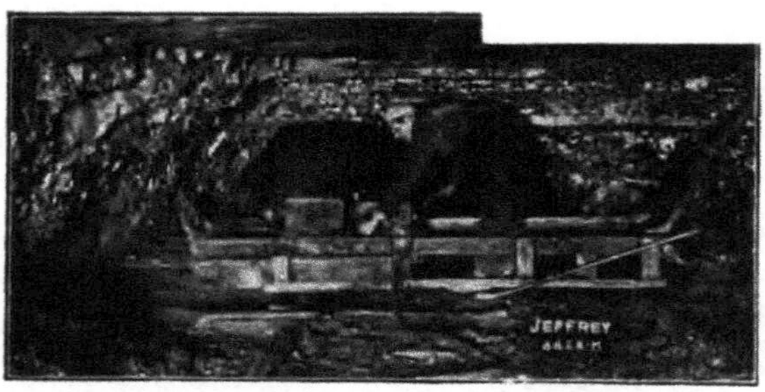

Jeffrey 27-B Low Vein Co Cutter in Mine of The Wilbern Coal Co.

Especially adapted for sean 2½ to 4 feet in height.

Jeffrey Air Power Coal Cutter.

This machine makes less fine coal and less dust than any other type of Air Machine on the market.

THE STEVENS MINE FAN is an improved type, combining the highest efficiency with economy in operation. It is constructed entirely of steel and iron and is therefore absolutely fire-proof. The fan wheel is so designed and enclosed that the air passes through the fan without concussion, thus avoiding loss of power and obtaining the highest efficiency, whether operated at a low speed under ordinary conditions, or at a high speed when the resistance to the air within the mine is increased.

The bearings are of the ball and socket, pivotal, chain oiling type, which secures perfect lubrication and alignment of the shaft in case of any unequal settling of the fan foundation.

All Stevens fans are designed to be used as reversible fans. However, by omitting the side housing and reversing doors, they can be used as straight blowing or exhaust fans.

The above cut shows a 7½ ft. Stevens fan, completely housed for reversing the air. The fan rests on a plain, rectangular foundation and as it is constructed entirely of steel and iron, completely erected in the shop, the cost of installation is very small, not over $60.00 for fan and engine foundation complete.

The Stevens Fan is furnished in sizes to meet special conditions and requirements, and may be used either as medium or high speed machines, as desired. For large quantities of air, or for overcoming unusual resistances at a slow speed the Stevens Fan 10 ft. in diameter or over is recommended. The 7½ ft. fan shown in the above cut has an actual mine test of 154,440 cubic feet of air per minute, at a 3 inch water gauge, at 345 RPM. This is less than half the maximum speed at which the fan is designed to operate continuously.

The Stevens Fans may be operated by any kind of power either directly connected to the fan shaft or pulley driven by means of belt or rope. With sizes less than 10 ft. in diameter direct connection is not recommended.

Catalog and complete information will be furnished on request by the Stevens Mine Fan Company, Chicago, Illinois.

MORGAN GARDNER—Standard Type Short-Wall Machine mounted on truck.

Complete information regarding all of our Machinery and supplies will be cheerfully furnished upon **request.**

MORGAN-GARDNER Steel Frame Locomotive. This cut shows the two-motor type Gathering Crab can be furnished with this locomotive if desired.

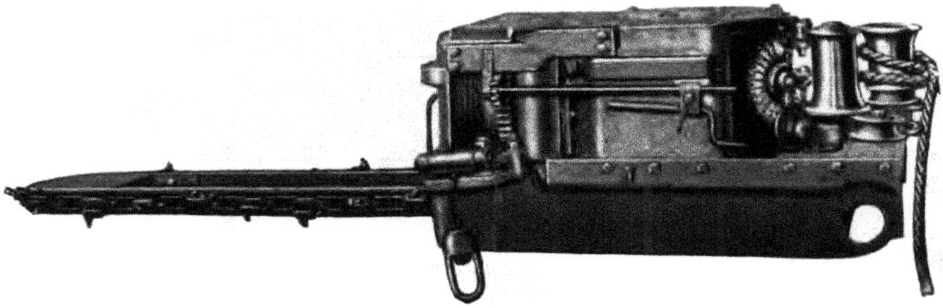

MORGAN-GARDNER Low-Vein Type Short Wall Machine off truck. This Machine can be equipped with Self-Propelling Steel Truck if so desired. This Machine is especially adapted to work in mines where the props are set close to the face of the coal.

STANDARD TYPE GOODMAN CHAIN BREAST MINING MACHINE
with Flame Proof Electrical Parts and with Chain Guards.

SHORTWALL TYPE GOODMAN ELECTRIC CHAIN MACHINE,
in Cutting Position, Showing Cutter arm, Feed Cable and Completely Inclosed Electrical Parts.

TYPE 2600 GOODMAN GATHERING LOCOMOTIVE,
with "Unbreakable" Frame Construction—a Cast Center as a Housing for the Working Parts; Plate Steel Sides; Cast Steel Ends.

"UNIVERSAL" GOODMAN GATHERING LOCOMOTIVE,
with Electric Conductor Cable Reel and an Auxiliary Steel Wire Haulage Rope on a Power Operated Drum in the Motorman's Cab.

SINGLE-MOTOR GOODMAN HAULAGE LOCOMOTIVE,

Having One Large Motor, Geared Directly to Both Axles, and therefore giving Greatest Possible Pulling Power per Ton of Weight, because No Wheel Can Slip until they All Slip.

SINGLE-MOTOR LOCOMOTIVE DISMANTLED.

All the Working Parts are Made Perfectly Accessible by Lifting off the Top Magnet or Motor Shell. No Work to be Done Underneath the Locomotive, so no Pit is Required in the Shop.

GOODMAN RACK RAIL SYSTEM OF HAULAGE,

for Hilly Mines. Plain Rack Rail or Combination Rack-and-Traction System. Locomotives Built on the Unit System, for Operating Singly as above, or in Multiple Units.

A RACK-RAIL LOCOMOTIVE OF 200 H. P.

Made Up of Two 100-H. P. Units, with Cab and Controlling Devices between. Rack Rail Equipment is Made to Suit the Requirements of Each Individual Situation.

TABLE OF MINING MACHINERY.

113

TABLE SHOWING THE NUMBER AND MAKE OF MINING MACHINES IN USE IN THE STATE, AND POWER BY WHICH THEY ARE OPERATED

Counties	Electric							Compressed Air				
	Jeffrey	Morgan Gardner	Goodman	General Electric	Ingersoll	Sullivan	Total Electric	Jeffrey	Harrison	Ingersoll	Total Compressed Air	Grand Total
Athens	[illegible]	[illegible]	[illegible]				[illegible]					[illegible]
Belmont	[illegible]	[illegible]	[illegible]				[illegible]		[illegible]		[illegible]	[illegible]
Carroll	[illegible]	[illegible]					[illegible]					[illegible]
Columbiana	[illegible]	[illegible]	[illegible]				[illegible]			[illegible]	[illegible]	[illegible]
Coshocton	[illegible]	[illegible]					[illegible]					[illegible]
Guernsey	[illegible]	[illegible]	[illegible]			[illegible]	[illegible]	[illegible]		[illegible]	[illegible]	[illegible]
Harrison	[illegible]	[illegible]				[illegible]	[illegible]					[illegible]
Hocking	[illegible]	[illegible]	[illegible]				[illegible]					[illegible]
Jackson	[illegible]	[illegible]	[illegible]				[illegible]					[illegible]
Jefferson	[illegible]	[illegible]	[illegible]			[illegible]	[illegible]					[illegible]
Lawrence	[illegible]					[illegible]	[illegible]					[illegible]
Mahoning		[illegible]					[illegible]					[illegible]
Meigs	[illegible]	[illegible]	[illegible]				[illegible]					[illegible]
Morgan	[illegible]	[illegible]					[illegible]					[illegible]
Muskingum	[illegible]	[illegible]					[illegible]					[illegible]
Noble	[illegible]	[illegible]					[illegible]					[illegible]
Perry	[illegible]	[illegible]	[illegible]				[illegible]					[illegible]
Portage	[illegible]						[illegible]			[illegible]		[illegible]
Stark			[illegible]				[illegible]			[illegible]		[illegible]
Summit			[illegible]				[illegible]					[illegible]
Tuscarawas	[illegible]	[illegible]					[illegible]		[illegible]	[illegible]	[illegible]	[illegible]
Vinton	[illegible]	[illegible]					[illegible]					[illegible]
Wayne	[illegible]		[illegible]				[illegible]					[illegible]
Total	[illegible]	[illegible]	[illegible]	[illegible]	[illegible]	[illegible]	[illegible]	[illegible]	[illegible]	[illegible]	[illegible]	[illegible]

Note—

Total machines of all kinds in use in [illegible] [illegible]

Total machines of all kinds in use in [illegible] [illegible]

Showing [illegible] [illegible]

TABLE SHOWING THE NUMBER AND MAKE OF HAULAGE MOTORS IN USE IN THE VARIOUS COUNTIES OF THE STATE IN 1910.

Counties.	Jeffrey.	Morgan-Gardner.	Goodman.	Link Belt.	General Electric.	Westinghouse.	Total Motors
Athens	22	19	28		2	2	73
Belmont	37	39	23			21	120
Carroll	5	1	1				7
Columbiana		8	2			1	11
Coshocton	2	1					3
Guernsey	17	22	14		2	1	56
Harrison	5	2				1	8
Hocking	6	6	1	1			14
Jackson	4	2					6
Jefferson	18	13	23	1	1	17	73
Lawrence	2						2
Mahoning		1					1
Meigs	1	10					11
Morgan	2	1					3
Muskingum		4					4
Noble	2	2					4
Perry	22	12	1				35
Portage							
Stark			2				2
Summit			1				1
Tuscarawas	8	7			1		16
Vinton		1					1
Wayne							
Total	153	151	96	2	6	43	451

NOTE: —

Total number motors in use in 1910	451
Total number motors in use in 1909	405
Gain over 1909	46

MINES AND MODE OF VENTILATION.

TABLE SHOWING NUMBER OF MINES OPENED, SUSPENDED AND ABANDONED DURING THE YEAR 1910, AS REPORTED BY THE DISTRICT MINE INSPECTORS.

Counties.	New Mines.	Suspended.	Abandoned
Athens	4	3	4
Belmont	5	1	1
Carroll	7	3	2
Columbiana	3	.....	.....
Coshocton	5	.....	3
Gallia	2	1	.....
Guernsey	1	4	2
Hocking	3	2	1
Jackson	2	4	6
Jefferson	2	2	3
Lawrence	1	2	1
Medina	.....	1	2
Meigs	1	2	.....
Muskingum	5	1	4
Noble	1	.....	.....
Ottawa	1	.....	2
Perry	.....	1	2
Scioto	.....	.....	1
Stark	7	6	2
Tuscarawas	5	.....	2
Vinton	.....	13	1
Wayne	.....	1	2
Total	55	47	41

DETAILED LIST OF MINES OPENED UP, SUSPENDED AND ABANDONED DURING THE YEAR 1910.

ATHENS COUNTY.

New Mines.	Suspended.	Abandoned.
C. & H. C. & I.	Sunday Creek No. 210.	Sedalia No. 14.
New York No. 35.	Sunday Creek No. 275.	Sunday Creek No. 212.
New York No. 36.	Sunday Creek No. 311.	Sunday Creek No. 252.
Poston & Fluhart.		Sunday Creek No. 312.

BELMONT COUNTY.

Boggs (re-opened).	Cochran.	M. T. Garrett.
Fairpoint.		
Pasco.		
Purseglove.		
Victor (re-opened).		

CARROLL COUNTY.

Big Four Slope.	Dorothy No. 2	Dorothy No. 1.
Dorothy No. 2.	Horse Shoe.	Magnolia Shaft.
Hazelwood.	Somers No. 2.	
Leesville No. 1.		
Mahanoy & Massillon Nos. 1 and 2.		

COLUMBIANA COUNTY.

Strabley No. 2.		
Vasey No. 2.		
West Pittsburg.		

COSHOCTON COUNTY.

Conesville No. 1.		Conesville No. 1.
Coshocton Clay No. 2.		Conesville No. 2.
Davis No. 1.		Forest Hill.
Davis No. 2.		
Fernell.		

GALLIA COUNTY.

Indian Guyan Coal Co.	Black Diamond.	
John Sumers.		

DETAILED LIST OF MINES OPENED UP, ETC. — Continued.

GUERNSEY COUNTY.

New Mines.	Suspended.	Abandoned.
Buffalo	Indian Camp. Leatherwood. Ohio No. 1. Union No. 1.	Kings. West Branch.

HOCKING COUNTY.

New Mines.	Suspended.	Abandoned.
Central Hocking. Essex Coal Co. Kramer Bros.	Gem Coal Co. Lost Run Coal Co.	New Pittsburg No. 2½.

JACKSON COUNTY.

New Mines.	Suspended.	Abandoned.
Booth Gilliland.	Armstrong Slope. Cameron. Washington. Woodrow No. 1.	Acorn Slope. Daisy. D. C. & I. No. 2. Holberg No. 4. Rempel. Reynolds.

JEFFERSON COUNTY.

New Mines.	Suspended.	Abandoned.
Nebo Union	Calumet. Congo.	La Grange. Pratt. Speaks.

LAWRENCE COUNTY.

New Mines.	Suspended.	Abandoned.
Lawrence Mill No. 2.	Buckhorn No. 4. Orchard Knob Clay.	Lawrence Mill No. 1.

MEDINA COUNTY.

New Mines.	Suspended.	Abandoned.
	Klondyke.	Long Shaft. Reichard.

MEIGS COUNTY.

New Mines.	Suspended.	Abandoned.
Ohio River Coal Co.	Harley Coal Co. Maynard North Hill.	

DETAILED LIST OF MINES OPENED UP, ETC.—Continued

MUSKINGUM COUNTY.

New Mines.	Suspended.	Abandoned
Garrett. German. Red Bud. Monitor. Wellers No. 3.	Walnut Hill.	No. 37 (Nos. 1 and 2). No. 16. Warners No. 1

NOBLE COUNTY.

Caldwell.		

OTTAWA COUNTY.

Fishack.		Consumers No. 2 Lea.

PERRY COUNTY.

	Pedlow—(S. C. No. 321).	Beech Grove Lyonsdale.

SCIOTO COUNTY.

		Globe Lime.

STARK COUNTY.

Arentz. Crescent. Elm Run No. 1. Evansdale. Hale. Moss Hill. Wise No. 2	C. H. B. Empire. Indian Run. Kime No. 2. Robertsville. West Brookfield.	Massillon-Crystal No. 17

TUSCARAWAS COUNTY.

Buckeye Slope. Dennison S. P. Coal Dennison S. P. Clay Goshen No. 4 Water Lilly		Beaverdam Somerdale

DETAILED LIST OF MINES OPENED UP, ETC.—Concluded.

VINTON COUNTY.

New Mines.	Suspended.	Abandoned.
	Alma Lime Nos. 51 & 52. Alma Lime Nos. 55, 56 & 57. Alma Coal. Alma Cement Limestone Mines Nos. 1 & 2. Mohr-Minton Nos. 3 & 4. Raccoon Valley Nos. 1 and 2. Raccoon Valley No. 3.	Inghams

WAYNE COUNTY.

New Mines.	Suspended.	Abandoned.
	Chippewa	Burton City Dalton No. 14.

TABLE SHOWING THE NUMBER OF LARGE MINES EMPLOYING TEN OR MORE MEN, AND THE NUMBER OF SMALL MINES WITH LESS THAN TEN MEN IN OPERATION DURING THE YEAR 1910; ALSO NUMBER OF LARGE MINES IDLE DURING THE YEAR.

Name of County.	Large Mines Ten or More Men in Operation.	Large Mines Idle in 1910.	Total Number of Large Mines.	Small Mines Less than Ten Men in Operation.	Total Mines in Operation in 1910.
Athens	47	6	53	13	60
Belmont	56	1	57	36	92
Carroll	8	4	12	15	23
Columbiana	18	0	18	23	41
Coshocton	11	1	12	20	31
Gallia	2	8	10	8	10
Guernsey	25	3	28	16	41
Harrison	5	0	5	36	41
Hocking	24	4	28	4	28
Holmes	0	0	0	9	9
Jackson	41	6	47	48	89
Jefferson	36	3	39	35	71
Lawrence	17	3	20	35	52
Mahoning	4	1	5	13	17
Medina	1	0	1	5	6
Meigs	15	2	17	27	42
Morgan	2	0	2	3	5
Muskingum	15	2	17	17	32
Noble	4	0	4	25	29
Perry	34	4	38	31	65
Portage	3	0	3	3	6
Scioto	1	0	1	1	2
Stark	22	4	26	33	55
Summit	2	0	2	6	8
Trumbull	0	0	0	9	9
Tuscarawas	35	1	36	47	82
Vinton	11	0	11	15	26
Wayne	6	0	6	5	11
Total	445	53	498	538	983

TABLE SHOWING THE NUMBER OF MINES USING THE VARIOUS METHODS OF VENTILATION AND THE THREE KINDS OF OPENINGS FOR THE YEAR 1910.

Name of County.	Drift.	Slope.	Shaft.	Total.	Fan.	Furnace.	Fire Basket.	Exhaust Steam.	Natural.	Total.
Athens	32	10	17	59	42	3	1	......	13	59
Belmont	72	11	5	88	48	22	2	1	15	88
Carroll	21	2	1	24	5	10	3	......	6	24
Columbiana ...	25	11	5	41	16	8	1	2	14	41
Coshocton	28	1	......	29	5	12	1	......	11	29
Gallia	9	......	......	9	......	1	......	......	8	9
Guernsey	15	11	15	41	24	3	1	......	13	41
Harrison	34	8	......	42	5	1	1	......	35	42
Hocking	27	2	......	29	17	7	1	......	4	29
Holmes	7	2	......	9	......	1	1	......	7	9
Jackson	72	6	12	90	24	34	5	......	27	90
Jefferson	51	6	8	65	33	14	......	......	18	65
Lawrence	51	1	......	52	3	16	......	......	33	52
Mahoning	3	10	3	16	4	3	......	1	8	16
Medina	......	5	1	6	......	2	......	3	1	6
Meigs	36	1	1	38	9	6	......	......	23	38
Morgan	4	1	......	5	2	1	......	......	2	5
Muskingum ...	40	9	2	51	7	12	6	......	26	51
Noble	24	2	3	29	4	1	......	......	24	29
Perry	46	8	6	60	27	6	1	......	26	60
Portage	......	......	6	6	5	......	......	1	......	6
Scioto	2	......	......	2	......	1	......	......	1	2
Stark	30	12	14	56	9	22	5	4	16	56
Summit	1	5	2	8	2	......	1	1	4	8
Trumbull	1	5	3	9	......	......	......	......	9	9
Tuscarawas ...	68	12	3	83	18	34	4	......	27	83
Vinton	21	3	1	25	6	4	......	......	15	25
Wayne	6	3	2	11	3	1	1	1	5	11
Total	726	147	110	983	318	225	35	14	391	983

TABLE SHOWING THE NUMBER OF MINES EMPLOYING THE VARIOUS METHODS OF VENTILATION, AND THE THREE KINDS OF OPENINGS FROM 1892 TO 1910, INCLUSIVE.

Year.	1892	1893	1894	1895	1896	1897	1898	1899	1900	1901	1902	1903	1904	1905	1906	1907	1908	1909	1910
Drifts	303	676	657	749	821	800	921	789	696	625	589	591	638	626	696	691	742	744	[illegible]
Shafts	91	121	149	150	149	153	143	145	122	133	140	142	153	130	168	140	140	130	110
Slopes	40	61	61	68	66	85	145	133	140	149	142	140	142	125	144	149	171	158	147
Small mines, kind of opening unknown	458	151	296	220	167	190	46	65	114	99	96	81	85	......	......	......	......	......	......
Total	892	1,009	1,163	1,187	1,203	1,228	1,255	1,132	1,072	1,006	967	954	1,018	881	1,008	980	1,058	1,032	983
Fans	127	141	139	134	134	149	149	147	171	182	219	259	282	289	299	322	314	302	318
Furnaces	253	323	264	278	281	280	317	274	264	258	222	244	254	239	252	235	236	240	225
Fire baskets	11	23	32	36	38	51	45	41	48	40	57	44	50	36	38	37	46	42	35
Steam jets and exhaust from pumps	30	39	43	48	52	49	47	34	33	44	45	32	34	13	13	19	14	19	14
Natural	205	316	378	452	528	516	636	523	458	389	336	302	320	304	401	367	443	429	391
Small mines, mode of ventilation unknown	266	167	309	242	179	200	73	107	103	98	88	78	78	......	......	......	......	......	......
Total	892	1,009	1,165	1,190	1,212	1,245	1,267	1,126	1,072	1,006	967	954	1,018	881	1,008	980	1,058	1,032	983

NOTE: — This department will henceforth classify all mines with more than one opening, and where all coal is dumped over one tipple, as one mine only.

DETAILED LIST OF MINES WHICH GENERATE LIGHT CARBURETED HYDROGEN GAS.

ATHENS COUNTY.

Canaanville
Eclipse No. 3
Hisylvania No. 23
Luhrig Nos. 1, 2 and 3
New Pittsburg Nos. 9 & 10
Northern Fuel No 24
Sunday Creek No. 10
Sunday Creek No. 10x
Sunday Creek No. 201
Sunday Creek No. 209
Sunday Creek No. 210
Sunday Creek No 211
Sunday Creek No. 212
Sunday Creek No. 254
Sunday Creek No. 255
Sunday Creek No. 256
Sunday Creek No. 266
Sunday Creek No. 267
Sunday Creek No. 275
Sunday Creek No. 281
Sunday Creek No. 311
Sunday Creek No. 312

BELMONT COUNTY.

Big Run
Black Diamond
Black Oak
Captina
Clifford
Dellora
Eleanor
Florence
Glen
Johnsons
Neff No. 1
Pittsburg-Belmont No. 3
Provident
Victor
Virginia Hill

COLUMBIANA COUNTY.

Big Walnut
Delmore
Garside
New Slope
Nieheisel
McNab
Salem
West Pittsburg

GUERNSEY COUNTY.

Black Top
Blue Bell
Buffalo
Cleveland No. 1
Detroit
Forsythe
Hartford
Imperial
Ideal
Kingston
Klondyke
Little Trail Run
Little Kate No. 1
Little Kate No. 2
Minnehaha
Midway
Murray Hill
Old Orchard
Ohio No. 2
Puritan
Trail Run No. 1
Trail Run No. 2
Valley
Walhonding No. 2

HOCKING COUNTY.

New Pittsburg No. 7

JACKSON COUNTY.

Domestic
Elk Fork No. 2
Globe
Superior No. 9
Superior No. 12
Wainwright

JEFFERSON COUNTY.

Amsterdam
Elizabeth
High Shaft
La Belle
Rice
Zerbe

DETAILED LIST OF MINES WHICH GENERATE LIGHT CARBURETED HYDROGEN GAS — Concluded.

MAHONING COUNTY.

Lowellville

NOBLE COUNTY.

Caldwell
Golden Rod
Laura
Noble

PERRY COUNTY.

Santoy No. 1
Santoy No. 2

PORTAGE COUNTY.

Hutson No. 4
Hutson No. 8

STARK COUNTY.

Fox No. 12
Geise No. 13
Pocock No. 3
Willow Grove No. 20

TUSCARAWAS COUNTY.

Beaver Dam No. 2
Goshen Shaft

WAYNE COUNTY.

No. 22

ACCIDENTS.

TABLE SHOWING THE TOTAL NUMBER OF FATAL, SERIOUS AND MINOR ACCIDENTS FROM JANUARY 1, 1910, TO DECEMBER 31, 1910, INCLUSIVE.

Counties.	Fatal.	Serious.	Minor.	Total.
Athens	11	78	31	120
Belmont	35	121	17	173
Carroll	1	2	3	6
Columbiana	5	10	5	20
Coshocton	1	6	7	14
Gallia	1	2		3
Guernsey	19	62	33	114
Harrison	5	9	1	15
Hocking	4	12	9	25
Jackson	10	10	4	24
Jefferson	47	82	29	158
Lawrence		3	1	4
Mahoning			1	1
Meigs	7	8	2	17
Muskingum	1	4	2	7
Morgan		2		2
Noble	3	7	7	17
Ottawa		2	23	25
Perry	3	15	10	28
Portage		3	2	5
Scioto	1	1		2
Stark	4	14	8	26
Summit		1		1
Tuscarawas	2	13	4	19
Vinton		2	1	3
Wayne	1	2	1	4
Totals	161	471	201	833

TABLE SHOWING THE NUMBER OF FATAL ACCIDENTS IN THE MINES OF THE STATE DURING THE YEAR 1910, AND CAUSES TO WHICH THEY WERE ATTRIBUTABLE.

Counties.	Falls of Roof.	Falls of Coal.	Mine Cars.	Motors.	Mining Machines.	Electricity.	Explosions of Gas.	Explosions of Powder.	Blown-out Shot.	Miscellaneous.	Total.	No. of Americans.	No. of Foreigners.	Per Cent. of Americans Killed.	Per Cent. of Foreigners Killed.
Athens	8	1	1	....	....	....	......	......	......	1	11	10	1	90.9	9.1
Belmont	25	1	2	1	....	4	......	......	......	2	35	12	23	34.3	65.7
Carroll	....	1	....	....	....	....	......	......	......	......	1	......	1	......	......
Columbiana	3	...	1	....	....	....	......	......	1	......	5	4	1	80.00	20.00
Coshocton	....	....	1	....	....	....	......	......	......	......	1	1	......	......	......
Gallia	1	....	....	....	....	....	......	......	......	......	1	1	......	......	......
Guernsey	11	1	5	....	....	2	......	......	......	......	19	12	7	63.2	36.8
Harrison	2	....	2	....	....	....	......	......	......	1	5	1	4	20.00	80.00
Hocking	3	....	....	1	....	....	......	......	......	......	4	3	1	......	......
Jackson	6	....	....	....	....	....	1	......	......	3	10	10	......	......	......
Jefferson	19	3	6	1	2	1	15	......	......	......	47	15	32	31.9	68.1
Meigs	5	....	1	....	....	....	......	1	......	......	7	7	......	......	......
Muskingum	1	....	....	....	....	....	......	......	......	......	1	1	......	......	......
Noble	3	....	....	....	....	....	......	......	......	......	3	1	2	......	......
Perry	2	....	....	....	....	....	......	......	......	1	3	3	......	......	......
Scioto	1	....	....	....	....	....	......	......	......	......	1	1	......	......	......
Stark	4	....	....	....	....	....	......	......	......	......	4	4	......	......	......
Tuscarawas	2	....	....	....	....	....	......	......	......	......	2	2	......	......	......
Wayne	1	....	....	....	....	....	......	......	......	......	1	1	......	......	......
Totals.	97	7	19	3	2	7	16	1	1	8	161	89	72	†55.3	*44.7

*Per cent. of Foreigners killed in the state.
†Per cent. of Americans killed in the state.

TABLE SHOWING PERCENTAGE OF EACH CAUSE TO WHICH FATAL ACCIDENTS WERE ATTRIBUTABLE.

	1909	1910
Falls of Roof	50.1	60.3
Falls of Coal	1.7	4.3
Mine Cars	17.4	11.8
Motors	3.5	1.9
Mining Machines	1.7	1.2
Fire Damp	.9	9.9
Premature Explosions	4.4	.7
Shocks from Electricity	1.7	4.3
Blown-out Shot	1.7	.7
Miscellaneous	7.9	4.9
	100.00	100.00

TABLE SHOWING THE NUMBER AND CHARACTER OF ACCIDENTS WHICH RESULTED FROM THE PRINCIPAL SOURCES AS REPORTED FROM EACH COUNTY FROM JAN'Y 1, 1910 TO DECEMBER 31, 1910 INCLUSIVE.

Name of County.	Falls of Roof.			Falls of Coal.			Mine Cars.			Motors and Mining Machines.			Exp. of Powder and Prem. Exp.			Explosions of Gas.			Electricity.			Miscellaneous.			Total			Grand Total.
	Fatal.	Serious.	Minor.	Fatal.	Serious.	Minor.	Fatal.	Serious.	Minor.	Fatal.	Serious.	Minor.	Fatal.	Serious.	Minor.	Fatal.	Serious.	Minor.	Fatal.	Serious.	Minor.	Fatal.	Serious.	Minor.	Fatal.	Serious.	Minor.	
Athens	8	22	5		6	2	1	24	13	....	*1 5 *2	*2 8	....	1	....	....	....	1		....	....	1	10	5	11	78	31	120
Belmont	25	53	4		6	3	2	35	3	1	10	3	....	....	....	....		2				2	15	2	35	121	17	173
Carroll	....	1	1			..	....	....	1	....	....	....	....	....	....	....						....	....	1	1	2	3	6
Columbiana	3	3	1				1	8	2	....	....	1	....	....	....	....						1	3	....	5	10	5	20
Coshocton	....	5	3			..	1	1	3	....	....	....	....	....	....	....						....	....	1	1	6	7	14
Gallia	1	1	..			..	....	....	....	....	....	....	....	1	....	....						....	....	....	1	2	....	3
Guernsey	11	29	6		5	3	5	12	12	....	*2 7	....	....	....	....	....						....	6	12	19	62	33	114
Harrison	2	6	1		1	..	2	2	....	....	....	....	....	....	....	....						1	....	....	5	9	1	15
Hocking	3	4	6		1	..	....	4	1	*1	*1	....	....	....	....	....							2	2	4	12	9	25
Jackson	6	7	1			..		....	1	....	....	....	....	....	....	1			....	....	....	3	3	1	10	10	4	24
Jefferson	19	42	12	3	4		6	17	9	*1 2	2 7	2	....	1	....	15	....	....	1	1	....	....	8	2	47	82	29	158
Lawrence	....	1	....	....	....	..		1	1	....	....	....	....	....	....	....	....	....	....	....	....	....	1	....	....	3	1	4
Mahoning	....	....	....	....	....	..		....	....	....	....	....	....	....	....	....	....	....	....	....	....	....	....	1	....	....	1	1
Meigs	5	5	1	....	1	..		1	..	....	*1	....	1	....	....	....	....	....	....	....	....	....	....	1	7	8	2	17
Morgan	....	1	....	....	....	..		1	..	....	....	....	....	....	....	....	....	....	....	....	....	....	....	....	....	2	....	2
Muskingum	1	2	1	....	1			1	..	....	....	....	....	....	....	....	....	....	....	....	....	....	....	....	1	4	2	7
Noble	8	2	3	....	2	....	....	....	3	....	*2 1	....	....	....	....	....	....	....	....	....	....	....	....	1	3	7	7	17
Ottawa	....	1	5	....	....	....	....	....		....	....	....	....	....	1	....	....	....	....	....	....	....	1	10	....	2	23	25
Perry	2	4	3	....	....	2	....	6	5	....	*1 2	....	....	....	....	....	....	....	....	....	....	1	2	....	3	15	10	28
Portage	....	1	1	....	....	....	....	....		....	....	....	....	....	....	....	....	....	....	....	....	....	[illegible]	....	....	3	2	5
Scioto	1	1	....	....	....	....	....	....	....	....	....	....	....	....	....	....	....	....	....	....	....	....	....	....	1	1	....	2
Stark	4	9	4	....	1	1	....	2	2	....	....	....	....	2	....	....	....	....	....	....	....	....	....	1	4	11	8	26
Summit	....	1	....	....	....	....	....	....	....	....	....	....	....	....	....	....	....	....	....	....	....	....	....	....	....	1	....	1
Tuscarawas	2	7	....	....	2	3	....	3	....	....	1	....	....	....	....	....	....	....	....	....	....	....	....	1	2	13	4	19
Vinton	....	....	....	....	....	....	....	2	....	....	....	....	....	....	....	....	....	....	....	....	....	....	....	1	....	2	1	3
Wayne	1	....	....	....	1	....	....	1	1	....	....	....	....	....	....	....	....	....	....	....	....	....	....	....	1	2	1	4
Total	97	208	68	7	83	20	19	116	66	5	15	11	1	5	1	16	1	1	7	1	....	9	62	12	161	471	291	883

*No. killed and injured by motors.

TABLE SHOWING THE NUMBER AND CHARACTER OF ACCIDENTS WHICH OCCURRED FROM JANUARY 1, 1910, TO DECEMBER 31, 1910, INCLUSIVE, TO WHAT CAUSES THEY WERE ATTRIBUTABLE, AND THE PERCENTAGE OF EACH.

Various Causes of Accidents	Fatal.	Serious.	Minor.	Total.	Percentage.
Falls of Roof	97	208	58	363	43.7
Falls of Coal	7	33	20	60	7.2
Mine Cars	19	116	65	200	23.9
Mining Machines	2	35	9	46	5.5
Motors	3	10	2	15	1.8
Electricity	7	1	....	8	.9
Premature Explosions	1	5	1	7	.9
Explosions of Gas	16	1	4	21	2.6
Miscellaneous	9	62	42	113	13.5
Totals	161	471	201	833	100.00

TABLE SHOWING PER CENT. OF INCREASE OF TONNAGE, PER CENT. OF INCREASE AND DECREASE IN NUMBER OF FATAL AND SERIOUS ACCIDENTS AND NUMBER OF TONS MINED FOR EACH FATAL AND SERIOUS ACCIDENT FOR THE YEARS 1904, 1905, 1906, 1907, 1908, 1909, AND 1910, AS COMPARED WITH 1903.

Years.	Number Tons Coal Produced for Each Year.	Per Cent. of Increase in Tonnage in 1904, 1905, 1906, 1907, 1908, 1909, and 910, as Compared with the Year 1903.	Number o Fatal Accidents for Each Year.	Decrease in the Number of Fatal Accidents in 1904, 1905, 1906, 1907, 1908, 1909, and 1910, as Compared with 1903.	Increase in the Number of Fatal Accidents in 1904, 1905, 1906, 1907, 1908, 1909, and 1910, as Compared with the Year 1903.	Per Cent. of Decrease of Fatal Accidents in 1904, 1905, 1906, 1907, 1908, 1909, and 1910, as Compared with the Year 1903.	Per Cent. of Increase of Fatal Accidents in 1904, 1905, 1906, 1907, 1908, 1909, and 1910, as Compared with 1903.	Number Tons of Coal Mined for Each Fatal Accident.	Number of Serious Accidents for Each Year.	Per Cent. of Increase of Serious Accidents in 1904, 1905, 1906, 1907, 1908, 1909, and 1910, as Compared with 1903.	Number of Tons Mined for Each Serious Accident.	Decrease in the Number of Tons Mined for Each Serious Accident in 1904, 1905, 1906, 1907, 1908, 1909, and 1910, as Compared with 1903.
1903	24,573,266	....	124	....	....	....	....	198,170	309	....	79,525	....
1904	24,583,815	.04%	118	6	....	4.8%	....	208,337	316	2.2%	77,797	1,728
1905	25,834,657	5%	114	10	....	8%	....	226,620	372	20%	69,448	10,077
1906	27,213,495	11%	127	....	3%	....	2%	214,279	384	24%	70,868	8,657
1907	32,365,949	32%	153	....	29%	....	23%	212,196	493	59%	65,854	13,671
1908	26,287,800	7%	112	12	....	9%	....	234,713	426	37.9%	61,708	17,817
1909	27,755,032	13%	115	9	....	7%	....	241,348	467	51.1%	59,433	20,092
1910	34,424,951	10%	161	....	37%	....	30%	213,819	473	53%	72,780	6,745

TABLE SHOWING THE NUMBER OF FATAL AND SERIOUS ACCIDENTS, NUMBER TONS OF COAL PRODUCED, NUMBER OF EMPLOYES, MINING MACHINES, AND MOTORS IN THE YEARS 1904, 1905, 1906, 1907, 1908, 1909 AND 1910, AS COMPARED WITH THE YEAR 1903.

Years.	Number of Employes.	Per Cent. of Increase of Employes in 1904, 1905, 1906, 1907, 1908, 1909 and 1910, as Compared With 1903.	Number of Employes for Each Fatal Accident.	Number Fatal Accidents.	Per Cent. of Increase in the Number of Fatal Accidents in 1904, 1905, 1906, 1907, 1908, 1909 and 1910, as Compared with 1903.	Per Cent. of Decrease in Number of Fatal Accidents in 1904, 1905, 1906, 1907, 1908, 1909 and 1910, as Compared With 1903.	Number of Employes for Each Serious Accident.	Per Cent. of Increase for Each Serious Accident for the Number Employed in 1904, 1905, 1906, 1907, 1908, 1909 and 1910, as Compared With 1903.	Per Cent. of Decrease for Each Serious Accident for the Number Employed in 1904, 1905, 1906, 1907, 1908, 1909 and 1910, a Compared with 1903.	Number Mining Machines in Operation.	Increase in Number Mining Machines in 1904, 1905, 1906, 1907, 1908, 1909 and 1910, as Compared With 1903.	Number of Mine Motors in Operation.	Increase in Number of Motors in 1904, 1905, 1906, 1907, 1908, 1909 and 1910, as Compared With 1903.
1903	41,396		334	124			134			774		143	
1904	45,834	10%	388	118		4.8%	145	8%		975	210	186	43
1905	44,193	6%	388	114		8%	119		11%	1,146	372	214	71
1906	46,501	12%	366	127	2%		121		10%	1,266	492	275	132
1907	47,876	13%	313	153	23%		97		28%	1,396	622	359	216
1908	50,267	21%	449	112		9%	118		12%	1,445	671	383	240
1909	47,019	13%	409	115		7%	101		25%	1,395	621	405	262
1910	48,830	18%	303	161	30%		103		23%	1,473	699	451	308

NOTE: —

Per cent. increase of fatal accidents in 1910 over 1909 .... 40%

Per cent. of increase in tonnage in 1910 over 1909 .... 24%

TABLE SHOWING THE NUMBER OF TONS OF COAL MINED TO THE LIFE LOST, TO THE SERIOUS INJURY AND TO THE TOTAL NUMBER OF FATAL AND SERIOUS ACCIDENTS FOR EACH YEAR SINCE THE CREATION OF THE DEPARTMENT.

Years	Number of Fatal Accidents.	Number of Serious Accidents.	Number of Tons Mined to the Persons Killed or Seriously Injured and Number of Tons to the Total.			Name of Chief Mine Inspector
			Fatal.	Serious.	Total.	
Fiscal 1874	20	80	108,919	4,844	31,419	Andrew Roy.
" 1875	23	40	202,667	121,606	77,210	"
" 1876	13	70	269,999	50,000	42,168	"
1877	30	39	175,000	134,615	76,087	"
1878	20	......	......	......	......	Jas. D. Posten.
1879	......	......	......	......	......	David Owen.
1880	22	61	292,624	114,754	84,217	Andrew Roy.
1881	29	......	283,621	......	......	"
1882	25	......	378,000	......	......	"
1883	26	......	316,516	......	......	"
1884	26	40	226,636	143,433	86,932	T. B. Bancroft
1885	51	32	244,258	153,258	94,170	"
1886	43	65	194,308	194,772	78,104	"
1887	36	75	286,158	137,356	92,808	"
1888	29	79	376,239	138,113	100,934	R. M. Haseltine
1889	33	52	330,527	209,757	128,322	"
1890	42	52	280,687	226,708	125,413	"
1891	44	66	296,595	197,730	118,636	"
1892	42	93	347,929	157,129	108,170	"
1893	32	123	463,378	120,553	95,655	"
1894	45	116	364,672	102,674	73,976	"
1895	52	152	263,151	90,025	67,078	"
1896	41	159	314,942	81,211	64,563	"
1897	40	142	311,221	87,668	68,400	"
1898	52	155	270,463	90,736	67,913	"
1899	59	204	269,643	77,985	60,490	"
1900	68	207	285,686	93,848	70,643	E. G. Biddison
1901	72	276	282,240	73,627	58,394	"
1902	81	298	293,818	80,299	63,138	"
" 1903	114	324	215,555	75,843	56,103	"
*Nov. 15-Dec. 31, 1903	22	26	......	......	......	"
Calendar year 1904	118	316	208,337	77,797	58,984	Geo. Harrison
Calendar year 1905	114	372	226,628	69,448	53,158	"
Calendar year 1906	127	384	214,279	70,868	53,255	"
Calendar year 1907	153	493	211,542	65,651	50,102	"
Calendar year 1908	112	426	234,713	61,708	48,862	"
Calendar year 1909	115	467	241,348	59,433	47,689	
Calendar year 1910	161	473	213,819	72,780	54,298	

NOTE:—Fatal accidents in calendar year 1903 were 124. Serious accidents in calendar year 1903 were 309.

* The 22 fatal and 26 serious accidents are not included in the fiscal year 1903 nor in the calendar year 1904.

DETAILED SYNOPSIS OF FATAL ACCIDENTS OCCURRING IN THE STATE OF OHIO FOR THE YEAR 1910.

ATHENS COUNTY.

FALL OF ROOF.

January 29.—Charles Coakley, American, 19 years old. Killed by fall of slate in Juniper No. 1 mine at the face of 1st E. entry. Boy was warned not to go into the place, that it was not safe. Entry was 12 feet wide, with a row of timbers about the center of the entry, one post being set close to the face, and other loose ones close by. This accident seems to have been due to carelessness as well as to some impracticability.

MINE CAR.

June 18.—Peter Bartels, German, 37 years old. Killed in Sunday Creek No 256 mine in a collision of mine car trips. Forest Withain, another driver, misunderstood the signal of the trapper and left the switch with an empty trip, meeting the trip of Bartels on the curve. Unfortunately deceased was riding on the front end of his trip.

FALL OF COAL.

June 20.—John Henderson, English, 70 years old. Injured by fall of coal in the Juniper No. 2 mine and died five hours later. He was working in a room running parallel with a north entry, which was being driven for air. A rib-shot had been fired, which stood and was working the coal out from under it, when the top turned over, catching him. The place seemed to be in fairly good order

FALL OF ROOF.

June 27.—Tod Tittle, American, 26 years old. Killed by fall of slate in room 15, on 9th west, at the face of the working place; room was well timbered within 15 feet of the face. The top is good throughout the mine, and this much space is left between the face and timbers for the machine to cut, but in this case the strata beetween the rock and coal was cut out at the face by the rock coming down on the coal, which gave the slate a loose end at the face unknown to the men who were working under it.

FALL OF ROOF.

Injured July 14; *died July* 16.—Herman Kemnitz, German, 54 years old Injured in New York No. 31 mine, in the face of room No. 19, on 6 east off second north by a fall of roof coal. He had loaded his last car in the room and had sent for the slate man to take the loose top down at the face of room in order for the machine man to cut it. He requested the slate man to wait until he finished drilling a hole which was under the loose piece of cannel coal He finished drilling the hole and while wedging down a piece of bone coal it released the cannel coal, falling on him and injuring him so that he died.

FALL OF COAL.

August 3.—Raymond Walker, American, 17 years old. Killed by fall of coal in Luhrig No 3 mine, in room No. 5, on main west south. Employed as a miner and was working with his brother; they had fired a rib shot the day before going home. The next morning deceased began to take some coal out from under the shot when it turned over on him, killing him instantly.

FALL OF ROOF.

October 25.—Clarence and Walter Beal, Americans, 21 and 28 respectively Killed by a fall of slate in Sunday Creek No. 201 mine at face of first east entry. north off of first east south. Entry was 12 feet wide and a break through at the face, causing considerable space; fairly well timbered, but the fall tripped the post The roof is of a very bad nature — full of slips and joints

FALL OF ROOF.

Injured November 4; *died November* 5.—George E. Glover, American, 30 years old. Injured in the Imperial mine by a small piece of slate weighing not to exceed from 50 to 75 pounds, which fell from the roof while he was preparing to drill a hole in room 21 on second east entry, and died from his injuries November 5. Everything indicated that this man was a good practical miner and no one was to blame.

FALL OF ROOF.

Injured August 25; *died December* 17.—Anthony Wuksi. Finlander, 40 years old. Injured in Northern Fuel No. 24 mine, by fall of slate on fourth east entry, north, about 20 feet from face. From the testimony it appears that deceased was warned that the roof was bad and to be careful. It is claimed that when the top fell deceased was working in some other part of the mine and was about to finish his place and it is supposed he was looking for another place.

FALL OF ROOF.

Injured December 15; *died December* 20.—Wm. Wearn, American, 36 years old. Injured in the New Pittsburg No. 9, by fall of slate at the face of No. 3 room, on 6th west entry, which fell out of left hand corner of a double track room in front of the track. There was a slip running diagonally across the corner of the room between face and timbers, and gave the top a loose end. It is claimed that only his foot was caught, but that blood poison developed and caused his death.

BELMONT COUNTY.

FALL OF ROOF.

January 11.—George Zumalatch, Greek, 45 years old. Killed in the Kirkwood mine, in No. 5 room, 5 H entry, by fall of stone, while carelessly working under same. Room was well posted and posts well set.

FALL OF ROOF.

February 2.—John Kroker, German, 37 years old. Killed in the Wheeling Creek mine, room No. 9, on fourth east entry, off of 6 face, 14 feet back from face of room. The stone fell out between the road posts and gob posts which were only 4 feet 3 inches apart; nearest post to face was 9 feet, with one post lying loose at the neck of room. Deceased and partner were waiting on posts to further post closer to the face, while Joe Kenick, his partner, was in the entry, he heard the stone fall and on investigation found Kroker dead.

FALL OF ROOF.

Injured March 21; died March 22.—William Wiley, American, 51 years old Injured in Neff No. 2 mine by fall of stone at the face of No. 5 room on sixth west entry, and died March 22. Deceased was found by the driver about 3:30 P. M under a fall of stone. It appears he was digging down some coal along the face. when the stone gave way. No posts were under it; it reached about two-thirds of the way across the room, but any kind of a small timber would have held it up. he was working alone at the time.

FALL OF ROOF.

March 23—John Dobensky, Pole, 45 years old. Killed in the Lansing mine. by fall of stone, in No. 5 room, on 28 west, off of main north, while tamping a hole. He was working with his partner and although they knew the stone to be loose, Dobensky started to drill the hole, he using the tamping-bar and his partner putting the tamping in, when the stone fell

FALL OF ROOF.

Injured March 14; died March 21.—Frank Traby, Slav, 29 years old. Injured in the Pultney mine, by fall of stone, in No. 8 room, on ninth east entry. while loading out coal, with no post under the stone, on the side on which he was working. His leg was crushed and he was sent to the hospital; he persistently refused to have his limb amputated and died from blood poisoning on March 21 as a result of the accident.

FALL OF COAL.

Injured February 23; died April 24—Hezekiah Sims, Welsh, 54 years old Injured in the Kennon mine by fall of coal in room No. 6, on 13 east entry, and died April 24. A center shot had been fired in the room, which had sprung the coal and did not bring it down. He was in the act of shearing the coal where he had fired the shot, and some of it gave way, falling on his leg, breaking it near the thigh: it failed to knit properly and the limb was amputated, causing his death

FALL OF ROOF.

May 2.—Frederick Murphy, American, 14 years old. Killed by fall of slate in Media mine in No. 4 room on fourth east entry; employed as a loader and was at work in this room with his father; fall consisted of false top over the coal which comes down, or is taken down by the miners under special agreement. The top, after the false part is down, is unusually good, and consequently miners become careless about posting or taking this false roof down, which would have averted the accident The father presented a school certificate, in writing, over his signature, that his son was born July 7, 1895

FALL OF ROOF.

May 5—Peter DeArc, Italian, 37 years old Killed in Empire No. 1 mine This seems to have been an unforeseen accident, occurring in No. 3 room, eighth west entry. Deceased and partner were considered good and careful miners. The room had no stone in it at all, and had just been cut by the machine men; accident occurred on the right side of the room; between road post and rib there was a spot or slip; one shot was fired and loosened it, causing it to fall.

FALL OF ROOF.

May 25—August Donato, Italian, 31 years old. Killed in Empire No. 2 mine by fall of stone, in No. 11 room, on thirteenth west entry. Room was driven in 75 feet with no break-through, yet very little stone was in the room. No post was under the stone. Deceased was considered a good practical man and this seems to have been an unfortunate accident.

FALL OF ROOF.

May 27—Benjamin Symeski, Pole, 30 years old. Killed in the Lydia mine. Deceased and partner were working in No. 8 room on sixth butt entry, off of second face; they had fired a shot on the right rib and were loading a car when a small stone fell, striking deceased on the side, from which injury he died the same evening. No posts had been set; however, the only safe plan was to have removed the stone, as it was a loose piece across the front.

ELECTRIC WIRE.

June 2—Anthony Mieckodisky, Russian, 26 years old. Electrocuted in the Black Diamond mine while getting into a mine car to ride out of the mine and came in contact with an electric wire, carrying 500 volts. In attempting to get into the car the deceased stepped on the coupling between cars, when getting on car his face came in contact with trolley wire.

FALL OF ROOF.

Injured May 12; died June 3—Joseph Lorella, Italian, 49 years, injured in the Rail & River No. 2 mine by fall of stone, in room 11, on second east entry; room was well posted. On account of death resulting later from this accident the room had been worked since that time. The Inspector states that along the rib it was about a foot thick and no slips. The room was a fair one and well timbered.

FALL OF ROOF.

Injured June 27; died June 28—Harrison House, American, 22 years old. Injured in the Media mine. Deceased was employed as loader and was working with his father in room No. 7, driving south off of third west entry. There was an area of 8x24 feet of loose draw-slate in this room, which was unposted. The father was loading from the west side and the son from the east side; a machine man entered the room and noticed the draw-slate was badly sprung, and advising them to come from under it until it was made safe. Before they were able to do so the slate gave way, the father escaping, but the son was caught by it, causing death. Had it not been for the warning of the machine man there would probably have been a double fatality. The setting of three posts would have prevented the accident.

FALL OF ROOF.

July 2.—Erminio Gagliasso, Italian, 25 years old. Killed in Empire No. 2 mine while working in No. 7 west butt entry, over which there is a very heavy stone, measuring a little over two feet in thickness; this stone is very heavy, and when heavy is very dangerous and full of slips. His death was due to this cause. Several posts were in this entry, but no cap pieces. It is stated by the partner of the deceased that he had not had much experience as a miner.

FALL OF ROOF.

July 6.—George Marsek, Austrian, 24 years old. Killed in Empire No. 2 mine while working in room No. 3 on eighth west butt entry. Room was just up 43 feet from entry to face; stone very heavy, 2 1-2 feet thick; right hand side of stone had been taken down to track; left side being up from the road to the rib, 12 feet in length and about 5 1-2 feet in depth; two posts were under this stone, the coal having all been loaded out. There was no cause for his being under this stone unless to remove posts to let the stone down; five tons of stone fell, killing him instantly; his partner was so frightened that he could not explain how the accident happened.

FALL OF ROOF.

July 9.—Thomas Humphrey, American, 30 years old. Killed in Kennon mine, on main haulage way by fall of stone, while on his way out from work Where the accident occurred a set of timbers were knocked out. Eleven and twelve east entries are used for a passway; when the loaded trip went out he was at this passway; when motorman was coming in with trip of empties he and the mine boss found him under this fall of stone, about 700 feet from passway and about 2,000 feet from the mine entrance.

FALL OF ROOF.

June 10; *died August* 11.—George Borza, Roumanian, 44 years old, injured in the Florence mine while employed as a miner in room in 38 room neck, on fifth east, north side, while loading the fourth machine cut out of a 16-foot wide neck, and had a post under the middle of the stone; a piece fell between the post and rib, striking Borza on the back. The partner of deceased stated that there were plenty of loose posts in the room, but they did not deem it necessary to use them to make the place safe

FALL OF ROOF.

August 19.—John Pitcavitch, Pole, 40 years old, injured by fall of stone in the Kirkwood mine at the face of No. 15 room, on tenth H. entry. Deceased was working alone and had cleaned the coal all out and was removing the stone, into which he had placed a shot to bring it down; it seems as if he had been using a bar on it and either slipped on the stone back of him, or tripped in some way. He was crushed so badly that he died shortly after being taken out from under it

MINE CAR.

Injured August 18; *died August* 20.—Samuel Granstaff, American, 38 years old. Injured in the Clifford mine, and was employed as a motorman. While going to his work, riding on the rear bumper of an empty car, he was caught between two empty cars, which were run loose down the slope and caught him in such a way as to cause his death. The testimony shows that there was a man employed on the loading tipple, or trestle, whose duty it was to look after empty cars on this tipple, and carelessly permitted 11 loose cars to run to the top of the slope, or knuckle, and with the assistance of two or three other men succeeded in checking all of these empty cars, but the two first, which ran down the slope, causing injury which resulted in his death.

FALL OF ROOF.

August 23.—James McGonigle, American, 24 years Killed in Maple Hill mine, while engaged in drawing posts, 26 feet from entrance of room No 20 on thirty-third entry. All but the last post was drawn and the man working with him struck the post twice with a sledge and said they would let this post stand, that it was not safe. McGonigle said he would knock it out and get it out of the way. The post was set about the center of the slate that caught him. Two pieces fell, covering him completely.

MISCELLANEOUS.

Injured August 26; died August 27.—William Webster Berry, American, 28 years old. Injured in the Provident mine. Deceased was employed to push cars to the foot of the shaft on the day which he met with these injuries. He and three other men pushed one loaded car into the elevator and signaled the engineer to take the car to the top of the tipple; some time after this signal was given to hoist this car they decided to take the car off of the elevator, and while in the act of removing the car the elevator started up, and the deceased fell out of the elevator and was caught between same and side of shaft, after which he fell to the bottom.

NATURAL CAUSE.

September 1.—John Hendershot, American, 43 years old. Found dead in the S. C. Hardesty mine; death supposed to have been caused by hart failure. He was working alone at the time in this small country mine, and not returning home at the accustomed time, investigation was made and he was found dead on the floor. He had suffered with heart disease for two years at least. (Not mine accident.)

MOTOR.

September 2.—George Harris, trapper boy, American, 17 years old. Deceased was employed as trapper boy at Empire No. 2 mine and, according to witnesses, must have been asleep on his seat beside the door, with his feet near the track, and not hearing the motor coming out with 49 loaded cars, was struck and shoved in front of the motor for a distance of 15 or 20 feet, half severing his body and killing him instantly; he had been found asleep once before on this same day. The motorman, on seeing that something was wrong at the door, endeavored to stop his motor, but was unable to do so until the motor and one car passed through the door, breaking it down.

FALL OF ROOF.

September 6.—Andy Brier, Pole, 38 years old. Killed by fall of stone in the Provident mine. The room where deceased was killed was just up for the first break through, 40 feet from entry; both places were undercut and shot, room was shot in center and when loading the third car both coal and stone fell, killing him.

FALL OF ROOF.

September 8.—Mike Howarth, Pole, 29 years old. Killed in the Lansing mine by fall of stone in No. 3 room, 29 east entry. Deceased and partner had just started to work and fired a shot on the left rib, the other side having been fired the day previous, and after shooting started to load coal; partner of deceased claims he wanted to take the stone down; it was not practical to have posted this stone and it should have been taken down.

FALL OF ROOF.

October 5.—Joseph Digiorgi, Italian, 48 years old. Killed in the Columbia mine, by a fall of stone, 1,200 feet from entrance of mine on main haulway;

width of entry 8 feet 7 inches; distance from timbers that were knocked out by fall to the other set on one side, 7 feet 4 inches; on the other side 8 feet 4 inches; railroad rails weighing 65 pounds to the yard were used across the entry, resting on short posts cut in the stone on top of coal; coal gave way under the stone post, causing it to fall with no warning.

FALL OF ROOF.

October 17; *died October* 18.—Mike Morcith, Slav, 23 years, injured in the Empire No. 2 mine, by fall of stone, in room No. 14, on 13 west entry; the stone fell from the middle of the room, which was a block room, and in fair order, only being driven a short distance in; the stone which fell was partly cut off with a slip, running over the top, which the firing of the shot would loosen. The fall crushed one of his legs, so that amputation was necessary, and also injured him through the breast and arm.

FALL OF ROOF.

October 28.—Lefaine Fenelon, French, 45 years. Killed in Crescent No. 3 mine, and at the time of accident was working alone, and was not discovered until the next morning, when the driver went into the room and found him covered with stone; the room was well timbered, but he neglected to post the draw slate or take it down.

MINE CAR.

October 31.—Herbert Simmons, American, 13 years, 9 months and 24 days Killed at the Neff No. 1 mine, while employed on the tipple to catch and couple empty cars coming from the loading tipple to the mine entrance, and on the day of the accident jumped on the front end of an empty car to shut down the brake to stop it, when his foot slipped, throwing him in front of the car, killing him

FALL OF ROOF.

October 31.—Gelestini Silvestrini, Italian, 19 years. Killed in Empire No. 1 mine, by fall of coal, in room No. 20, on the fourth west entry, in what was considered one of the best rooms in the mine, with very little stone over the coal. first shot had been fired on the right hand side of the room, four or five cars had been loaded and he was working loose coal from the bottom, when a chunk of coal, weighing about 2000 pounds, fell, striking him on the head, bending him over, killing him instantly.

FALL OF ROOF.

November 4.—Barney Batisti, French, 35 years Killed in the Blaine mine Deceased and partner were working in No. 1 east entry off of north face, and had loaded a shot of coal and were taking up bottom coal, finishing the last car, when a large stone fell, crushing Batisti; mine boss had just been in the room and ordered them to cease working under the stone and take it down.

NATURAL CAUSE.

November 9.—Hamilton Davis, American, 50 years. Deceased dropped dead from heart failure at the Black Diamond mine, while engaged at his work as weighman on the tipple, with which he was said to have been affected for four years (Not mine accident.)

ELECTRICITY.

November 16.—Gabriel Cherry, Hungarian, 32 years. Employed at the Lansing mine Deceased was electrocuted by coming in contact in some unknown manner with a mining machine which he was operating in room No. 2, on 31 east entry, which was charged with 250 volts. The machine was in good working order and the cable, while worn in some places, had been re-taped. It is presumed that he came in contact in some way with the starting box, being found on the right side of the machine and partner on the left.

ELECTRIC WIRE.

December 14.—Steve Kocialk, Slav, 25 years. Pittsburg-Belmont mine No. 3. Deceased was employed as a coal miner and on the day of the accident he had gone into the entry way for an empty car. There were three empty cars standing in the entry way, two of which were made of iron and one of wood. While stooping over between these empty iron cars to uncouple them, he raised up, and in some manner his right shoulder came in contact with the trolley charged with 250 volts, causing his death instantly.

MISCELLANEOUS.

December 17.—John Covalodge, Greek, 45 years. Killed in the Provident mine, by being caught between first set of timbers and cage on which he attempted to get on after the cage had signaled to start, causing him to fall down the shaft 15 feet and killing him.

FALL OF ROOF.

December 29.—Octave Jeffers, Canadian, 60 years, killed in the Hall & Gillhooley mine, employed as a day man, usually as a driver, and when there was no coal to haul usually looked after the safety of the mine, and on the day of the accident walked to the place where it occurred, and finding small amount of roof coal down went a short distance and got a shovel and returned to clean up the fall without examining roof. As the first layer of roof coal was about one foot thick and then what is known as blackjack top, about one foot thick, laid between the first and second layer of roof coal, fell, causing his death.

ELECTRICITY.

December 29.—John Pollock, Hungarian, 23 years. Found dead in Crescent No. 2½ mine, in Room 12, off fourth east entry; was working alone on the day of accident. The machine had been unloaded and two runs had been made and machine moved to the place for third run. The bar he used in moving it was still in the machine, and he was found sitting on the right side of room, 17 feet from front end of machine, about two feet from the reel that winds the cable and 25 feet from entry. Death was, according to the coroner's inquest, due to electric shock of the machine carrying 250 volts.

CARROLL COUNTY.

FALL OF COAL.

October 31.—Joe Polide, Italian, 40 years. Killed in the Robinson-Clay mine No. 5, by fall of coal, while digging clay in the mine. The clay had been shot down, leaving the coal hanging over. This was sounded and thought to be perfectly solid. While engaged in pulling down some loose clay, which had been loosened by the shot, a piece of coal fell without warning, injuring him so that he died half an hour later.

COLUMBIANA COUNTY.

MINE CAR.

January 13.—Edward Yarwood, English, 58 years. Injured in the Klondyke mine and died the following day; with several others he was idling in the shanty, when two cars broke loose, coming down the incline with terrific speed. The men scattered in all directions, Yarwood running into the tipple, a distance of about 40 feet past the scales, the cars leaving the track knocked Mr. Yarwood through a solid board partition to the ground below, a distance of 25 feet. Cars were still coupled together and his body was found under one of these.

KILLED BY AN EXPLOSION OF A BLOW-OUT SHOT.

January 24.—James Blaemire, Scotch, 62 years. Killed in the Delmore mine. Deceased was employed as shot firer and was found dead on third right entry, beyond the ninth room. When found deceased was on his hands and knees, with head resting on hands crossed below his face, as though protecting himself from an expected danger. Deceased was not blown or moved by the force of explosion, but was protecting himself from the forces of concussion that came from heavy blasting. Cause of explosion seems to have emanated from the same room and in the same manner as the accident which occurred on December 16th, in which two other shot-firers met their death in the same mine. Orders of the Department were found disregarded, not only in this instance but in several others, and the repetition of the accident on December 16th occurred.

FALL OF ROOF.

February 9.—John Ludlam, American, 26 years. Killed in the Old Slope mine by a fall of slate in an abandoned room already caved in to east 20 off of face known as No. 4 off of Burns entry. Deceased and partner were machine cutters, and not having enough cutting to make a full day, asked the mine boss to find them a place to load a few cars. He took them to this room, but on examination found it unsafe; took them to another place and it was found to be creeping, and he advised them to go home. This they started to do, but returned to the place and while partner of deceased had gone for a rail to post he took his pick and released some large chunks, causing the rock to fall on him.

FALL OF ROOF.

May 18.—Sam Mastrorania, Italian, 29 years. Killed in the Newhouse mine by fall of slate in room 43 on ninth east entry. 'Conditions point to an unforeseen accident. Deceased was shoveling coal from center shot, when the shoveling, or removing, of coal must have released the roof. There is a five-inch draw slate which comes down; this was down and removed; nearest post to face on side of room where accident occurred was 6 feet 9 inches; nearest road post on same side was 12½ feet from face; on the right side of car the nearest post to face was 9 feet 10 inches

FALL OF ROOF.

December 24.—John Baker, American, 48 years. Killed in the Strabley mine; employed as a loader after a machine, and the room they were loading in was nearly loaded out and was in a faulty territory where numerous slips and rolls are encountered. The left hand rib shot left a strip of coal about one foot in thickness next to the roof and concealed the edge of the pot, or slip, and provided [redacted] support for the roof slate, which later fell on deceased.

COSHOCTON COUNTY.

MINE CAR.

September 23.—Ira Dawson, American, 30 years. Killed at the Davis No. 2 mine, 112 feet outside of the mine on the tramway from the mine to the tipple about 1800 or 1400 feet. It appears upon coming on the outside of the mine the driver was accustomed to putting a blinder over the eyes of the mule while the trip was in motion and then jumping on the front of trip until he passed around the curve, when he would jump in between the first two cars. While doing this he tripped and fell in front of his trip of three cars, passing entirely over him. Brakes are on all cars and the trip could have been stopped if necessary; a pile of coal was lying on the north side of the track where he fell, which had been deposited there before the railroad switches were put in, and it is thought he tripped on some of this coal.

NATURAL CAUSE.

November 4.—Lorenze Faus, Frenchman, 40 years. Found dead in the Warwick No 4 mine. Death was due to organic heart trouble, superinduced by excessive cigaret smoking and a recent attack of the grip; he was found at about 11 A. M. by his fellow workmen in room No. 6 on 2 west entry in a dying condition and removed to the office outside of the mine, where means to resuscitate him were renewed, but he died two hours later. Everything in the room indicated normal condition. (Not mine accident.)

GALLIA COUNTY.

FALL OF ROOF.

October 2[illegible] – [illegible] American, [illegible] years. Killed [illegible] Guyan Mine, where he was [illegible] to open a small mine [illegible] when they expected [illegible] timbers on the gr[illegible]

[illegible]

[illegible]

January [illegible] cross-timbering [illegible] ceased being foreman [illegible] preparatory to [illegible] Inspector states [illegible] prevented the fa[illegible]

[illegible]

January 2[illegible] mine; he and [illegible] room, which ha[illegible]

Head-over was being driven 13 feet west and had advanced 21 feet. From the position in which deceased was found indicated that he had been shoveling the small coal from under the edge in view of turning the lump over when the top coal separated from a parting above the bench, the slate rolling over, knocking its victim down, covering his head and body.

NATURAL CAUSE.

February 22.—Harper J. Devore, American, 25 years. Died in the Imperial No. 1 mine, death being due to natural causes from an attack of angina pectoris while at work in room No. 5 on first west entry. While in the act of prying down some coal he staggered and fell dying almost instantly. (Not mine accident.)

ELECTRIC WIRE.

April 7.—John Patrigo, Slav, 23 years. Met death in the Minnehaha mine by coming in contact with an electric wire on No. 10 west entry, at 4th neck Deceased had gone out of his room on the entry and finding two empty cars on the track he decided to take them to his room, and in so doing one of them jumped the track. In attempting to place it back on the track, his chest up against the end of a car, his back in some way came in contact with the trolley wire above, producing a short circuit through his chest and heart, which was up against the iron on the car, producing instant death, with 250 volts, compounded to 300. Inspector Turner states the only unusual feature connected with this accident was the fact that the cross-timber had pulled considerable coal from loaded cars, which had been removed from the track and piled along the north rib of the entry

FALL OF ROOF.

April 25.—William Fiske, American, 27 years. Met death in Senecaville Mine, while employed as a water hauler, and had entered the mine previous to being examined by the fire boss, and was using an open light, both of which was contrary to law. He was killed by fall of slate on No. 7 entry at the parting of No. 35 room. Accident occurred some time during the early morning; the place had not been examined from the time the loaders quit work on Saturday until the fire boss discovered the accident on Monday morning, during which time the slate had cut, beginning at a pot in the roof opposite the east rib of the room neck, about the center of the entry and gave sufficient vent to break the slate along the south rib a distance of 9 feet and across the entry west of the room neck a distance of 10 feet 7 inches to a point where the slate had loosened by the cut and fell with little warning.

FALL OF ROOF.

June 11--John Kuti, Hungarian, 27 years. Employed as loader in the Forsythe mine, in 23 east entry, which was being driven four runs wide. Loaders were ordered to post the crossing of stone while loading out the coal; three unset posts were found in the entry

ELECTRIC WIRE.

June 20.--Michael Kalchmarick, Slav, 33 years Employed as loader in Little Kate No 2 mine, removing coal from No. 4 west entry, and taking two shots from all room necks turned south off of said entry, being in advance of the trolley wire This entry had been stopped to permit laying heavy iron track and he was transferred back to room neck. He had drilled and fired the shot on the west rib of the neck. In some way, it is presumed, in passing around his car, he came in contact with the trolly wire, killing him instantly. 4½ inch hangers were in use 14 feet apart, at the point where the accident occurred. The tension was slack over the point where the body lay, letting the wire eight inches from entry top; the two inch hangers east of where the body was found were pulled loose. It is probable that deceased was accustomed to working on entry where wires did not exist and forgot about them, and there being more room on that side of the car than on the south; he dodged around and accidently came in contact with wire.

MINE CAR.

June 23.—Charles Steinbrook, American, 23 years. Killed in Little Kate No. 2 mine, while employed as trip rider, and while attempting to jump on a trip was caught between the car and a narrow place. The car rolled him between the cars and rib, an entire distance of 32 feet while four cars were passing; he fell helpless on the track and died same day from injuries received.

FALL OF ROOF.

July 8.—Joseph Thomas, American, 16 years. Employed as trapper boy in the Detroit mine, and was killed on 26 west entry, 47 feet from his trap door. Accident was witnessed by two men who were stationed one on each side of the loose rock to arrest travel under it until it could be removed and loaded into cars; the boy standing by one of these men and wanting to get on the other side ran through and was caught.

FALL OF ROOF.

July 13.—Andy Babash, Slav, 32 years. Employed as an entry man, at the Hartford mine and was killed at the face of his working place. The top of this entry had always been good and did not require timbering; the machine had cut a neck and the entry; both places had been shot and loaded from; this was the first shot cut in the neck, and in drilling the first hole in the neck for his cutting shot it was extended into the roof and shot loose the rock that caught him

MOTOR.

July 26.—David Foster Bates, American, 27 years. Killed in Little Kate No. 2 mine, while employed as trip rider, and was riding the front end of trip when the accident occurred. He must have either lost his balance or been knocked off the front end of the motor while rounding a curve in the mine, and was dragged about 47 feet by the moving motor, causing injuries from which he died same day

MINE CAR.

September 1.—Frank Maleya, Slav, 23 years. Killed in the Little Trail Run mine, by falling in front of his two car trip in a haul way through an old room leading to 11 and 12 east entries without any apparent cause. He was employed regularly as a loader, but having no coal on this day, and the regular driver being off, the mine boss asked him to drive extra. There was plenty of room on either side of the track for a man to jump off. There is a very slight grade but not enough to cause a mule to go out of a walk.

MINE CAR.

September 7.—George Szilagyi, Hungarian, 32 years. Employed at the Minnehaha mine and was killed by having his head caught between post and rib on 9

west entry, while attempting to get in the clear of an empty car, pushed by a motor, coming down grade, which jumped the track, striking post, knocking it out, and resulting in death to this man. No definite cause could be ascertained as to why the car left the track, unless it was due to switch point or frog not being properly laid, and also to the fact that the empty was pushed ahead of the motor.

FALL OF ROOF.

October 6. *Died October* 15.—Clark Padget, American, 37 years. Injured in the Klondyke mine, while employed as fire boss, and general day hand, and was cleaning up slate in No. 2 butt room, out of No. 6 face room, on 26 east entry, off of No. 3 south face. Room was approaching a fault and the top was rolling and full of seams near the face, while cleaning some loose slate that had already fallen, four other men came in and started to talk and he sat down under the slate which fell and injured him so he died October 15th.

MINE CAR.

November 7. *Died November* 8.—Leander McConaha, American, 26 years. Injured in Trail Run No. 1 mine, by an empty car jumping track and catching his leg between it and loaded cars on the opposite track; cause of the car jumping was due to the dilly rope, catching over one of the wheels along the side of a loaded track and pulling car off of the track toward the loaded one

FALL OF ROOF.

November 8.—David Smith, American, 40 years. Killed in the Minnehaha mine by a fall of slate in room No. 1 on 12 west and at time of accident was working alone; he had been warned by the machine men of the danger of the slate that killed him, but in his haste to load he neglected to post it.

FALL OF ROOF.

November 15. *Died November* 16.—Isaac Fluhart, American, 62 years Injured in the Imperial No. 1 mine, in No. 8 room, on 4 east entry, by a pot falling out at the face of his working place. The roof in the place had always been good and was well posted, he being an old and experienced miner.

FALL OF ROOF.

November 16. *Died November* 17.—Henry Abrams, American, 22 years Employed at the Minnehaha mine, and at the time of accident was running a gathering motor, and was coming out of 11 east entry with a loaded car and stopped at No. 5 room and pulled a load out of it and was backing his motor and load back to couple onto the other load, and the trolley wire being hung too close to a timber caused the wheel to catch the timber and knock it out, causing the slate to fall, injuring him so he died the next day. Examination of the timber showed that the trolley wheel had been dragging the timber previous to this trip. and a number of timbers was in the same condition. On some of them the wire was tight up against them, which would make it a very dangerous proposition to run the pole the wrong way

FALL OF ROOF.

December 7. *Died December* 13.—William Gallagher, American, 47 years Employed as a coal loader in the Forsythe mine, but at the time of accident was engaged in drawing posts out of No. 9 room on 21 east entry, in an abandoned room. The roof in this room was exceptionally good, but the piece that caught him was what is commonly known as a wheel or pot, and probably not noticed by deceased when the post was knocked out from under it, as it suddenly fell and caught him.

FALL OF ROOF.

December 8. *Died December* 18.—Edward Landman, American, 25 years. Injured in the Old Orchard mine, employed as a machine man, cutting the widening shot in 41 room on 28 west entry, and it appears to have been a case of starting to work without first examining the roof which fell and caused his death

---

HARRISON COUNTY.

FALL OF ROOF.

April 26. *Died May* 23.—John Vinckit, Pole, 55 years.—Injured in the Roby No. 2 mine, in room No. 9, at the face of 10 northwest entry, by fall of stone while loading coal. Deceased and partner were just finishing loading a car when a piece of stone fell, injuring him so he was removed to the hospital and died from injuries received, on May 23rd. Room was driven 88 feet from entry on the breakthrough, or right hand side, 41 feet from face.

MINE CAR.

June 30.—Mike Mulitzski, Pole, 25 years. Employed as trip rider in the Majestic mine; while coupling cars he was caught between car and rib just beyond the breakthrough; at this point there is only about four inches between car and rib on this side; on the other side of car was a space of 2½ feet. However, the accident would not have occurred had he been on the other side of the car, or if the necessary space had been made on both sides of the track. It is claimed the victim was very ambitious and did not always display good judgment in the performance of his duties.

MISCELLANEOUS.

July 2.—Oscar C. Adams, American, 26 years. Employed as an engineer in the boiler room at the Adena mine. Little is known of the accident, as he was working alone; he had blown the whistle to start to work; the supposition is that after blowing the whistle for some reason he had gone on top of the boiler, and while up there the main steam line, which is a ten-inch pipe, separated at the flange union, and the steam rushing out struck him on the chest, scalding him and blowing him to the hard cement floor below at the back of the boiler, where he was found a few minutes later with his skull fractured

MINE CAR.

September 23. *Died September* 25.—Mike Uhrich, Austrian, 21 years. Employed at the Majestic mine as a driver. Accident occurred on 10 left room entry. He hitched his mule to the trip and started, but discovering only one car, the others not being coupled on, he got off of the trip and tried to get to the brake and stop it, when he was caught between car and rib; the narrowest place between car and rib was nine inches, and the widest place twelve inches. Width of entry was 7 feet, height 6 feet.

FALL OF ROOF.

November 17. *Died November* 18.—Andy Zetinchinski, Pole, 37 years. Injured in Roby No. 3 mine, No. 9 room, on 4th left entry. The breaking shot in the middle part of the room was partly loaded. The draw-slate should have either been taken down or posted: there were plenty of posts and caps in the room.

HOCKING COUNTY.

FALL OF ROOF.

January 27.—George Shannon, American, 28 years. Killed in the Jobs No. 2 mine, near face of No. 15 room, on 4th west, off of 3rd south, by fall of draw-slate. Deceased came out of No. 16 room, in which he was employed; two of the slate men knocked the post out, but the slate did not fall; they then drove a bar over the top of it until they saw it give and shouted for everybody to get in the clear. Mr. Shannon, in some way, was caught under the fall; room was driven in 46 feet and 30 feet wide at face; he was standing 19 feet from the face, two breakthroughs were marked off at face to be cut at this crossing.

FALL OF ROOF.

March 9.—Samuel McConnaha, American, 20 years. Killed by fall of slate in Star No. 1 mine, in North hill, on northeast entry. Deceased was employed as trip rider. There had been a small fall of slate, which had been cleaned up. McConnaha undertook to knock the post out with a sledge in order to let the rest of it fall, although he was advised not to do so, as he was standing under the loose slate when it was released, it fell on him, breaking his neck.

MOTOR.

August 19. *Died August* 22.—Frank Swyers, American, 20 years. Injured in Jobs No. 2 mine by falling off of front end of motor on long north entry, near second west latches, or switch stand. The point where he fell was an old abandoned switch, which was 22 feet, 3 inches wide, with a row of posts through the center. He was in the habit of getting off and throwing the latches, and opening a door and cutting off a portion of the empty cars for the second west, the other portion going to second east. On this occasion they had twenty empties, with the latches thrown for the west, intending to take the front section east. Mr. Swyers knowing the latches were thrown for the west it is supposed he was going to get off and run ahead to throw the latches. He just raised up off of the seat when he fell forward in front of the motor, falling on the left hand rail, the motor passing over his right leg, just below the knee, cutting it off. It is supposed he tripped his foot on the draw-bar, although deceased made a statement that he had just raised up and the motorman shut the power off, which checked the motor, and he lost his balance, but the motorman, and the man in the front car, both state they saw him falling and the motorman shut the power off, set the brake and jumped out and caught him

FALL OF ROOF.

October 26—Peter Hegye, Hungarian, 32 years. Killed by fall of draw-slate in Jobs No. 1 mine, in room No 4, on 2 east, in south hill, while drawing pillars. Deceased was warned to post the slate, that it was dangerous, but he appears to have been very careless, which, in this instance, proved fatal.

JACKSON COUNTY.

MISCELLANEOUS.

January 11.—Willard Norman, American, 18 years. Killed by shot blown through the pillar in the Harper mine, which was fired by Harry Gentil, who was working in the next room and failed to notify deceased when he was ready to fire. He considered the pillar was thick and that there was no danger; room of deceased was 31 feet wide, that of Gentil's 26 feet wide. Coroner in his finding, states: "Carelessness was shown, as these adjoining rooms were being worked at an angle, which required rigid supervision over same."

MISCELLANEOUS.

January 27.—Wm. Clyburn, Novascotian, 50 years. Killed in the Alma No. 2 mine; he was driving first west entry, on north, it being pick or solid shooting. Deceased had drilled and tamped hole, using a blasting barrel in place of a needle. When the report of the shot was heard by other miners working near by, and not hearing the shout "fire" they started to investigate and found him lying unconscious in the roadway, 46 feet from face of entry, having been hit by flying coal from the shot.

FALL OF ROOF.

February 5.—Henry Booth, American, 58 years. Killed in D. C. & I. No. 2 mine, on straight east entry. Deceased and partners were slabbing or taking a skip off the entry pillar, and was mining on a shot which they had fired, when the draw-slate fell; twelve feet of bottom had been taken up, making it very high and a ladder is used to reach the working place; he was injured 3 feet from edge of bottom.

FALL OF ROOF.

February 10.—Edward Bartz, German, 41 years. Killed in Superior No. 3 mine, by a circular piece of slate in room No. 16, on 6 west entry, measuring 4½ feet in diameter and 6 inches thick. From position in which he was found indicated that he was returning to face of the room where his supply of powder was kept, as a tamping bar, needle and cartridge, filled with powder, were found under the same slate, when he was caught by the fall.

FALL OF ROOF.

May 23.—Henry Stewart, American, 52 years. Killed in the Emma No. 2 mine. Deceased and his son were working in a cut-off on third west entry on the north, taking a narrow breast, or skip, across the face of a room to reach a block of coal. He was cutting on a shot which they had fired when the slate fell

FALL OF ROOF.

August 12. *Died August* 15.—Charles A. Gatewood, American, 50 years. Injured by fall of slate in Superior No. 9 mine, in face of his room on first east entry on the north. On the evening before a shot had been prepared; he had been warned not to go under the slate, but on next morning he proceeded to mine on a shot when the slate fell. The rock above the slate is good, and the slate should have been taken down.

NATURAL CAUSE.

September 9.—Harry Shuff, American, 37 years. Deceased was found dead in the Springfield mine, about 7:40 A. M. at the mouth of 3rd east entry on the north, lying on the top of the front car of his trip; he was driving two mules and had two loaded cars on the trip; judging from the position in which he was found, he was sitting on top of the front end of the car when stricken and fell back on top of the car; he had been subject to heart trouble for a year and was unable to perform hard work. (Not mine accident.)

MISCELLANEOUS.

September 12.—Thomas Oiler, American, 38 years Killed in the Harper mine, while attempting to attach a hoist rope to a platform, which was suspended 51 feet from the bottom of the shaft, which had been sunk to the workings of the mine, 102 feet deep, and which penetrated a part of the mine inundated with water; a pump was to be installed above the level of the water in the shaft; a wooden platform was to be placed at the bottom of shaft; the distance was miscalculated as to where the ropes and tackle would reach. While stepping on the platform the rope which was placed on the platform, and on which the rope and tackle were to be hooked, broke, precipitating him to the bottom below, causing his death five hours later.

EXPLOSION OF GAS.

September 27. Died September 28.—James Duane, American, 49 years. Deceased was burned by gas igniting with his open light at the cut-off door, between 5th and 6th entries. The superintendent and assistant superintendent of the mine were with him at the time. The mine had been suspended for several months, and arrangements were being made to resume; an examination was being made The superintendent asked deceased if it was safe to go with an open light, and was informed that it was. They went through the door on the cut-off on the 6th east entry and when returning through the door, the assistants in the lead, the deceased, while in the act of closing the door, ignited the gas; the mine officials dropped down into the water in the roadway and escaped; deceased failed to do so and received injuries from which he died next day. At the time of the accident ventilation was partly cut off on account of water in a dip in the return airway, and probably caused the gas to accumulate there.

FALL OF ROOF.

November 12.—Emmet Walton, American, 23 years. Killed in the Domestic mine by fall of roof, on the outer switch of the motor pass-way, on the north entry, while the miners were riding to their working places. When they arrived at the switch the mule stopped and the miners noticing the roof tumbling made an attempt to get to safety. The mule at the same time pulled the car from under the loose roof, but it fell before deceased could get from under it, killing him instantly.

MISCELLANEOUS.

November 23.—Andrew Tolbert, American, 34 years. Killed in the Superior No. 3 mine, by being struck by flying coal from ignited shot; it is not known whether accident was the result of a defective squib or whether deceased lighted both shots together and failed to wait the lawful time after hearing the first shot fired before going back

JEFFERSON COUNTY.

FALL OF ROOF.

January 3. *Died January* 9.—Andy Bloghy, Bohemian, 33 years. Injured in Jefferson No. 3 mine while working in room 15, on 10 right entry; the coal had been cut in at the bottom to a depth of 7 feet. The coal had been shot and deceased had a rod with a hook on the end of it, the other end of which was chisel shaped; while engaged in pulling down the coal a huge block loosened, causing the rod to puncture the bowels, from which injury death resulted.

FALL OF COAL.

January 11. *Died January* 12.—Frank Zalesky, Pole, 36 years. Killed in the Amsterdam mine, in room 8, first southwest entry; room was 24 feet wide and 5 feet high; the coal had not been properly prepared before shooting, and it was necessary to undermine it, when a huge block of coal loosened, falling on him, causing death.

FALL OF COAL.

January 17.—John Yocum, Pole, 40 years. Killed in the United States No. 4 mine, while working in room No. 11, off 9 east, which was driven a distance of 180 feet from the entry, which was fairly well timbered. The coal had been shot, but all of it had not been removed; deceased took a pick and tried to pull the coal down, when part of the cut of coal fell, catching him, breaking both legs and crushing his body; he died two hours later.

MINE CAR.

January 19. *Died January* 22.—David Young, English, 40 years. Injured in the Dunglen No. 2 mine, while employed in room 18, 1st south west entry; five cuts had been loaded out of the neck, and the sixth was being loaded; place was 9 feet wide and deceased was caught between the car he was loading and the face of the coal, due to the fact that he or some unknown person had left the switch of track leading to his room, open, causing the cars to be thrown off of No. 1 east entry into his room. Coroner states, accident was due to carelessness of person, or persons, whose duty it was to operate the switch leading off of entry into room at the time empty car was taken from entry to room.

FALL OF ROOF.

January 22.—John Gaza, Slav, 23 years, killed in the Connor No. 2 mine, in room No. 5, 10 N. W. entry, 80 feet deep, 24 feet wide, and breakthrough on both sides 10 feet from face; nearly all the coal had been removed when the stone fell, which killed him. There was one post under it, 7 feet from the right hand rib; stone was 10 inches thick and full of slips.

MINE CAR.

January 25.—William Taylor, American, 33 years. Killed in the Jefferson No 3 mine, employed as mule driver and was in the act of hitching the mule to the car of coal, when at a point in the entry (being down grade) he undertook to pass from back of car to front; the car moved, catching him between car and entry, causing him to sustain such injuries that death resulted immediately. Deceased was aware that the passage was too narrow on this side, there being an abundance of room on the other side.

FALL OF ROOF.

February 28.—Ignag Davis, Hungarian, 45 years. Injured in the Roby No 3 mine, in room 3, first S. E. entry, dying two hours later; room was driven a distance of 200 feet from entry, with breakthrough on right hand side, 20 feet from face. Place had good roof and fairly well posted; coal was all loaded out but two cuts, with no posts under the stone Deceased and partner were ordered to take the stone down, but failed to do so.

FALL OF ROOF.

March 15.—Wm. Johnson, English, 44 years. Killed in the United States mine No. 6, by fall of slate, at the face of the No. 4 N. W. entry. The entry originally is 9 feet wide, but was widened out to 12 feet at the face for the purpose of turning the machine around to cut a breakthrough; they were waiting until they loaded out the car to take the stone down, but the stone fell on the right hand side of entry, striking Mr. Johnson, resulting in his death four hours later.

FALL OF ROOF.

March 17; died on 18th.—Joe Brunslik, Bohemian, 34 years. Injured in Dillon No. 2 mine, in No. 3 room, 8 west entry on 7 north face. Deceased and partner were working together and cut was about all loaded out but about three cars; stone was all down, except what was over the coal on the left hand side of room. This coal, it seems, had settled down on the bottom, and in order to let it roll over Mr. Brunslik was punching the bottom out with a bar, when the coal and stone fell over on him, crushing him so that he died in the hospital from his injuries on March 18th

MINING MACHINE.

March 23. Died March 24.—Vince Millinger, Bohemian, 35 years. Injured in Plum Run No. 1 mine, in room No. 2; left entry, off No. 6 right face. While operating a mining machine, the front jack became loose in some way, causing the machine to break and threw it to one side, deceased being caught in the bits, injuring him so that he died on March 24. The coroner, in his verdict states that the accident was due to negligence on the part of deceased for the following reasons: 1st, failure to properly set jacks; 2nd, when jack was discovered to be loose, in not notifying the runner to shut the motor off at once; 3d, in working alone without the aid of a helper, as was the custom Deceased had been working with a partner, but he had occasion to go home some time after noon, and deceased attempted to cut the room alone instead of getting some one to assist him—machine was a Goodman; shields are made of 3-8 inch steel; right shield is 2 feet 8 inches long; left shield 3 feet 3 inches long; on the right side, where deceased was caught, 3 bits are exposed when the machine is back,—that is, 16 inches of the chain The first bits extend beyond the frame 3-4 inches, next 1½ inch, and the other almost 3 inches

FALL OF ROOF.

March 24 Died April 12.—Joe Augustine, Pole, 27 years. Injured in the U. S. No 5 mine, District No 2, by a fall of stone in room No. 9 on first left entry Room was well posted up to the point where accident occurred. A shot had just been fired, and they were working down the coal in the middle, when the stone gave way, breaking his back, causing death April 12.

FALL OF ROOF.

April 12.—Wm. C. Harris, American, 21 years. Killed in the Jean mine Accident occurred in room 15, on 3 west entry. Deceased had carried a post up to the face to put under the stone, but as it was not the right length, did not set it. intending to finish loading the car, which lacked about 200 pounds of being full; about a ton and a half of stone fell, but was broken up and was of a slippery nature.

MINE CAR.

April 18.—Clarence Cline, American, 20 years. Killed in the Amsterdam mine. Deceased was dropping a railroad car out from under the tipple at the time of the accident; he was on the front end of car and had a piece of churn drill about 3 feet long run through the brake wheel, which he was using for the purpose of tightening the brake. It is evident that the piece of drill which he was using to tighten the brake must have slipped, causing him to lose his balance and fall; car having moved 20 feet when he fell and car had not attained any speed

EXPLOSION OF GAS.

April 21.—Charles Howarth, American, timberman, and fourteen others. Killed by an explosion of gas on the night of April 21st, in the Amsterdam mine, caused, it is believed, by an investigation of the accident, by a door being propped open. causing a short circuit of air that permitted gas to accumulate in the part of the mine where the explosion took place. A full account and detailed description of this explosion will be found on pages 20-27 of this report.

FALL OF ROOF.

May 26.—Louie Coleffia, Italian, 40 years. Killed in room No. 5, 16th right in Connor No. 1 mine by a fall of stone. Deceased was a machine man, and was engaged in cutting the last cut. Room was properly posted when machine was taken into the room, but were removed in order to cut the room, and they failed to re-set them as the cutting progressed.

MINE CAR.

June 13. *Died June* 15.—Jno. Pesek, Pole, 32 years. Injured in the Dillon No. 4 room, while engaged in driving a mule hooked to two cars of coal. At the place where he was injured there is a cross-over in which the mule was supposed to be turned, and un-hooked from cars, but as the place was new, the mule failed to respond to the driver. The pass-way is not very wide at this place, and in his effort to direct the mule, was caught between cars and rib and crushed This was a new pass-way, and it was the intention to widen it to provide more room for cars to pass. Had this been done, the accident would probably have been averted.

MINE CAR.

June 14.—Grover Smith, American, 21 years. Killed in the Jefferson No 1 mine, by being caught and run over by two railway cars at the tipple. He and two other men were engaged in placing two rails of track, said track being used to take dirt away from the bottom of the tipple. There seems to have been a misunderstanding between Smith and his partner, his partner dropping the cars down while Smith went on placing the temporary track across railroad track and did not hear the approaching car until he in some way was caught, failing to get off the track. Coroner states that from the testimony the men had not been properly warned and it is his opinion that when brake is on the rear end of first car there should be some one to ride front end of the car to give warning to man at brake to see that the track is clear.

FALL OF ROOF.

June 22.—Anthony Samasewski, Pole, 48 years. Killed by a fall of stone in the Piney Fork No. 2 mine, in the No. 2 face entry on the left in the new hill He had been preparing a shot in the face entry, and had loaded car in the entry Whether he heard the stone working, and endeavored to run out or was going back along there for something else, is not known. He was working alone, and was found under the stone just outside of his loaded car.

FALL OF ROOF.

June 25.—Olinto Doncinlli, Italian, 46 years. Injured in Connor No. 1 mine at the face of working place in room No. 4 on 14th left entry by fall of stone. Room was just about finished except about two cars. Deceased was using a pick digging some of it loose when a large stone fell injuring him so that he died while being removed to his home. There was no post under the stone that fell; several posts were in the room but no cap pieces had been cut.

FALL OF ROOF.

July 19.—Julius Felice, Italian, 39 years. Killed in the Plum Run No. 1 mine, by a fall of stone; employed as a miner in room No. 25, on 11 right entry While stooping over picking up a lump of coal, the stone fell on him throwing him against a post breaking three or four ribs. There were 16 fairly good props in the room, but no caps furnished for them. The cut of coal was almost loaded out, with no props under the stone.

FALL OF ROOF.

August 30.—Wadislaw Zavoski, Pole, 20 years. Killed in the Piney Fork No 2 mine, while he and his partner were employed in room No. 13, on 11th left He was an inexperienced man, and his partner agreed to look after him. While he was getting a post, deceased, against the warning of his partner, went under the stone which fell killing him instantly. Room was well supplied with caps and posts.

FALL OF ROOF.

September 11.—Michael Kosic, Bohemian, 50 years. Killed in the Edgar No. 2 mine, while employed as a timberman, by a fall of roof on 10 left motor line, while putting up I beam cross timbers near the pass-way. While driving a wooden wedge by the side of one timber, the stone fell, crushing deceased on the head, against one of the loose I beams. This was a very narrow escape for the remainder of the party, and temporary posts should have been put up to support the roof, while places for the timbers were being made and placed

FALL OF ROOF.

September 12.—T. E. Allbright, American, 54 years. Killed in the U. S. No. 9 mine, while employed as a motorman. He was taking in an empty trip, and while engaged in conversation with the trip rider, who was riding on the front empty, a stone fell. The entry is timbered nearly all the way through; at the point where deceased was struck, there were no cross timbers broken, but the stone had come through the lagging breaking them. It is not known whether he saw the stone and jumped or whether he was knocked off.

FALL OF ROOF.

September 26.—Henry Rankin, Scotch, 46 years. Killed in the Zerbe mine by a fall of stone, while working in room No. 21 and 22 off 7th. N. W. Deceased was notified by fire boss that there was a fall near the face of 21 room; on reaching the place he and his son started to clean up this fall, so the machine could cut it. It appears that the place had not been well examined as they were just about to break the stone, when about three or four tons of roof came down, and caught deceased, striking him on the head and killing him instantly.

FALL OF ROOF.

September 24. *Died October* 2.—Nicholas Ratkowsky, Russian, 37 years. Injured by a fall of stone in the Rush Run No. 2 mine, in room on 11 right entry, while working in a cut-through on right hand side of room. Partner of deceased stated that there were plenty of caps and posts in the room at the time of accident.

FALL OF ROOF.

October 3.—Steve Grajek, Pole, 41 years. Killed in the Rush Run No. 2 mine by a fall of stone in room No. 4, 11 right entry. Coal had been shot on right hand side of room, and four cars loaded out; they then fired a rib shot, and car taken in and commenced to load, and when about one-third loaded, stone and coal fell. There was one post under the stone. Room was driven 76 feet from break-through. Boss stated that room was done after this cut was loaded out.

ELECTRICITY.

October 17.—Louis Bescey, Hungarian, 36 years. Killed in the U. S. No. 7 mine, and was employed as a pumper. The mine at the time of the accident had been idle for about three weeks. The deceased was with the mine boss, and they were looking the mine over. They had been up to the pump, which is located on the main face entry. They had proceeded about 175 feet away when Bescey remarked that the jumper used in connecting the wires was not right and that he would change it. He heard him call twice, and on reaching him found him lying across the track, his head having probably struck the rail and fractured it at the base. The theory advanced as to cause of death was that he in some way came in contact with the electric current, and fell striking his head. Voltage carried was 500 volts.

MINE CAR.

October 12. *Died October* 23.—Injured in Jefferson No. 1 mine. Frank Cantridge. By slipping and falling in front of trip. He was driving on main face pass-way; there were 16 loaded cars on the pass-way, and he was coming with 2 more loaded cars and riding on the front end in readiness to cut the mule loose, when he slipped and fell. His spine was dislocated, and he died on October 23

MINING MACHINE.

October 27. *Died October* 30.—Martin Kady, Hungarian, 34 years. Injured in the Wabash mine, by a mining machine in room No. 9 on 8 left. Four runs had been cut, and the machine set up for the 5th. When the machine was started deceased went along on the right side to oil the chain, when the bits hit the coal, and caused the front jack to give way, and caused the machine to veer around to the right, catching him in the legs, terribly lacerating them, and causing his death October 30.

FALL OF ROOF.

November 4.—Kotanty Bokaski, Pole, 25 years. Killed in the Jefferson No. 3 mine, by a fall of stone in room 25, on 12 left entry. There were three posts under the crossing of stone, and they had just finished loading out all the coal, and were going to take the stone down, when the partner of deceased, who had gone back to breakthrough to eat lunch, heard the stone fall. He does not know whether he knocked the post out, causing stone to fall, or whether it was tripped by the fall of stone.

FALL OF ROOF.

November 11.—Jos. Dominick, Austrian, 22 years. Killed in the McLain Fire Brick mine, where both coal and clay are mined. The clay had been removed from the room in which the accident occurred, and deceased was engaged in removing the coal from the face of the room toward the entry, when a piece of roof slate dropped, killing him instantly. The slate was entirely unsupported by timbers, not a single timber being used.

MOTOR.

December 8.—Lawrence Donavan, American, 15 years. Killed at the Dunglen mine, the accident occurring on the outside of the mine, (when both mines were idle), between the mouth of No. 1 mine, and top of incline. He was employed as a trapper, but was not working this day. It is presumed that this boy, who was on the motor, which is used on idle days to shift cars, jumped off to throw switch, and in some way slipped and fell across the track, the motor running over him, and killing him instantly.

FALL OF ROOF.

October 27. *Died December* 28.—Jno. Banyek, Pole, 29 years. Employed as loader in the Amsterdam mine, and had just reached his place of work, and had gone back some 35 feet to fill his lamp with oil, when a stone 2 x 5 x 1 fell striking deceased and crushed him to the ground causing death on December 28. Room was fairly well posted, but on examining the roof a clay slip running up into it was found, which cut the roof in such a manner that it was liable to break off at the posts, which it did.

MEIGS COUNTY.

FALL OF ROOF.

February 10.—James France, American, 20 years. Killed in the Hobson mine by fall of slate in room No. 1 neck on 6th north; place was driven 28½ feet and 7 feet wide with five posts set near the face; mine boss was in the room that morning and told them slate was loose, and to take it down, but as there was only one more car of coal to load, they decided to load it out before taking the slate down

MINE CAR.

February 15. *Died February* 16.—George Cline McFarland, American, 17 years. Injured in the Maynard mine on hoppers by a loaded car breaking loose at top of incline which came down on the hoppers like a flash, jumped the track running over the ties probably 120 feet before it left the loaded track; it then took a westward course across the light track, landing on the K. & M. R. R. Mr. McFarland on seeing the cars approaching car jumped off his trip down on the light car track, a distance of 6 feet and ran back toward the running car; just as he got even with the car it left the loaded track, and the car either struck him or a flying timber or a chunk of coal crushed his skull.

EXPLOSION OF POWDER.

February 28. *Died March* 1.—Fred Smith, American, 26 years. Injured in the Charter Oak mine on 16th west in jaws of 22nd room by spark from his lamp which was on his head igniting a keg of powder, which he had on his knee, filling his cartridge. Accident was due to criminal negligence, on part of victim.

FALL OF ROOF.

March 4.—Jacob Darst, German, 55 years. Killed in Charter Oak mine by a fall of roof on motor switch; the place had been examined the day before, by the mine boss and the District Inspector as the water had broken through the slate, and the Inspector advised that cross timbers be taken down, and the loose slate removed and larger cross timbers used, and lagged over top. The mine being idle the rest of the week work was started on it next morning when part of it had fallen during the night. Mine boss told Mr. Darst to take some men and set more timbers on switch and then knock the timbers out from under the loose slate, and take it down. Most of the timbers had been knocked out and Mr. Darst told Mr. Ebersbach to hand him a bar, and he would knock out post on west side of fall. He was advised not to use bar but to use bank rail and knock it out; he thought it safe and that there was no danger; he used it causing the roof to fall and break his neck.

FALL OF ROOF.

September 15.—Ray Rupe, American, 22 years. Killed at the Maynard mine by a fall of top coal in No. 26 room at face of 8th east entry. The top coal is left in this mine for roof, which was about 15 inches thick at this point. There had been a roll which ran across the room 10 feet from face, and the roof coal had been broken clear across the room; the last row of posts was set under this roll; which would have been within 5 feet of face; before the room was shot down a hole had bee ndrilled in the center of this room which was being worked on th esolid, the powder flying in the roof coal. It appears that deceased must have been digging when the hole was on the solid as it seemed that a small piece of coal which had held the top which in digging caused the coal to fall without warning. Another piece caught his brother Worley but it struck the car first and lodged on a chunk of coal on the fioor probably saving his life.

FALL OF ROOF.

December 21.—S. P. Farley, American, 57 years. Killed in the Silver Run mine by fall of slate while working in No. 1 west entry in the room neck. His partner, who was also injured, states that they had just pulled down all the loose slate and loaded it out; then shot the room neck down. The top was then sounded and seemed to be solid.

FALL OF ROOF.

December 30.—Levi Dodson, American, 64 years. Injured in Maynard No. 2 mine by fall slate in No. 18 room on No. 1 north, and died two and one-half hours later. After deceased had shot the last hole in the breakthrough he commenced to load a car without first examining the top and had not loaded more than 100 pounds in the car when he was caught. Son of deceased who, at the time of the accident, was employed with his father, stated that he was very careless, and no one was to blame but himself.

MUSKINGUM COUNTY.

FALL OF ROOF.

March 1.—Norman C. Smith, American, 25 years. Killed in Elk Mine by fall of roof while in the act of loading a car of coal in room No. 3 off first west entry which was driven 28 feet from entry and 18 feet wide at place where accident occurred. The fall took place between face of room and post, deceased was shovelling coal in car when fall came. There were 12 posts in room.

NOBLE COUNTY.

FALL OF ROOF.

February 21.—Michael Kocik, Slav, 45 years. Killed in the Golden Rod mine by fall slate in No. 4 north entry, driven about 11 feet wide; deceased was working single and was found dead under fall about 11:20 A. M., holding pick in his hand, and it is presumed he was killed shortly after driver delivered first car, as no work had been done in the place towards drilling the west rib hole. The place was not properly timbered to meet conditions as revealed by the fall.

NATURAL CAUSE.

March 14.—John Boyd, American, 60 years. Found dead in the Imperial No. 3 mine; death was due to natural causes; employed as stable boss and while engaged in wheeling bales of hay to cars for use in the mine, was seen to sink down on his knees, dying while being carried into the engine room. Death was due to acute dilation of the heart. (Not mine accident.)

FALL OF ROOF.

October 8.—Simon Storosko, Slav, 26 years. Killed in the Noble mine by fall slate; employed as a day hand and worked at night; they were engaged in shooting down top and filling a swale, and had prepared two holes, and powder ready to blast. There was a cross timber across the entry about ten feet from these holes and supported the rock which killed him. He was cautioned by the mine boss not to knock out the post under the end of the cross-timber but failed to heed the warning, and knocked the post out, the slate falling and killing him.

FALL OF ROOF.

December 13.—G. W. Love, American, 40 years old. Killed in Curtis mine. Mine where accident occurred was an old one, and had not been worked for years, and was cleaned up with the intention of starting an entry south near the mouth but went further back to get some pillars which were accessible and could be removed with safety. While cleaning up a pillar slate fell and caught him.

PERRY COUNTY.

MINE CARS.

September 28.—Alex Angle, American, 46 years. Killed in the Central mine by being struck by a trip of empty mine cars; deceased was standing on passway by the side of the loaded trip of coal about 80 feet from switch, when cars were cut loose from motor. There were 14 empty cars in trip, and front car jumped the track about 20 feet from where Angle stood, and caught him between loaded cars and empties and injured him so that he died the same day

FALL OF ROOF.

October 17.—Walter Snedden, Scotch, 21 years. Killed in No. 9 mine by fall of top coal and slate while loading a car of coal in a room 16 feet from entry; was 9 feet wide within 10 feet of face, and was widened to 16 feet. Killed within 8 feet of face.

MISCELLANEOUS.

December 19. *Died December* 27.—Chas. Reed, American, 33 years. Injured in Chapman No. 1 mine, in a machine shop while in the act of putting a belt on the pully wheel while the motor was running, which caused the ladder on which he was standing to slip by a sudden jerk given it, and his arm was caught between belt and wheel, dislocating his arm and shoulder and causing his death on December 27.

SCIOTO COUNTY.

FALL OF ROOF.

September 15.—Jno Fulk, American, 54 years. Killed in the Globe Lime mine, deceased and partner were loading limestone in neck of a room which had rock roof; a strata of slate 10 inches thick overlays the limestone, and is always taken down, if not shot down with the limestone. A shot had been fired, leaving a large piece of slate hanging at the face; assistant mine boss ordered these men to take slate down; they tried to pull it down with a bar and failed; then started to load a car under it; the car was nearly loaded when the slate fell catching deceased causing injuries from which he died, the same day.

STARK COUNTY.

FALL OF ROOF.

January 18.—Jos. Eckway, American, 38 years. Killed in the Canton Fert. Lime mine; was employed as a miner driving second east entry. This is the No. 4 seam of coal and is overlaid with limestone roof, in which crevices are numerous and dangerous at times; deceased was barring in at the face of the entry when stone fell, striking him on the head.

FALL OF ROOF.

January 19.—Jas. Evans, Welsh, 23 years. Killed in Fox No. 12 mine; was employed as a miner and was barring off a shot. There were slips in the stone that was over-hanging where he was working, which came down killing him instantly. He was working on the north side of shaft in room No. 1, parallel to face entry, and room was driven 150 feet from entry; nearest post to face, 10 feet. Breakthrough at face; room 19 feet wide; 18 posts in room not in use.

FALL OF ROOF.

February 8.—Fred'k Whittman, German, 50 years. Killed in mine No. 20 in No. 8 room No. 1 entry. Room was driven 14 yards from entry. There were four rows of posts in room which was 24 feet wide, nearest post to face was 14 feet. These were the road posts. Deceased was working on left side of room between face and post.

NATURAL CAUSE.

September 3.—Arch Wagner, American, 22 years. Killed in Davis Mine. Employed as day hand; mine had been idle for about five months. He and his brother were cleaning up and had commenced to pump the water out. Deceased was to run the pump on Friday night. On the morning of September 3 Jno Wagner went into the mine and found him about 15 feet from the pump in the place where they had left. Death was supposed to have been due to heart failure. (Not mine accident.)

FALL OF ROOF.

September 29. *Died September* 30.—Conrad Byfuse, German, 50 years. Injured in Massillon City mine, by fall of stone in room No. 3 2nd west butt entry. Room was driven about 50 feet from entry, a breakthrough was at the left hand side of room; the nearest post to face on left side was 10 feet on the right side, nearest post 40 feet. The stone which came down and caused death of deceased fell between posts and face of coal; roof is very dangerous in this mine, and places are visited every other day by the man in charge.

NATURAL CAUSE.

November 12.—Ray McDonald, American, 16 years. Killed in the Clay Pit, while visiting a grand-parent; the deceased and some companions visited an abandoned clay pit, and while in the act of mining some of the coal, which had out-cropped, four tons of shale came down on him killing him instantly. (Not mine accident.)

TUSCARAWAS COUNTY.

FALL OF ROOF.

March 5.—Jno. Baker, American, 68 years. Killed in the Advance Coal mine by fall of stone, in a small mine employing five men. This was an unforeseen accident and happened in the first room in the cut-off entry which had only been driven 160 feet from face entry The room neck had just been driven in 10 feet

6 inches from entry at a uniform width of 12 to 13 feet. The width of place at face was 13 feet 7 inches; a slip in the roof had crossed the entry from the old room causing stone to fall.

FALL OF ROOF.

April 23.—Matthew Hawkins, American, 54 years. Killed in the Royal Goshen No. 3 mine, in a room on the left of the main air-course, by a fall of stone. Nearest rooms had been driven in a good distance and have, on account of bad stone, been cut off in many places. The room was well posted, to within 5 feet 4 inches of the face, in center of room; a shot had been fired from a center shot and also from the rib shot. From appearances the powder from the center shot had entered the roof at a slip, the rib shot seems not to have knocked, and evidently in working at this rib shot it weakened the roof causing the stone to fall instantly killing him.

WAYNE COUNTY.

FALL OF ROOF.

February 26.—James H. Humble, English, 24 years. Killed in No. 21 mine in room No. 4 2nd east entry. Room 28 feet wide, the nearest post to face being 5 feet. Deceased was in the act of shovelling under a piece of draw slate which had not come down. It gave way killing him instantly.

LIST OF SERIOUS ACCIDENTS OCCURRING IN THE MINES OF THE STATE FROM JANUARY 1, 1910, TO DECEMBER 31, 1910, INCLUSIVE.

ATHENS COUNTY.

Date.	Name.	Nationality.	Age.	Character of Injury.	Cause of Accident.	Name of Mine.
Jan. 5	Lester McNamee	American	25	Hand and face injured	Ignited squib	New York 34.
Jan. 24	Harry Cooper	American	72	Collar bone broken	Prop under mine car, which gave way	254.
Jan. 24	Edw. Sohn	German	25	Arm broken	Thrown from mine car	Imperial.
Jan. 27	Joe Molnar	Hungarian	32	Hips and back injured	Caught between water box and roof	207.
Feb. 2	Wm. Linton	American	62	Hips injured	Fall soapstone	Doanville No. 1.
Feb. 3	Chas. Garlinger	American	32	Arm broken	Thrown under water-box	No. 31.
Feb. 23	Harry Dishong	American	24	Hips squeezed	Fall bone coal	No. 203.
Feb. 23	Wm. Dishong	American	21	Leg broken	Fall bone coal	No. 203.
Feb. 24	Web Norris	American	43	Left leg broken	Dropping railroad cars	No. 254.
Mar. 4	Fred South	American	26	Collar bone broken	Caught between cars	No. 209.
Mar. 4	Wm. Clester	American	26	Bones in foot broken	Starting engine	No. 212.
Mar. 16	Lafe McQuade	American	40	Left hand cut	Fall slate	No. 204.
Mar. 21	Daniel A. Sams	American	48	Right leg fractured	Fall roof slate	Canaan.
April 13	Fred Turner	American	33	Right hand broken	Caught in mining machine	Luhrig.
May 6	Bert Riley	American	47	Foot injured	Caught between bumpers	No. 211.
May 7	Julius Krakofski	Hungarian	55	Little finger injured	Caught between mine cars	No. 256.
May 9	Jos. Barber	American	52	Hips injured	Falling from tipple	No. 254.
May 9	Amzy Pritts	Foreigner	44	Legs and back injured	Fall coal	Imperial.
May 10	Jas. Quich	American	26	Right foot cut	Caught in chain of mining machine	Luhrig.
May 19	H. C. Graham	American	46	Leg broken	Fall roof	No. 203.
May 23	Robert Stevenson	American	25	Foot sprained	Car jumping track	Carbondale No. 2.
May 31	Robert Hodges	American	24	Right leg and hips injured	Caught between mine car and shaft	No. 254.
May 31	Wm. Hawk	American	54	Right leg broken	Falling from mine trip	No. 254.
June 4	Amos Collins	American	29	Back and head injured	Fall slate	No. 201.
June 7	Thos. Shipley	American	60	Hips injured	Fall coal	Luhrig.

June 8	Jesse Cassler	American	20	Hips injured	Squeezed between mule and mine car	Hisylvania.
June 9	Joe Davis	American	23	Finger cut	Coupling motor	Imperial.
June 14	Hugh Andrews	American	38	Right arm and hand injured	Moving mining machine	No. 31.
June 20	Chas. Bagley	American	42	Small bone in leg broken	Moving mining machine	No. 204.
June 24	Fred Kelley	American	18	Back, face and hands burned	Explosion of powder in keg	No. 266.
June 29	D. A. Presta	American	34	Left foot mashed	Caught by mining machine	Eclipse.
July 12	J. A. Robinson	American	48	Breast injured	Running into empty car	No. 267.
July 14	Lewis Butterworth	American	28	Leg injured	Car jumping track	No. 204.
July 20	Jno. Pierson	American	35	Foot injured	Changing trolley, flange wheel struck foot	New York C. & M.
July 29	Jas. Webb	American	56	Wrist injured	Fall slate	No. 204.
Aug. 2	Andy Cavanaugh	Irish	45	Right leg broken	Fall coal	Canaan.
Aug. 11	Henry Becktold	American	45	Face and back scalded	Boiler pipe burst	Imperial.
Aug. 15	Pearl Hunter	American	37	Back and legs injured	Fall draw-slate	Imperial.
Aug. 18	Geo. Moeth	American	51	Ankle broken	Fall clay	Clay Mine.
Aug. 18	Ira Sennings	American	65	Fingers taken off at first joint	Machinery connected with high speed engine	No. 256.
Aug. 19	Ed Grosvenor	American	17	Leg and ankle injured	Fell off mine car	Canaan.
Aug. 19	Ed Grosvernor	American	16	Right leg and ankle injured	Falling of mine car	Canaan.
Aug. 23	Guy Stewart	American	30	Foot injured	Fell in motor pit	Canaan.
Aug. 24	Lewis Habant	Pole	17	Right leg injured	Fell between mine cars	No. 254.
Aug. 26	Anthony Wuski	Finlander	40	Back and four ribs broken	Fall slate	N. F. 24.
Aug. 30	Harry Matheney	American	16	End of right thumb taken off	By mine cars	No. 204.
Sept. 1	Pearl Steele	American	22	Foot and ankle injured	Caught in tail chain	Canaan.
Sept. 7	Robt. Grimes	American	37	Hip and ankle injured	Fall soapstone	Black Diamond.
Sept. 8	Rol Holcomb	American	43	Leg injured	Thrown in front of mine car	No. 204.
Sept. 10	Jno. Bufalo, Sr	Hungarian	50	Head and hand injured	Fall coal	Canaan.
Sept. 12	Harry Sutton	American	23	Foot injured	Fall in coal from mine car	Canaan.
Sept. 13	Max Habant	Pole	51	Collar bone and two ribs broken	Caught between pot and mine car	No. 254.
Sept. 18	T. Griffin	American	38	Toes crushed	Run over by mine cars	266.
Sept. 20	Earl Barber	American	18	Leg broken below knee	Thrown under mine car	No. 204.
Sept. 21	Jas. Murray	American	30	Hips injured	Fall draw-slate	N. Y. Clay.
Sept. 23	Oland Craner	American	28	Left arm broken	Caught by mine car	No. 209.
Sept. 25	Robert Wright	American	37	Left arm broken	Thrown from a derailed motor	No. 10.
Sept. 30	Abe Kite	American	18	Leg broken, and head cut	Falling from motor	Canaan.
Oct. 1	Frank Smith	American	24	Right hip and leg injured	Fall draw-slate	No. 31.

LIST OF SERIOUS ACCIDENTS—Continued.

Date.	Name.	Nationality.	Age.	Character of Injury.	Cause of Accident.	Name of Mine.
Oct. 3	Jno. Surie	Hungarian	42	Ankle injured; body bruised	Fall slate	Eclipse.
Oct. 5	Long Hill	American	65	Leg injured	Fall coal	Carbon.
Oct. 10	Jno. Sarina	Hungarian	24	Toes crushed	Caught under mine cars	No. 266.
Oct. 18	Wm. Dryer	American	52	Hips injured	Fall slate	No. 204.
Oct. 21	Wm. Ervin	American	32	Leg injured	Fall slate	No. 211.
Oct. 27	Saml. Donahoe	American	22	Arm broken	Oiling fan shaft	C. & H. C. & No. 1A.
Nov. 12	Fred Russell	American	17	Thumb injured	Coal falling down shaft	No. 254.
Nov. 14	Jno. Turvey	American	54	Hand injured	Fall slate	No. 204.
Nov. 14	Jas. Jeffries	Mexican	50	Finger injured	Caught in mining machine	Canaan.
Nov. 18	Francis Kesterson	American	17	Legs injured	Caught under mine car	No. 201.
Nov. 19	Jno. Cline	American	40	Five ribs broken	Fall roof	New Monarch.
Nov. 22	Chester Hilt	American	20	Wrist injured	Struck by an ax	N. Y. No. 36.
Nov. 25	Mose Evans	Welsh	39	Five ribs broken	Fall coal	Imperial.
Nov. 25	N. J. Foley	American	64	Left leg broken	Mine car jumping track	No. 254.
Nov. 28	Daniel Bateman	American	60	Back and bowels injured	Struck by mine car	N. Y. No. 36.
Dec. 2	Frank Evans	American	18	Head, breast and hand injured	Fall slate	Imperial.
Dec. 6	Pat Curtis	American	38	Left foot injured	Fall roof	No. 254.
Dec. 16	Geo. Beckley	American	55	Back injured	Fall slate	Luhrig.
Dec. 28	Wm. Styler	American	23	Toe mashed	Unloading mining machine	S. C. No. 209.

BELMONT COUNTY.

Date.	Name.	Nationality.	Age.	Character of Injury.	Cause of Accident.	Name of Mine.
Jan. 5	Edw. Murray	Irish	27	Hip and knee injured	Struck by falling timber	Neffs No. 2.
Jan. 7	Jno. Keith	American	30	Right leg broken	Caught between chain and mine car	Pultney.
Jan. 12	Elias Stanford	American	24	Shoulder dislocated	Thrown from mine car	St. Clair.
Jan. 12	Sam Solovich	Austrian	22	Head injured	Fell, striking rail	Rail & River No. 3.
Jan. 17	Abraham Johnson	American	31	Leg broken	Fall coal	Neffs No. 2.

Jan. 21	Dominic Lauzi	Italian	30	Back injured	Fall stone	St. Clair.
Jan. 27	Val. [illegible]ski	Pole	32	Toes mashed	Fall coal and stone	Neffs No. 2.
Feb. 1	Carroll Dalin	Swede	24	Foot mashed	Injured by mining machine	Dellora.
Feb. 2	Fred Elslager	German	34	Back and hips injured	Fall stone	Empire.
Feb. 6	Paul Whitard	Pole	25	Hip injured	Fall coal	Troll No. 1.
Feb. 8	Tom Devine	Hungarian	45	[illegible]de, leg and head injured	Fall coal	Barton.
Feb. 16	Jno. Poyett	Pole	22	Head injured	Fall stone	Neffs No. 2.
Feb. 18	Jos. Jeffers	American	63	Two ribs broken	Caught by loaded mine car	West Wheeling.
Feb. 21	H[illegible]iah Sims	American	48	Leg broken	Fall roof coal	Kennon.
Feb. 21	Wm. Hall	American	20	Right leg broken	Chain on mine cars struck leg	Maple Hill.
Feb. 22	Frank Powell	German	46	Leg injured	Fall coal	Schicks.
Mar. 7	Geo. Howath	Hungarian	23	Left foot injured	Fall stone	Maple Hill.
Mar. 8	Andy Stadnijenko	Slav	30	Foot injured	Mining machine	Franklin.
Mar. 23	[illegible]is Pag[illegible]no	Hungarian	30	Right foot injured	Fall slate	Barton.
Mar. 24	Harry Beyers	American	24	Leg injured	Caught between mine cars	Glen.
Mar. 28	Rudy Lisk	Bohemian	24	Jaw bone broken	Caught between car and rib	Maple Hill.
Mar. 29	Tom B[illegible]yacho	Montenegro	21	Three fingers amputated	By mine motor	Glen.
April 9	Jos. [illegible]dy	[illegible]ian	27	First finger amputated	Putting rope over pulley wheel	Neffs No. 2.
April 14	Wm. Tusken	Pole	28	Left leg broken	Fall stone and coal	West Wheeling.
April 16	Chas. Pazzuia	Italian	27	Left ankle fractured	Fall stone	Rail & River No. 2.
April 18	Teofilo Megnain	Austrian	29	Great toe on right foot cut	Caught in chain of mining machine	Wheeling Creek No. 1.
April 21	Joe Slovitch	Pole	40	Head and ankle injured	Fall slate	Pittsburg - Belmont No. 1.
April 25	Joe Briton	American	23	Left foot injured	Fall stone	Rail & River No. 2.
April 26	Wm. Dunn	American	36	Arm broken	Trimming [illegible], brake slipped	Virginia Hill.
April 27	Mike Skolets	Austrian	25	Hips and back injured	Caught between car and rib	Dellora.
April 27	Andy Tuncoe	Slav	30	Left arm amputated at elbow	Caught in mining machine	Taggart.
April 28	Jno. W. Smith	American	69	Wrist dislocated	Struck by mine car	West Wheeling.
April 29	Jno. Tommolnes	Slav	24	Thigh and ankle injured	Caught in mining machine	Ellora.
May 6	Chas. Barnett	American	22	Hips injured	Caught by mine car	Big Run.
May 6	Wm. Pelkey	American	38	Leg broken	Fall stone	West Wheeling.
May 12	Andy Pulogo	Slav	22	Right leg cut	Shot through rib	Pittsburg - Belmont No. 3.
May 19	Mike Zipko	Slav	41	Rib broken and head bruised	Fall stone	Florence.
May 19	Jos. Wachelon	Lithuanian	39	Arm broken	Caught between car and rib	St. Clair.
May 20	Jno. Marcus	Austrian	46	Back injured and leg broken	Fall stone	Wheeling Creek.

LIST OF SERIOUS ACCIDENTS OCCURRING IN THE MINES OF THE STATE FROM JANUARY 1, 1910, TO DECEMBER 31, 1910, INCLUSIVE.

ATHENS COUNTY.

Date.	Name.	Nationality.	Age.	Character of Injury.	Cause of Accident.	Name of Mine.
Jan. 5	Lester McNamee	American	25	Hand and face injured	Lighted squib	New York 34.
Jan. 24	Harry Cooper	American	72	Collar bone broken	Prop under mine car, which gave way	254.
Jan. 21	Edw. Sohn	[illegible]man	25	Arm broken	Thrown from mine car	Imperial.
Jan. 27	Joe [illegible]	Hungarian	32	Hips and back injured	Caught between water box and roof	207.
Feb. 2	Wm. Linton	American	62	Hips injured	Fall [illegible]	Doanville No. 1.
Feb. 3	Chas. Garlinger	American	32	Arm broken	Thrown [illegible] water-box	No. 31.
Feb. 23	Harry [illegible]	American	24	Hips squeezed	Fall bone coal	No. 203.
Feb. 23	Wm. Dishong	American	21	Leg broken	Fall bone coal	No. 203.
Feb. 24	Web Norris	American	43	Left leg broken	Dropping railroad cars	No. 254.
Mar. 4	Fred South	American	26	Collar bone broken	Caught between cars	No. 209.
Mar. 4	Wm. [illegible]	[illegible]	26	Bones in foot broken	Starting engine	No. 212.
Mar. 16	[illegible]	[illegible]	40	Left hand cut	Fall slate	No. 204.
Mar. 21	[illegible] A. Sams	American	48	Right leg fractured	Fall roof slate	Canaan.
April 13	Fred Turner	American	33	Right hand broken	Caught in mining machine	Luhrig.
May 6	Bert Riley	American	47	Foot injured	Caught between [illegible]	No. 211.
May 7	Julius [illegible]ki	Hungarian	55	Little finger injured	Caught between mine cars	No. 256.
May 9	Jos. Barber	American	52	Hips injured	Falling from tipple	No. 254.
May 9	Amzy Pritts	Foreigner	44	Legs and back injured	Fall coal	Imperial.
May 10	Jas. Quich	American	26	Right foot cut	Caught in chain of mining machine	Luhrig.
May 19	H. C. Graham	American	46	Leg broken	Fall roof	No. 203.
May 23	Robert Stevenson	American	25	Foot sprained	Car jumping track	Carbondale No. 2.
May 31	Robert Hodges	American	24	Right leg and hips injured	Caught between mine car and shaft	No. 254.
May 31	Wm. Hawk	American	54	Right leg broken	Falling from mine trip	No. 254.
June 4	Amos Collins	American	29	Back and head injured	Fall slate	No. 201.
June 7	Thos. Shipley	American	60	Hips injured	Fall coal	Luhrig.

June 8	Jesse Gasler	American	20	Hips injured	Squeezed between mule and mine car	Hisylvania.
June 9	Joe Davis	American	23	Finger cut	Coupling motor	Imperial.
June 14	Hugh Andrews	American	38	Right arm and hand injured	Moving mining machine	No. 31.
June 20	Chas. Bagley	American	42	Small bone in leg broken	Moving mining machine	No. 204.
June 24	Fred Kelley	American	18	Back, face and hands burned	Explosion of powder in keg	No. 266.
June 29	D. A. Presta	American	34	Left foot mashed	Caught by mining machine	Eclipse.
July 12	J. A. [illegible]n	American	48	Breast injured	Running into empty car	No. 267.
July 14	Lewis Butterworth	American	28	Leg injured	Car jumping track	No. 204.
July 20	Jno. Pierson	American	35	Foot injured	[illegible]g trolley, [illegible]wheel struck [illegible]ot	New York C. & M.
July 29	Jas. Webb	American	56	Wrist injured	Fall slate	No. 204.
Aug. 2	[illegible]ly C[illegible]gh	Irish	45	Right leg broken	Fall coal	Do.
Aug. 11	Henry Becktold	American	45	Face and back scalded	Boiler pipe burst	Imperial.
Aug. 15	[illegible]rl Hunter	American	37	Back and legs injured	Fall [illegible]-slate	Imperial.
Aug. 18	Geo. [illegible]th	American	51	Ankle broken	Fall clay	Clay Mine.
Aug. 18	Ira Sennings	American	65	Fingers taken off at first joint	Machinery connected with high speed engine	No. 256.
Aug. 19	Ed Grosvenor	American	17	Leg and ankle injured	Fell off mine car	Gen.
Aug. 19	Ed [illegible]r	American	16	Right leg and ankle injured	Falling of mine car	Do.
Aug. 23	Guy Stewart	American	30	Foot injured	Fell in motor pit	Gen.
Aug. 24	[illegible]wis Habant	Bl[illegible]c	17	Right leg injured	Fell between mine cars	No. 254.
Aug. 26	Anthony Wuski	Finlander	40	Back and [illegible]r ribs broken	Fall slate	N. F. 24.
Aug. 30	[illegible]ry Matheney	[illegible]	16	End of right thumb taken off	By mine cars	No. 204.
Sept. 1	[illegible]rl Steele	American	22	Foot and ankle injured	Caught in tail chain	Do.
Sept. 7	Robt. Grimes	A[illegible]	37	Hip and ankle injured	Fall soapstone	Black Diamond.
Sept. 8	[illegible]dl Holcomb	American	43	Leg injured	Thrown in front of mine car	No. 204.
Sept. 10	Jno. Bufalo, Sr.	Hungarian	50	[illegible] injured	Fall coal	Do.
Sept. 12	Harry Sutton	American	23	Foot injured	Fall in [illegible]el from mine car	Do.
Sept. 13	Max [illegible]t	Pole	51	Collar bone and two ribs broken	Caught between pot and mine car	No. 254.
Sept. 18	T. Griffin	American	38	Toes crushed	Run over by mine cars	86.
Sept. 20	Earl Barber	American	18	Leg broken below knee	Thrown under mine car	No. 204.
Sept. 21	Jas. Murray	American	30	Hips injured	Fall draw-slate	N. Y. Clay.
Sept. 23	Ol[illegible]d Craner	American	28	Left arm broken	Caught by mine car	No. 209.
Sept. 25	Robert Wright	American	37	Left arm broken	Thrown from a derailed motor	No. 10.
Sept. 30	Abe Kite	American	18	Leg broken, and head cut	Falling from motor	Gen.
Oct. 1	Frank Smith	American	24	Right hip and leg injured	Fall draw-slate	No. 31.

LIST OF SERIOUS ACCIDENTS—Continued.

Date.	Name.	Nationality.	Age.	Character of Injury.	Cause of Accident.	Name of Mine.
Oct. 3	Jno. Surie	Hungarian	42	Ankle injured; body bruised	Fall slate	Eclipse.
Oct. 5	Long Hill	American	65	Leg injured	Fall coal	Carbon.
Oct. 10	Jno. Sarina	Hungarian	24	Toes crushed	Caught under mine cars	No. 266.
Oct. 18	Wm. Dryer	American	52	Hips injured	Fall slate	No. 204.
Oct. 21	Wm. Ervin	American	32	Leg injured	Fall slate	No. 211.
Oct. 27	Saml. Donahoe	American	22	Arm broken	Oiling fan shaft	C. & H. C. & No. 1A.
Nov. 12	Fred Russell	American	17	Thumb injured	Coal falling down shaft	No. 254.
Nov. 14	Jno. Turvey	American	54	Hand injured	Fall slate	No. 204.
Nov. 14	Jas. Jeffries	Mexican	50	Finger injured	Caught in mining machine	Canaan.
Nov. 18	Francis Kesterson	American	17	Legs injured	Caught under mine car	No. 201.
Nov. 19	Jno. Cline	American	40	Five ribs broken	Fall roof	New Monarch.
Nov. 22	Chester Hilt	American	20	Wrist injured	Struck by an ax	N. Y. No. 36.
Nov. 25	Mose Evans	Welsh	39	Five ribs broken	Fall coal	Imperial.
Nov. 25	N. J. Foley	American	64	Left leg broken	Mine car jumping track	No. 254.
Nov. 28	Daniel Bateman	American	60	Back and bowels injured	Struck by mine car	N. Y. No. 36.
Dec. 2	Frank Evans	American	18	Head, breast and hand injured	Fall slate	Imperial.
Dec. 6	Pat Curtis	American	38	Left foot injured	Fall roof	No. 254.
Dec. 16	Geo. Beckley	American	55	Back injured	Fall slate	Luhrig.
Dec. 28	Wm. Styler	American	23	Toe mashed	Unloading mining machine	S. C. No. 209.

BELMONT COUNTY.

Date.	Name.	Nationality.	Age.	Character of Injury.	Cause of Accident.	Name of Mine.
Jan. 5	Edw. Murray	Irish	27	Hip and knee injured	Struck by falling timber	Neffs No. 2.
Jan. 7	Jno. Keith	American	30	Right leg broken	Caught between chain and mine car	Pultney.
Jan. 12	Elias Stanford	American	24	Shoulder dislocated	Thrown from mine car	St. Clair.
Jan. 12	Sam Solovich	Austrian	22	Head injured	Fell, striking rail	Rail & River No. 3.
Jan. 17	Abraham Johnson	American	31	Leg broken	Fall coal	Neffs No. 2.

Jan. 21	Dominic Lauzi	Italian	30	Back injured	Fall st ne	St. Clair.
Jan. 27	Val. Yalkowski	Pole	32	Toes rhd	Fall el and stone	Ns No. 2.
Feb. 1	Carroll Dalin	Swede	24	Foot rhd	Injured by mining machine	Dellora.
Feb. 2	Fred Elslager	German	34	Back ad hips injured	Fall stone	Empire.
Feb. 6	Paul Whitard	Pole	25	Hip injured	Fall el	Troll N. 1.
Feb. 8	Tom Devine	Hungarian	45	N, dg ad head injured.	Fall el	Barton.
Feb. 16	Jno. Poyett	Pole	22	Hd injured	Fall stone	Neffs N. 2.
Feb. 18	Jos. Jeffers	American	63	Two ribs broken	Caught by dd mine car	West Wheeling.
Feb. 21	Hesekiah Sims	American	48	leg broken	Fall oof coal	Kdn.
Feb. 21	Wm. Hall	American	20	Right dg broken	Chain on mine ars struck leg	Maple Hill.
Feb. 22	Frank Powell	German	46	leg injured	Fall el	Schicks.
Mar. 7	G. Howath	Hungarian	23	Left ot injured	Fall stone	Maple Hill.
Mar. 8	Andy Stadnijenko	Slav	30	Foot injured	Mining mhine	Franklin.
Mar. 23	Lewis Bn	Hn	30	Right ot injured	Fall slate	Barton.
Mar. 24	Harry Beyers	American	24	leg injured	Gt between mine cars	Glen.
Mar. 28	Rdy Lisk	Bohemian	24	Jaw be broken	Gt between car and rib	Maple Hill.
Mar. 29	Tom Boyach	Ngro	21	Three fingers amputated	By mine motor	Glen.
April 9	Jos. O'Grady	American	27	First gr amputated	Putting pe over pulley wheel.	Ns No. 2.
April 14	Wm. Tusken	Pole	28	Left dg broken	Fall stone ad coal	West Wh eling.
April 16	G. Pazzuia	Italian	27	Left ankle fractured	Fall stone	Rail & Ri er No. 2.
April 18	Teofilo Me gain	Austrian	29	Great toe on right foot cut.	Caught in chain of mining machine	Wheeling Creek N. 1.
April 21	Joe Slovitch	Pole	40	Head and ankle injured	Fall slate	Pittsburg - Belmont No. 1.
April 25	Joe Briton	American	23	Left foot injured	Fall stone	Rail & River No. 2.
April 26	Wm. In	Ameri an	36	Arm broken	Trimming cars, brake slipped.	Vgia Hill.
April 27	Mike Skolets	Austrian	25	Hips and back injured	ught between ar and rib	Dellora.
April 27	Andy Tuncoe	Slav	30	Left arm aped at elbow	Caught in mining mchine	Taggart.
April 28	Jno. W. Smith	ri an	69	Wrist dislocated	Struck by me car	Wst Wheeling.
April 29	Jno. Tmolnes	Slav	24	Thigh and kle i ujed	ught in mining mchine	Dellora.
May 6	Chas. Barnett	ri an	22	Hips injured	Caught by mine car	Big Run.
My 6	Wm. Pelkey	ri an	38	Leg broken	Fall one	West Wheeling.
May 12	Andy Pulogo	Slav	22	Right leg cut	Shot through rib	Brg - Belmont N. 3.
May 19	Mike Zipko	Slav	41	Rib broken and head bruised.	Fall stone	Florence.
May 19	Jos. Wachelon	In	39	Arm broken	Caught between car and rib	St. Clair.
My 20	Jo. Marcus	Austrian	46	Back injured and leg broken.	Fall stone	Wheeling Creek.

LIST OF SERIOUS ACCIDENTS—Continued.

Date.	Name.	Nationality.	Age.	Character of Injury.	Cause of Accident.	Name of Mine.
May 21	Lem Yoho	American	40	Body injured	Caught by fall coal and stone	[illegible] - Belmont No. 1.
May 25	Stiney Mutoisk	Pole	24	Both legs and two ribs broken	Fall [illegible]	Black Diamond.
May 26	Chas. Weisicoski	Pole	19	Leg broken	Fall stone	Neffs No. 2.
June 1	Jno. Bokoca	Austrian	45	Toe mashed	Fall stone	Knob.
June 3	Moxey Orco	Slav	26	Leg broken	Falling from r. r. flats	[illegible] No. 2.
June 4	Joe Rokoskey	Pole	24	Shoulder blade broken	Caught between car and rib	St. Clair.
June 4	Joe Switcher	German	40	Foot mashed	Fall coal	Knob.
June 6	Jean Able	American	21	Leg crushed	[illegible] cars	Bannock.
June 10	Geo. Berza	Hungarian	44	[illegible] injured	Fall stone	[illegible]
June 11	Alex. Brown	Pole	26	Shoulder broken	Fall stone	Black Diamond.
June 14	Joe Moore	[illegible]		Two ribs broken	Fall stone	[illegible]
June 18	Jno. Reckia	Italian	32	Both feet injured	Coupling mine cars	Lafferty.
June 19	Toldio Godusky	Pole	24	Leg broken	Fall draw-slate	Troll No. 2.
June 24	Mike Eika	Bohemian	47	Right hip [illegible]	Fall coal	Wheeling Creek.
June 27	Harrison House	[illegible]	22	Hips injured, and arms	Fall slate	[illegible]
June 30	Steve Hydo	Hungarian	25	Head and back injured	Fall slate	Barton.
July 6	Dominic Domichel	Italian	22	Collar bone fractured	Squeezed between car and rib	Florence.
July 7	Dominic [illegible]	Pole	28	End of finger cut off	Fall coal	Neffs No. 2.
July 8	Sherd Brown	American	43	Right foot [illegible]	Fall slate	Glen.
July 8	Wilbur [illegible]	American	19	Great toe mashed	Caught between motor and mine car	Florence.
July 12	Joe Koshick	Pole	28	Foot injured	Run over by mine car	St. Clair.
July 17	Lawrence Cola	Pole	23	Collar bone broken	Caught between car and rib	St. Clair.
July 20	Joe [illegible]	American	23	Leg broken	Trestle gave way	Rail & River.
July 21	Jos. Red	[illegible]	34	Right rib broken	Fall stone	Florence.
July 22	[illegible] Adianni	Montenegro	32	Foot mashed	Fall slate	Glen.
July 27	David Thomas	Welsh	40	Back injured	Fall slate	Gaylord.
July 28	Wm. Franklin	American	50	Foot injured	Run over by mining machine	[illegible]
Aug. 24	[illegible] Donlarish	Greek	30	Left foot injured	Fall stone	Kirkwood.

Aug. 25	Jas. Minetes	Foreigner	41	Body injured	Fall roof	Empire No. 1.
Aug. 26	Simon [illegible]	Italian	42	Body injured	Fall slate	Rail & River No. 1.
Aug. 30	Andy Bracen	Slav	27	Leg broken	Fall soapstone	Pittsburg - Belmont No. 3.
Aug. 31	Jno. McFayden	American	21	[illegible]	Falling under mine cars	[illegible]
Sept. 2	Albion Fondeist	German	35	[illegible] and [illegible] injured	Fall stone	St. Clair.
Sept. 10	Joe Prosperi	Italian	28	Leg broken	[illegible] mine car	Rail & River No. 1.
Sept. 12	Volke Vingenzi	Italian	39	Leg broken	Fall coal	Rail & River No. 1.
Sept. 14	Frank Cyski	Pole	23	[illegible] and [illegible] mashed	Fall coal	Taggart.
Sept. 20	Albert Tronko	Slav	19	Finger taken off at first joint	Coupling mine cars	Black Diamond.
Sept. 27	Saml. [illegible]	[illegible]	57	Leg broken	Fall draw-slate	Franklin.
Oct. 4	Fred Porter	[illegible]	42	Side and hip [illegible]	Fall slate	Big Run.
Oct. 5	Jno. Payne	American	40	Left hand and right hand injured and one rib broken	Jumping off mine car	Crescent No. 3.
Oct. 6	[illegible] Vila	Italian	26	Left shoulder injured	Fall slate	Rail & River No. 2.
Oct. 6	Bop Pozain	Italian	29	Back and left arm broken	Fall slate	Johnson.
Oct. 6	J. Davidson	Scotch	60	[illegible] injured	Fall stone	[illegible] No. 2.
Oct. 8	R[illegible] White	American	25	Hip and ankle injured	Fall stone	Big Run.
Oct. 9	Phil [illegible]	American	52	[illegible]	Caught between car and refuse pile	Rail & River No. 2.
Oct. 14	[illegible]	[illegible]	20	Leg injured	Run over by mine car	Rail & River No. 2.
Oct. 15	Robt. [illegible]	Slav	39	Left knee cap broken	Riding mine cars	Puritan.
Oct. 22	Anton Molke	Pole	34	Foot injured	Stepping between cutter and face of coal	Pittsburg - Belmont No. 3.
Oct. 24	[illegible] Hood	American	20	Leg broken	Falling under mine cars	Belmont.
Oct. 28	Saml. [illegible]	American	19	Left leg broken	Fall slate	Lucy.
Oct. 31	Thos. Beasley	American	42	Finger injured	Coupling mine cars	Pittsburg - Belmont No. 2.
Nov. 1	Lulce Papas	Roumanian		Three ribs and collar bone broken	Caught between mine car and rib	Kirkwood.
Nov. 3	Joe Bailley	American	22	[illegible] injured	Caught between car and rib	Rail & River No. 6.
Nov. 3	Geo. Marks	Slav	37	Leg broken	Bracing mining [illegible]	Florence.
Nov. 7	Joe Lukannee	Pole	20	Arm and leg fractured	Stepped in front of moving trip	St. Clair.
Nov. 8	Sam Toney	Italian	22	Hip fractured and dislocated	Fall slate	Rail & River No. 6.
Nov. 11	Martin Leis	German	61	Ankle bone broken	Fall roof	Knob.
Nov. 11	E. Enneis	American	35	Leg broken	Struck by drill [illegible]	[illegible] No. 2.
Nov. 18	Ellis Dunfee	American	16	Wrist broken	Caught between mine cars	[illegible]
Nov. 22	Chas. Sindledecker	American	22	Head injured	Fall stone	Capti[illegible]

LIST OF SERIOUS ACCIDENTS—Continued.

Date.	Name.	Nationality.	Age.	Character of Injury.	Cause of Accident.	Name of Mine.
Nov. 27	Albert Ba[illegible]k	[illegible]ngarian	34	Foot injured	Fall [illegible]	[illegible] No. 1.
Nov. 28	John [illegible]	[illegible]	25	Right foot injured	Fall stone	[illegible]
Dec. 1	Albert [illegible]nickey	Slav	33	Head injured	Fall stone	Black [illegible]nd.
Dec. 2	Joe Bol[illegible]sh	[illegible]	19	Breast bruised	Caught [illegible] mine [illegible] and rib	[illegible] Hill.
Dec. 3	Vincin [illegible]	[illegible]	35	Left foot injured	Caught in mining [illegible]	Barton.
Dec. 5	Walter [illegible]	[illegible]	43	Foot injured	Falling [illegible]	Kennon.
Dec. 5	Fred Levy	Italian	25	Thigh injured	Collision of mine [illegible]	Rail & River.
Dec. 6	Sam Zabrunski	Pole	26	Leg and hips injured	Caught between [illegible] and rib	[illegible]rg - Belmont No. 1.
Dec. 9	Jas. [illegible]	[illegible]	42	Two ribs fractured	Caught by stone on stone pile	Barton.
Dec. 9	Joe Kurczmarczyka	Pole	23	Legs and hips injured	Jumping on motor	Pittsburg - Belmont No. 1.
Dec. 12	Frank Cross	[illegible]	45	Right foot injured	Mining machine	Barton.
Dec. 12	Chris J[illegible]n	American	24	Left ankle and hip bruised	Caught between mine cars	Johnson.
Dec. 12	Chas. Day	American	25	Three fingers on left hand injured	Run over by mine car	J[illegible]n.
Dec. 15	Leo Selargir	Hungarian	39	Leg broken	Fall stone	[illegible]
Dec. 15	Jno. Weaver	English	22	Hip injured	Caught between mine car and door	Rail & River.
Dec. 19	E. Lewis	[illegible]	18	Forehead injured	Kicked by mule	Hall & Gilhooley.
Dec. 24	Tom Souders	Negro	58	Face cut, knee and hip injured	Fall roof	Florence.
Dec. 28	Mike [illegible]itch	Pole	41	Thumb injured	Fall coal	Florence.
Dec. 28	Sam [illegible]	[illegible]	45	Ankle bone broken	Fall stone	[illegible]el.
Dec. 29	[illegible] [illegible]n	American	21	Head and right arm cut, and body bruised	Fall stone	Barton.
Dec. 31	Andy [illegible]r	[illegible]	20	Foot injured	Caught between motor and mine car	[illegible]
[illegible] 31	Frank Christy	Italian	34	Leg and ribs injured	Caught by mine cars	[illegible]d.

CARROLL COUNTY.

Jan. 27	Phil Lasso....	Belgian	42	Leg broken	Fall coal	Magnolia.
Oct. 22	Jos. Ruie.....	American ..	24	Ankle injured	Fall roof	Kirks.

COLUMBIANA COUNTY.

M. 19	Frank ...e..	American ..	42	Small toe ...l en...........	M...hine jack fell.............	...e.
M. 26	Jno. R...s.......	Welsh	40	...ht limb injured..........	Spragging mine car............	...e.
My 21	Jno. Brooks.......	...n ..	27	Ankle ...d	...ll ...oal	O. & P.
July 8	Thos. ...h....	Scotch	38	Hand injured	Caught in mine car wheel......	Big Walnut.
...y 22	H. Williams.......	Welsh		Body injured	Coal falling down shaft........	...e.
Aug. 10	David Hanl...y......	I...h	60	B...th limbs broken.........	...ll bone ...oal ...d slate........	O. & P.
Sept. 1	Jas. Jones.........	...ican ..	26	...eg in...d	S...k by rail................	Jones.
Oct. 28	G. Bryan.........	...ican ..	38	Right foot ...l.........	Fall top coal..................	O. & P.
...c. 2	Joe Hutchison.....	American ..	45	...eg ...d arm ...d........	...t between cars...........	Sal...m.
...c. 3	J...n Feyock.......	G...n	42	Jaw bone broken............	Fall ...e	...el.

COSHOCTON COUNTY.

Feb. 8	Ignatz Pongrat....	Hungarian ..	45	Left leg broken............	Fall ...e	Warwick No. 5.
Feb. 11	Jno. Jenkins.......	Welsh	51	Back injured	Fall sl...te	Franklin.
Aug. 29	Oliver Stiner......	American ..	24	Leg broken	Fall ...of	Locust Grove.
Sept. 20	Patrick White.....	American .	18	Leg broken	Fall ...e	Morgan Run No. 3.
Nov. 21	Rich'd Holdsworth.	American ..	62	Shoulder injured	Fall s...le	Conesville No. 4.
Nov. 28	Warner Sherrod...	American		Foot injured	...ght between car and ...r stick	Powers.

GALLIA COUNTY.

Jan. 13	Geo. Ellis.........	American ..	20	Hands and face burned.....	Explosion of powder..........	Carl.
Nov. 2	Elijah Frasure.....	American ..	58	Foot and back injured......	Fall slate	Carl No. 1 & 2.

LIST OF SERIOUS ACCIDENTS—Continued.

GUERNSEY COUNTY.

Date.	Name.	Nationality.	Age.	Character of Injury.	Cause of Accident.	Name of Mine.
Jan. 3	Jno. Hall	English	55	Leg broken	Fall slate	Trail Run No. 1.
Jan. 6	Earl Grier	American	26	Leg broken	[illegible]	Kings.
Jan. 12	Jno. Shipola	Slav	28	Bone in ankle broken	Fall coal and slate	Ideal.
Jan. 12	Jas. Allen	American	27	Back injured	Fall slate	Imperial.
Jan. 13	[illegible]	Slav	36	Head and body injured	Fall coal	Klondyke.
Jan. 17	Mike Sapko	Slav	21	Bone in left foot broken	Riding rear end of car	Black Top.
Jan. 18	Mike Potchin	Slav	38	Small bone in leg broken	Fall coal	Forsythe.
Jan. 28	Jas. [illegible]	American	22	Face injured	Kicked by mule	Kings.
Jan. 31	Geo. [illegible]	American	17	Left leg broken	Fall slate	Walhonding.
Feb. 2	Geo. Brown	American	27	Finger injured	Caught in chain of mining machine	Trail Run No. 2.
Feb. 2	Pete Maliska	Slav	40	Ribs broken	Falling under mining machine	[illegible] No. 2.
Feb. 10	Frank Barton	[illegible]	40	Back and shoulder bruised	Fall slate	Hartford.
Feb. 19	Martin Linovic	[illegible]	33	Arm broken & chest bruised	Fall slate	Klondyke.
Feb. 19	Wm. Wade	American	55	Leg broken	Fall slate	Clinton C. & M.
Feb. 26	[illegible] Fluhart	American	58	Leg broken	Fall slate	Derwent.
Feb. 28	Chas. Hockenberry	American	32	Right leg fractured	Mining machine, operating	Old [illegible]
Mar. 1	Andy Konalcheck	Slav	21	Ankle injured	Fall slate	Little Kate.
Mar. 9	Joe Fabish	Slav	38	Foot injured	Caught in chain of mining machine	Little Kate No. 2.
Mar. 9	Ralph Heskett	American	21	Legs and hips injured	Caught between car and post	Little Kate No. 2.
Mar. 9	Thos. Trott	American	45	Back injured & legs bruised	Fall slate	Forsythe.
Mar. 17	Jno. Wires	American	54	Head injured	Fall slate	Minnehaha.
Mar. 23	Jas. N. Ferren	American	28	Foot injured	Moving mining machine	Black Top.
April 8	Jos. Glen	American	31	Two ribs fractured and ankle sprained	Fell in front of mine car	Walhonding No. 2.
April 11	Thos. Gibbons	Irish	43	Four ribs fractured and back sprained	Fall slate	Walhonding No. 2.
April 18	Jno. Payne	American	43	Leg injured	Caught between car and motor.	Imperial.
April 19	[illegible] Sikora	Slav	42	Hand and side injured	Fall slate	Trail Run No. 2.

April 22	[illegible] Coleman	American	34	Two bones in hand broken	Fall slate	Forsythe.
April 25	Jos. [illegible]	American	34	Ankle injured	Fall roof	Imperial.
April 30	Jno. Ellis	Welsh	52	Left arm injured	Caught by mine car	Old Orchard.
May 2	Henry Woodson	American	32	Right hand injured	Caught between post and sprag.	Black Top.
May 17	R. Wilson	American	32	Foot injured	Caught by chain of mine car	Old Orchard.
June 3	Ellis Albright	American	21	Hand injured	Caught between car and motor.	[illegible]n.
June 13	Chas. Unkelshey	American	23	Arm, face and back burned	Struck a body of gas	[illegible]land.
June 28	Sam Allen	[illegible]	30	Arm broken	Caught by moving car	L. T. R.
July 10	Albert Sherrard	American	35	Back injured	Fall slate	[illegible]ha.
July 30	Jas. McCall	American	32	Hip dislocated	Fall slate	[illegible]
Aug. 17	Jesse Walker	English	37	Right foot amputated	Fall slate	[illegible] City.
Aug. 19	Hugh Collins	American	49	Back [illegible]	Caught by descending cage	Black Top.
Aug. 23	Paul Kermont	Lithuanian	44	Breast injured	Fall slate	[illegible]o No. 2.
Aug. 25	Ruel Sarber	American	30	Arm broken	Fall stone	Ideal.
Aug. 30	Jno. Parinchat	Slav	18	Leg broken	Fall coal	Trail Run No. 1.
Sept. 17	Mike Sapko	Slav	35	Right leg broken	Fall slate	Ideal.
Sept. 17	Jno. Hlard	Slav	45	Hips and head injured	Fall slate	Little Kate No. 1.
Sept. 20	[illegible] Phillips	American	51	Hips and back bruised	Fall slate	Forsythe.
Sept. 21	Thos. Scott	American	19	Right foot injured	Caught by mine car	[illegible]an.
Sept. 24	Sam Miller	American	45	Head injured	Falling down shaft	Little Kate No. 1.
Oct. 5	[illegible] Ramage	American	23	Back broken	Fall stone	Klondyke.
Oct. 5	J. P. Geese	American	50	Ankle injured	Prying car	Minnehaha.
Oct. 8	Archer Cook	American	28	Two toes broken	Caught by mine car	Trail Run No. 1.
Oct. 13	Jas. Messer	American	35	Leg broken	Fall coal	Minnehaha.
Oct. 13	G. Kundrat	Slav	29	Right leg injured	Fall slate	Trail Run No. 2.
Oct. 20	Jas. Evans	American	45	Foot injured	Fall slate	Puritan.
Oct. 28	Jas. Hoey	American	18	Left leg injured	Run over by motor	Old [illegible]d.
Nov. 3	Jno. Black	Scotch	29	Right thigh [illegible]	Fall coal	Puritan.
Nov. 10	Jno. Kozal	Slav	27	Left leg broken	Fall slate	Little Kate No. 1.
Nov. 15	Jas. Watkins	American	47	Foot injured	Caught by mining machine	Klondyke.
Nov. 15	Herman Brugh	American	17	Right leg broken	Run over by mine car	Black Top.
Nov. 21	Jno. Jeffrey	American	......	Head and right limb injured.	Hoisting rope broke	[illegible]ey.
Nov. 21	E. Bi[illegible]	American	19	Hips and foot injured	Fall rock	Little Kate No. 1.
Nov. 25	Chas. Nagel	American	29	Left arm broken	Fall slate	Ideal.
Dec. 6	Jno. [illegible]per	Slav	26	Left leg injured	Caught by mining machine	Little Kate No. 1.
Dec. 13	Wm. Parker	Scotch	41	Left hand injured	Car jumped track	Black Top.

LIST OF SERIOUS ACCIDENTS — Continued.

HARRISON COUNTY.

Date.	Name.	Nationality.	Age.	Character of Injury.	Cause of Accident.	Name of Mine.
Jan. 6	Andy Cheh	Magyar	21	Back and shoulder injured	Fall draw-slate	Roby No. 1.
Mar. 22	Jno. Clark	American	36	Head and hips injured	Fall slate	Newton C. & M.
April 14	Wm. Chance	American	43	Arm broken	Fall stone	Oliver.
April 21	Chas. Lulash	Russian	23	Shoulders, hips and leg injured	Fall stone	Roby No. 2.
April 26	Jno. Vincheh	Pole	55	Back injured	Fall roof	Roby No. 2.
May 13	Frank Griski	Pole	28	Left leg injured	Fall stone	Roby No. 1.
Sept. 15	Steve Nemthe	Hungarian	47	Back injured	Fall stone	Roby No. 1.
Oct. 25	Chas. Bricker	German	35	Shoulder injured	Riding mine cars	Newton C. & M. Co.
Dec. 14	Peter Ledger	American	28	Finger amputated	Caught between chain and hook.	Oliver No. 1.

HOCKING COUNTY.

Date.	Name.	Nationality.	Age.	Character of Injury.	Cause of Accident.	Name of Mine.
Feb. 18	Frank Hanning	American	45	Back injured	Fall roof	Star-Hocking.
Feb. 19	Stanley Beard	American	27	Leg injured	Fall coal	Jobs No. 1.
Feb. 28	Chas. Foster	American	22	Arm broken	Caught in paddle of fan	Jobs No. 1.
Mar. 22	Adam Furnell	German	55	Back injured	Caught between motor and roof	Rockquarry.
June 4	Phillip Savage	German	54	Left leg injured	Fall slate	Jobs No. 1.
July 4	Joe Howot	Hungarian	62	Leg broken	Fall slate	Jobs No. 1.
Aug. 13	Chas. Levering	American	21	Right leg cut off	Fell between mine cars	Starr.
Oct. 22	Hamel Bunting	American	27	Leg broken	Struck by mine car	New Pittsburgh No. 7.
Oct. 28	Robert Maffin	American	35	Crushed through hips and bowels	Caught between car and post	New Pittsburgh No. 5.
Nov. 4	Wm. Robison	American		Hands injured	Using torch	No. 207.

Nov. 23	A. Kolich	American	22	Leg broken	Stepping in front of mine cars	New Pittsburgh No. 10.
Dec. 12	Robert Coffy	American	45	Side and back injured	Fall slate	Carbon Hill.

JACKSON COUNTY.

Feb. 3	Chas. Bogg	[illegible]rican	30	Index finger injured	Fall stone	Superior No. 9.
Mar. 22	Thos. D. Davis	[illegible]sh	54	Back injured	Fall slate	Globe.
April 11	Eugene [illegible]ce	American	30	Jaw broken	Kicked by mule	Jisco.
June 1	Stephen King	American	42	Collar bone broken	Fall slate	D. T. & I. No. 3.
July 21	Bone Smith	American	40	Left foot injured	Fall slate	Superior No. 9.
Aug. 6	[illegible]. Hadler	American	35	Hip and foot injured	Fall [illegible]late	Wellston Colliery.
Sept 22	Michael Holtz	German	45	Hip injured	Fall slate	Laura No. I.
Oct. 19	Wm. [illegible]st	American	42	Hand injured	Caught in weigh box	Superior No. 9.
Oct. 24	Jno. Elkins	American	42	Leg broken	Fall stone	Superior N. 1.
Nov. 9	Thos. Brislin	American	45	Four ribs broken	Fall rock	D. T. & I. No. 3

JEFFERSON COUNTY.

Jan. 3	Bonner Press	American	30	Left ear burned off	Operating mining machine	Plum Run.
Jan. 6	Jno. Bealstoy	Pole	33	Right leg broken	Front jack caused mining machine to skid	LaBelle.
Jan. 6	Jno. Petroski	Pole	45	Right arm and leg injured	Fall roof coal	Dillon No. 2.
Jan. 6	W. Czyszowski	Pole	22	Right arm and ankle injured	Fall roof coal	Dillon No. 2.
Jan. 14	Andy Costanik	Slav	47	Toes crushed	Fall coal	Elizabeth.
Jan. 18	Chas. Pasenia	Italian	42	Back sprained	Fall slate	Jefferson No. 2.
Jan. 22	Joe [illegible]	Italian	42	Knee cap fractured	Foot struck by a sharp piece of coal	Jefferson No. 2.
Jan. 22	Joe Fetzer	Hungarian	40	Head cut and upper jaw broken	Fall slate	Plum Run.
Jan. 22	Jno. Joscosky	Pole	31	Back injured	Fall stone	Jefferson No. 2.
Jan. 28	Jno. Wicus	Russian	32	Knee injured	Fall coal	Walnut Hill No. 1.
Feb. 5	Mike Solusky	Slav	28	[illegible] bruised	Fall slate	X. L.
Feb. 9	Chas. Emery	English	40	Back [illegible]ed	Fall slate	Forest City.
Feb. 16	Harry Hicks	American	26	Right hand injured	Coupling mine car to motor	U. S. Dist. No. 1
Feb. 19	Frank Hol[illegible]s	Bohemian	33	Back injured	Fall stone	U. S. No. 9.

LIST OF SERIOUS ACCIDENTS—Continued.

Date.	Name.	Nationality.	Age.	Character of Injury.	Cause of Accident.	Name of Mine.
Nov. 28	Joe Trurzak	Italian	20	Arms broken	Fall slate	Kelley.
Dec. 3	Thos. Murray	American	16	Arm broken	Caught by mine car	Zerbe.
Dec. 6	Joe Antonette	Italian	19	Collar bone broken	Caught between car and roof	U. S. No. 1.
Dec. 10	Ernest Baker	American	28	Great toe crushed	Caught between mine cars	Zerbe.
Dec. 10	Joe Carter	American	21	Leg and two ribs broken	Falling under mine car	Elizabeth.
Dec. 19	Batist Zaney	American	18	Leg broken	Falling under motor	Elizabeth.

LAWRENCE COUNTY.

Date.	Name.	Nationality.	Age.	Character of Injury.	Cause of Accident.	Name of Mine.
Jan. 31	Chas. Kiser	American	38	Bone in arm broken	Mattock slipped	Pine Grove Lime.
May 16	Isaac Delander	American	26	Ankle bone broken	Fall slate	Limestone No. 2.

MAHONING COUNTY.

Date.	Name.	Nationality.	Age.	Character of Injury.	Cause of Accident.	Name of Mine.
May 20	Jno. Fieldhouse	American	53	Two fingers injured	Caught between car and rib	Fairview.

MEIGS COUNTY.

Date.	Name.	Nationality.	Age.	Character of Injury.	Cause of Accident.	Name of Mine.
Jan. 9	Jno. C. Ripley	American	49	Back and leg injured	Fall roof coal	Buckeye Splint.
Jan. 30	Val. Brown	American	23	Hips injured	Jumping on motor	Charter Oak.
Feb. 1	Vint. King	American	28	Face and shoulder injured	Fall coal	Buckeye Splint.
Feb. 10	Henry Ebersbach	American	61	Hip dislocated	Fall slate	Logan.
April 26	Jno. Payne	American	55	Finger broken	Caught between car and roof	Hobson.
July 12	Wm. Davis	American	50	Back and face injured	Fall slate	Hobson.

Sept. 15	Worley Rupe	American	29	Leg broken	Fall slate	Buckeye Splint No. 1.
Nov. 3	Chas. Howell	American	45	Hip and breast injured	Fall slate	Maynard.

MORGAN COUNTY.

Feb. 8	Jas. Williams	American	28	Finger injured	Coupling mine cars	Rose.
Dec. 19	Isaac Erwin	American	44	Right leg broken	Fall slate	Tropic.

I [illegible]M COUNTY.

Feb. 25	Gilbert H. Barlow	American	28	Right foot mashed	Run over by empty cars	Pan-American.
Mar. 10	Harry Smith	American	27	Collar bone broken	Fall coal	Pan-American.
Sept. 3	Val. Palmer	American	45	Back injured	Fall coal	McGarvey.
Nov. 9	Geo. Ickley	German	43	Shoulder and arm injured	Fall slate	Pan-American No. 1.

NOBLE COUNTY.

Feb. 12	Jno. Sawetska	Slav	19	Ankle injured	Falling off motor	Laura.
Mar. 5	Geo. Mezick	Slav	31	Breast injured, and one rib broken	Fall coal	Noble.
Mar. 22	Jno. Sklenar	Slav	24	Foot injured	Ran into mining machine	Noble.
Mar. 22	Mike Berice	Slav	39	Back and hips injured	Fall slate	Noble.
June 13	Frank Dennis	American	33	Hip and ankle injured	Fall slate	Noble.
July 6	Harry Porter	American	32	Leg injured	Caught between car and motor.	Golden Rod.
Aug. 18	Wm. Wheeler	American	35	Foot injured	Fall coal	Noble.

OTTAWA COUNTY.

May 3	Geo. Kuharick	Hungarian	29	Left foot mashed	Caught under tipple	U. S. Gypsum.
July 29	Paul Husivat	Hungarian	34	Left leg broken	Fall stone	West No. 3.

LIST OF SERIOUS ACCIDENTS—Continued.

PERRY COUNTY.

Date.	Name.	Nationality.	Age.	Character of Injury.	Cause of Accident.	Name of Mine.
Jan. 3	Thos. Storts	American	50	Back injured	Fall coal	Bear Run No. 1.
Jan. 6	Wade Savage	American	36	Left foot injured	By mine car	Rend No. 1.
Jan. 11	Chas. Stevenson	American	36	Finger injured	Riding on motor	Dixie.
Jan. 15	Jas. Johnson, Jr.	American	16	Left foot injured	Caught by mine car	Rend No. 1.
Feb. 22	Frank Nelson	American	32	Leg broken	Struck by cage	Captain.
Feb. 25	R. L. McNulty	American	28	Hand injured	Collision of mine cars	Keystone No. 2.
June 10	Wm. Angle	English	43	Toes mashed	Slipped under wheels of mining machine	Congo 301.
June 14	Frank Korting	German	27	Left arm and leg bruised	Struck by rod on cage	Congo 301.
June 16	H. Steele	American	40	Little finger on left hand mashed	Struck by jack	Greeley.
July 2	Jas. McLaughlin	American	29	Top of head cut and back injured	Shooting down rock	S. C. 268.
Aug. 1	Frank Metrosetz	Bohemian	19	Right hip and left ankle injured	Fall slate	No. 302.
Sept. 21	Paul Murray	American	26	Back injured	Fall slate	No. 301.
Nov. 3	Jas. Deems	American	......	Right hand injured	Caught between car and door	Greeley No. 3.
Dec. 1	Raymond Dennis	American	17	Right foot mashed	Caught between mine cars	No. 4.
Dec. 15	Emerson Loegard	American	20	Foot mashed	Running into empty car	Greeley No. 2.

PORTAGE COUNTY.

Date.	Name.	Nationality.	Age.	Character of Injury.	Cause of Accident.	Name of Mine.
Aug. 25	Robert Johns	American	28	Toes broken	Coal falling from mine car	Hutson No. 8.
Oct. 18	Jos. Evans	Welsh	30	Left eye injured	Flying rock	Hutson No. 4.
Dec. 9	A. Sewell	American	31	Arm broken	Fall slate	Mullins.

SCIOTO COUNTY.

Dec. 27	....	....	.....	....	Fall slate	Portsmouth Ref.

STARK COUNTY.

Jan. 17	Wm. Hamner......	American ..	24	Back bruised and hip cut....	Fall [illegible]	Pocock.
Jan. 19	Jno. Keller........	German	58	Left knee dislocated.........	Fall [illegible]	P c [illegible].
Feb. 8	J. Lewis...........	[illegible]sh	40	Head, back and hips injured.	Fall stone	P [illegible].
Feb. 23	Lewis H [illegible]......	German	61	Head, shoulder and arm injured	Fall slate	Massillon City.
Mar. 21	Jos. Williams......	Welsh	63	Right arm broken..........	Expl[illegible]sion of powder.........	Massillon Elm Run No. 5.
Mar. 21	Frank Rohn.......	German	33	Arms burned	From a missed shot..........	Elm Run No. 5.
[illegible] 28	Jno. Featheringham	Scotch	57	Bone in little toe broken.....	Fall slate	Massillon City.
July 14	[illegible]	Italian	35	Leg broken	Fall clay	National.
Sept. 13	Chas. Gardner.....	American ..	44	Ankle injured	Fall stone	West [illegible] No. 1.
Sept. 17	Edw. Kouk........	American ..	25	Foot injured	Car [illegible]	Massillon City.
Sept. 17	Jno. Switser.......	American ..	17	Arm broken	Fall coal	[illegible]ssillon City.
Oct. 22	Ambrose Williams.	American ..	38	Foot injured	Mine car jumping track........	Taggart No. 3.
Nov. 16	Jas. Collanero.....	Italian	21	Thigh broken	Fall stone	Taggart No. 3.
[illegible] 27	Julius [illegible]na....	German	40	Toe broken	Fall slate	Whittacre F. P. No. 5.

SUMMIT COUNTY.

Dec. 22	Wm. Houseman...	American ..	41	Back and ankle injured.....	Fall roof	Orchard Grove.

TUSCARAWAS COUNTY.

Jan. 4	Chas. Oler.........	American ..	33	Collar bone broken, shoulder bone cracked	Fall coal	Veleney No. 5.
Jan. 6	Geo. Goldhern.....	American ..	47	Hip injured	Fall coal	Royal Goshen.

LIST OF SERIOUS ACCIDENTS—Concluded.

Date.	Name.	Nationality.	Age.	Character of Injury.	Cause of Accident.	Name of Mine.
Jan. 14	Jno. Reniker	American	50	Leg broken	Fall slate	East Goshen No. 2.
Jan. 16	Oren Stauffer	American	26	Ankle injured	Fall coal	Midvale Goshen.
Feb. 21	Chas. Henderson	American	37	Back and hips injured	Fall rock	Royal Goshen.
Mar. 6	Alex Finkey	Hungarian	21	Left foot amputated.	Caught in mining machine	Mullins No. 2.
Mar. 15	Chas. Matthrus	English	24	Hand injured	Fall slate	Beaver Dam No. 1.
Mar. 25	Raymond Halters	American	17	Head and face injured	Fall slate	Royal Goshen No. 1.
May 13	Chas. Roe	American	35	Hip and arm broken	Fall sulphur	Beaver Dam No. 1.
May 14	Jno. Roberts	American	36	Hips injured	Fall roof	Central Valley.
May 21	Jno. Ginlinni	Italian	20	Wrist injured	Placing mine car on track	Midvale Goshen No. 7.
May 29	Frank Lantrain	Italian	38	Finger cut off	Spragging mine car	Beaver Dam No. 1.
Aug. 9	Wales Colers	American	34	Hip injured	Caught under mine car	Beaver Dam No. 1.

VINTON COUNTY.

Date.	Name.	Nationality.	Age.	Character of Injury.	Cause of Accident.	Name of Mine.
July 6	F. E. Bolar	American	29	Back and hip injured	Caught between mine car and door	McArthur.
Sept. 16	Elmer Napper	American	35	Ribs fractured	Caught between trip and rib	Clarion.

WAYNE COUNTY.

Date.	Name.	Nationality.	Age.	Character of Injury.	Cause of Accident.	Name of Mine.
Oct. 1	Thos. Jones	Welsh	24	Index finger cut off	By mine cars	No. 21.
Nov. 25	Wm. Bogle	German	35	Leg injured	Removing coal	No. 21.

IMPROVEMENTS.

TABLE SHOWING THE NUMBER AND CHARACTER OF THE PERMANENT IMPROVEMENTS MADE IN THE MINES OF THE STATE BY COUNTIES DURING THE YEAR 1910.

Counties.	Furnaces.	Fans.	Air Shafts.	Second Openings.	Additional Openings.	Safety Catches.	Stairways.	Speaking Tubes.	Ventilating Baskets.	Totals.
Athens	1	10	5		4		4			24
Belmont	2	10	3	5	17		2	1		41
Carroll	2		2		2		2			8
Columbiana		4		1	3		1	2		11
Coshocton	6		8	2			4			20
Guernsey		2		1	4	1		1		9
Harrison	1		1	1	2					5
Hocking	6	11	1	5	2					25
Jackson	2		1	5	1					9
Jefferson		8	1	2	17	2	2	1		33
Lawrence	2	3		1						6
Mahoning		1								1
Medina			2				1			3
Meigs		5		3			1		1	10
Muskingum		3								3
Ottawa		1	1							2
Perry	1	6		3						10
Portage		1	1				1			3
Scioto				1						1
Stark	1	5	4			2	4	1		17
Summit			1							1
Tuscarawas	4	2	8	7	1		4		1	27
Vinton							1			1
Wayne		2	2			2	2	2		10
Totals	28	74	41	37	53	7	29	8	2	279

TABLE SHOWING THE NUMBER AND CHARACTER OF PERMANENT IMPROVEMENTS MADE IN THE MINES OF THE STATE FROM 1884 TO 1910, INCLUSIVE.

Years.	Furnaces.	Fans.	Air Shafts.	Second Openings.	Additional Openings.	Safety Catches.	Stairways.	Speaking Tubes.	Ventilating Baskets.	Totals.
1884	43	10								53
1885	45	19	45			13				122
1886	13	6	22	10			12			63
1887	39	9	50	7			8			113
1888	43	4	52	17		13	12			141
1889	42	13	57	21		7	3	3		146
1890	57	20	66	46		8	11	4		212
1891	53	17	55	26		19	19	5		194
1892	37	26	65	27		13	7	4	2	181
1893	77	35	131	67		16	19	5	4	354
1894	55	18	106	60		7	11	3	9	269
1895	66	17	105	60		9	11	3	13	284
1896	56	21	93	81		5	7	3	14	280
1897	40	22	75	44		4	7	3	9	204
1898	44	17	73	45		7	11	1	15	213
1899	36	25	60	45		11	13	7	3	200
1900	24	27	69	31		1	9	1	8	170
1901	40	45	66	31		11	5	7	3	208
1902	50	59	98	37		21	20	10	8	303
1903	56	71	94	49		17	19	10	9	325
1904	31	54	63	55		21	18	12	3	257
1905	22	55	32	121		12	42	6		290
1906	26	48	37	80		24	23	3	4	245
1907	28	61	34	91		35	22	15	4	290
1908	29	66	51	82		32	25	8	5	298
1909	30	38	41	72		11	28	7	5	232
1910	28	74	41	37	53	7	29	8	2	279
Totals	1,110	877	1,681	1,242	53	324	391	128	120	5,926

WEIGH SCALES.

TABLE SHOWING TOTAL NUMBER AND KIND OF SCALES TESTED IN EACH COUNTY, ALSO NUMBER FOUND CORRECT AND NUMBER FOUND INCORRECT.

Counties.	Railroad		Platform.		Hopper.		
	Correct.	Incorrect.	Correct.	Incorrect.	Correct.	Incorrect.	Total.
Athens	3	2			5		10
Belmont					12	3	15
Carroll			1		2		3
Columbiana				1	2	2	5
Guernsey					4		4
Hocking					1		1
Jackson	2	1	1		3	1	8
Jefferson					6		6
Lawrence					2		2
Mahoning					1		1
Meigs					2		2
Noble					1		1
Perry	3				1		4
Stark			1		4	1	6
Summit					1		1
Tuscarawas		1	1				2
Wayne					3	1	4
Total	8	4	4	1	50	8	75

Total number of railroad scales tested	12
Percent found correct	67%
Percent found incorrect	33%
Total number of platform scales tested	5
Percent found correct	80%
Percent found incorrect	20%
Total number of hopper scales tested	58
Percent found correct	86%
Percent found incorrect	14%
Percent found correct of total number tested	83%
Percent found incorrect of total number tested	17%

62 sets correct; 13 sets incorrect; total 75 sets tested.

TABLE SHOWING THE NUMBER OF SCALES TESTED, AND RESULT OF THE EXAMINATION FROM 1887 TO DECEMBER 31, 1910, INCLUSIVE.

Years	Number of Sets of Scales Tested.	Number of Sets Found Correct.	Number of Sets Found Incorrect.
1888	55	41	14
1889	48	33	15
1890	59	46	13
1891	61	37	24
1892	86	62	24
1893	120	81	39
1894	64	37	27
1895	96	65	31
1896	93	65	28
1897	77	59	18
1898	99	82	17
1899	112	93	19
1900	131	115	16
1901	139	115	24
1902	154	131	23
1903	188	157	31
1904	230	208	22
1905	225	205	20
1906	163	150	13
1907	149	131	18
1908	69	60	9
1909	82	66	16
1910	75	62	13
Totals	2,575	2,101	474

PRODUCTION OF FIRE CLAY.

TABLE SHOWING THE PRODUCTION OF FIRE CLAY FOR THE YEAR 1910 AS COMPARED WITH 1909, AND THE NUMBER OF PERSONS EMPLOYED.

Counties.	Average Number Days, 8 Hour Basis, Worked in 1909.	Number Men Employed in 1909.	Number Tons Mined in 1909.	Average Number Days Worked in 1910.	Number Men Employed in 1910.	Number Tons Mined in 1910.	Gain in Men.	Loss in Men.	Gain in Tons.	Loss in Tons.
Athens ...	309	93	206,815	340	90	205,974	....	3	....	841
Belmont ..	373	11	27,508	350	12	23,875	1	....	....	3,633
Carroll ...	268	101	182,588	274	115	189,301	14	....	6,713	....
Columbi'a	248	74	109,575	220	94	140,119	20	....	30,544	....
Coshocton	242	13	16,843	303	13	16,800	....	....	....	43
Guernsey ..	280	9	6,400	300	9	8,000	....	....	1,600	....
Hocking ..	267	86	128,239	274	49	88,583	....	37	....	39,656
Holmes ...	300	1	1,500	188	1	600	....	....	....	900
Jackson ...	238	47	40,736	232	14	10,068	....	33	....	30,668
Jefferson .	241	196	344,697	228	167	311,055	....	29	....	33,642
Lawrence .	145	63	36,264	194	72	43,566	9	....	7,302	....
Mahoning	38	13	1,950	129	14	1,950	1	....	....	....
Musk'gum	261	39	66,554	224	40	75,480	1	....	8,926	....
Perry	210	85	96,097	244	92	132,898	7	....	36,801	....
Scioto	242	76	182,742	196	76	51,730	....	....	....	131,012
Stark	370	153	187,876	300	170	255,980	17	....	68,104	....
Summit ...	312	70	180,278	306	73	227,125	3	....	46,847	....
Tuscara's	288	177	287,426	271	141	245,748	....	36	....	41,678
Vinton ...	257	12	185,000	....	....	....	....	12	....	185,000
Total .	266	1,319	2,289,088	259	1,242	2,028,852	73	150	206,837	467,073

NOTE: —

Total number tons produced in 1910........................	2,028,852
Total number tons produced in 1909........................	2,289,088
Net Loss	260,236
Average days worked in 1910..............................	259
Average days worked in 1909..............................	266
Net Loss	7
Total number men employed in 1910........................	1,242
Total number men employed in 1909........................	1,319
Net Loss	77

TABLE SHOWING THE FIRE CLAY PRODUCTION OF THE STATE FROM JANUARY 1, 1884, TO DECEMBER 31, 1910, INCLUSIVE.

Years.	Output Tons.	Gain.	Loss
1884	168,208	....	....
1885	153,756	....	14,452
1886	266,709	112,953	....
1887	366,476	99,767	....
1888	471,794	105,313	....
1889	574,129	102,335	....
1890	833,159	259,030	....
1891	1,087,560	254,401	....
1892	1,253,110	165,550	....
1893	1,032,348	....	220,762
1894	942,913	....	89,435
1895	844,832	....	97,081
1896	827,450	....	17,382
1897	822,727	....	4,723
1898	1,026,922	204,195	....
1899	1,173,697	146,775	....
1900	1,473,088	299,391	....
1901	1,337,181	....	135,907
1902	1,528,829	191,648	....
1903	1,567,603	38,774	....
1904	2,045,848	478,245	....
1905	2,039,292	....	6,556
1906	2,126,179	86,887	....
1907	2,177,174	....	50,995
1908	2,004,019	....	252
1909	2,289,088	285,069	....
1910	2,028,852	....	260,236

PRODUCTION OF LIMESTONE.

TABLE SHOWING LIMESTONE PRODUCTION IN OHIO DURING 1910; NUMBER OF PERSONS SO EMPLOYED; AVERAGE NUMBER DAYS WORKED ON THE EIGHT-HOUR BASIS.

Counties.	No. Days Worked.	No. Men Employed.	No. Tons, 2,000 lbs. Each, Burned for Lime.	No. Tons, 2,000 lbs. Each, Burned for Fluxing.	No. Cu. Ft. Dimension Stone.	No. Cu. Yds. Ordinary Building Stone.	No. Cu. Yds. Piers and Protection.	Sq. Ft. Flagging.	Sq. Ft. Paving.	Lineal Ft. Curbing.	Cu. Yds. Ballast and Macadam.	No. Cu. Yds. Concrete.
Allen	253	127	...	6,000	...	500	...	...	...	...	258,424	...
Belmont	304	5	4,500	...	...	...	...	...	...	...	...	...
Butler	130	2	...	...	...	500	...	...	...	...	...	...
Clark	334	144	72,812	26,187	2,030	8,991	704	...	...	1,733	19,122	...
Clermont	150	6	...	...	...	...	...	...	...	...	785	...
Clinton	162	21	...	...	...	16	...	...	...	...	11,248	...
Crawford	164	90	14	450	...	...	...	...	...	...	67,817	...
Delaware	276	104	29,388	...	...	2,295	...	...	...	...	106,960	...
Erie	311	591	103,707	250,084	...	5,000	15,918	...	...	...	547,152	2,000
Franklin	332	553	...	703,026	...	12,506	...	...	...	...	629,158	...
Greene	151	57	3,000	...	...	2,000	...	...	...	...	12,400	...
Hamilton	155	33	...	...	...	2,335	...	...	...	...	4,390	...
Hancock	248	37	...	...	...	15	...	...	...	...	35,673	...
Harding	246	62	19,552	...	...	200	...	...	...	...	245,979	500
Harrison	86	3	1,200	...	...	...	...	...	...	...	...	
Highland	36	13	7	...	...	29	...	200	...	...	400	...
Lawrence	263	266	...	60,419	...	...	...	...	...	...	142,920	53,674
Logan	156	24	...	...	...	100	...	...	...	...	18,500	...
Lucas	375	50	...	...	...	...	...	...	...	...	101,055	...
Marion	350	329	102,030	24,737	...	19,319	...	...	...	...	240,500	...

Mercer	30	6	31	....	....	....	....	....	....	....	400	....
Miami	241	101	....	101,100	20,950	3,258	1,500	....	....	....	71,118	17,600
Montgomery	291	80	3,375	....	12,505	9,283	1,200	....	....	....	12,603	....
Ottawa	310	193	293,118	1,151,932	....	....	....	....	....	....	247,151	....
Paulding	150	60	....	....	....	....	....	....	....	....	30,000	....
Preble	278	78	....	....	159	300	....	....	....	....	121,263	....
Putnam	195	82	....	....	200	65	1,675	....	....	....	19,908	6,575
Ross	250	20	....	33	14	12	....	....	....	....	18,900	....
Sandusky	311	213	38,195	....	35,219	22,379	....	....	....	....	177,354	10,532
Scioto	292	20	....	11,380	....	....	413	....	....	....	....	....
Seneca	192	139	36,197	15	....	3,718	....	....	16,400	....	117,306	....
Stark	240	32	11,754	....	....	....	....	....	....	....	....	87,175
Van Wert....	192	64	....	68,000	....	....	....	....	....	....	178,892	....
Wood	238	153	14,127	....	....	....	....	....	....	....	289,020	....
Totals	287	4,361	733,307	2,406,963	71,377	92,821	21,110	200	16,400	1,733	3,819,698	178,056
1909	285	4,705	924,244	1,071,855	115,608	123,634	13,520	9,643	....	4,770	3,086,882	373,519
1910	287	4,361	733,307	2,406,963	71,377	92,821	21,410	200	16,400	1,733	3,819,698	178,056
Gain over '09.	2	....	....	1,335,108	....	....	7,890	....	16,400	....	732,816	....
Loss from '09.	....	344	190,937	....	44,231	30,813	....	9,443	....	3,037	....	195,463

TABLE SHOWING THE COMPARATIVE PRODUCTION OF LIMESTONE IN OHIO FROM 1886 TO 1906 INCLUSIVE

Years	Average Number Days Worked	Number of Men Employed	Number of Tons of 2,000 Pounds Each Burned for Lime	Number of Tons of 2,000 Pounds Each Burned for Fluxing	Cubic Feet of Dimension Stone	Cubic Yards of Ordinary Building Stone	Cubic Yards for Piers and Protection Purposes	Square Feet of Flagging	Square Feet of Paving	Lineal Feet of Curbing	Cubic Yards of Ballast and Macadam	Cubic Yards for Cement and Concrete
1886	140	2,383	517,270	328,080	566,697	295,231	61,050	187,000	151,630	60,650	186,810	
1887	182	2,767	619,027	178,674	950,393	385,247	78,942	350,054	380,105	130,171	416,018	
1888	165	3,025	602,071	666,481	1,795,048	......	78,381	580,001	318,855	305,237	115,770	
1889	165	2,631	849,142	245,298	898,886	364,685	60,876	413,400	586,361	309,330	351,544	
1890	171	2,445	689,827	308,521	333,076	270,367	81,411	673,850	507,313	165,431	132,650	
1891	143	3,286	744,046	284,178	634,901	361,637	65,395	417,855	1,018,030	290,750	623,104	
1892	132	3,353	641,049	217,981	1,057,157	323,600	18,402	171,567	2,883,308	101,820	701,781	
1893	149	2,929	396,690	108,476	747,712	200,614	57,371	226,654	303,883	300,337	757,142	
1894	138	2,484	349,631	340,173	1,393,702	181,723	22,830	296,736	312,868	111,012	145,701	
1895	127	3,829	1,175,088	429,633	500,648	253,000	18,675	573,634	640,836	152,873	650,217	
1896	132	3,186	397,162	623,544	260,280	215,000	20,111	137,570	163,373	71,230	553,330	
1897	131	3,308	481,871	320,437	371,741	348,303	97,548	115,331	118,095	55,108	630,011	
1898	132	3,119	624,921	571,030	605,172	308,343	17,762	71,600	43,950	52,040	730,800	
1899	142	3,165	626,274	701,701	405,412	261,640	87,000	100,183	81,706	57,001	801,340	
1900	141	3,680	547,046	883,426	166,270	374,019	120,201	131,837	61,170	40,550	1,308,416	
1901	154	4,135	551,523	1,410,087	318,095	304,312	134,781	103,177	48,512	37,838	1,551,378	
1902	181	3,946	652,000	1,480,074	93,186	273,140	108,074	65,001	13,337	25,331	1,380,104	
1903	167	3,848	548,068	1,501,638	106,861	386,683	88,114	14,330	204,018	16,730	1,371,087	
1904	229	3,076	604,070	1,402,820	102,044	323,200	148,407	44,038	146,634	20,303	1,580,805	54,130
1905	245	4,728	740,203	2,143,001	937,702	300,368	77,230	16,308	36,403	14,700	3,087,100	387,102
1906	246	5,131	655,503	1,333,538	16,541	305,120	131,006	10,863	115,320	63,175	3,105,805	114,551

1907	218	5,420	844,726	2,718,820	92,331	160,468	96,850	15,060	31,121	223,382	2,834,820	401,775
1908	225	4,678	658,182	1,459,588	99,100	132,513	19,881	4,117	38,125	6,275	2,937,802	357,120
1909	285	4,705	924,244	1,071,855	115,608	123,634	13,520	9,643	....	1,770	3,086,882	373,519
1910	287	4,361	733,307	2,406,963	71,377	92,821	21,110	200	16,400	1,733	3,819,698	178,056
Gain over 1909 ...	2	....	....	1,335,108	....	....	7,890	....	16,400	....	732,816	....
Loss from 1909 ...	......	344	190,937	....	44,231	30,813	....	9,443	....	3,037	....	195,463

PRODUCTION OF IRON ORE.

TABLE SHOWING THE PRODUCTION OF IRON ORE BY COUNTIES DURING THE YEARS 1909 AND 1910 AND THE GAIN AND LOSS IN EACH COUNTY.

Counties.	Tonnage 1909.	Tonnage 1910.	Gain.	Loss.
Jackson	2,080	....	....	2,080
Lawrence	392	2,521	2,129	....
Perry	8,837	....	....	8,837
Scioto	79	7,198	7,119	....
Tuscarawas	1,004	....	....	1,004
Totals	12,392	9,719	9,248	11,921

Note — Net loss, 2,673.

TABLE SHOWING THE IRON ORE PRODUCTION OF THE STATE FROM 1884 TO 1910 INCLUSIVE.

Years.	Blackband. Output Tons.	Blackband. Loss.	Blackband. Gain.	Hematite. Output Tons.	Hematite. Loss.	Hematite. Gain.	Total.
1884	....	....	....	....	....	....	276,286
1885	70,931	....	....	188,646	....	....	259,577
1886	83,947	....	13,012	260,537	....	71,891	344,484
1887	87,965	....	4,018	289,500	....	28,963	377,465
1888	82,054	5,911	....	171,298	118,202	....	253,352
1889	70,398	11,656	....	182,011	....	10,713	252,409
1890	41,848	28,550	....	127,240	54,771	....	169,088
1891	15,540	26,308	....	52,444	74,796	....	67,984
1892	8,680	6,860	....	81,042	....	28,598	89,722
1893	3,837	4,843	....	64,423	16,619	....	68,260
1894	....	3,837	....	58,043	6,380	....	58,043
1895	....	....	....	93,051	....	35,008	93,051
1896	....	....	....	70,765	22,286	....	70,765
1897	....	....	....	50,267	20,498	....	50,267
1898	....	....	....	51,659	....	1,392	51,659
1899	....	....	....	25,359	16,800	....	25,359
1900	....	....	....	52,266	....	26,907	52,266
1901	....	....	....	41,325	10,941	....	41,325
1902	....	....	....	10,681	30,644	....	10,681
1903	....	....	....	12,995	....	2,314	12,995
1904	....	....	....	20,652	....	7,657	20,652
1905	....	....	....	14,207	6,445	....	14,207
1906	....	....	....	8,515	5,692	....	8,515
1907	....	....	....	2,423	6,092	....	2,423
1908	....	....	....	2,120	303	....	2,120
1909	....	....	....	12,392	....	10,272	12,392
1910	....	....	....	9,719	2,673	....	9,719

PRODUCTION OF GYPSUM.

TABLE SHOWING COMPARISON OF GYPSUM PRODUCTION OF 1910, COMPARED WITH 1909; NUMBER OF EMPLOYES; DAYS WORKED DURING 1910.

County and Companies.	Number Tons Produced in 1909.	Number Tons Produced in 1910.	Gain.	Loss.	Number Employes in 1909.	Number Employes in 1910.	Number Days Worked in 1909.	Number Days Worked in 1910.
Ottawa County.								
American Gypsum Co	108,517	115,800	7,283	....	85	130	285	280
United States Gypsum Co...	120,287	97,525	....	22,762	115	275	250	305
Totals	228,804	213,325	....	15,479	200	405	......	......

NOTE.

Average days worked.................................... 297
Average tons produced for each man for the year 1910.... 527
Average tons produced for each man per day.............. 1.8
Loss in tonnage as compared with 1909.................. 15,479

MINE MAPS.

DEPARTMENT OF MINES AND MINING.

STATE OF OHIO,

OFFICE OF

CHIEF INSPECTOR OF MINES.

COLUMBUS, OHIO.

The designing of the accompanying schedule has been found necessary, owing to the lack of conception on the part of mining engineers, operators and mine managers as to what a map shall exhibit in order to possess some value. This is evidenced by the continued filing with the Department of maps that are either so carelessly delineated, inaccurately drawn, or that many of the essential elements are either omitted or are so poorly set forth as to render the maps almost worthless.

It is the desire of the Department that hereafter maps designed for filing shall be compared with this schedule and made to conform with its requirements as closely as possible.

WHAT A MAP SHALL EXHIBIT IN ORDER TO BE COMPLETE AND COMPLY WITH THE REQUIREMENTS OF THE DEPARTMENT AND THE LAW.

THE MAP MUST SHOW—

The name of the mine..........
The name of the company..........
Their postoffice address..........
Township, county and state where located..........
Name and address of mining engineer..........
Date on which survey was made..........
The top of the map to the north, with a north point..........
The scale on which the map is drawn..........
Scale to be not less than two hundred feet per inch..........
Streams and bodies of standing water..........
Kinds of openings and their locations..........
Lines of railroad, public highways, oil and gas wells, magazines, and buildings, plainly marked with the name of each..........
Direction of air current or currents indicated by arrows..........
Boundary lines and names of owners of surface..........
Boundary lines of the territory and for not less than 500 feet contiguous thereto..
Township and county lines, with the name of each plainly marked close to and parallel with such lines..........
Section lines and their numbers..........
Excavations and connections with the surface survey..........
Location and extent, as far as known or obtainable, of the excavation of any other mine or mines within the limits of the map..........
Boundary lines of tracts of coal owned or leased within the limits of the map.. ..

Elevation of floor of excavation at or near the boundary line or lines.........
Valleys which displace the coal..
The line and extent of the entries.......................................
The course and extent of the rooms.......................................
The drawing of pillars...
The limit of the coal deposit or basin...................................
The name or numbers of the vein as it is geographically known................
If above drainage, the outcrop...
The location of the fan or furnace.......................................
The location of pumps, boilers, or other machinery in the mine...............
The line and extent of horsebacks or faults..............................
The line and extent of any interruption in the coal basin....................
Indicate the working places which are approaching the workings of an abandon mine, the limits of which are not known by actual survey................
Map must show breakthroughs in entries and rooms.
The wagon roads should show what points they connect.

SUGGESTIONS.

If the excavation of your mine does not exceed 15,000 cubic yards, the l requiring a map of it being filed with the Department does not apply to you, a upon receipt of this notice you should reply at once.

Your map should show the amount of coal left in the entry ribs and ro pillars.

Lines of entries should be shown by double lines.

All maps must bear the following certificates and acknowledgments, prope signed:

All extensions of entries and leading places to maps, in whatever directi they are added, should bear the year and date in which they were made, indicati the beginning and ending of all additional extensions.

FORM OF CERTIFICATE OF ENGINEER.

I, the undersigned, hereby certify that this map is correct, and shows the information required by section nine hundred and thirty-five of the Gene Code, and covers the period ending......................, ...

....

Engineer.

Acknowledged before me a.......................... this ....
day of ...., ...

FORM OF CERTIFICATE OF MINE-FOREMAN.

I, the undersigned, hereby certify that I am a mine-foreman at the mi represented by this map, and to the best of my knowledge and belief the sa correctly represents the excavations of the mine for the period ending..........

....................., ...

Mine-Foreman.

Acknowledged before me a.........................., this............
day of ... ., ...

....

NOTE — These certificates should be copied on your original tracing wit blank line spaces so that the signature of the engineer and mine boss could b inserted on the blue-prints filed with this office

NOTICE.

On and after June 11, 1910, all maps filed must conform with the following section of the Mining Laws before they can be accepted by the State Mining Department.

Section 935. The owner, lessee or agent of a mine having an excavation of fifteen thousand cubic yards, or more, shall cause to be made, on a scale of not less than two hundred feet per inch, an accurate map thereof, which shall show the following: The boundary lines and names of the owners of the surface of each tract under which excavation is made, and for not less than five hundred feet contiguous thereto, and under which excavations are likely to be made during the ensuing year, together with all streams and bodies of standing water; the township and county lines coming within the limits of such map, with the name of each plainly marked close to and parallel with such lines; the title, the name or number of the mine, or both, the township and county in which located; the section lines, with the number of each, marked plainly within the sections: the location of the mine openings, railroad tracks, public highways, oil and gas wells, magazines and buildings, and plainly marked with name of each; the location and extent of the excavations and connection with the surface survey; the direction of the air current, or air currents, by arrows; the location and extent, so far as known or obtainable, of the excavation of any other mine or mines within the limits of the map; the boundary lines of the tracts of coal owned or leased within the limits of the map; the elevation of the floor of the excavation, above mean tide at Sandy Hook, at or near the boundary line or lines of the coal owned or leased where the coal is adjacent to coal owned by a person, firm or corporation, other than the owner or lessee of such mine, and where the excavations of such mine cease or may be approached by another mine, at points not exceeding three hundred feet apart, and references to some permanent monument near the main opening of such mine, and shown on the map and plainly marked bench mark, with the elevation of same.

"CIRCULAR LETTER MAILED TO MINING ENGINEERS AND COAL COMPANIES RELATIVE TO THE FILING OF COMPLETE MAPS."

STATE OF OHIO,

STATE MINING DEPARTMENT

COLUMBUS, OHIO

DEAR SIRS. —

Owing to the incompleteness of many of the maps received at this office, and also to frequent inquiries which are made in regard to information required on maps under the new Mining Laws, we have been able, through the courtesy of one of our leading coal operators and member of the late Ohio Mining Commission, Mr. J. J. Roby, to publish a map which we consider reasonably complete in detail as required by Section 935, and which we would suggest as a guide in making maps to be filed in this office.

Especially do we desire to call to the attention of engineers the importance of showing the Government bench marks and elevations which Section 935 requires, and for lack of which it has been necessary to return many of the maps filed with this department.

We also desire to suggest that blank forms of certificates of the mining engineer and mine-foreman be made on the original tracing so that they will be shown on the blue print, and save time and trouble and the possibility of printed ones becoming detached and lost.

The new Mining Laws having now been in effect nearly a year, future maps positively cannot be accepted and must of necessity be returned, unless complying with the full requirements of this Law as exhibited on the enclosed map.

Yours very truly,

GEO. HARRISON,
Chief Inspector of Mines

APPOINTMENTS.

CHIEF INSPECTORS APPOINTED SINCE THE CREATION OF THE DEPARTMENT.

Name of Inspector.	County.	Governor by whom appointed.	Term began.	Term expired.	Time served.	Remarks.
Andrew Roy, D.	Trumbull	Wm. Allen, D.	ril 6, 1874	April 6, 1878	4 years	Resigned.
Jas. D. Poston, D.	Hocking	R. M. Bishop, D.	l 6, 1878	Nov. 15, 1879	1 yr. 7 mo.	Not confirmed by Senate.
David Owens, D.	Trumbull	R. M. Bishop, D.	16, 1879	Feb. 12, 1880	3 months	
Andrew Roy, R.	Jackson	Chas. Foster, R.	12, 1880	Feb. 16, 1884	4 years	Resigned.
Thos. B. Bancroft, D.	Gallia	Geo. Hoadley, D.	16, 1884	April 1, 1888	4 yrs. 1½ mo.	Reappointed.
Robt. M. Haseltine, R.	Mahoning	Joseph B. Foraker, R.	April 1, 1888	Apr. 30, 1888	1 month	Reappointed.
Robt. M. Haseltine, R.	Mahoning	Joseph B. Foraker, R.	May 1, 1888	Apr. 30, 1892	4 years	Reappointed.
Robt. M. Haseltine, R.	Mahoning	Wm. McKinley, Jr., R.	y 1, 1892	Apr. 30, 1896	4 years	Reappointed.
Robt. M. Haseltine, R.	Mahoning	Asa S. Bushnell, R.	y 1, 1896	Apr. 30, 1900	4 years	Resigned.
Elmer G. Biddison, R.	Athens	George K. Nash, R.	y 1, 1900	Apr. 30, 1904	4 years	
George Harrison, R.	Jackson	Myron T. Herrick, R.	1, 1904	Apr. 30, 1908	4 years	Reappointed.
George Harrison, R.	Jackson	Andrew L. Harris, R.	1, 1908	Apr. 30, 1912	....	Incumbent.

DISTRICT MINE INSPECTORS APPOINTED SINCE THE CREATION OF THE DEPARTMENT.

Name of Inspector.	County.	Governor by whom Approved.	Chief Inspector by whom Appointed.	Term Began.	Term Expired.	Time Served.	Remarks.
Jacob P. Klein, R.	Stark	Chas. Foster, R.	Andrew Roy, R.	6- 4-81	1-26-83	2 y, 7 m, 15 d.	Resigned.
Jno. P. Williams, R.	Trumbull	Chas. Foster, R.	Andrew Roy, R.	1-26-83	2-16-84	1 y, 21 d.	
Austin P. King, Jr., D.	Columbiana	Geo. Hoadley, D.	Thos. Bancroft, D.	2-16-84	4-30-86	2 y, 2 m, 15 d.	Resigned.
Wm. Dalrymple, D.	Athens	Geo. Hoadley, D.	Thos. Bancroft, D.	5- 1-84	3- 1-88	3 y, 10 m.	Resigned.
Wm. A. Davis, D.	Guernsey	Geo. Hoadley, D.	Thos. Bancroft, D.	5- 1-84	2-15-86	1 y, 9 m, 15 d.	Resigned.
Jos. L. Morris, R.	Coshocton	Jos. B. Foraker, R.	Thos. Bancroft, D.	2-15-86	5- 1-87	3 y, 2 m, 15 d.	Resigned.
Jos. L. Morris, R.	Coshocton	Jos. B. Foraker, R.	Thos. Bancroft, D.	5- 1-87	4-30-90	1 yr.	Dist. changed

DISTRICT MINE INSPECTORS APPOINTED SINCE THE CREATION OF THE DEPARTMENT — Continued.

Name of Inspector.	County.	Governor by whom Approved.	Chief Inspector by whom Appointed.	Term Began.	Term Expired.	Time Served.	Remarks.
Jos. L. Morris, R.	Coshocton	Jos. B. Foraker, R.	R. M. Haseltine, R.	5- 1-88	4-30-91	....	
Robt. Bell	Stark	J. B. Foraker, R.	T. B. Bancroft, D.	5- 1-86	4-30-87	1 y.	Reappointed
Robt. Bell	Stark	J. B. Foraker, R.	T. B. Bancroft, D.	5- 1-87	4-30-88	1 y.	Reapp and redist.
Robt. Bell	Stark	J. B. Foraker, R.	R. M. Haseltine, R.	5- 1-88	4-30-91	2 y. 3 m, 10 d.	Resigned.
D. J. Harry	Jackson	J. B. Foraker, R.	R. M. Haseltine, R.	4- 1-88	4-30-88	1 m.	Reappointed
D. J. Harry	Jackson	J. B. Foraker, R.	R. M. Haseltine, R.	5- 1-88	4-30-91	3 y.	
David E. Evans	Meigs	J. B. Foraker, R.	R. M. Haseltine, R.	5- 1-88	4-30-91	3 y.	
Jas. W. Haughee	Athens	J. B. Foraker, R.	R. M. Haseltine, R.	5- 1-88	4-30-91	3 y.	
Jas. W. Haughee	Athens	Wm. McKinley, R.	R. M. Haseltine, R.	7-15-92	7-14-95	No time on this term.	Reappointed. & resigned
Ebenezer Lewis	Summit	Jas. E. Campbell, D.	R. M. Haseltine, R.	8-11-90	4-30-91	8 m, 20 d.	Reappointed
Ebenezer Lewis	Summit	Jas. E. Campbell, D.	R. M. Haseltine, R.	5- 1-91	4-30-94	3 y.	
Thos. H. Love	Carroll	J. B. Foraker, R.	R. M. Haseltine, R.	6- 1-89	5-31-92	2 y, 2 m.	Resigned
Thos. H. Love	Carroll	Wm. McKinley, R.	R. M. Haseltine, R.	7-15-92	4-30-94	1 y, 9 m, 15 d.	Redistr. and Reapp.
Thos. H. Love	Carroll	Wm. McKinley, R.	R. M. Haseltine, R.	5- 1-94	4-30-97	3 y, 9 m, 15 d.	Held over reg. time.
Wm. B. Rennie	Tuscarawas	Jas. E. Campbell, D.	R. M. Haseltine, R.	8- 1-91	4-30-94	11 m, 15 d.	Resigned.
Jno. E. Short	Hocking	Jas. E. Campbell, D.	R. M. Haseltine, R.	5- 1-91	4-30-94	3 y, 7 d.	
A. P. McDonald	Perry	Jas. E. Campbell, D.	R. M. Haseltine, R.	5- 1-91	4-30-94	1 y, 2 m, 14 d	Resigned.
Robt. H. Miller	Perry	Wm. McKinley, R.	R. M. Haseltine, R.	7-15-92	4-30-94	1 y, 9 m, 15 d	Reappointed.
Robt. H. Miller	Perry	Wm. McKinley, R.	R. M. Haseltine, R.	5- 1-94	4-30-97	4 y, 2 m, 15 d.	Held over reg. time.
W. H. Turner	Guernsey	Jas. E. Campbell, D.	R. M. Haseltine, R.	5- 1-91	4-30-94	3 y.	
Alex Beattie	Athens	Wm. McKinley, R.	R. M. Haseltine, R.	7-15-92	7-14-95	3 y.	Reappointed.
Alex Beattie	Athens	Wm. McKinley, R.	R. M. Haseltine, R.	7-15-95	7-14-98	3 y.	
Jno. P. Jones	Stark	Wm. McKinley, R.	R. M. Haseltine, R.	7-15-92	7-14-95	3 y.	Reappointed.
Jno. P. Jones	Stark	Wm. McKinley, R.	R. M. Haseltine, R.	7-15-95	7-14-98	2 y, 5 m, 15 d.	Resigned

Wm. K. Moore	Stark	Asa S. Bushnell, R.	R. M. Haseltine, R.	1-17-98	7-11-98	6 m.	Reappointed.
Wm. K. Moore	Stark	Asa S. Bushnell, R.	R. M. Haseltine, R.	7-15-98	7-14-01	1 y 10 m 15 d.	Resigned.
Saml. Llewellyn	Jackson	Wm. McKinley, R.	R. M. Haseltine, R.	5- 9-94	4-30-97	3 y, 12 d.	Reappointed.
Saml. Llewellyn	Jackson	Asa S. Bushnell, R.	R. M. Haseltine, R.	5- 1-97	4-30-00	3 y.	
Thos. McGough	Belmont	Wm. McKinley, R.	R. M. Haseltine, R.	5- 1-94	4-30-97	3 y.	Reappointed.
Thos. McGough	Belmont	Asa S. Bushnell, R.	R. M. Haseltine, R.	5- 1-97	4-30-00	3 y, 1 m.	Reappointed.
Rees T. Davis	Columbiana	Wm. McKinley, R.	R. M. Haseltine, R.	5- 1-94	4-30-97	3 y, 21 d.	Reappointed.
Rees T. Davis	Columbiana	Asa S. Bushnell, R.	R. M. Haseltine, R.	5-21-97	4-30-00	2 y, 11 m, 9 d.	Resigned.
Jas. P. Davis	Carroll	Asa S. Bushnell, R.	R. M. Haseltine, R.	2-15-98	4-30-00	2 y 10 m 16 d.	Reappointed.
L. W. Hull	Athens	Asa S. Bushnell, R.	R. M. Haseltine, R.	7-15-98	7-15-01	1 y.	Resigned.
[illegible] H. Williams	Athens	Asa S. Bushnell, R.	R. M. Haseltine, R.	7-15-99	7-15-01	2 y.	Reappointed.
D. B. Wilson	Perry	Asa S. Bushnell, R.	R. M. Haseltine, R.	7-15-98	4-30-00	1 y, 10 m, 15 d	Reappointed.
D. B. Wilson	Perry	Geo. K. Nash, R.	E. G. Biddison, R.	6- 1-00	4-30-03	2 y 10 m 29 d	Resigned.
Thos. McGough	Belmont	Geo. K. Nash, R.	E. G. Biddison, R.	6- 1-00	4-30-03	2 y 10 m 29 d	Reappointed.
Thos. McGough	Belmont	Geo. K. Nash, R.	E. G. Biddison, R.	5- 1-03	4-30-06	3 y 4 m 15 d.	Held over.
Jas. P. Davis	Carroll	Geo. K. Nash, R.	E. G. Biddison, R.	1- 1-01	4-30-03	2 y, 4 m.	Reappointed.
Jas. P. Davis	Carroll	Geo. K. Nash, R.	E. G. Biddison, R.	5- 1-03	4-30-06	2 y, 7 m.	Resigned.
W. H. Turner	Guernsey	Geo. K. Nash, R.	E. G. Biddison, R.	6- 1-00	4-30-03	3 y.	Reappointed.
W. H. Turner	Guernsey	Geo. K. Nash, R.	E. G. Biddison, R.	6- 1-03	4-30-06	3 y.	Reappointed.
W. H. Miller	Stark	Geo. K. Nash, R.	E. G. Biddison, R.	7- 1-00	7-15-01	1 y, 15 d.	Reappointed.
W. H. Miller	Stark	Geo. K. Nash, R.	E. G. Biddison, R.	7-15-01	7-15-04	3 y.	Reappointed.
R. M. McMillan	Hocking	Geo. K. Nash, R.	E. G. Biddison, R.	5-21-00	4-30-03	2 y, 11 m, 9 d.	Reappointed.
R. M. McMillan	Hocking	Geo. K. Nash, R.	E. G. Biddison, R.	5- 1-03	4-30-06	3 m, 15 d.	Resigned.
Ed. S. Smith	Licking	Geo. K. Nash, R.	E. G. Biddison, R.	8-15-03	4-30-06	9 m, 16 d.	Resigned.
Jno. Winefordner	Muskingum	Geo. K. Nash, R.	E. G. Biddison, R.	6-11-03	4-30-06	11 m, 20 d.	Resigned.
D. H. Williams	Athens	Geo. K. Nash, R.	E. G. Biddison, R.	7-15-01	7-15-04	3 y.	Reappointed.
D. H. Williams	Athens	Myron T. Herrick, R.	Geo. Harrison, R.	7-16-04	7-15-07	10 m.	Resigned.
Jno. L. McDonald	Athens	Myron T. Herrick, R.	Geo. Harrison, R.	5-16-05	7-15-07	2 y, 29 d.	Reappointed.
Jno. L. McDonald	Athens	Andrew L. Harris, R.	Geo. Harrison, R.	7-16-07	7-15-10	10 m, 15 d.	Law changed, [illegible]
Jno. L. McDonald	Athens	Andrew L. Harris, R.	Geo. Harrison, R.	6- 1-08	5-31-11		Incumbent.
Lucius W. Hull	Hocking	Myron T. Herrick, R.	Geo. Harrison, R.	6- 1-04	4-30-06	7 m, 23 d.	Resigned.
Jno. T. Dolan	Hocking	Myron T. Herrick, R.	Geo. Harrison, R.	1-21-05	4-30-06	1 m, 23 d.	Resigned.
Jas. Pritchard	Perry	Myron T. Herrick, R.	Geo. Harrison, R.	3-17-05	4-30-06	1 y, 1 m, 13 d	Reappointed.
Jas. Pritchard	Perry	Andrew L. Harris, R.	Geo. Harrison, R.	5- 1-06	4-30-09	2 y, 3 m.	Resigned.

DISTRICT MINE INSPECTORS APPOINTED SINCE THE CREATION OF THE DEPARTMENT — Concluded.

Name of Inspector.	County.	Governor by whom Approved.	Chief Inspector by whom Appointed.	Term Began.	Term Expired.	Time Served.	Remarks.
W. C. Wiper	Morgan	Andrew L. Harris, R.	Geo. Harrison, R.	8- 1-08	4-30-09	11 m	Held over, regular time, resigned.
Ebenezer Jones	Jefferson	Andrew L. Harris, R.	Geo. Harrison, R.	9-15-06	4-30-09	2 y 7 m 16 d	Resigned.
Isaac Hill	Muskingum	Judson Harmon, D.	Geo. Harrison, R.	7- 1-09	6-30-12		Incumbent.
Thos. Waters	Jackson	Myron T. Herrick, R.	Geo. Harrison, R.	6- 1-04	4-30-06	1 y, 11 m	Reappointed.
Thos. Waters	Jackson	Andrew L. Harris, R.	Geo. Harrison, R.	5- 1-06	4-30-09	3 y, 3 m	Held over regular time, resigned.
Jno. Burke	Jackson	Judson Harmon, D.	Geo. Harrison, R.	8- 1-09	7-31-12		Incumbent.
W. H. Miller	Stark	Myron T. Herrick, R.	Geo. Harrison, R.	7-16-04	7-15-07	3 y	Reappointed.
W. H. Miller	Stark	Andrew L. Harris, R.	Geo. Harrison, R.	7-16-07	7-15-10	10 m, 15 d	Law changed, reapp.
W. H. Miller	Stark	Andrew L. Harris, R.	Geo. Harrison, R.	6- 1-08	5-31-11		Incumbent.
W. H. Turner	Guernsey	Andrew L. Harris, R.	Geo. Harrison, R.	5- 1-06	4-30-09	4 y, 2 m	Held over regular time, resigned.
Abel Elwood	[illegible]	Judson Harmon, D.	Geo. Harrison, R.	7- 1-10	6-30-13		Incumbent.
Thos. Morrison	Carroll	Andrew L. Harris, R.	Geo. Harrison, R.	7- 5-06	5-30-09	3 y 11 m 26 d	Held over reg. time, reapp.
Thos. Morrison	Carroll	Judson Harmon, D.	Geo. Harrison, R.	7- 1-10	6-30-13		Incumbent.
Alex Smith	Tuscarawas	Andrew L. Harris, R.	Geo. Harrison, R.	6- 1-08	5-31-11		Incumbent.
Lot Jenkins	Belmont	Andrew L. Harris, R.	Geo. Harrison, R.	6- 1-08	5-31-11		Incumbent.
Edw. Kennedy	Hocking	Andrew L. Harris, R.	Geo. Harrison, R.	6- 1-08	5-31-11		Incumbent.
L. D. Devore	Belmont	Judson Harmon, D.	Geo. Harrison, R.	5- 1-09	4-30-12		Incumbent

Jas. Hennessy	Belmont	Judson Harmon, D...	Geo. Harrison, R..	6-11-10	6-10-13		Incumbent. (add. insp.)
Robt. Wheatley	Columbiana .	Judson Harmon, D...	Geo. Harrison, R..	7- 1-10	6-30-13	....	Incumbent. (add. insp.)

DISTRICTS AND DISTRICT MINE INSPECTORS.

INSPECTORS AND DISTRICTS INTO WHICH THE STATE IS DIVIDED.

1910.

GEO. HARRISON,

Chief Inspector of Mines, Wellston, Ohio.

FIRST DISTRICT.

Composed of the Counties of Jackson, Lawrence, Scioto, Vinton, and a portion of Gallia.

JOHN BURKE, INSPECTOR,

Wellston, Jackson County, Ohio.

SECOND DISTRICT.

Composed of the Counties of Hocking, Meigs, and a portion of both Athens and Gallia.

EDW. KENNEDY, INSPECTOR,

Carbon Hill, Hocking County, Ohio.

THIRD DISTRICT.

Composed of the County of Athens, (excepting New York Coal Company's mines, No. 10 X, Maple Hill, and York C. & M. Co's mines, which are in charge of Edw. Kennedy.)

JOHN L. McDONALD, INSPECTOR,

Glouster, Athens County, Ohio.

FOURTH DISTRICT.

Composed of the Counties of Perry, Muskingum and Morgan.

ISAAC HILL, INSPECTOR,

Zanesville, Muskingum County, Ohio.

FIFTH DISTRICT.

Composed of the Counties of Guernsey, Noble and Washington

W. H. TURNER, INSPECTOR,

Cambridge, Guernsey County, Ohio.

Succeeded July 1, 1910, by Abel Ellwood, Cambridge, Guernsey County, Ohio.

SIXTH DISTRICT.

Composed of the Counties of Coshocton, Tuscarawas, and Columbiana until July 1, 1910, when it was included in Twelfth District.

ALEX. SMITH, INSPECTOR,

New Philadelphia, Tuscarawas County, Ohio.

SEVENTH DISTRICT.

Composed of the Counties of Holmes, Medina, Ottawa, Portage, Stark, Summit, Trumbull and Wayne.

W. H. MILLER, INSPECTOR,

Massillon, Stark County, Ohio.

EIGHTH DISTRICT.

Composed of the Counties of Belmont and Jefferson.

LOT JENKINS, INSPECTOR,

4777 Jefferson St., Bellaire, Belmont Co., Ohio.

NINTH DISTRICT.

Composed of Carroll County, excepting Sterling No. 1, Strip Vein and Kirk mines; a portion of Jefferson County, and the Newton mine in Harrison County; also all oil and gas wells.

THOMAS MORRISON, INSPECTOR,

Sherodsville, Carroll County, Ohio.

TENTH DISTRICT.

Composed of a portion of Belmont County; the United States Mines, the Glens Run Coal Co's Mines in Jefferson County, and the Media and Cochran Mines of Belmont County.

L. D. DEVORE, INSPECTOR,

R. F. D. No. 2, Bellaire, Belmont Co, Ohio.

ELEVENTH DISTRICT.

Composed of a portion of Jefferson, Belmont and Harrison Counties.

JAMES HENNESSY, Inspector.

Barton, Belmont County, Ohio.

TWELFTH DISTRICT.

Composed of the Counties of Columbiana, Mahoning, the fire clay mines of Jefferson County; and the Sterling No. 1, Strip Vein and Kirk Mines in Carroll County.

ROBERT WHEATLEY, Inspector,

Salineville, Columbiana County, Ohio.

Born December 19, 1829. Died July 12, 1910.

Wm. Smurthwaite, the subject of this sketch, died at his home in Steubenville, Ohio, on July 12, 1910.

Mr. Smurthwaite was one of the pioneer men when the coal industry of this country was practically in its infancy, having emigrated here in the year 1858.

He was born in Philadelphia, Durham County, England, on December 19, 1829. At about the age of 16 years he assisted his father in a colliery at that place. In the year 1844 the family removed to Cassop, where he again assisted his father, who was mine foreman. In the year 1848, having married, he took his family to Quarington Hill, where he, himself, was employed as a mine foreman.

In the year 1858 he sought new fields of labor and came to the United States, and in the year 1859 located at Steubenville, Ohio, where he was employed as mine foreman at the shaft of the Steubenville Coal and Mining Co. A few years later he was appointed superintendent, a position he held for forty-seven years, retiring at the age of 77 years.

During this period of his stewardship in such capacity but three fatal accidents occurred in the operation of this plant. He at all times kept himself in touch with all new and improved methods used in the production of coal in this country, and at the age of 70 years superintended the installation of an electric plant for mining and hauling coal without even suspending the operation of the mine. During this span of life he witnessed the mining of coal in its crudest form, that of hand pick mining, to that produced by the most modern and advanced methods, by powerful machinery operated by electricity, both for cutting the coal, and for the speedy delivery of it to the surface by high speed electric motors, which have played such a part in the keen competition encountered in what appears to be, one of the most fascinating of business enterprises.

He was a good practical miner, mining engineer, a good chemist, a good draftsman, and a good geologist, and brought to this country the excellent methods of mining practiced in England, the country where he was born. He was not only a practical man, but he was a fair-minded one, and just in all of his dealings with all persons, and enjoyed the confidence of miners and operators alike in the many years of his activity and duties of mine foreman and mine superintendent.

The loss of such a man in the complex industrial situation as it exists today, is indeed to be deplored, when all the diplomacy and good sound judgment that can be brought to bear are such necessary requisites in adjusting matters pertaining to capital and labor, and it will be difficult to fill the place he so capably occupied as an employer of labor as well as man and citizen.

INSPECTIONS.

TABLE SHOWING NUMBER OF VISITS TO MINES MADE BY THE CHIEF INSPECTOR AND DISTRICT INSPECTORS IN THE VARIOUS COUNTIES OF THE STATE FROM JANUARY 1, 1910, TO DECEMBER 31, 1910, INCLUSIVE.

	1st Dist.—Burke.	2nd Dist.—Kennedy.	3rd Dist.- McDonald.	4th Dist. Hill.	5th Dist. Turner.	5th Dist.- Ellwood.	6th Dist.- Smith.	7th Dist.- Miller.	8th Dist.- Jenkins.	9th Dist.--Morrison.	10th Dist.- Devore.	11th Dist. Hennessy.	12th Dist. Wheatley.	Chief Inspector.	Total.
Athens		24	213	6										3	246
Belmont					7				158	5	142	94		4	410
Carroll										31			9		40
Columbiana							42	4		1			81	4	132
Coshocton							75								75
Gallia		21													21
Guernsey					65	104								5	174
Harrison									1	17		32			50
Hocking		167	1												168
Holmes								7							7
Jackson	218													7	225
Jefferson	9	8	6	3	4		5	4	82	123	106	21	45	7	425
Lawrence	52														52
Mahoning							1	10					16		27
Medina								9							9
Meigs		89													89
Morgan				3											3
Muskingum				49										1	50
Noble					6	14								2	22
Ottawa								15							15
Perry				151											151
Portage								18							18
Scioto	15														15
Stark								154						1	155
Summit								17							17
Tuscarawas							137								137
Vinton	12	15													27
Wayne								40							40
Total	306	324	222	212	82	118	260	278	241	177	248	147	151	34	2,800

NOTE: — The above table includes visits made to investigate fatal accidents. One week in June was spent by the inspectors at Chicago, Illinois, attending the Mine Inspectors' Institute. Sixty-four (64) days were spent by Inspector Morrison in the oil and gas fields of the State.

REPORT OF DISTRICT MINE INSPECTORS.

FIRST DISTRICT.

JOHN BURKE.

Composed of the Counties of Jackson, Lawrence, Scioto, Vinton and a portion of Gallia.

HON. GEO. HARRISON, *Chief Inspector of Mines, Columbus, Ohio.*

DEAR SIR: — In compliance with the mining laws, I herewith submit to you my second annual report of the First Mining District, from January 1, 1910, to December 31, 1910, inclusive. During the time covered by this report 17 permanent improvements have been made, consisting of 4 furnaces, 3 fans, 8 second openings, 1 air shaft and 1 stairway. Three new mines were opened, 14 remained suspended during the year, 9 were abandoned, 9 sets of scales were tested, 7 were found correct, 2 incorrect. I regret to report 11 fatal accidents and 1 death from natural causes in the mines; 10 of the fatalities occurred in Jackson Co., 1 in Scioto Co. The investigations show that a majority of the victims lost their lives through neglect on their part or others; two of the fatal accidents were the result of impracticability on the part of the mine foreman.

The mines, with few exceptions, have worked fairly well from the time work was resumed after the suspension in April to the close of the year, the scarcity of cars being the great drawback.

While several of the operators have complied fairly well with the new mining code, the majority have been very slow in putting their mines in condition to meet the requirements of the law.

There are a great many small openings in the district; quite a number of them are opened into territories of mines which have been abandoned years ago, which are working in the coal on the crop, and in some instances drawing the pillars which were left when the mine was abandoned; the life of these mines are necessarily of a very short duration.

In conclusion, I desire to thank you and the other members of the Mining Department for courtesies shown, and information given, during the year.

Respectfully yours,

JOHN BURKE,

Inspector First District,

December 31, 1910. Wellston, Ohio.

JACKSON COUNTY.

The following mines are owned and operated by the Superior Coal Co., Wellston, Ohio. S. H. Wilson, Supt., succeeded August 1st, by Jno. E. Baumgartner, both of Wellston, Ohio.

Superior No. 1.

Located near Wellston, on the D. T. & I. Ry. Evan A. Thomas, Coalton, O., mine foreman. Shaft opening, 100 · ft. deep, No. 2 seam of coal, 3 ft. thick. Double entry system; fan ventilation; employs 14 miners and 9 day hands. Visited March 14th, requested a check door hung on 6th west entry. May 7th and June 6th, ordered loose slate and rock on the main haulway taken down or timbered; order was partially complied with. August 31st, stopped 4 men working on an entry stump on account of the unsafe condition of the roof. November 16th, ordered the hauling stopped on the 2nd west entry until all loose slate and rock was taken down or timbered. This mine has a great amount of bad roof and water with which to contend. The final robbing of the pillars has begun, and the mine will soon be abandoned.

Superior No. 3.

Located 2 miles northwest of Wellston, on a switch of the B. & O. S.-W. Ry. George Ebberts, Wellston, O., mine foreman. Shaft opening, 47 feet deep, No. 2 seam of coal, 3½ ft. thick. Double entry system; fan ventilation; employs 56 men and 32 day hands. Visited January 5th, requested the working places on 6th west entry properly ventilated. February 11th, called to investigate a fatal accident to Edward Bartz, who was killed at the face of his working place by a fall of slate. On this visit W. B. Montgomery was mine foreman, having succeeded Geo. Ebberts. August 9th, found mine in fair condition. August 25th, ordered the haulway on the south side of the mine timbered. Sept. 20th, requested a check door hung on the 6th west entry; on this visit Wm. Pollock was mine foreman. Nov. 25th, called to investigate fatal accident to Andrew Tolbert, who was injured by a coal shot in his working place on the 23rd of November and died same day. Ordered loose slate taken down on the north and 5th west entries; otherwise, the mine was in fair condition. The solid coal is all worked out.

Superior No. 4.

Located near Ironton Junction, on the C. H. & D. Ry. Virgil Callahan, Coalton, O., mine foreman. Shaft opening, 84 ft. deep. No. 2 seam of coal, 32 in. thick. Double entry system; fan ventilation. Employs 65 miners and 36 day hands. Visited March 24th, requested a check door hung on 3rd east entry; otherwise mine was in fair condition. May 26th, found the ventilation fair; roads in a wet and muddy condition. Aug. 12th, requested that not less than three resting places be built in the Meadow Run opening, which has a straight ladder for means of ingress and egress. The mine foreman readily agreed to this request. Otherwise, the mine was in fair condition.

Superior No. 9.

Located 3 miles southeast of Wellston, on the C. H. & D. Ry. Chas. G. May, Wellston, O., mine foreman. Shaft opening, 150 ft. deep. No. 2 seam of coal, 3½ ft thick. Double entry system. Fan ventilation. Pick and machine mining; employs 35 pick miners, 21 loaders, 4 machine men and 45 day hands. Visited March 3rd, requested the breakthroughs cleaned out and check doors hung on 3rd and 4th east entries. July 26th, ordered an escapement way made from the interior of the mine to the surface. August 16th, called to investigate a fatal accident to Chas. A. Gatewood, who was injured by a fall of slate at the face of his working place on the 12th of August and died on the 15th. November 21st and 22nd, Theodore Waters in charge of the mine, having succeeded Chas. G. May, as mine foreman. Found the mine in an improved condition; the escapement ways from all working places to the surface have been opened up, and the volume of air increased in all parts of the mine.

Superior No. 10, or Florence.

Located 7 miles southeast of Wellston, on C. H. & D. Ry. S. H. Wilson, Wellston, O., mine foreman. Drift opening, No. 5 seam of coal, 3 ft. thick. Double entry system. Fan ventilation; pick and machine mining; employs 20 pick miners, 30 loaders, 6 machine runners and 43 day hands. Visited Oct. 25th, ordered the trolley wire over traveling ways guarded, and the feed wires which are carried through the escapement way, put up in compliance with the law. Tested scales and found incorrect; otherwise mine was in fair condition. Nov. 3rd, tested scales, found them weighing correctly.

Superior No. 11, or Laura.

Located about 9 miles southeast of Wellston, on the C. H. & D. Ry. W. B. Montgomery, Wellston, O., mine foreman. Drift openings, Nos. 4 and 5 seams of coal, 4 ft. thick. Double entry system; fan ventilation. Pick and machine mining; employs 18 pick miners, 85 loaders, 12 machine runners and 53 day hands. Visited Sept. 21st, ordered the electric wire guarded; otherwise the mine was in satisfactory condition. October 25th, tested the scales, found them weighing correctly. December 27th, Gab McNaeil was in charge of the mine, having succeeded W. B. Montgomery; ordered all small coal in the machine cuttings removed from the mine; otherwise the mine was in good condition.

Superior No. 12.

Located on the D. T. & I. Ry., 3 miles east of Wellston. James Duane, Coalton, O., mine foreman, until his death, which occurred Sept. 28; succeeded by Chas. May, Wellston, O. Shaft opening system, 155 ft. deep, No. 2 seam of coal, 28 inches thick. Double entry, fan ventilation; pick and machine mining; employs 10 pick miners, 25 loaders, 6 machine runners and 20 day hands. Visited Feb. 5th, mine found idle. March 7th, mine found idle. The water bailer is allowed to enter the mine without an examination being made by a fire boss; ordered the mine examined before any person was allowed to enter. October 3rd and 4th, visited to investigate fatal accident to James Duane, mine foreman, who was injured by an explosion of gas on the 27th of September and died on the 28th. October 28th, visited the mine in company with Chief Inspector of Mines for the purpose of examining the daily report of the fire boss. November 4th, ordered the mine foreman to have the water, which is standing in the return airway, pumped out and kept out at all times.

The following mines are owned and operated by The Chapman Coal Co., Jackson, O. John E. Hayes, Chapman, O., General Superintendent.

Springfield.

Located on the Springfield switch, D. T. & I. Ry. W. J. Eisnagle, Chapman, O., mine foreman. Shaft opening, 54 feet deep, No. 2 seam of coal, 3 ft. thick. Single entry system. Fan ventilation; pick and machine mining; employs 20 pick miners, 31 loaders, 8 machine runners and 30 day hands. Visited January 20th, ordered loose slate taken down on 6th and 7th east and south entries. May 16th, only part of the mine working. Conditions fair. August 1st and 8th, requested an interior opening made on the south side of mine. Sept. 10th, called to investigate the death of Harry Shuff, who died from natural causes in the mine on the 9th of September. Oct. 24th and 26th, found the interior opening on the south side of the mine completed, pipe lines and hose in the tipple, boiler room and at the elevators. Dec. 1st, ordered loose slate taken down on 3rd west and 4th east entries. Otherwise the mine was in fair condition.

Grace.

Located on Ada switch, D. T. & I. Ry. Frank Pierpont, Wellston, O., mine foreman. Shaft opening, 100 ft. deep, No. 2 seam of coal, 34 in. thick. Single entry system. Fan ventilation; pick and machine mining. Employs 4 pick miners, 40 loaders, 8 machine runners and 34 day hands. Visited January 25th, found the refuge holes on the north motor haul, which I requested to be made on former visit, completed. July 21st, requested the blacksmith shop removed from between the shaft house and boiler room, and the refuge holes on the motor haul, whitewashed. October 10th, found requests of former visit complied with; otherwise, the mine was in satisfactory condition. November 22nd, tested the scales, found them weighing correctly.

Chapman.

Situated near Chapman, on the D. T. & I. Ry. Jacob Houser, same place, mine foreman. Drift opening, No. 2 seam of coal, 32 in. thick. Single entry system. Fan ventilation. Employs 18 miners and 5 day hands. Visited October 7th, found in good condition.

The following mines are owned and operated by the Emma Coal Co., Jackson O. Edwin Jones, same place, general superintendent:

Emma No. 2.

Located near Glenroy, on the D. T. & I. Ry. John Rockwell, same place, mine foreman. Shaft opening, 80 ft. deep, No. 2 seam of coal, 3 ft. thick. Double entry system; fan ventilation; employs 7 miners and 3 day hands. Visited March 28th, found ventilation fair. Otherwise the mine was in poor condition. May 24th, called to investigate a fatal accident to Henry Stewart, who was killed on the 23rd by a fall of slate at the face of his working place. May 27th, ordered loose slate taken down or timbered on north and 2nd west entries. July 13th, found mine in poor condition. November 19th, ordered the mine shut down until all loose slate was taken down on the haulway, and slope put in condition for traveling: order complied with. The mine is all pillar work and will soon be abandoned.

Emma No. 3.

Located on Springfield switch, D. T. & I. Ry. J. D. Richards, Jackson, O., mine foreman. Drift opening, No. 2 seam of coal, 3 ft. thick. Single entry system;

furnace ventilation. Employs 40 miners and 13 day hands. Visited January 21st and Sept. 15th, found in fair condition.

Emma No. 4.

Located two miles west of Coalton on the C. H. & D. Ry. John Rockwell, Glenroy, O., mine foreman. Drift opening, No. 2 seam of coal, 3 ft. thick. Single entry system; furnace ventilation. Employs 5 miners and 7 day hands. Visited November 23rd, ordered loose slate taken down on the main entry. The mine had just started to work after a suspension of over two years; mine was in poor condition.

Wellston Colliery.

Located two miles east of Wellston, O., transportation, C. H. & D. Ry. Operated by the Wellston Collieries Co., Wellston, O. W. S. McCloud, Wellston, O., Supt., Thos. Waters, same place, mine foreman. Shaft opening, 97 ft. deep, No. 2 seam of coal, 3 ft. thick. Double entry system; fan ventilation; pick and machine mining; employs 31 pick miners, 20 loaders, 6 machine runners and 34 day hands. Visited January 17th, found mine in good condition. January 26th, ordered the management not to allow any of the employes to enter the mine when the waters of the meadow run creek overflowed the low grounds overlaying the territory of this mine. Feb. 17th, mine found idle. June 10th, found in satisfactory condition. July 19th, requested the hoisting signal code observed and fire protection for shaft house and other buildings. Sept. 16th, tested scales, found incorrect. December 22nd, John Yeager, mine foreman, found requests made on July 19th complied with. Ordered the building, which is situated between the second opening and boiler room, removed, and the wooden building on top of second opening replaced with a non-inflammable structure. Otherwise, the mine was in good condition.

Domestic.

Located two miles east of Wellston, on the D. T. & I. Ry. Operated by the Domestic Coal Co., Wellston, O. H. A. Goddard, Supt., Cal. Littlejohn, mine foreman, same place. Shaft opening, 97 ft. deep, No. 2 seam of coal, 3 ft. 4 in. thick. Double entry system; fan ventilation; pick and machine mining; employs 4 pick miners, 55 loaders, 10 machine runners and 36 day hands. Visited March 7th, ordered the management not to allow any person to enter the mine before it was examined by the fire boss. May 10th, found the mine undergoing repairs. July 26th, requested escapement ways made from the interior of the mine to the surface. Aug. 24th, ordered refuge holes on north motor haul. Aug. 27th, found no supply of caps at the mine. Ordered the mine foreman to remove the men from the mine until caps were procured and delivered to the men. November 12th, visited to investigate fatal accident to Emmet Walton, who was killed by a fall of slate on the motor passway on the north. Nov. 14th, ordered all loose slate taken down or timbered. Nov. 18th, visited in company with Chief Inspector Harrison. Nov 30th, found a force of men timbering the haulways. Dec. 5th, requested the men removed from the 2nd east entry on the north, on account of a squeeze, and having only one traveling way from the working places; request was complied with.

D. C. & I. No. 2.

Located at Wellston. Transportation, B. & O. S. W. Ry. Operated by the Dayton Coal and Iron Co., Wellston, O. Herbert Poore, Wellston, O., Supt. Robert Pope, same place, mine foreman. Shaft opening, 53 ft deep, No. 2 seam of coal, 3½ ft. thick. Double entry system; fan ventilation; pick and machine mining; employs 12 pick miners, 24 loaders, 6 machine runners and 19 day hands. Visited Jan. 7th, mine found in good condition. Feb. 7th, called to investigate fatal accident to Henry Booth, who was injured in his working place by a fall of drawslate on the 6th of February, and died same day. Mine has since been abandoned.

D. C. & I. No. 3.

Located at Wellston, transportation, C. H. & D. Ry. Operated by the Dayton Coal and Iron Co., Wellston, O. Herbert Poore, Wellston, O., Supt., Robert Pope, same place, mine foreman. Shaft opening, 85 ft. deep, No. 2 seam of coal, 4 ft. thick; double entry system; fan ventilation; employs 14 miners and 7 day hands Visited May 28th, mine found in good condition. Aug. 24th, found that the second opening had become unavailable on account of the final robbing of the pillar. Requested that a competent person be kept at the mine at all times when men were in the mine, as a protection against fire; otherwise the mine was in satisfactory condition.

Tom Corwin No. 1.

Located near Glenroy, on the C. H. & D. Ry. Operated by the Tom Corwin Coal Co., Dayton, O. E. J. Harper, Glenroy, O., Supt., D. R. Welsh, same place, mine foreman. Shaft opening, 105 ft. deep, No. 2 seam of coal, 3 ft. thick. Double entry system; fan ventilation; employs 14 miners and 15 day hands. Visited January 26th, found in fair condition. Feb. 25th, found poor ventilation on 5th and 6th west entries on the south; requested the breakthroughs opened up. March 5th, found requests of former visit complied with. Aug. 4th, ordered the men removed from the pillar workings on the north until the haulway was properly timbered. Aug. 12th, found orders of former visit complied with, haulway timbered as requested. Oct. 8th, found in fair condition.

Elk Fork No. 2.

Located three miles east of Wellston, on the D. T. & I. Ry. Operated by the Elk Fork Coal Co., Wellston, O. W. P. Porter, Supt., Frank Craggs, mine foreman, both of Wellston, O. Shaft opening, 124 ft. deep, No. 2 seam of coal, 28 in. thick. Double entry system; fan ventilation; pick and machine mining; employs 5 pick miners, 25 loaders, 8 machine runners and 17 day hands. Visited January 28th, to investigate a fatal accident, which occurred on the 27th, to Wm. Clyburn, who was injured by flying coal from his own shot, dying the same day. Feb. 4th, mine in good condition May 31st, mine found idle. July 29th, ordered a blackboard put at entrance to mine for fire boss to report on. Aug. 19th, requested the building, which is located between the shaft house and boiler room, removed, and the fan put in operation two hours earlier each morning, so as to clear the mine of gases and give the fire boss sufficient time to make a thorough examination of all working places before the employes enter the mine. November 28th, W. B. Montgomery, mine foreman, having succeeded Frank Craggs; mine found in good condition.

Elk Fork No. 3, or Dewitt.

Situated on the D. T. & I. Ry., three miles east of Wellston. Operated by the Elk Fork Coal Co., Wellston, O. W. P. Porter, Supt., Frank Alberts, mine foreman, both of Wellston, O. Drift opening, No. 5 seam of coal, 3 ft. thick. Double entry system; furnace ventilation; employs 10 miners and 4 day hands. Visited Jan. 10th, July 7th and Nov. 4th, found in fair condition. The final robbing of the pillars is begun; mine will soon be abandoned.

Twinada.

Located near Glenroy, on the D. T. & I. Ry. Operated by the Twinada Coal Co., Coalton, O. W. J. Harper, Wellston, O., Supt. and mine foreman. Shaft opening, 90 ft. deep, No. 2 seam of coal, 3 ft. thick. Single entry system; fan ventilation. Visited Dec. 2nd; a force of men was cleaning up the mine, preparing to begin operation. This was formerly the Ada No. 1 mine; it has been suspended for several years.

Sun.

Located three miles west of Jackson, on the D. T. & I. Ry. Operated by the Sun Coal Co., Jackson, O. Wm. Rhody, Supt., Chas. Booth, mine foreman, both of Jackson. Drift opening. Jackson Hill seam of coal, 30 in. thick. Single entry system; furnace ventilation; employs 32 miners and 11 day hands. Visited March 11th, found idle. July 6th, found only the entries working. Ordered the volume of air increased in the mine. Aug. 30th, found ventilation deficient, reduced the force to 8 men. Aug. 31st, found conditions improved. October 24th, found ventilation deficient on 1st right entry; reduced the force to 8 men. Dec. 6th, T. T. Hughes, mine foreman. Ventilation deficient. Ordered the men removed from the mine; order was complied with. Dec. 12th, found ventilation improved.

Acorn Slope.

Located near Glenroy, on the D. T. & I. Ry. Operated by the Jones Coal Co., Jackson, O. E. T. Jones, Supt., M. M. Morgan, mine foreman, both of Jackson, O. Slope opening, 140 ft. long, No. 2 seam of coal, 3 ft. thick. Double entry system; fan ventilation; employs 6 miners and 3 day hands. Visited Jan. 4th, found in fair condition. Mine has since been abandoned.

Lucy No. 3.

Located on Armstrong switch, D. T. & I. Ry. Operated by the Armstrong Coal Co., Jackson, O. John Armstrong, Supt., Gus. Smales, mine foreman, both of Jackson. Drift opening, No. 2 seam of coal, 3 ft. thick. Single entry system; furnace ventilation; employs 24 miners and 8 day hands. May 20th, visited the mines, found no supply of timber, ordered a supply for use at the mines at once which was complied with, before I left the mine. Visited Aug. 11th and Oct. 22nd, found in satisfactory condition.

Mohawk.

Located seven miles southeast of Wellston, transportation, C. H. & D. Ry. Operated by the Mohawk Coal Co., Wellston, O. John A. Lockard, same place, supt. Perry Lucas, R. D. No. 2, Wellston, O., mine foreman. Drift opening, No. 5 seam of coal, 3½ ft. thick. Double entry system; furnace ventilation; employs 22 miners and 10 day hands. Visited March 29th, found in fair condition. October 5th, requested brick and cement stoppings built in all breakthroughs on the main inlet and outlet; otherwise the mine was in good condition.

Jackson Iron & Steel.

Located near Jackson, transportation, D. T. & I. Ry. Operated by the Jackson Iron & Steel Co., Jackson, O. Daniel C. Jones, same place, Supt. and mine boss. Shaft opening, 50 ft. deep, No. 1 seam of coal, 3 ft. Double entry system; fan ventilation. Employs 33 miners and 15 day hands. Visited May 11th, found in good condition. August 15th, John Jones, mine foreman. Requested a pipe line and hose placed in the tipple and boiler room, and breakthroughs opened up on the 2nd and 3rd right entries. Otherwise the mine was in satisfactory condition.

Globe.

Located near Jackson, on B. & O. S. W. Ry. Operated by the Globe Iron Co Jackson, O. J. E. Jones, Supt., Ross L. Lewis, mine foreman, both of Jackson. Shaft opening, 103 ft. deep, No. 1 seam of coal, 3 ft. 8 in. thick. Double entry sustem; fan ventilation; machine mining; employs 36 loaders, 6 machine runners and 15 day hands. Visited March 31st, found in good condition. April 13th, found in good condition June 22nd, requested the management to procure the required number of safety lamps and recording pressure gauge. Otherwise the mine was in satisfactory condition. Sept. 23rd and December 2nd, found in satisfactory condition. Dec. 24th, ordered the ice removed from the stairway in the second opening.

Rowe.

Located near Coalton, on the D. T. & I. Ry. Operated by Wm Rowe, Coalton, O., who is Supt., J. R. Maddox, same place, mine foreman. Drift opening, No. 2 seam of coal, 30 in. thick. Single entry system; ventilated by the return air from the Springfield mine. Employs 13 miners and 3 day hands. Visited March 14th, found the second opening closed up. No ventilation on the left entry. Ordered the mine foreman to remove the men from the entry, which was complied with. March 19th, found the second opening cleaned out and mine in fair condition. August 17th, found in fair condition.

Price.

Located on Price's switch, D. T. & I. Ry. Operated by W. A. [illegible] & Co., Toledo, O. J. C. Hurd, Jr., Jackson, O., Supt. [illegible] Mapes, same place, mine foreman. Drift opening, No. 2 seam of coal, [illegible] thick. Single entry system, furnace ventilation; employs 36 miners and [illegible] day hands. Visited [illegible] and August 3rd. Mine found in good condition. [illegible] requested [illegible] timbers put up at entrance to the mine. Otherwise [illegible] condition.

Harper.

Located on Ada switch, D. T. & I. Ry. Operated by the Harper Coal Co., Coalton, O. John E. Harper, Supt. [illegible] mine foreman, both of Coalton. Slope opening, [illegible] feet long, No. 2 seam of coal, [illegible] thick. Single entry system; fan ventilation; employs [illegible] miners and [illegible] day hands. Visited [illegible], requested a check door hung in [illegible] entry. January [illegible], called to investigate a fatal accident which occurred on the [illegible] of January [illegible], who was killed by a slate [illegible] through the [illegible]. March [illegible], mine found in good condition. May [illegible], ordered the mine foreman to remove [illegible] from south entry, which was done, found no ventilation in the entry. September [illegible], called to investigate a fatal accident which occurred on the [illegible] of September to Thomas [illegible], who was injured by falling down a shaft and died the same day. October [illegible], mine found idle. [illegible]

Jackson & Decatur No. [illegible]

Located six miles west of Jackson on the [illegible] Ry. Operated by the Jackson & Decatur Coal Co., Jackson, O. [illegible] Campbell, same place, Supt., John Newport, [illegible], mine foreman. [illegible] opening, No. [illegible] seam of coal, [illegible] ft. thick. Double entry system; furnace ventilation; employs [illegible] miners and 11 day hands. Visited May [illegible], mine found idle. September [illegible], found the ventilation deficient, the result of the furnace being neglected.

Jackson & Decatur No. 2.

Located three miles west of Jackson, wagon transportation. Operated by the same company. Robert S. Campbell, Jackson, O., Supt., Geo. Young, same place, mine foreman. Drift opening, No. 1 seam of coal, 3 ft. thick. Single entry system; furnace ventilation; employs 4 miners and 1 day hand. Visited May 25th, found in poor condition. Ordered the furnace repaired and fired within eight days. June 6th, found orders issued on May 25th not complied with and shut down the mine. July 5th, found improvements made.

McKittrick.

Located near McKittrick Sta., C. H. & D. Ry. Operated by Fred J. Hall, Dayton, O. A. E. Howell, Jep., Ohio, Supt., Murley Bates, Oak Hill, O., mine foreman. Drift opening, No. 5 seam of coal, 3 ft. 8 in. thick. Double entry system; furnace ventilation; employs 23 miners and 6 day hands. Visited July 15th and October 6th. On last visit requested the work on the escapement way pushed as rapidly as possible. Otherwise the mine was in good condition. Tested the scales and found them correct.

Commercial.

Located near Madison Furnace, C. H. & D. Ry. Operated by C. W. Hammerstein, Remple, O., who has full charge of the mine. Drift opening, No. 5 seam of coal, 3 ft. thick. Single entry system; furnace ventilation. Visited October 6th, found a force of eight men cleaning up the mine, preparatory to commencing operations.

Northern.

Located near Glenroy, on the D. T. & I. Ry. Operated by the Northern Coal Mining Co., Jackson, O. Edwin Jones, same place, Supt., John Rockwell, Glenroy, O., mine foreman. Shaft opening, 40 ft. deep, No. 2 seam of coal, 3 ft. thick. Single entry system; fan ventilation; employs 12 miners and 6 day hands. Visited June 1st, ventilation fair; roads in wet and muddy condition. September 24th, found in fair condition. October 13th, ordered the men working on the pillars on the north to suspend work until they were supplied with the proper lengths of timber. Order was complied with; also requested the fan put in operation in time to remove the blackdamp from the working places before the employes entered the mine.

Diamond.

Located near Oak Hill, O. Operated by the Diamond Firebrick Co., Oak Hill, O. C. D. Shephard, same place, has full charge of the mine. Drift opening, No. 4 seam of coal, 4 ft thick. Single entry system; furnace ventilation; employs 5 miners and 1 day hand. Visited March 4th, found in fair condition. The product of this mine is used at the brick yard.

Thomas Davis.

Located at Oak Hill. Operated by Thomas and Davis, Oak Hill, O. T. J. Davis, Oak Hill, O., Supt., John J. Jones, same place, mine foreman. Drift opening, No. 4 seam of coal, 4 ft. thick, single entry system; furnace ventilation; employs 6 miners and 1 day hand. Visited March 15th, found a gasoline pump on the main entry; ordered it removed at once. June 8th, mine found idle, found the gasoline pump removed from the mine. Tested the scales; found them weighing correctly.

Ohio Fire Brick.

Located at Oak Hill. Operated by the Ohio Fire Brick Co., Oak Hill, O. David Davis, Supt., Geo. Sharp, mine foreman, both of Oak Hill. Drift opening, No. 5 seam of coal, 3 ft. 8 in. thick; single entry system; furnace ventilation; employs 7 miners and 2 day hands. Visited March 4th, found in fairly good condition. Sept. 9th, mine found idle. Requested a second opening made, and the boiler removed to the lawful distance from the entrance to the mine.

Evans.

Located at Oak Hill, on the B. & O. S. W. Ry. Operated by the Ward Coal Co., Oak Hill, O. Chas. Bowman, Supt., H. E. Bowman, mine foreman, both of Oak Hill, O. Drift opening, No. 5 seam of coal, 3 ft. 8 in. thick. Single entry system, furnace ventilation; employs 11 miners and 5 day hands. Visited September 9th, ordered all hauling stopped on the main entry until loose slate was taken down; order complied with. The roads were in a wet and muddy condition; otherwise the mine was in fair condition.

Davis Fire Brick

Located at Oak Hill. Operated by the Davis Fire Brick Co., Oak Hill, O. Evan Davis, Supt., Frank Raynor, mine foreman, both of Oak Hill. Drift opening, No. 5 seam of coal, 2 ft. thick. Double entry system; furnace ventilation; employs 13 miners and 3 day hands. Visited March 2nd, found in poor condition; ventilation was deficient and polluted with fumes from a gasoline pump which was located on the inlet. Ordered the men removed from the mine at once, which was complied with. March 12th, found the gasoline pump removed from the mine, and a compressed air pump installed. August 18th, mine found in poor condition. Ordered all loose slate taken down on the main haulway.

Oak Hill Fire Brick.

Located at Oak Hill. Operated by the Oak Hill Fire Brick Co., Oak Hill, O. T. J. Davis, same place, Supt., Edward Harrison, Kitchen, O., mine foreman. Drift opening, No. 4 seam of coal, 3½ ft. thick. Single entry system; furnace ventilation; employs 6 miners and 2 day hands. Visited July 15th, ordered a second opening made, and furnace repaired. Otherwise the mine was in satisfactory condition.

Rempel.

Located near Limestone Furnace, on the C. H. & D. Ry. Operated by the John F. Hall Coal Co., Dayton, O. A. E. Howell, Jep., O., Supt., Oscar Silvey, Rempel, O., mine foreman. Drift opening, No. 4 seam, 3½ ft. thick. Single entry system; furnace ventilation; employs 22 miners and 5 day hands. Visited February 24th, mine found idle, requested breakthroughs opened up and brattices repaired. March 1st, found in fair condition. June 8th, ordered a supply of timber put at the mine. Mine has since been abandoned.

Pyro.

Located near Oak Hill Sta., on the C. H. & D. Ry. Operated by the Pyro Fire Brick Co., Oak Hill, O. Wm. Griffiths, Oak Hill, O., Supt., Mitchell Tope, same place, mine foreman. Drift opening, No. 5 seam of coal, 3½ ft. thick. Double entry system; furnace ventilation; employs 4 miners and 1 day hand. Visited July 15th, ordered a second opening made. Otherwise the mine was in good condition.

Rhodes & Sell.

Located three miles west of Coalton, on the C. H. & D. Ry. Operated by the Rhodes & Sell Coal Co., Coalton. Ohio. E. A. Rhodes, Supt., H. R. Milliken, mine foreman, both of Coalton. Drift opening, No. 2 seam of coal, 4 ft. thick. Double and single entry system; fan ventilation; employs 14 miners and 5 day hands. Visited June 1st, found in poor condition. August 2nd, requested the escapement way from the interior of the mine to the second opening cleaned out and made safe for traveling. November 23rd, found in poor condition.

Midway.

Located two miles southeast of Wellston. Operated by V. A. Pittenger, Wellston, Ohio, who has full charge of the mine. Slope opening, No. 4 seam of coal, 4½ ft. thick. Single entry system; natural ventilation; employs 4 miners and 1 day hand. Visited October 5th, found small steam boiler, not the lawful distance from the mine opening. Ordered the men removed from the mine until an interior opening is made and the mine ventilated by artificial means; order was complied with.

Victor Royal No. 2.

Located near Lincoln Furnace, D. T. & I. Ry. Operated by J. H. Browne, Wellston, O. T. B. Patrick, same place, has full charge of the mine. Slope opening, No. 4 seam of coal, 4 ft. thick. Double entry system; fan ventilation. Employs 11 miners and 7 day hands. Visited July 7th, found in good condition.

Pastor.

Located near Lincoln Furnace, D. T. & I. Ry. Operated by the Pastor Coal Co., Wellston, O. Robert Kirkley, Supt., I. B. Wilson, mine foreman, both of Wellston, O. Drift opening, No. 4 seam of coal, 4 ft. thick. Double entry system; fan ventilation; employs 32 miners and 10 day hands. Visited February 15th, mine found in good condition. Tested the scales, found them weighing correctly. April 14th, found in satisfactory condition. September 7th, requested escapement ways made from the interior of the mine to the surface; otherwise the mine was in fair condition.

Wainwright.

Located three miles southeast of Wellston. Transportation, C. H. & D. Ry. Operated by the Jackson Mining Co., Wellston, O. Frank C. Morrow, Supt., Cornelius Coyle, mine foreman, both of Wellston, O. Shaft opening, 96 ft. deep, No. 2 seam of coal, 28 in. thick. Double entry system. Fan Ventilation; pick and machine mining; employs 32 pick miners, 14 loaders, 4 machine runners and 25 day hands. Visited July 25th, ordered the mine examined by a competent person with a safety lamp before any person was allowed to enter the mine. August 23rd, ordered the management not to allow the employes to enter the mine whenever the water in Raccoon Creek rises above normal stage. October 15th found the ventilation deficient. November 14th, ordered the wooden building, in which the generator is located, replaced with a non-inflammable structure. December 3rd, found in poor condition. December 16th, ordered advance holes bored in rooms approaching the old workings. This mine has been inundated for several years, the result of a cave-in to the surface under Raccoon Creek.

Kessler.

Located near Lincoln Furnace, D. T. & I. Ry. Operated by the Kessler Coal Co., Wellston, O. J. E. Kessler, same place, had full charge of the mine. Drift opening, No. 4 seam of coal, 4½ ft. thick. Double entry system. Fan ventilation; employs 15 miners and 4 day hands. Visited June 21st, found in fair condition. Visited November 10th. The Advance Coal Co., Dayton, O., was operating the mine. Thomas Kelly, Wellston, O., had charge; found in fair condition.

Star Furnace.

Located near Jackson, on the D., T. & I. Ry. Operated by the Star Furnace Co., Jackson, O. L. V. Brown, Supt., Frank Patton, mine foreman, both of Jackson. Drift opening, No. 1 seam of coal, 3½ ft. thick. Double entry system; fan ventilation; employs 8 miners and 5 day hands. Visited March 11th and August 31st; found in fair condition. The mine is nearly exhausted and will soon be abandoned.

Cochran.

Located six miles west of Jackson, on the D. T. & I. Ry. Operated by the Cochran Coal Co., Jackson, O. A. J Cochran, same place, has charge of the mine. Drift opening, No. 1 seam of coal, 3 ft. thick. Single entry system; fan ventilation; employs 6 miners and 4 day hands. Visited May 25th, found in fair condition. The pillars are being drawn and will soon be abandoned.

Gem City.

Located five miles west of Jackson, on the D. T. & I. Ry. Operated by Williams & Roland, Jackson, O. Joseph Roland, same place, has full charge of the mine. Drift opening, No. 1 seam of coal, 3 ft. thick. Single entry system, furnace ventilation. Employs 7 miners and 2 day hands. Visited December 14th, found in fair condition.

Central No. 2.

Located four miles west of Jackson, O., on the D. T. & I. Ry. Operated by the Central Coal Co., Jackson, O. John Armstrong, same place, Supt., Sherman Walker, Coalton, O., mine foreman. Drift opening, No. 1 seam of coal, 3 ft thick. Single entry system. Fan ventilation. Employs 14 miners and 5 day hands. Visited February 10th, mine found idle. September 13th, ordered a second opening made. Otherwise the mine was in fair condition.

Victor.

Located near Coalton, on the C. H. & D. Ry. Operated by T. J. Evans, Coalton, O, who is Supt. of the mine, Linn Freeman, same place, mine foreman. Drift opening, No. 2 seam of coal, 26 in. thick. Single entry system; natural ventilation; employs 9 miners and 1 day hand. Visited July 8th, found in fair condition.

Browne.

Located three miles southeast of Wellston, on the D. T. & I. Ry. Operated by J. H. Browne, Wellston, O., who is Supt., P. H. Doody, same place, mine foreman. Drift openings, No. 4 seam of coal, 4 ft. thick. Double entry system. Furnace ventilation. Employs 32 miners and 12 day hands. Visited January 11th, found in fair condition. April 20th, Frank Downard, mine foreman. Mine found in fair condition. June 23rd, conditions fair in Nos. 1 and 2 openings. No. 3 opening was worked over the 100 ft. limit in advance of the air. Ordered it stopped until ventilated, which was complied with.

Crescent.

Located near Jackson, on the D. T. & I. Ry. Operated by the Crescent Coal Co., Jackson, O. S. J. Jones, Supt., C. M. Brunton, mine foreman, both of Jackson. Drift opening, No. 2 seam of coal, 26 in. thick. Single entry system; furnace ventilation; employs 5 miners and 1 day hand. Visited August 22nd, requested loose slate taken down in traveling way to second opening; otherwise the mine was in fair condition.

Jones and Morgan No. 3.

Located near Glenroy, on the D. T. & I. Ry. Operated by the Jones & Morgan Coal Co., Jackson, O. Moses Morgan, Jackson, O., Supt., D. R. Jones, same place, mine foreman. Slope opening, 150 ft. long, No. 2 seam of coal, 34 inches thick. Single entry system; fan ventilation; employs 12 miners and 6 day hands Visited February 8th, found ventilation deficient on 8th right entry, requested a breakthrough made and others stopped up. February 11th, found requests complied with, mine in fair condition. Visited May 9th, July 11th and November 7th, found mine in fair condition.

Daisy.

Located on Armstrong switch, D. T. & I. Ry. Operated by F. M. Kirkendall, Coalton, O.. Edward Fair, same place, had charge of the mine. Drift opening, No. 2 seam of coal, 3 ft. thick: Single entry system; natural ventilation; employs 4 miners and 1 day hand. Visited August 11th, found in fair condition; it has since been abandoned.

Goodrich.

Located two miles west of Coalton, on the C. H. & D. Ry. Operated by J. J. Goodrich, Wellston, O., R. F. D. No. 1, Walter Goodrich, same place, has charge of the mine. Drift opening, No. 2 seam of coal, 3 ft. thick. Single enrry system; natural ventilation; employs 6 miners and 1 day hand. Visited December 20th, found in fair condition.

Shook.

Located one mile west of Coalton, on the C. H. & D. Ry. Operated by Shook & Meyers, Coalton, O. Jacob Shook, same place, has charge of the mine. Drift opening, No. 2 seam of coal, 25 in. thick. Single entry system; furnace ventilation; employs 4 miners and 1 day hand. Visited July 8th, found in safe condition.

Hamilton.

Located near Jackson, wagon transportation. Operated by Mrs. Belle F. Hamilton, Jackson, O. John Hamilton, same place, has charge of the mine. Drift openings, No. 2 seam of coal, 30 inches thick. Single entry system; natural ventilation; employs 9 miners. Visited July 22nd, found in safe condition.

Holberg No. 4.

Located near Jackson, wagon transportation. Operated by Howard & Marsh, Jackson, O. Frank Howard, same place, has charge of the mine. Drift opening, No. 2 seam of coal, 26 inches thick Single entry system. Ventilated by a fire basket; employs 4 miners. Visited February 14th, found in fair condition. This mine has since been abandoned.

Pritchard.

Located near Coalton, on the H. V. Ry Operated by the Glenroy Coal Co., Jackson, O., Geo. House, Coalton, R. D. No. 1, has charge of the mine. Drift opening, No. 2 seam of coal, 26 in. thick Single entry system; furnace ventilation;

machine mining. Visited July 25th, found a force of men cleaning up the mine, preparatory to beginning operations.

Rhodes.

Located near Coalton. Wagon transportation. Operated by Thomas Rhodes, Coalton, O., who has full charge of the mine. Drift opening, No. 2 seam of coal, 30 inches thick. Single entry system; furnace ventilation; employs 8 miners and 2 day hands. Visited February 9th, ventilation poor. September 24th, found the inlet closed up, no ventilation in the mine; ordered the men removed from the mine until the inlet was opened up; order was complied with.

Grimes.

Located on Springfield switch, D. T. & I. Ry. Operated by Humphreys & Grimes, Coalton, O. E. C. Humphreys, same place, has charge of the mine. Drift opening, No. 2 seam of coal, 28 inches thick. Single entry system; natural ventilation; employs 3 miners and 1 day hand. Visited December 9th, found in safe condition.

Collard.

Located near Chapman Station, D. T. & I. Ry. Operated by Frank Collard, Coalton, Ohio, who has charge of the mine. Drift opening, No. 2 seam of coal, 3 ft thick. Single entry system; natural ventilation; employs 3 miners and 1 day hand. Visited December 9th, found in fair condition.

Humphreys.

Located on Springfield Switch, D. T. & I. Ry. Operated by Humphreys & Stevens, Coalton, Ohio. E. C. Humphreys, same place, has charge of the mine. Drift opening, No. 2 seam of coal, 28 inches thick. Single entry system; natural ventilation; employs 2 miners. Visited December 9th, found in safe condition.

Turner.

Located on Springfield Switch, D. T. & I. Ry. Operated by the Coyan Coal Co., Coalton, Ohio. Harley Turner, same place, has charge of the mine. Drift opening, No. 2 seam of coal, 30 inches thick. Single entry system; ventilated by a small fire; employs 4 miners and 1 day hand. Visited October 7th, found in fair condition.

Bloomfield.

Located near Ridgeland Sta., C. H. & D. Ry. Operated by the Bloomfield Mining Co., Jackson, Ohio, R. D. No. 7. Geo. Eagle, same place, has charge of the mine. Drift opening, No. 4 seam of coal, 4½ ft. thick. Double entry system; furnace ventilation; employs 1 miner. Visited December 21st, mine found idle.

Burris.

Located near Ridgeland Sta. Wagon transportation. Operated by Stanton & Norman, Berlin Crossroads, Ohio. Chas. Norman, same place, has charge of the mine. Drift opening, No. 3 seam of coal, 20 in. thick. Single entry system; ventilated by a fire basket; employs 6 miners and 2 day hands. Visited December 21st, ordered a second opening made. Otherwise the mine was in fair condition.

Wills.

Located three miles west of Coalton, on the C. H. & D. Ry. Operated by the Evans Coal Co. Coalton, O. Fred Rice, Glenroy, O., has charge of the mine.

Drift opening, No. 1 seam of coal, 3 ft. thick. Single entry system; furnace ventilation; employs 3 miners. Visited November 23rd, found in fair condition.

Gilliland.

Located on Price's switch. Wagon transportation. Operated by Roy Gilliland, Jackson, O., who has charge of the mine. Drift opening, No. 2 seam of coal, 30 in. thick. Single entry system. Natural ventilation; employs 6 miners. Visited July 22nd, found in safe condition.

Oliver.

Located on Springfield Switch, D. T. & I. Ry. Operated by the Oliver Coal Co., Chapman, O. James Oliver has charge of the mine. Drift opening, No. 2 seam of coal, 28 in. thick. Single entry system. Natural ventilation. Visited December 9th, found the old opening abandoned and a new opening being made.

Fred Jones.

Located on the C. H. & D. Ry., three miles west of Coalton. Operated by Patterson & Frisbie, Coalton, O. Wm. Patterson, Supt., John Frisbie, mine foreman, both of Coalton. Drift opening, No. 2 seam of coal. 32 in. thick. Single entry system; furnace ventilation; employs 5 miners and 2 day hands. Visited August 2nd, found in fair condition.

VINTON COUNTY.

Elk Fork No. 1.

Located at Elk Fork, on H. V. Ry. Operated by the Elk Fork Coal Co., Wellston, O. W. P. Porter, same place, Supt., John Foit, Elk Fork, O., mine foreman. Shaft opening, 95 ft. deep, No. 2 seam of coal, 30 in. thick. Double entry system; fan ventilation: pick and machine mining; employs 5 pick miners, 15 loaders, 4 machine runners and 15 day hands. Visited July 18th, in company with Inspector Kennedy. Requested that the blacksmith shop and part of building in which the hoisting engine is located be removed from between the boiler house and shaft, pipe line and hose placed in the shaft house and boiler room, remove the wooden structure from around the fan engine and replaced with a non-inflammable structure; place a ladder in the fan shaft with not less than three resting places. October 17th, found requests of former visit complied with, except the pipe line and hose had not been placed in the tipple and boiler room, and the ladder had not been placed in the fan shaft. Mine foreman stated that he would attend to these matters at once Conditions otherwise fair.

Clarion.

Located near Clarion Sta. on the H. V. Ry. Operated by the Clarion Coal & Limestone Co., Columbus, O., W. H. Johnson, Clarion, O., Supt. and mine foreman. Drift opening, No. 4 seam of coal, 4 ft. thick. Double entry system; fan ventilation; pick and machine mining; employs 4 pick miners, 27 loaders, 4 machine runners and 16 day hands. Visited October 18th, ordered all dust and small coal removed from the mine. Otherwise condition was fair.

Lawler.

Located near Minerton, on the H. V. Ry. Operated by John L. Lawler & Son, Columbus, O. John C. Lawler, Minerton, O., Supt. and mine foreman. Drift opening, No. 4 seam of coal, 4 ft. thick. Double entry system; fan ventilation; pick and machine mining; employs 3 pick miners, 32 loaders, 4 machine runners and 10 day hands. Visited October 18th; ordered a light carried on front of motor, signal light on rear car of motor trip and the trolley wire guarded over the traveling ways. Otherwise, the mine was in satisfactory condition.

Tompkins No. 1.

Located at Minerton, on the H. V. Ry. Operated by the Fobes Tompkins Coal Co., Columbus, O. James J. Murphy, Minerton, O., Supt. and mine foreman. Drift opening, No. 4 seam of coal, 4 ft. thick. Double entry system; fan ventilation; employs 30 miners and 11 day hands. Visited September 21st, requested a check door hung on the right entry, and a supply of props and caps kept at the entrance to the mine Otherwise the conditions were fair.

Puritan.

Located two miles east of Hamden Junction, on the H. V. Ry. Operated by the Puritan Brick Co., Hamden Junction, O. F. C. Morgan, same place, Supt., A. K. Williams, Wellston, O., mine foreman. Drift opening, No. 4 seam of coal, 4 ft. thick. Double entry system; fan ventilation; employs 19 miners and 4 day hands. Visited October 19th, found in good condition.

Star No. 2.

Located near Hawk Sta., on the H. V. Ry. Operated by the Star Coal Co., Hawk, O. Henry Jones, same place, has charge of the mine. Drift opening, No. 4 seam of coal, 4 ft. thick. Single entry system. Furnace ventilation; employs 4 miners and 3 day hands. Visited October 20th; mine found idle.

McArthur Fire Brick.

Located near McArthur, on the H. V. Ry. Operated by Boler & Irwin, McArthur, O. F. E. Boler, same place, Supt., and mine foreman. Drift opening, No. 4 seam of coal, 4 ft. thick. Double entry system; furnace ventilation; employs 16 miners and 2 day hands. Visited Sept. 6th, found the ventilation deficient at the face of the north entries, and standing water in second opening. Ordered the doors repaired and water removed. December 8th, found the mine inundated with water. Visited the mine in regard to an application from the management of the mine to the Chief Mine Inspector to install a gasolene pump in the mine; found that if the pump was located so as to comply with the mining laws, it would not remove the water; pump was not installed in the mine.

Goode.

Located near Lincoln Furnace, on the D. T. & I. Ry. Operated by the J. W. Goode Coal & Mining Co., Dayton, O. Warren McKinness, Wellston, O., Supt. and mine foreman. Drift opening, No. 4 seam of coal, 4 ft. thick. Double entry system; fan ventilation; employs 18 miners and 7 day hands. Visited June 21st, found in fair condition. Visited November 10th, found the mine operated by the DeWitt Coal Co., Wellston, O., Willard DeWitt, same place, had charge of the mine. Conditions fair.

Kirkendall.

Located near Lincoln Furnace, D. T. & I. Ry. Operated by the Kirkendall & Piatt Coal Co., Coalton, O. Albert Piatt, same place, has charge of the mine Drift opening, No. 5 seam of coal, 3 ft. thick. Single entry system; furnace ventilation; employs 17 miners and 6 day hands. Visited January 19th, found in fair condition. May 31st, ordered loose slate taken down on the main entry.

LAWRENCE COUNTY.

Cobb No. 2.

Located near Etna Sta., D. T. & I. Ry. Operated by the Halley Coal Co., Pedro, O. O. S. Callahan, same place, Supt. and mine foreman. Drift opening, No. 5 seam of coal, 3½ ft. thick. Single entry system; furnace ventilation; employs 56 miners and 15 day hands. Visited February 3rd, ordered loose slate taken down on the main and 2nd right entries. March 26th, found the ventilation poor, the result of breakthroughs being partially filled up and doors leaking. Tested the scales, found them weighing correctly. June 28th, found the ventilation deficient on the right entries. Ordered the breakthroughs opened up and loose slate on the entries taken down. A gasoline pump which was located in the mine has been removed to the outside October 14th, mine found idle.

Cobb No. 3.

Located near Etna Sta., D. T. & I. Ry. Operated by the Halley Coal Co., Pedro, O. O. S. Callahan, same place, Supt., James Potts, mine foreman. Drift opening, No. 5 seam of coal, 3 ft. thick. Single entry system; furnace ventilation; employs 28 miners and 6 day hands. Visited March 18th, ordered a regular attendant kept at the furnace, and the brattices and doors repaired. March 21st, found brattices and floors repaired, and attendant at the furnace. May 13th, ordered a new furnace built closer to the workings. June 30th, found order of former visit not complied with; the superintendent agreed to start on the work at once. July 14th, found the volume of air in the mine sufficient for 13 men and 1 animal: reduced the working force to that number. September 8th, found a heavy squeeze on the main entry, which is the only traveling way from the interior of the mine. Ordered the men removed from the mine at once, which was done. October 14th, found the left entry working. Conditions fair.

Hall.

Located at Campbell Sta. on the C. H. & D. Ry. Operated by V. E. Hall, receiver for the J. F. Hall Coal Co., Dayton, O. Edward Brohard, Jep, O., has full charge of the mine. Drift opening, No. 4 seam of coal, 4 ft. thick. Single entry system; furnace ventilation; employs 24 miners and 7 day hands. Visited February 23rd, ordered a supply of timber kept at the mine. June 9th, found a gasolene pump installed on the intake, ordered it removed. August 5th, found the mine in fair condition and gasolene pump removed from the mine.

Buckhorn No. 5.

Located near Buckhorn Sta., C. H. & D. Ry. Operated by the Buckhorn Coal Co., Buckhorn, O. Isaac Day, same place, Supt. and mine foreman. Drift opening, No 5 seam of coal, 3 ft. 4 in. thick. Double entry system; furnace ventilation; employs 27 miners and 7 day hands. Visited September 22nd, mine found idle, no inspection made.

Kelly.

Located at Ironton. Operated by the Kelly Nail & Iron Co., Ironton, O. Conrad Klein, same place, Supt. and mine foreman. Drift opening, No. 5 seam of coal, 3 ft. thick. Single entry system; furnace ventilation; employs 30 miners and 9 day hands. Visited April 22nd, found an entry working over 60 ft. in advance of the air; ordered it stopped until the ventilation was brought within the lawful distance from the face. September 2nd, found the mine in fair condition.

Oliver No. 4.

Located near Olive Furnace, on the C. H. & D. Ry. Operated by R. H. McGugin, Olive Furnace, O. Jacob Stevenson, same place, has charge of the mine. Drift opening, No. 4 seam of coal, 4 ft. thick. Single entry system; furnace ventilation; employs 14 miners and 2 day hands. Visited December 30th, found in fair condition.

Ginn.

Located at Lagrange Sta., on the D. T. & I. Ry. Operated by the Ginn Co., Ironton, O. H. H. Keyes, same place, Supt., John Beanard, Ironton, O., R. D. No. 2, mine foreman. Drift opening, No 5 seam of coal, 3 ft. thick. Single entry system; furnace ventilation; employs 32 miners and 13 day hands. Visited March 16th, found idle. March 25th, found one working place over the 60-ft. limit in advance of the air; ordered it stopped, which was done. July 29th, found mine working, furnace not properly fired. Ordered the mine foreman to remove the men from the mine; order was complied with. October 21st, mine found idle. October 31st, tested the scales and found them weighing correctly. November 1st, found the miners using miners' oil which did not comply with the mining laws; ordered the superintendent to remove the men from the mine, and take all the oil out of the mine, which he readily agreed to do.

Lawrence Mill No. 2.

Located at Royersville Sta., on the D. T. & I. Ry. Operated by John Deer, Ironton, O., R. D. No. 2. O. S. Callahan, Pedro, O, Supt., John Deer, mine foreman. Drift opening, No. 5 seam of coal, 4 ft. thick. Single entry system; natural ventilation; employs 10 miners and 1 day hand. Visited July 14th, ordered a furnace built, and a second opening made. Otherwise the mine was in fair condition.

Etna Pine.

Located near Lisman Junction, on the D. T. & I. Ry. Operated by W. R. Maxey, Pedro, O. James Kelly, Culbertson, O., has charge of the mine. Drift opening, No. 5 seam of coal, 3 ft. thick. Single entry system; natural ventilation; employs 15 miners and 2 day hands. Visited December 23rd, ordered the mine foreman to remove the men from the mine, with the exception of those working on the right, until an interior opening was made, which was complied with.

Irish Hollow No. 2.

Located at Blackfork, on the B. & O. S. W. Ry. Operated by the Black Fork Co., Black Fork, O. Edward Dayler, Portsmouth, O., Supt., Frank Alberts, Black Fork, mine foreman. Drift opening, No. 5 seam of coal, 2 ft. 8 in. thick.

Double entry system; furnace ventilation; pick and machine mining; employs 2 pick miners, 58 loaders, 12 machine runners and 19 day hands. Visited March 9th, found in fair condition. The mine has been suspended since March 31st.

Clarion No. 4.

Located at Black Fork, on the B. & O. S. W. Ry. Operated by the Black Fork Co., Biack Fork, O. Edward Dayler, Portsmouth, O., Supt., John M. Jenkins, Eifort, O., mine foreman. Drift opening, No. 4 seam of coal, 4 ft. thick. Double entry system; fan ventilation; employs 28 miners and 24 day hands. Visited February 28th, found in fair condition. September 24th, found four men working in the mine without any ventilation, the fan not being in operation; ordered the mine foreman to remove them at once, which was done.

Black Fork No. 5, Clay.

Operated by the Black Fork Co., and under the same management. Drift opening, into a seam of clay 5 ft. thick. Double entry system; furnace ventilation; employs 7 miners and 1 day hand. Visited September 14th, found in fair condition.

Black Fork, Clay.

Operated by the same company, James Riley, Black Fork, O., in charge of the mine. Drift opening, into No. 5 seam of coal and clay. Double entry; natural ventilation; employs 4 miners and 1 day hand. Visited August 18th, ordered an air shaft sunk, furnace and second opening.

Portsmouth Refractories.

Located on York Switch, on the B. & O. S. W. Ry. Operated by the Portsmouth Refractories Co., Portsmouth, O. M. C. Dickens, Oak Hill, Ohio, R. D. No. 3, Supt. and mine foreman. Drift opening, No. 5 seam of coal, 40 in. thick. Double entry system; natural ventilation; employs 17 miners and 7 day hands. Visited December 20th, ordered the furnace and second opening completed as soon as possible. Otherwise conditions were satisfactory.

York Portland Cement, Lime Mine.

Located on York Switch, on the B. & O. S. W. Ry. Operated by the York Portland Cement Co., Portsmouth, O. Drift opening, into a seam of limestone 7 ft. thick. Double entry system; furnace ventilation. Visited December 20th, found the mine suspended.

Superior Portland Cement, Limestone.

Located at Superior, on the D. T. & I. Ry. Operated by the Superior Portland Cement Co., Superior, O. E. C. Switzer, Supt., W. E. Crothers, mine foreman, both of Superior, O. Drift opening into a seam of limestone, 6 ft. thick. Double entry system; fan ventilation; electric haulage; employs 34 miners and 30 day hands. Visited March 30th, found in good condition. June 24th, ordered the guards on the trolley wire over the traveling ways repaired. July 28th, found in fair condition. December 13th, E. E. Whitlatch, mine foreman; mine found in satisfactory condition.

Superior Portland Cement, Coal Mine.

Located at Superior. Operated by the same company. Ben Reaper, mine foreman, Steece, Ohio. Drift opening, No. 5 seam of coal, 28 in. thick. Double entry system; fan ventilation; machine mining; electric haulage; employs 7 loaders, 2 machine runners and 5 day hands. Visited December 13th, ordered the trolley wire guarded over the traveling ways. Otherwise the mine was in satisfactory condition.

Pine Grove, Lime.

Located near Pine Grove Furnace. Operated by the Hanging Rock Iron Co., Hanging Rock, O. D. B. Meacham, Cincinnati, O., Supt., Hugh Shields, Hanging Rock, O., mine foreman. Drift opening, into a seam of limestone, 6 ft. thick. Single entry system; furnace ventilation; employs 12 miners and 4 day hands. Visited March 21st and May 13th, found in fair condition.

Ironton Portland Cement.

Located near Ironton. Operated by the Ironton Portland Cement Co., Ironton, O. John H. Lynd, same place, Supt., and mine foreman. Drift opening, into a seam of limestone, 6 ft. thick. Single entry system; fan ventilation; employs 35 miners and 20 day hands. Visited April 21st, found in fair condition. Visited July 28th and October 31st, ordered the haulways timbered.

Riley Lime.

Located at Center Station, on the D. T. & I. Ry. Operated by Michael Riley, Ort, O., Chas. Cable, same place, has charge of the mine. Drift opening into a seam of limestone, 8 ft. thick. Single entry system; natural ventilation; employs 10 miners and 5 day hands. Visited March 22nd, ordered the working place on the right stopped; it had no pillars for support and no timbers set.

Kelly Lime.

Located at Bartles Station, on the D. T. & I. Ry. Operated by the Superior Portland Cement Co., Superior, O. Mine has been suspended since the fore part of the year.

Willard.

Located near Bartles Sta., on the D. T. & I. Ry. Operated by E. B. Willard, Ironton, O. Robert Aldridge, Steece, O., Supt., Chas. Depriest, same place, mine foreman. Drift opening into a seam of limestone, 6 ft. thick. Double entry system; natural ventilation; employs 23 miners and 9 day hands. Visited December 29th, found in fair condition. Preparations are being made to sink an air-shaft and build a furnace in the new opening.

New Castle.

Located near Pine Grove Furnace. Operated by the Hanging Rock Iron Co., Hanging Rock, O. D. B. Meacham, Cincinnati, O., Supt., Hugh Shields, Hanging Rock, O., mine foreman. Drift opening, No. 5 seam of coal 3 ft. thick. Single entry system; natural ventilation; employs 12 miners and 2 day hands. Visited April 12th, found in fair condition.

Keating.

Located near Lagrange Sta., wagon transportation. Operated by Henry Keating, Ironton, O., who has charge of the mine. Drift opening, No. 5 seam of coal, 3 ft. thick. Single entry system; natural ventilation; employs 7 miners. Visited March 25th, found the escapement way closed up. Ordered the men removed from the mine, which was complied with.

Scherer.

Located near Coal Grove. Operated by Scherer & Hughes, Ironton, O. Chas. Hughes, same place, has charge of the mine. Drift opening, No. 5 seam of coal, 3 ft. thick. Single entry system; furnace ventilation; employs 7 miners and 1 day hand. Visited July 28th, mine found idle.

Hunter.

Located near Coal Grove, O. Operated by Hunter & Geil, Ironton, O. A. D. Hunter, Coal Grove, O., has charge of the mine. Drift opening, No. 5 seam of coal, 3½ ft. thick. Single entry system; natural ventilation; wagon transportation. Visited July 28th, ordered an escapement way made and furnace built. Otherwise the mine was in fair condition. The mine employs 3 miners.

Ryan.

Located near Coal Grove. Operated by Ben Ryan, Coal Grove, O., who has charge of the mine. Drift opening, No. 5 seam of coal, 3 ft. thick. Single entry system; furnace ventilation; wagon transportation; employs 3 miners. Visited December 31st; mine found idle.

Maxey.

Located near Etna Sta. Operated by W. R. Maxey, Pedro, O. Drift opening, No. 5 seam of coal, 3 ft. thick. Single entry system; natural ventilation; employs 6 miners. Mine has wagon transportation. Found in fair condition.

Perry Bailey.

Located near Etna Sta. Operated by Perry Bailey, Pedro, O., who has charge of the mine. Drift opening, No. 5 seam of coal, 3 ft. thick. Single entry; natural ventilation; employs 4 miners. Visited December 29th, found in fair condition.

Black Fork No. 3.

Located near Black Fork. Operated by Chas. Smith, Black Fork, O. Drift opening, into No. 5 seam of coal and clay. Single entry system; natural ventilation; employs 4 miners and 1 day hand. Visited August 8th, requested an escapement way made.

SCIOTO COUNTY.

Sugar Camp.

Located on a switch of the B. & O. S. W. Ry. Operated by the Harbison-Walker Refractories Co., Pittsburg, Pa. H. B. Campbell, Portsmouth, O., Supt., C. W. Stumpf, South Webster, O., mine foreman. Drift opening into a seam of fire clay, 5 ft. thick. Double entry system; furnace ventilation; employs 10 miners and 3 day hands. Visited May 18th, found in fair condition. August 10th, mine found idle. Found a boiler located 24 ft. from entrance to the mine; ordered it removed to the lawful distance from the mine opening.

Adkins.

Operated by same company, and under same management as Sugar Camp mine. Drift opening into a seam of fireclay, 4 ft. thick. Double entry system;

furnace ventilation; employs 4 miners. Visited February 10th, found the first right and first left entries over the 60-ft. limit in advance of the air. Ordered them stopped until the air was brought within the lawful distance from the face. May 19th, found in fair condition.

Eifort Lime.

Located near Eifort Sta. on the B. & O. S. W. Ry. Operated by Morgan & Horton, Eifort, O. W. H. Horton, Supt., Edward Queen, mine foreman, both of Eifort, O. Drift opening into a seam of limestone, 6 ft. thick. Single entry system; furnace ventilation; employs 19 miners and 14 day hands. Visited June 27th, found in fair condition.

Globe Lime.

Located near Eifort Sta., B. & O. S. W. Ry. Operated by the Globe Iron Co. and Star Furnace Co., Jackson, O. O. F. Hughes, Eifort, O., Supt. and mine foreman. Drift opening into a seam of limestone, 7 ft. thick. Single entry system; natural ventilation; employs 28 miners and 12 day hands. Visited August 22nd, requested the entrance to the No. 3 opening timbered. Otherwise the mine was in fair condition. September 19th, visited to investigate a fatal accident, which occurred on the 15th of September to John Fulk, who was injured in his working place by a fall of slate and died the same day. This mine has since been abandoned.

Buckeye Fire Brick & Clay No. 1.

Located at Scioto Furnace, on the B. & O. S. W. Ry. Operated by the Buckeye Fire Brick & Clay Co., Scioto Furnace, O. A. C. Pyles, same place, Supt. and mine foreman. Drift opening into a seam of fireclay 3½ ft. thick. Double entry system; furnace ventilation; employs 12 miners and 3 day hands. Visited May 19th; found in satisfactory condition.

South Webster Clay.

Located at South Webster, on the B. & O. S. W. Ry. Operated by the South Webster Face Brick Co., South Webster, O. Harry Strong, Supt., John Jenkins, mine foreman, both of South Webster. Drift opening into a seam of fireclay, 5 ft. thick. Single entry; furnace ventilation; employs 8 miners and 2 day hands. Visited August 10th; found in fair condition.

Scioto Fire Brick.

Located at Gephart Sta., B. & O. S. W. Ry Operated by the Scioto Firebrick Co., Sciotoville, O. Herman Held, Lilly P. O., Ohio, Supt. and mine foreman. Drift opening into a seam of fireclay, 6 ft. thick. Single entry system; furnace ventilation. Employs 7 miners and 4 day hands. Visited May 19th; requested a door erected on the main entry to force the air into the working places on the left. Otherwise the mine was in fair condition.

Nagel.

Located on a switch on B. & O. S. W. Ry. Operated by Fortner & Slack, Scioto Furnace, O. Joseph Fortner, same place, has charge of the mine. Drift opening into a seam of fireclay 7 ft. thick. Single entry; furnace ventilation; employs 4 miners. Visited August 10th; found in safe condition.

Hanging Rock Iron Ore.

Located at Ohio Furnace. Operated by the Hanging Rock Iron Co., Hanging Rock, O. Chas. Lawless, Supt., C. G. Etterling, mine foreman, both of Hanging Rock, O. Drift opening into a seam of iron ore, 12 inches thick. Single entry system; furnace ventilation; employs 8 miners and 2 day hands. Visited September 1st. The miners are supplied with props, but no caps are furnished, the old system of having the miner to make his own caps being still in existence. Ordered a supply of caps kept at the mine and delivered to the miner. Otherwise the mine was in fair condition.

MINES VISITED IN JEFFERSON COUNTY.

Visited the Y. & O. mine on the following dates:
April 23rd, 1910.
April 28th, 1910.
April 29th, 1910.
April 30th, 1910
May 2nd, 1910.
May 3rd, 1910.
Visited the Zerbe mine on the following dates:
April 25th and 27th, 1910.
Visited the Elizabeth mine, April 26th, 1910.

Visits, Jackson County	207
Visits, Lawrence county	52
Visits, Vinton County	12
Visits, Scioto County	14
Visits, Jefferson County	9
	294

SECOND DISTRICT.

EDWARD KENNEDY.

Composed of Counties of Hocking, Meigs, and a portion of Athens, Vinton and Gallia.

HON. GEORGE HARRISON, *Chief Inspector of Mines, Columbus, O.*

DEAR SIR:—In accordance with the laws of Ohio, and the usual custom of the Mining Department, I have the honor of submitting to you my third annual report of the mines of the Second Mining District, for the year commencing January 1, 1910, and ending December 31, 1910, inclusive.

The Second Mining District includes the counties of Hocking, Meigs, and a portion of Athens, Vinton and Gallia.

Three hundred and fifteen visits were made during the year, as follows: 162 in Hocking, 94 in Meigs, 15 in Vinton, 16 in Gallia and 20 in Athens. Eight visits were made in Jefferson County, a full report of which will be found in District Inspector Morrison's report.

During the time covered by this report, seven new mines were opened in the district; 3 remained suspended and 1 abandoned. Three sets of scales were tested during the year, all of which were found correct. Thirty-eight permanent improvements covered by this report, are as follows: Furnaces, 6; fans, 19; air shaft, 1. Second and additional openings, 10. Ventilating baskets, 1.

I regret to note 13 fatal accidents charged to my district during the year, an increase of 5 over the previous year. Four were credited to Hocking County, 7 to Meigs, 1 to Gallia and 1 to Athens, as follows: At Jobs No 2. mine in Hocking County, January 27, 1910, George Shannon was killed by fall of slate at face of working place. At Star No. 1, or North Hill, on March 9, 1910, Samuel McConnaka was killed by knocking a post out from under loose slate, allowing it to fall on him. At Jobs No. 2 mine, on August 19, 1910 Frank Swyers fell off the front end of motor, cutting his leg off and died on August 22, 1910. At Jobs No. 1 mine, on October 26, 1910, Peter Heyge was killed by fall of roof while drawing pillars.

In Meigs County, at Hobson mine, on February 10, 1910, James France was killed by fall of roof at face of working place. At Maynard No. 1 mine, on February 15, 1910, Clarence McFarland was injured by car breaking loose on incline, jumping the track on hoppers and catching him; died February 16, 1910. At Charter Oak mine, on February 28, 1910, Fred Smith, by spark from lamp on head, igniting a full keg of power on his lap. Died from burns on March 1, 1910. At Charter Oak, on March 4, 1910, Jacob Durst was tripping timbers on motor switch to take loose slate down, was caught by falling slate. At Maynard No. 1 mine, on September 15, 1910, Ray Rupe was killed by fall of top coal at face of working place. At Silver Run mine, on December 21, 1910, Simon P. Farley was killed by fall of slate at face of working place. At Maynard No. 2 mine, on December 30, 1910, Levi Dodson was killed by fall of slate at face of working place.

In Gallia County, at John Summers' mine, on October 27, 1910, Mathew F. Hazelet was killed by fall of slate at face of working place. This was a new opening, only in 17 feet and only two sets of timbers set and no extra timber on the ground. Swore out affidavit for mine boss, John Summers, for not furnishing an adequate supply of timber; he plead guilty, was fined $10 and cost.

In Athens County, at New York No. 31 mine, Herman Kunnitz was killed on July 16, 1910, by fall of cannel coal at face of working place, which makes 69 and 3-13 per cent. of men in this district were killed at face of working place by falls of roof.

It has been my highest aim in the discharge of my duties to protect the lives of the men entrusted to my care, and to impress on the minds of all who work in the mines the dangers that exist in following their usual occupation. Yet notwithstanding my many admonitions for watchfulness and care, you will note that 10 of the fatal accidents out of the 13 were falls of roof, 9 of which occurred at the working face. These to a great extent could be avoided, if the miners would use more precaution and examine the roof on entering the mine and after shooting. Quite often when the inspector makes an investigation of a fatal accident he is told by the victim's partner that they were aware that the top was loose, and that they were going to take it down or timber it as soon as they loaded a car.

While it is an impossibility to eliminate all fatalities in coal mines, they could be materially reduced by operating companies if they could be induced to put traveling bosses, or inspectors, in their mines, whose whole duty would be to travel through working places and look after timbering and loose top. The top in most parts of this district is bad. In Hocking County a great many of the mines are working faulty coal that was left in the mines years ago. In Meigs County several mines are taking down from two to three feet of slate in both entries and rooms. With few exceptions the mines in this district have worked almost steady the entire year.

With but very few exceptions we have secured the enforcement of the new mining code, which went into effect on June 11, 1910, in all of the mines under our supervision. Some of the companies complied readily, and their managements gave every assistance in maintaining discipline and rigid enforcement of the rule, for which I wish to extend my appreciation.

While my labor for the last year has been arduous, it has nevertheless been very pleasant. I have endeavored to perform my duty honorably and fearlessly, treating all concerned justly and respectfully, and I acknowledge with pleasure that, with few exceptions, I have been very respectfully received by both operators and miners, with whom my duty brought me in contact. Thanking them for their courteous treatment, and you, and the other members of the department, especially for the many favors and kindly advice at all times, I am,

Very respectfully,

EDWARD KENNEDY, *Inspector Second District.*

Carbon Hill, Ohio, December 31, 1910.

HOCKING COUNTY.

Deweye.

Located in Lost Hollow, on the Lost Run branch of the H. V. R. R. Operated by Geo. Price, New Straitsville, O., who is superintendent and mine boss. Drift opening, penetrating the No. 6 seam of coal, which runs from 4 to 8 ft. in thickness. Employs 14 pick miners and 2 day hands. Visited January 25th, June 21st, August 29th and November 16th. During the early part of the year a furnace was built and second opening made, found in fair condition on each visit.

Star Nos. 1 and 2.

Located at Coonville, on the River Division of the H. V. R. R. Operated by Starr Hocking Coal Mining Co., Bay City, Michigan. Wm. Wiper, Starr, O., Supt. and mine boss up to November; was succeeded by John Murphy, Nelsonville, O., as Supt. and W. Sidle, Starr, O., mine boss. Drift opening, penetrating No. 6 seam of coal, 4 ft. thick. Machine mining and motor haulage. Employs 65 loaders, 12 machine cutters, 24 day hands. Visited March 7th, found in poor condition. Ventilation was poor, canvas being used for brattices on main entry in South Hill, which were found down; requested them replaced with brick and cement brattices, a good furnace built and fan installed in North Hill. March 10th, investigated fatal accident of Samuel McConnaha, day hand. May 26th, stopped dark south entry until a breakthrough was made and north entries in North Hill until door was erected. August 8th, ventilation was weak in west entries in South Hill, due to brattices leaking, which were ordered repaired. November 22nd, mine was found in an improved condition.

Prosperity.

Located at Sand Run, O., on the H. V. R. R. Operated by the Carbon Coal Co., Carbon Hill, O. B. F. Sheron, Carbon Hill, O., Supt. and mine boss. Drift opening, penetrating No. 6 seam of coal, from 3 to 6 ft. in thickness. Employs 54 loaders, 4 cutters and 13 day hands. Visited March 18th, requested door on main west, above motor switch, and door between 1 and 2 east. May 18th and 21st, they had made new second opening and installed a 6 ft. electric Jeffrey fan. On first named date ventilation was deficient. Requested 5 brattices built; on the 21st brattices had been built and ventilation was satisfactory. August 26th, ordered No. 4 on 4 east, which was stopped up to the limit, and loose slate taken down in No. 6 room on 2 west. September 23rd requested 2 doors and 3 brattices built on 2 west south and fan moved to south entries.

Stalters No. 1.

Located at Longstreth, O., on the Monday Creek branch of the H. V. R. R. Operated by the Carbon Hill Mining Co., Carbon Hill, O. Frank Hawk, Carbon Hill, O., Supt. and mine boss. Drift opening, penetrating the No. 6 seam of coal, 6 ft. thick. Machine mining. Employs 6 loaders, 2 cutters and 3 day hands. Visited January 24th, June 22nd, August 25th and October 28th. The latter part of August the Central Hocking Coal Co. had installed a fan, which drove the damps in this mine, causing them to be idle for some time. Advised Mr. Stalters to install a fan, which was done, and proved successful. On my last visit the mine was found in good condition

Stalters No. 2.

Located at Longstreth, O., on the Monday Creek branch of the H. V. R. R. Operated by the Big Six Coal Co., Carbon Hill, O. Drift opening, penetrating No 6 seam of coal, 6 ft. thick. Employs 5 pick miners. Visited January 24th, was found satisfactory. On December 2nd mine had changed hands, was being operated by Kepler and Symes, of Nelsonville, O. Timbering on this date was poor and no extra supply on the ground; gave orders that supply of timber must be kept at working place. Otherwise, mine in fair condition.

Stalters No. 3.

Located at Longstreth, O., on the Monday Creek branch of the H. V. R. R. Operated by R. Cable, Nelsonville, O., who is Supt. and mine boss. Drift opening, penetrating No. 6 seam of coal, 6 ft. thick. Single entry system. Machine mining; furnace ventilation. Employs 10 loaders, 2 cutters and 3 day hands. Visited January 24th and May 18th, mine satisfactory. On June 22nd, ventilation was poor, requested fan installed, but owing to electric power being limited they installed a furnace. August 23rd and December 2nd, mine in fair condition.

Royal.

Located at Longstreth, O., on the Monday Creek branch of the H. V. R. R. Operated by the Royal Coal Co., Nelsonville, O. John Lax, Nelsonville, O., Supt. and mine boss. Drift opening, penetrating the No. 6 seam of coal, 7 ft. thick. Pick mining. Double entry system and basket ventilation. Employs 21 pick miners and 8 day hands. Visited March 16th and June 7th. On latter date ventilation at head of north entries was deficient, due to brattices leaking, which were ordered repaired. On August 25th and October 28th, general condition fair.

Union Furnace Clay.

Located at Union Furnace, O., on the River Division of the H. V. R. R. Operated by the Columbus Brick and Terra Cotta Co., Columbus, O. B. S. Fisher. Supt., and James Beckel, mine boss, both of Union Furnace, O. Drift opening, penetrating the No. 3 seam of fire clay, 10 ft. thick. Employs 3 drillers and shooters, 9 loaders and 10 day hands. Worked on double entry system. Furnace ventilation. Visited March 21st, May 26th, and September 12th, mine in good condition on each visit.

Kachelmacher Coal.

Located one mile north of Kachelmacher, on the H. V. R. R. Operated by the C. & H. C. & I. Co., Columbus, O. Fred Weymueller, New Straitsville, O., Supt, John Weymueller, Nelsonville, O., mine boss. Drift opening, penetrating No. 6 seam of coal, 6 ft. thick. Pick mining, basket ventilation. Employs 6 miners and 2 day hands. Visited February 9th, mine found in good condition. Some time after this date, the plant closed down and mine was suspended the balance of the year.

Kachelmacher Clay Nos. 1, 2, 3, 4 and 5.

Located one mile north of Kachelmacher, O. Operated by the Columbus and Hocking Clay & Construction Co., Columbus, O. Drift openings, penetrating the Nos. 3, 4 and 5 seams of fire clay from 4 to 6 feet in thickness. Fred Weymueller, New Straitsville, O., Supt., George Davis, Kachelmacher, O., mine boss. Employs 14 miners, 2 cutters and 4 day hands. Visited February 9th, stopped Nos. 1 and 2 rooms ahead of air in No. 2 Hill, and ordered brick brattices on main entry in same Hill. The plant closed down shortly after my visit and remained suspended the remainder of the year.

No. 53, Beatty Bros.

Located near Buchtel, on H. V. R. R. Owned by the C. & H. C. & I. Co., Columbus, O. Operated by Dave Keeny & Son, Buchtel O. Fred Weymueller, New Straitsville, O., Supt. and Dave Keeny, Buchtel, O., mine boss. Slope opening, penetrating No. 6 seam of coal, 6 ft. thick. Ventilated by a steam fan. Employs 9 pick miners and 2 day hands. Visited March 16th, June 23rd, August 30th and November 27th. Pillars and main entry stumps are being drawn, and owing to the many breaks to the surface the ventilation has not been the best.

Gem.

Located in Lost Hollow, on the lost Run branch of the H. V. R. R. Operated by the Gem Coal Co., Nelsonville, O. H. B. Summers, Nelsonville, O., Supt. and mine boss. Drift opening, penetrating No. 6 seam of coal, from 3 1-2 to 10 feet in thickness. Double entry system. Machine mining; fan ventilation. Employed the forepart of the year, 35 loaders, 4 cutters and 12 day hands. Visited January 25th, June 21st and August 29th. On June 25th, ordered door between 1 and 2 south and door between the 3 and 4 east, and sink an air shaft in the last room turned off No. 1 on 1 east. August 29th, former request had been complied with and mine was found in an improved condition. Mine closed down after this date and was suspended the rest of the year.

Black Diamond Coal Nos. 1 and 2.

Located two miles from Haydenville, O. Operated by the National Fire-proofing Co., Pittsburg, Pa. H. L. Elliot, Supt., Henry Snoke, mine boss, both of Haydenville, O. Drift openings, penetrating the No. 6 seam of coal, 4 ft. thick. Worked on double entry system. Furnace ventilation and pick mining. Employs 43 pick miners and 10 day hands. Visited February 16th. Ventilation was not sufficient for the number of men employed. Ordered them to reduce force to 28 men and build brattices in room which broke into old works, build new door at mouth of mine, repair brattices between 3 and 4 west, hang door in old works so as to make air cut faces of rooms. February 23rd, mine was found in improved condition and permission given to work full force. May 27th, new opening made, furnace installed, and second opening made; ventilation was found deficient in No. 2 Hill, ordered the mine boss to take men out, and drive the 1st west entry outside, so as to make that point the inlet. May 31st, No. 1 west had not yet reached outside, but work was continued day and night; 2 or 3 cuts more would complete the work. September 2nd and December 5th, mine was satisfactory.

Black Diamond Clay.

Located near coal mine. Operated by same company and under same management. The product of both coal and clay are used at the plant. Drift opening, pentrating the No. 5 seam of clay, 7 ft. thick. Worked on double entry system. Pick mining and furnace ventilation. Employs 9 miners and 3 day hands. Visited February 16th, May 27th, September 2nd and December 5th, mine was found in good condition.

NOTE.

R. S. Weitzell, Nelsonville, O., was district superintendent for Sunday Creek Co., Columbus, for all mines in Hocking Valley, up to November. Mr. Weitzell resigned on this date and was succeeded by Harry Kelly, of Congo, O.,

Frank Knox, Nelsonville, O., inspector. M. M. Kassler, Nelsonville, O., is district superintendent for all New Pittsburg Coal Co. mines in Hocking County, and Frank Knox, Nelsonville, O., is mine manager.

New Pittsburg Nos 1 and 1½.

Located at Blackford, O., on the H. V. R. R. Owned by the New Pittsburg Coal Co., Columbus, O. Operated by George Douglas, Jobs, O. George Douglas, Jobs, O., Supt., Herb Edgell, same place, mine boss. Drift openings, penetrating No. 6 seam of coal, 6 ft. thick. Machine and pick mining; fan ventilation. Employs 70 miners, 6 machine men, 22 day hands. Visited March 15th, mine had been idle for 14 months. Ventilation was poor. Requested fan installed in south entries. May 17th, previous orders complied with and ventilation improved. July 7th, ordered loose slate taken down on rope road and broken timbers taken out and replaced with new ones, slate cleaned up at Big South, air being choked. August 16th, ordered check door at No. 8 room on second west to conduct the air to face of rooms; and clean up fall at entrance to Big South, as ventilation was impeded. October 10th, No. 1 was found in fair condition, No. 1½, ordered door across main entry above face to shut off short circuit of air back to fan, and gave orders for management to see that hands kept door shut.

New Pittsburg No. 2.

Located at Blatchford, on the H. V. R. R. Operated by the New Pittsburg Coal Co., Columbus, O. Wm. Lanning, Jobs, O., mine boss. Drift opening, penetrating No. 6 seam of coal, 6 ft. in thickness. Pick mining; furnace ventilation; employs 24 pick miners and 2 day hands. Visited February 10th, ordered two doors put up and breakthrough cut at face of east entry. After this date they drew the entry stumps in First Hill and abandoned the mine.

New Pittsburg No. 2 1-2.

Abandoned.

New Pittsburg No. 3.

Located at Blatchford, O., on the H. V. R. R. Operated by the New Pittsburg Coal Co., Columbus, O. Wm. Bowers, Jobs, O., has supervision. Drift opening, penetrating the No. 6 seam of coal, 6 ft. thick. Pick mining; fan ventilation. employs 23 pick miners and 2 day hands. Visited August 16th, mine was idle, waiting for an electric pump. December 1st, they had installed pump and electric fan. Mine was in good condition.

New Pittsburg No. 5.

Located at Murray City, O., on the H. V. R. R. Operated by the New Pittsburg Coal Co., Columbus, O. John Slater, Murray, O., Supt. and mine boss. Slope opening, penetrating No. 6 seam of coal, 6 ft. thick. Machine mining; rope and motor haulage. Ventilated by 1 steam fan and 2 electric fans. Employs 187 loaders, 20 cutters and 74 day hands. Visited January 20th and 21st, March 29th, May 19th and 20th, July 27th and 28th, September 21st and 22nd, and December 13th and 14th. Mine was usually found in fair condition.

New Pittsburg No. 7.

Located at Murray City, O., on the H. V. R. R. Operated by the New Pittsburg Coal Co., Columbus, O. Henry Freriks, Murray, O., Supt. and mine boss.

Drift opening, penetrating No. 6 seam of coal, from 6 to 8 ft. in thickness. Ventilated by a 14 ft. steam fan and 2 electric fans. Machine mining; rope and motor haulage; employs 225 loaders, 22 cutters and 80 day hands. Visited on January 18th and 19th. There was a squeeze on 2 and 3 and 4 west on 3 north, and 2 and 3 and 4 east off 2 north, cutting that part of the mine off. Brattices were leaking on 1 and 2 east on 4 north, were ordered plastered. March 30th, ordered loose top taken down on main east, fall cleaned up and water pumped out of manway. April 22nd, was called by mine committee to look after gas well located on 1 east on 4 north. While taking this matter up with committee, received message to go to Amsterdam, where an explosion had taken place. May 2nd and 3rd, visited mine to take up complaint in regard to the gas well. The miners had held a meeting and passed a resolution not to go to work until some disinterested person had made survey and located the well. Mr. Farms, president of the mine, insisted that the Mining Department have this survey made; informed him that the Department had no engineer and no appropriation for the employment of one. Mr. Knox proposed to the committee to call a meeting that evening and he would have both sets of engineers at the meeting and they could explain how the lines were run. At the meeting the men reconsidered their former motion and went to work, Mr. Knox agreeing to fill neck near well with concrete. June 10th, mine in fair condition. August 4th and 5th, found they were running motor trips without markers; ordered them stopped until markers were placed on them, and to remove loose slate in No. 2 room on 2 west, cross-timber face of No. 2 room on 1 west; otherwise in fair condition. October 11th and 12th, ordered door on motor road kept shut so as to throw more air in pillar work in old north. November 12th, made inspection of No. 1 room on dark east, considered dangerous by committee and man who worked room. Advised the mine boss to give the man another place, which he did. December 15th and 16th, requested more air on 1 and 2 east on 3 south; check door on 2 east on 6 north; take loose slate down in No. 13 room on 4 east on 4 south. Otherwise mine was in fair condition.

New Pittsburg No. 8.

Located near Orbiston, on the H. V. R. R. Operated by the New Pittsburg Coal Co., Columbus, O. John Murphy, Supt., Wm. Sidle, mine boss, both of Nelsonville, O., were succeeded the latter part of year by Dan Shay, Supt., and Robert Eddy, mine boss, both of Nelsonville, O. Drift opening, penetrating No. 6 seam of coal from 4 to 6 ft. thick. Ventilated by steam and electric fans; machine mining; employs 175 loaders, 18 cutters and 70 day hands. Visited January 27th and 28th. Former request in regard to cement stopping on 1 north and protection of wire not complied with. Ventilation in this section was poor. Management agreed to make improvements at once. May 4th and 5th, former request complied with and mine in good condition. August 2nd and 3rd, stopped No. 11 on 1 east, where there was loose top and dangerous. Check door at pillars on dark west. Hoppers burned down and all buildings surrounding it on May 23rd and were rebuilt and mine started up; on July 23rd mine was found in fair condition. November 9th and 10th, ordered wire at heads of entries protected, breakthroughs made regular and boy 14 years of age taken out of mine. Otherwise mine was satisfactory.

New Pittsburg No. 11.

Located at Blackford, O., on the H. V. R. R. Owned by the New Pittsburg Co., operated by Davis & England, Jobs, O. Charley England, Nelsonville, O., has supervision. Drift, No. 6 seam of coal, 7 ft. thick. Pick mining; natural ventilation. Employs 15 pick miners, 2 day hands. Visited July 7th, August 16th and December 1st. Mine was closed down the forepart of the year, were drawing the entry stumps. On last visit mine was almost exhausted and stumps were being drawn near mouth of mine; found in fair condition on all three visits.

Jobs No. 1.

Located near Jobs, O., on the Brush Fork branch of the H. V. R. R. Operated by the Sunday Creek Co., Columbus, O. C. W. Farrel, Jobs, O., Supt., Arthur Stiff, Murray, O., mine boss. Drift opening, penetrating No. 6 seam of coal, from 4 to 6 ft. thick. Furnace and fan ventilation; machine and pick mining; employs 60 miners, 6 cutters and 30 day hands. Visited January 13th, mine in fair condition. May 6th, ventilation was sluggish at face of rooms No. 6 west; ordered check door on this entry to carry air to face of rooms, and stopped 1 west entry ahead of air. July 6th, ordered loose slate taken down on 1st west entry and on 2 west at No. 1 room neck, and set more posts in rock roof rooms. August 19th, requested more air at face of 1 and 2 west; shortage was due to leaking brattices, which were ordered repaired. September 19th, brattices up, two breakthroughs between Nos. 1 and 2 room on 6 west and plaster brattices in North Hill on 1 west. October 27th, investigated fatal accident of Peter Hayge, who was killed by fall of draw slate in No. 4 pillar on 2 east. Mine was usually found in fair condition.

Jobs No. 2.

Located at Jobs, O., on the Brush Fork branch of Hocking Valley R. R. Operated by the Sunday Creek Co., Columbus, O. C. W. Farrell, Jobs, O., Supt., Wm. Morgan, Murray, O., mine boss. Drift opening into No. 6 seam of coal, from 4½ to 6 ft. thick. Ventilated by two electric fans; machine and pick mining; employs 10 pick miners, 14 cutters, 130 loaders, 48 day hands. Visited January 17th, requested breakthroughs stopped between No. 2 and 3 on 12 east. Otherwise mine as seen was satisfactory. January 28th, investigated fatal accident of Geo. Shannon, who was killed by fall of slate at face of No. 15 room on 4 west, on 3 south. February 14th and 15th, on first named date made inspection of brattices surrounding the fire territory and saw no cause for alarm. On last named date made joint inspection with John L. McDonald, inspector third district, and two members of mine committee, and so far as we could see mine was as safe as had been at any time since it had been sealed. March 28th, requested lock door put on north end of 3 south rope switch and to cease putting electric wire across last breakthroughs in rooms. April 13th, 14th and 18th, opened fire zone and found no indications of any fire; the brattice was left open the remainder of the year. June 18th, requested check door at No. 18 room on 3 east, mud brattices on 3 and 4 east and 3 and 4 west on 3 south; take men out of 8 south until ventilation was restored, which would require the rebuilding of 17 brattices on the 6 east entry on 8 south. August 1st, requested they speed west fan up, put regulator on 8 south so as to force more air to second west and 1 and 2 east; otherwise satisfactory. August 23rd, investigated fatal accident of Frank Swyers, who was injured August 19th by falling off front end of motor and motor passing over his legs, and died from injuries on August 22nd. November 7th, requested loose top taken down in No. 23 on 4 east, check door on 4 east, put more air in pillar work on 12 east, on 8 south. Taking into consideration that all the coal mined in this mine this year was coal that had been around and left years ago on account of it being faulty, it was found in as good condition as could be expected.

Jobs No. 3.

Located at Jobs, O., on the H. V. R. R. Operated by the Sunday Creek Co., Columbus, O. C. W. Ferrell, Supt. and mine boss. Drift opening, penetrating No.

[illegible]

[illegible] in good condition. [illegible] the outlet. [illegible]

[illegible]

[illegible] on the H. V. R. R. Operated by [illegible] Frank Patton, Nelsonville, O., [illegible] seam of coal, from 6 to 8 [illegible] ventilation. Employs 4 cutters, 48 [illegible] was idle and in fair condition. [illegible] Hill until air shaft was sunk, not [illegible] installed. September 20th, in- [illegible] North Hill for new furnace. [illegible] Hill, door and brattice [illegible] furnace in North

Hill. Ordered door on north entry at 1 west, and make second opening in No. 1 Hill. Otherwise mine in fair condition.

Copperhead.

Located two miles east of Gore, O., on the Straitsville branch of the H. V. R. R. Operated by the Hocking Fuel Co., Columbus, O. Harry Irvin, Columbus, O., Supt. and mine boss. Machine and pick mining; fan ventilation; employs 4 cutters, 31 loaders, 6 pick miners, 13 day hands. Visited January 25th, mine was idle, took up matter of water and mud in mine; the management agreed to install an electric pump. March 11th, installed pump and siphon, but were still unable to take care of water. January 21st, mine was idle, no inspection. July 8th, mine was idle, water was under control and water-way being driven at head of 2 east. September 6th, mine was practically dry and most all mud taken out of mine, was satisfactory. November 16th, mine was found in good condition; located place at head of 2 east to move fan.

Rock Quarry.

Located one mile west of Carbon Hill, O., on the H. V. R. R. Operated by Nelsonville Coal Co., Nelsonville, O., managed by Receiver, E. D. Carr, Columbus, O. Wesley Miskell, Nelsonville, O., had supervision up to September, was then succeded by John McMillen, Nelsonville, O., Wm. Thomas, Carbon Hill, O., mine boss. Drift openings into No. 6 seam of coal, 4 ft. thick. Machine mining. Fan ventilation. Employs 100 loaders, 10 cutters, 39 day hands. Visited February 7th, mine in fair condition. March 4th, tested scales and found correct. Ordered trapper put at southwest door, repair Nos. 1 and 3, 5 and 6 brattices on 3 west; protect wire at head of all entries. June 1st, previous improvements asked for had not been made; mine in poor condition. Took the matter up with Receiver E. D. Carr. On June 6th, Mr. Carr came to mine and accompanied me through. I pointed out needed improvements to him and he ordered mine boss to put force of men at work to make them at once. July 15th, previous orders complied with; mine in fair condition. Septmber 1st, requested loose slate taken down on cut-off in south off 8 east; timber loose slate in main south; cross-cap loose slate in 6 west entry, and put trapper on 5 west door. November 11th, requested check door at No. 1 room on second south, check door between No. 1 and 2 rooms on 8 west, check air to face of rooms on 8 west cut off. Otherwise mine in fair condition.

Edgell.

Located at Sand Run, O., on the H. V. R. R. Operated by the Edgell Coal Co., Carbon Hill, O. John Carter, Nelsonville, O., Supt. and mine boss. Drift opening, into No. 6 seam of coal, 6 ft. thick. Machine mining. Furnace ventilation. Employs 7 cutters and loaders and 1 day hand. Visited January 26th, May 18th and October 27. During the year an air shaft was sunk and new furnace installed. Mine satisfactory on each visit.

Sunday Creek No. 513.

Located at Consol, O., on the Brush Fork branch of the H. V. R. R. Operated by the Green Coal Co., Nelsonville, O. Aaron Green, same place, has supervision. Drift openings into No. 6 seam of coal, 6 ft. thick. Fan and furnace ventilation. Pick mining. Employs 12 pick miners and 3 day hands. Visited March 16th, mine in fair condition. June 23rd, requested two brattices in north entries. July 29th, stopped four places in east off north; ventilation deficient. Furnace was too small to conduct air from that point; advised fan installed. September 26th, they installed fan in North Hill and furnace in East Hill. Mine in fair condition.

Esco.

Located 2½ miles northwest of Murray City, O., on the H. V. R. R. Operated by the Essex Coal Co., New Straitsville, O. Calvin Essex, New Straitsville, O., Supt. and mine boss. Drift opening, pentrating the No. 6 seam of coal, 6 ft. thick. Machine mining. Motor haulage; fan ventilation. Employs 6 cutters, 31 loaders, 14 day hands. Visited March 17th, mine was just starting to operate and were driving two face entries. June 20th, main entries had struck rock fault, which had almost cut the coal out. Requested they change electric wires to comply with law, and use brick brattices on main entries. July 29th, ordered two cross-caps at face of second east, one cross-cap at face of second west. Otherwise mine in fair condition. September 20th, north entries were just going out of fault. Mine was in good condition.

C. & H. C. & I. Co No. 15

Located at Sand Run, O., on the H. V. R. R. Operated by the Central Hocking Coal Co., Columbus, O. T. J. McLeish, Carbon Hill, O., Supt., Charles James, New Straitsville, O, mine boss. Drift opening, penetrating the No. 6 seam of coal, 6 ft. thick. Machine mining; motor haulage; fan ventilation. Employs 4 cutters, 50 loaders, 19 day hands. Visited August 17th, made partial inspection, for the purpose of finding a suitable location to place fan, and it was decided to set fan at head of 5 west entry. September 23rd, fan installed, which was giving good results Mine was in good condition. November 15th, ordered door on 6 west cut off and door on 6 west at south entry. Otherwise, mine in fair condition.

Butterfly.

Located at Payne's crossing, on the H. V. R. R. Operated by Kramer Bros., New Straitsville, O. John P. Kramer, New Straitsville, O., has supervision. Drift opening into the No. 6 seam of coal, 6 ft. thick. Pick mining; employs 2 miners. Visited August 29th, mine was satisfactory.

Diamond Clay.

Located near Haydenville, O., on the H. V. R. R. Operated by the Diamond Clay Co., Nelsonville, O. John Rhutter, Nelsonville, O., Supt., E. Campbell, same place, mine boss. Drift opening. Employs 1 diggers and 1 day hand. Visited December 5th, mine was satisfactory

---

MEIGS COUNTY.

Log-n.

Located at Pomeroy, O Operated by Martin Ebersbach, Pomeroy, O. George Ebersbach, Supt., Walter Ebersbach, mine boss, both of Pomeroy, O. Machine mining. Natural ventilation Employs 2 cutters, 5 loaders and 3 day hands. Visited March 8th and October 19th, mine in fair condition.

Red Bird.

Located near Silver Run, on the H. V. R. R. Operated by the Pomeroy Fuel Co., Columbus, O J. E. Dorsey, Middleport, O., Supt. and mine boss. Drift opening, penetrating the No. 8 seam of coal, 4½ ft. thick. Fan ventilation. Machine mining. Employs 6 cutters, 26 loaders and 10 day hands. Visited March 2nd, requested wire protected at head of 1 west entry, cut breakthroughs in No. 8 and 9 rooms on second west; put brick brattices in north entries. June 20th, they installed electric fan. Mine was satisfactory. October 6th requested more timber set in rooms, otherwise mine was satisfactory. December 29th, they were opening the third hill and sunk shaft; will install furnace at once. Requested they stop main entry until dark is driven up in breakthrough made, cut breakthrough in 4th west entry: check door on second east. Otherwise mine in fair condition.

Rockville No. 2, Kings & Buckeye Splint, North Hill.

Remained suspended the entire year.

Maynard No. 1.

Located at Rutland, O., on the K. & M. R. R. Operated by the Maynard Coal Co., Columbus, O. Wm. Williams, Rutland, O., Supt., John True, same place, mine boss. Drift opening, penetrating No. 8 seam of coal, 5 ft. thick. Fan ventilation. Machine mining. Employs 12 cutters, 95 loaders and 37 day hands. Visited February 17th, investigated fatal accident to Clem McFarland. Advised safety switch placed at top and bottom of incline. March 23rd, ordered loose top taken down on motor road and in manway, and on 8th and 11 west entries, where marked. June 30th, ordered breakthroughs cut in Nos. 1, 6, 7, 8, 9 and 10 rooms on 9 east, timber loose slate in No. 18 room on 9 east, see that timbering in rooms is set in more practical way throughout mine August 11th, requested loose top taken down on 8 west and 9 east; put check door on 8 east. Otherwise mine in fair condition. September 15th, investigated fatal accident of Roy Rupe, who was killed by fall of top coal at face of No. 26 room on 8 east. November 3rd, check air to face of rooms on 8 east. Otherwise mine in fair condition.

Maynard No. 2.

Located three miles north of Middleport, O., on K. & M. R. R. Operated by Maynard Coal Co., Columbus, O. Wm. Williams, Rutland, O., Supt., Dayton Thomas, Pomeroy, O., mine boss, up to October, was then succeeded by G. W. Miller, Pomeroy, O. Drift opening, pentrating No. 8 seam of coal, 4½ ft. thick. Fan ventilation. Machine mining; motor and mule haulage. Employs 10 cutters, 65 loaders and 35 day hands. Visited February 1st and March 24th, mine was in fair condition on both visits. July 19th, they had made new second opening and had new wires from No. 1 mine into this mine; requested same be changed to comply with the law; otherwise, mine in fair condition. October 5th, ventilation was poor all over mine, due to leaky and decayed brattices and doors. Ordered force put on at night to plaster brattices and repair doors. December 21st, stopped three places in dark south up the limit, check door at 1 place working on main south to force air to face of working places; reduce men in this section of mine to suit air conditions: check door at No. 2 room on 1 north; double shift breakthrough from No. 2 on 1 north to 5th west entry; double shift air course at head of 1st north. Otherwise mine was satisfactory. December 30th, investigated fatal accident of Levi Dodson.

Dabney.

Located between Middleport and Pomeroy, O., on the H. V. R. R. Operated by T. W. Jones, Middleport, O., T. W. Jones, Middleport, O., Supt., Adam Scholl, Pomeroy, O., mine boss. Drift openings, penetrating the No. 8 seam of coal, 5 ft thick. Pick mining. Furnace ventilation. Employs 11 pick miners, 6 day hands.

Visited February 18th, requested breakthrough cut in 1st 5 rooms working on 1 east; loose slate taken down on 1st east entry. July 22nd, ordered loose slate removed on sides in second hill; clean up slate on escapement way; repair trestle between 2 and 3 hill, and see that furnace has more attention. October 21st, mine in fair condition.

Rolling Mill.

Located at Pomeroy, O., on the H. V. R. R .Operated by Martin Ebersbach, Pomeroy, O. Wm. Ebersbach, Pomeroy, O., Supt. and mine boss. Drift opening, penetrating No. 8 seam of coal, 4½ ft. thick. Double entry system. Fan ventilation. Machine mining; motor and mule haulage. Employs, on last visit, 92 loaders, 10 cutters and 32 day hands. Visited on August 9th, the mine had just started up, after an idleness of 5 or 6 months. They purchased a tract of coal laying next to face of north entry, were driving nothing but entries on this visit, and was found satisfactory October 19th, changes were being made at power house and power was poor, ordered fan speeded up; brattices on north entry were leaking; ordered them cemented at once. Otherwise mine was in fair condition.

Ohio River Coal Co. Nos. 1. and 3.

Located at Pomeroy, O., on the H. V. R. R. Operated by the Ohio River Coal Co., Columbus, O. Wm. Kauff, Middleport, O.. Supt. and mine boss. Drift openings, penetrating No. 8 seam of coal, 5 ft. thick. Fan and natural ventilation. Pick mining. Employs 30 pick miners and 8 day hands. Visited February 3rd; mine in good condition. May 12th, had put basket in shaft, in No. 1 hill, which gave poor results; ventilation was poor. August 12th, ventilation was still poor in No. 1 hill; gave the management two weeks to install fan at mouth of mine. September 16th, fan installed, which gave good results. Mine in good condition. December 23rd, mines were in good condition.

Noble Summit.

Located 3 miles north of Middleport, O., on K. & M. R. R. Operated by the Noble Summit Coal Co., Middleport, O. John Kauff, Middleport, O., Supt. and mine boss, up to April 1st, was succeeded by C. M. Hennesy, Supt., Millard Zerkle, mine boss, both of Middleport, O. Drift opening, penetrating No. 8 seam of coal, 5 ft. thick. Double entry system. Pick mining. Furnace ventilation. Employs 34 pick miners and 7 day hands. Visited February 1st, ordered check door between first two rooms, working on 2 east, leakage stopped around door on second opening. December 21st mine had closed down on March 15th and was allowed to fill up with water, starting a squeeze, which closed the two entries up They took up the bottom in first east and started mine October 15th. Stopped 1 and 2 south entries until breakthrough was completed. Otherwise mine was in fair condition.

Charter Oak.

Located at Pomeroy, O., transportation Ohio River and H. V. R. R. Operated by the Peacock Coal Co.. Pomeroy, O. Fred Ebersbach, Pomeroy, O., Supt., Wm. Ebersbach, same place, mine boss up to about August 1st was then succeeded by H. V. Carl, Pomeroy, O. Drift opening, penetrating No. 8 seam of coal, 4 ft. thick. Double entry system. Coal is mined and hauled by electric power and ventilated by electric fans. Employs 24 cutters, 155 loaders and 80 day hands. Visited February 2nd and 3rd, found they had a squeeze on 12 and 13 and 14 west, which was affecting the ventilation somewhat; ordered doors reversed to meet new conditions on west side. March 3rd, investigated fatal accident of Fred Smith, miner, who was burned February 28th in jaws of No. 22 room on 16th west by igniting a keg of powder on his lap from spark off lamp on his head and died March 1st. March 8th, investigated fatal accident of Jacob Durst, day hand, who was caught by fall of roof on motor switch, while taking timbers out to pull loose slate on March 4th. June 28th and 29th, requested check door on 7 east; open break-through in No. 8 room on 9th east choked, and make manholes larger on motor road and whitewash same. Made trip through dark north entry, which was in poor condition and not safe for men to travel. The top had fallen from 9 west to 15th, and many places entry was almost closed. Requested air shaft sunk at head of 18th west, or clean up dark north entry from 9th west to 18th west, which they agreed to do. September 14th and 15th, ventilation was choked on west side in the squeeze territory; requested two brattices torn down on dark north, where there is a switch to store mixed coal, and build two cement brattices between main and dark north, which would give them the dark norrn as well as rooms through territory affected by the squeeze for return air way, which would relieve the choke to some extent. Ordered cement brattices built in jaws ot 11th, 12th, 13th and 14th west entries. December 28th, shaft sunk to coal, but entry lacks about 40 ft. of being to shaft, which was ordered double shifted. Ordered check door on 10 east. Ventilation was weak all over mine, due to choke on return air way; other conditions, as seen, were fair.

Pittsburg.

Located at Minersville, O., transportation, Ohio River and H. V. R. R. W. H. Miller, Pomeroy, O., Supt., Earl Ewing, Syracuse O., mine boss. Drift opening, penetrating No. 8 seam of coal, 4½ ft. thick. Double entry system. Fan ventilation. Coal is hauled and mined by electric power. Employs 16 cutters, 90 loaders and 30 day hands. Visited March 1st, ordered dust loaded out of rooms, loose slate taken down on 5 west entry, wire protected at head of north and main east, and trapper placed on 5 east door. May 11th and 12th, tested scales and found correct. Requested shaft sunk at head of main east for escapement way and release choke on ventilation. July 21st, considerable loose slate was found through the working places on this visit, which was ordered taken care of at once; otherwise mine in fair condition. October 20th, tested scales, which were found correct. Force was at work sinking shaft, and an 18-in. hole has been drilled from surface to inside of mine and all the slate and rock is handled from shaft on inside of mine through this hole. Mine was in fair condition.

Silver Run.

Located at Silver Run, O., on the H. V. R. R. Operated by the Silver Run Coal Co., Middleport, O. W. C. Russell, Middleport, O., Supt., John E. Reese same place, mine boss. Drift opening, penetrating No. 8 seam of coal 4½ ft thick. Double entry system. Ventilated by two electric fans. Machine mining employs 4 cutters, 25 loaders and 12 day hands. Visited March 2nd, May 10th, August 10th and 17th. Mine was usually found in fair condition. December 22nd, investigated fatal accident of Simon P. Farley, who was killed at face of 1 west entry in 3 hill by fall of bastard coal. On December 21st and 28th, requested air checked to face of No. 15 room on 2 west and see that timbering was done in a more practical way; otherwise satisfactory.

Hobson.

Located near Hobson railroad yards, on the K. & M. R. R. Operated by Pomeroy Coal Co., Little Washington, Pa. George Jenkins, Supt., T. A. Harly, mine boss, both of Middleport, O., up to April, was then succeeded by Jos. McGill,

Middleport, O., who had full supervision. Drift opening into No. 8 seam of coal. 4½ ft. thick. Double entry system. Fan ventilation. Machine mining; motor and mule haulage. Employs 6 cutters, 35 loaders and 20 day hands. Visited February 11th, investigated fatal accident of James France, who was killed in No. 1 room neck on 6 north by fall of draw slate, place was 7 ft. wide; requested No. 2 room on 2 south stopped on account of being ahead of air and wire protected at heads of entries. Visited March 9th, May 13th, July 20th, August 10th, October 7th and December 30th. The top in this mine is very poor, from 2 to 3 ft. is taken down in most all places in the mine. Hills are narrow, making it impossible to work the mine with any system. Slate is continually falling, which makes it impossible to keep electric wire hung to comply with the law. Air courses are usually found full of falls of slate, which keeps a choke on the ventilation. Some insulated wire is being used which is giving good results; are driving place on south and one on north to outside for inlet and outlet of air; when completed all old works can be cut out behind those points; under these conditions, the mine has not been found in very good condition.

Thomas Shaft.

Located on Ohio River, near Racine, O. Transportation, electric railway and H. V. R. R. Operated by Thomas Coal Co., Racine, O. J. W. Thomas, Supt., David Lawson, mine boss, both of Racine, O. Shaft opening, 112 ft. deep, penetrating the No. 8 seam of coal, 4 ft. 8 in. thick. Double entry system. Machine mining; fan ventilation. Employs 2 cutters, 13 loaders and 5 day hands. Visited March 25th, requested fan installed and stairway built in second opening and partition in shaft. August 9th, former request complied with, mine in good condition. November 4th, mine in fair condition.

Schlaegel.

Located at Pomeroy, O. Operated by the Schlaegel Salt Co., Pomeroy, O. George Gress, Mason City, W. Va., Supt., George Olinger, Pomeroy, O., mine boss. Drift opening into No. 8 seam of coal, 5 ft. thick. Coal is mined with pick, and consumed at salt plant Employ 15 pick miners and 4 day hands. Visited February 4th and July 1st. On last named date requested broken timbers replaced in second hill with new ones, and brush top and sides in same hill. The management claimed he was not able to make needed repairs and closed mine down, which has been suspended since that date.

Headley.

Located near Middleport, O. Operated by John Headley, Middleport, O., who is superintendent and mine boss. Drift opening into No. 8 seam of coal, 4½ ft. thick. Pick mining. Furnace ventilation. Employs 6 miners, 1 day hand and 2 teamsters. Coal is mostly consumed at brick plant. Visited October 18th, mine in fair condition

---

SMALL MINES VISITED.

Scotts.

Located at Pomeroy, O. Operated by Henesy & Sauer, Pomeroy, O. Employs 8 miners and 2 day hands.

Ficks.

Operated by Philip Fick, Pomeroy, O. Employs 6 miners, 2 teamsters.

Albert Frazier, Carlton, O.	4 miners
Charley Dixon, Middleport, O.	4 miners
Charley Densmore, Middleport, O.	2 miners
James Saulsberry, Middleport, O.	3 miners
Jack Grogan, Middleport, O.	2 miners
Hordon Bros., Middleport, O.	2 miners
James Russell, Middleport, O.	2 miners
Dave Owens, Middleport, O.	2 miners
George Lewis, Pomeroy, O.	6 miners
Richland Needs, Pomeroy, O.	2 miners
Edward Weeks, Pomeroy, O.	2 miners
August Voss, Pomeroy, O.	4 miners
James Roush, Pomeroy, O.	3 miners
Lawrence Guinther, Pomeroy, O.	2 miners
Marion Boss, Pomeroy, O.	2 miners
John Fohmer & Sons, Pomeroy, O.	3 miners
George Baer, Minersville, O.	5 miners

VINTON COUNTY.

Note.

Mines covered by this report will date from January 1, 1910, to July 18, 1910.

Alma Cement Limestone Mines, Nos. 1 and 2, and 51, 52, 55, 56 and 57 suspended.

Alma Coal, located at Oreton, suspended.

Mohr-Minton No. 4.

Located 2 miles from McArthur, O., on the H. V. R. R. Operated by Busner Coal Co., Cleveland, O. J. M. Moor, McArthur, O., Supt., Wm. Crow, Elk Fork, O., mine boss. Drift opening into No. 3 seam of coal, 5 ft. thick. Double entry system. Fan ventilation. Pick mining. Employs 17 miners and 7 day hands. Visited March 22nd, mine was starting up on this date, had been idle for 3 months. Ventilation was weak, due to mine being idle so long and decayed and settled condition of brattices all over mine, which were ordered repaired at once. Mine closed down a few days after my visit and was suspended balance of year.

Mohr-Minton No. 3 and Mohr-Minton Clay suspended the entire year.

Elk Fork.

Located at Elk Fork, O., on H. V. R. R. Operated by Elk Fork Coal Co., Elk Fork, O. Shaft opening, 95 ft. deep, penetrating No. 2 seam of coal, 30 inches thick. Double entry system. Machine and pick mining. Fan ventilation. Employs 14 pick miners, 2 cutters, 4 loaders and 15 day hands. Visited January 31st, ordered check door between No. 2 and 3 room on 7 west on north; brattices built on 8 west and 8 east, face cleaned up on 8 west, which impeded and choked ventilation, and to send men through dark south and north to level falls of slate where air was choked. July 11th and 12th, found buildings between boiler house and shaft not in compliance with law. Called Chief Inspector Harrison and Inspector Burke to mine for consultation; after viewing the situation it was agreed that the matter be taken up at Nelsonville, with Inspectors Hill and McDonald. July 18th, made inspection, with John Burke, Inspector from 1st District; requested that blacksmith shop and part of building in which the hoisting engine is located be moved from between the boiler house and shaft, a pipe line, with hose attached, placed to top of tower of hoppers; also pipe line, with hose attached, kept at boiler house, and to remove wooden structure from around fan and replace with an inflammable structure; also to place ladder in fan shaft, with three resting places to make it an escapement way. Ordered a loose piece of slate taken down on 5th west entry, door erected on south side of fan shaft to produce more air on north side. Found a force of men cleaning up the escapement way on north side of shaft. The south side was not working. W. P. Porter, Wellston, O., Superintendent, John Foit, Elk Fork, mine boss.

Tompkins No. 1.

Located at Minerton, O., on H. V. R. R. Operated by Fobes-Tompkins Coal Co., Columbus, O. James Murphy, Minerton, O., has supervision. Drift opening into No. 4 seam of coal, 4 ft. thick. Double entry system. Fan ventilation. Pick mining. Employs 35 pick miners and 10 day hands. Visited February 17th, mine had been idle for one year and was just starting up, found in fair condition. June 27th, ordered door on west repaired, two test weights provided; also stretchers and blankets kept on hand, and a new second opening made through county mine; otherwise satisfactory.

Clarion.

Located at Clarion, O., on H. V. R. R. Operated by S. S. McDonald, Columbus, O. W. G. Bennet, Clarion, O., has supervision. Drift opening into No. 4 seam of coal, 4 ft. thick. Double entry system. Machine mining. Fan ventilation. Employs 6 cutters, 44 loaders, 18 day hands. Visited February 24th, requested three machines stopped until they were lawfully shielded; open breakthrough at face of rooms; make breakthroughs larger in 24 and 25 rooms on 6 east; finish breakthrough between 26 and 27 rooms on 6 east; check door on 6 west and one on 5 east; wire placed on suitable insulators all over mine, and same protected with boards; repair doors on cut off on 6 east; plaster brattices between 5th and 6th east. March 4th, improvements asked for on previous visits made, except some little wire not protected; ordered same done at once. May 24th, requested brick brattices on north entry from mouth of mine to 6th east entry; otherwise in fair condition.

Raccoon Valley.

Located at Minerton, O., on H. V. R. R. Operated by John L. Lawler, Columbus, O., who is Superintendent., John W. Lawler, Minerton, O., mine boss. Drift opening into No. 4 seam of coal, 4 ft. thick. Double entry system. Machine mining. Fan ventilation. Employs 4 cutters, 25 loaders and 8 day hands. Visited May 9th, requested they open ditch in mouth of mine; build two brick brattices in north entry and tighten belt on fan. Otherwise mine was satisfactory.

Puritan.

Located two miles east of Hamden, O., on H. V. R. R. Operated by the Puritan Brick and Cement Co., Hamden Junction, O. Harry Cole, Supt., C. S. Cunningham, mine boss, both of Hamden Junction, O. Drift opening into No. 4 seam of coal, 4 ft. thick. Double entry system. Pick mining. Fan ventilation. Employs 19 pick miners and 4 day hands. The product of mine is consumed at plant. Visited February 28th and May 25th, mine found in good condition on both visits.

Star No. 2.

Located at Hawks Station, O., on H. V. R. R. Operated by A. C. Tipton, Logan, O., David Eberst, Oreton, O., has supervision. Drift opening into No. 4 seam of coal, 4 ft. thick. Single entry system. Pick mining. Furnace ventilation. Employs 12 pick miners and 5 day hands. Visited February 25th, mine had been idle a year and was just starting up. Requested new door at mouth of mine and door repaired at air shaft. Otherwise mine was satisfactory.

Brick Yard.

Located near McArthur, O., on H. V. R. R. Operated by Bolar & Irvin, McArthur, O. F. E. Bolar, McArthur, O., has supervision. Drift opening into No. 4 seam of coal, 4 ft. thick. Double entry system. Furnace ventilation. Employs 19 pick miners and 3 day hands. Visited March 22nd., requested they open ditch in mouth of mine; put more grate bars in furnace; raise stack 8 or 10 feet on furnace; repair door on east and remove mud from mine. May 23rd, requested loose slate taken down in No. 1 and 6 rooms, on 1st north, put check doors on Nos. 1 and 2 north entries. Outside of mud and water, was satisfactory.

Raccoon Valley Nos. 1, 2 and 3, suspended the entire time covered by this report.

Inghams, or Valley Coal Co., suspended the entire time covered by this report.

GALLIA COUNTY.

Swan Creek.

Located 12 miles below Gallipolis, O., on the Ohio River. Operated by John Scherschel, Bladen, O. Employs 3 diggers and one day hand.

Mayflower.

Located 10 miles below Gallipolis, O., on the Ohio River. Operated by the Indian Guyan Coal Co., Napoleon, O. A. L. Sheldon, Middleport, O., has supervision. Drift opening into No. 7 seam of coal, 6 ft. thick. Visited September 13th. This is a new mine. The tipple is not yet in operation at the river, nor at the mine. Grade has not been made from river up to mine, which is about three-fourths of a mile. Railroad ties are on the ground and portion of rails. Closed down on July 30th, for some unknown cause. Mine was full of water and no inspection made. .

Carl Nos. 1 and 2.

Located at Carlton, O., on H. V. R. R. Operated by the Riverside Coal Co., Carlton, O. W. D. Edwards, Carlton, O., Supt., C. M. Little, same place, mine boss. Drift opening into No. 7 seam of coal, 4 ft. thick. Furnace ventilation. Employs, the latter part of year, 26 pick miners and 11 day hands. Visited March 9th, requested air checked to face of last rooms on 1 east in No. 2 hill; furnace installed in No. 1 hill at once. Otherwise mine was satisfactory. May 10th, mine was satisfactory. October 6th, the property was taken over by the

Carbon Hill Coal Co., Columbus, O. J. W. Miskell, Supt., James Thomas, mine boss, both of Carlton, O. Mine was idle. This company has cleaned up the mine and it was found in good condition.

Summers.

Small house coal mine, located on the Indian Guyan Coal Company's property. Operated by J. H. Summers, Gallipolis, O., who had full supervision. Employed 4 miners. This was a new mine and had only been developed 17 ft. from mouth. Visited October 31st and November 1st, to investigate fatal accident of Mathew F. Hazelett, who was killed on October 27th, by fall of roof. Found mouth of mine very poorly timbered; only two sets of timbers being set in mine and they were very poorly constructed, and no suitable timber on hand. November 17th and 18th served affidavit for John H. Summers, owner and manager of mine, for not supplying a sufficient amount of suitable timber, who plead guilty in Squire Bradbury's court, at Gallipolis, on November 18th and was fined $10.00 and cost.

SMALL MINES.

John Scott, Cheshire, O.	2 miners.
Orestis Roush, Cheshire, O.	3 miners.
Elzy Mullford, Cheshire, O.	1 miner.
Scott & Jacobs, Cheshire, O.	2 miners.
Howard Shuler, Cheshire, O.	2 miners.
Alex Scott, Cheshire, O.	3 miners.
Ellis Rife, Cheshire, O.	1 miner.
Miss Virginia E. Myers, Gallipolis, O.	3 miners.
Peter Brechtel, Middleport, O.	3 miners.

ATHENS COUNTY.

NOTE: — Mines covered by this report will date from July 13th to December 31st, 1910.

New York No. 31.

Located near Buchtel, O., on the H. V. R. R. Operated by the New York Coal Co., Columbus, O. P. C. Morris, Nelsonville, O., Supt., E. G. Woody, same place, mine boss. Drift opening, penetrating the No. 6 seam of coal, 6 ft. thick. Double entry system. Fan ventilation. Coal is mined and hauled by electric power. Employs 20 cutters, 194 loaders and 91 day hands. Visited July 13th, with Inspector McDonald. Requested breakthroughs cut in Nos. 11, 12, 13 and 14 rooms on 6 east north up the limit. Nos. 1 and 2 rooms stopped on 5 west on north, which men had driven up to the limit; otherwise mine in fair condition. July 16th, investigated fatal accident of Herman Kemnitz, who was injured at face of No. 19 room on 6 east by a fall of cannel coal on July 14th and died July 15th. September 7th and 8th, ordered air checked to face of rooms on 1, 2, 3 and 4 east on 4 north; build brattices in jaws of 2 east on No. 2 north, so as to throw more air in 3rd and 4th west on 3rd north. December 7th, check air to face of rooms on 5th and 6th east on second north; see that dust is loaded out cleaner; double shift second west on 3rd south so as to break it through for traveling way for that section of mine. Otherwise mine in fair condition.

THIRD DISTRICT.

JOHN L. McDONALD.

COMPOSED OF ATHENS COUNTY.

HON. GEO. HARRISON, *Chief Inspector of Mines, Columbus, Ohio*

DEAR SIR:—I herewith submit the annual report of the Third Mining District of Ohio, for the year beginning January 1, 1910, and ending December 31, 1910.

The district is composed of Athens County, the mines are operated in the number 6, 7 and 8 seams of coal, the number 6 varying from 4 to 6½ ft. in thickness, consisting in the main of shaft mining, at a depth of from 80 to 450 ft., has formerly been overlayed with a splint coal top, but has been gradually developing into a very bad white slate top, which is full of slips and joints, rendering the occupation of the miner more hazardous, and great vigilance will have to be exercised on the part of both miner and the management, and with an increased cost of mining, to be mined with any reasonable degree of safety. The No. 7 seam is about 4 ft. in thickness, and is being developed mainly in Trimble township, on the Hocking Valley side, where it is mined in the hill tops. Two new mines have been opened in the No. 7 seam during the year, operations being comparatively small as compared with the No. 6 seam. The No. 8 seam is not very extensively worked, on account of poor transportation and a large amount of refuse found in the vein. This seam is from 5 to 9 ft. in thickness, separated with a natural strata of 15 inches of slate in the middle, and a large amount of other impurities. The mines, with the exception of a few small ones, are equipped with electric mining machinery. Rope and motor haulage, with large steam driven fans, are installed at most of the mines, with sufficient capacity to produce the required amount of ventilation, and is well distributed into the inner sections, when brick or substantial material is used for that purpose, except in mines which are rapidly being exhausted.

Three mines were indefinitely abandoned, 3 remained suspended the entire year, 2 small mines were closed down the latter part of the year, on account of financial failure.

The provision of the new code requiring an additional traveling way has been a marked improvement to the ventilation, as it provides two ways to be kept open from the interior to the openings. Very little opposition was encountered in order to secure the enforcement of the new code, which went into effect June 11th; a majority of the owners readily complied, and their management gave every assistance in maintaining a rigid enforcement, for which they are to be commended.

Central openings were made into the interior workings, for ready escape in case of an emergency, in the most extensive mines. Recording pressure gauges were provided at all mines generating fire damp, and daily records kept of the air pressure; also test weights on the tipple to test the weigh scales.

The coal trade has been exceptionally good during the year, the mines worked a little better than two-thirds time, compared with less than one-half time any previous year, notwithstanding they were all idle during the month of April, while a wage scale was being adjusted; only minor troubles of local importance disturbed the operations and they were quickly disposed of. In all, the year has been a prosperous one.

It is to be regretted that I am compelled to report 9 fatal accidents to our fellow craftsmen: 2 by fall of slate in Sunday Creek Mine No. 201; one by fall of slate in Juniper No. 1; one by fall of slate in New Pittsburg No. 9; one by fall of slate in Northern Fuel No. 24; one by fall of coal in Lubrig No. 3, one by fall of coal in Juniper No. 2; one by colliding with a trip of cars in Sunday Creek No. 256; making a total of six by fall of slate, two by fall of coal and one by colliding with mine cars, a more complete report of which will appear in another part of the annual report. No explosions of gas occurred during the year. One mine fire which broke out in Sunday Creek mine

No. 209, on March 9th, from a shot in the coal, which ignited a feeder of gas, at the face of 3rd east, at quitting time, and was not discovered until about three hours later ,by the night man, and was then beyond his control. The officials of the mine were notified, but when they arrived on the scene the fire was beyond all control. They proceeded to confine the fire to a small space by sealing it, when an explosion occurred, apparently at the bottom of the up cast shaft, about 3000 ft. from where the fire originated; the gases from the fire had gathered at the outlet and were ignited by the trolley wheel at that point, while supplies were being taken into the mine. There is no doubt in my mind, but what the explosion originated at or near the outlet, as the force of it damaged the fan and main shaft to some extent. The persons who were near the fire at the time, say it was very indistinct; this placed a fear on some of the persons in charge and they were advised by the chief engineer to seal the shafts. Two months later the seal was removed and the fan operated about eight hours, there being no signs of any fumes in the return air; with a party of the Company's officials we entered the mine to close first west door; before reaching that point there was a reaction in the current, indicating a light explosion, or a large fall. The following morning, there being no fumes or signs of fire at the outlet of air, we again entered the mine and reached the main south within 1000 ft. of where the fire started, and found black smoke coming slowly out of the fire district. Mr. Monsarrat, manager of mines, advised that the shafts again be sealed. Two months later, they were opened and the seal placed inside of main south entry, reducing the fire district to about three acres; the enclosure generated gas until the pressure became so great that the gas oozed through under the walls into the mine. I advised that a drill hole be sunk into the enclosure from the surface, but instead a 3 inch pipe line inserted into the seal at the top, running to the surface was installed, which answered the purpose, releasing the pressure to the surface. December 10th, the seal was removed and the fire was found entirely extinguished; it had scarcely burned into solid coal, which indicated that very little air had made its way to the fire to support combustion. We are pleased to compliment the management and those in charge for the effective way in which the matter was handled.

In conclusion I desire to state that my relations with both miners and operators have been of the most pleasant character, and the assistance of both in securing better conditions around the mines is fully appreciated. In addition I desire to thank you for the valuable and timely advice given at all times during the year, and for the many courtesies shown by yourself and members of the Department.

Very respectfully,

JNO. L. MCDONALD,
Inspector 3rd District.

December 31st, 1910.

ATHENS COUNTY.

New Pittsburg No. 9.

Situated one mile southwest of Chauncey, Ohio, on the H. V. R. R. Operated by the New Pittsburg Coal Co., Columbus, Ohio. M. M. Kassler, Nelsonville, O., Dist. Supt.; George Butts, same place, mine foreman; Charles Walters, assistant. Shaft opening, 102 ft. in depth; No. 6 seam; 6 ft. thick; equipped with electric power; machine mining; motor haulage; fan ventilation; 208 loaders, 20 machine men, 53 day men, employed. February 26th, found mine in good condition. July 8th, requested door placed between 3 and 4, east north, and fine coal removed from the tracks; also breakthroughs between rooms kept free from obstructions; otherwise conditions satisfactory. October 4th in good condition. December 22nd was called to investigate the death of William Wearn, who was injured December 15th at the face of No. 3 room, on 6th west entry, by fall of slate; died December 20th; his foot was badly injured. blood poison set in. Made partial inspection of mine, conditions found good.

New Pittsburg No. 10.

Situated 3 miles north of Athens, Ohio, on the H. V. R. R. Operated by the New Pittsburg Coal Co., Columbus, Ohio. M. M. Kassler, Nelsonville, O., Dist. Supt.; Joseph Slater, Athens, O., mine forman; Fred Slater, same place, assistant. Shaft opening, 187 ft. in depth; No. 6 seam: 4 to 6 ft. thick; double and triple entry system: equipped with electric power: machine mining: motor haulage: fan ventilation; 149 loaders, 14 machine men, 63 day men, employed. January 26th, in good condition. June 9th, requested that doors be repaired so they would close of their own accord; also requested doors placed on the outside end of motor switches. August 24th, visited mine, in company with Chief Inspector Harrison, to examine cages, on which a rack is used while lowering and hoisting men; a more substantial arrangement was advised to be used instead of the rack. October 14th, conditions satisfactory, except the cages were not equipped with the safety appliances on the sides, as requested on my former visit.

Sunday Creek No. 10.

Situated two miles west of Glouster, Ohio, on the K. & M. R. R. Operated by the Sunday Creek Co., Columbus, O. D. H. Williams, Glouster, O., Dist. Supt.: J. F. Roberts, Derthic, O., mine foreman; Walter Hayden, same place, assistant. Shaft opening, 110 ft. in depth; No. 6 seam; 6 ft. thick; double entry system; equipped with electric power; machine mining; motor haulage; fan ventilation; 198 loaders, 22 machine men, 70 day men, employed. February 27th, the management was advised to investigate the speed with which the man trip was run, while taking the men in before starting time, and to prevent men from congregating on the switches; also see that miners timbered better; otherwise conditions were satisfactory. May 4th, in good condition. July 22nd, requested that stoppings be repaired on south side, which is not in actual course of working, and to place brick stoppings between 5 and 6 north; mine generally in good order. October 17th, advised that loose top, at bottom of stairway, be taken down or securely timbered, also refuge holes made on motor pass switch; otherwise conditions satisfactory.

D. S. Weitzell, district superintendent, resigned; succeeded by Harry Kelley.

Sunday Creek No. 10 X.

Situated near Orbiston, Ohio, on the H. V. R. R. Slope opening; No. 6 seam. Harry Kelley, Supt.; Nelsonville, O.; Wm. Berwell, Glouster, O., (R. D. No. 5), mine foreman; C. C. Garlic, Orbiston, assistant. Double entry system; equipped with electric power; motor haulage; fan ventilation; 200 loaders, 18 machine men, 54 day men. March 1st, east side in fair condition, except ventilation; advised that the stoppings be repaired, and brick, or substantial material, used between 1 and 2 east; also an escapement way made. July 7th, ventilation improved; mine generally in fair order; an opening has been made to the adjacent mine, New Pittsburg No. 5. This mine was assigned to Mr. Kennedy of second district.

Sunday Creek No. 201.

Situated at Floodwood, Ohio, on the H. V. R. R. Operated by the Sunday Creek Co., Columbus, O. Harry Kelley, Dist. Supt.; Asa Hammond, mine foreman, resigned, succeeded by D. L. Nutter, resigned, succeeded by Chas. Monks; Matt Bradenburg, assistant, all of Nelsonville, O. Shaft opening, 90 ft. in depth; No. 6 seam; 6 ft. thick; double entry system; equipped with electric power; machine mining; motor haulage; fan ventilation; 150 loaders, 14 machine men, 56 day men. March 8th, in good condition. July 12th, inspected by Mr. Hill of the Fourth district. October 13th, in good condition. October 26th, was called to investigate the cause of the death of Clarence and Walter Beal, brothers, who were instantly killed by a fall of slate at the face of 1st east entry.

December 30th, visited mine in company with Mr. Kelley, district supt., in regard to top on east side, which is very bad and which will require close attention on part of both miner and management; they were requested to do so.

Mr. D. L. Nutter, mine foreman, was found under the influence of liquor, reported to the Mayor of Nelsonville, and was fined $10 and costs.

Sunday Creek No. 203.

Situated near Old Floodwood, on the H. V. R. R. Operated by the Sunday Creek Co., Columbus, O. Harry Kelley, Nelsonville, O., Dist. Supt.; Frank Murphy, same place, mine foreman. Drift opening; No. 6 seam; 6 ft. thick; equipped with electric power; all pillar work; machine and pick mining; motor haulage; fan ventilation; 30 loaders, 21 pick men, 6 machine men, 30 day men. March 8th, made partial inspection, ventilation fair and, generally, conditions as good as could be expected, as the mine is being rapidly exhausted; room No. 19 on 10 west, stopped on account of being ahead of air. June 2nd and September 20th, conditions satisfactory, except ventilation, which is becoming deficient on account of location of fan; preparations are being made to install a larger steam driven fan, as requested on former visit. December 22nd, found fan installed and giving good results. Mine generally in fair order.

Sunday Creek No. 204.

Situated near Kimberly, on the H. V. R. R. Operated by the Sunday Creek Co., Columbus, O. Harry Kelley, Nelsonville, O., Dist. Supt.; Joe Barber, same place, mine foreman; resigned December 15th, succeeded by Asa Hammond, Nelsonville, O. Drift opening; No. 6 seam; 6 ft. thick; double entry system; equipped with electric power; machine mining; motor and rope haulage; fan ventilation; 160 loaders, 16 machine men, 75 day men, employed. March 3rd and October 6th, found in good condition. July 13th, inspected by Mr. Hill of 4th district. December 9th, tested scales on request of miners, found correct and in good condition.

Sunday Creek No. 209.

Situated on Sugar Creek, about 4 miles north of Athens, Ohio, on the H. V. R. R. Operated by the Sunday Creek Co., Columbus, O. Field Scott, Athens, O., Supt.; Wm. Altman, same place, mine foreman. Shaft opening, 260 ft. in depth; No. 6 seam; 4 to 6 ft. thick; double and triple entry system; equipped with electric power; machine mining; motor haulage; fan ventilation; 145 loaders, 12 machine men, 53 day men, employed. January 25th, in good condition; requested that check be placed on 4 east to ventilate cut-off properly. March 10th, visited mine on account of fire, which started at the face of 3rd east entry, main south, from a shot that was fired at quitting time the day previous; found the mine sealed. May 12, 13 and 14th, visited the mine, when the seal was removed, signs of fire was found and the mine was again sealed. August 11th, made inspection on account of the seal having been removed, July 12th, and placed inside of main south entry, confining the fire district to about 3 acres, and they were preparing to operate the other sections of the mine; found the fire district sealed with 4 good substantial brick and cement stoppings; conditions throughout the rest of the mine were found normal, the ventilation was traveling its regular course and no standing gas. October 10th, found pressure of gas oozing through, under and over the walls, from the fire district; advised that the walls be repaired and the current of air increased which passes the walls, and the men taken out of the return current, beyond that section; otherwise conditions satisfactory, except that permanent connections were made, where rooms are wired; advised that this be discontinued. October 11th, found walls repaired and current of air increased. November 10th, visited mine in company with Chief Inspector, on request of miners to investigate the surroundings of fire district; no signs of imminent danger were found, but recommendations were given to watch the walls and no men to be employed on the return, near the fire section. A four inch pipe was inserted into the wall near the top, running to the surface, which released the pressure of gas from flowing into the mine. December 20th, inspected fire district which was opened December 10th and ventilated, and no fire was to be found; a good current of air was traveling through all sections and no standing gas discovered; surrounding territories were in good order. A more detailed report will be given in my editorial.

Sunday Creek No. 210.

Remained suspended the entire year.

Sunday Creek No. 211.

Situated on Sugar Creek, 3½ miles northeast of Athens, on the H. V. R. R. Operated by the Sunday Creek Co., Columbus, O. Field Scott, Athens, O., Supt.; Herman Theisen, same place, mine foreman. Shaft opening, 240 ft. deep, to the No. 6 seam, varying in thickness from 4½ to 6 ft; double entry system; equipped with electric power, machine mining; motor haulage; fan ventilation; 213 loaders, 19 machine men, 81 day men. January 4th and 5th, was found in good order, except, requested ventilation be increased on the 4th east cut off. March 17th, in good condition. May 11th, inspected old works, and sections not in operation, was found well ventilated and no standing gas. August 10th and 17th, and November 16th, found in good condition; on the latter date scales were tested and found incorrect.

Sunday Creek No. 212.

Situated on Sugar Creek, about 4½ miles northeast of Athens, O. Operated by the Sunday Creek Co., Columbus, O. Field Scott, Athens, O., Supt.; W. M.

Pritchard, Athens, O., mine foreman. Shaft opening, 300 ft. in depth; No. 6 seam, varying in thickness from 3 to 6 ft.; equipped with electric power; machine mining; horse haulage; fan ventilation; 13 loaders, 2 machine men, 9 day men. January 5th, was found in good order; location of fan was changed, as requested on my former visit, and ventilation improved. March 25th, in good condition. The mine was later indefinitely abandoned, on account of faults and irregular height of coal.

Sunday Creek No. 252.

Mine has been indefinitely abandoned since 1905.

Sunday Creek No. 254.

Situated at Jacksonville, O., on the K. & M. R. R. Operated by the Sunday Creek Co., Columbus, Ohio. D. H. Williams, Glouster, O., Dist. Supt.; Dan McBride, same place, mine foreman; Pat. McCann, Jacksonville, O., assistant. Shaft opening, 110 ft. in depth; No. 6 seam, 6 ft. thick; double entry system; equipped with electric power; machine mining; rope haulage; fan ventilation; 150 loaders, 12 machine men, 66 day men. February 11th requested that trappers be placed at cross over door between 17 and 18 west, and 11 and 12 east; also dust removed from haulage roads and stairways repaired in escapement shaft, otherwise in fair order. May 31st, rooms No. 7 and No. 8 on 12 east and 11 and 12 on 9 east, also 2 and 3 on 20 west, not properly ventilated; advised checks placed on entries to conduct a current into these rooms; found that the dust had been removed from the east side; the west side still found dusty. Ordered the same loaded out at once. August 4th, mine idle, inspected old works, found them well ventilated and free from standing gas. Made partial inspection of the workings and found ventilation improved. November 2nd, requested trapper placed at 13 and 14 west; also stable constructed to comply with the law and dust removed from haulage roads.

S. C. No. 255.

Situated 3 miles southwest of Jacksonville, on the K. & M. R. R. Operated by the Sunday Creek Co., Columbus, O. D. H. Williams, Glouster, O., Dist. Supt.; Robt. Snyder, same place, mine foreman; Carl Fierce, assistant. Shaft opening, 150 ft. in depth; No. 6 seam, 6 ft. thick; double entry system; equipped with electric power; machine mining; motor haulage; fan ventilation; 120 loaders, 18 machine men, 56 day men employed. March 14th, in good condition; also June 23rd, September 12th and December 12th, mine found in good condition.

S. C. No. 256.

Situated at Glouster, Ohio, on K. & M. R. R. Operated by the Sunday Creek Co., Columbus, O. D. H. Williams, Glouster, O., Dist. Supt.; Harry Cunningham, same place, mine foreman; Thos. Hope, assistant. Shaft opening, 90 ft. in depth; No. 6 seam, 6 ft. thick; double entry system; fan ventilation; equipped with electric power; machine mining; motor haulage; 217 loaders, 26 machine men, 83 day men employed. February 24th and 25th, conditions were found satisfactory, except advised that the ventilation be increased on 5th and 6th west north, and check placed on back entry; also requested that a man way be made to No. 2 air shaft and a stairway installed. May 16th and June 1st, found former requests complied with, and the mine generally in good condition; requested brick stoppings placed between north split of air. June 20th, was called to investigate cause of the death of Peter Bartels, a driver, who was killed on the 18th, by colliding with another trip, while coming onto the 5 west motor switch, becoming confused with the signals. July 25th, visited mine on request of miners, to test the scales, which were found correct, inspected old works, they were found well ventilated and free from standing gas. August 1st, in good order; advised that a check be placed between 5 and 6 rooms on 5th west. October 31st and November 1st, conditions satisfactory, except an accumulation of dust and fine coal along the northwest haulway; advised that the same be given attention at once.

S. C. No. 266.

Situated at Hollister, O., two miles west of Glouster, on the K. & M. R. R. Operated by the Sunday Creek Co., Columbus, O. D. H. Williams, Glouster, O., Dist. Supt.; John Collins, same place, mine foreman; Thos. Cox, assistant. Shaft opening, 90 ft. in depth; No. 6 seam, 6 ft. thick; double entry system; equipped with electric power; machine mining; motor haulage; fan ventilation; 170 loaders, 15 machine men, 59 day men employed. Four inspections made. February 14th, May 10th, August 3rd and October 27th. No recommendations were made, mine generally in good condition.

S. C. No. 267.

Situated at Hunterdon, Ohio, three miles west of Glouster, O., on the K. & M. R. R. D. H. Williams, Glouster, O., Dist. Supt.; John Yaw, same place, mine foreman; Phil. Blower, Glouster, O., assistant. Slope opening, 450 ft. in length; No. 6 seam, 6 and 6½ ft. thick; double entry system; equipped with electric power; machine mining; motor haulage; fan ventilation; 205 loaders, 20 machine men, 68 day men employed. January 27th, found in good order, requested that a check be placed between rooms 4 and 5 on 20th west. May 5th and 6th, and July 29th, also October 28th, in good condition, no recommendations were made.

S. C. No. 275.

Remained suspended the entire year.

S. C. No. 281.

Situated about 3½ miles northwest of Jacksonville, O., branch of the K. & M. R. R. Operated by the Sunday Creek Co., Columbus, O. D. H. Williams, Glouster, O., Dist. Supt.; D. S. Williams, Jacksonville, O, mine foreman; Chas. Dusy, same place, assistant. Shaft opening, 125 ft. in depth; No. 6 seam, 5 and 6 ft. thick; double entry system; fan ventilation; equipped with electric power; machine mining; motor haulage; 72 loaders, 20 machine men, 62 day men employed. June 30th, owing to the mine being suspended for a long period, and started on short notice, found the ventilation deficient, but the necessary improvements being made to restore the mine to its former condition. Requested a trapper placed at 3 and 4 east on south, and fine coal and dust removed from haulage roads. September 19th, in an improved condition; advised that a west entry be driven off the south to connect with air shaft, to be used as an additional traveling way. December 16th, in fair condition; requested a traveling way made on west side of mine for the north end. December 28th, visited the mine in company with D. H. Williams, Dist. Supt. for consultation in regard to making changes in the course of the ventilation; it was decided to use the west side for the inlet to north end of mine, which had formerly been the return, and which is to be made a traveling way, as requested.

Sunday Creek Nos. 311 and 312.

. Indefinitely abandoned.

New York Nos. 31 and 32.

Situated near Buchtel, O., on the H. V. R. R. Operated by the New York Coal Co., Columbus, O. P. C. Morris, Nelsonville, O., Supt.; E. G. Woody, same place, mine foreman. Drift opening, No. 6 seam, 5 to 6 ft. thick; double entry system; fan ventilation; equipped with electric power; machine mining; motor haulage; 189 loaders, 24 machine men, 72 day men employed. March 4th, found in fair condition; also March 30th, except the ventilation, which is not reliable, on account of fan being located inside of mine; requested that a more reliable ventilating medium be installed. July 13th, visited mine in company with Mr. Kennedy, inspector 2nd dist., who was assigned the mines and will visit same in the future. We advised that an additional traveling way be made, to conform with the new code.

New York No. 33.

Situated near Buchtel, O., on the H. V. R. R. Operated by the New York Coal Co., Columbus, O. P. C. Morris, Nelsonville, O., Supt.; A. E. Harold, same place, mine foreman; John Shepard, assistant. Drift opening, No. 7 seam, about 5 ft. thick; equipped with electric power; machine mining; gathering and haulage motor; fan ventilation; double entry system; 81 loaders, 8 machine men, 40 day men employed. February 28th, conditions found satisfactory, except the doors, which were in bad order and not attended; advised that the matter be given attention at once. June 21st, called to test the scales; found correct. July 5th, ventilation insufficient; a new air shaft is under construction and almost completed, which will improve conditions. Mr. Kennedy, of 2nd district, was also assigned this mine on July 12th.

New York No. 34.

Situated at Old Floodwood, O., on the H. V. R. R. Operated by the New York Coal Co., Columbus, O. P. C. Morris, Nelsonville, O., Supt.; E. W. Jones, same place, mine foreman. Drift opening, No. 6 seam, 5 to 6 ft. thick; double entry system; furnace ventilation; pick mining; rope and mule haulage; 35 pick miners, 7 day men employed. January 31st, found in fair condition. July 5th, August 29th, found the mine suspended. September 22 and December 7th, conditions satisfactory.

New York No. 35.

Situated near Buchtel, O., on the H. V. R. R. Operated by the New York Coal Co., Columbus, O. P. C. Morris, Nelsonville, O., Supt.; C. L. Milligan, Buchtel, O., mine foreman. Drift opening, No. 7 seam, 4½ ft. thick; double entry system; fan ventilation; electric mining; motor haulage; 40 loaders, 4 machine men, 17 day men employed. March 29th and July 5th, conditions found satisfactory, except the trolley wire branches were not porperly guarded; requested same remedied at once. This mine has been assigned to Mr. Kennedy, of the 2nd district.

Eclipse No. 3.

Situated about three miles north of Athens, on H. V. R. R. Operated by the Lorain Coal and Dock Co., Columbus, O. John H. Morefield, Athens, O., Supt.; Carl Miller and John Brewer, same place, mine foremen. Shaft opening, 187 ft. deep; No. 6 seam, 5 and 6 ft. thick; double and triple entry system; equipped with electric power; machine mining; motor haulage; fan ventilation;

211 loaders, 22 machine men, 70 day men employed. January 6th, March 18th, May 25th, conditions throughout the mine were found satisfactory, except requested that the rubbish be removed from under ground stable. June 28th, was called to investigate the cause of the death of Tod Tittle, who was killed by a fall of slate in room No. 15, on 9 west entry. August 12th and 18th, mine found in good condition; requested some safety devices placed on side of cage, to be used instead of a rack, while lowering and hoisting men. August 23rd, visited mine in company with Chief Inspector, to advise something to be used on cages instead of a rack. November 3rd and 4th, mine found in good condition. December 13th, visited mine by order of Chief Inspector to consult with the management in regard to placing boiler plate on sides of cage, permanently, while lowering and hoisting men. Mr. Jackson, the manufacturer of the cage, was present and advised a device that was approved.

Luhrig Nos. 1 and 2.

Situated at Luhrig, O., on the B. & O. S. W. Operated by the Luhrig Coal Washing and Mining Co., Charleston, W. Va. Sherman Shull, Luhrig, O., Supt.: John Gibbs, same place, mine boss. Shaft opening, 150 ft. deep; No. 6 seam, 5 to 7 ft. thick; double entry system: fan ventilation; equipped with electric power; machine mining; motor haulage; 159 loaders, 16 machine men, 72 day men employed. May 18th and 19th, inspected mine, requested safety hole made at the 19th, west switch stand; ventilation fair considering the long distance it travels, and the choked conditions of air course; advised that an additional opening be made in the interior workings of No. 1, for an escapement way, and to increase the ventilation; otherwise conditions satisfactory. August 16th, mine generally in fair condition; an order was given to provide an interior opening, to conform with the provisions of the new code, which requires two traveling ways; also an increase in volume of air, and control openings in old extensive mines. It was agreed between Company, Mr. Harrison, Chief Inspector, and myself, that if an opening was commenced at once and finished within 60 days, that mine would be permitted to operate while improvement was being made. November 11th, found new shaft, 12 by 8 ft. in the clear, 204 ft. in depth, 12000 ft. from the original openings, with two compartments and a winding stairway in one, the other to be used for an upcast for the ventilating current. We are pleased to report that this is a great improvement to the property, as well as a relief to everyone concerned. Conditions generally were satisfactory.

Luhrig No. 3, or South Side of No. 2.

Operated by the same Company, same management: employs 103 loaders, 10 machine men, 51 day men. March 15th and July 18th and 19th, conditions were found satisfactory, except, ordered an additional traveling way be made. August 6th, was called to investigate the cause of the death of Raymond Walker, a miner, who was killed by a fall of coal, while working down a standing shot, in Room No. 5, on main west entry. October 18th, former order complied with: mine generally in good condition.

Canaanville No. 1.

Situated at Canaanville, O., on the B. & O. S. W. R. R. Operated by the Canaan Coal Co., Athens, O. Geo. Welsh, Canaanville, O., Supt.; Chas. Coleman, same place, mine foreman, resigned, succeeded by Henry Shires, resigned, succeeded by Geo. Bell. Shaft opening, 450 ft. deep; No. 6 seam, 4 to 6 ft. thick; double and triple entry system; fan ventilation; equipped with electric power; machine mining; motor haulage; 129 loaders, 16 machine men, 74 day men employed. March 16th, north side found in fair order. May 20th, found ventilation becoming deficient; ordered brick stoppings built between north and south entries, also the doors renewed and hung so they would close of their own accord. May 27th, found orders complied with and ventilation doubled in the interior of mine. July 20th, in good condition. September 21st, south side in good condition. October 19th, made partial inspection and found conditions satisfactory. December 21st, south side found in good condition, an additional boiler has been installed, separate from the main steam plant, to be used in case of an emergency, as the only means of escape is derived from steam power. This mine generates considerable gas, but it is well taken care of.

Hisylvania No. 23.

Situated at Trimble, O., on the K. & M. R. R. Operated by the Hisylvania Coal Co., Columbus, O. Enoch Blower, Trimble, O., Supt.; Chas. Jones, Glouster, O., mine foreman. Slope opening, 450 ft. long; No. 6 seam, 6 ft. thick; double entry system, fan ventilation: electric mining and haulage; 90 loaders, 8 machine men, 31 day men employed. Four inspections were made. February 9th, May 3rd, July 26th and October 25th, conditions were found good.

Northern Fuel No. 24.

Situated one mile southwest of Jacksonville, O. Operated by Chas. Cohenour, receiver for the Northern Fuel Co., Columbus, O. D. L. Wallace, Glouster, O., Supt.: John Cox, Trimble, O., mine foreman. Shaft opening, No. 6 seam, 6 ft. thick; double entry system; fan ventilation; equipped with electric power; machine mining; motor haulage; 155 loaders, 16 machine men, 55 day men employed. February 8th and 10th, the mine generally was in fair condition: requested that check be placed between rooms Nos. 11 and 12, on the 7th west, and also dust removed from the haulage roads. May 9th, in fair condition. July 28th, advised that a door be placed at outside end of 6th east north switch, and man holes made along motor road; also obstructions removed on the way leading to the escapement shaft. September 26th, my former orders were complied with, except man holes were only partially made; the mine generally was in fair order. November 14th, was in fair condition. December 27th, visited mine to investigate the cause of the death of Anthony Wuksi, who was injured August 26th by a fall of slate, on 4th east entry, and died December 17th. Made partial inspection and conditions were satisfactory.

Bailey Run.

Situated one mile south of Jacksonville, O., on the K. & M. R. R. Operated by Bailey Run Coal Co., Corning, Ohio. C. R. Monsarrat, Corning, O., Supt.; Wm. Dixon, Millfield, O., mine foreman. Slope opening, 100 ft. in length; No. 7 seam, 4 ft. thick; double entry system; fan ventilation; equipped with electric power; machine mining; mule haulage; 35 loaders, 4 machine men, 8 day men employed. January 14th, visited mine on complaint of miners, in regard to air, was found in good condition, except one room, which was beyond the limit without breakthrough, the same was stopped. March 23rd, in good condition, also June 24th, ordered that stretchers be provided, and that substantial material be used for stoppings between inlet and outlet of air. September 14th and December 15th, in good condition.

Poston & Fluhart.

Situated near Millfield, Ohio, on the K. & M. R. R. Operated by Poston & Fluhart Coal Co., Athens, O. Joseph Smith, Millfield, O., has supervision.

Slope opening; No. 7 seam, 4 ft. thick; double entry system; equipped with electric power; machine mining; slope equipped with a chain hoist; fan ventilation; 10 loaders, 2 machine men, 7 day men employed. September 14th, found this a new opening; are making connections with the second opening, which is a shaft, 70 ft. deep, with two compartments, the main opening being equipped three compartments. The mine is being made modern in every respect, equipped with the best machinery. December 15th, conditions were found satisfactory, except too many men were found working inside of last breakthrough in main north entry, and the number was reduced. Connections have been made with the air shaft and the installing of a large fan is almost completed, and a winding stairway is being placed in one of the compartments of air shaft.

Carbondale No. 2.

Situated at Carbondale, Ohio, on the B. & O. S. W. R. R. Operated by the Carbondale Coal Co., Carbondale, Ohio. M. H. Doolittle, Carbondale, O., Supt.: Ford Doolittle, same place, mine foreman. Drift opening; No. 6 seam, 5½ ft. thick; double entry system; fan ventilation; equipped with electric power; machine mining; motor haulage; 83 loaders, 8 machine men, 29 day men employed. February 3rd, was found in good condition, also June 7th, requested that loose top be taken down, on old north, at 8th west, also on main east motor road, near cut-off door. August 31st and December 1st, conditions were satisfactory throughout the mine, except requested that 1st and 2nd east and 3 and 4 east entries be cross-timbered.

Carbondale Nos. 1 and 3.

Situated at Carbondale, Ohio, on the B. & O. S. W. R. R. Operated by Carbondale Coal Co., Carbondale, O. M. H. Doolittle, Carbondale, O., Supt.; Jacob Pollock, same place, mine foreman. Drift opening; No. 6 seam, 4½ to 5½ ft. thick; double entry system; fan ventilation; equipped with electric power, machine mining, motor haulage; 54 loaders, 6 machine men, 29 day men employed. February 4th, in good order. June 8th, mine not in operation on account of no trade; made partial inspection. August 30th, found in good condition. Requested stairway repaired in escapement shaft. December 1st, found No. 1, which is a new opening, in good condition, the coal is dumped over No. 3 tipple; conditions throughout No. 3 were found satisfactory.

Hocking or Moore.

Situated at Carbondale, Ohio, on the B. & O. S. W. R. R. Operated by the Hocking Mining Co., Athens, O. G. W. Arnold, Carbondale, O., Supt.; James Gascoyne, same place, mine foreman. Slope opening; No. 6 seam, 4½ ft. thick; double entry system; fan ventilation; equipped with electric power; machine mining; both gathering and motor haulage; 160 loaders, 18 machine men, 50 day men employed. February 2nd, was found in good condition. June 8th, made partial inspection, found in good order, except the ventilation, which is fair. The Company is making preparations to install a 15 ft. Jeffrey fan. September 1st and November 30th, conditions throughout the mine satisfactory. Requested that loose top be taken down at the entrance to No. 9 and 19 rooms on 5 west; we find on the latter date the new fan is in operation, giving the best satisfaction.

Winchester.

Situated at Carbondale, Ohio, on the B. & O. S. W. R. R. Operated by Wm. Shingler, Carbondale, O., who has full supervision Slope opening; No.

6 seam, 4 ft. thick; double entry system; fan ventilation; equipped with electric power; machine mining; mule and rope haulage; Loaders 3, machine men 2, and 5 day men employed. February 4th, found ventilation, wiring, drainage and means of escape bad; a specific order was given to have the mine put in a lawful condition. June 8th, found mine suspended, on account of financial failure, and has since been indefinitely abandoned.

Doanville No. 1.

Situated near Myers Crossing, on the H. V. R. R. Operated by the C. & H. C. & I. Co., Columbus, O. R. E. McClain, Nelsonville, O., Supt.; resigned, succeeded by Wm. Reybold, same place, who was formerly mine boss, resigned, succeeded by R. E. McClain, who, at present, has full supervision. Slope opening; No. 6 seam, 5 to 6 ft. thick; double entry system; fan ventilation; equipped with electric power; machine mining; rope and motor haulage; 82 loaders, 10 machine men, 60 day men employed. March 10th, conditions satisfactory, except in old south, in which a specific order was given to have the ventilation increased, and man holes made along haulage road; also better attention given to the top, which is very bad. August 30th, found the mine had been suspended about three months previous, and resumed operation in the north, the old south being abandoned; requested that the wires be arranged to comply with the law, and haulage roads cleaned and cross timbered, and properly drained. November 29th, conditions have been improved, my former orders complied with. Mine generally in fair condition.

Doanville No. 1 A.

Situated at same place as No. 1. Operated by same Company. F. W. Weymueller, New Straitsville, O., Supt.; J. W. Jones, Doanville, O., mine foreman. Drift opening; No. 7 seam, 5 to 6 ft. thick; double entry system; fan ventilation; equipped with electric power; machine mining; motor haulage; 130 loaders, 12 machine men, 29 day men. March 2nd found a large fan has been installed, escapement way made as ordered on my previous visit, also brick stoppings placed between inlet and outlet. Mine generally in an improved condition. May 26th, September 15th, in fair condition, except the wiring, ordered same properly hung. December 8th, in fair condition, except, requested that obstructions be removed from breakthroughs, between rooms.

Imperial.

Situated near Myers Crossing, on the H. V. R. R. Operated by the Imperial Mining Co., Columbus, O. Pearl Barrell, Nelsonville, O., Supt.; Noah Matheney, same place, mine foreman. Drift opening; No. 6 seam, 5 to 6 ft. thick; double entry system; fan ventilation; equipped with electric power; machine mining; motor haulage; 135 loaders, 8 machine men, 43 day men employed. March 9th, found in fair condition. July 12th, found ventilation wasting through surface breaks, requested same closed; also stoppings repaired. October 5th, found satisfactory, except, advised that a door be placed between 14 and 15 rooms to improve the ventilation in working places on second east. November 7th, was called to investigate the death of Ed. Glover, who was injured November 4th, died the following day from a small fracture of the skull, caused by fall of slate in room No. 21 on second east. December 29th, in fair condition.

Maple Hill.

Situated 3 miles northeast of Nelsonville, on the H. V. R. R. Operated by the Maple Mining Co., Nelsonville, Ohio. Geo. Silcott, Nelsonville, O., Supt.; Thos. Matheney, same place, mine foreman. Drift opening; No. 6 seam, 5½ ft. thick; double entry system; equipped with electric power; machine mining; rope haulage; fan ventilation; 40 loaders, 2 machine men, 15 day men employed. March 22nd, in fair order. Mine was assigned to Mr. Kennedy of 2nd District, in July.

Juniper No. 1.

Situated at Buchtel, Ohio, on the H. V. R. R. Operated by Geo. McKee, Nelsonville, O., who has supervision. Owned by the York Clay Mining Co., Nelsonville, O. Drift opening; No. 7 seam, 5 to 6 ft. thick; double entry system; furnace ventilation; equipped with electric power; machine mining; mule haulage; 21 loaders, 4 machine men, 7 day men. February 1st, was called to investigate the cause of the death of Chas. Coakley, who was killed January 29th, by fall of slate, at the face of 1st east entry. Made inspection of mine, found in bad condition. Ordered that the entries be cross timbered, and a more substantial means of ventilation be installed. The mine was later suspended, and assigned to Mr. Kennedy, in July.

Juniper No. 2.

Situated at Buchtel, Ohio, on the H. V. R. R. Operated by the York Clay Mining Co., Nelsonville, O. John Murdy, Buchtel, O., Supt.; Hugh Mallen, same place, mine foreman. Drift opening; No. 6 seam, 4 to 6 ft. thick; double entry system; fan ventilation; equipped with electric power; machine mining; motor haulage; 80 loaders, 10 machine men, 25 day men employed. March 28th, fair condition. June 21st, was called to investigate the cause of the death of John Henderson, who was killed by fall of coal in room No. 1, on north territory, while working down a standing shot. This mine was also assigned to Mr. Kennedy of 2nd district, in July.

Poston No. 65.

Situated at Nelsonville, Ohio, on the H. V. R. R. Operated by J. M Lama, Nelsonville, O., who has supervision; L. G. Dollison, same place, mine foreman. Drift opening; No. 6 seam, 6 ft. thick; pick mining; natural ventilation; mule haulage; 23 pick miners, 4 day men employed. July 11th, November 17th, conditions are as well as could be expected, owing to the work being all in stumps and pillars. November 28th, visited mine on complaint of miner, in regard to working too many men in a place; owing to shortage of places arrangements were made to work the men alternate shifts, at their request.

Broadwell.

Situated at Broadwell, Ohio, on the M. C. & C. R. R. Operated by the Federal Coal Co., Marietta, O. O. B. Gard, Marietta, O., Supt.; J. D. Smith, Broadwell, O., mine foreman. Slope opening; No. 8 seam, 4 to 8 ft. thick; double entry system; fan ventilation; rope and mule haulage; 23 loaders, 4 machine men, 7 day men employed. February 17th, in fair condition. June 22nd, ordered an escapement way made in the interior of the workings. July 6th, was called to consult in regard to location for an opening, which was begun at once. November 25th, was suspended on account of financial failure, was later leased by the Big Four Coal Co.

Federal Valley No. 1.

Situated at Broadwell, Ohio, on the M. C. & C. R. R. Operated by the Federal Hocking Coal Co., Columbus, O. J. C. Adams, New Lexington, O., has full supervision. Slope opening; No. 8 seam, 5 to 8 ft. thick; double entry system: fan ventilation; equipped with electric power; machine mining; rope haulage; 18 loaders, 2 machine men, 5 day men employed. January 24th, visited mine to test scales, which were found correct. Ordered doors and brattices repaired, obstruction removed from air course to improve ventilation. June 6th, conditions were not improved and men were removed until the mine could be placed in proper condition. August 22nd and November 21st, in fair condition.

Black Diamond.

Situated at Lathrop, Ohio, on the M. C. & C. R. R. Operated by the Black Diamond Coal & Coke Co., Columbus, O. A. E. Lafferty, Sharpsburg, O., Supt.; T. O. Day, same place, mine foreman. Drift opening; No. 8 seam, 7 and 8 ft. thick; double entry system; fan ventilation; equipped with electric power; machine mining; motor haulage; 72 loaders, 8 machine men, 24 day men employed. May 24th, in good order. August 8th, was called to test scales, which were found incorrect. August 26th, conditions were found satisfactory, except ordered brick stoppings placed between inlet and outlet of air. November 22nd, former order complied with. Mine in good order. On the following day the tipple, steam and power plant were burned down, from some unknown cause.

Schuler.

Situated at Sharpsburg, O., on the M. C. & C. R. R. Operated by Jacob Schuler, same place, has full supervision. Drift opening; No. 8 seam, 6 to 8 ft. thick; double entry system; furnace ventilation; machine mining; mule haulage; 10 loaders, 2 machine men, 3 day men employed. March 22nd, found satisfactory, except ventilation, ordered that some artificial means be installed. June 27th, found small furnace installed and condition satisfactory. October 3rd, in fair condition.

Carbon or Wells.

Situated at Lathrop, Ohio, on the M. C. & C. R. R. Operated by the Carbon Coal Mining Co., Amesville, O. T. E. Clark, Amesville, O., Supt. and mine boss, resigned, succeeded by Geo. Brown. Drift opening; No. 8 seam, 6 to 8 ft. thick; double entry system; fan ventilation; electric mining; mule haulage; 38 loaders, 2 machine men, 8 day men employed. February 16th, in fair condition. May 23rd, found suspended, on account of lack of trade. August 26th and November 23rd, found in fair condition.

ATHENS COUNTY.

SMALL MINES EMPLOYING LESS THAN TEN MEN.

Glouster Domestic.

Situated at Glouster, Ohio, on the K. & M. R. R. Operated by Sidney Hildrick, Glouster, O., who has full supervision. Shaft opening, 48 ft. deep; No. 7 seam, 4 ft. thick; double entry system; ventilated by fire basket; equipped with air plant; machine mining; 6 miners, 2 day men. February 10th, fair order. Requested safety catch placed on cage. September 13th, mine had just resumed operation after 5 months suspension; found in fair order; later, suspended on account of financial failure.

Edgell & Young.

Situated at Nelsonville, Ohio, on the H. V. R. R. Operated by Edgell & Young, Nelsonville, O. Output consumed by the Nelsonville Brick Co. Shaft opening; No. 6 seam, 5 an 6 ft. thick; fan ventilation; machine mining; 4 loaders, 2 machine men, 2 day men employed. July 14th, we find new opening made close to the workings. Mine generally in fair order.

Silcott.

Situated at Old Floodwood, Ohio, on H. V. R. R. Operated by Geo. Silcott, Nelsonville, O., who is Supt.; O. M. Reynolds, Floodwood, O., mine boss. Drift openings; No. 6 seam, 5 and 6 ft. thick; Furnace and natural ventilation; 9 miners, 2 day men employed. The operations are exclusively in stumps and pillars, in several crop openings. July 14th, in fair condition.

Pig Skin.

Situated at Nelsonville, O., on the H. V. R. R. Operated by T. S. Rosser, same place, who has supervision. Drift opening; No. 6 seam. The operations are in pillar work. Output consumed by the Nelsonville Brick Co. Machine mining; natural ventilation; 4 loaders, 1 day man employed. July 14th, in fair condition.

Wells, New Opening.

Situated at Kimberly, Ohio, on the H. V. R. R. Operated by J. M. Lama, Nelsonville, O., who has supervision. Slope opening; No. 6 seam, 6 ft. thick; furnace ventilation; 6 pick miners, 2 day men employed. July 14th, inspected by Mr. Hill, inspector of 4th district. December 9th, found in good condition. Tested scales, found correct. Mine was not in operation the forepart of year.

Nixon No. 4.

Situated at Myers Crossing, on the H. V. R. R. Operated by Nixon Coal Co., Nelsonville, O.; L. H. Nixon, Nelsonville, O., Supt. Drift opening, No. 6 seam, 6 ft. thick; natural ventilation; pick mining; 6 miners, 2 day men employed. July 14th, visited mine on complaint of miners to investigate air conditions, which were found bad; men were taken out until some artificial means could be installed. October 7th, furnace has been installed and in fair order.

ATHENS COUNTY CLAY MINES.

Nelsonville Clay Mine No. 1.

Situated at Nelsonville, O. Operated by the Nelsonville Brick Co. C. Colegrove, Nelsonville, has supervision. Drift opening; No. 5 seam, 6 ft. thick; furnace ventilation; new opening; 14 miners, 6 day men employed. July 14th, inspected by Mr. Hill, of 4th district. October 20th, was found in fair condition.

Nelsonville Clay Mine No. 2.

Situated at Nelsonville, O. Operated by the Nelsonville Brick Co., Nelsonville, O. Joe Roscoe, same place, has full charge. Drift opening; No. 5 seam, 7 to 9 ft. thick; fan ventilation; motor haulage; 20 miners, 14 day men employed.

July 14th, inspected by Mr. Hill, of the 4th district. October 20th, found in good condition.

Hocking Valley Clay Mine.

Situated at Nelsonville, O. Operated by the Hocking Valley Fire Clay Co., Nelsonville, O. Jos. Spencer, same place, has supervision. Drift opening; No. 5 seam, 8 ft. thick; natural ventilation; 8 miners, 2 day men employed. July 14th, found in fair condition.

MINES VISITED OUTSIDE OF DISTRICT NO. 3.

HOCKING COUNTY, DIST. NO. 2.

Jobs No. 2.

Operated by the Sunday Creek Co., Columbus, O. February 15th, visited mine on request of Mr. Kennedy, in whose district the mine is situated, to investigate the surroundings of fire district, which had been sealed on account of fire since last June. The walls were in good condition, and no imminent danger appeared.

JEFFERSON COUNTY, NINTH DISTRICT.

Amsterdam.

Located at Amsterdam, O. Operated by the Y. & O Coal Co., Cleveland, O. Richard Jones, Amsterdam, O., Supt.; Edwin Lee, same place, mine foreman. April 22nd, 23rd and 24th, visited the mine, by order of Chief Inspector, on account of gas explosion, in which 15 men lost their lives, for the purpose of assisting in the rescue work, and to restore the ventilation, so an examination could be made, to determine the cause of the explosion. An examination was made later by Chief Inspector, a full account of which will no doubt appear in the Annual Report, by Mr. Morrison, in whose district the mine is situated.

Zerbe.

Situated at Amsterdam, O. Operated by the Ohio and Pennsylvania Coal Co., Cleveland, O. Geo. Wagner, Supt.; John Lee, mine foreman, both of Amsterdam, O. April 25th, visited mine, in company with Mr. Burke and Mr. Kennedy, also Mr. Morrison, in whose district the mine is situated. Made partial inspection.

Elizabeth.

Located at Amsterdam, O. Operated by Wolf Run Coal Co. R. T. Price, Cleveland, O., Supt.; Harry Marson, Wolf Run, mine foreman. April 27th, visited, in company with Inspectors Kennedy, Burke and Morrison; made partial inspection. A report will be given by Mr. Morrison, in whose district the mine is situated.

FOURTH DISTRICT.

ISAAC HILL.

COMPOSED OF THE COUNTIES OF MUSKINGUM, PERRY AND MORGAN.

Hon. George Harrison, *Chief Inspector of Mines, Columbus, O.*

Dear Sir:—In compliance with custom of the Mining Department, I herewith submit to you my second annual report of the Fourth Mining District, composed of the counties of Muskingum, Perry and Morgan, beginning January 1st and ending December 31, 1910.

During the early part of the year the coal trade was very good in southern part of Perry county, and continued so with several mines during the entire year, but in the Crooksville district work was suspended April 1st and remained so until November 5th, which represented the largest portion of my district.

One hundred and ninety-two (192) visits were made. Improvements were as follows: Fans, 9; second openings, 2; furnaces, 1. Four sets of scales tested and found all weighing correctly. Five days were spent in oil fields. Forty-six visits were made to mines in Muskingum County and three days spent in oil fields. In Perry County one hundred and thirty mines were visited and two days spent in the oil fields, and in Morgan County, three visits at mines. In Athens County, six visits were made and two days were spent in Jefferson County.

In discharging my duty as District Mine Inspector, I have visited mines as often as the duties of my office would permit, considering the time mines were in operation.

I regret to report four fatalities during the year: Norman Smith was killed by fall of roof in the Elk Mine, March 2nd; Alex. Angle was killed by empty cars on motor switch in Central mine, September, 28th; Walter Snedden was killed by fall of roof in No. 9 mine at New Straitsville, O., October 17th; Charles Reed, killed in machine shop at Chapmans No. 1, December 17th.

My official dealings with both operators and miners have been pleasant. There have been some small grievances, but they were amicably settled.

In conclusion, I desire to extend my thanks to you, and all the Mining Department, for the advice rendered me in the discharge of my duties.

Respectfully submitted,

Isaac Hill, Zanesville, O.,

Inspector Fourth District.

December 31, 1910

MUSKINGUM COUNTY.

Ables.

Located one mile south of Buckeye, on a branch of the Cannelville Division of the Z. & W. R. R. Operated by the Muskingum Coal & Ry. Co., Zanesville, O. C. I. Butts, S. Zanesville, Supt. and mine boss, until April 1st. Drift opening to No. 6 seam of coal, 3 ft. 6 in. thick; fan ventilation; machine mining, employs 30 loaders, 8 machine men and 13 day hands. Visited February 21st, found mine in fair condition, except main south motor road. There were no man holes, protecting men from passing motor trips. Mine was suspended April 1st to November 1st, when the mine resumed operation, under the Jonathan Creek Coal Co., Pittsburg, Pa. L. D. Able, Zanesville, O., Supt.; B. H. Harlan, Philo, O., mine boss. Visited November 29th, found mine in fair condition.

Elk.

Located near Roseville, on the C. & M. V. R. R. Operated by the Elk Coal Co., Columbus, O. S. E. Raney, Columbus, O., Supt.; Al. Caton, Roseville, O., mine boss. Drift opening to No. 6 seam, 3½ ft. thick; machine mining; fan ventilation; motor haulage; employs 48 loaders, 10 machine runners and 12 day hands. March 2nd, was called to investigate fatal accident of Norman Smith, killed by fall of slate in room No. 3, on 1st west entry. Visited November 15th, mine in fair condition.

Granger.

Located near Buckeye Station, on the O. & L. R. R. R. Operated by Victoria Coal Co., Cleveland, O. Jos. Baker, Zanesville, O., Supt.; C. L. Harris, S. Zanesville, mine boss. Drift opening to No. 6 seam of coal, 3½ ft. thick; machine mining; fan ventilation; employs 47 loaders, 8 machine runners and 20 day men. Two visits were made. March 15th, in fair condition; a new second opening had been made. On November 30th, found ventilation very poor on account of fan being too small; a new fan was being installed, to be in operation in three days.

Maynard No. 38.

Located at Cannelville, on the Z. & W. R. R. Operated by Maynard Coal Co., Columbus, O. Elmer Bratton, Cannelville, O., Supt.; Ed. Morgan, same place, mine boss. Drift opening to No. 6 seam of coal, 3 ft. 8 in. thick; furnace ventilation; coal is mined by solid shooting; employs 50 pick miners, 10 day men and 2 shot firers. January 4th, found mine in fair condition for small force of men; requested company if they increased the number of men in mine that fan must be installed. On December 30th, visited mine; found Ed. Hysell, of Cannelville, O., Supt., and Grant Norrigan, same place, mine boss; 70 miners and 17 day men. Had installed a 6 ft. Sackett fan, giving good results.

McGarvey's.

Located at Cannelville, O., on the Z. & W. R. R. Operated by J. A. McGarvey Coal Co., Cannelville, O. J. A. McGarvey, Cannelville, O., Supt. and mine boss. Slope opening to No. 6 seam of coal, 3½ ft. thick; furnace ventilation; rope haulage; employs 30 miners and 10 day men. Coal is mined by solid shooting. Two visits made. March 11th, mine in fair condition. November 17th, mine in fair condition. Requested second opening cleaned out.

Pan-American.

Located at Cannelville, O., on the Z. & W. R. R. Operated by the Pan-American Coal Co., Newark O. John Walker, Cannelville, O., Supt.; Harry Anders, same place, mine boss. Slope opening to No. 6 seam of coal, 3 ft. 10 in. thick; rope haulage; fan ventilation; coal is mined by solid shooting; employs 80 miners and 20 day men. Two visits made. May 23rd, found mine in fair condition, except in slope no safety holes were provided for men; requested safety holes made at once and two doors at main entry side track, and one at first north entry in place of curtains. November 18th, found system of mining changing from pick mining to machine. Mine in fair condition.

Red Bud.

Located at Cannelville, O., on the Z. & W. R. R. Operated by Red Bud Coal Co., of Cannelville, O. W. H. Blaney, Cannelville, O., Supt.; Frank Blaney, Cannelville, O., mine boss. Drift opening to No. 6 seam of coal, 3⅜ ft. thick ; furnace ventilation; rope haulage; coal is mined by solid shooting; employs 19 miners and 7 day men. One visit was made December 28th, mine in fair condition.

Monitor.

Located one mile south of Darlington, O. Operated by the Monitor Coal Co., of Zanesville, O. C. A. Case, Zanesville, O., Supt.; Enos Miller, S. Zanesville, O., mine boss. Drift opening to No. 6 seam of coal, 3½ ft. thick; fan ventilation; motor haulage; machine mining; employs 16 loaders, 4 machine runners and 4 day men. Visited November 21st, in fair condition.

Weller No. 3.

Located one-half mile south of South Zanesville, O. Operated and superintended by W. H. Weller, S. Zanesville, O.; J. C. Wagoner, same place, mine boss. Drift opening; No. 6 seam of coal, 3½ ft. thick; furnace ventilation; dog haulage; coal is mined by solid shooting; employs about 20 miners and 1 day man. Six visits made. March 14th, new opening made, fair condition. May 2nd, requested furnace built. June 10th, mine in fair condition. Requested check on main entry to force air in rooms. June 24th, fair condition. September 9th, found mine in very poor condition, stoppings leaking and curtains between 1st and 2nd south entries were very poor; requested men taken out of mine until conditions were improved.

Stone.

Located near Stone Station, on the O. & L. K. Division of the B. & O. R. R. Operated by Blue Rock Coal Co., of Gaysport, O. J. Souders, Gaysport, Supt. and mine boss. Drift opening to No. 7 seam of coal, 4 ft. thick; furnace ventilation; pick mining; employs 9 miners and 4 day men. Two visits made. August 25th, found mine in fair condition. September 23rd, mine idle.

Garretts.

Located at Garretts Station, on O. & L. K. Division of the B. & O. R. R. Operated by Denhaur Bros., Philo, O. A. C. Denhaur, Philo, Supt. and mine boss. Drift opening to No 6 seam of coal, 3 ft. thick; coal is mined by solid shooting; furnace ventilation; employs 12 miners and 3 day men. Visited September 23rd, mine in fair condition; requested door put up in place of curtain at entrance of furnace

L. Fisher's No. 2.

Located at Sorghum Hollow, on South River road. Operated by L. Fisher, Zanesville, O., who is Supt. Wm. Ray, Zanesville, O., mine boss. Drift, to No. 6 seam of coal, 3 ft. thick; furnace ventilation; dog haulage; picks are used to mine the coal. Three visits made. January 28th, found mine in poor condition, at entrance of mine one foot of water was found over track, being the only avenue of ingress or egress, with no circulation of air and furnace not fired. Ordered men out of mine and not to return to work until water was taken out and ventilation restored by firing furnace and cleaning up airway. January 30th, was called to mine by operator who was desirous of resuming operation, found water removed, but no ventilation. Requested furnace fired every day mine was operated. Visited June 23rd, found mine in fair condition.

F. Fisher.

Located two miles south of Zanesville, O., on South River road. Operated and superintended by F. Fisher, Zanesville, O.; Charles Anderson, same place, mine boss. Drift opening in No. 6 seam of coal, 3 ft. thick; pick mining; furnace ventilation. February 23rd, employed 13 miners and 2 day men; mine in fair condition. Visited September 15th, found 9 miners and 1 day man; mine in fair condition.

Germans.

Located one mile and a half south of Zanesville, O., on South River road. Operated and superintended by W. A. Werner, Zanesville, O.; C. Huey, same place, mine boss. Drift opening to No. 6 seam of coal, 3 ft. thick; pick mining; furnace ventilation; employs 12 miners and 1 day man. Visited January 17th and April 26th; mine in fair condition. August 30th, ventilation poor; requested stoppings repaired.

S. Wigdon.

Located near Roseville, O. Operated and managed by S. Wigdon, Roseville, O. Drift to No. 6 seam of coal, 3½ ft. thick; pick mining; natural ventilation. Two visits were made. July 29th, mine in fair condition, except a gasoline pump was placed in mine so the fumes reached the men while at work. Visited August 19th, by request of Chief Inspector Geo. Harrison, and requested pump removed from mine at once.

SMALL MINES EMPLOYING LESS THAN TEN MEN.

Salt Run No. 2.

Located at Romine Station, on the O. R. & W. R. R. Owned by the Fair Oaks Coal Co., Columbus, O. A. B. Mullen, Zanesville, O., Supt. and mine boss. Drift, No. 7 seam, 6 ft. thick; pick mining; natural ventilation; employs 7 miners and 1 day man. Visited mine September 28th, found in fair condition.

Porter Bros.

Located one mile southeast of Mt. Sterling, O., on national pike. Operated by Porter Bros., Hopewell, O., Route No. 2. G. L. Porter, Hopewell, O., Supt. and mine boss. Drift, No. 7 seam, 6 ft. thick; pick mining; employs 7 miners and 2 day hands; furnace ventilation. Visited October 6th, mine in fair condition

Pierce & Greiners.

Located four miles northeast of Zanesville, O. Operated by Pierce & Greiner, Zanesville, O. J. A. Pierce, Zanesville, O., mine boss. Drift, No. 7 seam, 4 ft. thick; natural ventilation; pick mining; employs 8 miners. Visited October 14th, mine in fair condition.

Morehead.

Located one mile east of Zanesville, O. Operated by W. A. Werner, Zanesville, O. C. Huey, same place, mine boss. Drift, No. 6 seam, 3 ft. thick; pick mining; furnace ventilation; employs 9 miners and 1 day hand. Visited August 4th, found mine in fair condition, except very muddy; requested mud removed, or top shot, so men would not have to crawl through mud to push coal.

Greiners.

Located about two miles northeast of Zanesville, O. Operated by H. L. Greiner & Son, Zanesville, O. Drift, No. 5 seam of coal, 4½ ft. thick; a fire basket is used for ventilation; employs 8 miners and 2 day men. Visited September 12th, found ventilation fair, but found a gasoline pump on intake air; ordered it moved at once on return air; management of mine started to do so at once.

F. J. Paul.

Located three and one-half miles south of Zanesville, O. Operated by F. J. Paul, Zanesville, O. Drift opening; furnace ventilation; employs 7 miners and 1 day hand. Visited September 14th, conditions approved.

Lutz.

Located two miles east of Zanesville, O. Operated by Lutz Bros., Zanesville, O. Three miners and 1 day hand employed. Visited September 12th, mine in fair condition.

W. Fisher.

Located three miles east of Zanesville, O. Operated by W. Fisher, Zanesville, O. Drift opening; furnace ventilation; employs 8 miners and 1 day hand. Visited September 13th, mine in fair condition.

MINES SUSPENDED IN MUSKINGUM COUNTY.

Walnut Hill.

Located at Cannelville, on Z. & W. R. R. Operated by the Walnut Hill Coal Co., Detroit, Mich. Visited December 31st, as they were repairing to operate, and requested fan put on top of air shaft instead of in center of mine.

Dewey.

Located near Sealover Station, on the O. & L. K. Division of the B. & O. R. R. Owned by Duncan Run Coal Co., Detroit, Mich. Visited August 19th, by request of company, as they expected to operate soon, but mine is still idle.

Kings.

Located near Ellis Station, on the C. & M. V. R. R. Owned by R. J. King, Zanesville, O.

COAL MINES ABANDONED DURING YEAR.

No. 37, (1 and 2).

Located at Cannelville, O. Owned by Fobes & Thompkins Coal Co., Columbus, O

No. 16.

Located at Cannelville, O. Owned by Maynard Coal Co., Columbus, O.

Werner No. 1.

Located three-fourths of a mile east of Zanesville, O. Owned by W. A. Werner. Zanesville, O.

CLAY MINE.

Lehigh No. 2.

Located at Ironspot, on the C. & M. V. R. R. Operated by the Hydraulic Pre/. Brick Co., Ironspot, O. R. F. Wallace, Roseville, O., Supt. and mine boss. Drift openings, Nos. 5 and 6 seams of clay, 8 ft. thick; fan ventilation; employs 16 miners and 3 day hands. Two visits made, May 20th and August 29th, found mine in fair condition.

PERRY COUNTY.

Union.

Located near Crooksville, O., on a branch of the C. & M. V. R. R. Operated by Union Coal Mining Co., Columbus, O. George Carding, Rose Farm, O., Supt.; N. W. Spencer, Crooksville, O., mine boss. Drift, No. 6 seam of coal, 3½ ft. thick; fan ventilation; machine mining; employs 20 miners, 4 machine runners and 13 day men. Visited January 25th, found mine in fair condition. Mine has been suspended since April 1st.

Keystone No. 1.

Located at Crooksville, on C. & M. V. R. R. Operated by Zanesville Coal Co., Crooksville, O. Thomas Opie, Crooksville, O., Supt.; George McClellan, same place, mine boss. Drift, No. 6 seam of coal, about 3 ft. 6 in. thick; fan ventilation; machine mining; employs 116 loaders, 16 machine runners and 40 day men. Three visits were made. March 21st and 22nd, mine in fair condition. November 25th, mine in fair condition for force of men working; suggested a larger fan before force of men was increased.

Keystone No. 2 and 1 Off No. 2.

Located at McLuney, O., on the C. & M. V. R. R. Operated by Zanesville Coal Co., Crooksville, O. Thos. Opie, Crooksville, O., Supt.; Thos. Ward, McLuney, O., mine boss. Drift, No. 6 seam, 3½ ft. thick; two fans are used for ventilation; machine mining; employs 85 miners, 12 machine runners and 23 day men. Visited February 16th and November 28th, mine in fair condition on both visits.

Keystone No. 3.

Located at Crooksville, O., on the C. & M. V. R. R. Operated by Zanesville Coal Co., Crooksville, O. Thos. Opie, Crooksville, O., Supt.; C. A. Mullen, same place, mine boss. Drift, No. 6 seam, 3 ft. 8 in. thick; fan ventilation; pick mining; employs 30 miners and 6 day men. Visited January 21st and November 22nd, found mine in fair condition. Requested by miners to test scales and found them correct.

Keystone No. 4.

Located at Roseville, O., on a branch of the C. & M. V. R. R. Operated by the Zanesville Coal Co., Crooksville, O. Thos. Opie, Crooksville, O., Supt.; Thos. Evans, Roseville, O., mine boss. Drift, No. 6 seam, 3½ ft. thick; machine mining; fan ventilation; employs 40 loaders, 10 machine runners and 10 day hands. Three visits made. January 1st, visited in regard to machine feed wire being on opposite side of trolley; requested the use of this wire, as a feed wire, discontinued. March 29th and November 16th, mine in fair condition.

Rends.

Located at Crooksville, O., on C. & M. V. R. R. Operated by the Standard Hocking Coal Co., Chicago, Ill. N. B. Snell, Supt.; James Murphy, mine boss, both of Crooksville, O. Drift, No. 6 seam, 3½ ft. thick; fan ventilation; machine mining; employs 75 loaders, 12 machine miners and 33 day men. Five visits were made. Visited February 2nd, in company with Chief Inspector Harrison, found mine in very poor condition. Orders were given to clean motor road and place wire in lawful position, and brick stoppings on main air way. Visited on February 18th, found ventilation improved and mine in better condition. Mr. Rend, general manager of company, was at mine and requested me to eliminate brick stoppings; we agreed that he install a fan in the interior of mine at man way, and carry brick stoppings from that point, on main air ways. March 18th and 28th, was still repairing and new fan not running. November 23rd, mine just resuming work since April 1st. December 28th, mine in fair condition, new fan running and brick stoppings in, and other conditions fair.

Dixie.

Located at Dixie, on Shawnee Division of B. & O. R. R. Operated by Upson Coal & Mining Co., Newark, O. W. F. Upson, Newark, O., Supt.; John Bell, Dixie, O., mine boss. Drift opening, No. 6 seam, 3 ft. 8 in. thick; ventilated by two 5 ft. Sackett fans, machine mining; motor haulage; employs 60 loaders, 12 machine runners and 24 day men. Two visits made March 30th and December 19th, mine in fair condition on both visits.

C. & E, or Simons No. 5.

Located on branch of the Z. & W. R. R. Operated by A. C. Simons & Son, Redfield, O. A. C. Simons, Supt. and mine boss. Drift opening, No. 5 seam, 4 ft. thick; fan ventilation; machine mining; employs 28 loaders, 4 machine runners and 17 day hands. Three visits made. February 15th, November 14th and December 12th, mine in fair condition.

Davis Bros.

Located at Shawnee, O., on Z. & W. R. R. Operated by Davis Bros., Shawnee, O. T. L. Davis, Shawnee, O., Supt. and mine boss. Drift, No. 6 seam, 5 ft. thick; fan ventilation; machine mining; employs 26 loaders, 4 machine runners and 10 day men. Six visits made. March 25th, mine in fair condition. April 28th, mine in poor condition; loose rock and trolley wire in poor condition. Ordered men taken out of mine until repairing was done. May 5th and 18th, mine idle, still repairing. August 17th and October 26th, mine in fair condition.

Jones Bros.

Located at New Straitsville, O., on H. V. R. R. Operated by Jones Coal Co., New Straitsville, O. Evan Jones, same place, Supt. and mine boss. Drift opening to No. 6 seam of coal, about 12 ft. thick; natural ventilation; machine mining; employs 72 loaders, 6 machine runners, 20 day hands. Four visits were made. January 27th, May 24th, July 21st and October 25th, mine in fair condition on each visit.

B. & O. No. 3.

Located on Rock Run branch of B. & O. R. R. Operated by C. & H. C. & I. Co., Columbus, O. Fred Weymueller, New Straitsville, O., Supt.; Robert Nealson, same place, mine boss. Fan ventilation; machine mining: employs 22 loaders, 4 machine runners, 18 day hands. Two visits made. August 16th, tested scales. August 22nd, found mine workings in fair condition.

Greeley Nos. 1, 2, 3 & 4.

Located one mile east of McCuneville, O., on Shawnee Division of B. & O. R. R. Operated by Peabody Coal Co., Chicago, Ill. H. N. Young, New Lexington, O., Supt.; Oscar Tom, mine boss at Nos. 1 and 2, and Link Morrow, mine boss at Nos. 3 and 4, both of New Lexington, O. All coal from the four openings is handled over one Hopper scale. Drift openings to No. 6 seam, 3 ft. 8 in. thick; fan ventilation; machine mining; motor haulage; employs 138 loaders, 20 machine runners and 48 day hands. Ten visits made. Visited Nos. 1 and 2 January 27th, May 24th, July 21st and October 25th; found in fair condition. Visited Nos. 3 and 4 January 31st; found squeeze in No. 4 opening. May 31st, mine in fair condition. July 25th and 26th, requested a shaft sunk in interior of mine and fans for both openings placed there. November 2nd and 3rd, found shaft down and fans were being moved.

Central No. 3.

Located at New Straitsville, O., on the H. V. R. R. Operated by the C. & H. C. & I. Co., Columbus, O. Fred Weymueller, New Straitsville, O., Supt.; John Achauer and John Neilson, New Straitsville, O., mine boss. Drift, No. 6 seam, 8 ft. thick; fan ventilation; machine mining; employs 330 loaders, 22 machine runners and 80 day men. Nine visits made. On May 11th and 12th, mine ventilation poor; requested a new fan placed in an opening in the interior of mine. Visited again May 17th and 18th, found fan installed, with good results. August 2nd and 3rd, found mine in fair condition. August 15th, tested scales. October 3rd and 4th, investigated fatal accident of Alex. Angel, and found mine conditions improved.

XX Nos. 1 & 2.

Located at Shawnee, O., on Z. & W. and B. & O. R. R. Operated by Shawnee Coal Mining Co., Shawnee, O. D. C. Jenkins, Supt.; W. K. Redfern, mine boss, both of Shawnee, O. Drift, No. 6 seam, about 7 ft. thick; fan ventilation; machine mining; employs 40 loaders, 6 machine runners and 17 day hands. Four visits were made. June 21st and September 20th, mine in fair condition, all pillar work, almost complete.

Sunday Creek No. 268.

Located near Rendville, O., on T. & O. C. R. R. Operated by the Sunday Creek Coal Co., Columbus, O. Andrew Wilson, Corning, O., Supt. and mine boss. Slope, 400 ft. long; No. 6 seam of coal, 12 ft. thick; ventilated by two fans; machine mining; employs 230 loaders, 18 machine runners and 69 day men. Three visits made. May 6th, June 24th and September 21st; mine in fair condition. Ordered some minor repairs on each visit.

Sunday Creek No. 301.

Located at Congo, O., on the Z. & W. R. R. Operated by Sunday Creek Coal Co., Columbus, O. J. J. Murray, Congo, O., Supt. and mine boss. Shaft opening, 28 ft. to No. 6 seam of coal, about 13 ft. thick; fan ventilation; machine and pick mining; employs 40 miners, 250 loaders, 18 machine runners and 77 day men. Eight visits made. June 26th and 27th, mine in fair condition, except some wiring not in compliance with law. Visited May 25th and 26th, August 23rd and 24th, December 20th and 21st, found mine in fair condition.

S. C. No. 302.

Located at Congo, O., on Z. & W. R. R Operated by Sunday Creek Coal Co., Columbus, O. A. H. Braidwood, Congo, O., Supt. and mine boss. Shaft, 20 ft. to No. 6 seam of coal, 13 ft. thick: fan ventilation: machine mining: employs 275 loaders, 16 machine runners and 75 day hands. Five visits made. February 1st and June 8th, found mine in fair condition, except some breaks between rooms partly filled up with bone coal. Visited September 2nd and December 21st and 22nd, mine in fair condition.

S. C. No. 9, East Side.

Located at Carrington, O., on Z. & W. R. R. Operated by Sunday Creek Coal Co., Columbus, O. John Wiles, Hemlock, O., Supt.: E. W. Roberts, Hemlock, O., mine boss. Drift, No. 6 seam, 7 ft. thick: fan ventilation; machine mining: employs 26 loaders, 2 machine runners and 5 day hands. Four visits made. January 11th, May 19th and August 25th; found mine in fair condition. September 22d, tested scales, found weighing correctly.

S. C. No. 9, West Side.

Located at Carrington, O., on Z. & W. R. R. Operated by Sunday Creek Coal Co., Columbus, O. John Wiles, Hemlock, O., Supt.; E. W. Roberts, Hemlock, O., mine boss. Drift, No. 6 seam of coal, 5½ ft. thick: fan ventilation; machine mining; employs 180 loaders, 16 machine runners and 57 day hands. Four visits made; January 12th and May 19th, mine in fair condition. July 7th, mine in fair condition for force of men working. Requested a larger fan, or some change, for more ventilation. Visited October 11th, found a larger fan house built, furnishing a larger discharge for air, doubling the volume.

Hazelton.

Located near Shawnee, O., on Z. & W. R. R. Operated by George Gibbs, New Straitsville, O., who is Supt. and mine boss. Drift, No. 6 seam, 8 ft. thick; fan ventilation; machine mining: employs 34 loaders, 4 machine runners and 6 day hands. Four visits made. February 9th and March 16th, found mine in fair condition. Visited June 1st, found some dangerous roof and some wiring not in compliance with law. Visited September 1st, mine in fair condition.

Essex No. 37.

Located at New Straitsville, O., on H. V. R. R. Operated by Essex Coal Co., New Straitsville, O. H. H. Essex, Supt., and L. Essex, mine boss, both of New Straitsville, O. Drifts, No. 6 seam, about 7 ft. thick; natural ventilation; machine mining; employs 33 loaders, 4 machine runners and 7 day hands. Two visits made. July 18th and October 24th, mine in fair condition.

Santoy No. 1.

Located at Santoy, O., on the Santoy Division of the B. & O. R. R. Operated by New England Coal Co., Columbus, O. C. S. Wheeler, Santoy, O., Supt. and mine boss. Shaft, 185 ft. deep, to No. 6 seam, about 4 ft. thick; fan ventilation: machine mining; employs 32 loaders, 4 machine runners and 17 day hands. Visited December 13th, found mine in very bad condition, air-ways filled up with water and slate until too small; motor road was filled up until men could not pass motor trips, and stoppings in bad condition. Requested them put in with brick and cement and mine to cease operation until repair work was over.

Santoy No. 2.

Located one mile north of No. 1, on same railroad, and operated by same company as Santoy No. 1. C. S. Wheeler, Santoy, O., Supt. and mine boss. Shaft, 214 ft. deep, No. 6 seam, about 4 ft. thick; fan ventilation; machine mining; employs 40 loaders, 6 machine runners and 13 day hands. Two visits were made. January 20th, mine idle. Visited February 10th, found mine in fair condition.

Northwest No. 26.

Located one-half mile south of Corning, O., on the T. & O. C. R. R. Operated by the Chicago & Hocking Coal Co., Toledo, O. Daniel Cook, Corning, O., Supt. and mine boss. Slope, 300 ft. long, to No. 6 seam of coal; fan ventilation; machine mining; employs 30 loaders, 4 machine runners and 10 day hands. Two visits made. Visited October 5th, found idle, repairing to operate. Visited November 1st, mine in fair condition.

Chapman No. 1, Nos. 1 and 2 Openings.

Located one mile west of Moxahala, O., on branch of the T. & O. C. R. R. Operated by the Chapman Mining Co., Moxahala, O. H. N. Rose, Supt.; James Fleming, mine boss, both of Moxahala, O. No. 1 opening is a slope, 160 ft. long, to No. 6 seam of coal, 4 ft. thick; fan ventilation; machine mining; employs 18 loaders, 4 machine runners and 9 day hands. Three visits made. March 17th and December 14th, mine in fair condition. December 29th, investigated the fatal accident of Chas. Reed.

No. 2 opening is a drift, to same seam of coal, the coal being dumped over the same hopper, and practically the same conditions as No. 1; employs 70 loaders, 8 machine runners and 22 day hands. Visited March 17th and December 29th, found mine in fair condition.

Chapman No. 2, Nos. 3 and 4 Openings.

Located one mile west of No. 1, on same railroad. Operated and superintended by same company as No. 1. C. W. Holmes, New Lexington, O., mine boss. Slope openings to No. 6 seam, about 4 ft. thick. Both openings practically in same condition; fan ventilation; machine mining; employs 45 loaders, 6 machine runners and 20 day hands. Two visits made. Visited January 24th, mine in fair condition. April 1st, mine temporarily abandoned.

Bear Run No. 1.

Located at Goston, O., on the C. & M. V. R. R. Operated by W. A. Gosline & Co., Toledo, O. E. W. Lewis, New Lexington, O., Supt.; C. Priest, same place, mine boss. Shaft, 64 ft. deep, No. 6 seam of coal, 3½ ft. thick; fan ventilation; machine mining; employs 60 loaders, 12 machine runners and 33 day hands. Visited February 8th and December 15th, found mine in fair condition on both visits.

Peerless.

Located at Saltillo, O., on Z. & W. R. R. Operated by Hamilton & Wallace Coal Co., Saltillo, O. Wm. Wallace, Saltillo, O., Supt.; Edward Moore, same place, mine boss. Drift, to No. 6 seam, about 3½ ft .thick; fan ventilation; machine mining; employs 15 loaders, 4 machine runners and 9 day hands. Two visits made. February 17th, mine idle. Visited December 27th, mine in fair condition.

Wilbren.

Located at Wilbren, O., on the C. & M. V. R. R. Operated by Wilbren Coal Co., New Lexington, O. C. Priest, New Lexington, O., Supt. and mine boss; fan machine wire not in compliance with law. Visited June 9th, found mine idle. hands. Three visits made. February 14th, mine in fair condition, except some ventilation; machine mining; employs 30 loaders, 6 machine runners and 17 day December 16th, mine being operated by the G. M. Wilson Coal Co., Pittsburg, Pa. G. W. Brown, New Lexington, Supt. and mine boss. Mine was in poor condition, present mine boss only having been in charge of mine one week, and will soon have mine in fair condition.

Rock Run Coal.

Located on Rock Run, a branch of the B. & O. R. R. Operated by Iron Clay Brick Co., Columbus, O. O. F. Grimes, Shawnee, O., Supt.; Wm. Davett, same place, mine boss. Drift, No. 6 seam, 7 ft. thick; natural ventilation; employs 10 miners and 3 day hands. Two visits made. April 27th and September 19th, mine in fair condition.

Simons No. 2.

Located on Redfield branch of Z. & W. R. Operated by A. Simons & Son, Redfield, O. A. Simons, Supt. and mine boss. Drift, No. 5 seam, 4 ft. thick; furnace ventilation; pick mining; employs 13 miners and 4 day hands. One visit made. February 11th, mine in poor condition, very wet and no second opening. Requested mine repaired and management suspended it and has remained so since.

Lilly.

Located three-fourths of a mile east of New Lexington, on C. & M. V. R. R. Operated by Lilly Hocking Coal Co., Starr, O. W. O. Davis, New Lexington, O., Supt. and mine boss. Drift, No. 5 seam, 4½ ft. thick; furnace ventilation; pick mining; employs 33 miners and 10 day hands. Four visits made. May 27th, ordered second opening put in and furnace built, and gasoline pump moved on return air. Visited June 22nd, found mine in much better condition and still repairing. July 28th, found second opening completed and furnace built. Visited October 13th, mine in fair condition.

SMALL MINES IN PERRY COUNTY.

Perry No. 1.

Located on Redfield branch of the Z. & W. R. R. Operated by Perry Coal Co., Somerset, O. J. C. Williams, Somerset, O., Supt. and mine boss. Drift, No. 6 seam, 3½ ft. thick; furnace ventilation; pick mining; employs 8 miners and 3 day hands. Visited February 11th, mine in fair condition.

20th Century Nos. 1 and 3.

Located at Redfield, on the Z. & W. R. R. Operated by the 20th Century Coal Co., Columbus, O. J. C. Davis, Redfield, O., Supt. and mine boss. Pick mining and natural ventilation in both openings. No. 3 employs 7 miners and 2 day hands. No. 1 employs 6 miners and 1 day man. Two visits made. Visited December 23rd, all pillar and crop coal; mine in fair condition.

Sines Bros.

Located at New Straitsville, O. Operated by Sines Bros., New Straitsville, O. Drift, No. 6 seam, 6 ft. thick; natural ventilation; employs 7 pick miners and 1 day man. Visited March 24th.

A. Gibbs.

Located on Rock Run, on B. & O. R. R. Operated and managed by A. Gibbs, New Straitsville, O. Drift, No. 6 seam, 6 ft. thick; machine mining; natural ventilation; employs 7 loaders, 2 machine runners and 2 day men. Visited July 20th.

Garretts.

Located on Rock Run, on B. & O. R. R. Operated and managed by Garretts Coal Co., Shawnee, O. Drift, No. 6 seam, 6 ft. thick; natural ventilation: pick mining; employs 7 miners and 2 day men. Visited July 20th.

Webbs.

Located on Rock Run, on B. & O. R. R. Operated by Webb Coal Co., New Straitsville, O. Drift, No. 6 seam, 6 ft thick; natural ventilation; employs 7 miners and 2 day men. Visited July 20th.

Abrams.

Located at New Straitsville, O. Operated and managed by Abrams Bros., New Straitsville, O. Drift, No. 6 seam, 6 ft. thick; natural ventilation; employs 4 miners and 1 day man. Visited August 1st, mine in fair condition.

No. 9.

Located at New Straitsville, O., on H. V. R. R. Operated by Richardson Coal Co., New Straitsville, O. John Richardson, New Straitsville, O., Supt. and mine boss. Drift, on No. 6 seam, 6 ft. thick; natural ventilation; employs 6 miners and 1 day man. Visited October 17th, to investigate fatal accident to Walter Snedden. killed by fall of slate.

Underwood.

Located one mile west of New Lexington, O., on Shawnee road. Operated by Underwood Bros., New Lexington, O. Drift, No. 6 seam, 3 ft. thick. Furnace ventilation; machine mining; employs 4 loaders, 2 machine runners and 2 day men. Visited July 29th, requested some minor repairs.

Woods.

Located near Underwood. Operated by W. Woods, New Lexington, O. Drift, No. 5 seam, 4 ft. thick; natural ventilation; employs 5 miners and 1 day man. Visited July 29th, mine in fair condition.

Teals.

Located at Rehoboth, O. Operated by H. Teal, of Rehoboth, O. Drift, No. 5 seam, 4 ft. thick; natural ventilation; employs 2 miners and 1 day man. Visited January 17th, to see about installing a gasoline pump; found conditions fair.

MINE SUSPENDED IN PERRY COUNTY.

Pedlow, or S. C. No. 321.

Located at Misco, O., on Z. & W. R. R. Owned by Sunday Creek Coal Co., Columbus. O.

ABANDONED MINES IN PERRY COUNTY.

Beech Grove.

Located at McLuney, O., on C. & M. V. R. R.

Lyondale.

Located at Green Valley, O., on C. & M. V. R. R.

CLAY MINES IN PERRY COUNTY.

Rock Run.

Located on Rock Run branch of B. & O. R. R. Operated by Iron Clay Brick Co., of Columbus, O. O. F. Grimes, Shawnee, O., Supt.; R. D. Jones, same place, mine boss. Drift; furnace ventilation; employs 10 miners and 6 day men. Visited April 27th, mine in fair condition; second opening just completed. August 31st, ventilation very poor, requested a fan in place of furnace; was installed in five days.

Shawnee Flash Brick.

Located at Shawnee, on Z. & W. R. R. Operated by Shawnee Flash Brick Co., Columbus, O. E. M. Starner, Shawnee, O., Supt. and mine boss. Shaft, 90 ft. deep; fan ventilation; employs 6 miners and 2 day men. Visited June 6th and August 16th, mine in fair condition.

Impervious Clay.

Located at New Straitsville, O. Operated by Straitsville Impervious Brick Co., New Straitsville, O. J. D. Martin, Supt.; J. W. Call, mine boss, both of New Straitsville, O. Fan ventilation; employs 7 miners and 3 day men. Visited June 28th, mine in fair condition.

O. M. & M. C. Clay.

Located at Shawnee, Ohio. Operated by Ohio Mining & Mfg. Co., Shawnee, Ohio. E. W. Davis, Shawnee, O., Supt. and mine boss. Two shafts, 82 ft. deep. Fan ventilation; employs 25 miners and 6 day men. Three visits were made. May 4th, July 19th and October 10th. Requested stopping repaired on each visit.

Reeds Clay.

Located at Crooksville, Ohio. Employs 5 men. Visited November 4th.

Stoneburners Clay.

Located near Crooksville, Ohio. Employs 4 men. Visited November 4th.

Moore Bros. Clay.

Located near Crooksville, Ohio. Employs 4 men. Visited November 4th.

MORGAN COUNTY.

Tropic.

Located at Tropic, Ohio, on Z. & W. R. R. Operated by Tropic Mining Co., Toledo, Ohio. C. Spring, Rose Farm, O., Supt.; C. James, same place, mine boss. Slope, 900 ft. long; No. 6 seam of coal, 4 ft. thick; machine mining; fan ventilation; employs 170 loaders, 20 machine runners and 65 day hands. Three visits made, February 24th and 25th, found mine ventilation fair, but fan too small for force of men working, requested larger fan. Visited December 1st, found mine in fair condition, an 8 ft. Jeffrey fan having been installed, giving good results.

Rose.

Located near Tropic Station, on Z. & W. R. R. Operated by Carding Coal Co., Columbus, O. Geo. Carding, Rose Farm, O., Supt. Mine operated a short time the first of the year and suspended the remainder of year.

MINES VISITED IN THIRD DISTRICT.

ATHENS COUNTY.

Sunday Creek No. 201.

Located at Floodwood, Ohio, on the H. V. R. R. Operated by Sunday Creek Coal Co., Columbus, Ohio. Asa Hammond, Nelsonville, O., Supt.; Mat. Brandenburg, Floodwood, O., mine boss. Shaft, 90 ft. deep to No. 6 seam, 6 ft. thick; fan ventilation; machine and pick mining; employs 18 pick miners, 155 loaders, 14 machine runners, and 50 day men. Visited this mine July 11th and 12th, found mine in fair condition.

S. C. No. 204.

Located near Kimberly, Ohio, on the H. V. R. R. Operated by Sunday Creek Coal Co., Columbus, Ohio. Jos. Barber, Nelsonville, O., Supt. and mine boss. Drift, No. 6 seam, 6 ft. thick; fan ventilation; employs 6 pick miners, 160 loaders, 16 machine runners and 70 day men. Visited mine July 13th; mine in fair condition, except 3rd north entry, found a stopping out and short of ventilation; went to repairing at once.

Lama.

Located at Kimberly, Ohio, on the H. V. R. R. Operated by J. M. Lama, Nelsonville, O., who has supervision. Drift, No. 6 seam. Natural ventilation; employs 6 pick miners and 2 day men. Visited July 14th, mine in fair condition.

CLAY MINES IN ATHENS COUNTY.

Nelsonville Clay No. 1.

Same as No. 2. Furnace ventilation; employs 14 miners and 6 day men. Visited July 14th, mine in fair condition.

Nelsonville Clay No. 2.

Located at Nelsonville, O., on the H. V. R. R. Operated by Nelsonville Brick Co., Nelsonville, O. Jos. Roscoe, same place, has supervision. Drift opening to No. 5 seam of clay; fan ventilation; employs 24 miners and 10 day men. Visited July 14th, found mine in fair condition.

JEFFERSON COUNTY.

Amsterdam.

Visited this mine April 22nd, 23rd, and 24th, on account of explosion. A detailed report will be found in Thomas Morrison's report.

FIFTH DISTRICT.

W. H. TURNER.

COMPOSED OF GUERNSEY, NOBLE AND WASHINGTON COUNTIES.

(Succeeded by Abel Ellwood, Cambridge, Ohio, July 1, 1910.)

HON. GEORGE HARRISON, *Chief Inspector of Mines, Columbus, Ohio.*

DEAR SIR: — I herewith present my report of six months service, commencing January first and ending July first, 1910. Mr. Abel Ellwood, who succeeded me, took charge of the district, whom I accompanied through some of the important mines, imparting information concerning pending orders for improvements which had been ordered, and other desired instructions.

During the months of April and May, mining affairs continued in a perplexing state, pending the continued effort to amicably adjust the wage agreement, which was accomplished about June 1st, in all its phases. While some idleness was incurred on account of the miners becoming impatient during the delay, no strikes were inaugurated in this District.

During the period herein reported, I have had the co-operation of operators and miners, in the enforcement of laws, and preparing to conform to the new code, effective June 11th. During the sixty days grace following April 11th, when His Excellency, Governor Judson Harmon, attached his signature, a general activity was exercised in preparing to conform to the law, when it became effective, and some were successful in securing the important changes, while others were delayed by their inability to secure the necessary results, owing to the prevailing demand. All express their approval of the law, and desire to conform to its demands at their earliest convenience, which, if enforced, will increase the safety of both life and property, and reduce accidents to a minimum.

I wish to commend the members of the Mining Commission, who fearlessly performed their arduous duties, and judiciously framed and recommended laws, regulating all the dangers incident to modern mining, which were enacted without a dissenting voice.

With the advanced mining developments in the state, which are now provided with a full complement of miners who are daily becoming more practical in the duties of the avocation, and are being followed by their male posterity in the mining affairs, promises to place us upon a level with the older countries, with practical, experienced workmen, which will undoubtedly decrease the human slaughter that can only be charged to the incompetency of the victim or victims.

I regret to note that during my thirteen years experience in investigating fatal accidents, I found impracticability on one hand and over-confidence in the experienced miner on the other, have contributed to the larger per cent. of accidents we have recorded, and believe that a rigid enforcement of Section 952 on experienced and unexperienced men alike, by the mine managers, that many accidents would be averted, and workmen will become better disciplined through custom and cease trusting their judgments as to the strength of a hanging rock and place timbers underneath to make the place secure.

It is gratifying to us that during all these years no calamity of any nature has occurred under our jurisdiction, yet we have spent many restless hours when we knew the safety of men depended wholly upon the faithful performance of duty on the part of the managers, and the accuracy of maps of abandoned mines, fearing the possibility of error. We sincerely hope that our successor will be equally fortunate.

Eternal vigilance along all lines is the only reliable safeguard to avert similar calamities to that of Amsterdam. Conditions in many of our mines would produce the same results if neglected. This lurking danger must be recognized and treated accordingly, if we avoid heartrending catastrophies, destroying both life and property, impoverishing widows and orphans.

Some complaints are offered by the miners concerning the legal grade of oil, claiming it fails to burn fast enough, which is the greatest evidence of its desired quality. We readily recognize, while traveling the mine, since the new oil was introduced, that the smoke from lamps has decreased and the air is much superior in quality. Time will convince the miner that the small lamp and the improved oil is essential for safe and healthy ventilation, and remove the false desire to use the torch, fed by impure oils, diluting the air with poisonous fumes, unfitting it for healthy respiration.

In severing our official connection with the Department of Mines, we feel honored with the distinction of serving under seven different Governors, and three different Chief Inspectors, who never reversed an order given by us, and insisted that we should enforce the laws, regardless of fear or favor. We realize that this Department has made its greatest advancement toward securing adequate laws, and the uniformity of the enforcement of same throughout the State during *the past six years,* due to the untiring efforts of a practical miner as Chief, a practical Mining Commission and practical District Inspectors. Our associations have been pleasant with all whom our work brought us in contact. We have never resorted to law in securing the enforcement of same, from either operator or miner, and we retire with good will to all and malice toward none.

Thanking you for the wise counsel rendered, and wishing you every success,

Respectfully submitted,

W. H. TURNER, *Cambridge, Ohio,*

July 1, 1910. *Inspector 5th District.*

BELMONT COUNTY.

NOTE: Warren Township, No. 8 coal, 4½ ft. thick.

Media.

Drift, located on the B. & O. R. R., near Baileys Mills, O. Owned by the Colburg Coal Co., Columbus, O. Charles Elliott, Supt.; Joseph Shooter, mine boss, both of Baileys Mills. Fan ventilation; electric haulage; employing 80 miners and 24 day hands. May 3rd, investigated the accidental death of Edward Murphy. Ordered the posting done more promptly, under the draw slate, cared for by the miner, under our agreement. Otherwise conditions approved. June 30th, investigated the death of Harrison House, caused by deficient posting. Called the attention of the managers to section 952 of the mining law, and ordered them to enforce it strictly. Gathering motors were installed. Ordered a fender placed outside of the trolley wire, opposite switch points entering working places. Conditions were approved along other lines.

Cochran.

Drift, situated on the B. & O. R. R., near Baileys Mills, O. Controlled by the W. A. Werner Coal Co., Zanesville, O. J. E. Morris was manager while the mine was operating. 72 miners and 30 day hands employed. February 9th, found the shields broken off the machines. Ordered the boss to cease operating them until the shields were replaced. February 17th, found the machines properly shielded. Advised that an adequate fan displace the furnace. May 3rd, found the mine idle since April 1st and still idle June 30th. Mr. Morris has secured a position elsewhere and Thomas Davy was looking after the property. The fan had not been installed, which will be essential to meet the requirements of the late law before operation can resume.

Captina.

Shaft, situated on the O. R. & W. R. R. in Washington township, Belmont County, owned by the Captina Coal Co., Armstrongs Mills, O. Wm. Rankin, same place, manager. Visited this mine in company with Mr. Lot Jenkins, inspector in charge, who had closed the mine until it was placed in condition to conform to the law, and we found his action justifiable to avert a probable calamity.

GUERNSEY COUNTY.

NOTE: All mines are working No. 7 coal, which varies in thickness from 5 to 7 ft., excepting Indian Camp and Union, which penetrates No. 6 coal seam, varying from 2 ft. 4 in. to 3½ ft.

The following nine mines, beginning with Ideal and ending with Buffalo, are electrically equipped, have fan ventilation, and are operated by the Cambridge Collieries Co., of Cleveland, O. P. Y. Cox, General Manager, assisted by Harry Cameron, with main office in Cambridge, Ohio.

Ideal.

Shaft 75 ft. deep. Situated on the Penna. R. R., near Byesville, O. D. B. Morse, Supt.; Robt. Robison, L. A. Scott, are mine foremen on the south section, and J. B. Dawson on the north section of the mine. 258 miners and 114 day hands employed. March 21st and May 24th, conditions approved. Overcasts were being erected to split the air to the south and to increase the volume to conform to the new law. July 6th, accompanied Mr. Ellwood, our successor; found the overcasts completed and ventilation in satisfactory condition in the south section, which was the only territory examined on this occasion; the reconstruction of the stable had not reached completion. Requested Mr. Morse to perfect the work at his earliest convenience.

Walhonding No. 2.

Shaft, 161 ft. deep. Situated near Buffalo, Ohio, with transportation over both the B. & O. and Penna. R. Rs. Employs 141 miners and 73 day hands. J. C. Henderson, Supt., Buffalo, O.; Charles O. Morrow, mine foreman, Pleasant City, O. January 11th, tested two sets of scales, finding them accurate. May 5th, conditions commendable. The stable under construction surpassed the demands of the statute.

Hartford.

Shaft, 85 ft. deep. Located at Buffalo, Ohio, with transportation over the B. & O. and Penna. R. Rs. H. S. Gander, Supt.; O. P. Moss, mine foreman, both of Buffalo, O. Employs 136 miners and 64 day hands. January 31st, investigated the death of William Cooper, killed by a lump of coal rolling over on him while loading a car. Found general conditions satisfactory. May 25th, the fan house had burned during the night; the inspection was omitted. June 29th, requested repairs made on the stairs in the third opening, and the reconstruction of the stable, excepting the air-split, completed. The connection now made to the Buffalo mine provides the fourth outlet, as soon as the cages are in operation, making ready escape for both mines, in case it is needed.

Trail Run No. 1.

Shaft, 72 ft. deep. Located on the Penna. R. R., near Trail Run, O. Matt Straugh, Supt.; Geo. Slay, mine foreman, both of Robins, O. Employs 156 miners and 62 day hands. March 25th, owing to a recent fall in the main air course, ventilation was deficient; a part of two stoppings were removed, giving vent to the current around the obstruction, until it could be removed. Advised the fan house remodeled and the air shaft cribbing renewed.

Trail Run No. 2.

Shaft, 112 ft. deep. Situated on the same railroad switch, near No. 1. A. L. Black, Supt.; Joseph Wootton, mine foreman, both of Robins, O. Employs 164 miners and 88 day hands. March 28th, conditions approved. Extensive changes were being made by erecting overcasts to shorten the air travel, when the rock entry pierces the north workings, which will assure the best and most reliable ventilation, and meet the requirements of the new law, and it is evidence of the exceptional ability of the management.

Detroit.

Shaft, 185 ft. deep. Located on the Penna. R. R., near Ava, Ohio. Jerry Oldroyd, Supt.; O. Fowler, mine foreman, both of Ava, O. Employs 121 miners and 68 day hands. February 11th, ordered the use of insulators and refuge holes made on 21st west entry. January 14th, investigated the death of John Brondus, timber man, who was killed by a fall of slate while preparing to cross timber same. April 27th, conditions were approved. Owing to unusual conditions surrounding this mine much additional expense is incurred in advancing with reasonable safety.

Midway.

Slope, 100 ft. long. Situated on the Penna. R. R., near Byesville, O. Geo. E. Hall, Supt.; Thomas Bradbury, mine foreman, both of Byesville, O. Employs 100 miners and 50 day hands. February 7th, ordered the electric wires removed from the last breakthroughs, between working places, in three instances, and leakages repaired that partially supplied the fan with air from the north shaft and surface breaks, without traveling the working sections. May 18th, ordered all inlets of air closed off, excepting the south shaft and obstructions removed from some of the refuge holes along the main motor lines and the practice of carrying the tools up and down the stairway abolished.

Blue Bell.

Shaft, 85 ft. deep. Situated on the B. & O. R. R., near Blue Bell, Ohio. J. M. Burt, Supt.; M. L. Kaehley, mine foreman, both of Pleasant City, O. Employs 106 miners and 45 day hands. March 28th, conditions were approved.

Buffalo.

Shaft, 82 ft. deep, situated on the Penna. R. R., one mile north of Derwent, O. Coal was struck March 23, 1910. Joseph Sharp, Supt.; D. H. Thomas, mine foreman, both of Byesville, O. April 12th, stone from the shaft was being crushed, preparatory to starting the foundations for machinery and buildings. June 23rd, they were laying off the foundation. We informed them that all buildings must be at least 60 ft. from the shaft. This promises to be one of the most modern of mines, and will afford an escape-way for both Hartford and Trail Run No. 1 mines, the former mine is already connected and the latter is driving in close proximity to connect. A slope, with an independent travel way, is going down. Every move indicates an honest desire on the part of the company and managers to reduce all dangers to a minimum and conform strictly with the statutes.

The following four mines, beginning with Kings and ending with Cleveland No. 1, are owned by the Morris Coal Co., Cleveland, O. John Simpson, with main office in Cambridge, Ohio, is general manager. These mines are electrically equipped and ventilated with modern fans:

Kings.

Shaft, 100 ft. deep, located on the B. & O. R. R., near Lore City, O. A. J. Lafferty, Supt, Cambridge, O.; Walter Snedden, mine foreman, Lore City. O. 242 miners and 121 day hands were employed. February 8th, being informed that the tipple, boiler house, power house and fan house had been consumed by fire during the night, we proceeded to the scene, finding the night men encountered no difficulty in reaching the surface through the escape shaft and the mules were safe and sound in the stable below. We recommended that a power line be extended from Black Top mine and a fan installed at an early date for the protection of the mules and attendants. March 28th, learning that the mine was to be dismantled, and no fan yet in operation, ordered a fan installed before the work should commence; the orders were complied with, and the material removed from the mine. The writer does not know what the future procedure with this mine will be.

Old Orchard.

Shaft, 48 ft. deep, located on B. & O. R. R., near Mineral Siding, A. J. Lafferty, Supt.; J. S. Hughes, mine foreman, both of Cambridge, O. Employs 180 miners and 60 day hands. This mine resumed operation February 23rd, 1910, after a continued idleness extending from March 31, 1908. March 2nd, conditions approved, with recommendation that an air interior opening be secured through the old abandoned Wilson mine.

Black Top.

Shaft, 120 ft. deep, situated on the B. & O. R. R., near Lore City, O. A. J. Lafferty, Supt., Cambridge, O.; Walter Snedden, mine foreman, Lore City, O. Employs 156 miners and 56 day hands. March 29th, ordered cement stoppings continued to the face of the main airways, all wires strung on insulators, and the stable reconstructed to conform with the law, the partition between the down and upcast repaired.

Cleveland No. 1.

Shaft, 198 ft. deep, situated on the B. & O. R. R., near Senecaville, O. Edward Lynch, Supt.; Wm. Sellers, mine foreman, both of Senecaville, O. Employs 164 miners and 64 day hands. April 26th, investigated the death of William Fiske, a water hauler, who was killed by a fall of slate. The general condition of the mine was approved, excepting the stable, which was ordered reconstructed to conform to the new regulations. June 29th, investigated complaint, charging persons with violating Section 959, by passing a danger signal, finding the charge true, we ordered the mine foreman to perform his duties, as prescribed in Section 952, by prosecuting the violators. A drill hole was being sunk on the north side in the abandoned works to permit the escape of a constant generation of carburetted hydrogen gas in that section of the mine. Mr. Simpson informed us that after the completion of this hole the gas accumulations disappeared. The stable was being remodeled to conform to the law.

The following three mines named, beginning with Ohio No. 1 and ending with Imperial No. 1, are owned by the O'Gara Coal Co., Chicago, Ill. James Orr, general manager, with main office located in Byesville, Ohio. All are electrically equipped, with fan ventilation, but Ohio No. 1, which has furnace ventilation, pick mining and mule haulage:

Ohio No. 1.

Drift, located on the Penna. R. R., near Cambridge, O. Joseph Alloway, mine foreman, Cambridge, O. Employs from 3 to 6 miners. Since March 31, 1908, this mine has operated for domestic trade alone. May 27th, conditions approved.

Ohio No. 2.

Shaft, 65 ft. deep, located on the Penna. R. R., near Byesville, O. Harry Dudley, Supt.; Alex. Sigman, mine foreman, both of Byesville, O. Employs 48 miners and 27 day hands. This being a limited coal field motor haulage was never installed. The pillars are being removed and nearing exhaustion. March 24th, conditions approved.

Imperial No. 1.

Shaft, 110 ft. deep, located on the Penna. R. R., near Derwent, O. W. A. Oliver, Supt., Byesville, O.; Alex. Sigman, mine foreman, Byesville, O. Employs 166 miners and 84 day hands. February 8th, we gave instructions concerning the reconstruction of the underground stable. February 24th, visited the mine to investigate a death. Found mine idle on account of the bottom lands being flooded. We accompanied Mr. Ort and the mine committee over the bottom lands to agree upon a danger line, and decided so long as the creek and the tributaries thereto contained the waters in bank the men were allowed to enter the mine, under the previous ruling of the Mining Department. We returned on the 25th, finding the mine working, and the death above referred to due to natural causes. Our examination of the rock entry section of the mine proved satisfactory. We advised that the reconstruction of the stable be completed as soon as possible. June 8th, the stable was completed, excepting the inch siding on stalls and mangers, and the air split from the inlet. A splendid system of hose and pipe is provided for use in case of fire. On this occasion the west side of the mine was found in compliance with law. July 5th, accompanied our successor, Abel Ellwood, finding the stable about completed and ventilation satisfactory, but could not consider the two ways from the interior on the west side safe and available for travel, as demanded by the statutes, effective June 11th. We ordered such provisions made, either by sinking an interior air shaft, or clearing a road, making travel available.

The National Coal Co., of Akron, Ohio, operate the following three mines, which are electrically equipped and have fan ventilation, beginning with Little Kate No. 1 and ending with Minnehaha. G. L. Walkinshaw is general manager, main office at Byesville, O.

Little Kate No. 1.

Shaft, 100 ft. deep, located on the Penna. R. R., near Byesville, O. G. W. Chambers, mine foreman, Byesville, O. Employs 180 miners and 75 day hands. March 17th, operation had resumed recently after an extended suspension; repairs had been made during the idleness, and the mine was found in compliance with the law. June 28th, being notified through the Mining Department that pillar drawing would begin at an early date, we examined the territory, methods and systems to be employed by Mr. Chambers while removing same, and fully approved them with the understanding that practical men only would participate. Advised the speed of the fan increased 15 revolutions per minute to assure the amount of air determined by the new law at the inlet.

Little Kate No. 2.

Slope, 300 ft. long, situated on the B. & O. R. R., near Blue Bell, O., with transportation over the Pennsylvania R. R. James Martin, mine foreman, Pleasant City, O. Employs 175 miners and 38 day hands. March 15th, tested the scales, found them accurate. May 19th, gave orders to abolish the practice of lowering powder in the slope with the electric haulage, and an additional fire boss employed in order to examine the mine in the time limited. June 21st, investigated the death by electrocution of Michael Katchmarack. Ordered the trolley wire shielded in front of all partings leading to working places. We found the orders issued on our previous visit were executed. June 24th, investigated the death of Chas. Steinbrook, trip rider, who was running along the rib, trying to board a moving trip and was caught between the cars and rib and rolled, dying from the injury received a few hours later. The general condition of the mine was approved on this occasion.

Minnehaha.

Slope, 115 ft. long, situated at the terminus of a five mile switch, leading from the Penna. R. R., near Byesville, O. C. B. Llewellen, Byesville, O., mine foreman. Employs 222 miners and 64 day hands. April 11th, investigated the death of John Patrigo, from electrocution. Ordered shields placed along the trolley wires of the gathering motors, opposite switch points, leading to working places. Otherwise conditions were approved.

Forsythe.

Slope, 110 ft. long, located on the B. & O.. near Mineral Siding, O. Operated by the Forsythe Coal Co., Cambridge, Ohio. J. P. Davis, Supt.; W. A. Alderman, mine foreman, both of Cambridge. Fan ventilation; electrical equipments; employing 153 miners and 58 day hands. March 30th, we approved of conditions under the existing laws. Advised that an interior shaft be sunk to enable them to meet the requirements of the law, becoming effective June 11th, and protested against the idea offered, to place a fan inside the mine, as a booster. Our experience has convinced us that all fans should be located either at the inlet or outlet of air for safe and reliable ventilation.

Klondyke.

Slope, 150 ft. long, located on the B. & O. R. R., near Klondyke, O. Operated by the Loomis-Moss Coal Co., Akron, O. Harry Moss, general manager; James Moss, Supt., both of Cambridge, O.; Allen Treherne, mine foreman, Kipling, O. Electrically equipped, with cable haulage; fan ventilation; employing 90 miners and 31 day hands. January 28th, conditions approved.

Murray Hill.

Slope, located on the B. & O. R. R., near Klondyke, O. Operated by the Akron Coal Co., Akron, O. Wm. Rigby, Supt., Cambridge, O.; Clarence Long, mine foreman, Kipling, O. Employs 40 miners and 15 day hands. January 28th, conditions were in compliance with law. Fan ventilation; electric mining and haulage; cable hoist.

Puritan.

Shaft, 106 ft. deep, situated on the Penna. R. R., near Derwent, O. Operated by the Puritan Coal Co., Cambridge, O. W. A. Lucas, Supt., Cambridge, O.; Chas. Haskins, mine foreman, Byesville, O. Electrically equipped; fan ventilation. Employs 129 miners, 47 day hands. February 24th, recommended the reconstruction of the stable to comply with orders. Otherwise conditions approved.

Union No. 1 and Indian Camp Mines.

Drifts, situated on the Penna. R. R., near Birds Run, O. U. G. Williams, Birds Run, Ohio, receiver. Made no effort to operate during the period covered by this report.

Little Trail Run.

Slope, 160 ft. long, situated on the Penna. R. R., near Byesville, O. Operated by the Byesville Coal Co. Harry Davis, Supt.; Benjamin Morris, mine foreman, all of Byesville, O. Has electrical mining, haulage and pumping; fan ventilation.

Employs 73 miners and 19 day hands. March 9th, ordered one machine shield replaced; insulators used in stringing wires; stoppings, repaired, directing air to 11 and 12 east entries. June 23rd, found mine idle. The inspection was omitted.

Guernsey Brick.

Drift, situated on the Penna. R. R., near Byesville. O. Operated by the Guernsey Clay Co., Byesville, O. Adam Bates, Cambridge, O., succeeded Chas. Rabe, who resigned on account of ill health, about February 1st, as mine foreman. Employs 9 miners and 1 day hand. March 10th, conditions approved, with the understanding that the forces could not be increased until an available escapeway is provided.

Red Oak.

Drift, located near Byesville, O., on the Penna. R. R. Operated by the Domestic Coal Co., Cambridge, O. Furnace ventilation. Compressed air mining and pumping; mule haulage. John Wilson, manager, Cambridge, O. Employs 11 miners and 5 day hands. February 21st, ordered the mine map corrected and returned to the office of the Mining Department. April 27th, conditions approved.

West Branch.

Slope, 66 ft. long, located on the Penna. R. R., near Byesville, O. Operated by the Clinton Mining Co., Cambridge, O. Edgar Collier, manager, Byesville, O. Fan ventilation; electric mining; mule haulage and cable hoist. Employs 44 miners and 14 day hands. March 3rd, ordered three drill holes, carried in advance of 1 and 2 west entries approaching the abandoned Sugar Point mine, and the manway cleared of obstruction. March 6th, Sugar Point was tapped by one cut of the machine, and all men escaped with little difficulty. Mine remained idle about three weeks, while getting control of the water emitted. An investigation proved that only one three foot hole had been drilled before cutting the entry.

Valley.

Slope, 119 ft. long, situated on the Penna. R. R., near Byesville, O. Operated by the Cambridge Valley Coal Co., Cambridge, O. E. W. Stalter, manager, Byesville, O. Fan ventilation; electrical mining and pumping; mule haulage. Employs 17 miners and 7 day hands. February 5th, advised that all places be stopped before reaching high water mark; an adequate fan to displace the steam jet in use, and the mules stabled on the surface. April 21st, previous orders, excepting with reference to the fan, were enforced. We again urged an early construction of the fan, believing the jet would prove deficient on the approach of extreme hot weather. May 25th, the fan was in operation much to our gratification, and ventilation commendable. A piece of unowned coal land had been passed with 1 and 2 west entries, reaching the territory belonging to this Company, which was being speedily developed into territory; the roads were being relaid with heavy iron preparatory for motor haulage, which will be in operation before the close of this year, and so reported by my successor.

Leatherwood No. 2.

Drift, located on the B. & O. R. R., near Cambridge, O. Edward Alexander, Cambridge, Ohio, receiver Fan ventilation; electrically equipped, and with the exception of producing boiler fuel and a little domestic coal, this mine remained suspended during the time herein reported.

GUERNSEY COUNTY.

Small mines, employing less than ten men, located near Cambridge, Ohio, working No. 7 coal seam.

Burris.

Operated by James Burris, Cambridge, O., employing from 2 to 6 men.

Briar Hill.

Owned by Wm. Nicholson, operated by Elmer Wharton, both of Cambridge, O., employing from 2 to 4 men.

Wild Cat.

Operated by Jas. Stoner, Cambridge, O., employing from 2 to 4 men.

The following small mines are located near Quaker City and Salesville, O. Pierce No. 8 coal seam, which is 4 ft. thick.

Keenan.

Operated by C. E. Keenan, Quaker City, O.

Carter.

Operated by J. B. Carter, Quaker City, O.

Holensworth.

Operated by Dr. Holensworth, Quaker City, O.

B. L. Galloway.

Operated by B. L. Galloway, Quaker City, O.

E. B. Galloway.

Operated by E. B. Galloway, Quaker City, O.

Webster No. 1.

Operated by Waldo Webster, Quaker City, O.

Webster No. 2.

Operated by Clyde Hays, Quaker City, O.

Montgomery.

Operated by J. W. Montgomery, Quaker City, O.

Sayer.

Operated by Samuel Sayer, Quaker City, O.

Hall.

Operated by Jabo Cleary, Spencer Station, O.

Spencer.

Operated by Richard Spencer, Quaker City, O.

McCormick.

Operated by Clarence McCormick, Quaker City, O.

Bates.

Operated by Richard Bates, Quaker City, O.

NOBLE COUNTY.

Laura.

Shaft, 185 ft. deep, situated on the Penna. R. R., near Coal Ridge, O. Operated by the Belle Valley Coal Mining Co., Cambridge, O. T. E. Richards, Supt., Cambridge, O.; J. B. Morris, mine foreman, Coal Ridge, O. Employs 164 miners and 34 day hands. May 4th, conditions approved, with the understanding that the stable would be reconstructed to conform to the recently enacted statutes. Fan ventilation; modern electrical equipments are employed.

Caldwell.

Shaft, now being sunk by the Belle Valley Coal Mining Co., Cambridge, O., situated on the Penna. R. R., near Caldwell, O. T. E. Richards is superintendent, Cambridge, O.: W. J. Metheney, mine foreman, Caldwell, O. July 8th, when visited by Hon. George Harrison, Chief Inspector of Mines, Abel Ellwood, District Inspector, and the writer, the shaft was down about 16 ft., the switches were being graded and the location of the buildings were determined. Indications are that this will be one among the modern mines of the State, and the producing of the experience of our extensive mining business.

Imperial No. 3.

Shaft, 189 ft. deep, located on the Penna. R. R., near Belle Valley, O. Operated by the O'Gara Coal Co., Chicago, Ill. James Orr, Supt., Byesville, O.; J. A. Collins, mine foreman, Belle Valley, O. Fan ventilation; modern electrical equipments. Employs 133 miners and 56 day hands. February 8th, advised upon the reconstruction of the underground stable. February 14th, tested scales, found them accurate. March 16th, investigated the death of John Boyd, stable boss, who dropped dead on the surface, near the hay barn; found death due to natural causes. June 7th, conditions were approved, with the understanding that the stable would fully conform to the law, when effective, and the trolley wire would be set 6 inches outside and parallel with the rail on the run around.

Coal Run.

Drift, situated on the O. R. & W. R. R., near Hiramsburg, O. Robert Aultman, manager, Hiramsburg, O. Furnace ventilation; pick mining; mule haulage; employs 10 miners and 2 day hands. Conditions satisfactory, considering the small force employed.

Marion.

Slope, 75 ft. long, situated on the O. R. & W. R. R., near Steam Town. Operated by the Marion Coal Co., Whigsville, O. J. W. Young, manager, Sarahsville, O. Employs 14 miners and 2 day hands. Furnace ventilation; pick mining; mule haulage and cable hoist. Conditions were approved. Mr. Young informed me that a fan was ordered and would be installed soon. We are advised that this company has changed since our last visit.

JEFFERSON COUNTY.

Y. O. Mine (Amsterdam), Located near Amsterdam, Ohio.

In obedience to orders received by 'phone, at 1 o'clock, A. M., April 22nd, we met Hon. Geo. Harrison, Chief Inspector of Mines, at Newcomerstown, and proceeded to the Y. & O. Mine, at Amsterdam, where a local explosion had occurred on the south side of the mine. We joined the rescuers upon our arrival, and at 3 P. M. the following day the last body was removed from the mine, 15 in all; 12 deaths being due to suffocation from after damps and 3 deaths due to force and burns. After examining the interior of the mine we were of the opinion that the explosion was first started by two machine men igniting gas, at the face of the south entries, which carried flame, igniting the latent gases over the worked out territory between 1 and 2 and 3 and 4 west entries, which extended force and destruction to the main shaft, wrecking stoppings, disarranging fan and the air current. All who attempted to escape from the south section were suffocated. Three men who were rescued alive are entitled to due credit for returning to the interior of the mine beyond the point where the after damps were traveling to the upcast. The writer had jurisdiction and inspected this mine, periodically, for about one year, during 1906. Realizing this, like many other mines in this State, was generating sufficient gas to cause destruction of life and property at any time if eternal vigilance was neglected; and we trust that the death and destruction produced by this explosion will be accepted as a warning to all concerned in mining, and every precaution exercised to avert similar calamities in the future. The State is to be commended for the prompt action taken for the relief of the families that were robbed of their support by this unwelcomed event.

Respectfully,

W. H. TURNER, *Cambridge, Ohio,*
Inspector Fifth District.

July 1, 1910.

FIFTH DISTRICT.

ABEL ELLWOOD.

Composed of the Counties of Guernsey, Washington and Noble.

CAMBRIDGE, OHIO, December 31, 1910.

HON. GEO. HARRISON, *Chief Inspector of Mines, Columbus, O.*

DEAR SIR:—I have the honor of submitting to you my first annual official report of the Fifth Mining District, covering the period from the date of my appointment July 1, 1910, to December 31, 1910, which embraces the counties of Guernsey, Washington and Noble.

During the time covered by this report two new mines were opened, one abandoned and four remained suspended.

With but few exceptions the mines of this district have worked very steady during the time covered by this report, and all permanent improvements have been made when conditions demanded them.

With but few exceptions, the recently enacted law relating to the construction of underground stables was observed and complied on or before the law took effect, and the new mining code, in general, has been reasonably well observed.

It has been my highest aim in the discharge of my duties to protect the lives and health of the miners of this district by registering a strong complaint against any matter, thing or practice, that in my opinion, would be dangerous to employes, yet I regret very much to record 14 fatal accidents in this dictrict for the 6 months covered by this report, as well as a large number of serious accidents, some of which may yet prove fatal, as some have sustained a fracture of the spine. Twelve of the fatal accidents occurred in Guernsey County and 2 in Noble.

Four arrests were made in this district during the time covered by this report; two charged with violating the law governing the crossing of a danger signal of the fire boss, and were fined $25.00 each, and one charged with violating the law governing the selling of impure oil, who was also fined $25.00.

One mine superintendent was arrested, charged with violating the law governing the running of trips of cars ahead of motor without a signal light on the front car. I also regret to state that the same trip rider and motorman who furnished the statements that led to the arrest, when the fatal accident of one of their fellow workmen was investigated, who was killed by the violation, refused to testify against the management and the case had to be withdrawn. We are unable to determine why employes would refuse to testify in court in a case which so directly concerned them, and where the object of the arrest was for the betterment of their conditions in regard to the safety, and the stamping out of an unlawful and dangerous practice that cost the life of one of their fellow craftsmen only a few days previous.

A large percent of the operators and mine foremen of this district take pride in keeping their mines in the best possible condition and observe the mining laws and rules of the Department, and see to it that others do so, while the remaining few who disregard the laws and rules of the Department encourage their employes to do likewise, resulting in no discipline which is essential to safety, and the result is an unnecessary number of fatalities.

In conclusion I desire to state that my official dealings with both miners and operators have been of the most pleasant character, and the assistance of both in securing better and safer conditions throughout the mines of this district is fully appreciated.

Extending to you my hearty appreciation for your ever ready and valuable advice rendered in the complicated affairs that have confronted me in the discharge of my duties.

Respectfully,

ABEL ELLWOOD, *Cambridge, Ohio,*
Inspector Fifth District.

December 31, 1910.

GUERNSEY COUNTY.

NOTE: All mines not otherwise mentioned are located in the No. 7 seam of coal which runs from 5 to 7 ft. in thickness. The following nine mines are operated by the Cambridge Collieries Company, Detroit, Michigan.

P. Y. Cox is the general superintendent and Harry Cameron, assistant superintendent, with office at Cambridge, Ohio.

Blue Bell.

Shaft, 85 ft. deep, situated on the B. & O. R. R., near Blue Bell, Ohio. J. M. Burt, Supt.; M. L. Kachley, mine foreman, both of Pleasant City, O. Fan ventilation, modern electric equipments, employing 120 loaders and 47 day men. July 28th, ordered the report of the fire bosses kept at mine office, and test weights provided. November 15th, conditions approved.

Buffalo.

Shaft, 92 ft. deep, situated on the Penna. R. R., near Buffalo, Ohio. This is a new mine and was not fully equipped on this visit. Fire proof building and steel tipple are being erected; indications are that this will be a modern mine in every respect. October 27th, mining was progressing satisfactorily and the mine is ventilated from the Hartford mine fan. Joseph Sharp, Buffalo, O., Supt.; D. H. Thomas, Byesville, O., mine foreman. Employs 34 miners, 53 day men. Conditions fair.

Detroit.

Shaft, 185 ft. deep, situated on the Penna. R. R., near Ava, Ohio. Jerry Oldroy, Supt.; and Oscar Fowler, mine foreman, both of Ava, O. Fan ventilation and electrical equipments; employs 103 miners and 56 day men. July 8th, investigated fatal accident of Joseph Thomas, trapper boy, killed by fall of slate while on his road from his door to parting. July 14th, ordered refuge holes along motor line whitewashed; other conditions fair. August 23rd, ordered a refuge hole made at trap door on 20 east entry for the safety of trapper. November 23rd, conditions approved.

Hartford.

Shaft, 75 ft. deep. Located on the B. & O. R. R., at Buffalo, Ohio. Fan ventilation, electrical equipments; employs 147 loaders and 70 day men. H. F. Gander, Supt.; John Moss, mine foreman, both of Buffalo, O. July 15th, investigated fatal accident of Andy Robish, loader, killed by fall of slate. August 29th, ordered obstruction removed and refuge holes whitewashed. November 22nd, again ordered refuge holes whitewashed and additional ones made on 21 west, where some new work was being started, and ordered the waste hay taken out of stable and the dust and fine coal cleaned off of a portion of the main motor road.

Ideal.

Shaft, 70 ft. deep, situated on the Penna. R. R., near Byesville, Ohio. Fan ventilation, electrical equipments; employs 265 miners and 112 day men. D. B. Morse, Supt.; Robert Robison, L. A. Scott and Pete Thompson, mine foremen, all of Byesville, O.

July 6th, the underground stable was not yet completed on this visit, which was ordered rushed to completion at the earliest possible date. September 14th. The stable was completed on this visit and conditions approved. December 6th.

The ventilation on the south side of the mine was found deficient on this visit, and 11 and 12 east entries were stopped and orders given to keep the men out until the difficulty could be found and a lawful amount of air furnished. Orders were also given to remove from the mine the dust and fine coal that had been deposited along the track on the main south, and to keep the power off the wire in rooms when not in use, and requested an attendant placed at 14 east motor door. December 12th, returned on this visit to investigate the conditions of the air on the entries that showed such a deficiency on December 6th. The ventilation had been improved, but was still short of a lawful amount in some parts, and as this part of the mine has advanced almost an unreasonable distance from an opening an air shaft was requested sunk, which would afford an escapement way for employes and also solve the problem of ventilation; this matter was taken up at the Cambridge office with the proper officials and they agreed to sink a shaft at the earliest possible date.

Midway.

Slope, 90 ft. long, situated on the Penna. R. R., near Byesville, Ohio. G. E. Hall, Supt.; Thos. Bradberry, mine foreman; both of Byesville, O. Fan ventilation, electrical equipments; employs 95 miners and 50 day men. July 25th, ordered safety gate made and fence around manway and the electric wires changed on bottom of manway where employes were forced to travel under and cease the dangerous practice of carrying tools down the man way. September 26th, the requests made on the previous visit had been complied with and general conditions approved. December 16th. Conditions fair and approved .

Trail Run No. 1.

Shaft, 72 ft. deep, situated on the Penna. R. R., at Trail Run. Matt Strauch, Supt.; Geo. Slay, mine foreman, both of Robins, O.; fan ventilation electric mining and pumping, cable haulage. August 19th, ordered signal lights carried on rope haulage trips; other conditions fair. November 9th, investigated the accidental death of Leander McConneha, driver, caused by empty trip jumping track, which caught him between empty trip and loads on parting. General condition satisfactory.

Trail Run No. 2.

Shaft, 106 ft. deep, situated on the Penna. R. R., near Trail Run. A. L. Black, Robins, O., Supt.; and Joseph Wooton, Cambridge, O., mine foreman; Fan ventilation, electrical equipments; employs 165 miners and 75 day men. August 17th, conditions fair and approved. October 31st, mine found in excellent condition.

Walhonding No. 2.

Shaft, 160 ft. deep, situated on the B. & O. R. R., near Hartford, Ohio. Fan ventilation, modern electrical equipments, J. C. Henderson, Supt.; Buffalo, O., Charles O. Marrow, Pleasant City, O., mine foreman; Employs 160 miners and 100 day men. August 22nd., ordered emergency signal placed in shaft and test weights provided. Other conditions fair. November 16th, conditions commendable.

Black Top.

Shaft, 100 ft. deep, located on the B. & O. R. R., near Lore City, Ohio. Owned and operated by the Morris Coal Co., Cleveland, O. Fred Hornicle, Cambridge, O., Supt.; Walter Snedden, Lore City, O., mine foreman; Fan ventilation, electrical equipments; employs 155 miners and 60 day men. July 11th, ordered guards placed along trolley wire at crossings of travel ways, and to insist on loaders providing boxes for their powder. Other conditions fair. October 12th, general conditions fair and approved. December 13th, ventilation found deficient, both at the inlet and in the interior workings, but on inquiry from the miners developed the fact that this condition did not always exist, and that the ventilation was generally good; a reasonable time was granted to restore the ventilation to the required standard; a force of men immediately started to overhaul the stoppings and doors.

While at the mine on this visit, Wm. Parker, boss hauler, had the misfortune to lose his left hand in a motor wreck.

Cleveland.

Shaft, 180 ft. deep, situated on the B. & O. R. R., near Senecaville, O. Owned by the Morris Coal Co., Cleveland, O.; Fan ventilation, modern electrical equipments. Fred Hornicle, General Supt.; Cambridge O., Edward Lynch, Supt.; and Wm. Sellers, mine foreman, both of Senecaville, O. Employs 150 miners and 65 day men. August 15th, conditions approved. October 28th, a strong feeder of oil had broken into the mine at the head of 7 and 8 west entries and work in the entries had been suspended; the oil was being taken out as fast as it collected in order to avoid the danger of fire; otherwise the mine was in good condition. December 21st, conditions commendable.

Old Orchard.

Shaft, 45 ft. deep, situated on the B. & O. R. R., near Mineral Siding. Owned by the Morris Coal Co., Cleveland, O.; Fred Hornicle, Cambridge, O., Supt.; and John Hughes, Cambridge, O., mine foreman; Fan ventilation, electrical equipments; employs 125 miner and 46 day men. July 20th, conditions approved. October 17th, a shortage of air was found on 29 and 30 west entries, due to leaking brattices and trap doors, which were ordered repaired at the earliest possible date. November 1st, returned for the purpose of ascertaining whether the previous orders had been complied with, and finding the conditions of the air worse than before, the doors and stoppings on 29 and 30 west entries not repaired, ordered the mine foreman to cease work on enough places at the head of the two entries to reduce the number of men in accordance with the amount of air traveling the entries; also ordered them kept out until such time as a lawful amount of air could be supplied. December 20th, investigated the accidental death of Edward Landman, caused by a fall of slate on December 8th and died on December 18th. The ventilation on this visit on 29 and 30 west was excellent and conditions commendable.

Little Kate No. 1.

Shaft, 100 ft. deep, situated on the Penna. R. R., near Byesville, O. Owned by the National Coal Co., Cleveland, O.: G. L. Walkinshaw, Supt.; and G. W. Chambers, mine foreman, both of Byesville, O. Fan ventilation, electrical equipments; employs 175 miners and 70 day men. August 12th, mine found in good condition. October 19th, conditions fair and approved.

Little Kate No. 2.

Slope, 300 ft. long, situated on the B. & O. R. R., near Blue Bell, O. Owned by the National Coal Co., Cleveland, O.: G. L. Walkinshaw, Byesville, O., Supt.; James Martin, Pleasant City, O., mine foreman: Fan ventilation, electrical equipments entirely: employs 200 miners and 45 day men. August 1st, a shortage of air was found at the inlet, which was ordered increased and the machine wires which were hung on road posts in rooms were ordered changed and the refu[illegible] holes on motor lines cleaned out. Strict orders were given to carry signal lig[illegible] on motors, and a travel way ordered made around a parting where employes w[illegible] forced to travel between trips and under the trolley wires. July 27th, investiga[illegible] the accidental death of David Foster Bates, trip rider, caused by falling off of t[illegible] front end of motor. August 9th, returned for the purpose of seeing if t[illegible] requests made on the first were being complied with. Found the conditions [illegible] the intake air current very much improved and the other orders complied with an[illegible] conditions approved. November 3rd; James Martin had been succeeded by Wm Wilson, as mine foreman. Ordered the stoppings between permanent inlet and outlet air ways built of brick and cement; ordered the pressure gauge repaired and put in use and the refuge holes cleaned.

Minnehaha.

Slope, 135 ft. long, situated on the Penna. R. R., on a 5 mile switch, leaving main line near Byesville, O. Owned and operated by the National Coal Co., Cleveland, O. Electrical equipments. G. L. Walkinshaw, Byesville, O., Supt.; C. B. Llewellyn ,Claysville, O., mine foreman; Employs 220 miners and 76 day men. August 8th, ordered signal lights promptly put on all motors and trolley wire overhauled and made to conform to the law, and guards placed along same at travelways; a travel way was ordered made around a parting where employes were forced to travel between trips and under trolley wire, and refuge holes ordered whitewashed. September 7th, investigatd fatal accident of George Felida, killed by empty car jumping track that was being pushed ahead of motor and crushing him between car and corner of room neck. Visited 9 and 10 east entries, which we were unable to reach on previous visit; condition of same fair. November 10th, investigated fatal accident of David Smith, loader, killed by fall of slate. November 18th, investigated fatal accident of Henry Abrahams, motorman, killed by trolley pole knocking out timber and causing the slate to fall on him. November 28th, on this visit the wiring of the mine for the application of electric power for the operation of electric motors was carefully examined and showed considerable deviation from the general code. Gave a specific order, and returned December 2nd, and, with but few exceptions, the trolley lines and appliances of the power had been made to conform to the law and rules of the Department; general conditions were commendable.

Imperial No. 1.

Shaft, situated on the Penna. R. R., at Derwent, Ohio, controlled by the O'Gara Coal Co., Chicago, Ill.; fan ventilation, electrical mining and pumping; rope and electric haulage; employs 160 miners and 82 day men. J. C. Orr, Supt.; W. A. Oliver, mine foreman, both of Byesville, O. July 5th, ordered refuge holes whitewashed, signal light carried on rope haulage trips and hand rail put on stairway leading into tipple. August 26th, found a shortage of air at the inlet, and orders were given to reduce the force of men accordingly until such time as the volume of air could be increased. Recommended that a larger fan be installed. November 17th, investigated fatal accident of Isaac Fluehart, loader, killed by a fall of slate. December 1st, the ventilation was found greatly improved and the mine in good condition.

Ohio No. 1.

Drift, situated on the Penna. R. R., near Cambridge, Ohio. Owned by the O'Gara Coal Co., Chicago, Ill. Furnace ventilation. J. C. Orr, Byesville, O., Supt.;

Joseph Alloway, Cambridge, O., mine foreman; Employs 4 miners, 1 day man; supplies wagon trade only. Operation was suspended March 31st, 19[illegible]. October 18th, conditions approved.

Ohio No. 2.

Shaft, 65 ft. deep, situated on the Penna. R. R., near Byesville, O. Owned by the O'Gara Coal Co., Chicago, Ill.; J. C. Orr, Supt.; Harry Dudley, mine foreman, both of Byesville, O. Employs [illegible] miners and 27 day men; fan ventilation, electric mining and haulage. July 21st, conditions fair and approved. October 21st, conditions met with approval.

Clifton.

Slope, [illegible] ft. long, situated on the Penna. R. R. on local switch, near Byesville, O. Controlled by Jamie Freeman; Edgar Collier, Byesville, O., mine foreman. Fan ventilation, electric mining and pumping, mule haulage and cable hoist; employs [illegible] miners and [illegible] day men. August [illegible], conditions fair and approved. October [illegible], the mine being about finished on this visit orders were given to have a correct map made to file with the Chief Inspector of Mines and County Recorder when abandoned. Abandoned November 3rd, [illegible].

Forsythe.

Slope, [illegible] ft. long, situated on the B. & O. R. R., near Mineral Spring. Operated by the Forsythe Coal Co., Cambridge, O.; J. P. Davis, Supt.; [illegible] Alderman, mine foreman, both of Cambridge, O. Fan ventilation, modern electrical equipments, employing [illegible] loaders and [illegible] day men. July [illegible]th, ordered refuge holes whitewashed and guards placed along the trolley wire at crossings. August 30th, tested the hopper scales and found correct. October [illegible]th, found there had been a change in the management since the last visit, Superintendent James P. Davis having been succeeded by Wm. Sheehan. Ordered refuge holes whitewashed, guards placed along trolley wires at traveling crossings and the wire changed on No. 1 face where the trolley wire was on one side and machine wire on the other. Otherwise, conditions fair. December 14th, investigated the accidental death of Wm. Galligher, caused by the fall of slate while drawing posts.

Guernsey Clay Mine.

Drift, situated on the Penna. R. R., near Byesville, Ohio. Owned and operated by the Vigo Clay Co., Cambridge, O. Adam Bates, Cambridge, O., Supt.; and mine foreman. Furnace ventilation, mule haulage; employs 10 miners and 8 day men. July 22nd, ordered stoppings repaired and door hung on man-way. September 23rd, ordered test weights secured. Conditions of mine fair and approved. November 26th. This visit was made by request of Company, as an old test oil and gas well had been broken into and it was thought the mine was filling with gas. After a careful examination with a safety-lamp (and no trace of gas being found), the mine was reported safe and the men returned to work. Ordered a brick wall built around the opening for a form and filled with cement to dam the opening off from the mine. December 5th, returned to investigate the condition and status of the test well and found it had been closed, as requested, which was a complete success. Conditions of mine fair and approved.

Klondyke.

Slope, 165 ft. long, situated on the B. & O. R. R., near Klondyke, Ohio, controlled by the Loomis & Moss Coal Co., of Akron, Ohio. James Moss, Cambridge,

O., Supt.; Allen Treherne, Kipling, O., mine foreman. Fan ventilation, electrical mining and pumping; cable haulage; employs 100 miners and 32 day men. July 13th, mine found in good condition. October 10th, investigated the accident of Clark Padget and Israel Ramage, who were caught by a fall of slate on October 6th, both sustaining a broken back. Clark Padget died from the injuries on October 14th, 1910. Conditions of mine fair and approved.

Little Trail Run.

Slope, 160 ft. long, located on the Penna. R. R., near Byesville, Ohio. Operated by the Byesville Coal Co., Byesville, O. Fan ventilation, electrical equipments and cable hoist. Hiram Davis, Supt.; and Benjamin Morris, mine foreman, both of Byesville, O. Employs 50 loaders and 19 day men. July 19th, ordered the test weights provided and to see that the loaders provide boxes for powder. September 1st, investigated the accidental death of Frank Maley, extra driver, caused by falling in front of his trip. September 22nd, ordered signal light placed immediately on motor, signal light carried on front car of empty trip which is pushed ahead of motor from bottom to the interior of mine. October 25th, ordered some stoppings, which were leaking, repaired; other conditions fair and approved.

Leatherwood.

Drift, situated on the B. & O. R. R., near Cambridge, Ohio. Was operated by the Leatherwood Consolidated Coal Co., Toledo, O. Fan ventilation, electric mining, haulage and pumping. With the exception of a little domestic coal the mine has been idle since March 31st, 1908

Murray Hill.

Slope, 165 ft. long, situated on the B. & O. R. R., near Klondyke. Operated by the Akron Coal Co., Akron, O. William Rigby, Cambridge, O., Supt.; C. E. Long, Kipling, O., mine foreman.' Fan ventilation, electric mining, mule haulage, cable hoist. July 12th, with the exception of the muddy haulways the mine was in good condition. October 13th, conditions met with approval.

Puritan.

Shaft, 110 ft. deep, situated on the Penna. R. R., near Derwent, O., controlled by the Puritan Coal Co., Cambridge, O. Wm. Lucas, Cambridge, O., Supt.; C. E. Haskins, Byesville, O., mine foreman. Fan ventilation, electrical equipments; employs 153 miners and 60 day men. August 2nd, ordered refuge holes whitewashed, and power kept off the wire in rooms when not in use. August 6th the underground stable not being completed and very little work accomplished on it, ordered the mules kept on the outside until same could be completed. October 26th stable was completed and the mine in good condition.

Red Oak.

Drift, situated on the Penna R. R., near Byesville, O. Owned and operated by the Domestic Coal Company, Cambridge, O. J. R. McBurney, Supt.: J. F. Wilson, mine foreman, both of Cambridge, O. Furnace ventilation, compressed air mining and mule haulage. Employs 11 miners and 5 day men. September 16th, mine found in good condition. November 2nd, orders were given to see that the men provide boxes for their powder. Conditions of mine fair and approved.

Valley.

Slope, 119 ft. long, situated on the Penna. R. R., near Byesville, Ohio. Operated by the Cambridge Valley Coal Co., Cambridge, O. Otis Moss, Buffalo O., Supt.; E. V. Stalter, Byesville, O., mine foreman. Fan ventilation; electrical equipments and cable hoist; employs 42 miners and 15 day men. July 26th, conditions fair. October 4th, ordered test weights provided. Mine in fair condition. December 15th, conditions approved.

Indian Camp & Union No. 1.

Located near Birds Run, O., has remained suspended during the entire year.

SMALL MINES EMPLOYING LESS THAN TEN MEN, WORKING NO. 7 COAL.

Briar Hill.

Drift, operated by W. F. Nicholson, Cambridge, O. Employs from 3 to 5 men.

Deep Cut.

Drift, operated by J. E. Burris, Cambridge, O. Employs from 4 to 5 men.

Lloyd.

Drift, operated by John Lloyd, Cambridge, O. Employs 5 men.

Ross Scott.

Drift, operated by Siras Lafollete, Cambridge, O., Employs 2 men.

Sugar Tree.

Drift, operated by Gable & Frame, Byesville, O. Employs 7 men.

SMALL MINES EMPLOYING LESS THAN TEN MEN, LOCATED NEAR QUAKER CITY, OHIO, WORKING NO. 8 COAL, WHICH IS 4 FEET IN THICKNESS.

Galloway.

Drift, operated by E. B. Galloway, Quaker City, O. Employs from 2 to 3 men.

Montgomery.

Drift, operated by J. W. Montgomery, Quaker City, O. Employs 2 men.

Sears.

Drift, operated by Samuel Sears, Quaker City, O. Employs from 2 to 4 men.

Webster.

Drift, operated by Waldo Webster, Quaker City, O. Employes 2 men.

NOBLE COUNTY.

Caldwell.

Shaft, 209 ft. deep, situated on the Penna. R. R., near Caldwell, O. This is a new mine that is just being equipped with the best and latest improved machinery and fire proof buildings. Indications are that this will be a modern mine along all lines. It is owned by the Belle Valley Coal Mining Co., of Cambridge, O. T. E. Richards, Cambridge, O., Supt; W. J. Matheny, Caldwell, O., mine foreman. One visit was made to this mine while it was being sunk; conditions satisfactory.

Laura.

Shaft, 185 ft. deep, situated on the Penna. R. R., near Coal Ridge, O. Operated by the Belle Valley Coal Mining Co., Cambridge, O. T. E. Richards, Cambridge, O., Supt.; J. B. Morris, Belle Valley, O., mine foreman. Fan ventilation, electric equipments employs 150 loaders, 55 day men. August 10th, ordered the stock stabled on the surface until such time as the underground stable could be completed; other conditions fair. November 14th, found a lawful stable erected, and the mine in good condition.

Golden Rod.

Shaft, 200 ft. deep, located on the Penna. R. R., near Coal Ridge, O. Operated by the Guernsey Coal & Mining Co., Newark, O. George A. Blood, Newark, O., Supt.; L. M. Haskins, Pleasant City, O., mine foreman. Fan ventilation, electrical equipments, employs 30 miners and 15 day men. July 7th, found in fair condition. September 6th, ordered the pressure gauge and test weights provided, and refuge holes whitewashed. November 25th, conditions approved.

Noble.

Shaft, 187 ft. deep, located on the Penna. R. R., near Belle Valley, O. Operated by the O'Gara Coal Co., Chicago, Ill. J. C. Orr, Byesville, O., Supt.; J. A. Collins, Belle Valley, O., mineforeman. Fan ventilation, electrical equipments; employs 115 loaders and 52 day men. August 11th, ordered the mules stabled on the surface until such time as the underground stable was made to meet the requirements of the law. Other conditions fair. October 8th, investigated the accidental death of Simon Strosko, day hand, caused by the fall of slate. November 11th, found in good condition.

Coal Run.

Drift, in the No. 8 seam of coal, situated on the O. R. & W. R. R., near Hiramsburg, O. Operated by G. W. Figgins, Cumberland, O. Furnace ventilation, mule haulage; employs 10 miners and 2 day men. December 23rd, mine found in good condition.

Marion.

Slope, 70 ft. long, located on the O. R. & W. R. R., near Summerfield, O., working No. 8 coal. Operated by the Marion Coal Co., Columbus, O. Grover Lauenstine, Columbus, O., Supt.; C. T. Hague, mine foreman. Fan ventilation, pick mining, mule haulage, cable hoist. Employs 10 miners and 3 day men. September 1st, conditions approved. November 1st, ordered some brattices repaired, and recommended that larger pillars be left between rooms to prevent a squeeze.

Upholds.

Drift, No. 8 seam, operated by J. A. Upholds, Cumberland, O. Employs 4 men.

Curtis.

Visited for the purpose of investigating fatal accident to G. W. Low, who was killed by a fall of roof, December 13, 1910.

SIXTH DISTRICT.

ALEX. SMITH.

COMPOSED OF THE COUNTIES OF COSHOCTON, TUSCARAWAS, ALSO COLUMBIANA, FOR A PERIOD OF SIX MONTHS.

HON. GEORGE HARRISON, *Chief Inspector of Mines, Columbus, O.*

DEAR SIR:—In conformity with the long established custom of the Mining Department, I herewith submit for your approval the report of the Sixth Mining District. This report embraces the period from January 1st, to December 31st, 1910, inclusive, and the Counties of Columbiana, Coshocton and Tuscarawas, until July 1st, thereafter Coshocton and Tuscarawas only, Mr. Robert S. Wheatley, of Salineville, Ohio, having been appointed, Columbiana County was placed in the 12th District July 1st.

During the period covered by this report, ten new mines were opened, five abandoned and four resumed operation. Five pairs of scales were tested, 3 were found correct and 2 incorrect; fifty permanent improvements are recorded, as follows: 3 fans, 12 furnaces, 16 air-shafts, 11 second openings, 7 stairways and 1 fire basket.

I regret to have to record 7 fatal accidents; also one death from unknown or natural causes: 4 in Columbiana County, 1 in Coshocton County and 2 in Tuscarawas County, and one death, at the Warwick No. 4 mine, Coshocton, Ohio, due to natural causes; 4 were killed by falls of stone, one by dust explosion, one by runaway cars on incline, and one by falling in front of his trip of cars.

There were two prosecutions, at Newcomerstown, O., for selling oil in violation of law, both parties pleading guilty and were fined $25.00 and costs.

Work throughout the district for the year was only very moderate. In the early part work was very much interrupted by mines being flooded with water. Some mines which had been in operation for years were laid idle for the first time in their history. The mining scale between operators and miners expired April 1st. This, in many places, caused mines to cease operation April 1st, for several weeks; the miners in Tuscarawas County after being idle three or four weeks in April, resumed work, pending a settlement of their sub-district scale, and at a joint conference of operators and miners, held in Canton, the first week in June, they failed to reach a settlement on the machine scale, for cutting and loading, and a strike was declared, beginning June 11th, and the mines in the whole county, with few exceptions, have been idle since, no settlement having been reached at this writing. This strike has had a very detrimental effect on the county in many ways, for many of the best miners, with their families, have moved to other States; others have moved to other counties, thus affecting the moral as well as the commercial and industrial condition of the county.

I am pleased to note the ready response to the new Code of Mining Laws, which was submitted by the Mining Commission to the 78th General Assembly and passed without a dissenting vote. The present as well as future generations are already reaping benefits long denied their forefathers. Yet, in speaking of the new Code, it is not so perfect as to cover every condition to be met in mines; this, I observe, was also noted by the Commission, when the matter of systems of mining was considered; the dangerous system of solid shooting is still the same dangerous element that it was, even though it has been attended with such dire results, the two explosions at the Delmore Mine in Columbiana County following each other within forty days, and claiming three victims as a sacrifice, emanating from the same causes and conditions, it would seem that these two terrible catastrophes would have made a lasting impression, and would have been a warning to all men to cease such a vicious system. Notwithstanding these frequent occurrences we found mines in the Washingtonville district still indulging in these same methods of producing coal. Written notices were served on the management and miners of the Big Walnut and McNab mines March 16th and 17th, respectively, that at least one-half of their coal must be mined, that no hole be drilled past cutting or shearing, and all holes drilled on a line with shots so made; that shot firers, if such were employed, should tamp all holes, or see them tamped; and that no drill dust or dry material should be used as tamping; these were the same orders that had been given at Delmore mine before the last explosion and which, upon investigation, were found to have been disregarded and violated, and at each mine where the above orders were given men came on strike against them and stayed out for four weeks.

At a request of operators and miners, Chief Inspector Harrison, Inspectors Miller and Morrison and myself, met the operators and miners of the Big Walnut and McNab mines, at Salem, April 12th, and fully discussed the conditions and dangers in those mines to men and property, but after hearing their arguments the Department could not agree with them so far as to revoke the orders, but insisted that the orders must stand.

This system of solid shooting which came with the introduction of the drilling machine, and the importation of men with little experience in mining has since been fostered by miners and encouraged by some coal companies because of the profits in the sale of powder, and the large percent of screenings, until it has become one of the most dangerous elements in some of the dry mines, and we shall hail the day when shots will be properly prepared and tamped, and the danger reduced or eliminated.

In conclusion permit me to say that, as a whole, my official relations with the operators and miners have been most pleasant, considering the changes demanded by the new Code, which went into effect June 11th last; also with the members of the Department, and especially do I appreciate your advice and counsel, and ever ready assistance at all times.

Respectfully submitted,

ALEX SMITH,

150 Minnich Ave., New Philadelphia, O.,

December 31, 1910. *Inspector Sixth District.*

COLUMBIANA COUNTY.

Garside.

Located two miles from Salineville, on a branch of the C. & P. R. R. Owned and operated by the Big Vein Coal Co., Cleveland, Ohio. T. R. Lewis, Alliance, O., Supt.; James Campbell, Salineville, O., mine boss. Two inspections made by me during the first half of the year, February 1st and May 11th. On February 1st found the mine in reasonably fair condition, considering the conditions to be met. A small quantity of gas was found in No. 11 face entry, and in 41 butt entry, but air was in good circulation; safety catches tested at both shafts; No. 1 was in good working order, but at the No. 2 they failed to work, and were ordered repaired immediately. On my second visit found a new superintendent in charge, Mr. W. P. Crookson, of Massillon; found mine in fair condition; three new automatic doors had just arrived to be placed on the north side of mine. Ordered pressure gauge placed and stables built to conform to new code. Having been relieved of Columbiana County July 1st, subsequent inspections will be reported by Mr. Wheatley, who was appointed to take charge of that county.

Strabley.

Located at Salineville, on C. & P. R. R. Operated by the Strabley Mining Co., Salineville. O. J. S. Strabley, Supt. and mine boss. Drift opening to No. 7 seam, 5 ft. thick. Fan ventilation; machine mining; motor and mule haulage; 29 miners and 13 day hands employed. Two visits made, May 13th and June 10th. On the former visit the mine in poor condition, air in very poor circulation; gave orders to place doors, stoppings and trolley wires as provided by law as soon as possible. June 10th, found orders carried out and the mine in fair condition.

Old Slope.

Located at Salineville, on the C. & P. R. R. Operated by Ohio & Penna. Coal Co., Cleveland, O. Joseph Nelms, Supt., and Wm. Beynon, mine boss, both of Salineville, O. Slope opening to No. 6 seam, 4½ to 5½ ft. thick. Machine and hand pick mining; 66 miners and 28 day hands employed; motor and mule haulage. Three visits made, February 2nd, 10th, and May 12th. On the former and latter visits found the mine in fair condition, at least in as fair a condition as the system of operation would permit, as all work being done was the robbing of pillars. February 10th, was called to investigate the fatal accident of John Ludlam, who met his death in No. 4 room, off Burns entry, on February 9th, a full account of which was sent to the office of the Department.

Big Walnut.

Located about two miles from Washingtonville, on the Y. & O. R. R. Operated by the Card & Prosser Coal Co., Cleveland, O. Thomas Prosser, Lisbon, Ohio, Supt.; J. F. Waters, Washingtonville, O., mine boss. Slope opening to No. 3 seam of coal, 3 ft. 3 in. thick. Fan ventilation; rope and mule haulage; single entry system; pick mining, or solid blasting; 57 miners and 17 day hands employed. Three visits made; March 16th, fairly good condition, but very dry and dusty; miners were blasting about all coal off the solid, nothwithstanding they had previously been requested to mine part of their coal. Shot-firers are employed, but a goodly number of miners were still tamping their own shots. A written order was given that all shots in future must be mined at least one-half; that no hole be drilled beyond the cutting or shearing; and all holes drilled on a line with shots so made, and that shot-firers should fire no shots unless they tamped them themselves, or saw them tamped. On the following day the miners refused to obey the order and the mine was idle as a result until April 18th. On April 12th, in company with Chief Inspector Harrison, Inspectors Miller, of Massillon, and Morrison, of Sherodsville, we met the operators and miners of the Big Walnut and McNab mines, in Salem, Ohio, for the purpose of reaching some agreement whereby the mines could be safely operated and the lives of the employes guarded against the evils of solid shooting; this meeting, however, failed to accomplish any definite conclusion. On May 5th we found the mine operating and the orders of the Department reasonably well carried out and dust well sprinkled. July 13th, we visited mine in company with new inspector, Robert Wheatley, and found it in fair condition, with air in good circulation, and the mine much more damp and safe than previously; this visit will doubtless be reported in detail by Mr. Wheatley.

State Line No. 3.

Located at East Palestine, on P. Ft. W. & C. R. R. Operated by the National Fireproofing Co., Pittsburg, Pa. W. F. Kocher, Supt.; Charles Jones, mine boss, both of E. Palestine, O. Drift opening to No. 7 seam of coal, 2½ ft. thick, clay beneath coal 3½ to 4 ft. thick, both of which are mined. Visited March 25th, and found the management experiencing much trouble on account of water, but mine was again getting into fair condition; 16 miners and 7 day hands employed; rope and mule haulage; conditions approved.

State Line No. 1.

Located at East Palestine, O., on P. Ft. W. & C. R. R. Operated by the State Line Coal Co., Cleveland, O. Hugh Laughlin, Supt.; Geo. Southern, mine boss, both of East Palestine, O. Employs 150 miners and 30 days hands; rope and mule haulage. Two visits made, March 25th, conditions in our territory approved. June 7th, tested scales and found correct.

Beech Grove.

Located on C. & P. R. R., at Salisbury, Ohio. Operated by Robert Bursner, Cleveland, O. Edward Hart, Supt.; Jacob Ehlenbach, mine boss, both of Salisbury, O. Slope opening to No. 3 seam of coal, 3 ft. 3 in. thick. Fan ventilation; pick and machine mining; rope and mule haulage; 20 miners and 8 day hands employed. Visited March 14th, found in poor condition; a squeeze had shut off 4th, 5th and 6th, right entries; timbers inside passage way were ordered renewed and two doors placed to aid circulation of air.

Klondyke.

Located at Lisbon, Ohio, on the Erie R. R. Operated by the Card & Prosser Coal Co., Cleveland, O. Thomas Prosser, Lisbon, Supt. Drift opening to No. 6 seam, 2 ft. thick; single entry system; electric machine mining; motor and mule haulage inside, rope haulage outside. Visited January 18th, to investigate fatal accident to Edward Yarwood, who was killed by runaway cars between the mine and the tipple, on January 13th; this was a very unfortunate accident; two cars had broken away from the trip and came one-fourth of a mile down a steep grade; Mr. Yarwood, who was Check weighman at the tipple, was running away to safety, as he supposed, when the cars jumped the track and forced him through the side of the tipple, where he fell 22 ft. below the cars, the cars falling on him.

Salem.

Located three miles east of Salem, on the Y. & O. R. R. Operated by the Salem Co., Salem, O. Wm. Dunn, Salem, O., Supt.; R. J. Borden, Salem, R. F. D. No. 6, mine boss. Drift opening to No. 3 seam of coal, 3 ft. thick. Electric machine mining; motor and mule haulage; fan ventilation; single entry system; 70 miners and 22 day hands employed. Three visits made: January 21st, found mine in fair condition, except air, which was ordered given immediate attention. May 4th, found mine fair, but ordered ventilation increased to meet requirements of new law. July 12th, visited in company with Mr. Wheatley, inspector of that district; found a Booster fan had been installed to aid circulation, but soon after entering the mine we discovered the belt had broken on the new fan. Inspector Wheatley will no doubt report this inspection in detail.

Fairfield No. 3.

Located at New Waterford, on P. Ft. W. & C. R. R. Operated by the Fairfield Coal Co., Cleveland, O. Hugh Laughlin, East Palestine, Supt.; Wm. Shasteen, New Waterford, mine boss. Drift opening to No. 6 seam, 3 ft. thick. Rope and mule haulage; furnace ventilation; single entry system; 103 miners and 22 day hands employed. Visited June 9th, found in good condition, both in regard to ventilation and travel. Ordered a fan installed at the earliest possible moment to meet requirements of new law. Superintendent Laughlin consented to do so immediately, and in about three weeks received word from him that the fan had been placed and was in operation, giving good results.

Prospect Hill No. 1.

Located at East Palestine, Ohio, on P. Ft. W. & C. R. R. Operated by the Prospect Hill Coal Co., East Palestine, O. Grant Hill, Supt.; Thos. Stackhouse, mine boss, both of E. Palestine, O. Slope opening to No. 6 seam, 3 ft. 4 in. thick. Compressed air machine mining; fan ventilation; rope and mule haulage; single entry system; 61 miners and 15 day hands employed. Visited March 24th and conditions approved; tested scales and found them incorrect; ordered them put in condition at once.

Prospect Hill No. 2.

Located two miles west of East Palestine, Ohio, on the P. Ft. W. & C. R. R. Operated by same company as No. 1, same superintendent, James Fleming, mine boss. Drift opening to No. 6 seam, 3 ft. 4 in. thick. Furnace ventilation; mule haulage; hand pick mining; single entry system. This mine was visited June 8th, and found in very poor condition. Ordered that if this mine continued to operate, a proper furnace must be built and the mine placed in condition to meet the requirements of new code; 14 miners and 4 day hands employed.

McNab.

Located near Salem, Ohio, and operated by the Buck Coal Co., Salem, O. Grant Hill, E. Palestine, Supt.; M. J. Flinn, Salem, O., mine boss. Shaft opening, 250 ft. deep, to No. 3 seam, 3 ft. thick. Exhaust steam ventilation; single entry system; hand pick mining, or solid shooting. March 17th, there were 25 miners and 12 day hands employed, on this visit. Found miners shooting almost all coal off the solid and using great charges of powder; also found quantities of dust on the roadways and in the rooms, greatly enhancing the grave danger to this system of operation. Ordered company to sprinkle and remove dust; gave written notice as to the method of shooting, drilling of holes and firing of shots.

Miners took exception to our orders and ceased work for several weeks, but finally decided to resume work and to adopt the system. On our next visit, May 6th, only 12 miners and 5 day hands were employed, but the system of operation was found much safer. July 11th, visited, in company with Inspector Robert Wheatley, who had been appointed to that district, and who will likely report that inspection in detail.

Newhouse.

Located at New House, on the P. L. & W. R. R. Operated by the Herriott Coal Co., Lisbon, O. C. C. Herriott, Lisbon, O., Supt. and mine boss. Drift opening to No. 6 seam, 3 ft. thick. Furnace ventilation; single entry system; electric machine mining; motor and mule haulage; mine was found in fair condition, excepting ventilation, which was ordered placed in condition to meet requirements of new code; also investigated cause of fatal accident to Samuel Masteoranni, 29 yrs. of age, who was killed by a fall of slate in 43 room on No. 9 entry, on May 18th; a large amount of stone had fallen, but the car which was being loaded caught the main part of it; a brother was working with the deceased at the time of the accident, but he escaped unhurt, though the stone fell almost across the entire room. Twenty-six miners and 7 day hands employed.

Delmore.

Located one and one-half miles southwest of Leetonia, O., on the Erie R. R. Operated by the Delmore Coal Co., Cleveland, O. H. D. Hileman, Cleveland, O., Supt.; Daniel McGrath, Leetonia, O., mine boss. Slope opening, 360 ft. long, to No. 3 seam, 3 ft. thick. Fan ventilation; single entry system; hand pick mining or solid shooting. December 16, 1909, an explosion occurred in this mine, which killed the two shot-firers and wrecked the mine, a full report of which is given in the Chief Inspector's annual report for 1909, and which also contains the orders given by the Department on December 27, 1909, as to how shots should be placed and coal mined and holes tamped and dust removed from the mine. We visited this mine again on January 19th, soon after it had resumed operation, found mine in fair condition, with tile stoppings between the main inlet and outlet, as provided by law; also found entries well sprinkled and dampened. Cautioned miners to be careful in preparing shots, and the management was ordered to keep roadways and entries sprinkled with water and to see that our previous orders were carried out. Permissible explosives had been tried by experts, but it appears did not give the results expected. On the evening of January 24th, was called by telephone by Inspector Miller, of Massillon, who informed me that an explosion had again occurred and that the shot-firer was in the mine; started immediately for the mine, reaching there next day at noon; the shot-firer had not yet been found, although searching parties of volunteer miners aided the management under greatest difficulties, that of having to face the after damp, which emanated from the mouth of the mine, owing to the main entrance being the return air way. The body was found on the 3rd right entry, just a little beyond No. 9 room, apparently having died of suffocation. This was the second explosion within forty days, both occurring at the same place and resulting from the same cause, which will be found in a joint report elsewhere in this annual report. January 26th, again, in company with Chief Inspector Harrison and Inspector Miller, of Massillon, visited the mine but found nothing had been done, except the operation of the fan and we were unable to make an investigation. February 17th, in company with Chief Inspector Harrison, Inspectors Miller of Massillon, and Morrison of Sherodsville, Sub-district Prest. Tetlow, of Washingtonville, and Mine Boss McGrath, we made a thorough inspection of the mine and found in many cases our previous orders disregarded and violated; shots placed and fired without the use of a pick, and holes drilled much heavier behind than in front, and some holes tamped with drill dust. No trace of gas could be found in the mine. May 3rd, found the mine still idle and being equipped with electric apparatus to cut coal and for haulage purposes. May 16th, was requested to visit the mine, preparatory to commencing operation; the work was almost completed and approved; found the air on this visit circulating nicely and no trace of standing gas could be found, but ordered the mine cleaned of all dust and well sprinkled before starting work. July 15th, mine was found in fair condition, air in fair circulation; all mining is now done by electrical machines and all coal gathered by electric motors. This visit was made with Inspector Robert Wheatley, who will report this visit more fully.

McLain.

Located at New Salisbury, on C. & P. R. R. Operated by the Colonial Coal and Clay Co., Pittsburg, Pa. George Dando, Beaver, Pa., Supt.; R. W. Nicholson, Irondale, O., mine boss. Drift opening, No. 6 seam, 3 ft. 8 in. thick. Fan ventilation; rope and mule haulage; 14 miners and 3 day hands employed. This mine had been suspended for over two years; it was formerly known as the Norris mine and resumed work November, 1909; found part of mine being cleaned up and part of it working; the 12 ft. fan was not running, owing to the fact that gasolene had given out (fan is run by gasoline engine); gave orders that a supply must always be kept on hand, instead of depending on the dealer to deliver it at a given time; other conditions approved.

Hoon.

Located at East Palestine, Ohio, on branch of P. Ft. W. & C. R. R. John Jones, Sr., Supt.; Thos. Jones, mine boss, both of East Palestine. Drift opening to No. 7 seam, 3 ft. thick. Furnace ventilation; mule haulage; single entry system; pick mining; 10 miners and 2 day hands employed. A new air shaft had just been sunk, supplying the miners with fresh air almost at head of workings; conditions approved.

Average.

Located at Washingtonville, Ohio, on Y. & O. R. R. Owned and operated by John D. Smith, who is also Supt. and mine boss. Slope opening to No. 4 seam, 2½ ft. thick. Fan ventilation; rope and mule haulage. Found a gasoline engine and electric generator had recently been installed in the mine for the purpose of cutting coal with an electric machine. Owing to the danger connected with the gasoline engine where it was located, advised that it be removed and placed outside of the mine. Six miners and 4 day hands employed.

Andelusia.

Located about two miles north of Salem, O. Operated by Jesse Shepherd, Salem, R. F. D. 4. Shaft opening to No. 3 seam, 3 ft. thick. Natural ventilation; single entry system; mule haulage; 5 miners and 2 day hands employed. Mine is very wet and a gasoline engine is used for pumping purposes. Advised the uttermost caution exercised on account of men inside.

Beech Hollow.

Located two miles northwest of Salem, O. Operated by Reese Bros., Salem, O. Thos. G. Reese, Supt. and mine boss. Drift to No. 3 seam, 3 ft. thick. Six miners and 2 day hands employed. Visited January 27th, ordered ventilation improved by building a furnace.

Vasey.

Located at Salineville, O. Operated by S. J. Vasey, Salineville, O. Chas. Feasey, Supt. and mine boss. Visited this mine May 13th, found air in poor condition; ordered furnace built in thirty days; mine again visited June 10th, found no effort had been made toward carrying out our orders and the ventilation in even worse condition than on our former visit; in consequence written notice was posted at the mine and the miners ordered out until furnace was built and ventilation improved. Six miners and 1 day hand employed.

Oak Hill Clay.

Located on Y. & O. R. R., near Washingtonville, O. Operated by the Columbia Fire Clay Co., Cleveland, O. J. M. Davis, Washingtonville, Supt. and mine boss. Slope opening to No. 3 clay. Rope and mule haulage. Found great quantities of dynamite stored in the mine. Ordered this practice to cease and the law complied with. Also ordered a 2nd opening made for escape way for men. Mr. Davis had just taken charge of the mine. Ten miners and 7 day hands employed.

Colonial Clay.

Located at New Salisbury, Ohio, on the C. & P. R. R. Operated by the Colonial Coal and Clay Co., Pittsburg, Pa. R. E. Lloyd, Supt., and M. B. Henry, mine boss, both of Irondale, O. Mine in good condition, excepting dynamite was being taken into mine in large quantities. Ordered this stopped at once. Shaft opening 91 ft. deep. Seven miners and 1 day hand employed. Fan ventilation. Safety catches tested and found correct.

COSHOCTON COUNTY.

Franklin No. 1.

Located near Franklin Station, on the Pan Handle R. R. Operated by the Columbus Coal and Mining Co., Coshocton, Ohio. R. N. Barnes, Coshocton, O., Supt.; J. S. Kitchen, Coshocton, R. F. D. 5, mine boss. This mine is fast being worked out, only 5 miners and 2 day hands employed. The drawing of pillars is the only work being done. Visited September 13th; condition fair.

Franklin No. 2.

Coal from this mine is hauled through No. 1, to same tipple, and is under same management. Drift opening to No. 6 seam, 3 ft. 8 in. thick. Furnace ventilation; mule haulage; pick mining, 24 miners and 6 day hands employed. Four visits made: March 31st, July 8th, September 13th and December 13th; on each inspection mine was found in fair condition, but is fast approaching an end: main work is the robbing of pillars.

Franklin No. 3.

Near No. 1, and the coal is being brought to same tipple, is under same management. Furnace ventilation; mule haulage; solid blasting, or pick mining; single entry system; 26 miners and 6 day hands employed. Four visits made: March 31st, found in fair condition, especially the ventilation. A new second opening had just been made and will be used on the resumption of work after April 1st.

July 8th, found mine in fair condition, but air which was brought in at two openings was not working satisfactory and orders were given to take all air in at new opening. September 13th and December 13th, mine found much improved, but it is a difficult matter to maintain perfect ventilation in these single entry solid shooting mines, owing to heavy blasting and the poor condition of doors and stoppings.

Barnes No. 1.

Owned and operated by the Barnes Coal & Mining Co., Coshocton, O. R. N. Barnes, Coshocton, O., Supt.; John Ford, Conesville, O., mine boss. Drift opening to No. 6 seam, 4 ft. 2 in. thick. Transportation, W. & L. E. R. R. Fan ventilation; pick and machine mining; mule haulage; double entry system; miners and 19 day hands employed. This mine was idle most of the summer. Two visits were made: August 18th and November 4th, on each visit mine found in good condition. A second opening had been made directly through the hill and the air was taken in at this new opening, giving fresh air at the head of the workings and putting the mine in good condition.

Barnes No. 2.

Located on W. & L. E. R. R., 1½ miles from Conesville, O. Operated by the Barnes Coal & Mining Co., Coshocton, O. C. C. Hudson, same place, Supt. and mine boss. Drift opening to No. 6 seam, 4 ft. thick. Fan ventilation; motor and mule haulage; electric machine mining; 47 miners and 18 day hands employed. Four visits made: March 30th, mine found in poor condition, but undergoing many changes. July 7th, September 16th and December 15th, mine was found much improved and in fair condition.

Conesville No. 1.

Located near Conesville, O., on the Pan Handle R. R., has been abandoned, except the main haulway, which runs directly through the hill to a new opening, owned and operated by James G. Davis, and known as new No. 1. Drift opening to No. 6 seam, 4 ft. thick. Visited December 15th; 14 miners and 4 day hands employed. The mine is just beginning development, a new air shaft has been sunk and an entry is being driven to a second opening; conditions were approved.

Conesville No. 4.

Owned and operated by David Davis, Conesville, O., who is also Supt. Coal goes to same tipple as No. 1. J. F. Murphy, Conesville, O., is mine boss. Slope opening to No. 6 seam of coal, 3 ft. 4 in. thick. Fan ventilation; rope and mule haulage; compressed air machine mining; single entry system. This mine covers a very large territory and coal is hauled about a mile by mules, whence it is taken by cable about one mile more to tipple. Four visits made: February 4th, May 26th, September 14th and December 14th; on each visit mine was found in fair condition, although it only worked poor time during a large part of the year. 50 miners and 17 day hands employed.

Davis No. 1.

This is a new mine, located eight miles west of Coshocton, transportation on the C. A. & C. R. R. Owned and operated by David Davis, Conesville, Ohio, who is also Supt.; J. W. Larr, Sr., Coshocton, R. F. D. No. 6, mine boss. Drift opening to No. 6 seam of coal, 3½ ft. thick. Fire grate ventilation; mule haulage;

single entry system; 18 miners and 7 day hands employed; mine found in good condition. Orders given to build stoppings of brick or cement, as provided by law. Mine began shipment of coal August 15th. Two visits made: September 15th and December 16th.

Davis No. 2.

Located near No. 1, coal goes to same tipple and is under same management, is drift opening to No. 6 seam of coal, 3½ ft. thick. Furnace ventilation; mule haulage; single and double entry system; 36 miners and 16 day hands employed Three visits made: September 15th, orders were given to enlarge entrance to furnace and provide test weights, stretchers and blankets, etc. September 24th, we investigated fatal accident of Ira Dawson, a driver, who was killed by his trip of cars running over him, tripping and falling in front of it, or mule, about 112 ft. outside of the mine on the tramway, while he was putting the blinder over the head of his mule; he was an American, 30 years old and married. December 16th, mine in good condition, but all the provisions of the new code had not yet been provided; these were ordered provided at once

Warwick No. 4.

Located about 4 miles southeast of Coshocton, on the W. & L. E. R. R. Drift opening to No. 6 seam of coal, 3 ft. 8 in. thick. Machine mining; fan ventilation; double entry system; 30 miners and 8 day hands employed. Six visits made: February 8th, May 24th, August 16th; on these visits Mr. Wm. Powers, of Coshocton, was managing the mine. On October 19th, found Emery Aukney, New Philadelphia, Supt., and Geo. Deans, mine boss A new air shaft was being sunk and the mine generally being overhauled November 4th, investigated the death of Lawrence Faust, Frenchman, who died on that day, having taken sick in the mine about 11 A. M. and died soon after being removed from the mine; he worked in No. 6 room on 2nd west entry; found his place in good condition and nothing could be found as evidence to cause either accident or death, and concluded deceased had died from natural causes December 20th, found mine much improved and air being brought in at the new shaft opening, with a ladder placed for an escape way for men

Warwick No. 5.

This mine is located near No 4, coal goes to same tipple and is under same management as No. 4, except Mr Ed Golder, was found as mine boss on our last two visits. Fan ventilation; motor and mule haulage; pick and machine mining. 73 miners and 31 day hands employed During the early part of the year a shaft opening was made for air and manway Five visits were made: February 8th, May 25th, July 21st, October 19th and December 20th On my last visit found the mine had undergone many improvements; the motor haulage had been extended to new passways in three different directions and the air was much improved which is very creditable to the new management

Morgan Run.

Located about 8 miles from Coshocton, on the W. & L. E. R. R. and Pan Handle. Operated by the Morgan Run Coal Co., Cleveland, O. R. B. Deans, Supt.; Robt McCormick, mine boss, both of Coshocton O. Drift opening to No 6 seam. Furnace ventilation, motor and mule haulage; double entry system 7[illegible] miners and 30 day hands employed Three visits made March 1st mine was idle flooded with water; July 6th and October 18th, mine was found in good condition

Wade No. 2.

Located on the W. & L. E. and Pan Handle R. R., three miles from Coshocton, O. Owned and operated by the Wade Coal Co., Cleveland, O. H. D. Dennis, Cleveland, Supt.; James Perkins, Coshocton, O., mine boss. Drift opening to No. 6 seam, 2 ft. 10 in. thick. Pick mining; mule haulage; furnace ventilation; 20 miners and 10 day hands employed. A new furnace and a new shaft opening for man-way was made during the year. Three visits made: March 2nd., August 19th, and December 1st. Conditions fair.

Oden Valley No. 2.

Located on branch of Pan Handle R. R., two miles from Conesville, Ohio. Operated by the Oden Valley Coal Co., Coshocton, O. G. W. Cassingham, Coshocton, Supt.; James Ford, was mine boss on my first two visits of the year; on August 17th, a new mine boss was in charge, Charles C. Winkler. On November 3rd, found James H. Fitch in charge. Drift opening to No. 6 seam, 3½ ft. thick. Rope haulage and a new furnace were installed during the year; found in poor condition on each visit, notwithstanding the improvements the management were making. On November 3rd, found the pillars being robbed, and from present appearances the mine will soon be finished. Eighteen miners and 7 day hands employed, on my last visit.

Oden Valley No. 3.

Located near No. 2 and under same management. Drift opening to No. 6 seam, 3 ft. 4 in. thick. Fire grate ventilation; single entry system; mule haulage. Visited March 29th, found 11 miners and 3 day hands employed, mine in poor condition. On November 3rd again visited to find the mine just being cleaned up, preparatory to resuming operation, the mine having been suspended since April 1st; 4 day hands employed. Material was on hand to build new furnace.

Locust Grove.

Located about 4 miles from Coshocton, on W. & L. E. R. R. Owned and operated by John Williams, Coshocton, O., who is also Supt.; Geo. Doney, same place, mine boss. Drift opening to No. 6 seam, 4 ft. to 4½ ft. thick. Hand pick mining; 18 miners and 5 day hands employed. Furnace ventilation; mule haulage. Five visits made: March 30th, found mine in poor condition; July 20th, ordered new furnace built in 15 days to assist circulation of air; November 2nd, in fair condition and new furnace in operation, but ordered number of men reduced until a second opening was made; November 29th, found orders of November 2nd had not been carried out, and after consultation with Chief Inspector Harrison, returned to mine November 30th to put into effect the orders of November 2nd, but found orders complied with.

Powers.

Located near the Warwick mines on the W. & L. E. R. R. Owned and operated by the Powers Coal Co., Coshocton, O. Drift opening to No. 6 seam, 3 ft. 3 in. thick. Pick mining; single entry system; mule haulage; 27 miners and 6 day hands employed. During the former part of the year coal was brought out of the old opening, but is now brought out of the new. A new tipple has been built and is also in operation. A new furnace and shaft in operation. On my first two visits mine was in poor condition; on two latter visits mine was in good condition.

Rock Run.

Located three miles southwest of Coshocton, on the W. & L. E. R. R. Operated by M. S. Wolford, Coshocton, Ohio, who is also Supt. and mine boss. Drift to No. 6 seam, 4 ft. thick. Mule haulage; furnace ventilation; pick mining; 10 miners and 2 day hands employed; 2 visits made; conditions fair.

Comly No. 1.

Located near Coshocton, domestic mine. Operated by Thomas Williams, who is also superintendent, Peter Ingham, mine boss, both of Coshocton, O. Mule haulage; natural ventilation; 7 miners and 2 day hands employed. Visited March 2nd and found in poor condition. Visited December 22nd, conditions fair.

Nichols.

Located about one mile from Coshocton. Domestic mine. Operated by A. C. Nichols, who is also superintendent, Geo. Burdock, mine boss, both of Coshocton, O. Drift to No. 6 seam, 3½ ft. thick; mule haulage; 4 miners and 1 day hand employed. Visited November 2nd and found conditions fair.

Hudson.

Located one and one-half miles from Coshocton, Ohio. Operated by Hudson Brothers, Daniel Hudson, Supt.; Edward Hudson, mine boss, both of Coshocton, O. Furnace ventilation; mule haulage; 4 miners and 1 day hand employed. Visited December 1st, conditions good.

Saxton.

Located 2½ miles east of Coshocton, Ohio; coal is hauled by team to W. & L. E. R. R. Operated by Chas. Saxton, Coshocton, O., Willard West, same place, mine boss; five miners employed. Visited December 21st, conditions fair.

Garfield Wood.

This is a domestic mine, located two miles east of Coshocton, Ohio. Operated by Garfield Wood, Coshocton, O. Three miners and 1 day hand employed. Found in fair condition November 2nd.

Drake No. 1.

Owned and operated by Thos. Williams, Coshocton, O. Drift to No. 6 seam, 3 ft. 4 in. thick. Mule haulage; furnace ventilation; 4 miners and 1 day hand employed. A new second opening (new shaft) has been made at head of workings. Visited December 2nd, conditions good.

Eckels.

Located two miles east of Coshocton, Ohio. Operated by R. M. Eckels, Coshocton, Ohio, who is also superintendent and mine boss. Drift opening to No. 6 seam, 3½ ft. thick. Furnace ventilation; mule haulage; 7 miners employed Visited December 21st, conditions fair.

Lear.

Located one mile east of Coshocton, O., Operated by Henry Lear, Coshocton, Ohio, who is also superintendent; James Lear, mine boss. Drift to No. 6 seam, 3½ ft. thick. Furnace ventilation; mule haulage; 6 miners and 2 day hands employed. Visited December 22nd, conditions fair.

West No. 1.

Located near Coshocton, brick plant. Operated by Chas. West. Drift opening to No. 6 seam, 3 ft. thick. Six miners employed. Visited March 3rd, found in bad condition, and ordered men removed. December 2nd, found men working on opposite side of mine, which was only in poor condition. Orders were given Mr. West to repair doors and stoppings at once, or it would be necessary to close the mine.

West No. 2.

Located one-fourth mile from No. 1. Chas. West owner and superintendent. Drift to No, 6 seam. Mule haulage; natural ventilation; 5 miners and one day hand employed. Visited March 3rd and December 2nd, conditions good.

Furnell.

Located near old Cassingham No. 2. This is a new mine, opened during the summer. Owned and operated by Thos. Furnell, Coshocton, O., who is also manager. It was intended to ship coal over W. & L. E. R. R., from Cassingham No. 2 tipple, but R. R. Co. condemned the branch; hence, the mine can only be used for domestic purposes; 4 miners employed; coal 4 ft. thick. Visited December 21st, conditions good.

Coshocton Clay.

Located near Coshocton Brick Plant. Operated by Coshocton Brick Co., Coshocton, O. Frank Cotter, Supt.; Roy Harden, mine boss, both of Coshocton, O. Visited March 3rd, found 10 clay miners and 2 day hands employed. Visited again August 19th, found the old mine being fast worked out, but a new opening made and furnace shaft sunk. Eight miners and 2 day hands employed. Found conditions fair in both mines.

Note: Since visiting this mine August 19th, a new furnace has been built in the new mine and is in operation.

TUSCARAWAS COUNTY.

Mullins No. 1.

Located on a branch of the C. & P. R. R., about six miles from New Philadelphia, O. Operated by the James Mullins Coal Co., Cleveland, O. A. E. Norkes, Supt.; Robt. Sewell, mine boss, both of New Philadelphia, O. Drift to No. 6 seam, 3 ft. 8 in. thick. Fifteen miners and 7 day hands employed; fan ventilation; motor haulage; pick mining. Visited March 8th, found the mine in poor condition. Compressed air plant had been abandoned and removed men were scattered over large territory, with gathering motors in very low entries. Since my last visit in December, miners have been reduced from 47 to 15. The mine is fast being depleted.

Mullins New No. 2.

Located near No. 1 and operated by the same company. A. E. Norkes, Supt. and mine boss. Drift to No. 6 seam, 3 ft. 10 in. thick. Electric machine mining; rope and motor haulage; fan ventilation; 55 miners and 17 day hands employed. Visited March 8th, found conditions fair, a new second opening just made, found Alex Finkey had lost his foot by having it inside of machine frame while running his motor back till it almost cut his foot off at the ankle. This accident happened on March 7th. Found machine still in place as left by the cutter at time of accident.

Reeves No. 1.

Located on C. & P., 2½ miles from New Philadelphia, O. Operated by the Reeves Coal Co., Canal Dover, O. On February 24th, Richard Clemens was superintendent; on June 6th, Ebenezer Jones was superintendent and Charles Ledky, mine boss. Drift opening to No. 6 seam, 4 ft. thick. Pick and electric machine mining; fan ventilation; motor and mule haulage; 36 miners and 15 day hands employed. This mine was suspended for almost two years, resumed operation January 15th. Mine found on first visit fair, considering long suspension. On second visit mine was found in poor condition. Five days were given to put mine in shape, but a strike began on the latter date and is still in effect.

Reeves No. 2.

Located on same branch as No. 1, but a mile further up. Operated by same company. Richard Clemens, Canal Dover, Supt.; Abraham Richardson, New Philadelphia, R. F. D. No. 4, mine boss. Drift to No. 6 seam, 4 ft. thick. Fan ventilation; motor and mule haulage; compressed air machine mining; 81 miners and 35 day hands employed. Visited April 26th, conditions approved.

East Goshen No. 1.

Located on C. & P. R. R. Operated by the Goshen Coal Co., Cleveland, O. Emery Ankney, Supt.; John Horger, mine boss, both of New Philadelphia, O. Drift to No. 6 seam, 4 ft. 10 in. thick. Hand pick mining; 56 miners and 19 day hands employed on January 28th. May 27th, found 70 miners and 25 day hands employed. Rope and mule haulage. This mine was suspended from February 28th, 1908 to January 1, 1910, and in consequence was found in poor condition. On our first visit requested furnace replaced with a fan, which was located in poor location for results. On our second visit found a 7 ft. fan installed and mine very much improved, which in the short space of time was very commendable to the management..

East Goshen No. 2.

Located on same railroad, about one mile from No. 1. Operated by same company and under same management, except mine boss, Edward Golder, in charge. Slope opening to No. 6 seam, 4 ft. thick. Fan ventilation; compressed air machine mining; motor and mule haulage; 93 miners and 36 day hands employed. Mine found in fair condition, except second opening. Requested a new second opening made as soon as it could reasonably be done. Visited April 18th.

Goshen Hill.

Located at Rosewell and operated by the Goshen Coal Co., Cleveland, O. T. G. Brooks, Supt.; Peter Kirk, mine boss, both of New Philadelphia, O. Slope to No. 6 seam, 4½ ft. thick. Hand pick mining; furnace ventilation; rope and mule haulage; double entry system; 60 miners and 17 day hands employed. Visited April 19th, found in poor condition, air polluted with black damp from old works, on the inlet air course, just outside of main passway. Ordered this taken care of, either by sinking an air shaft near head of workings or building overcast to carry it over main intake into return airway.

Goshen Shaft.

Operated by same company as Goshen Hill, and under same management, except Ed Graham, Jr., is mine boss. Located on C. & P. R. R., near Rosewell, O. Shaft opening to No. 6 seam, 105 ft. deep, coal 4 ft. thick. Double entry system; compressed air machine mining; fan ventilation; rope and mule haulage; 42 miners and 23 day hands employed. Visited February 15th, found in poor condition, owing to a squeeze which cut off a very large working part of the mine. Visited May 31st and found mine in fair condition; found standing gas in No. 2 room on 8 west entry cut off; a fire boss was ordered to examine places before men entered mine in the morning and report, as provided by law.

Beaver Dam No. 1.

Located at Rosewell, O., and operated by same company as Goshen shaft and under same management, except Evan Phillips, of New Philadelphia, is mine boss. Shaft opening, 75 ft. deep to No. 6 seam, 4 ft. thick. Fan ventilation; electric machine mining; motor and mule haulage; double entry system. This mine was visited May 18th and found in poor condition, owing to water breaking into mine; this mine has been flooded with water the greater part of the winter and spring. Since the strike began in this county, June 11th, this mine has been abandoned and dismantled.

Beaver Dam No. 2.

Located about two miles from Midvale, Ohio, on the B. & O. R. R. Operated by same company as No. 1, and under same management, except Elmer Tidrick, of Midvale, O., is mine boss. Shaft opening, 84 ft. deep to No. 6 seam, 4 ft. thick; double entry system; pick mining; 50 miners and 26 day hands employed. Fan ventilation; motor and mule haulage. Two visits made: January 17th, mine found in fair condition. April 27th, mine was found in poor condition, air deficient in several entries. Ordered this remedied at once, and crossovers and dust given immediate attention.

West Goshen.

Operated by the Goshen Coal Co., Cleveland, O. Located at Joyce, Ohio, on the C. & M. R. R. Emery Ankney, New Philadelphia, O., Supt.; Wesley Grimm, New Philadelphia, R. F. D. No. 2, mine boss. Drift opening to No. 6 seam, 4 to 5 ft. thick. Hand pick and electric machine mining; double entry system; fan ventilation; motor and mule haulage. Visited April 21st and found mine in good condition.

Goshen Central.

Located on C. & P. R. R., and operated by Goshen Central Coal Co., Massillon, O. W. K. Moore, New Philadelphia, O., Supt. and mine boss. Drift to No. 6 seam, 3½ to 5 ft. thick. Double entry system; fan ventilation; motor and mule haulage; electric machine mining; 68 miners and 22 day hands employed. Visited June 1st, conditions fair.

Houk.

Located at Stillwater, O., on B. & O. R. R. Operated by the American Sheet & Tin Plate Co., Canal Dover, O. J. L. Houk, Supt.; Emmet Carnes, mine boss, both of Stillwater, O. Drift opening to No. 7 seam, 5 ft. thick. Fan ventilation; motor and mule haulage; double entry system; hand pick mining. Three visits made: February 21st, August 8th and November 7th; on each visit found conditions fair. Forty miners and 25 day hands employed.

Wainwright No. 4.

Located at Wainwright, O., on B. & O. R. R. Operated by the Midvale Goshen Coal Co., Cleveland, O. Frank McIntosh, New Philadelphia, Supt.; Wm. McIntosh, Wainwright, O., mine boss. Slope opening to No. 6 seam, 4 ft. 4 in. thick. Rope and mule haulage; fire basket ventilation; double entry system; hand pick mining; 24 miners and 7 day hands employed. Visited March 10th and found inner workings flooded with water; men are at present crowded into two entries. Conditions poor.

Midvale Goshen No. 6.

Located at Wainwright, O., on B. & O. R. R. Operated by same company as No. 4, and under same management, except Robt. Reichman, Wainwright, O., is mine boss. Slope opening to No. 6 seam, 4 ft. thick. Fan ventilation; motor and mule haulage; machine mining; double entry system; 82 miners and 24 day hands employed. Visited February 23rd, conditions fair.

Midvale Goshen No. 7.

Located near No. 6 and operated by same company and management, except Chas. Lorenz, Wainwright, O., is mine boss. Drift to No. 6 seam, 4 ft. thick; double entry system; pick and machine mining; 92 miners and 26 day hands employed. Furnace ventilation; rope and mule haulage. Visited January 24th, ordered dust and stone taken care of; other conditions fair.

Hazel No. 6.

Located about one mile from Midvale, on B. & O. R. R. Operated by the Royal Goshen Coal Co., New Philadelphia, O. H. C. Cole, Supt.; C. B. Fox, mine boss, both of Midvale, O. Drift to No. 6 seam, 4 ft. thick. Furnace ventilation; rope and mule haulage; pick mining; double entry system; 38 miners and 13 day hands employed. Visited April 28th, conditions fair.

Veleney.

Located at Barnhill, O., on B. & O. R. R. Operated by same company as Hazel No. 6, and same management, except Ralph Beatty, mine boss. Drift to No. 6 seam, 4½ ft. thick. Mule haulage. Visited May 17th, found the mine being rapidly depleted, but a new opening is being made into the hill beyond.

Royal Goshen No. 2.

Located near Midvale, on the B. & O. and Pan Handle R. R. Operated by same company as the Veleney mine and same management, except C. C. White, Midvale, O., is mine boss. Drift to No. 6 seam, 4½ ft. thick. Furnace ventilation; mule haulage; 11 miners and 3 day hands employed. Two visits made: May 23rd and September 20th, conditions fair.

Royal Goshen No. 3.

Located near Midvale, on B. & O. R. R. Operated by same company as Hazel No. 6, and same management, except Wm. Fairless, Midvale, O., is mine boss. Drift to No. 6 seam, 4½ ft. thick. Furnace ventilation; rope and mule haulage; double entry system; 33 miners and 13 day hands employed. Visited April 25th, stone on left side of this mine is very dangerous. The management and men were cautioned and advised to give special attention to it. On this visit also investigated the fatal accident of Matthew Hawkins, who was instantly killed on the morning of April 23rd by a fall of rock in his room; it was a very large pot stone. Found the room well timbered; the accident was to al appearances accidental.

Water Lily.

Located near Hazel No. 6, operated by same company and under same management. Drift to No. 6 seam, 1½ ft. thick. Furnace ventilation; rope and mule haulage; double entry system; 11 miners and 5 day hands employed. This is a new opening into old works of No. 2 Midvale Goshen mine; found conditions fair.

Goshen No. 2.

Located at Goshen, on the B. & O. R. R. Operated by the Goshen Valley Coal Co., Massillon, O. Herman Schneider, New Philadelphia, O., Supt.; Gibson Carlisle, Beidler, O., mine boss. Slope opening to No. 6 seam 4 ft. thick. Fan ventilation; rope and mule haulage; pick mining; 40 miners and 11 day hands employed. Visited February 22nd, found all the old workings cut off by a squeeze which was effecting the entire mine. All men were found working near the bottom of slope in coal left years ago. Conditions fair.

Goshen No. 3.

Located near Goshen, on B. & O. R. R. and operated by same company as No. 2. Herman Schneider, supt. and mine boss. Drift to No. 6 seam, 4½ feet thick. Double entry system. Furnace ventilation; mule haulage; 18 miners and four day hands employed. Visited March 11th, found most men robbing pillars. Conditions fair.

Goshen No. 4.

Located near No 2 and operated by same company and same management, except Herman Schneider is also mine boss. This is a new drift opening to No. 6 seam, 4½ feet thick. Furnace ventilation; mule haulage; 22 miners and five day hands employed. Visited February 22nd, conditions good.

Indian Hill.

Located one mile west of Uhrichsville, on Pan Handle R. R. Operated by the Bursner Coal Co., Cleveland, O. John Ronalds, Uhrichsville, O., supt. and mine boss. Drift to No. 6 seam, 4 feet thick. Fan ventilation; motor and mule haulage; electric machine mining; double entry system; 48 miners and 23 day hands employed. Visited March 28th, mine was in poor condition and air in poor circulation, mixed with quite an amount of black damp. Orders were given to improve the ventilation at once.

Central Valley.

Located near New Cumberland, O., on the W. & L. E. R. R. Operated by the Massillon Tuscarawas Coal Co., Massillon, O. C. C. Smith, Somerdale, O., superintendent and mine boss. Drift opening to No. 6 seam, 3½ feet thick. Fan ventilation; rope and mule haulage; compressed air machine mining. Double entry system. 61 miners and 19 day hands employed. Visited April 29th, found conditions fair, except in 7 and 8 and 9 and 10 left entries, which has been caused by No. 10 left entry squeezing.

Huff Run No. 1.

Located at Mineral City, on the B. & O. R. R. Operated by the Ridgeway-Burton Co., Cleveland, O. Alex Lindsay, Mineral City, superintendent and mine boss. Drift to No. 5 seam, 3 feet, 4 inches thick. Fan ventilation, rope and mule haulage; pick mining. Two visits made. February 3rd, found mine in fair condition, with 50 miners and 22 day hands. May 9th, mine was only in poor condition, with air in poor circulation, only 34 miners and 18 day hands employed.

South Side.

Located at Mineral City, O., on B. & O. R. R. Owned and operated by C. E. Holden, Mineral City, O., Harry Wood superintendent, William G. Smith mine boss, both of Mineral City, O. Drift opening to No. 5 seam, 3½ feet thick. Furnace ventilation; mule haulage; single entry system. Four visits made. January 31st, mine found in fair condition; May 9th, found the air polluted with black damp and the men driven from the mine while I was present. A written notice was given the management that no work would be permitted until black damp was overcome and controlled. August 23rd, found mine free from black damp and overcast had been put in to carry part of it off and prevent it from passing into the air, but the same trouble will be encountered as soon as Huff Run No. 1 again resumes operation. November 10th, found A. H. Jones in charge as mine boss, Mr. Smith having resigned. Mine in fair condition, except near head of workings. Ordered air-way made larger for the free circulation of air.

Massillon Peacock.

Located at Mineral City, O., on B. & O. R. R. Operated by the Peacock Coal Mining Co., Mineral City, O. John Puncheon, Mineral City, O., manager. Drift to No. 5 seam, 3½ to 5 feet thick. Furnace ventilation; rope and mule haulage; pick mining, 40 miners and 14 day hands employed. Three visits made: February 10th and August 24th, mine found in fair condition. November 11th, coal was being hauled from a new opening recently made. Mine in very bad condition, being very much cut up on account of rolls and heavy dips.

Acme No. 2.

Located one mile east of Mineral City, Ohio, on B. & O. R. R. Operated by George J. Markley, Mineral City, O. C. L. Jones, same place manager. Drift to No. 5 seam, 3 feet thick. Furnace ventilation; mule haulage; pick mining. Double entry system. 12 miners and 3 day hands employed. Visited February 4th, found in fair condition. October 5th, found mine idle on account of black damp. Orders were given to fire furnace the day previous to resumption, after mine had been idle. Otherwise conditions fair.

Federal Coal.

Located at Factory No. 1, on B. & O. R. R. Operated by the Federal Clay Product Co., Mineral City, O. C. L. Jones, same place, superintendent and mine boss. Drift to No. 5 seam, 3 feet thick. Furnace ventilation. Mule haulage. Two visits made. February 4th, mine was found in fair condition. October 4th, in poor condition, and air in poor circulation, owing to furnace not being on in the mine, which ventilates the mine also. We had previously suggested a furnace for this mine alone. Orders were given to place mine in better condition.

Novelty No. 1.

Located near Newcomerstown, on the C. & M. R. R. Operated by the Novelty Brick and Coal Co., same place. R. L. Shoemaker, superintendent; George Adams, mine boss; both of Newcomerstown, O. Drift to No. 6 seam, 3 feet thick. Fan ventilation; mule haulage. Three visits made: March 4th and September 1st, found mine being fast depleted, but in fair condition. December 7th, found mine in charge of Charles Smith, as mine boss, and in fair condition, but the left side of mine entirely abandoned. 6 miners and 2 day hands employed.

Novelty No. 2.

Located about one-half mile south of No. 1 on same R. R. Operated and managed by same parties until recently. Drift to No. 6 seam, 2½ feet thick. Furnace ventilation; rope and mule haulage; compressed air machine mining; single entry system. Three visits made: March 4th and September 1st, found mine in fair condition. December 7th, found mine had been leased to Dan Harrison, Newcomerstown, who is also superintendent. J. M. Stoffer, same place, mine boss. Conditions fair, but air not well distributed; gave orders to improve this defect immediately. 14 miners and 2 day men employed.

Diamond Coal.

Located at Diamond Sewer Pipe Plant on B. & O. R. R., Uhrichsville, O. Operated by the American Sewer Pipe Co., Akron, O. J. M. McClave, superintendent; Levi Ross, mine boss; both of Uhrichsville, O. Furnace ventilation; mule haulage; pick mining; 10 miners and 5 day hands employed. Three visits made: June 22nd, September 21st, and December 27th; on each visit mine was found in fair condition; on last visit found J. W. Moore, Uhrichsville, superintendent. Visited this mine also February 28th. No inspection made owing to the mine being flooded.

Buckeye Coal.

Located one mile west of Uhrichsville, Ohio, on Pan Handle R. R. Operated by the Buckeye Fire Clay Co., Uhrichsville, O. W. B. Stevens, same place, superintendent; J. M. Shank, Tracy, O., mine boss. This is a new slope opening, 430 feet to No. 6 seam, 3½ feet thick. Fan ventilation; rope and mule haulage; double entry system. 15 miners and 5 day hands employed. Five visits made: March 9th, June 21st, August 30th, November 21st and December 5th. On each visit found mine fair. A new air shaft was sunk during the summer and a new fan installed between my last two visits. December 5th, tested scales and found them correct.

Robinson-Graves Coal.

Located on B. & O. R. R. about two miles from Uhrichsville, O. Operated by the Robinson-Graves Clay Co., Uhrichsville, O. Wm. Tanzie, Dennison, O., superintendent and mine boss. Drift to No. 6 seam, 4 feet thick. Furnace ventilation; mule haulage; 12 miners and 2 day hands employed. Conditions fair.

Eureka.

Located one-half mile northeast of New Philadelphia, O. Operated by the Goshen Mining Co., New Philadelphia, O. C. R. Klein, superintendent and mine boss. Drift to No. 6 seam, 4 feet thick. Furnace ventilation; mule haulage; pick mining; 11 miners and two day hands employed. Visited August 9th and November 9th. Conditions fair.

Rufenacht.

Located two miles southwest of New Philadelphia, O. Operated by Fred Rufenacht, same place, who is also superintendent, John Swihart, same place, mine boss. Drift to No. 6 seam, 3 feet 8 inches thick. Furnace ventilation; mule haulage; pick mining. Three visits made: May 2nd, August 5th and October 11th. Fourteen miners and 2 day hands employed. Conditions fair.

Pleasant Hill.

Located about two and one-half miles west of New Philadelphia, O. Operated by Davis and Mathias, both of New Philadelphia, O. J. G. Davis, mine boss. Drift to No. 6 seam, 4 feet thick. Fire basket ventilation; mule haulage; 9 miners and 3 day hands employed. Visited October 11th, conditions fair.

This company recently purchased the mine and at once commenced to repair it. A new air shaft was sunk during the summer.

Horn.

Located about two and one-half miles southwest of Canal Dover, O. Operated by Bryer and Rufner, New Philadelphia, R. F. D. 2. Frank Bryer, mine boss. Drift to No. 6 seam, 3 1-2 feet thick. Fire basket ventilation; mule haulage; 5 miners and 1 day hand employed. Two visits made, August 5th and November 17th. Conditions approved.

Royal No. 3.

Located at Royal Sewer Pipe Works, Midvale, O. Operated by J. S. Scott, Jr., who is also mine boss. Drift to No. 6 seam, 4 1-2 feet thick. Natural ventilation; mule haulage; visited October 13th, but found no one in the mine, but conditions very bad.

Advance Coal.

Located at Advance Brick Plant, near Urichsville, O. Operated by the Advance Fire Clay Co., Urichsville, O. Geo. Ross, Sr., superintendent and mine boss, Urichsville, O. Drift to No. 6 seam, 3 feet 8 inches thick. Furnace ventilation; mule haulage; 6 miners and 1 day hand employed. Three visits made: March 7th, July 25th and November 22nd. March 7th, investigated the fatal accident of John Baker, who was killed on March 5th, in first room on cut-off entry; room was well timbered; the place where he was killed was posted within 4 feet 3 inches of face; room was only 13 feet, 7 inches wide; stone fell out between two slips, which evidently were unseen to the deceased. On other visits found conditions fair.

Laughlin.

Located 2 1-2 miles east of Mineral City, Ohio. Operated by Wm. Laughlin, Mineral City, O. Drift to No. 5 seam, 4 feet thick. Fire basket ventilation; mule haulage; 5 miners and 3 day hands employed. Robbing pillars is the only work being done. Visited November 25th, conditions fair. This mine has been idle all summer.

Dennison.

Located one mile east of Dennison, O. Operated by Howell Williams and Sons, same place. Drift to No. 6 seam, 4 feet thick. Furnace ventilation; mule haulage; 7 miners and 2 day hands employed. Visited October 28th, conditions approved.

Stettler.

Located one mile north of New Philadelphia, O. Owned and operated by S. H. Banks, New Philadelphia, Ohio, who is also manager. Drift to No. 6 seam, 4 feet 8 inches thick. Furnace ventilation; mule haulage; 5 miners and 1 day hand employed. Visited July 26th, found old opening almost done. November 14th, found a new opening to same mine; also new furnace and air shaft. Conditions approved.

Tuscarawas Electric Light.

Located one mile north of New Philadelphia, O. Operated by Tuscarawas Light & Power Co., New Philadelphia, O. H. R. Brown, superintendent, and mine boss. Drift to No. 6 seam, 4 1-2 feet thick. Furnace ventilation; mule haulage; compressed air machine mining; 8 miners employed. Four visits made: July 26th and 30th, August 4th and September 9th. During the early part of the year a gasoline engine had been installed for power very near the mouth of mine, which was a violation of law, and a grave danger to men in the mine. After a joint conference, in Columbus, with Chief Inspector Harrison, Manager Barnard of the Electric Co., Mr. Brown and myself, we arrived at a solution by having a fire wall built on end of engine, and a new second opening made to supply ventilation and remove gasoline to a distance, all of which was done within the time specified. Other conditions fair.

N. O. T. & L.

Located four miles east of New Philadelphia, O. Owned by Northern Ohio T. & L. Co., Akron, O. Patrick Selby, same place, mine boss. Drift to No. 6 seam, 4 feet thick. Four miners and 1 day hand employed. Furnace ventilation; mule haulage. Three visits made: February 25th, mine was in poor condition August 11th and December 8th, mine was in charge of Anthony Brick, also of New Philadelphia. Mine on both of these visits was found fair.

Twin City.

Located near Dennison, on Pan Handle R. R. Operated by the Dennison Coal & Fuel Co., Dennison, O. Harry Hirst, superintendent, Joseph Hirst, mine boss. Drift opening to No. 6 seam; 4 feet thick. This mine has been suspended for almost three years; it has been equipped with rope haulage and a new tipple, and it is just about ready for operation. Visited December 29th, found mine being put into very good shape.

Ridge Road.

Located near the Eureka mine. Owned and operated by Lewis Bucher, of New Philadelphia, O. Drift opening, to No. 6 seam, 3½ feet thick. Visited August 9th, found in poor condition; gave orders for improvements.

Burgis No. 1.

Located 2½ miles southeast of Canal Dover, O. Operated by David M. Wigfield, Canal Dover, O., who is also manager. Drift to No. 6 seam, 4 feet thick. Furnace ventilation; mule haulage; 4 miners and 1 day hand employed. Visited November 17th, found conditions fair.

Burgis No. 2.

Located near No. 1. Operated by James Burgis and John Border, the latter being mine boss. Drift to No. 6 seam, 4 feet thick. Furnace ventilation; mule haulage; 3 miners employed. Visited November 17th, conditions approved.

Evans Coal.

Located near Uhrichsville, on B. & O. R. R. Operated by Enos Hibbs and Sons, Uhrichsville, O., Enos Hibbs, superintendent and mine boss. Drift to No. 6 seam, 3½ feet thick. Furnace ventilation; mule haulage; 9 miners and 2 day hands employed. Three visits made. February 7th mine was in fair condition. Orders were given to put mine in better condition. July 18th, found a new drift opening being made. October 24th, found new opening being used and old one abandoned, except for escape way. Conditions fair.

National Coal.

Located near Strasburg, O. Operated by the National Fire Brick Co., Strasburg, O. Thomas Kemp, Canal Dover, superintendent, Martin Clapper, Strasburg, O., mine boss. Drift to No. 5 seam, 3 feet 3 inches thick. Furnace ventilation; mule haulage; 6 miners and 1 day man employed. Visited June 23rd, found conditions fair.

Beers.

Located near Newcomerstown, O. Operated by C. R. Scheafe, who is also superintendent, Geo. Tufford, mine boss. Drift to No. 6 seam, 2 feet thick. Furnace ventilation; mule haulage; 8 miners and 2 day hands employed. Three visits made: September 19th, found mine without air, air-course was caved shut. Men were ordered from the mine until a furnace could be built and air-course cleaned. October 3rd, mine was found not just ready for work. October 20th, found new furnace in operation, giving fair results and mine in fair condition.

Scotts.

Located about two miles from Dennison, O., on the Ridge Road to Midvale. Operated by Walter O. Scott, of Dennison, O., who is also superintendent and mine boss. Furnace ventilation; mule haulage; 5 miners and 1 day hand employed. Visited September 22nd, conditions good. This mine generally employs 15 miners in winter. Drift to No. 7 seam, 5½ feet thick.

Morey Ridge.

Operated and managed by C. J. Nungesser, Beidler, O. Located near Beidler, on B. & O. R. R.; 7 miners and 2 day hands employed. Drift to No. 6 seam, 4½ feet thick. Furnace ventilation; mule haulage. Visited February 25th, found in poor condition, has since been abandoned.

Dennison Sewer Pipe, Coal.

Located near Dennison, O., is a new drift opening to No. 6 seam, to supply a new sewer pipe plant near by; will be operated by the Dennison Sewer Pipe Co., Uhrichsville, O. J. J. Maguire, superintendent, Alex Matters, mine boss, both of Uhrichsville, O.

Minnich.

Located one and one-half miles west of Uhrichsville, O. Operated by Banner Minnich. Drift to No. 6 seam, 4 feet thick. Nine miners and 1 day hand employed. Two visits made: October 26th, ordered men removed from the mine until it could be put into working condition. Called by Mr. Minnich October 31st, found no improvement in the ventilation and ordered no more men employed until the mine could be properly ventilated

Shindler.

Located one mile west of Uhrichsville, O. Operated by H. A. Shindler, Tuscarawas, O., who is also manager. Drift to No. 6 seam, 4 feet thick. Natural ventilation; mule haulage; 4 miners employed. Visited October 26th, conditions fair.

Rothacher.

Located two and one-half miles west of Canal Dover, O. Operated by Rothacher Brothers, Canal Dover, R. F. D. No. 1. Drift to No. 5 seam, 4 feet thick. Natural ventilation; mule haulage; 7 miners and 1 day hand employed. Two visits made: May 2nd and October 12th. Air was only in poor circulation on each visit, but a second opening was almost completed through the hill on my last visit; this will place the mine in good condition.

Lenharz.

Located near Rothacher mine. Operated by W. A. Lenharz, Canal Dover, O., R. F. D. No. 1. Drift to No. 5 seam, 4 feet thick. Furnace ventilation; mule haulage; 6 miners and 1 day hand employed Two visits made, May 2nd and October 12th. On each visit found conditions fair.

Royal Clay.

Located near Midvale, O., on B. & O. and Pan Handle R. R.'s. Operated by the Robinson Clay Product Co., Akron, O. S. P. Myers, Uhrichsville, O., superintendent, John Hale, New Philadelphia, O., mine boss. Shaft 80 feet deep. Fan ventilation; mule haulage; electric machine drilling. Two visits made: October 13th and December 6th. This mine has been idle since December, 1909, on account of a boiler explosion, which happened on the 17th of that month, wrecking the plant. On my last visit the mine had just resumed operation. Condition fair.

Robinson-Graves Clay.

Located near Robinson-Graves plant on B. & O. R. R. Operated by Robinson-Graves Sewer Pipe Co., Uhrichsville, O. Wm. Tanzie, Dennison, O., superintendent, T. W. Harding, Uhrichsville O. mine boss. Drift opening. Furnace ventilation; rope and mule haulage. Three visits made: March 7th, July 12th and October 6th. On each visit found conditions fair. Usually 12 men are employed. Rope haulagé was recently installed.

Diamond Clay.

Located at Diamond plant, on B. & O. R. R. at Uhrichsville, O. Operated by the American Sewer Pipe Co., Akron, O. J. M. McClave, superintendent and Wm. Trueshal, mine boss, both of Uhrichsville, O. Drift, furnace ventilation; mule haulage; 8 miners and 1 day hand employed. Four visits made: February 28th, June 22nd, September 21st and December 27th. A second opening has recently been made for manway and air. Have requested a fan placed for ventilation, which will put this mine in good condition. On last visit J. W. Moore, Uhrichsville, O., was found in charge as superintendent.

Buckeye Clay.

Located at the Buckeye Fire Clay plant. Operated by the Buckeye Fire Clay Co., Uhrichsville, O. W. B. Stevens, superintendent, Henry Adamson, mine boss, both of Uhrichsville, O. Slope opening: furnace ventilation; rope hoist and mule haulage; 10 miners employed. Five visits made: March 9th, mine in poor condition, June 21st, fair condition, August 30th, poor condition; on this visit a fan was requested placed and a shaft sunk; November 21st, was compelled to order mine closed down until air could be put into circulation. November 23rd, was called to examine mine to ascertain if conditions warranted a resumption of work; found air in fair circulation and ordered men to work. A new air-shaft has recently been sunk.

Federal Clay.

Owned and operated by the Federal Clay Product Co., Mineral City, O. E. L. Jones, same place, superintendent and mine boss. Drift opening; furnace ventilation; mule haulage. Three visits made: February 4th, June 24th and October 5th. On each visit found mine in fair condition. This has been a very dangerous mine for men to work, but the system has been largely changed by making flint clay the roof. Ten miners and 2 day hands employed.

South Side Clay.

Owned and operated by C. E. Holden, Mineral City, O., and under same management as south side coal. Six miners and one day hand employed. Visited January 31st, May 9th, August 23rd and November 10th. On each visit found conditions fair.

Evans Clay.

Located near Uhrichsville, O. Operated by the Evans Clay Mfg. Co., Uhrichsville, O. W. S. McMillen, same place, superintendent and mine boss. Drift. Furnace ventilation; mule haulage; 6 miners and 1 day hand employed. Visited February 7th, July 18th and October 24th. Conditions fair.

Dover Fire Brick Clay.

Located near Strasburg, O., on B. & O. R. R. Operated by the Dover Fire Brick Co., Strasburg, O. P. Arnold, superintendent, Robert Bowen, mine boss, both of Strasburg, O. Drift. Furnace ventilation; mule haulage. Visited June 23rd, found in poor condition. October 25th, found in fair condition.

Dennison Sewer Pipe Clay.

Located near Dennison, and under same management as Dennison Sewer Pipe Coal. New slope, just ready to operate, to supply new sewer pipe plant.

Advance Clay.

Located near Uhrichsville, O., on B. & O. R. R. Operated by the Advance Fire Clay Co., Uhrichsville, O. Geo. Ross, Sr., superintendent and Geo. Ross, Jr., mine boss, both of Uhrichsville, O. Drift. Natural ventilation; mule haulage. Visited March 7th, July 25th and November 22nd. Last visit found a new air shaft sunk; a new furnace will soon be built; conditions approved.

National Clay.

Located near Strasburg, O. Operated by same company and same management as National Coal; 5 men employed. Visited June 23rd, found conditions fair

NOTE: Visits made outside of Sixth District.

Zerbe, Jefferson Co.

Visited this mine in company with Inspectors Miller and Morrison April 18th to inspect conditions of shaft and cages; found north side cage in fair condition, south side cage damaged. Shaft was being repaired, but not completed. Orders were given to repair cage and complete work in shaft before resuming operations, or permitting any one to ride up or down on them.

Rice Mine, Jefferson Co.

Visited this mine April 14th, in company with inspectors Miller and Morrison to inspect the location and construction of dams in the mine, also location of a shaft for escapement way for men; found two dams completed and approved the same; requested the others pushed to completion as soon as possible; also favored locating shaft on 12 butt as the most accessible point for all concerned.

April 22nd, was called by Chief Inspector Harrison to go to Amsterdam at once to aid in the work of rescue at the Y. & O. mine, where an explosion occurred the night of the 21st, in which 15 men were killed. With Chief Inspector Harrison, and all the other members of the Department, and many others, we entered the mine several times until all of the bodies were recovered, as well as three rescued alive, a full account of which will be found in Chief Inspector Harrison's annual report.

Was also called to meet Chief Inspector Harrison and Inspector Morrison at Amsterdam June 27th, for the purpose of looking into the matter of closing off part of the Y. & O. mine, which was being abandoned, a full account of which will doubtless be found in Mr. Morrison's report.

The second week in July we spent with Mr. Wheatley, the new Inspector, in Columbiana County, which visits are recorded in this report.

SEVENTH DISTRICT.

W. H. MILLER.

COMPOSED OF THE COUNTIES OF HOLMES, MEDINA, OTTAWA, PORTAGE, STARK, SUMMIT, TRUMBULL AND WAYNE.

HON. GEORGE HARRISON, *Chief Inspector of Mines, Columbus, Ohio*:

DEAR SIR:—In compliance with the mining laws of the State of Ohio, and custom of the Mining Department, I have the pleasure of submitting to you for your approval my annual report of the Seventh Mining District, for the year beginning January 1, 1910, and ending December 31, 1910, inclusive.

My district composes the counties of Holmes, Medina, Ottawa, Portage, Stark, Summit, Trumbull and Wayne.

During the time covered by this report, 36 permanent improvements were made, as follows: 1 furnace, 9 fans; 11 second openings; four pair of safety catches; 8 stairways and 3 speaking tubes. Eight mines were opened, 8 suspended and 8 abandoned.

Eleven sets of scales were tested, 9 of which were accurate and 2 inaccurate.

I regret that it is necessary to report 6 fatal accidents and one death, from natural causes, in connection with the operation of mines in the district, attributed to counties, as follows: Stark, 5; Joseph Eckway, who was killed by a fall of stone at the face of his entry, in the Canton Fertilizer Lime and Clay Company's mine. Fred Whitman was killed in No. 20 mine near the face of his room, by a fall of slate. James Evans was killed in Fox No. 12 mine by a fall of slate, near the face of his room. Conrad Byfus was injured by a fall of slate near the face of his room, in the Massillon City mine, near East Greenville, O., and died the same evening, from injuries received. Alex Gravo was injured in the McGinty mine, by a premature blast, on December 15, 1909, and died from the injuries on December 20, 1909. The accident was not reported until February 1st. I made an investigation on February 2, 1910, which was filed with the department. Archie Wagner was employed as a pump tender at the Harris mine, at night; he was found near the pump in the morning in a sitting posture, death resulting from natural causes. Wayne county, James Humble was killed in No. 21 mine by a fall of slate, near the working face of his room.

It will be observed that five of the fatalities out of the six which occurred during the year occurred near the working faces and will bear out the statement in my former report; i. e., that carelessness is responsible for a great number of the fatalities which occur in the mines. The mines of this district were in operation about eight months of the year.

I am pleased to state that the provisions of the new Mining Code, which went into effect on June 11, 1910, has worked out very successfully, both in its relation to miners and operators, and much credit is due the Mining Commission for their efforts to improve conditions in and around the mines.

At the request of Chief Inspector of Mines, George Harrison, six visits were made outside of my district during the year; Columbiana county three, and Jefferson county three

On January 24th an explosion occurred at the Delmore mine, in Columbiana county. Being at the time in that vicinity I went immediately to the mine to render assistance. In the meantime notified Chief Inspector of Mines, George Harrison, and District Inspector Alex Smith, who had charge of this mine. Mr. Smith arrived the following morning at the mine. James Blaemire, who was employed as a shot-firer, was in the mine when the explosion occurred; and was killed. The body was not recovered until about 2:00 P. M., on the 25th by Inspector Alex Smith and a party of explorers. February 17th, George Harrison, Chief Inspector if Mines; Morrison and Smith (District Inspectors), Percy Tetlow, (District President of U. M. W. of A.), Daniel McGrath, mine foreman, and the writer, made a thorough inspection of the mine to determine the cause of the explosion, which was filed with the Mining Department, and will appear in this report.

On the morning of April 22nd, I received a telephone message from District Inspector, Thomas Morrison, stating that an explosion had occurred at the [illegible] mine, near Amsterdam, [illegible] on April 21st, [illegible] requested me to come at once, and I immediately went [illegible] Chief Inspector of Mines, George Harrison, and [illegible] district inspectors at the time, [illegible] engaged searching [illegible] bodies. The work was continued until all the bodies were recovered, [illegible] Saturday, April 23rd. [illegible] detailed account [illegible] report.

In conclusion, I desire to state that my [illegible] have been [illegible] appreciate [illegible] Mining Department, and [illegible] valuable assistance and [illegible]

Respectfully submitted,

[illegible]

[illegible] 1911 [illegible]

MEDINA COUNTY.

Birbeck.

Located near Wadsworth, O. Operated by the Birbeck Coal Co., Wadsworth, O. J. P. Birbeck, Wadsworth, O., has full charge. Slope opening, 210 feet in length, entering the No. 1 seam of coal, which is 4 feet thick. Ventilated by exhaust steam; 8 miners and 2 day-men employed. Two inspections made: March 23rd, August 23rd. Ventilation deficient in No. 3 room, No. 1 entry. Ordered air course cleaned out.

Pleasant View.

Situated near Wadsworth, O. Owned and operated by Gerstenslager and Son, Wadsworth, O. O. V. Gerstenslager, Wadsworth has full charge. Slope opening, 196 feet in length, entering the No. 6 seam of coal, which is 3½ feet thick; 6 miners and 2 day men employed. Two visits were made: March 22nd mine found in good condition. August 24th, visited and found idle. Exhaust steam is used as a ventilating medium.

Star.

Located near Wadsworth, O. Operated by the Hutchinson Coal Co., Wadsworth, O. John Hutchinson, superintendent, Wadsworth, O., John Malaney, mine foreman, Wadsworth, O. This is a slope opening 65 feet in length, entering the No. 1 seam of coal, which is 4 feet thick. Exhaust steam is used as a ventilating power, 5 miners and 1 day man find employment here. Visited August 23rd. Mine found in fair condition.

Pleasant View.

Situated near Wadsworth, Ohio, on a branch of the Erie Railroad. Operated by the James Coal Co., Wadsworth, O. Thomas James, Wadsworth, O., has full charge. This is a slope opening 228 feet in length entering the No. 1 seam of coal, which is 4 feet thick. Exhaust steam is used as a ventilating medium. Worked on the double entry system. Three visits made during the year: March 23rd, former orders complied with. Ventilation deficient in No. 2 entry; ordered it stopped until a break-through was cut. May 20th, August 25th, former orders complied with; ventilation deficient in No. 1 entry. Ordered a break-through cut and a door put up; 16 miners and 4 day men find employment here.

Hambleton.

Located near Wadsworth, O. Operated by the Hambleton Coal Co., Wadsworth, O. Geo. Hambleton, Wadsworth, O., has full charge. Drift opening into the No. 1 seam of coal, which is 4 feet thick. Furnace ventilation. Employes from 6 to 10 miners and 2 day men. Visited August 23rd; mine in good condition.

Klondyke.

Remained suspended throughout the year.

MAHONING COUNTY.

Lowellville.

Located near Lowellville, O. Operated by the Lowellville Coal Co., Youngstown, O. Richard Hoon, Lowellville, O., has full charge. Shaft opening, 75 feet deep, entering the No. 1 seam of coal, which is from 2½ to 4 feet thick. Has fan ventilation; worked on the single entry system. Employs from 15 to 20 miners and 5 day men. Three visits were made: July 24th, ventilation deficient in the main entry, caused by the air course being blocked with gob; ordered it removed, and a check door put on No. 1 room. April 25th, visited and found idle; no inspection made. July 18th, visited this mine in company with R. S. Wheatley of District No. 12, who has taken charge of this county. The mine not being in operation for several months, no inspection was made.

Fair View.

Situated on the Erie R. R., near Washingtonville, O. Operated by the Ohio Coal and Clay Co., Cleveland, O. Chas. Abblett, Leetonia, O., has full charge. Slope opening, 300 feet in length, penetrating the No. 3 seam of coal, which varies in thickness from 3 to 3½ feet. Is ventilated by two fans; worked on the single entry system; 40 miners and 13 day men employed. Two visits made: February 9th, mine found in good condition. April 27th, while making my inspection, found considerable water on the main haulway, the cause being a shortage of steam power. They are installing two new boilers: when this is completed they will be able to take care of the water.

Allison.

Situated near Salem, O. Operated by Callihan and Allison Coal Co., Salem, O. John Allison, same place, has full charge. Slope opening, No. 3 seam, 3 feet thick. Fan ventilation; employs 10 miners and 2 day men. Visited February 7th, found in good condition.

Fisk.

Located near Canfield, O., on the Erie R. R. Operated by the Mahoning and Lake Erie Coal Co., Youngstown, O. W. H. Hunter, Calla, O., has full charge. Slope opening 215 feet in length, penetrating the cannel seam of coal, from 2½ to 4 feet thick; employs from 20 to 30 miners and 9 day men. Exhaust steam is the ventilating power. Three visits were made during the year: February 8th, ventilation deficient in No. 1 south entry. Ordered three sets of timber replaced by new ones in the slope. April 26th, found Mr. Hunter had made a number of improvements, but the ventilation was still deficient; the matter was taken up with the company, and they agreed to install a fan. July 18th, visited this mine, in company with R. S. Wheatley, of District No. 12, and found the ventilation deficient, the Company failing to comply with their promise of April 26th. An order was given that unless a fan was installed and the mine put in compliance with the Mining Law by August 10th, the mine would be closed. Mr. Wheatley has taken charge of this mine.

OTTAWA COUNTY.

American No. 1.

Located near Port Clinton, O., on the L. S. & M. S R. R. Owned and operated by the American Gypsum Co., Port Clinton, O. Arthur Chase, same place, has full charge. Shaft opening, 42 feet deep, entering the Gypsum seam, which varies in thickness from 5 to 6 feet. Fan ventilation. Employs 50 loaders, 28 drillers and 35 day men. Four visits made during the year: February 22nd, May 3rd, July 26th, and October 11th; on each visit the mine was found in good condition.

Consumer No. 2.

Abandoned.

Fishack.

Located near Gypsum, O., on the L. S. & M. S. R. R. Owned and operated by the Fishack Gypsum Co., Port Clinton, Ohio. E. J. Hughes, Gypsum, O., has full charge. This is a new slope opening, 125 feet in length, penetrating the Gypsum seam, which is 7 feet thick. Has force fan ventilation. Employs 4 miners, 2 day men. October 11th, found in good condition.

No. 1 North.

Located near Gypsum, O., on the L. S. & M. S. R. R. Owned and operated by the United States Gypsum Co., Chicago, Ill. Erhard Holm, Gypsum, O., has full charge. Drift opening into the No. 1 Gypsum seam, which is 5 feet thick, and has fan ventilation; 4 drillers, 14 loaders, 8 day men employed. Four visits made: February 23rd, May 4th, mine in good condition; July 27th and October 12th, mine in good condition for pillar work.

No. 2 West.

Located near No. 1 North, on the same R. R. Owned and operated by the same Company, under the same supervision. Drift opening, entering the Gypsum vein, which is 5 feet thick; ventilated by fan, and worked on the double entry system. Employs 4 drillers, 6 loaders and 2 day men. Two visits were made: July 27th, found the mine in operation after a suspension of several months. Ventilation deficient; an order was given to improve the ventilation. October 12th, former order complied with, mine in good condition.

No. 3 West.

Located near Gypsum, O. Operated and under the same supervision as No. 1 North and No. 2 West. Drift opening, penetrating the Gypsum seam, which is 5 feet thick; has fan ventilation. Employs 20 drillers, 20 loaders and 10 day men. Four inspections were made: February 23rd, May 4th; mine found in good condition, July 27th, October 12th, I found the main entry had struck into some bad roof, which was dangerous. Mr. Holm, who is in charge, is exercising great care for the safety of the men.

PORTAGE COUNTY.

Hutson No. 4.

Situated on the L. E. A. & W. R. R., New Deerfield, O. Owned and operated by the Huston Coal Co., Cleveland, O. T. J. Williams, Lloyd, O., is superintendent, J. P. Williams, Deerfield, O., mine foreman. Shaft opening 214 feet deep, penetrating the No. 1, or Palmyra seam of coal, which varies in thickness from 3½ to 4 ft. Worked on the single entry system; has fan ventilation; employs 28 pick miners, 6 cutters, 30 loaders and 38 day men. Four visits made: March 30th, while making my inspection of this mine, I noticed Mr. Williams had been replacing quite a number of old timbers with new ones, along the main haulway. Conditions were good. June 21st, found Section 928 had not been complied with; ordered the same corrected. September 14th, former order complied with. December 9th, mine in good condition.

Hutson No. 8.

Located near Davis, Ohio, on the L. E. A. & W. R. R. Owned and operated by the same company as No. 4 mine, under the same supervision, with R. Lewis Lloyd, as mine foreman. Shaft opening, 130 feet, No. 1 seam of cannel coal, which is of a fine quality and is from 3 to 4 feet thick, ventilated by a fan; worked on the single entry system; 55 miners and 23 day men employed. Four inspections made during the year: March 29th, June 22nd, on examining the report of fire boss, found small traces of gas in parts of the mine recorded; made a thorough inspection, in company with the fire boss, and no traces of gas were found. Ordered report of fire boss placed on black-board, also section 928 of the Mining Laws complied with. September 13th, December 6th, found only portion of my former orders complied with; repeated the order. Found small traces of gas on my last visit in Sullivan's room, and a number of miners using the carbide lamps; notified the mine foreman that carbide lamps were dangerous and must not be used in the mine; this order will be complied with.

Mullins.

Located near Deerfield, O., on the L. E. A. & W. R. R. Operated by the South Palmyra Coal Co., Cleveland, O. J. S. Davis, Deerfield, O., is superintendent, Thomas Davis, same place, mine foreman. Shaft opening, 225 feet deep, entering the No. 1 or Palmyra seam of coal, 4 feet thick. Fan ventilation, single entry system; motor and mule haulage, and employs 15 pick miners, 6 cutters, 25 loaders and 28 day men. Four visits made during the year: March 28th, June 23rd, in good condition. Ordered Section 928 complied with. September 15th, former orders complied with. December 7th, found electricity installed. The Morgan Gardner mining machine being used, giving general satisfaction.

Strong.

Located near Atwater, O. Owned and operated by the Strong Bros. Coal Co., Atwater, R. D. No. 14, O. W. A. Strong, Atwater, has full charge. Shaft opening, 31 feet deep, entering the No. 4 seam, which is 4 feet thick. Exhaust steam is used as a mode of ventilation; employs 8 miners and 2 day men. Two inspections made: September 16th, December 8th; found the mine in operation after a suspension; the condition was good.

Beveridge.

Located near Atwater, O. Operated by J. Wilson, Atwater, O., has full charge. Shaft opening, 31 feet, penetrating the No. 4 seam, which is 3½ feet thick; ventilated by exhaust steam; employs from 5 to 8 miners and 1 day man. Two visits made: September 16th, visited and found idle. December 8th, mine found in fair condition.

Black Diamond.

Situated near Lloyd, O. Operated by the Black Diamond Coal Co., Lloyd, O., Thomas Jones, same place, has full charge. Shaft opening 90 feet, entering the No. 1 seam, or Palmyra block coal which is 2½ feet thick. Has fan ventilation and worked on the single entry system; employs 8 miners and 1 day man. Two visits made: September 16th, December 8th, found former orders complied with; second opening completed, stairway built, fan erected, and the mine in good condition.

STARK COUNTY.

Fox No. 12.

Located near Navarre, O., on the W. & L. E. R. R. Operated by the Massillon Coal Mining Co., Cleveland, O. Wm. Baumgardner, Sr., Massillon, O., is superintendent, P. H. Harney, Navarre, O., mine foreman. Shaft opening 200 feet deep penetrating the No. 1 seam of Massillion coal, which is 5 ft. thick at this point, worked on the double entry system; fan ventilation; motor and mule haulage; employs 70 pick miners, 4 cutters, 22 loaders and 52 day men. Nine visits made during the year. January 19th, called to investigate fatal accident of James Evans, who was killed by fall of stone at the face of his room. March 1st, called to test scales, tested and found incorrect. May 23rd. I found Mr. Harney in charge. Mr. Baumgardner, former mine foreman having resigned; part of my former orders were complied with; ventilation was deficient on the south side. Notified Mr. Harney to place the mine in compliance with the law. July 13th and 15th, former orders complied with; ventilation deficient in Nos. 2 and 3 entries, south side. Ordered light carried on motor trip. September 23rd and 24th, former orders complied with; ordered a door put up in No. 1 entry, a break-through closed in No. 3 entry and a check on No. 5 room. December 13th and 14th, former orders complied with. While making my inspection, learned from the miners of there being a shortage of timber, notified the mine foreman and also the superintendent that miners must be supplied with ample timber.

Gelse No. 13.

Located near Stanwood, O., on the B. & O. R. R. Owned and operated by the same company, as No. 12, same supt. with Wm. Moffet, Massillon, O., as mine foreman. Shaft opening, 200 feet deep, entering the No. 1 seam of coal, which is 5 feet thick. Fan vantilation, double entry system; mule haulage; employs 35 miners and 14 day men. Four visits made; January 3rd, March 15th, mine found in good condition, September 1st. visited and found idle, no inspection made. November 25th, found this mine in operation after a suspension of seven months; ventilation deficient, on account of air course being blocked by the removing of pillars; a new air course is being opened up, which will require about two days work; when this is completed the ventilation will be much improved.

No. 17.

Located near West Brookfield, O. Operated by the Massillon Coal Mining Co., Cleveland, O. Wm. Baumgardner, Massillon, O., Supt., P. H. Harney, Navarre, O., mine foreman. Shaft opening, 225 feet into the No. 1 seam of coal, which is 5 feet, thick. Fan ventilation, double entry system; employed 38 miners and 18 day men. January 5th, ordered a number of timbers set at the bottom of the shaft. This mine was worked out and abandoned the forepart of the year.

No. 20.

Situated near Canal Fulton, O., on the Penna. R. R. Owned and operated by the Massillon Coal Mining Co., Cleveland, O. Wm. Baumgardner, Massillon, O., Supt; J. Hogden, Canal Fulton, O., mine foreman; shaft opening, 214 feet deep into the No. 1 seam, which is from 4 to 5 ft. in thickness; double entry system; fan ventilation and mule haulage; employs 45 pick miners, 12 cutters, 24 loaders and 28 day men. Seven visits were made: January 17th, made a partial inspection of the mine and found the haulways very dry, ordered them sprinkled. January

28th, completed my inspection of the south side, found the haulways dry and dusty; repeated the sprinkling order. February 10th, called to investigate fatal accident of Fred Whittman, who was killed by fall of stone at the face of his room. June 24th, found 4 men doing repair work; ordered section 928 of the mining laws complied with, August 16th, former orders complied with. September 8th, ventilation deficient in Nos. 3 and 4 rooms in No. 1 entry, south side; ordered door erected and breakthrough closed, also check on No. 2 entry. Tested scales, in company with mine committee and found accurate. November 18th, former orders complied with; ventilation deficient in No. 1 room, No. 1 entry; ordered break-through closed; ventilation deficient in No. 4 entry, which was bad, not being driven to the 60 foot limit, but a break-through was being made, which will require about two cuts.

Elm Run No. 5.

Situated on the W. & L. E. R. R., near Elton, O. Operated by the Massillon Elm Run Coal Co., Cleveland, O. Philip Sonnhalter, Massillon, O., superintendent. Lewis Brenkamp, Navarre, O., mine foreman; shaft opening 110 feet, into the No. 1 seam of coal, which is 4 feet thick; double entry system, fan ventilation; mule haulage; employs 35 miners and 15 day men. Three visits made: March 7th, May 5th, ventilation deficient, caused by the removing of pillars. July 29th, mine in good condition for pillar work.

Elm Run No. 7.

Located south of Navarre, O., on the W. & L. E. R. R. Operated under the same supervision as No. 5 mine, with M. Davis, Massillon, O., as mine foreman; shaft opening, 214 feet deep, penetrating the No. 1 seam, which is 5 feet thick; fan ventilation, double entry system; mule haulage; employs 25 miners and 10 day men. February 16th, mine in good condition. They are making preparations to remove the pillars. Worked out and abandoned during the year.

Elm Run No. 11.

Located nearly 5 miles southwest of Massillon, O., on the W. & L. E. R. R. Operated by the Massillon Elm Run Coal Co., Cleveland, O. Philip Sonnhalter, superintendent, Massillon, O., M. Davis, Massillon, O., mine foreman. Shaft opening, 165 feet into the No. 1 seam of coal which is 4 feet thick; has exhaust steam as ventilating power double entry system; mule haulage; employs 20 miners and 10 day men. Four visits made: July 29th, September 20th, on my visit found 12 men engaged in making the bottom and shooting a sump; notified Mr. Davis, who is in charge, to commence work on second opening; a sinking engine was on the ground and the order will be complied with. November 25th, found 14 miners and 2 day men at work; they had driven the main entry about 220 feet from the inside of the bottom; notified Mr. Davis that the law was not being complied with, and it became my duty to order operations to cease until the second opening was completed. Posted a notice to this effect. The second opening has reached a depth of 100 feet, when completed it will be 165 feet. The mine ceased operation and will remain so until the law is complied with.

Pocock No. 3.

Located near East Greenville, O., on the B. & O. R. R., and W. & L. E. R. R. Operated by Pocock Coal Co., Massillon, O. Wm. Kutz, Massillon, O., has full charge. Shaft opening 245 feet deep into the No. 1 seam of coal, which is 5 feet thick; worked on the double entry system; mule haulage; fan ventilation;

employs 70 pick miners and 37 day men. Six visits were made: March 11th, May 13th, mine found in fair condition. July 12th, September 26th, mine in good condition for pillar work. October 4th, called to examine and test scales; made test of same, in company with mine committee, and found correct. November 10th, pillars are being removed from the old part of the mine. The rock tunnel has reached a distance of about 1300 feet. Conditions are good.

Hipp.

Located near Newman, O., on the Penna. R. R. Operated by the Massillon Stone & Fire Brick Co., Massillon, O. S. J. Preece, Massillon, O., R. D. No. 1, has full charge. Drift opening, into the clay seam, which is 5 feet thick; furnace ventilation; employs 2 drillers, 4 loaders and 2 day men. Four visits were made: February 11th, June 6th; ventilation good; haulage very muddy. Ordered a number of timbers replaced by new ones along the main haulage. August 17th, December 30th, former orders complied with; mine in fair condition.

Sippo No. 2.

Situated near North Lawrence, O., on the Penna. R. R. Operated by the Everhart Co., Massillon, O. John Yast, Massillon, O., has full charge. Drift opening into the clay seam, which is 5 feet thick; furnace ventilation, double entry system. Employs 12 miners and 2 day men. Four visits made: March 8th, May 26th, ventilation good; haulage muddy. August 18th, November 11th, mine in good condition.

McGinty.

Located near Louisville, O., on the Penna. R. R. Operated by the Louisville Brick & Tile Co., Louisville, O. Frank Duplin, Louisville, O., has full charge. Drift opening into the No. 6 seam of coal and clay; coal 3 feet, clay 6 feet. Furnace ventilation; employs 25 miners and 12 day men, worked on the single entry system. Six visits were made; January 27th, former orders complied with; ventilation deficient in No. 4 entry, No. 3 room; ordered breakthrough cut; noticed a scarcity of timber at this time; notified the mine foreman to keep a sufficient supply of timber on hand at all times. February 2nd, called to investigate fatal accident of Alex Gravo, who was injured by a premature blast on December 15th and died December 20th. May 31st, August 9th, former orders complied with; ventilation deficient in No. 2 room, in No. 2 entry; ordered several sets of timber replaced by new ones in No. 2 entry. October 5th, former orders complied with; ordered second opening retimbered. December 1st, former orders complied with, found 4 men removing pillars in No. 4 entry; the roof being dangerous, I stopped them until the place was retimbered and made safe.

Taggart No. 3.

Located near Navarre, O., on the B. & O. R. R. Operated by the Taggart Coal Co., Massillon, O. George Bullock, Massillon, O., has full charge. Shaft opening, 135 feet deep, entering the No. 1 seam of coal, which is 3½ to 4 feet thick; has fan ventilation; double entry system; mule and rope haulage; employs 52 miners and 24 day men. Four visits were made during the year. February 11th, mine in fair condition. August 29th, mine in operation after a suspension of nearly five months; a larger fan has been installed, the former fan being insufficient to furnish the amount of ventilation required by the new law; found a number of brattices that needed repairing and an order was given to repair them. October 17th, former orders complied with; mine in good condition. December 29th, ventilation deficient in Nos. 1 and 2 rooms; ordered breakthrough cut.

Summit Hill.

Located near Greentown, O., on the B. & O. R. R. Operated by Mrs. L. E. Smith, Greentown, O. George Traxler, Greentown, O., has full charge. Drift opening into the No. 4 seam, which is 5 feet, including a strata of stone in the center, which varies in thickness from to 2 to 4 inches; has furnace ventilation, single entry system; employs 14 miners and 3 day hands. Four visits made during the year. March 3rd, mine found in good condition. June 9th, found a main door standing open which cut off the ventilation from the interior of the mine; notified the mine foreman that the driver must attend to this door, or otherwise to place an attendant there; order complied with August 22nd. November 17th, mine in good condition.

Willow Grove.

Located near West Brookfield, O. Domestic mine, operated by the Willow Grove Coal Co., Massillon, O. C. F. Smith, same place, has full charge. Shaft opening, 147 feet deep, penetrating the No. 1 seam of coal, which is from 3 to 3½ feet thick. Fan ventilation, worked on the double entry system; mule haulage; employs 9 miners and 3 day men. Three visits were made, March 18th, former orders complied with; ordered door put up on No. 2 room. September 21st, former orders complied with. December 5th, ventilation deficient in No. 3 room, No. 2 entry; ordered breakthrough cut.

North Berlin.

Located near New Berlin, O. Operated by G. F. Smith, New Berlin, O F. Smith, New Berlin, O., has full charge. Shaft opening, 40 feet deep, into the No. 4 seam of coal, which is 5 feet thick, including a strata of stone, varying in thickness from 2 to 4 inches. Has furnace ventilation; employs 13 miners and 3 day men. Four visits were made. March 2nd, June 7th, mine in good condition. September 26th, ventilation deficient in No. 1 entry, south side, caused by the furnace not being in use; notified Mr. Smith that the furnace must be kept in use while the mine was in operation. December 15th, former orders complied with.

Wise No. 2.

Located near North Industry, O. Operated by Wise Bros. Coal Co., Canton, O. Clark Wise, Canton, O., has full charge. Drift opening, into the No. 4 seam, which is 4 feet thick; has furnace ventilation. Employs 7 miners and 1 day man. November 21st visited and found ventilation deficient in No. 2 room. Ordered a breakthrough cut and a check door put up.

West Brookfield.

Remained suspended throughout the year.

Lahmiller No. 1.

Located near Waco, Ohio. Operated by J. G. Lahmiller, Canton, O., who has full charge. Drift opening into No. 5 seam of coal, which is 3 feet thick. Furnace ventilation; employs from 10 to 15 miners and 2 day men. Four visits made. February 1st, May 9th, mine in good condition. August 1st, visited and found idle; 2 men were cleaning up the entries, so the mine could resume operation. November 1st, ventilation deficient in No. 3 room in No. 2 entry. Ordered a breakthrough cut. Aside from this conditions good.

N. F. P. No. 1.

Located on the W. & L. E. R. R., near Osnaburg, O. Owned and operated by the National Fire Proofing Co., Canton, O., John Murley, Canton, O., is generai manager; Daniel Plotner, Osnaburg, O., mine foreman. Drift opening, into No. 6 seam of coal, 4 feet thick; furnace ventilation, double entry system; mule haulage; employs 25 miners and 9 day men. Four visits made, March 9th, May 11th, ventilation good; haulage muddy; August 4th, November 4th, mine in good condition.

N. F. P. No. 2.

Located near Waynesburg, Ohio, on the Penna. R. R. Owned and operated by the National Fireproofing Co., Canton, O. John Murley, general manager; Wm. Smith, Waynesburg, O., mine foreman. Slope opening, into No. 5 seam, which is 3 feet of coal and 5 feet of clay; fan ventilation, worked on the single entry system; employs 14 miners and 5 day men. Three visits were made. May 10th found the traveling way to the second opening in bad shape, ordered it cleaned out and re-timbered, also stairway repaired; ventilation deficient in No. 1 entry. Ordered breakthrough cut. August 3rd, former orders complied with. November 3rd, found the ventilation deficient in No. 2 entry. Mr. Smith stated that he would erect a door in the course of a day or two, which will improve conditions.

Whittacre No. 5.

Situated near Waynesburg, O., on the Penna. R. R. Operated by the Whittacre Fireproofing Co., Waynesburg, O. J. Milner, Waynesburg, O., has full charge. Drift opening, into No. 5 seam of coal, which is 3 feet thick, clay 6 feet. Fan ventilation, 18 miners and 6 day men employed. Four visits were made. March 10th, ventilation deficient in No. 3 room, No. 2 entry. Ordered breakthrough cut. May 10th, former orders complied with. August 2nd, ventilation deficient in No. 2 entry; ordered a door put up. November 2nd, former orders complied with. Ordered breakthrough cut in No. 1 entry and a door built in No 2 entry.

Whittacre No. 6.

Located near No. 5, on the same R. R. and under the same supervision. Drift opening, into No. 6 seam of coal, which is 3 feet, clay 6 feet. Fan ventilation; employs 33 miners and 13 day men, and worked on the double entry system. Four visits were made. March 27th, former orders complied with. Mine in good condition. May 10th, found the ventilation deficient, owing to the inadequacy of the furnace to furnish ventilation. Notified the Company to this effect, and suggested installing a fan. August 2nd the Company has purchased two Brazil fans, one for each mine; the fan houses were in the course of erection and the fans will be placed in operation as soon as possible. November 2nd, found fans in operation and mine in good condition.

Indian Run.

Remained suspended throughout the year.

Keim No. 1.

Located near Mapleton, O., on the W. & L. E. R. R. Operated by the Keim Brick & Tile Co., Louisville, O. George Hoover, Osnaburg, O., has full charge. Drift opening, into No. 6 seam of coal and clay, coal 3 feet, clay 6 feet. Furnace ventilation, worked on the double entry system. Employs 8 miners and 4 day men. Three visits were made. March 31st former orders complied with; ventilation good; haulage muddy, caused by the surface water. August 3rd, ventilation deficient in Nos. 1 and 2 rooms, in No. 2 entry. Ordered two breakthroughs closed and a check door erected between Nos. 1 and 2 rooms. November 3rd, former orders complied with. Ordered breakthrough closed between Nos. 1 and 2 entries also two sets of timber replaced by new ones at the neck of No. 1 room, in No. 2 entry.

Keim No. 2.

Remained suspended throughout the year.

Robertsville.

Remained suspended throughout the year.

Edgefield.

Located near Edgefield, O. Operated by John Wynn & Sons, Canton, O John Wynn, Sr., Canton, O., has full charge. Slope 150 feet in length, entering the No. 4 seam of coal, which is 4 ft. thick; furnace ventilation; employs 11 miners and 3 day men. Three visits made during the year. February 25th, ventilation deficient in No. 1 room; ordered breakthrough cut. September 26th, December 15th, former orders complied with; mine in good condition.

C. H. B.

Remained suspended throughout the year.

Canton Sparta Clay.

Located near Sparta, O., on the B. & O. R. R. Operated by the Canton Sparta Clay Co., Mineral City, O. James Hutchinson, Sandyville, O., has full charge. Drift opening, into a clay seam, which is 6 feet thick. Furnace ventilation; employs 7 miners and 4 day men. Two visits made. April 19th. This is a new drift opening; on my visit found it in good condition. November 22nd, the roof is very dangerous in this mine; there is a shale that varies in thickness from 2 to 4 feet between the clay and sand rock. Mr. Hutchinson, who is in charge, works the place narrow, which is a protection to the roof and makes it much safer for the miners.

Fox Run.

Located near North Industry, O., on the B. & O. R. R. Operated by Fox Run Coal Co., North Industry, O. W. B. Myers, North Industry, has full charge. Drift opening, into No. 4 seam, which is 4 feet thick. Furnace ventilation; employs 14 miners and 4 day men. Two visits made. June 29th, ordered traveling way to second opening cleaned out. August 31st, former orders complied with Mine idle, made inspection and found conditions fair.

Sonnhalter.

Located north of Canton, O. Operated by the Sonnhalter Coal Co., Massillon, O. Adam Sonnhalter, Canton, O., has full charge. Shaft opening, 60 feet deep, entering No. 4 seam of coal, which is 4½ feet thick. Ventilated by exhaust steam, worked on the double entry system. Compressed air is in use here, with the Ingersoll Punching Machine. Employs 8 loaders, 2 cutters and 3 day men. Four visits made. February 25th, order manway leading to second opening enlarged. April 20th, visited and found idle; made inspection and found my former orders complied with. July 14th, ordered hand-holds and sides on cage. October 18th, former orders complied with. Ordered breakthrough cut in No. 1 room, check door put up between Nos. 1 and 2 rooms, in No. 2 entry.

Massillon Crystal.

Located near Crystal Springs, O., on the Penna. and B. & O. R. R.'s. Operated by the Massillon Crystal Coal Co., Massillon, O. John Mitchel, McDonaldsville, O., has full charge. Shaft opening, 150 feet deep, entering No. 1 seam of coal, which is 4 feet thick; worked on the double entry system; fan ventilation and mule haulage; employs 34 miners and 15 day men. Four visits made. January 6th, March 17th. Mine in good condition. May 27th, visited and found idle; made inspection and found 4 men mining boiler fuel. July 8th, found 7 men engaged in removing pipes and taking up track to abandon the mine.

Booth.

Located near Justus, O. Operated by the Booth Coal Co., Navarre, Ohio. B. H. Evans, Navarre, O., has full charge. Drift opening, into the No. 3 seam, which is 3 feet thick. Furnace ventilation, double entry system; employs 9 miners and 1 day man. Three visits made during the year. March 1st, ventilation deficient, furnace not in use, was the cause; ordered furnace fired, while the mine was working. September 9th, December 13th, former orders complied with; mine in good condition.

Arntz.

Located near North Industry, O. Operated by Charles Arntz, North Industry, O., who has full charge. Drift opening into No. 6 seam of coal, which is 3 feet thick, double entry system; natural ventilation; employs 14 miners and 1 day man. One visit. November 24th. Mine found in good condition.

Massillon City.

Located near East Greenville, O., on the W. & L. E. R. R. Owned and operated by the Massillon City Coal Co., Massillon, O. Wm. Penman, same place, has full charge. Shaft opening, 250 feet deep, entering No. 1 seam of Massillon coal, which is 5 feet thick, worked on the double entry system; fan ventilation; employs 69 miners and 19 day men. Six visits were made. February 24th, May 16th, mine found in good condition. July 5th, ventilation deficient in No. 6 room, in No. 2 entry. Ordered two breakthroughs closed and a check door built to force the ventilation up to the working place. August 19th, former orders complied with. Ventilation deficient in No. 4 room, in No. 2 entry. Ordered check door built. October 3rd, called to investigate fatal accident of Conrad Byfus, who was injured by a fall of slate, near the face of his room. December 2nd, former orders complied with. Ventilation deficient in room No. 2, No. 3 entry. Ordered breakthrough cut; aside from this conditions good.

H. B. Camp.

Located near Altman, Ohio, on the B. & O. R. R. Operated by H. B. Camp Clay Co., Altman, O. Edward Babb, same place, has full charge. Drift opening, into a clay seam, which is 9 feet thick; worked on the single entry system; employs 10 miners and 2 day men. Four visits made. March 3rd, when I arrived at this mine found the miners eating their lunch in a shanty close to the mouth of the mine; the stove was red hot and there were four boxes of dynamite stored around it; notified the mine foreman that this was a violation of the law, and that it would have to be removed immediately, which was done. Visited June 7th, August 22nd, November 17th, on each occasion the mine was found in good condition.

Massillon City B.

Located near West Brookfield, O. Operated by Swier & Llewellyn Coal Co., Massillon, Ohio. Wm. Llewellyn, same place, has full charge. Shaft opening, 77 feet deep, entering the No. 1 seam of coal, which is 4 feet thick; ventilated by exhaust steam, and worked on the double entry system; employs 9 miners and 3 day men. Four visits were made. March 14th, visited and found idle, made inspection and found in good condition. Ordered stairway in second opening; June 6th, former orders complied with. September 21st, December 30th, conditions were good.

B. & B.

Located near Canal Fulton, Ohio. Operated by Blank & Bliler Coal Co., Canal Fulton, O. L. Bliler, same place, has full charge. Slope opening, 156 feet in length, entering the No. 1 seam of coal, which is 4 feet thick; ventilated by exhaust steam, worked on the double entry system; employs 7 miners and 3 day men. Four visits made. January 28th, April 20th, found in good condition. August 30th, ventilation deficient at face of No. 1 entry; ordered breakthrough cut. December 16th, former orders complied with; mine in good condition.

Lahmiller No. 2.

Operated by J. G. Lahmiller, Canton, O. Drift opening, No. 6 seam, 3 feet thick; employs 3 miners and 1 day man.

Sunnyside.

Operated by Wm. Lahmiller, North Industry, O. Drift opening, No. 6 seam, 3 feet thick; employs 5 miners.

Hale.

Operated by Albert Hale, Osnaburg, O. Drift opening, No. 6 seam, 3 feet thick; employs 5 miners and 1 day man.

Eli No. 2.

Operated by Ed. Eli, Alliance, O. Shaft opening, 55 feet deep, No. 3 seam, 2 feet 8 inches. Employs 5 miners and 1 day man.

Krunlauf.

Operated by Wm. Krunlauf, Osnaburg, O. Drift opening, No. 6 seam, coal 3 feet. Employs 5 miners and 1 day man.

Fisher.

Operated by T. Savage, Justus, O. Drift opening, No. 3 seam of coal, 3 feet thick. Employs 3 miners and 1 day man.

Sheatzley.

Operated by E. O. Blough, North Industry, O. Drift opening, No. 6 seam, 3 feet thick. Employs 6 miners.

St. Elmo.

Operated by L. C. Johnson, Canton, O. Slope opening, into No. 4 seam of coal, which is 4 feet thick. Employs 5 miners and 1 day man.

Urban Hill.

Operated by J. Longsworth, North Lawrence, O. Slope opening, 60 feet deep, No. 1 seam, 3½ feet thick. Employs 3 miners and 1 day man.

Newman.

Operated by the Newman Coal Co., Massillon, O., R. R. No. 2. Slope opening, into the No. 1 seam of coal, which is 5 feet thick. Employs 3 miners and 1 day man.

Orchard Hill.

Operated by Maggie Currey, Minerva, O. Slope opening, into No. 6 seam, coal 28 inches thick. Employs 6 miners and 1 day man.

Harris.

Operated by David Harris, Canton, O. Drift opening, No. 4 seam, 5 feet thick; employs 6 miners and 2 day men.

Kester.

Operated by Kester Coal Co., Osnaburg, O. Drift opening, No. 6 seam, coal 3 feet thick. Employs 5 miners.

C. F. L.

Operated by the Canton Fertilizing Lime Co., Canton, O. Drift opening, No. 6 seam. Employs 3 miners and 1 day man.

Stemwinder.

Operated by Ed. Myers, Massillon, O. Slope opening, into No. 1 seam, coal 3 feet thick. Employs 2 miners.

Evansdale.

Situated on the B. & O. R. R., near North Industry, O. Operated by Evansdale Lime and Clay Product Co., Canton, O. John Morledge, N. Industry, O., has full charge. Drift opening, into the No. 4 seam, which is 4 feet thick, worked on the double entry system; furnace ventilation. Employs 33 miners and 10 day men. Five inspections were made. February 3rd, found the mine dry and dusty; ordered it sprinkled. April 18th, since my former visit to this mine, found separate traveling way had been made, in compliance with the law. June 28th, October 20th, mine found in good condition. December 23rd, found idle, inspected and found Nos. 1 and 2 west entries very dry and dusty; ordered them sprinkled.

Moss Hill.

Located near Howenstine, O., on the B. & O. R. R. Operated by the Farmers Lime & Fertilizing Co., Canton, O., C. M. Miller, N. Industry, O., has full charge. Drift opening into No. 4 seam, which is 4 feet thick; worked on the single entry system; furnace ventilation; employs 14 miners and 2 day men. Two visits were made. June 27th. This is a new mine; on my visit found the ventilation deficient in No. 3 entry, on account of the air course being blocked with gob. November 22nd, visited and found idle, made inspection, found former orders complied with.

Crescent.

Located near Paris, O., on the L. E. A. & W. R. R. Operated by the Tippecanoe & Goshen Coal Co., Canton, O. J. P. Jones, Canton, O., superintendent. E. O. Jones, Paris, O., mine foreman. Slope opening, 60 feet in length entering the No. 5 seam of coal, 3 feet in thickness. Fan ventilation; employs 18 miners and 5 day men, on November 16th. This is a new slope; on this visit found the haulage very muddy; ventilation deficient in No. 4 room, in west entry. Ordered breakthrough cut, also guard railing on tipple, and safety block on top of slope.

SUMMIT COUNTY.

Turkey Foot No. 2.

Located near Manchester, O., on the C. A. & C. R. R. Operated by the Turkey Foot Mining Co., Akron, O. J. D. Jones, Barberton, O., has full charge. Slope opening, 340 feet long, coal 3½ to 4½ feet thick, worked on the double entry system; fan ventilation; mule haulage; employs 50 miners and 14 day men. Five visits made. March 24th, found a number of the brattices needed repairing; ordered them repaired. May 19th, former orders complied with; ventilation deficient in No. 3 entry. Ordered check door put up. July 21st, October 7th, former orders complied with. Mine in good condition. Tested scales and found correct. December 20th, while making my inspection learned from a number of the miners that there was a scarcity of timber, and notified Mr. Jones that a supply of timber must be kept at the mine at all times.

Beechwood-Massillon.

Located at Manchester, O., on the C. A. & C. R. R. Operated by the Beechwood-Massillon Coal Co., Cleveland, O. Ed. Penman, Clinton, O., has full charge. Shaft opening, 140 feet deep, into the No. 1 seam of coal, which is 5 feet thick, worked on the double entry system; motor and mule haulage; fan ventilation; employs 38 pick miners, 8 cutters, 43 loaders, and 34 day men. Four visits were made. February 4th, former orders complied with; ventilation deficient in No. 1 room, in No. 3 entry; had it stopped until a breakthrough was cut. May 18th, former orders complied with; found a number of brattices that needed repairing, ordered this done. August 11th, former orders complied with. October 21st, ventilation deficient in No. 6 entry; ordered a breakthrough cut in No. 3 room, No. 4 entry.

Hill.

Located near Mogadore, O., on the W. & L. E. R. R. Operated by the Robinson Clay Product Co., Akron, O. Wm. Lilley, Mogadore, O., has full charge. Drift opening, into the clay seam, which is 5 feet thick; furnace ventilation; employs from 10 to 12 miners and 3 day men. Three visits were made during the year. April 19th, August 10th and November 15th. On each occasion the mine was in compliance with the law.

Swinehart No. 1.

Suspended indefinitely.

Clinton Shaft.

Operated by A. Morrow, Clinton, O. Shaft opening, into No. 1 seam, coal 3 feet thick; employs 4 miners and 2 others.

Cottage Grove.

Located near Cottage Grove, O. Operated by Cottage Grove Coal Co., Akron, Ohio. Slope opening, 86 feet in length, into No. 1 seam, 3 feet thick; employs 7 miners and 2 day men. Mine in good condition.

Barberton.

Located near Hametown, Ohio. Operated by the Barberton Coal Co., Barberton, O. Slope opening, 85 feet in length, into the No. 1 seam of coal, which is 4½ feet thick. 7 miners and 3 day men employed; exhaust steam as a ventilating medium.

WAYNE COUNTY.

West Lebanon No. 2.

Located near West Lebanon, Ohio, on the C. A. & C. R. R. Operated by the Massillon Coal Mining Co., Massillon, O. William Baumgardner, superintendent, Massillon, O. D. W. Heinbuck, West Lebanon, O., mine foreman. Slope opening, 330 feet in length, penetrating the No. 1 seam of coal, which is 5 feet thick. Worked on the double entry system; fan ventilation; employs 46 miners and 15 day men. Four visits made during the year. January 4th, March 16th, former orders complied with, mine in fine condition; tested scales and found correct. September 1st, this mine has changed hands, and it is now the property of the M. C. M. Co. November 9th, mine in good condition for pillar work.

Dalton No. 14.

Located near Dalton, Ohio, on the W. & L. E. R. R. Operated by the Massillon Coal Mining Co., Massillon, O. Wm. Baumgardner, superintendent, Massillon, O.; John LaViers, Dalton, O., mine foreman. Shaft opening, 125 feet deep, entering the No. 1 seam of coal, which is 4 feet thick, worked on the double entry system; fan ventilation; employs 34 miners and 15 day men. Four visits were made March 25th, mine in good condition. July 6th, pillars were being removed; ordered Section 928 complied with. September 7th and October 31st, former orders complied with. Mine in good condition for pillar work.

No. 21.

Situated on the W. & L. E. R. R., near Dalton, Ohio. Operated by the Massillon Coal Mining Co, Massillon, O. Wm. Baumgardner, Massillon, O. superintendent; John Ryne, Dalton, O., mine foreman Shaft opening, 157 feet deep, entering No. 1 seam of coal, which is from 4 to 5 feet thick; worked on the double entry system; fan ventilation; employs 60 miners and 22 day men. Seven visits made. February 15th, former orders complied with; ventilation deficient in No. 2 entry, S. S. Ordered breakthrough cut, also gob removed from air course in No. 3 entry, N. S. February 28th, called to investigate fatal accident of James Humble, who was killed by a fall of stone near the face of his room. July 7th, this mine is in operation after a suspension of nearly five months. The principal work on this visit was the driving of entries. Ordered breakthroughs cut in No. 2 and 3 entries, and section 928 of the mining law complied with. September 7th, called to test scales; made test in company with mine committee, and found incorrect. September 12th, former orders complied with; ventilation deficient in No. 1 entry, S. S. Ordered breakthrough closed. Tested scales and found correct. October 28th, December 27th, former orders complied with; mine in good condition.

No. 22.

Located 3 miles south of Dalton, Ohio, on the W. & L. E. R. R. Operated by the Massillon Coal Mining Co., Massillon, O., under same supervision as No. 21, with Hugh Patterson, Dalton, O., as mine foreman. Shaft opening, 212 feet deep, entering No. 1 seam of coal, which is 5 feet thick, worked on the double entry system; fan ventilation; mule haulage; employs 15 pick miners, 6 cutters, 35 loaders and 26 day men. Four visits made during the year. May 25th, mine in good condition, tested safety catches and found them in good working order. July 11th, found second opening completed, stairway built, and fan in course of erection, which will be completed in a few days. Learned from the fire boss that he had found small traces of gas in No. 1, S. E. entry; on my inspection, no traces of gas were found. September 19th, mine in good condition. December 12th, ventilation deficient in No. 3 entry; ordered breakthrough cut, found traces of gas in No. 1 face entry, S. S.

No. 23.

Located near No. 22, on the same railroad. Owned and operated by the same Company, same superintendent. John LaViers, Dalton, O., mine foreman. Shaft opening, 120 feet deep, penetrating the No. 1 seam of coal, which is from 3½ to 4 feet thick; worked on the double entry system. Exhaust steam used as a ventilating medium. Two visits made. July 11th, visited and found idle; mine suspended indefinitely. December 28th, found the mine in operation, after suspension of about nine months. The water had just been pumped out and a few men employed; the mine will be in full operation in the course of a week. On December 16th, 1909, gave an order for a speaking tube and a back signal put in; my order was not complied with, owing to the mine shutting down; repeated my order; Mr. LaViers, who is in charge, assured me the order would be complied with.

Grute.

Located near North Lawrence, Ohio, on the Penna. R. R. Operated by the Minglewood Massillon Coal Co., Cleveland, O. C. A. Kouth, Massillon, O., has full charge. Slope opening, 280 feet, penetrating No. 1 seam of coal, which is from 3½ to 4½ feet thick; worked on the double entry system; fan ventilation; employs 76 miners and 19 day men. Five visits made during the year. March 4th, June 8th, and August 15th, mine found in good condition. October 14th, ordered a breakthrough closed in No. 2 entry, found a main door standing open, notified the mine foreman that the driver must attend to this door, or an attendant placed at it. December 22nd, former orders complied with; ordered and air course cleaned out in No. 4 entry; aside from this, conditions were good.

Hametown No. 2.

Located near Hametown, Ohio. Operated by Hametown Coal Co., Barberton, Ohio. J. D. Jones, Barberton, O., has full charge. Slope opening, 335 feet in length, into No. 1 seam of coal, which is 4 feet thick, work on the double entry system, ventilated by exhaust steam; employs 16 miners and 3 day men. Three visits were made during the year. March 22nd, August 24th, former orders complied with; mine in good condition. November 29th, they were driving the main entry towards an abandoned mine, known as the Old Negro Shaft, which is filled with water; test holes are being drilled and great caution exercised.

Kentucky.

Located near Fredericksburg, Ohio, on the C. A. & C. R. R. Operated by the Kentucky Fire Brick Co., Portsmouth, O. J. L. Leighew, Fredericksburg, O., has full charge. Drift opening into the No. 5 seam of coal, which is 3 feet thick: natural ventilation; employs 13 miners and 4 day men. Three visits made. May 24th, former orders complied with. August 12th, ventilation deficient; natural ventilation is relied on here, and it is insufficient; notified the superintendent that it would be necessary to increase the ventilation, and unless this was done his force of men would have to be reduced; he agreed to take the matter up with the Company. October 24th, suspended indefinitely and no inspection made.

Redett.

Operated by Wm. Redett and Son, Fredericksburg, O. Drift opening. No. 5 seam, 2 feet 8 inches thick; employs 7 miners and 1 day man.

Elm Run No. 9.

Located near Clinton, Ohio, on the C. A. & C. R. R. Operated by the Massillon Elm Run Coal Co., Cleveland, O. Philip Sonhaulter, Massillon, O., superintendent. H. Williams, Canal Fulton, O., mine foreman. Shaft opening, 110 feet deep, into No. 1 seam of coal, which is 4 feet thick; worked on the double entry system; fan ventilation; employs 46 miners and 17 day men. Five visits made. March 21st, second opening completed, stairway built and fan erected. June 10th, July 22nd, mine found in fair condition. Ordered section 928 of the mining laws complied with. October 6th, only a portion of my former orders were complied with; repeated my order for test weights. December 19th, orders complied with. Ordered breakthrough cut in No. 5 room, in No. 1 West entry.

Elm Run No. 10.

Located near Doylestown, Ohio, on the Erie R. R. Owned by the Massillon Elm Run Coal Co., Cleveland, O. Philip Sonnhalter, Massillon, O., superintendent, Massillon, O. M. Morris, Clinton, O., mine foreman. Shaft opening, 144 feet deep, into No. 1 seam of coal, which is 5 feet thick; worked on the double entry system; ventilated by exhaust steam. November 28th, this mine has been suspended since April, 1905; they have just got the water pumped out and are commencing to clean up. The mine will be in operation in the course of a week. I noticed there was no brake on the drum, ordered one put on.

Gilt Edge.

Operated by A. W. Laughlin, Fredericksburg, O. Drift, No. 5 seam; employs 4 miners.

HOLMES COUNTY.

Uhl No. 2.

Operated by B. Uhl, Millersburg, O. Drift opening, No. 6 seam, 3 feet. 7 miners, 1 day man, employed.

Horn.

Operated by John Horn, Killbuck, Ohio. Drift, No. 6 seam; 3 feet. 3 miners , 1 day man employed.

Bilderback No. 2.

Operated by D. M. Bilderback, Millersburg, O. Drift, No. 6 seam, 3 feet Employs 4 men.

Brooks.

Operated by Wm. Brooks, Millersburg, Ohio. Drift, No. 6 seam, 3 feet. Employs 4 men.

Chevellard.

Operated by E. H. Chevelard, Millersburg, Ohio. Drift, No. 6 seam; furnace ventilation, coal 3 feet. Employs 5 miners, 1 day man.

Quillen No. 1.

Operated by the Holmes County Coal and Clay Product Co., Millersburg. O. Drift opening, No. 4 seam, 4 feet. Furnace ventilation; employs from 7 to 12 miners and 2 day men.

Mast.

Operated by A. A. Echard, lessee, Millersburg, Ohio. Drift, No. 6 seam; natural ventilation; employs from 5 to 8 miners and 1 day man.

MINES VISITED OUTSIDE OF SEVENTH DISTRICT.

COLUMBIANA COUNTY.

Card & Prosser.

On July 20th, visited this mine, in company with R. S. Wheatley, Inspector of 12th District.

Klondyke.

On July 20th, visited with R. S. Wheatley, and found idle. No inspection was made.

JEFFERSON COUNTY.

Zerbe.

On April 13th, visited this mine, in company with District Inspection Morrison and Smith. A report of the findings was filed by Mr. Morrison.

Rice.

On April 14th, visited this mine, in company with above named Inspectors. A full report was filed by Mr. Morrison.

EIGHTH DISTRICT.

LOT JENKINS.

COMPOSED OF A PORTION OF THE COUNTIES OF BELMONT, JEFFERSON AND HARRISON.

HON. GEORGE HARRISON, *Chief Inspector of Mines, Columbus, Ohio:*

DEAR SIR: — In compliance with the custom of the Mining Department, I herewith submit for your approval, the official annual report of the Eighth Mining District, for the year commencing January 1, 1910, and ending December 31, 1910.

The Eighth Mining District, since July first of this year, was changed when two additional Inspectors were appointed in compliance with the new code of mining laws.

In the description of mines in my district, the majority will only be a six months' report, for the remaining half year of these reports will be found in district number nine, ten, or eleven, reported by the inspectors of those districts.

The condition of the coal trade throughout the year has been good, and a year of steady work has come to a close.

When the scale agreement between operators and miners expired on March 31st they were able to agree on a mining and day labor rate, which was the highest that has prevailed for a number of years, with only a few days of idleness and, with the exception of a few local strikes that effected a few of the mines at times, all the others have worked practically full time, affording a good opportunity for the miners.

Evidently Belmont and Jefferson counties will show an increase tonnage for the year. Several of the mines have increased the daily output during the year, and the majority of the mines are in better condition at the close of the year than they were at the beginning, which speaks well for the management of those mines and is much appreciated by the inspectors.

I have made 212 visits to the different mines; tested 11 sets of scales; reported 27 permanent improvements, as follows: 11 new fans; 12 additional openings; 2 safety catches and cages; 2 speaking tubes, and many other improvements that are not classed in the permanent list.

The new mining laws, which went into effect June 11th of this year, necessitated the installation of additional fans at several of the mines, or one that would produce a larger supply of air. This was done by all the companies as fast as could be reasonably expected, and all other changes that the new law called for have been put into force, and at the close of the year everything was running smoothly. It may be necessary for some changes to be made in the new code, but when the task of revising the entire mining law by a commission is taken into consideration, it is unreasonable to expect them to be absolutely perfect. They are a decided improvement over the former laws, especially so in that penalties are provided for all sections, and covering electrical appliances in all forms and places where the old law was silent it has been made plain in the new, so that inspectors can accomplish better results when giving orders at any mine.

Eighteen fatal accidents have been investigated this year: Eleven in Belmont and seven in Jefferson counties. Twelve by falls of stone, all of which occurred while working at the face; one by fall of coal; 2 due to electricity, one of which was due to coming in contact with an electric wire; the other occurred while a mining machine was being operated, and one by mine cars. This is a reduction of 10 when compared with that of last year in my district. A report of these will be found in the detailed synopsis of fatal accidents of this report.

On April 22nd, while at the Empire No. 6 mine, I was notified from the Columbus office of an explosion which had occurred at the Y. & O. mine at Amsterdam and to report there as soon as possible. In company with my colleague, L. D. Devore of the 10th district, we proceeded there as fast as transportation would carry us. Upon our arrival we found Chief Inspector Harrison, with others of the inspection force. All of the inspectors, including myself, gave assistance, and remained until all the bodies were removed from the mine, which was accomplished in a very systematic manner. A complete report will be found in the report of Thomas Morrison, in whose district the explosion and the rescue work took place.

Four warrants have been sworn out for violations of the mining laws, one against a mine boss for failing to make breakthrough at proper distance, to which he pled guilty and was fined according to the penalty provided for violation of that section.

Two retail grocery dealers were arrested for selling oil to miners below the standard required by the state law, one of whom pled guilty and was fined: the other demanded trial, but a verdict of guilty was rendered by justice of the peace, Isaac Newland, and a fine of $25 and costs was imposed. An affidavit was also sworn to for the arrest of J. B. Walker, a machine runner, for operating a mining machine in the Kelley mine that was not properly shielded, but before he could be served with the papers, he crossed the Ohio river into West Virginia. The warrant is still being held in readiness should he return to the Ohio side. There have been no mines abandoned this year, and two new ones have been opened up, in my district: one at Fairpoint, by the Fairpoint Coal & Coke Company, and one at Blaine, by the Lorain Coal & Dock Company.

In my description of mines it is to be understood that they are machine mines, with motor haulage, where it is not otherwise mentioned. Practically all the shipping mines have motors hauling from passways.

In conclusion I wish to say, that my relations with both management of mines and miners have been as pleasant as could be reasonably expected in filling a position that requires strict obedience to all laws, and I hereby take this opportunity of thanking you, and all the members of the Department, and the office force, for the courtesies shown me and the advice received during the year.

Respectfully submitted,

LOT JENKINS, Bellaire, Ohio,

December 31, 1910. *Inspector Eighth District.*

BELMONT COUNTY.

Black Diamond.

Located at Neff, Ohio. Operated by the Belmont Coal Mining Co., Pittsburg, Pa. E. H. Lace, Bellaire, O., Supt.; Lawrence Gardner, Neff, O., mine boss. Drift opening in No. 8 seam of coal, 5½ ft. thick. Employs 206 miners and 60 day men. Four visits made, one to investigate fatal accident. February 1st, ventilation in a few places was not very good, principally on account of stoppings not being carried forward far enough; these were ordered built immediately, and refuge holes made along 12 west motor line. March 30th, found previous orders complied with, but the stairs in the shaft opening on Snyder's entry were ordered repaired. May 26th, mine in fair condition. June 6th, investigated accident of Anthony Meickovesky. A new fan was on the ground, preparatory to replacing the inside fan. The mine is ventilated by two fans, one outside and the other inside; air is supplied from two different air shafts. Transportation, B. & O. and W. & L. E. R. R.

Glen.

Located near Glencoe, on the B. & O. R. R. Operated by the Belmont Coal Mining Co., Pittsburg, Pa. Slope opening, 100 ft. long, into No. 8 seam, 5 ft. high. John E. Barth, Glencoe, Supt.; Wm. Williams, same place, mine boss. The mine is ventilated by a 16 ft. Robinson fan. Employed, when last visited, 187 miners and 61 day men. Four visits made. January 13th, ventilation was not satisfactory; orders were left for improvement and I returned again January 24th, with Inspector L. D. Devore, of the Tenth District. The ventilation had been somewhat improved and fair readings of air were obtained at the he- of all entries. March 22nd, orders were left to clean out man-holes along motor lines and some dust taken out of the main motor line; also ordered men prohibited from working in 14 west until sufficient air was conducted to head of entry. May 15th and 16th, visited the mine by request of the management a few days previous to cutting through to a pair of entries that had been previously closed up on account of a squeeze along the first few rooms of it, which, when cut through some standing gas, was found; this coming to the knowledge of the miners they refused to work until the inspector made an examination of the mine. This was done, and found the management had taken all possible care for safety in that respect. All men had been ordered out while gas was being removed. The general condition of this mine is not as good as might be; entries are not as well timbered as they should be, filling roads with refuse from falls placed along the sides, when the district was changed and no more visits were made; an air shaft was being sunk at the interior of the mine, which should improve the ventilation. This mine will also be reported in District No. 10.

Knob.

Located one and one-half miles west of Bellaire, Ohio, on the B. & O. R. R. Operated by the Bakewell Coal Co., Bellaire, O. J. H. Pearsall, Bellaire, O., Supt. and mine boss. At the beginning of the year it was ventilated by a furnace and on February 24th and March 4th, found ventilation poor in some sections. Requested furnace replaced with a fan, or the working force of men reduced. May 12th, found a 6 foot Scott fan placed too near an additional opening that had been made, and ventilation good, which was very gratifying to all concerned, the inspectors, as well as all others. Scales tested and found correct

Buckeye.

Located two and one-half miles west of Flushing, on the C. L. & W. R. R. Drift opening in No. 8 seam, employing 26 miners and 12 day hands. Operated by the Harrison Coal Mining Co., Holloway, O. Wm. Harrison, Holloway, Supt.; John Harrison, same place, mine boss. Ventilated by a 10 ft. Brazil fan. Two visits made. February 22nd, mine idle, fan not being in operation, no inside inspection was made. March 10th, in company with Chief Inspector, Geo. Harrison, and district inspector, Thos. Morrison, of the 9th district, partial inspection was made. The mine is not in as good condition as should be and it remained suspended during the time it remained under my supervision, and will be found in district eleven at the close of the year. Coal is only 3½ ft. thick in this mine.

Taggart.

Located on the branch of the C. L. & W. R. R. from Barton to St. Clairsville, O. Operated by the Barton Coal Co., Cleveland, O. Geo. Green, St. Clairsville, O., Supt.; Jabez D. Goulding, same place, mine boss. Drift, No. 8 seam of coal, 5½ ft. thick; employing 97 miners and 33 day men. Two visits made, February 7th and April 12th, the ventilation was not very good in some places, caused by return air courses having fallen in until they were too small. A consultation was held with the management and they agreed to sink an air shaft on the south side and drive a place out to daylight on the other side immediately. It should, when completed, place the mine in good condition. Report of this mine will be found in District Inspector Hennessy's district for the last half of the year.

Bannock or Victor.

Located at Bannock, on the C. L. & W. R. R. Suspended during the time territory was covered by me in 1910.

Captina.

Located at Captina, Ohio, on the Ohio River and Western R. R. Operated by the Captina Coal Co., Armstrongs Mills, O. Wm. Rankin, same place, Supt. and mine boss. Shaft, 68 ft. deep, in the No. 8 seam of coal, 6 ft. high; employing 18 pick miners and 5 day men. This is one of the old mines, opened in 1880 and does not conform with the present mining laws in regard to location of the boilers and buildings around the top of the shaft. Seven visits made: January 7th and April 14th, between the April 14th visit and June 10th, there had been a section of old works abandoned and brattices were built for the purpose of improving the ventilation in the new section where the men were employed. On arriving at the mine June 10th was informed by Mr. Rankin what had been done and that he had thoroughly explored this section before sealing it up and had found no explosive gas. Examination of the mine was made and upon approaching these stoppings we found there was a body of standing gas back of them. The men were ordered out and those stoppings were tapped and a pipe with a valve put in. Returned June 20th, no work having been done since, only fan operating. I found there was still considerable pressure of explosive gas coming from the pipe and June 25th W. H. Turner, Inspector Fifth District, accompanied me to the mine by my request. It was found in the same condition as on June 10th and 20th, and he fully sustained my action in not allowing the mine to operate. August 24th, in company with Chief Inspector Harrison and L. D. Devore of the Tenth District, the mine was visited by request of the management for a conference as to what was necessary to be done in order that operations could be resumed. We insisted that the boilers and buildings be removed the required distance from the shaft and all other requirements covered by the new code of laws. August 19th, in company with Inspector L. D. Devore of the Tenth District, again visited by request of the management. They had decided to abandon that section and were putting in concrete stoppings with pipes inserted which would lead to the surface in order to conduct any gas that might accumulate at that point, and agreed to remove the boilers the required distance from shaft and open up a new section of work not far from bottom of shaft. This would make the mine as safe as any other mine and permission was granted to resume operations, the management was fully as anxious to safeguard the mine in a manner satisfactory to the Department as they possibly could be before resuming work.

Columbia.

Located at Fairpoint, Ohio, on the C. L. & W. R. R. Operated by Akron Coal Co., Akron, O. D. W. Selway, Fairpoint, O., Supt.; Ira Watkins, St. Clairsville, mine boss. Drift opening, No. 8 seam of coal, 5½ ft. high. Employs 151 miners and 57 day men. Three visits made. February 14th, in fair condition, excepting drainage in places: April 20th, in good condition. First west entry had been driven outside and was entering the other hill. Advised starting the other opening in that hill far enough apart to comply with the law. June 23rd, in company with the newly appointed inspector, James Hennessy, mine in good condition, excepting the new hill. We ordered it stopped until air shaft was sunk to provide ventilation for those men. The management started men to work immediately to sink shaft.

Fairpoint.

Located at Fairpoint, O., on the C. L. & W. R. R. Operated by the Fairpoint Coal & Coke Co., Wheeling, W. Va. Henry Selway, Fairpoint, O., Supt. and mine boss. This is a new mine that was just starting when visited February 14th, employing 2 miners and 5 day men. It is the intention to equip it with electrical appliances. It will be found in Mr. Hennessy's report of mines, as he had charge as inspector in that section during the latter part of the year.

Gaylord No. 1.

Located a mile east of Martins Ferry, O., on the C. & P. R. R. Operated by the Pittsburg and Cleveland Coal Co., Cleveland, Ohio. T. E. Sauters, Martins Ferry, Supt.; Wilfred Sowden, same place, mine boss. Drift opening, No. 8 seam of coal, about 5 ft. high, employing 146 miners and 37 day men. Visited three times. July 19th, found ventilation deficient for the number of men employed, roads dirty and places on entries not well timbered. Orders were left to employ no more men than the volume of air justified, and to cross-timber haulage way in places. October 10th, found considerable improvement had been made in condition of the mine; Mr. Sowden, who had just taken charge before my former visit, had put in an overcast, splitting the air so both sections were supplied with a separate current of air, increasing the total amount; back air course had been cleaned and the water removed from the roads; some timbering had also been done on haulage way. December 5th a new Robinson fan had replaced the two other fans and mine was in fairly good condition. The management works in harmony with the Department and any suggestion is given prompt attention, which is highly appreciated by the Department.

Gaylord No. 2.

Located two miles east of Martins Ferry, Ohio, on C. & P. R. R. Owned and operated by the same Company as No. 1, same superintendent; W. D. Scott, Bridgeport, O., mine boss. Drift, No. 8 seam of coal, 5 ft. high, ventilated by a 5 ft. Robinson fan. Three visits made: July 8th, September 16th and December 13th. This mine was found in good condition on each visit and no requests were necessary, as it is well taken care of. There had been an additional place driven outside close to mouth of mine on last visit. Most all the working places have none of the soapstone generally found overlaying this coal which causes so many accidents.

Tunnell.

Located at Flushing, Ohio, on the C. L. & W. R. R. Operated by the Flushing Coal Co., Elyria, Ohio. Drift opening, into No. 8a seam of coal, about 3½ ft. high. J. A. Trimbath, Flushing, O., Supt. and mine boss. Compressed air machines are used to cut the coal; 48 miners and 14 day men employed when last visited. Three visits made: February 22nd, ventilation was fair but drainage poor: a great deal of the water comes from the roof in this seam of coal and many of the places were wet. Three pumps were located in different places and the management was doing all in its power to keep places dry. May 3rd, advised that boards in place of gob be used for stoppings and a couple of doors substituted for canvas to improve the air along working faces. May 28th, scales tested and found correct.

Lucy.

Located between Neffs and Stewartsville, Ohio, on the B. & O. R. R. Operated by the Gordon Coal Co., Stewartsville, O. Hugh Ferguson, Stewartsville, O., Supt. and mine boss. Drift mine, employing 68 miners and 17 day men; ventilated with a 7 ft. Cole fan. Three visits made: January 20th, March 21st and June 1st. Found in fair condition first and second visits; June 1st, the doors and wires in a few places were not satisfactory, having been broken and wire being too low down in places. Mr. Ferguson willingly agreed to have them hung, as requested, at once.

Dellora.

Located at Glencoe, Ohio, on the B. & O. R. R. Operated by the Y. & O. Coal Co., Cleveland, O. H. S. Reppert, Glencoe, O., Supt.; E. F. Jones, same place, mine boss. Shaft, 67 ft. deep, in No. 8 seam of coal; ventilated with a 10 ft. Robinson fan. Three visits made. January 31st, ventilation was fair, excepting the trolley wire in places not in good condition. Also requested two machines stopped until shields were repaired; also requested cable on two machines repaired. March 14th, found wire in better condition and ventilation fair. May 4th, in fair condition, except the trolley wire, which in places had been broken down by falls of roof. It was ordered put up and the management said they would have it done at once. When last visited 197 miners and 78 day men were employed.

Maple Hill.

Located at Barton, on the C. L. & W. R. R. Operated by the Y. & O. Coal Co., Cleveland, Ohio. Wm. A. Williams, Barton, O., Supt.; Matthew Anderson, same place, mine boss. Drift opening, into No. 8 seam of coal, 5 ft. thick, employing 168 miners and 50 day men. Two visits made, February 15th and May 13th. A new Jeffrey 8 ft. fan had replaced the Stine fan at the head of the slope that had been made the latter part of the previous year, and ventilation was excellent all over the mine, and other conditions good. This Company has been using steel I beams in place of timber on motor haulage roads, which is very much of an improvement over the old wooden timbers and much more durable.

Barton.

Located at Barton, on the C. L. & W. R. R. Operated by the Y. & O. Coal Co., Cleveland, O. W. A. Williams, Barton, O., Supt.; W. C. Bartson, same place, mine boss. Drift opening into No. 8 seam of coal, 5½ ft. high. Ventilated by three fans, one Jeffrey, located on the outside and two Stine fans, placed on inside. Employed, when last visited, 253 miners and 76 day men. Three visits made; January 25th, March 3rd and May 19th; on each visit was found in fair condition. Conditions were much improved over that of last year; entries were much better timbered with steel I beams and at the time the district was changed, a place was being driven out to daylight on west side of mine to bring fresh air close to working face, which should put the mine in first-class condition.

Florence.

Located one and one-half miles northwest of Martins Ferry, Ohio, on the C. & P. R. R. Operated by the Y. & O. Coal Co., Cleveland, O. Lee Rankin, Martins Ferry, O., Supt.; Carl Ryan was succeeded as mine boss by John Gallagher, both of Martins Ferry, O. There were two drift openings in the No. 8 seam of coal, 5½ ft. high, both ventilated by fans. Three visits made, one to investigate fatal accident. August 2nd and 3rd the conditions of the motor road in the main opening was badly in need of timbering in places and the other opening was in poor condition on account of water and mud along the roads and motor line was not well timbered. Ventilation was fair. November 3rd and 4th, found one of the openings abandoned and being dismantled; the other motor line had been timbered as requested and was much safer than on previous visit. Ventilation was unsatisfactory along the working faces in a few entries. Upon investigation found the belt on the fan was slipping some: this was adjusted and on the 4th found somewhat better, but could not be considered up to the standard; but the fan from the other hill was intended to be placed so as to assist the other fan and should improve the ventilation of the mine. August 2nd, 227 miners and 68 day men were reported, but November 4th the number reported was 183 miners and 61 day men.

Whitaker-Glessner.

Located at Martins Ferry, Ohio. Owned and operated by the Whitaker-Glessner Co., Wheeling, W. Va. W. H. Kasley, Wheeling, W. Va., Supt.; Richard Walker, Martins Ferry, O., mine boss. Drift, into No. 8 seam of coal, 5 ft. high: fan ventilation. Two visits made. August 12th, 19 pick miners employed and 7 day men; mine in good condition. No orders necessary. November 28th, the mine was found idle The fan had been broken that morning and the four men then working were sent home until fan was repaired. I was informed the mine was in about the same condition as when visited on August 4th and that it was not the intention to work a larger force of men for some time and that the mill was then being fired principally by gas from the gas well near the town The mill was the market for coal mined and none was shipped.

Kennon.

Located one and one-half miles west of Flushing, Ohio, on the C. L. & W. R. R. Operated by the Kennon Coal Co., Cleveland, O. Frank Corey, Flushing,

O., Supt.: Geo. Millward, same place, mine boss. Drift opening, into No. 8 seam of coal, 4½ ft. high; fan ventilation; employs 72 miners and 30 day men. Two visits made. February 23rd, the mine was not in very good condition, as there was considerable water with which to contend in traveling to second opening, and quite a number of falls along that road, making airway small, so that air returned to fan without reaching working faces. Orders were left to clean them up. May 2nd, found they had cleaned up some falls along that road, but there was not volume enough reaching the distributing point for the number of men employed. Orders were left to put in brick stoppings to carry air to distributing point. This mine had one fatal accident during my time of inspection, due to a fall of coal, Hezekiah Sims having had a leg broken, which later caused his death.

Black Oak.

Located between Lafferty and Flushing, on the C. L. & W. R. R. Operated by the St. Clair Coal Co., Cleveland, O. John Moon, Supt.; Hugh Gaffney, same place, mine boss. Shaft, 87 ft. deep, into No. 8 seam of coal, 5 ft. high. Employs 152 miners and 38 day men. Two visits made. February 10th, mine in fair condition. April 19th and 20th, mine in fair condition. The ventilation at this time was practically up to the standard required by the law then in force, but the new laws, requiring an increase, having just passed, suggested another opening at the interior of the mine, which would furnish a good permanent improvement. This mine works a great many rooms with machines, retaining the original stone that lays over this coal and appears to be the most successful system in many places in the mine. Report of this mine will be in District Eleven for last six months of the year.

Lansing.

Located west of Bridgeport, on the C. L. & W. R. R. Operated by the Lorain Coal & Dock Co., Columbus, Ohio. James W. Johnson, Bridgeport, O., Supt.; Wm. Slater, Blaine, O., mine boss. Drift openings, into No. 8 seam of coal, 5½ ft. high; employing, when last visited, 362 miners and 110 day men. This is one of the largest mines in this district. Eight visits made during the year, three for the purpose of investigating fatal accidents. Mine was generally found in good condition, and any suggestions made by the Department are willingly complied with. April 23rd, found the brattice work not carried forward as close as it should be; ordered this corrected at once, and on June 28th and 29th, found another fan had promptly been installed to increase the ventilation to comply with the new code of mining laws and was in good condition. October 27th and 28th, ordered ventilation improved on 25 and 26 east first north; three fans are used to provide the ventilation. Two persons are employed to assist the mine boss and working places are visited very regularly; the stone over this coal in that locality is of a very slippery nature, requiring a great deal of care in posting in order to avoid accidents.

Wheeling Creek.

Located two miles west of Bridgeport, Ohio, on the C. L. & W. R. R. Operated by the Lorain Coal & Dock Co., Columbus, Ohio. Two drifts into No. 8 seam of coal, 5½ ft. high, being connected on the inside. J. E. Waters, Bridgeport, O., Supt.; Gilbert Hanson, same place, mine boss, employing 324 miners and 137 day men. Six visits were made. One fatal accident occurred during the year. The mine is well taken care of and is ably managed by those in charge, producing a large daily tonnage. It is generally found in satisfactory condition. When the new law went into effect June 11th it was necessary to provide a new fan to increase the quantity of air; this was promptly done, but the one installed proved inadequate for so large a mine and a large one was ordered and installed as soon as it could be gotten from the manufacturer, and when last visited, December 2nd, it was giving good results and the required amount of air was being furnished. No other requests were necessary at the mine during the year, everything was in lawful condition.

Crescent Nos. 2, 1-2, 3, 3 1-2, and 4.

All located at Crescent, on the C. L. & W. R. R. All drift openings, operated by the Lorain Coal & Dock Co., Columbus, Ohio. James R. Birkbeck, Bridgeport, Ohio, is Supt. over all those mines. The coal is brought to two tipples and the mines are generally found in good condition, it being seldom necessary to leave any orders, as anything suggested to mine bosses, when making inspections, are found complied with on return visit. All are drifts, No. 8 seam of coal, about 5 ft. high.

Crescent No. 2, 1-2.

Wm. Embleton, Blaine, Ohio, mine boss. Drift, No. 8 seam, employing 111 miners and 35 day men. Two visits made. January 27th and March 29th, both times found in good condition. Attention was called to the fact that the mine would require a greater volume of air under the new law.

Crescent No. 3.

Wm. Donley, mine boss, St. Clairsville, Ohio, R. F. D. 1. Drift, employing 90 miners and 31 day men. Three visits made: January 26th, March 23rd and June 21st, in company with the newly appointed inspector, James Hennessy. Each visit found in good condition; the only suggestion made was in regard to some trolley wire along motor line. Mr. Donley promised to give it prompt attention.

Crescent No. 3, 1-2.

Richard Delbridge, Maynard, O., mine boss. Drift, employing 44 miners and 21 day men. Three visits made, January 6th, March 2nd and May 18th, each time found in fair condition. On May 18th, suggested that larger quantity of air be carried to faces of right side of mine.

Crescent No. 4.

Same mine boss as No. 3. Drift, employing 50 miners and 24 day men. Two visits made. January. 27th, found brattice work was not carried forward as close as it should be; those were ordered put up immediately. March 28th, requested that more air must be carried to face of 5 and 6 north face and 1 and 2 east of south. Attention was called to increase quantity of air required by new law that was soon coming in force, and preparations were being made to put in a larger fan to ventilate this mine and the No. 2½; both are connected and ventilated by the same current of air. A report of these mines will be found in Inspector Hennessy's district.

Pascoe.

Located at Blaine, O., on the C. L. & W. R. R. Operated by the Lorain Coal & Dock Co., Columbus, O. This is a new mine being opened. James W. Johnson, Bridgeport, O., is superintendent; David Jack, Blaine, O., is mine boss. Openings have been started in both hills, north and south; a large brick engine and boiler room has been erected; a steel tipple is also being built, and preparations are being made to make it a very large and up to date mine, there being a large acreage of coal to work in this locality. Four visits were made, one to investigate fatal accident of Barney Ratasta, was killed by fall of stone while working in 1st west entry in north side hill. Fan ventilation is in use in both hills and when last visited employed [illegible] miners and 18 day men.

Laughlin.

Located at Martins Ferry, Ohio. Operated by the American Sheet & Tin Plate Co., Pittsburg, Pa. Edward Hite, Martins Ferry, O., superintendent and mine boss. Drift into No. 8 seam, 5 ft. high. Ventilated by fan. Two visits made. September 17th, mine just started, after a period of long idleness; found in fairly good condition. Requested some timbering done on motor line. When visited November 28th, it was again found idle, the mill having closed down and only four men employed. This mine has been practically suspended all year, only working a short while during September and October, but the mine is being well taken care of during its idleness.

Aetna Standard.

Located at Aetnaville, Ohio. Operated by the American Sheet & Tin Plate Co., Pittsburg, Pa. Wm. Fitzgerald, Tiltonville, O., superintendent and mine boss. Drift opening, No. 8 seam, employing 10 miners and 8 day men; furnace ventilation. When visited September 19th, found just in operation after a long suspension; found in fair condition. Visited again November 18th; found in good condition; roads had been cleaned up better, but shortly after the mill closed down and the mine is again suspended at close of year, as the mill is the only market for the coal, no shipping being done.

Edge Hill.

Operated by the A. J. Morgan Coal Co., Bellaire, O. Jacob Long, Bellaire, O., superintendent and mine boss. Drift into No. 8 seam of coal, 5½ ft. high. Fan ventilation; employs 90 miners and 14 day men. Two visits made: August 6th and October 24th; the mine was in good condition on both visits and no orders were necessary. All the coal is gathered by electric motors.

Kirkwood.

Operated by the Hutchinson Coal Co., Fairmont, W. Va. Earl McConnaughy, Bridgeport, O., Supt.; Wm. Heller, same place, mine boss. Drift into No. 8 seam, 5½ ft. high. Ventilated by two fans, one 11 ft. Brazil on the outside and by a 2 ft. Robinson on the inside. Six visits in all; two for the purpose of investigating fatal accidents, and partial inspections were made on each visit. The mine is generally found in good condition. When visited March 16th, advised abandoning two entries on account of dangerous roof, a squeeze was working on them, 8th entry on G. and 2nd entry on E. This was willingly done by management and equipment was taken out. On October 21st suggested splitting the air in two currents, as there was a section that could easily be given a fresh split of air at H. entry. Two fatal accidents occurred at the mine, both from fall of stone while working at the face of rooms, one on January 11th and one August 21st; other visits were made January 10th, March 16th, June 8th and October 21st. The management is prompt in complying with any orders left by the department. Scales tested January 10th and found correct.

Pittsburg-Belmont No. 1, or Neff No. 1.

Located at Neff, Ohio, on the B. & O. R. R. Operated by the Pittsburg-Belmont Coal Co., Columbus, O. Franklin Neff, Supt.; John Crawford, mine boss, Steel, Ohio. Drift opening, into No. 8 seam of coal, 5½ ft. high. Ventilated by a 7 ft. Capell fan, employing when last visited, 62 miners and 18 day men. This mine employs a much larger force, but was working over a temporary tipple while a steel tipple was being built, the old tipple having been burnt down November 9, 1909. Two visits were made, February 25th and April 28th, found in good condition on both visits.

This mine for last half of the year will be reported by L. D. Devore, District Ten.

Pittsburg-Belmont, or Neff No. 2.

Located at Neff, O., on the B. & O. R. R. Operated by Pittsburg-Belmont Coal Co., Columbus, O. Franklin Neff, Neff, O., Supt.; John W. Lovejoy, Steel, O., mine boss. Drift, into No. 8 seam of coal, 5½ ft. high. Ventilated by fan, employing 155 miners and 41 day men. Three visits made, one to investigate fatal accident. February 4th, mine in fair condition; May 27th, ventilation was deficient in a few places, and a violation of the breakthrough law was found in a few rooms; all such places were stopped and breakthroughs ordered made; also ordered ventilation improved where it was found deficient.

Pittsburg-Belmont No. 3.

Located on the Belmont Central R. R. about two miles from Lafferty, O. Operated by the Pittsburg-Belmont Coal Co., Columbus, O. James Pendergast, Lafferty, O., Supt.; John Atkinson, same place, mine boss. Slope opening, 283 ft. deep, into No. 8 seam of coal, 5 ft. high, employing, when last visited on May 10th, 65 miners and 24 day men. Three visits made. January 11th, mine in fair condition. Suggested small fan put in until permanent one could be placed at the shaft opening. Scales were tested and found they needed some adjusting; this was promptly given attention and made satisfactory. March 1st found small 3½ ft. Stine fan had been erected, and telephone communication from bottom of slope to tipple and office on surface have been put into operation. May 10th, mine in good condition, excepting no stairs in the shaft opening. Preparations were being made to have them put in at once. No other orders necessary, as the mine was being well looked after by the management.

Lydia.

Located one and one-half miles west of Maynard, O., on the C. L. & W. R. R. Operated by the Purseglove Coal Co., St. Clairsville, O. Samuel Purseglove, St. Clairsville, O., superintendent and mine boss. Drift opening, into No. 8 seam of coal, 5½ ft. high. When last visited in May, 166 miners and 28 day men were employed. Four visits made; one to investigate a fatal accident. January 17th, mine in good condition; March 15th, ventilation fair, but some violations of the breakthrough law were in evidence; all unlawful places were stopped until the law was complied with. April 27th, mine in fair condition; only orders left was for a few stoppings to be built at once. The management was also notified that the use of gasoline in connection with the operation of two pumps which were located on the inside of the mine would have to be dispensed with. May 31st, investigated a fatal accident that had occurred; also made partial inspection and found satisfactory. Preparations were being made to use electric power for the pumps in place of the gasoline before the new law came into effect June 11th.

Provident No. 1.

Located between St. Clairsville and Maynard, O., on W. & L. E. R. R. Operated by the Provident Coal Co., Cleveland, O. David Thomas, St. Clairsville, O., Supt.; Clyde L. Lutton, same place, mine boss. Shaft, 68 ft. deep, into No. 8 seam of coal, and when last visited by me, employed 301 miners and 82 day men. Three visits made and generally found in good condition. Any improvements suggested were willingly complied with by the management. May 28th requested refuge holes made along a south face motor line. Visited January 18th and 19th, March 17th, May 28th and 29th. This mine has capacity for a large tonnage and is under able management. There are some sections in it that have some very tender roof, requiring a great deal of cross-timbering on entries. Usually two days were spent inspecting the mine.

Empire No. 6.

Located three miles west of Bellaire, O., on the B. & O. and O. R. R. Operated by the Rail & River Coal Co., Pittsburg, Pa. Wm. Maloney, Bellaire, O., Supt.; Fred Kinder, same place, mine boss. Drift opening, employing 78 miners and 27 day men when last visited. February 8th, mine in good condition. April 25th, only orders given were for some cross-timbers to be placed on the motor line that had broken; the management agreed to have them changed immediately; no other orders necessary, as everything else was satisfactory.

Lorena.

Located between Maynard and St. Clairsville, O., on the W. & L. E. R. R. Operated by the Roby-Somers Coal Co., Cleveland, O. J. O. Somers, St. Clairsville, O., Supt.; Broney Ostroski, Maynard, O., mine boss. Drift opening, in No. 8 seam, 5½ ft. high, employing 99 miners and 24 day men, when last visited. Three visits made, one in company with the newly appointed inspector, James Hennessy. February 16th, mine found in good condition; entries had been well timbered; steel "I" beams having taken the place of wooden cross-timbers; but two machines were found with no shields on right side and were ordered stopped until shields were put on. April 11th, mine in good condition; only a few places driven over distance before breakthroughs were made; these were ordered stopped and requested the law strictly complied with. June 24th, in company with Inspector James Hennessey, found the mine in good condition; no orders being necessary.

Franklin.

Located at Stewartsville, O., on the B. & O. R. R. Operated by the Raven Coal Co., Wheeling, W. Va. Sim Reynolds, Stewartsville, O., Supt.; James Spence, same place, mine boss. Drift opening, employing 64 miners and 23 day men. Ventilated by furnace, when last visited. Three visits made: February 11th, found idle, no inspection made. February 23rd, ventilation fair, but there was a local squeeze affecting 11 and 12 east entries and a great amount of broken timber along them. Requested the men taken from these entries on account of it being dangerous. The management willingly complied and men were put to work removing material from them; also requested 10 west cross-timbered. May 11th, ventilation was not up to the standard along working faces; suggested a fan installed in place of the furnace. This, I believe to have been done, and report of it will be found in that of L. D. Devore, in whose district it was located during the latter part of the year.

Sheets.

Located at Martins Ferry, O. Domestic mine owned by Sheets Coal Co., Martins Ferry, O. Drift opening. Fan ventilation, with one mining machine used to cut coal. James Ralston, Martins Ferry, O., superintendent and mine boss; 12 miners and 3 day men were employed. Two visits made. October 20th ventilation was deficient for the number of men employed, caused by return airway having fallen in, in many places, and requested an improvement. November 9th, some improvement had been made and larger volume of air was reaching the working faces, but it was still inadequate and not up to the standard required by law. Requested the fan speeded faster. This was done by securing an electric motor with which to operate it in place of the gas engine which formerly furnished the power for the fan.

Shicks.

Located west of Bellaire, O., on the B. & O. R. R. Operated by the Schicks Coal Co., Bellaire, O. M. J. Schicks, Bellaire, O., Supt., and Ed Conoway, Klee, O., mine boss. Drift opening, to No. 8 seam of coal. Fan ventilation; employing 60 miners and 19 day men. Three visits made. January 21st, ventilation was somewhat weak on 6 west; this was ordered improved. March 31st, mine in fair condition, only where two rooms had cut through to old works of the Carnegie mill mine and foul air was coming out and polluting the current to some extent. This was ordered closed. June 22nd, in company with Inspector Hennessy, tested the scales and found them correct. The mine being idle, no fan was in operation, no inspection of inside was made.

Trolls No. 1.

Located at Maynard, O., on the W. & L. E. R. R. Operated by the Troll Coal Mining Co., St. Clairsville, O. Jesse S. Troll, St. Clairsville, O., Supt., and Geo. Findlay, mine boss, succeeded by R. E. Roush, both of Maynard, O. Mr. Evans was transferred to the No. 2 mine, which is a drift in No. 8 seam, 5½ ft. high; when last visited employed 268 miners and 47 day men. March 7th, in fair condition, and April 21st, when visited, found one entry had been driven out to daylight, when it reached the surface it was in too close proximity to No. 2 mine tipple, and it was the intention to use it as a haulage way and also for the purpose of dumping some of the coal mined over the No. 2 tipple. A request was left for additional refuge places made along a certain section of a motor line. otherwise the mine was in first class condition.

Trolls No. 2.

Located same place as No. 1, on the W. & L. E. R. R. Operated by the same company as No. 1, same superintendent, with Evan Evans, Maynard, O., mine boss. Drift, into No. 8 seam, about 5 ft. high. When last visited 121 miners and 28 day men were employed. When visited March 11th, advised the use of a drag on the rear end of motor trip on main entry where a heavy grade occurs. June 27th, mine had just started operation after remodeling the tipple and re-timbering part of the motor road. Requested stoppings carried forward a little better and some timbering done on the mule haulage entries.

West Wheeling.

Located at West Wheeling, on the C. & P. R. R. Operated by the West Wheeling Coal Co., Bridgeport, O. Wm. Johnson, Bridgeport, O., superintendent and mine boss. Drift, into No. 8 seam of coal, 5½ ft. high, employing 64 miners and 14 day men, has fan ventilation and motor haulage was installed during the latter part of the year. Four visits made. July 22nd found the mine effected by a local squeeze on 5 and 6 west, impairing the ventilation; as they were the intake airway a few stoppings were put in, in order to conduct the air through another channel, and when visited May 4th, the ventilation of the mine was up to the standard. November 18th; scales were tested and found binding, causing them not to work as sensitive as they should; this was soon adjusted by the management. December 14th, mine was in good condition. An additional opening had been made close to working faces, bringing fresh air near the working places. Stoppings in the mine are all made of brick, assuring good distribution of the air. A great many of the rooms are worked on the double track system, which proved very satisfactory. On my last visit a motor was being used to haul the coal from the passway.

Virginia Hill.

Located at Lafferty, Ohio, on the C. L. & W. R. R. Operated by the Virginia Hill Coal Co., Cleveland, O. Thos. J. Jordon, Lafferty, O., Supt.; Frank Jordon, same place, mine boss. Slope, 95 feet deep, No. 8 seam, 4½ ft. high. Three visits made, and when last visited 77 miners and 27 day men were employed. February 9th, ordered some of the electric wires protected with boards and suggested sumps made to improve the condition of the roads. February 28th, former orders were being complied with. Scales tested, found correct. May 9th, found the mine in better condition in many respects; several entries had been timbered with steel "I" beams and roads were considerably cleaned up, all cross over wires protected and no orders were necessary, as all was being done that could be expected by the management.

Lee Woods Mine.

Located at Martins Ferry, Ohio. This is a domestic mine, operated by Lee Woods & Son, Martins Ferry, O. Drift, in the No. 8 seam, about 5½ ft. coal; one mining machine cuts the coal; the working force is generally much larger in the fall and winter than during the summer. When last visited 9 miners and 2 day men were employed. The ventilation is scarcely kept up to the standard for the number of men employed on my last visit and the management was informed that it would be necessary to either secure a small fan or increase the size of the furnace, or the number of men decreased. Requested some electric wires in room removed. Mr. Woods willingly agreed to comply with the request. Visited August 1st and November 28th.

Riley Mine.

Located west of Bridgeport, Ohio. Domestic mine, operated by the Riley Brothers, Bridgeport, Ohio. Drift, in the No. 8 seam of coal, 5½ ft. high. Furnace ventilation; mule haulage; employs 8 miners and 2 day men. This mine is always found in first-class condition and is well taken care of. Andy Riley is superintendent and Mike Riley mine boss. Visited November 11th.

SMALL MINES IN BELMONT COUNTY, EMPLOYING LESS THAN TEN MEN.

Neff & Robinson.

Operated by G. H. Hamilton, Bellaire, O. Drift, employing 2 men. Another opening has been made to this mine and it was in good condition. Visited May 17th.

Nelan.

Operated by J. C. Nelan, Bellaire, O. Drift, employing 9 men. Employs furnace ventilation and mule haulage. In fair condition when visited May 17th.

Koehnline.

Located at Bridgeport, O. Drift opening, employing 5 men, the coal being cut with a compressed air machine; has natural ventilation and mule haulage. Mine in poor condition when visited October 20th. Was unable to reach the shaft opening and the haulage way in places was badly in need of timber and the roads very muddy. Informed the management the mine would have to be placed in an improved condition or cease operation. Mr. Koehnline stated he would start men to drive a place to the shaft and repair mine in general in order to place it in a satisfactory condition. Operated by the Koehnline Ice & Coal Co., Bridgeport, O. Geo. Koehnline has entire supervision.

Patterson.

Located at Lansing, O. Operated by John Hilt, Bridgeport, O. Drift, employing 5 men; natural ventilation; mule haulage; in fair condition when visited November 11th.

Davis.

Located at Lansing, O. Operated by John Davis, Lansing, O. Drift, employing 5 men; furnace ventilation; mule haulage; found in poor condition; return airway fallen in, being unable in places to get through it. Orders were left to make it large enough so it could be traveled or a new one made at once, or the mine would not be allowed to operate. Mr. Davis promised to have it attended to immediately. He had lately taken charge of the mine and intended putting it in good condition.

McGrail.

Located at Martins Ferry, O. Operated by Myers McGrail, Martins Ferry, O. Drift, employing 2 men; furnace ventilation. The coal is pushed out, as there is a natural grade from face of works. Orders were left that two ways must be provided from face of works, one of the present ones being in bad condition from falls. The management stated that it was their intention to make a new one around the fall.

Meister Brothers.

Located at Bridgeport, O. Operated by the Meister Brothers. Joseph Meister is in charge. Drift, employing 8 men, with a compressed air machine used in cutting the coal. Mine was in good condition; has furnace ventilation, and during the year made a connection with an opening on the opposite side of the hill and bringing the air in at the opening.

Edgar No. 1

Located two miles east of Du[illegible] [illegible] by the Glens Run Coal Co., Cleve[illegible] Henry W. Jack, same place [illegible] ft. high. Ventilated with a [illegible] men. Three visits made. [illegible] and haulage ways not well [illegible] vided with as many refuge [illegible] along working face [illegible] [illegible]

Piney Fork No. 1.

Drift opening, coal about 5 ft. high, and is ventilated by two fans since latter part of September, one 15 ft. Brazil outside, and a 6 ft. Stine fan inside. The ventilation is split into three different currents, each going to different sections of the mine. Four visits made; July 13th, October 6th and 26th, and December 29th, one to investigate fatal accident, and on each visit mine was found in fairly good condition, and special orders were not necessary. When last visited 180 miners and 46 day men were employed. H. D. Albaugh, Piny Fork, Ohio, is mine boss.

Piney Fork No. 2.

Wm. Bunney, Piney Fork, Ohio, mine boss. Drift opening, in No. 8 seam of coal, 3½ ft. high. Ventilated by a 15 ft. Brazil fan, employing in this hill 157 miners and 69 day men. Three visits made for inspection and one on account of a fatal accident. There are several inlet openings to this mine and the greatest difficulty is to regulate them so that the required amount of air is supplied to the different sections of the mine; this is generally carefully watched and on each visit was in good condition. Visited July 14th, August 31st, October 7th and December 28th. The coal from Cabbage Run is taken through this mine to the same tipple.

Cabbage Run (Piney Fork No. 2.)

Drift opening, coal 4½ ft. high, employing 54 miners and 7 day men, same mine boss as Piney Fork No. 2, 15 ft. Brazil fan providing ventilation. Visited three times; found in good condition on last visit. Requested stoppings carried forward a little closer in a few places .

Piney Fork No. 3.

Thomas Macallum, Harpersville, O., is mine boss. Drift opening, No. 8 seam, about 5 ft. high, ventilated by a 15 ft. Brazil fan; 167 miners and 48 day men employed. The air is split in two separate currents, going to either side of the mine. Visited July 27th, found in good condition. October 12th, ventilation was a little sluggish on main section and a few places. Breakthrough law was not strictly observed. Requested these stopped and air improved on the main section. December 30th, in good condition; a separate and distinct wire had been connected to the electric fan and no orders were necessary.

Piney Fork No. 4.

Suspended all the year.

Portland.

Located at Connor, Ohio, on the W. & L. E. R. R. Operated by the Rayland Coal Co., Pittsburg, Pa. Charles Miller, Connorville, O., Supt.; Hugh Boyle, Rayland, O., mine boss. Drift opening, fan ventilation; employing 98 miners and 23 day men. Two visits made: July 29th, mine in fair condition, except some of the stoppings along the main intake, which were in poor condition. Preparation was being made to replace them with cement stoppings. September 23d, several of the cement stoppings had been built and mine was in good condition. Some of the rooms off the back main air course were being started, which, in my opinion, appeared to be a wrong system, as it may have a tendency to cause a squeeze at this place.

Kelley.

Located one mile east of Warrenton, O., on the C. & P. R. R. The company has changed hands several times during the year, causing each time changes in management. It was operated for a time by the Shannon Run Coal Co., Pittsburg, Pa., and on last visit it was operated by the Kelley Mine Coal Co., Pittsburg, Pa. E. P. Tanley, Rayland, O., Supt.; Harry Leach, Warrenton, mine boss. Drift opening, No. 8 seam of coal, 4½ ft. high; fan ventilation; when last visited 34 miners and 22 day men were employed. Four visits made; the mine has an extensive development and has not been well taken care of; haulage ways are poorly timbered and electric wires had not been well put up; the ventilation at the working faces was not good, although some improvement was made in it, due to an additional opening being made during the year at the head of 6 west entry. There is an abundance of air entering the mine, but on account of a large amount of old workings along side of the intake airway a great portion of it is lost before reaching the working faces. The number of changes in the management has hampered the department in keeping the mine in as good condition as it would be if the same management had remained any length of time, as each new management wanted a little time to familiarize himself with the mine.

Wabash.

Located at Parlett, O., on the Wabash R. R. Operated by the Wabash Coal Co., Cleveland, O. Slope opening, in No. 8 vein, 5 ft. thick; ventilated by fan; 68 miners and 18 day men employed. Wm. Bates, Parlett, O., was succeeded by Geo. T. Odbert, same place, and Ed. Vacheresse was succeeded as mine boss by John Williams, both of Parlett, O. Three visits made, mine was not up to the standard in the matter of ventilation when first visited July 28th, and the wires were very poorly strung up. A shaft that former inspector, Mr. Morrison, had ordered sunk was being made. The electric wires were also ordered moved from the floor and to secure the proper appliances for the care of injured persons, and machinery in engine room protected. August 29th, found shaft completed and machinery satisfactory and a great deal of wire put up, but ventilation was not good in some places. October 31st, ventilation was not sufficient for the number of employes. Orders were given to reduce the working force commensurate with the amount of air provided; also investigated fatal accident on this visit.

Florence.

Located at Florencedale, O., on the L. E. A. & W. R. R. Operated by the Witch Hazel Coal Co., Youngstown, O.: Geo. Evans, Florencedale, O., Supt.; Julius Grimm, same place, mine boss. Drift opening, No. 8 seam of coal, 5 ft. thick; employing 71 miners and 22 day men: ventilated by a 7 ft. Stine fan. Three visits made; July 28th, the fan was not in good condition, one of the cog wheels being minus a few cogs, which impeded the progress of the fan. After being in the mine a short time requested the men sent out and fan repaired, in order that it could be depended upon. August 31st found in fair condition, except roads were wet. There is a very light surface covering the coal in this locality and much trouble is experienced with water coming in from the surface, making it difficult to keep places dry. December 27th, mine was found in fair condition, the management doing all that could be expected, taking into consideration the conditions with which they have to contend.

Dillon No. 2.

Located at Dillonvale, O., on the W. & L. E. R. R. Operated by the W. & L. E. Coal Co., Cleveland, O. Fred Hornickel, Dillonvale, O., was succeeded as superintendent by Fred Aspinwall during the latter part of the year, Mr. Hornickel removing to Guernsey county to take charge of mines. Geo. W. Chamberlain, Dillonvale, O., mine boss. Drift opening, 5 ft. thick; ventilated by three fans, one steam and two electric. Three visits made. July 25th, mine in fair condition, excepting a number of the electric return wires were not put up as the department required them, practically all over the mine. This was ordered remedied. October 5th, found former orders in regard to wires were being complied with, but a great deal of the wiring yet remained to be changed. December 22d, ventilation on the right side of the mine was not as good as on former visits; the electric fan, located on that side of the mine, was effected on account of not getting good current for some reason and ventilation was not regular. Orders were left to have the electric wires gone over and repaired in order to insure better power for the fans and to further speed the fans; the management agreed to have this done immediately. The mine has an extensive development, and employs 228 miners and 73 day men.

Connor No. 1

Located at Connorsville, O., on the W. & L. E. R. R. Operated by the W. & L. E. Coal Co., Cleveland, O. Fred Aspinwall, Dillonvale, O., Supt.; S. W. Ruckman, Connorsville, O., mine boss. Drift opening, coal 5 ft. thick; ventilated with a 10 ft. Brazil fan; employing 77 miners and 25 day men. My first visit to this mine was for the purpose of investigating a fatal accident. It was then in District No. 9; the man had been killed by a fall of stone while working at the face of his room, failed to take proper care in posting. Upon investigation the place was found to have been driven beyond the distance at which a breakthrough should have been made. A warrant was issued for the arrest of mine boss, S. W. Ruckman, and, at the hearing, he pled guilty and was fined according to law. Three other visits were made and the mine was found in fair condition on each visit; the only suggestion made was in regard to method of hanging wires and the management willingly agreed to place them as requested.

Connor No. 2.

Located same place as No. 1, same company and same superintendent, J. B. Ruckman, Connorsville, O., mine boss. Drift opening; ventilated by two fans; employing 172 miners and 40 day men. Three visits made. On July 6th, the ventilation was not up to requirements of the law, caused by the intake airway not being in good condition from falls and water, making it too small. Orders were left to improve it or reduce the working force for the amount of air provided. On return visit September 6th found the airway cleaned out and a wonderful improvement in the ventilation was apparent and the mine was in good condition. December 8th, mine in good condition and well taken care of by management.

Augusta.

Formerly known as Redmud, located at Warrenton, O., on W. & L. E. R. R. Operated by the Augusta Coal Co., Pittsburg, Pa. J. C. Robinson, Rayland, O., was succeeded as superintendent and mine boss by James Cook, same place. This mine has been equipped with electric machines and motors during the year. Drift opening; coal 5 ft. high; furnace ventilation was in use until late in the year, when it was replaced by a fan. Five visits made. The ventilaiton was not very good while the furnace was in use, but everything was being done by the management that could be done to improve conditions, and when last visited, November 30th, was informed that a fan would be delivered in a few days. This should place the mine in good condition, as it is not a very large mine; 48 miners and 15 day men were employed on last visit.

Russell.

Located at Tiltonville, O., on the C. & P. R. R. Operated by the Russell Coal Mining Co., Cleveland, O. Seth Williams, Tiltonville, O., is superintendent and mine boss. Drift opening, No. 8 vein; ventilated by a 6 ft. Scott fan, employing 99 miners and 21 day men. Two visits made; both times found in fair condition, excepting the roads on the north side were wet and muddy; some of the old works are located on that side of the mine, emitting water, causing the roads to be wet. On last visit a place was being driven to the outside to improve the drainage on that side of the mine.

Walnut Hill Nos. 1 and 2.

Located at Yorkville, O.; transportation on the C. & P. R. R. Charles Shockley succeeded Wm. Neath as superintendent, both of Yorkville, Mr. Neath having been transferred to one of the same company's mines at Bergholz, O. Operated by the Ohio & Pennsylvania Coal Co., Cleveland, O. Drift opening; ventilated by fan; employing 70 miners and 24 day men. Two visits made, August 11th and October 17th. The mine is a very long distance in and conditions of motor line are not very good, especially the timbering along it, which has been in use for a long time, some of which are not in the best condition, but the management change them whenever they become too dangerous. The roads are quite wet and muddy, but there had been considerable cleaning up done along them on my last visit, and about all that could be expected was being done. Ventilation along working faces has always been found good. John A. Evans, Yorkville, O., mine boss of both Nos. 1 and 2 mines.

No. 2.

Located same place, same company and management as No. 1. Drift opening; fan ventilation; employing 67 miners and 24 day men; coal taken to same tipple as No. 1. Two visits made, August 11th and October 18th; each time found in fair condition. On first visit requested some of the electric wires changed from overhead refuge holes along motor line. On next visit found this had been done; ventilation on both visits found good.

Jean.

Located at Salt Run, O., on the C. & P. R. R. Operated by the Blyth Coal Mining Co., Pittsburg, Pa. John Neal, Brilliant, O., Supt.; Frank Horn, same place, mine boss. Drift opening. No. 8 seam of coal; ventilated by a 12 ft. Brazil fan; mule haulage; employing 72 miners and 25 day men. Three visits made, August 16th, ventilation was found deficient along working faces, caused by a local squeeze that had previously been in existence on 1st and 2nd butts working over on to 3rd and 4th butts. There was an opening on the right side of the mine that was not being used for ventilating purposes; advised that it be used to improve ventilation. This was done, and on September 6th conditions were better, but the squeeze was working over on the 5th and 6th butt, 1st and 2nd had been cleaned up and new face entries were being driven inside to cut off the parts effected by the squeeze. December 9th, face entries had been driven across and it was practically a new section, and the mine at the close of the year is in much better condition than when first visited.

Goucher.

Located near Brilliant, on a switch of the C. & P. R. R. Operated by the Dexter Coal Co., Pittsburg, Pa. W. D. Gibson, Brilliant, O., Supt.; Wm. Pilkington, same place, mine boss. Drift opening, in No. 8 seam of coal, 5 ft. thick; ventilated by fan; employing 102 miners and 41 day men. Two visits made, and with exception of a few places where breakthroughs were not made at proper distance, otherwise the mine was in good condition, and on second inspection breakthrough law was strictly observed.

High Shaft.

Located at Steubenville, O. Operated by the Steubenville Coal Co., Steubenville, O. Shaft opening, 225 ft. deep, No. 6 seam of coal, 3½ ft. thick. The coal is used for domestic trade. Wm. Smurthwaite, Steubenville, O., Supt.; Matthew Cassner, same place, mine boss. Mine is ventilated with two fans, one at the bottom of the hoisting shaft and the other used as a booster on the inside close to working faces. The mine is one of the old mines opened long before the present mining laws were made;. Boilers located on outside, and buildings do not comply with present law. Three visits made. August 18th conditions not satisfactory; traveling way to second opening not in good condition and cages in main shaft in poor condition. Requested them to cease operation at working faces and to make repairs in general, which was done. Returned on August 26th, in company with Inspector L. D. Devore, of 10th District, and found a new cage had been put in and another one being made men had been working on the way to the second opening and everything being done to place the mine in better condition: permission was given to resume operation at the face. November 2nd, again visited and found that the previous orders were being complied with; two new cages were in use and a speaking tube had been put in from bottom of shaft and traveling way to other shaft was in fair condition. On this visit considerable water was found at the face of the workings, coming from an oil well that passed through the mine; a line of pipe was in readiness to take care of the water and keep working places dry. The management is very willing to comply with any orders left by the department.

LaBelle.

Located at Steubenville, O. Operated by the LaBelle Iron Works, Steubenville, O. Shaft, 200 ft. deep, No 6 seam of coal, averaging about 3½ ft. thick. R. W. McCasland, Steubenville, O., Supt.; David Love was succeeded by John Davis as mine boss, both of Steubenville, O. Ventilated with a 16 ft. Robinson fan; employing 146 miners and 25 day men The mine is opened on the Ohio side of the river, both hoisting, escapement, air shaft and fan, but all the coal recently mined is on the West Virginia side of the river, and it is not under the jurisdiction of the Ohio Mining Department as to how the ventilation should be. The jurisdiction of this Department extends to low water mark, which is in good condition. The hoisting shaft has been repaired during the year, equipped with new guides and cages repaired, which are often examined to see that safety catches are in good working condition, and no orders have been necessary, for the portion of the mine located on the Ohio side. The mine penetrates some explosive gas, and two fire bosses are employed, and on the Ohio side, where no work is being done, is examined by the fire bosses daily.

Sugar Hill.

Situated close to Steubenville, O. Operated by the Sugar Hill Coal Co., Steubenville, O. Elmer King, Steubenville, O., Supt. and mine boss. It is a drift in the No. 8 seam of coal, 5 ft. thick. This is a domestic mine, employing 21 men when visited, and was in first class condition; pick mining; furnace ventilation; mule haulage. A small shaft was sunk during the year close to the head of workings, by request of Inspector L. D. Devore, who had charge of this section until July of this year.

Coal Hill.

Located about a mile and one-half southwest of Steubenville, O. Operated by E. W. Vandine, Steubenville, O. This is a domestic mine. Drift, in No. 8 seam of coal, 5 ft. thick; employing 12 men; pick mining; furnace ventilation; mule haulage. Visited December 12th, found in fair condition.

SMALL MINES VISITED IN JEFFERSON COUNTY, EMPLOYING LESS THAN TEN MEN.

G. W. Jenrie.

Operated by F. J. Knoch, Rayland, O. Drift opening, in No. 8 seam of coal, 5 ft. high; employing 3 pick miners; furnace ventilation; mule haulage; in good condition.

P. R. Nicholson.

Operated by Mr. Nicholson, Dillonvale, O. Drift opening, No. 8 seam of coal, 5 ft. high; employing 5 pick miners; furnace ventilation; mule haulage; in good condition.

Brettell Bros. No. 1.

Located about a mile east of Mingo Junction, O. Operated by Brettell Bros. Robert Kingley, Mingo Junction, in charge of mine. Drift mine, in No. 8 seam of coal, 4½ ft. high; pick mining; only 3 men being employed when visited; has furnace ventilation and mule haulage. They have been rebuilding the tipple and putting in wider gauge road in the mine, and it appeared they were going to make a fine mine of it by the way they were fixing things up.

Brettell Bros. No. 2. (Pratt).

Located one mile northwest of Mingo Junction, O. Operated by Brettell Bros. Robert Kingley, mine boss, Mingo Junction, O. Drift; employing 8 pick miners: natural ventilation—putting coal out—ventilation was not good along faces. Advised that a furnace be built and was informed that it was the intention to take the majority of the men over to the other mine to work as soon as the tipple was ready, and only about two men would be employed in this mine.

Robert Hill.

Located one and one-half miles north of Mingo Junction, O. Operated by Henry Brickerstaff, Mingo Junction, O. Drift, with shaft on right side of mine where air was brought in and furnace at another opening close to haulage opening; employing 7 pick miners. Found in fair condition.

HARRISON COUNTY.

Hopedale.

Located at Hopedale, O., on the Wabash R R. Operated by the Lamberson Coal Co., Coshocton, O. Drift, in No. 8 seam of coal. August 24th, found no evidence of any operation whatever, no switch being built or tipple erected; no one at the mine to give any information, and am unable to say when operation will commence.

NINTH DISTRICT.

THOMAS MORRISON.

COMPOSED OF THE COUNTIES OF CARROLL, HARRISON, A PORTION OF JEFFERSON, AND ALL OIL AND GAS WELLS.

HON. GEORGE HARRISON, *Chief Inspector of Mines, Columbus, O.*

DEAR SIR: In compliance with the time honored custom of the Mining Department, I herewith submit for your approval the official annual report of the Ninth Mining District for the year beginning January 1, 1910, and ending December 31, 1910.

During the first six months of the year, the district was composed of Carroll, Harrison, and a portion of Jefferson County. About the first of July two additional inspectors were added to the force and the districts rearranged. Under the new arrangement the mines in Carroll County, and those in the Bergholz and Amsterdam districts, Jefferson County, in connection with the jurisdiction of all oil and gas wells, drilled or about to be drilled through a workable seam of coal, were placed under the jurisdiction of the inspector of the ninth district

The report shows the number of days devoted to mine inspections, the time devoted to the work of procuring records of oil and gas wells, duties in connection with the abandonment of wells, procuring maps and otherwise attending to the duties of my office, the number of visits made, mines opened, suspended and abandoned, scales tested and results, number and nature of permanent improvements.

It is to be regretted that 34 of our fellow craftsmen lost their lives while in the discharge of their duties in and around the mines, under my jurisdiction during the year. One mine alone is credited with the loss of 18 lives, 15 of which were lost on the night of April 21st, in the ill fated Amsterdam mine, due to an explosion which occurred about 9:15, while 23 men were working in the mine, only 8 out of the 23 escaping with their lives. A complete account of this disaster will be found in another part of this report.

The question of sealing up abandoned sections in gaseous mines, when they could not be properly ventilated, is one on which practical mining men have always differed, some claiming that they should be kept open, while others would claim that it was better to seal them up.

The writer has devoted much study to this subject in late years, principally due to the fact that conditions were arising in mines, under his jurisdiction, that in the near future would demand that abandoned parts of certain mines be either sealed up or the mine abandoned, as it would be a physical impossibility in the very near future to ventilate them so as to keep them free from standing gas. I concluded that under such conditions it would be much safer to seal up such sections, as without a supply of oxygen there can be no combustion; therefore, if the sealing was effectively done, so that no air could penetrate the part sealed up, and it should fill up with gas, generated in that part of the mine, which it undoubtedly would, it would be perfectly harmless in fact it would be the same thing as gas stored in a tank, conducted through a pipe, or that stored in a pocket in the strata it has to be exposed to the atmosphere or mixed with certain properties of air before it will even burn.

A section of the Amsterdam mine is being sealed up at the present time and is almost completed: heavy concrete walls are built about fifteen feet apart and packed between with dirt: this constitutes one stopping; these walls are built in the shape of an arch, the inside one being made to resist the pressure from the inside, and the outside one vice versa; pipes are built in this stopping, and if necessary additional pipes can be connected, and conducted to the return shaft to the surface. A great deal of coal is wasted where places have to be sealed up, as no place is allowed to be driven nearer than 100 ft. to the part sealed up. A system of mining could be adopted that would make it unnecessarry to seal up abandoned workings, as they would effectively seal themselves; this I have gone into thoroughly with the operators of this district, even to the extent of making a trip to the State of Illinois, in company with a number of them, for the purpose of investigating the longwall system of mining. The parties interested all agreed that it was the best and safest method of mining coal when the strata adjacent to the coal generated gas, but after figuring the additional cost of production, they concluded that it would be impossible for them to adopt this system and operate the mines at a profit.

As much of my time as was not taken up in the work of inspecting mines, was devoted to my duties connected with the oil and gas well fields, and we succeeded in having quite a number of the oil and gas companies file maps of their property with your office, also witnessed a number of wells when they were abandoned in order to see that the casing was left in as required by law.

For a time there was some apprehension and uneasiness in connection with wells being drilled through the Rice and Zerbe mines, but these were finally cased, so that there was very little danger in connection with their operation.

Five prosecutions were brought under the law; three in connection with the operation of mines, and two in connection with abandoned oil wells, a report of which has been filed in your office, and I presume will appear in another part of the report.

The coal trade throughout the district has been good, the mines, as a rule, working about full time.

In conclusion I wish to thank both miners and operators for their courteous treatment while in the performance of my duties, and wish to take this opportunity of thanking yourself, the other members of the department, and the office force, for the many courtesies shown.

Respectfully submitted,
THOMAS MORRISON,
Inspector Ninth District.

December 31 1910.

CARROLL COUNTY.

Big Four Drift.

Located one mile east of Malvern. Operated by the Big Four Clay Co., Canton, O., George Neidlinger, Malvern, Supt.; Bert Sanfts, same place, mine foreman. Drift opening to the No. 6 seam of coal and clay, the former being 2½ ft. and the latter 6 ft. thick. Mule haulage; furnace ventilation; 5 miners, 1 day man, employed. Visited February 9th and June 29th; found in very good condition.

Big Four Slope.

Under the same mangement as the drift. No. 5 seam of coal and clay, the former being 3½ ft. and the latter 5 ft. thick. Employs 6 miners and 2 day men. Visited June 29th. Boiler located too near the opening; ordered it moved to comply with the law. August 15th, airshaft completed and furnace being built; orders given to conduct ventilation closer to face of working places.

Sandy Valley.

Located at Malvern. Operated by the Deckman-Duty Brick Co., Cleveland, O. John Fisher, Malvern, Supt.; Mitchel Buck, same place, mine foreman. Drift opening to No. 6 seam of coal and clay; the former is 2½ ft. and the latter 7 ft thick; furnace ventilation, mule haulage. Employs 12 miners and 7 day men. Visited February 10th, June 29th, and October 6th. This mine is under good management, has a good roof and very little water with which to contend, and is generally found in excellent condition.

Greer Beatty.

Located near Magnolia. Operated by the Greer-Beatty Clay Co., Magnolia, O. J. J. Deganhard, Magnolia, has charge of the mine. Drift opening to the No. 5 vein of coal which is 3½ ft. thick; furnace ventilation; mule haulage; pick mining. Employs 6 miners and 4 day men. During the year an escapement shaft was sunk near the face of the workings, making a ready means of escape in case of accident on the main entry. Ventilation good.

Dorothy No. 2.

Located at Delroy. Operated by the Lincoln Coal Co., Delroy, O. J. F. Myers, Supt.; R. M. Campbell, mine foreman. Main slope and manway sunk to the No. 6 vein of coal, which is about 4 ft. thick.

Owing to some cause unknown to the writer operations were suspended after both openings had reached the coal.

Leesville.

Located at Leesville. Operated by the Leesville Mining Co., Carbondale, Pa. E. J. Thomas, Leesville, O., Supt.; Shaft opening, No. 6 vein. Visited December 14th. This shaft is 12′ x 6′ inside of the timbers; when visited it was down 25 ft. and when completed will be 146 ft. deep.

Magnolia.

Located at Magnolia. Operated by the Magnolia Coal Co., Akron, O. J. J Degenhard, Magnolia, Supt.; Hugh Patterson, mine foreman. Shaft 65 ft. deep.

to the No. 5 vein of coal, which runs from 4 to 5 ft. thick; ventilation by a 10 ft Brazil fan; motor and mule haulage; machine mining. Employed 22 miners and 19 day men. Visited February 11, pillars being drawn preparatory to abandonment. Mine abandoned March 31st.

Metropolitan.

Located at Pekin. Operated by the Metropolitan Paving Brick Co., Canton O. A. L. Currey, Minerva, Supt.; L. L. Buck, same place, mine foreman. Drift opening to the No. 6 seam of coal and clay, the former is 2½ and the latter 7 ft thick; ventilated by a 10 ft. home made fan; mule haulage. Employs 10 miners and 4 day men. Visited April 18th, July 12th, Dec. 12th, and on each occasion was found in very good condition.

National No. 6.

Located near Magnolia. Operated by the National Fire-proofing Co., Canton, O. Wm. Weaver, Magnolia, Supt.; John Williams, same place, mine foreman. Drift opening to the No. 6 seam of coal and clay, the former 3½ ft. thick and the latter 4 ft. thick. Mule haulage; furnace ventilation. Visited September 16th, orders given to make a second opening near the face of the workings. Employs 8 miners and 3 day men.

Horse Shoe.

Located at Lindentree. Operated by the Ohio Mining and Railway Co., Massillon, O. Operations suspended during the entire year.

Midway.

Located about two miles west of Malvern. Operated by the Pitts.-Malvern Clay Co., Pittsburg, Pa. Operations suspended the greater part of the year. No inspection made.

Robinson No. 5.

Located at Malvern. Operated by the Robinson Clay Product Co., Akron, O. Geo. Poland, Malvern, Supt.; Jasper Johnson, same place, mine foreman. Slope opening to the No. 5 coal and clay; the former is 2 ft. and the latter 6 ft. thick; ventilated by a 4 ft. electric driven Stine fan; has mule and rope haulage, with a steam locomotive to haul the clay from the mines to the sewer pipe plant; employs 10 miners and 8 day men. This mine was visited three times during the year; one fatality occurred during this time, due to coal falling off a corner which was being taken off to straighten the track. The roof is full of slips, but is generally well timbered.

Russell Hill.

Located at Delroy. Abandoned.

Sterling No. 1.

Located at Salineville. Operated by the Sterling Mining Co., Carbondale, O. Samuel Madison, Salineville, is Supt. Visited March 16th, posted a notice forbidding the men from entering the mine before the fan is put in operation, and ordered the rooms at the head of 8 west entry stopped, on account of an oil well which had not been located by survey. Strip vein, 3½ ft. thick; ventilated by a 10 ft. Brazil fan; rope and motor haulage; machine mining.

Somers No. 2.

Located at Sherodsville. Operated by the Somers Mining Co., Cleveland, O. Mark Coe, Sherodsville, Supt.; Harry Harris, same place, mine foreman. Shaft 71 ft. deep, No. 6 seam of coal, which is about 4 ft. thick; ventilated by a 12 ft. Brazil fan; motor and mule haulage; machine mining; about 135 miners and 52 day men are usually employed. Visited February 7th;. ventilation on the south side of the mine very poor; requested that the face entries be double shifted in order to reach a suitable place for an air-shaft as soon as possible. Owing to the inability of the miners and operators to agree upon a scale for the ensuing two years, operations were suspended March 31st, remaining so until the close of the year.

Hazelwood.

Located near Delroy. Operated by the Eastern Ohio Mining Co., Canton, O. B. F. James, Canton, Supt.; J. H. Thomas, Delroy, mine foreman. Drift opening to the No. 7 vein of coal, which is about 5 ft. thick; pick mining; mule haulage; furnace ventilation; employs about 35 miners and 6 day men. Visited February 8th; tipple and switch not completed. June 1st, ordered air shaft sunk and furnace built. July 8th, shaft sunk, but furnace not built; ordered this done at once. October 14th, ventilation limited to the number of men employed; gave orders not to employ any more men until ventilation was increased; posted notice limiting shot firing to once a day, and forbidding miners from drilling their holes beyond the shearing or undercutting, or shooting coal unless at least one-half of it was undercut. December 30th, mine idle, no inspection.

Mahanoy.

Located near Bowerston. Operated by the Mahanoy Massillon Mining Co., Mahanoy City, Pa. E. J. Thomas, Leesville, had charge of the mine, but toward the close of the year he was succeeded by George Wilthem, Bowerston, O. Two veins of coal are being opened on this property, a drift to the No. 7 vein and a shaft 170 ft. deep to the No. 6 vein of coal. The intention is to have one plant to operate both mines and bring all the coal to the same tipple. Up to the present time the shaft has not reached the coal, and there is no development in the drift. The work of erecting the tipple has not yet commenced, nor has the switch been laid.

HARRISON COUNTY.

Adena.

Located one mile west of Adena. Operated by the West Mining Co., Adena, O. R. C. West, Adena, is Supt.; John West, same place, mine foreman. Drift opening to the No. 8 vein of coal, which is 5 ft. thick;machine mining; mule haulage; furnace ventilation. Visited February 14th, condition good. July 6th, investigated accident which resulted in the death of C. C. Adams, engineer.

Majestic.

Located at Blairmont. Operated by the A. G. Blair Mining Co., Toledo, O. Wm Bunney was Supt. and R. H. Bunney, mine foreman; but on May 1st the management was changed, W. L. Moke, Adena, taking charge as Supt. and Anthony Wannacott as mine foreman. This mine was visited three times, the last visit being made July 6th to investigate a fatal accident. Conditions were very bad.

but after the change of management they began to improve conditions as rapidly as possible, using steel eyebeams to support the roof along the entry, also draining the haulways and traveling ways, and improving the ventilation by cleaning out the air courses and repairing the stoppings.

Newton.

Located at Fishers. Operated by the Newton Coal & Mining Co., Dennison, O. Frank Culley, Dennison, has full charge of the property. Slope opening to the No. 7 vein, which is 4½ ft. thick; machine mining; mule and rope haulage; fan ventilation; employs 56 miners and 20 day men. Visited four times during the year. As a rule, this mine is generally found in good condition, both in regard to ventilation, drainage and general security. On July 11th, the machine runners cut into an abandoned oil well while cutting the No. 2 room off the main entry; fortunately there was very little gas escaping, or the result might have been very serious; the cut was finished, the coal loaded out, and the following day I ordered the hole filled with cement, which was done, with good results. This shows the importance of having oil and gas wells accurately located on the map, so as to guard against cutting into them.

Roby No. 1.

DRIFTS 1 AND 2.

Located at Robyville. Operated by the Roby Coal Co., Cleveland, O. W. L. Moke, Adena, Supt.; Louis Murdock, Robyville, Asst. Supt.; Thomas Aspinwall, mine foreman No. 1, and Joseph Penman, mine foreman No. 2. No. 8 vein, coal 5 ft. thick; machine mining; motor and mule haulage. No. 1 is ventilated by an 18 ft. steam driven Brazil fan; No. 2 ventilated by a 12 ft, electric driven Brazil fan. No. 1 employs about 98 miners and 37 day men. Visited May 19th and found in excellent condition. No. 2 usually employs 106 miners and 37 day men. Visited May 18th and 27th; condition of haulage roads good, well drained and timbered; ventilation on the north side of the mine deficient, owing to the doors and stoppings not being properly looked after; ordered them to make the necessary repairs to properly ventilate this part of the mine.

Ginther.

Located at Kenwood. Operated by the Oliver Coal Co., Pittsburg. Pa. J. F. Thomas, Supt.; John Dailey, mine foreman. Drift opening to the No. 8 vein. which is 5 ft. thick; machine mining; motor and mule haulage; ventilated by a 12 ft. steam driven Brazil fan. Visited February 16th, orders given to make an escapement way at the face of the first right entry, and recommended that steel eyebeams be used to support the roof on the haulways.

JEFFERSON COUNTY.

Amsterdam.

Located near Amsterdam. Operated by the Y. & O. Coal Co.. Cleveland. O. Richard Jones, Amsterdam, Supt.: Edward Lee, same place, mine foreman. Shaft 276 ft. deep to the No. 5 seam of coal, which averages from 4 to 4½ ft. thick. Machine mining; motor and mule haulage; ventilated by a 14 ft. steam driven fan of the Robinson make. Usually about 115 miners and 65 day men are employed.

This mine has a poor roof and most of the rooms fall in before they can be worked out, and as the mine generates gas very freely, it is very important that a current of air be kept sweeping the old workings as well as the new, as gas would accumulate in places that had caved in if this was not done; even with the best of care this sometimes occurs, and it keeps the management continually on the watch, in order to detect these occurrences, and see that the ventilation is conducted so as to dilute any gas which may accumulate on top of the falls. Visited January 13th to investigate a fatal accident, made a partial inspection, recommended changing the system of working. March 24th, inspected the N. W., S. W., and second section of the South face entry, also a part of the old workings, found the ventilation good, ordered 3 and 4 N. W. sprinkled, intending to complete the inspection the following day, but was called to Plum Run to investigate a fatal accident. April 19th, called to investigate a fatal accident, which resulted in the death of Clarence Klein, who fell in front of a railroad car, while letting it out from under the tipple; completed the inspection commenced March 24th, found ventilation good in the south and east side. April 21st, an explosion occurred between 9 and 9:30 at night, resulting in the loss of fifteen lives, full account of which will be found in another part of the report. April 22nd, Chief Harrison, and all the members of the department, had arrived on the premises, and the work of rescue progressed as rapidly as circumstances would permit. April 23rd, last body recovered and work of rescue completed. April 28th, visited, in company with district inspectors McDonald, Kennedy and Burke. Fan was not yet in running order; returned the following day, entering the mine about 6 P. M., finding the air charged with gas, returned to the surface, and decided to return the following day, at which time we were able to reach the outer end of the second south west entry, again encountering gas charged air, temporary canvas stoppings were built and the last breakthrough reached at 4 P. M. May 2nd, in company with Inspector Burke, we reached the face of the south entry, the initial point of the explosion. May 3rd, in company with Chief Inspector Harrison, District Inspector Burke, who had remained with me from the time of the explosion, and J. W. Paul, of the Geological Survey, an investigation was made and a report filed, which no doubt will appear in another part of the report. Orders were then given to proceed to clean up the aircourses and build permanent stoppings, using nothing but closed safety lamps until the ventilation was restored. June 21st, 22nd, air courses cleaned up, stoppings built and ventilation good; permission was given to use open lights, except in workings. June 27th visited, in company with Chief Inspector Harrison and District Inspector Smith; conditions approved and permission given to resume operations. August 24th, 25th, made a thorough inspection, found the ventilation good, but suggested that it be increased on the S. W. entries.. September 24th, gas found in abandoned part of the south side, gave instructions in regard to removing it, with orders not to operate until, a thorough examination was made; 26th, south side of the mine clear; 27th, in company with the mine foreman and three committeemen, a complete inspection of all available parts of the mine was made, and conditions approved; all old workings found ventilated and free from standing gas, with the exception of a little in No. 12 room, 1st. west. October 12th, visited, in company with State's Attorney F. H. Kirtley, inspected part of the mine about to be sealed up. November 1st. investigated accident which proved fatal to John Banyek. December 21st, examined that part of the mine that was being sealed up; ordered all possible energy exerted to complete walls, as the air was gradually being cut off by falls; 22nd, completed the examination of the mine, found ventilation poor on the north side, fan running 90 revolutions per minute, producing 60,000 cu. ft., increased speed of fan at noon to 120 revolutions per. minute which increased the ventilation to 85,900 cu. ft. In the afternoon found the ventilation very good; gave orders not to operate the mine with the fan running less than 120 revolutions per minute, and ordered all stoppings cemented.

Connor Nos. 1 and 2.

Located at Connors. Operated by the W. & L. E. Coal Co., Cleveland, O. Fred Aspinwall, Supt.; Samuel Ruckman, mine foreman of No. 1, James Ruckman, mine foreman of No. 2. Drift opening, No. 8 vein 5 ft. thick. Machine mining; motor and mule haulage; fan ventilation. May 27th, investigated fatal accident in No. 1 mine. June 27th, investigated fatal accident in No. 2 mine; made an inspection of the mine, found it well ventilated and in good condition.

Dorothy.

Located at Warrenton. Operated by the J. F. Blair Co., Parkersburg, W. Va. J. C. Robinson, Rayland, mine foreman. Drift opening, No. 8 vein, 5 ft. thick. Pick mining; mule haulage; furnace ventilation. Employs 44 miners and 11 day men. Visited March 11th, conditions good.

Dillon No. 2.

Located at Dillonvale. Operated by the W. & L. E. Coal Co., Cleveland, O. Fred Hornickel, Dillonvale, Supt.; George Chamberlain, same place, mine foreman. Drift opening, No. 8 vein, 5 ft. thick; machine mining; motor and mule haulage; fan ventilation. Employs 260 miners and 50 day men. March 18th, investigated fatal accident. March 29th, ventilation good; parts of the mine dry and dusty. Ordered this sprinkled and removed from the mine.

Dillon No. 4.

Located at Herrick. Joe Bainbridge, Herrick, O., has charge of the mine. Employs 128 miners and 30 day men. March 31st, ventilation improved since former visit, ordered main entry re-timbered; found second opening made as previously ordered. June 20th, investigated fatal accident.

Dunglen Nos. 1 and 2.

Located at Dunglen. Operated by the Morris-Poston Coal Co., Cleveland, O. Charles Thomas, Dunglen, Supt.; Wilfred Souden, mine boss No. 1, Elmer Lyon, mine boss No. 2. Drift opening, No. 8 vein, 5 ft. thick; machine mining; motor haulage; fan ventilation. No. 1 employs 132 miners and 37 day men. January 28th, conditions fair; ordered manholes made on main entry. March 9th, visited, in company with Chief Inspector Harrison, main entry, inspected, and system of timbering approved. No. 2 employs 120 miners and 30 day men. January 24th investigated fatal accident. March 2nd, found mine in very good condition.

Diamond.

Located two miles west of Yellow Creek. Operated by W. E. Smith, Wellsville, O. Isaac Thomas, Irondale, O., mine boss. Slope opening, No. 3 vein, 3 ft. 3 in. thick. Machine mining; mule and rope haulage; fan ventilation. Employs 14 miners and 6 day men. Visited March 14th, condition good.

Irondale Brick Co. Mines.

Located at Irondale. Operated by the Irondale Brick Co., Irondale, O. Fred Danda, Irondale, Supt.

Dando Coal Mine.

Samuel Parsons, Hammondsville, O., mine boss. Drift opening; strip vein 28 in. thick. Pick mining; man haulage. Visited March 15th; orders given to install a fan to ventilate the mine.

Dando Clay Mine, No. 1.

Ed. Grimes, Vanport, Pa., mine boss; slope opening, No. 3 clay, 10 ft. thick, mule haulage; fan ventilation. Employs 3 miners and 2 day men. Visited March 15th, conditions very good.

Dando Clay, No. 2.

Duff Thompson, mine boss, Irondale, O. Shaft, 128 ft. deep, No. 1 seam of clay 15 ft. thick. Ventilated by fan. Employs 10 miners and 2 day men. Visited March 15th; ordered second opening completed as quick as possible; otherwise, conditions good.

Florence.

Located at Florencedale, O. Operated by the Witchazel Coal Co., Youngstown, O. George Evans, Florencedale, Supt.; Julius Grimm, same place, mine boss. Drift opening to the No. 8 vein, which is 4½ ft. thick. Machine mining; motor and mule haulage; fan ventilation. Visited February 14th; orders of previous visit complied with, and mine in very good condition.

Edgar Nos. 1 and 2.

Located near Dillonvale, O. Operated by the Glens Run Coal Co., Cleveland, O. C. W. Maurer, Dillonvale, Supt.; H. W. Jack, mine foreman No. 1, Robert Nicholson, mine foreman No. 2 mine. Drift opening to the No. 8 vein of coal, which is 5 ft. thick; motor and mule haulage; machine mining; fan ventilation. About 175 miners and 86 day men employed in the two mines. No. 1 visited March 30th, ventilation fair, haulway being timbered with steel eyebeams. Conditions improved since former visit, No. 2 May 12th, ventilation very unsatisfactory; main haulage dusty; ordered dust removed, independent line run to the fan and speed increased, and the necessary repairs made to properly conduct the ventilation through the workings.

Jefferson Nos. 1, 2, 3.

Located at Piney Fork and Harpersville, O. Operated by the Jefferson Coal Co., Cleveland, O. Wm. Simpson, Piney Fork, Supt.; Drift opening to the No. 8 vein, which is 5 ft. thick. Machine mining; motor and mule haulage. Each mine equipped with a 15 ft. Brazil fan.

No. 1.

Visited May 10th, 11th, very poorly ventilated on the west side. Suggested certain changes to overcome this for the present. Mr. Simpson stated that they had ordered a fan for this side of the mine, which would be placed at the opening; this no doubt will give good results.

No. 2.

Visited January 27th, found in excellent condition; no recommendation necessary.

No. 3.

Visited January 20th, investigated fatal accident, inspected the mine and found it in very good condition. January 26th again called to investigate fatal accident

Portland.

Located at Connors, O. Operated by the Rayland Coal Co., Pittsburg, Pa. Charles Miller, Rayland, Supt.: Drift opening to the No. 8 vein, 5 ft. thick. Machine mining; motor and mule haulage; ventilated by a 12 ft. Robinson fan Employs 73 miners and 20 day men Visited March 7th, ordered escapement way cleaned out and timbered, and brick stoppings built between main and back entry. Ventilation good.

Roby No. 2.

Drifts 3, 4, and 5.

Operated by the Roby Coal Co, Cleveland, O. W. L. Moke, Adena, Supt: W. J. Oxley, Ramsey, mine foreman No. 3; Louis Moke, mine foreman No 4 These are drift openings to the No. 8 vein, which is 5 ft. thick; machine mining; motor and mule haulage; ventilated by two 16 ft. fans.

No. 3.

Employs 128 miners and 34 day men. Visited March 1st. South and main entry very poorly ventilated; requested that brick stoppings be built between main inlet and return, and ventilation increased.

No. 4.

Employs 125 miners and 34 day men. Visited May 20th; conditions excellent; recommended that an escapement way be made by driving 13 and 14 S. W entry to shallow cover and sinking an air shaft.

No. 5.

Operations suspended.

Wabash.

Located at Parlett, O. Operated by the Wabash Coal Co., Cleveland, O W. P. Bates, Parlett, Supt. Slope opening to the No. 8 vein, which is between 4½ and 5 ft. thick. Machine mining; motor and mule haulage; fan ventilation. Visited May 13th, ordered an air shaft sunk near the face of the main entry, and requested that entry be properly timbered, and manholes whitewashed; ventilation very poor.

Rice.

Located near Bergholz, O. Operated by the Rice Coal Co., Cleveland, O Wm. Neath, Bergholz, Supt.; Abel Armitage, same place, mine foreman Slope opening to the No. 5 vein, which is 5 ft. thick; machine mining; motor and mule haulage; ventilated by a 15 ft. Brazil fan. Employs 170 miners and 60 day men Nine days were devoted to the inspection of this mine during the year, and on one of these occasions was accompanied by District Inspectors Miller and Smith for the purpose of having their advice in regard to the building of dams, which were deemed necessary for the protection of those employed in the mine, and also to decide upon a proper location for an escapement shaft. Owing to an oil well being drilled through a room, and not properly cased, oil and gas escaped into the mine, and before the mine could be operated an additional string of casing, with two rubber packers, had to be put in, the mine remaining idle for several days while this was being done. The stairway in the shaft has been repaired, as requested, and some improvement made in the distribution of the ventilation. On my last visit considerable coal dust was found along the third south and fifth north entry. Orders were given to remove this from the mine at once.

United States Coal Co. Mines.

Located at Bradley and Plum Run, O. Operated by the U. S. Coal Co., Cleveland, O. Drift opening to the No. 8 vein, which is 5 ft. thick; machine mining; motor and mule haulage; fan ventilation. Wm. Wagoner, Bradley, Supt. of the Bradley mines; Bert Keim, Supt. of the Plum Run mines. These mines have a very large output, all of the coal being handled over two tipples.

Bradley, Section 1.

Employs 130 miners and 44 day men. D. M. Harper, mine boss. Visited February 23rd. Ventilation very good; requested that third west be retimbered.

Section 2.

Employs 84 miners and 26 day men. Robert Lane, mine boss. Visited February 23rd. Ventilation good; requested that a new traveling way be made from the north face to the air shaft, by driving a pair of entries and turning no rooms. March 18th, was called to investigate fatal accident.

Section 3.

Employs 90 miners and 30 day men. David Jack, mine boss. Visited February 24th; requested that three shifts be put on in the main entry and driven out for a traveling way; conditions good.

Section 4.

Employs 87 miners and 27 day men. John Newton, mine boss. January 21st was called to investigate fatal accident; inspected the mine and found it in good condition.

Plum Run No. 1.

Employs 103 miners and 41 day men. H. W. Merriman, Rhodesdale, mine boss. Visited March 25th to investigate fatal accident. June 9th, gave orders to make 17 manholes on main west and clean out No. 2 drift for a traveling way; suggested that an overcast be built at first south and air split.

No. 3.

Employs 69 miners and 28 day men. June 9th, air shaft completed and stairway put in, as requested on former visit; gave orders to clean out manholes and whitewash them, and drain haulways; ventilation fair.

No. 4.

Employs 105 miners and 43 day men. Benj. Sweet was mine boss until June 1st, when he was succeeded by James Briggs. March 28th, ventilation fair; haulways neither properly drained nor timbered; ordered this done at once. June 10th, mine in about the same condition, but new mine boss promised to drain and timber the haulways.

Nebo.

Located at Bergholz. Operated by the Clover Leaf Coal Co., Bergholz, O. John Fisher, Bergholz, Supt. Shaft, 88 ft. deep to the number 5 vein, which is 3 ft. 8 in. thick. Visited August 1st, September 19th. Shaft completed; work of development not yet commenced.

Elizabeth.

Located two miles east of Amsterdam. Operated by the Wolf Run Coal Co., Cleveland, O. Harry Marson, Wolf Run, Supt.; J. A. Davin, same place, mine boss. Shaft opening, 193 ft. deep to the No. 5 vein, which is from 4 to 5 ft. thick; machine mining; motor haulage; ventilated by a 14 ft. steam driven Cappell fan; employs 170 miners and 60 day men. Ten days were devoted to the inspection of this mine during the year, and on one occasion I was assisted by District Inspectors McDonald, Kennedy and Burke. During the dry season the water became scarce, causing them to use mine water for the boilers; this caused a lot of trouble, as it would foam in the boilers and result in a low steam pressure; this would generally cause the speed of the fan to decrease, which is a serious affair in a mine of this kind. Requested that a dam be built large enough to hold enough water to supply them during the dry season. A start was made on this, but the writer does not know whether it has been completed or not. As a rule, the ventilation is very good, the management realizing that it is important to have it so, as the mine generates gas very freely, both from the coal and the strata above. As practically no brushing is done, the haulways are very low, and as the miner generally loads the fine coal on top, a great deal of dust is found strewn along the haulways. To overcome this I have always recommended that the entries be brushed. On my last visit I found ice accumulating in the inlet shaft and ordered the exhaust steam turned in; gave orders to keep all dust loaded out and cement all stoppings along the main entry.

X. L.

Located at Bergholz. Operated by the Bergholz Coal Co., Bergholz, O. J. S McKeever, Berholz, Supt.; John Peterson, same place, mine boss. Slope opening to the No. 6 vein, which is 3 ft. thick, worked on the single entry system; machine mining; motor haulage; fan ventilation; employs 90 miners and 29 day men. Visited three times during the year and generally found in good condition. Mr. McKeever is one of our most progressive mine managers and would readily change his system of mining to longwall, if the price paid would justify him in doing so. As it is, he spares no expense in keeping the mine in a safe and healthy condition.

Zerbe.

Located at Amsterdam. Operated by the O. & P. Coal Co., Cleveland, O George Wagoner, Amsterdam, Supt.; John Lees, same place, mine foreman. Shaft opening, 185 ft. deep to the No. 5 vein, which is 5 ft. thick; machine mining; motor and mule haulage; ventilated by a 20 ft. Brazil fan; employs 162 miners and 64 day men. Ten days were devoted to the inspection of this mine during the year. on one occasion I was assisted by Inspectors Miller and Smith, and some advice given in regard to the timbering of the lower section of the shaft. April 25th and 27th, Inspectors McDonald, Kennedy and Burke assisted in the inspection of the mine, the shaft examined and approved. On the 25th a body of gas was found in the old workings at the head of a face entry off the 4th west; on the 27th found this removed and all old workings ventilated and free from gas. Several oil wells have penetrated the workings during the year, causing some uneasiness for a time, but these have been cased and sealed on the outside with cement, and we cannot detect any escaping gas. As a rule, the mine is generally well ventilated, as the management realizes the importance of good ventilation, as the mine generates gas very freely. December 8th and 9th, all old workings available were examined, in company with the mine committee; found fairly well ventilated and free from standing gas.

Allens.

Located at Bergholz. Operated by C. C. Heckathorn, Bergholz, O. Drift opening to the No. 6 vein, which is 3 ft. thick; mule haulage; furnace ventilation; worked on the single entry system; employs 5 miners and 2 day men. Visited December 23rd; ventilation deficient; ordered four doors put up on room necks to conduct air to the face of the entry

TENTH DISTRICT

[illegible]

[illegible]

HON. GEORGE HARRISON, *Chief Inspector of Mines, Columbus, O.*

DEAR SIR: — In compliance with the law and in accordance with the custom, I herewith submit to you, for your approval, the official annual report of the Tenth Mining District for the year commencing January 1, 1910, and ending December 31, 1910. The Tenth District is composed of the southern section of Belmont and a portion of Jefferson Counties, the changes in the various districts taking effect July 1st. All mines on main line of C. & P. R. R., from Bellaire to Yellow Creek, formerly reported in District Ten, will be reported as follows: Bellaire to Steubenville, Lot Jenkins, District Eight; Steubenville to Yellow Creek, Robert S. Wheatley, District Twelve; all mines west of Bellaire on main line of B. & O. R. R., reported by Inspectors Jenkins and Turner up to July 1st, are from that date up to close of the year reported in District Ten. The United States Coal Co., mines, known as Bradley and Plum Run, formerly reported by Thomas Morrison of District Number Nine, have been reported from July 1st, to close of the year in District Ten.

We secured twenty-five permanent improvements, namely: Five ventilating fans and two furnaces, one stairway in shaft opening, and seventeen traveling and escapement ways, with many other improvements not permanent.

The new law is of much importance to the miner and an improvement to the mines. It has increased the volume of air, furnished props and caps for ready use, equipped all mines with more avaliable traveling and escapement ways and adding very materially to the safety of all concerned. Great credit is due to the promoters of the laws, but with all of the improved conditions the fatalities still continue. I very much regret to note the large number of our craftsmen that met death in and around the mines in the short period of time covered by this report, as it fell to my lot to investigate twenty fatalities, two outside of my district, one of which was caught by fall of stone, the other by being run over by railroad flat, while placing temporary rail under tipple; fourteen were caused by falling roof and stone, one by cars getting away and running down slope uncontrolled, one boy, while coupling up cars on tipple, one by coal falling, and one by coming in contact with electric wire. Six of these fatalities occurred in the month of October. Empire No. 2 mine, operated by the Rail & River Coal Co., was especially unfortunate, six fatalities occuring there in one year.

There are many unpleasant duties in connection with the work of an inspector. During the year we found it necessary to go before Justices of the Peace and swear out thirteen different affidavits, covering violations of law as follows: For operating machines without shields, 9; a mine foreman for not causing breakthroughs to be made, and one for not furnishing timber, employing boys under the school age, and one store-keeper for selling oil which was not up to the standard. Good judgment was exercised by operators and miners alike in not closing the mines while a contract was being negotiated. By this method of co-operation the operators placed themselves in a position to keep their mines in operation very steadily up to the close of the year. In most instances the mine managers and miners worked in harmony with the Inspectors to better conditions. Quite a number of the operators started improvements in order to meet the demands of the new law before it went into effect. Four sets of scales were tested, all of which were found correct.

In conclusion I desire to thank you for your ever ready and able advice, and, through you, to the office force and members of the Department for their many courtesies shown me while a member of the Mining Staff.

Respectfully yours,

L. D DEVORE, Bellaire, O., R. D. No. 2,

December 31, 1910. *Inspector Tenth District.*

Note: [illegible] understood [illegible] seam [illegible] average [illegible] thickness [illegible] mines [illegible] machine mines [illegible] ventilation [illegible] possible.

BELMONT COUNTY

[illegible]

Located at Pipe Creek. Owned and operated by the [illegible] Bellaire, O. Slope opening, 250 ft. long, on C. & P. R. R. [illegible] Bellaire, O., Supt. and mine boss. Five visits made during year. One hundred [illegible] miners and 14 day men are employed. February [illegible] conditions [illegible] stairs in escapement shaft had been completed in first class condition. [illegible] as usual conditions fair. August 22nd, [illegible] Cornek and Frank Marmino operating machine without [illegible] they appeared before J. W. Merrell, Bellaire, O., and were fined. October [illegible] condition of mine good. John E. Smith, Shadyside, O., mine [illegible] having succeeded H. W. Davis, resigned. It is the desire of this company to have the law complied with.

Big Run.

Located at Ash, C. & P. R. R. [illegible] Co., Alliance, O. Slope opening, [illegible] ft. long. Five visits made. February [illegible] ice found in stairs in escapement way, gave orders to not allow [illegible] otherwise conditions fair. Joseph Milner, Shadyside, O., Supt.; [illegible] same place, mine boss. April 19th, ordered manholes, which were [illegible] made larger, and stairs in escapement way repaired, otherwise conditions [illegible] July 18th found conditions of mine very much out of order, gave strict orders that law must be complied with. Isaiah Nichol, St. Clairsville, O., Receiver for Company. September 23rd, condition of mine very much improved. [illegible] Dillies Bottom, O., having succeeded Joseph Milner and Geo. Johnson as Supt. and mine boss. November 17th, conditions fair, mine very much improved. Sixty-two miners and 27 day men employed.

Clifford.

Located at Dille, C. & P. R. R. Owned and operated by the Fort Pitt Coal Co., Pittsburg, Pa. Slope opening, 420 ft. long. A. G. Leonard, Moundsville, W. Va., Supt.; Edward Cooley, mine boss. Seven visits made. One hundred miners and 27 day men employed. January 21st, mine idle, no inspection. January 25th, ordered fan speeded up, as mine generates fire damp, March 13th the conditions fair, May 2nd tested scales, found accurate, May 10th, ordered conditions improved, and breakthroughs made in accordance with the law. Mike Wasily having succeeded Edward Cooley as mine boss. June 20th, conditions improved in all respects. Wm. Wagnor having succeeded Mike Wasily as mine boss. August 8th, conditions fair. Geo. Dawson having succeeded Wm. Wagnor as mine boss. August 23rd, investigated fatal accident in which Samuel [illegible] staff lost his life by cars getting away at top of slope and running down on him. October 20th, conditions fair; Mike Wasily having succeeded Geo. Dawson as mine boss. December 8th, conditions good, work being confined in connection with old works and a nice territory being opened up, bore holes are kept in advance where they are approaching old works.

Pultney.

Located one mile south of Bellaire. Owned by the Cambria Mining Co., Toledo, O. Slope opening. George M. Jones, Bellaire, O., Supt.; Wm. Boring, Shadyside, O., mine boss. C. & P. R R. Two hundred and sixty-six miners and 85 day men employed. Five visits were made: February 7th, March 28th, June 22nd, August 24th, and November 14th. While this is a large mine everything is looked after in a systematic way, and the manner in which this mine was kept all the year is very commendable. March 28th, investigated fatal accident to Frank Traby, who was injured March 14th and died of his injuries March 24th. In my inspection of August 24th, Thomas Bennett, Mike Duskey and Stanley Kaspen were found operating machines without shields. This practice the Company desired abolished, as well as the Department. August 25th, all three were taken before Squire Morrell of Bellaire, and were fined according to law.

Empire No. 1.

Located at Bellaire. Owned and operated by the Rail and River Coal Co., Pittsburg, Pa. C. & P. R. R. Drift opening. Seven visits made during year. Wm. Maloney, Bellaire, O., Supt., Owen Donahue, same place, mine boss. January 14th and March 17th, mine conditions improving, cleaning up and re-removing dust according to orders. May 9th investigated fatal accident to Peter De Arc, who was killed by fall of roof coal in room No. 3 on 8 west entry. Tested scales, found correct. May 25th and 26th, conditions improved. Ordered ventilation increased. July 11th, was called to mine, as escapement way had been allowed to get in dangerous condition, ordered this attended to at once. August 11th and 12th, found mine very dusty; gave orders law must be complied with. Richard Jones having succeeded O. P. Donahue, as mine boss. November 1st, refuge holes cleaned, dust being removed. Improvements noted in many respects. Investigated fatal accident to Gelestine Silvestrini, who was killed by fall of coal. December 9th, mine in better condition than at any time during the year; ordered ventilation increased on 1 and 2 west entries; 213 miners and 67 day men are employed.

Empire No. 2.

Located at Bellaire, Ohio. Owned and operated by the same company as the No. 1 mine. Slope opening, on C. & P. R. R. Wm. Maloney, Bellaire, O., Supt.; John Eagen, same place, mine boss. Seven visits made. 175 miners and 56 day men are employed. January 12th, mine at workings fair, ordered dust removed from haulway. February 15th and May 11th conditions fair; May 26th investigated fatal accident to August Domato, who was instantly killed by fall of stone in No. 11 room on 13 west entry. June 6th investigated fatal accident to Joseph Larella, who was injured May 12th and died June 3rd; accident occurred in No. 11 room on 2nd west entry. July 6th condition of mine fair. Investigated fatal accident to Emilio Gogliosso, who was instantly killed by fall of stone in No. 8 west entry, and while in the mine, George Marsek was instantly killed in No. 3 room on 8th west entry. Stone in this section of the mine overlaying the coal is very heavy. September 2nd investigated fatal accident to George Harris, trapper boy, age seventeen years. He was trapping main entry door, mine had been idle for seven weeks and had just started up, this being the second day. In some manner he was caught by motor and instantly killed. September 15th conditions of mine fair, except too much dust had been allowed to accumulate, ordered this removed The mouth of slope had been re-timbered in first class order. October 19th, investigated fatal accident to Mike Marcithe, who was injured by fall of stone in room No. 14 on 13th west entry; Marcithe was removed to hospital and died shortly afterward. December 12th, mine in fair condition, having intersected with the No. 1 mine, making a good escapement way for men.

Empire No. 6.

Located two miles west of Bellaire, on main line of B. & O. R. R. Owned and operated by the Rail and River Coal Co., Pittsburg, Pa. Wm. Maloney, Bellaire, O., Supt.; Wm. Gulley, mine boss. Drift opening. Three visits were made. 115 miners and 34 day men employed. July 26th, in fair condition, except some timbering that was ordered on main haulage ways. October 6th, mine found in fair condition; refuge holes and main haulways cleaned up. Richard Foster, Bellaire, O., has succeded Wm. Gulley as mine boss. December 6th, condition of mine very satisfactory. The matter of timber is well looked after by Mr. Foster, who sees that the men are well supplied.

Hall & Gilhooley.

Domestic mine, located at Bellaire. Owned and operated by the above firm. John Hall, Bellaire, O., is superintendent and mine boss. Four visits made; 10 miners and 3 day men employed. Visited January 21st, September 20th, November 30th, December 30th. This is an old mine, but kept in first class condition at all times. December 30th, investigated fatal accident to Octah Jeffers, who was instantly killed by fall of top, known as black jack. Mr. Jeffers was employed as day man to look after the safety of the men and mine; he was walking into the mine; found a small amount of roof coal down, secured a shovel and started to clean up, when a piece of top gave way, killing him instantly.

Progressive.

Located at Bellaire, Ohio. Operated by Progressive Coal Co., formerly operated by Long & Winder. Domestic mine. Drift opening. Furnace ventilation. Pat Gilhooley, Bellaire, O., is superintendent and mine boss. September 2nd, mine found in good condition. November 30th, have installed electricity, with one mining machine in use, power being secured from electric light plant. Conditions were found good, except that timbers all along main entry are too close; 13 miners and 3 day men are employed.

Nail Mill.

Located at Bellaire, O. Owned and operated by the Carnegie Steel Co., Pittsburg, Pa. Drift opening; consume their own coal. Five visits made. B. F. Marling, Bellaire, O., is superintendent and mine boss. February 22nd, May 13th, July 29th, October 13th and December 22nd. Mine in first class condition. An ambulance placed on trucks is kept in the mine; also blankets and bandages are kept in case, which are removed from the mine for inspection daily. Any orders or suggestions given by the Department are complied with. 96 miners and 15 day men are employed. Conditions are commendable.

Captina.

Located at Captina, O. Owned and operated by the Captina Coal Co., Armstrongs Mills, O. Shaft opening, 68 ft. deep. At this point the No. 8 coal is 6 ft. thick; 12 miners and 5 day men are employed; transportation, O. R. & W. R. R. Wm. Rankin is superintendent and mine boss. August 4th, visited mine in company with Chief Inspector Harrison and Lot Jenkins, of District No. Eight. Mine was idle, as it had been allowed to get in such condition as to be unsafe and was ordered closed. On this visit the Department gave orders by which the mine could be reopened. August 19th, in company with Inspector Jenkins, visited mine; instructions of Department were being carried out and preparations being made to place boilers lawful distance from shaft. December 2nd, mine was in very satisfactory condition. New boilers had been erected to comply with the law

Nealon.

Located two miles west of Bellaire, O. Owned and operated by the Nealon Coal Co., Bellaire, O. Pick mine; furnace ventilation; 9 miners and 1 day man employed. Cook Nealon is superintendent and mine boss, Bellaire, O., R. D. No. 2. October 21st, mine in fair condition, excepting too much water had been allowed to accumulate on main haulway.

Schicks.

Located one mile west of Bellaire, on main line of B. & O. R. R. Owned and operated by the M. J. Schicks Coal Co., Bellaire, O. M. J. Schicks, Supt., Bellaire, O.; Edw. Conaway, same place, mine boss. Drift opening; 88 miners and 25 day men employed. September 1st, ordered timbering done on main haulway; otherwise in fair condition. November 4th, my orders of September 1st had been carried out and mine in excellent condition. This mine will be found reported up to July 1st in District Number Eight by Lot Jenkins.

Knob.

Located one and one-half miles west of Bellaire, on main line of B. & O. R. R. Drift opening. Owned and operated by the Bakewell Coal Co., Bellaire, O. J. H. Pearsall, Bellaire, O., is superintendent and mine boss; 112 miners and 26 day men employed. Two visits made. August 30th, mine was found in fair condition; gave orders that the law must be complied with regarding the furnishing of suitable timbers. November 7th, timbers being furnished in accordance with the law; ventilation good; conditions generally fair.

Neff No. 1.

Located at Neff, O., on main line of B. & O. R. R. Owned and operated by Pittsburg-Belmont Coal Co., Columbus, O. Drift opening. Franklin Neff, Neffs, O., Supt.; John Crawford, Steel, O., mine boss; 198 miners and 51 day men employed. July 27th, found mine in fair condition. October 31st, ordered wire guarded where men pass under it, otherwise mine in first-class condition. Investigated fatal accident to Herbert Simmons, who was killed on the tipple while coupling cars while I was at the mine; age 13 years, 9 months and 24 days. This was the third part of a day he had been employed at this work. November 28th, a warrant was issued by 'Squire Morrell, of Bellaire, for Mr. Crawford. He appeared and was fined according to law, under Section 953.

Neff No. 2.

Located at Neffs, O., on B. & O. R. R. Owned and operated by the Pittsburg-Belmont Coal Co., Columbus, O. Franklin Neff, Neffs, O., is Supt., and John Lovejoy, Steel, O., is mine boss. Drift opening. Two visits made; 153 miners and 51 day men employed. July 28th, found ventilation deficient; ordered 60 men removed from the mine; otherwise conditions fair. October 24th, ventilation increased, haulage ways cleaned up, timbering done according to orders and general conditions very satisfactory; law strictly complied with

Lucy.

Located at Stewartsville, on main line of B. & O. R. R. Owned and operated by the Gordon Coal Co., Bellaire, O. Hugh Ferguson, Stewartsville, O., superintendent and mine boss. Drift opening; 66 miners and 20 day men employed. Three visits were made. July 7th, condition of mine not very gratifying; gave instructions that the law must be complied with in regard to supply of caps and props September 14th, ventilation not up to the standard. Ordered brattices of substantial material built on main air lines. December 1st, considerable improvement noted, lawful material being used for brattices and general conditions fair.

Black Diamond.

Located at Neffs, O., on the B. & O. R. R. and W. & L. E. R. R. Operated by the Belmont Coal Mining Co., Pittsburg, Pa. Drift opening; 206 miners and 53 day men employed. C. H. Lace, Bellaire, O., Supt.; Lawrence Gardner, Neffs, O., mine boss. Four visits were made. August 3rd and 5th, condition of mine unsatisfactory; ventilation inadequate to meet the demands of the new law; refuge holes in bad condition; stairs in escapement shaft dangerous. September 19th, stairs in escapement shaft repaired; mine much improved, except ventilation was ordered made lawful, and brattices placed in a number of places in order to shut off black damp and strengthen the ventilation. September 26th, men being furnished, props and caps in compliance with the law: conditions somewhat improved. November 9th, new opening through the old Echo mine had been cleaned and opened up and side fan removed to this point and was doing good work. Fifty-one men employed on rooms on 7 and 8 and 9 and 10 west and 9 and 10 east off north Snyder entry. No air, owing to bad brattices and doors. Ordered men from mine; otherwise conditions good.

Glen.

Located at Glencoe, main line of B. & O. R. R. Owned and operated by Belmont Coal & Mining Co., Pittsburg, Pa. Slope opening; 192 miners and 60 day men employed. Six visits made. January 24th, visited at request of Lot Jenkins, of District Eight, during the time the mine was under his supervision; while mine was somewhat improved, it was found in very poor condition. J. E. Barth, Glencoe, O., Supt.; Wm. Williams, same place, mine boss. Drainage was bad, haulways wet and muddy, air-ways full of falls and choked and a great deal of timbering needed. With all the advice and moral suasion that Mr. Jenkins could command it seemed impossible to get conditions very much improved. August 2nd condition of mine at working faces fair; no improvement on main haulage ways and air ways. Mr. Barth stated that he could not comply with the orders of the Department when he could get no material. November 10th, main haulway much improved, mud and water removed and timbered in good condition. H. W. Davis, Bellaire, O., having succeeded J. E. Barth as Supt. Southwest section still in bad condition. November 21st air improved by sinking a shaft, provided with a good set of stairs for escapement way. Main west haulway very bad from mud and water; many timbers were broken, making it unsafe; No. 8 and 7 west entries dangerous; advised they cease operating them until timbered and made safe. December 5th main west entry unchanged; advised the hauling of coal through it to cease; 14th and 15th west off of the mains have intersected with faces off main west; this is an improvement and adds much to the safety of the men. Wm. Bertram having succeeded Wm. Williams as mine boss. December 14th, in company with Mr. George Harrison, Chief Inspector, T K Maher, General Manager and C. H. Lace, General Superintendent, visited the mine; No. 7 entry, complaint of which had been made, was abandoned and material removed; No. 3 was being timbered and made safe; the main west had been gone over and broken timber removed and replaced with new ones; mud and water removed. Improvements were such that it was very gratifying.

Franklin.

Located at Stewartsville, Ohio, on B. & O. R. R. Operated by the Franklin Coal Co., Stewartsville, O. F. L. Head, St. Clairsville, O., Supt.: James Spence, Stewartsville, O., mine boss. Drift opening. 84 miners and 27 day men employed. Five visits made. July 19th, ventilation deficient owing to the mine being driven a long way and ventilated by a furnace; ordered men removed to meet the requirements of the law. Refuge holes ordered made large. August 16th, a new Jeffrey 6 ft. electric fan was being installed. Refuge holes made larger according to orders; conditions fair. October 17th, timbering 10 west as directed: general conditions approved. December 13th, conditions of mine very satisfactory; much credit is due the management for the many improved conditions, as they were ever ready to take advice, their desire being to comply with the law.

Purseglove.

Located at Stewartsville, main line of B. & O. R. R. New mine, just opening up; owned and will be operated by the Big Five Coal Co. It is the intention of this Company to make this one of the model mines of eastern Ohio. Samuel Purseglove is general overseer and manager. This Company expects to be running coal by early spring.

Dellora.

Located at Glencoe, on main line of B. & O. R. R. Owned and operated by the Y. & O. Coal Co., Cleveland, O. Shaft opening 60 ft. deep. H. E. Reppert, Glencoe, O., Supt.; E. T. Jones, same place, mine boss. Two visits were made. August 18th condition of mine at working faces good. All back workings and air-ways in bad condition, as this mine had changed hands a number of times and there had been too much coal removed, with nothing left to protect the main entries and air courses. October 6th mine idle, men were on strike on account of some local differences. Mine still closed at close of year.

Florence.

Located one and one-half miles northwest of Martins Ferry, O., on C. & P. R. R. Owned and operated by the Y. & O. Coal Co., Cleveland, O. Drift opening. W. H. Sharp, Martins Ferry, O., Supt.; Carl Ryan, same place, mine boss. 204 miners and 60 day men employed. Three visits made. January 26th and 27th, mine in fair order, except ventilation was weak in south section of the mine; an outlet had been made in this section of the mine, but it was very small and had not been completed. Ordered it opened out at once. March 24th and 25th new outlet completed, ventilation much benefited; conditions fair. June 23rd and 24th, east, or No. 1 side of mine, very wet, top tender. Are driving to outside to get escapement way. Conditions generally fair. This mine generates a small percentage of gas, but it is closely looked after by supplying a good volume of air at the faces.

Eleanor.

Located at Warnock, on B. & O. R. R. Shaft opening, 142 ft. deep. Owned and operated by the Y. & O. Coal Co., Cleveland, O. Three visits made. H. E. Reppert, Glencoe, O, Supt.; John Reppert, same place, mine boss. No.-

vember 16th. mine had been idle seventeen months, working five men cleaning up, using safety lamps. Water had not been lowered sufficiently to make thorough inspection. November 23rd made thorough inspection of the mine: small traces of gas found in 1st and 2nd west entries: 2 miners and 6 day hands at work, using open lights. Gave instructions for fire boss to report on the outside of mine before men were permitted to enter and record kept in office. December 15th 4 miners and 5 day men employed getting mine pretty well cleaned up: the top is very tender and substantial brattices are being put up. Small traces of gas found in 1st and 2nd west entries and north faces off 1st west. The Company is preparing to equip this mine with electricity and modern machinery.

Media.

Located at Baileys Mills, on B. & O. R. R. Owned and operated by the Colburgh Coal Co., Columbus, O. Drift opening. No. 8 seam, at this point 4 ft. thick. Charles Elliott, Baileys Mills, O., Supt.; Otto Crumm, same place, mine boss. August 9th breakthrough law being violated in a number of places; ventilation good. Ordered wire guarded at room necks and where men were compelled to pass under it. November 3rd all orders had been complied with. Men well looked after; 71 miners and 29 day men employed. Conditions very commendable.

Cochran.

Located at Baileys Mills, on B. & O. R. R. Drift opening. Operated by the Quaker Coal Co., Columbus, O. G. W. Davis, Baileys Mills, O., Supt. and mine boss. No. 8 seam about 4 ft. thick at this point: 35 miners and 13 day men employed. Mine not in good condition, as it had been closed down since the 1st of April. November 11th, have installed a new 4 ft. electric fan of the Golonial type; doors and brattices were out of order: improvements were being made as rapidly as they could be. Ordered direct cables off of machines and work of improvement pushed until mine was placed in lawful condition. This, Mr. Davis agreed to do, as he stated it was the desire of the Company to comply with the law.

Edgehill.

Located at Bellaire, Ohio, on C. & P. R. R. Owned and operated by the A. J. Morgan Coal Co., Bellaire, O. Jacob Long, Bellaire, O., Supt. and mine boss. Drift opening; 80 miners and 15 day men employed: three visits made. January 28th, mine in good order; electric lights were placed at refuge holes on motor road. March 31st, condition of mine improved. Found Walter Sykes and Richard Kane operating machines without shields: as they had been properly warned by the Company and myself, they were brought before 'Squire Morrell, of Bellaire, and fined according to law. June 11th gave orders that new law must be complied with in regard to caps and props of lawful length. Taking all matters into consideration up to this time, the conditions were all that could be desired.

West Wheeling.

Located at West Wheeling, Ohio, on C. & P. R. R. Owned and operated by the West Wheeling Coal Co., Bridgeport, O. Wm. Johnson, Bridgeport, O., Supt. and mine boss. Drift opening; 58 miners and 12 day men employed. February 23rd fan moved to better location, giving good results. Condition of mine fair on this visit. April 28th, ordered timbering done on main haulway near mine opening, and drainage looked after. The old works were being approached and considerable trouble was being experienced on account of the water. Thomas Hughes and James Griffin were found operating machines without shields. On

May 3rd 'Squire Morrell, of Bellaire, issued warrants for their arrest, but before the constable could serve them Griffin had escaped; Hughes went before the 'Squire and by some arrangement was released until such time as Griffin could be apprehended.

Aetna Standard.

Located at Aetnaville, Ohio. Owned and operated by the American Sheet and Tin Plate Co., Pittsburg, Pa. Drift opening. Wm. Fitzgerald, Tiltonville, O., superintendent and mine boss. Closed during the time it was under my supervision, owing to strike at the mill.

Laughlin.

Located at Martins Ferry, O. Owned by same company as Aetna Standard. Edward Hite, Martins Ferry, O., superintendent and mine boss. Idle on account of strike at the mill.

Laughlin No. 2.

Located at Martins Ferry, O. Owned and operated by the Whitaker-Glessner Co., Wheeling, W. Va. Mill mine; drift opening; 26 pick miners and 8 day men employed. Harry Kasley, Wheeling, W. Va., Supt.; Richard Walker, Martins Ferry, O., mine boss. February 17th, condition of mine fair. May 12th, electricity installed and an electric punching machine in operation. Mr. Walker takes great pride in looking after the mine and the safety of his men.

Gaylord No. 1.

Located one and one-half miles north of Martins Ferry, O., on main line of C. & P. R. R. Owned and operated by the Pittsburg & Cleveland Coal Co., Cleveland, O. T. E. Santers, Martins Ferry, O., Supt.; John Gallagher, same place, mine boss. Three visits made; 147 miners and 48 day men employed. January 11th, in accordance with my request the main haulway was being cleaned up and timbered. March 14th, main motor road much improved; mine in first class condition at working faces. April 21st, haulways where dust had accumulated, being sprinkled. Condition on this visit very satisfactory, considering the mine is an old one.

Gaylord No. 2.

Located near the No. 1 mine, on C. & P. R. R. Owned and operated by same company as No. 1. Drift opening. T. E. Santers, Martins Ferry, O., Supt.; W. D. Scott, Bridgeport, O., mine boss. 55 miners and 14 day men employed. February 16th, all conditions approved. Visited April 22nd and 25th; April 22nd, while in this mine, received a call from the Columbus office to report at Amsterdam on account of an explosion which had taken place. April 25th, completed inspection. This is a model mine; conditions first class in every respect. This company, in my opinion, made no mistake in placing Mr. Scott in charge, as he takes great pains in looking after the company's interests and safety of the men.

SMALL MINES EMPLOYING LESS THAN TEN MEN.

Sheets.

Located at Martins Ferry, O. Domestic trade mine. Drift opening. Owned and operated by Sheets Coal Co., Martins Ferry, O. James Ralston, same place, mine manager. March 21st, 6 miners and 2 day men employed; mine in good condition; fan ventilation and electric machine mining.

Lee Woods.

Located at Martins Ferry, O. Owned and operated by Woods & Son. Drift opening; machine mining; furnace ventilation; 6 miners and 1 day man employed. Conditions not good. Lee Woods, Martins Ferry, O., superintendent and mine boss.

M. T. Garrett.

Located at Bellaire, O. Machine mine, 6 miners and 2 day men employed. Has since been abandoned.

Thos. Long.

Located at Bellaire, O. Domestic trade. Owned and operated by Long Coal Co., Shadyside, O. Machine mining; furnace ventilation. October 14th, 7 miners and 2 day men are employed; mine has been very much improved; hoist coal by way of new slope instead of shaft and by this comply with orders of the Department; in this they do away with boilers that were up against the shaft opening. Mr. Long expects to increase number of men as the trade warrants it. Thos. Long, Shadyside, O., superintendent and mine boss.

Beverage and Green.

Located at Powhatan, O. Slope opening; steam jet ventilation. Visited November 28th. Domestic mine; 4 miners and 2 day men employed.

Isaiah Owens.

Located at Powhatan, O. Three men employed.

Klee.

John Klee, Klee, O. Drift opening. Three men employed.

Weeks.

James Weeks, Bellaire, O. Three to 5 men employed.

Roush.

Andrew Roush, Klee, O. Two men employed.

Crozier.

John Crozier, Klee, O. From 1 to 2 men employed.

Koehnline.

Drift opening. Compressed air punching machine used to mine the coal; exhaust steam ventilation. Operated by the Koehnline Ice & Coal Co., Bridgeport, O. Three miners and one day man employed.

CLAY MINE IN BELMONT COUNTY.

Suburban Brick Co.

Located at Bellaire, O. Owned and operated by the Suburban Brick Co., Wheeling, W. Va. Drift opening; clay [illegible] to [illegible] ft. in thickness. C. H. Carpenter, Martins Ferry, O., Supt.; J. W. [illegible], Bellaire, O., mine boss. Mine kep[illegible] in good condition throughout the year. A new opening is being made which will soon intersect with inside workings. The sides are being walled with stone and timbering overhead being done with good substantial timbers. Nine miners and 3 day men employed.

JEFFERSON COUNTY.

Walnut Hill Nos. 1 and 2.

Located at Yorkville, O., on C. & P. R. R. Owned and operated by O. & P. Coal Co., Cleveland, O. Drift opening. Wm. Neath, Yorkville, O., Supt.; John Evans, same place, mine boss. 133 miners and 46 day men employed. January 20th, mine somewhat improved but conditions still bad. February 11th, conditions of haulways very bad; refuge holes filled up with fallen roof and dirt. February 18th, made inspection, meeting by appointment with Mr. Price, general manager for the company. Motor road somewhat improved, but still in bad condition; inlet airway nearly closed with ice. Mine continued to improve from this time on. April 15th, ventilation weak, as the No. 1 mine fan had been destroyed by fire. June 21st, ventilation good, the second fan being in operation; haulways and refuge holes improved; conditions fair; traveling way cleaned up for escapement way from No. 2 mine.

Russell.

Located at Tiltonville, O., on C. & P. R. R. Owned and operated by the Russell Coal and Mining Co., Cleveland, O. Drift opening. Seth Williams, Tiltonville, O., superintendent and mine boss; 88 miners and 19 day men employed. February 21st, mine very wet; ordered sumps blown out in order to remove water from off haulage and traveling ways; otherwise conditions fair. April 18th, in about the same condition as on previous visit. Ordered sump blown out at north side passway in order to remove water from passway. Aside from these irregularities, conditions fair.

Kelley.

Located one mile north of Rayland, O., on C. & P. R. R. Operated by Shannon Run Coal Co., Pittsburg, Pa. Drift opening. Val Cox, Warrenton, O., superintendent and mine boss. 51 miners and 15 day men employed. This is a very old mine, and as it has been idle for a long time it was naturally found in very poor condition. January 13th, ordered brattices repaired at once in order to get the air to the working faces. February 25th, found mine improved. Ordered fan reversed so as to make the new opening the inlet, which had been made near the workings. Ordered trolley wire moved in conformity with the law. April 27th, conditions improved and it is almost impossible to place the mine in lawful condition.

RUSH RUN MINES Nos. 1, 2, 3. Owned and operated by the Glens Run Coal Co., Cleveland, O., transportation C. & P. R. R.

Rush Run No. 1.

Located at Rush Run, O. Drift opening. Howard Ulrich, Rayland, O., Supt.; John Coss, Rush Run, O., mine boss. 90 miners and 30 day men employed. February 9th and April 12th, conditions fair. May 20th, met Mr. Thomas and

Superintendents Ulrich and Werker, in regard to the location of fan which they had proposed moving nearer to the workings. June 28th, conditions improved. August 31st, wiring unsatisfactory, as return wire was too near the bottom. Breakthroughs not in compliance with the law. November 18th, wiring improved: breakthroughs made at the proper distance and kept open at the faces; improvement very satisfactory; 3rd and 4th north faces have been worked to the surface, affording another traveling way.

Rush Run No. 2.

Located two and one-half miles west of No. 1. W. H. Werker, Rayland, O., Supt.; B. F. Roberts, same place, mine boss. Drift opening; 126 miners and 44 day men employed. Five visits made. February 10th, ventilation weak; gave orders to hasten work on entries which were being driven to intersect with No. 1 mine. April 14th, mine improved; top is very tender. July 8th, as new law provided for increased ventilation and nothing had been done by the company to meet the demands, it was necessary to order 75 men from the mine. September 16th, connections had been made with the No. 1 mine; both fans were being operated but results were not what they expected. A great deal of timbering will be required to make haulways safe. October 4th, investigated fatal accident to Steve Grayek, who was instantly killed by fall of stone in No. 4 room on 11th right entry. On same date investigated fatal accident to Nicholas Ratkowsky, who was injured in room No. 11 on 11th left entry by fall of stone. Accident occurred September 24th and resulted fatally October 2nd. November 22nd, a great deal of timbering being done and much remaining to be done, as it is necessary to timber almost every foot of all the right or west entries. Ventilation has been improved.

Rush Run No. 3.

Dumps over the same tipple as No. 2. W. H. Werker, Supt.; Jarvis Shanhan, Rayland, O., R. D. No. 1, mine boss. Drift opening; 27 miners and 11 day men employed. Mine just starting operations after a long idleness; top is tender. August 17th conditions bad. Forty-two rooms were open at the time the mine closed down, 41 of which caved in and all the entries. November 15th, the mine was being cleaned up and timbering done; ordered work on entry which was being driven to the outside hastened, as there was only a short distance yet to be finished; when this is completed conditions will be much improved

Jean.

Located at Salt Run, O., on C. & P. R. R. Owned and operated by the Blyth Coal Co., Pittsburg, Pa. Geo. Vandyke, Brilliant, O., superintendent and mine boss. Drift opening; 44 miners and 30 day men employed. Two visits made. March 1st, found in very poor condition; top in this mine is very bad and it is necessary to cross-timber the most of the rooms. Ordered a force of men put to work timbering, so as to place mine in safe condition. April [illegible] mine much improved, as most of the timbering has been finished all over mine. A new outlet has been made for traveling way. Investigated fatal accident to William Harris, who was instantly killed by fall of stone in room [illegible] on [illegible] west entry.

Goucher.

Situated two miles west of Brilliant, O., on C. & P. R. R. Owned and operated by the Dexter Coal Co., Brilliant, O. M. D. Gibson, Brilliant, O., Supt.; Wm. Pilkington, same place, mine boss. Drift opening; [illegible] miners and

31 day men employed. January 31st, conditions fair, except breakthrough law was being violated. Warned the mine boss to be careful in this respect. March 30th, ventilation good; conditions of mine fair; breakthrough not being made to comply with the law; again warned mine boss to be careful. Ordered safety switches placed on incline. May 27th, condition of mine was good, except no attention being paid to breakthroughs; found so many beyond the legal distance that I ceased counting them. All places were stopped until breakthroughs were made at the 60 ft. mark. May 31st, swore out warrant for mine boss before E. M. Weekly, justice of the peace, Brilliant, O. June 1st, Mr. Pilkington appeared, plead guilty and paid a fine of fifty dollars and costs, amounting to $54.45.

Sugar Hill.

Situated two miles southwest of Steubenville, O. Owned and operated by the Sugar Hill Coal Co., Steubenville, O. Drift opening, domestic trade. Chas. F. Schobert, Steubenville, O., superintendent and mine boss; 14 miners and 1 day man employed; pick mining; furnace ventilation. March 2nd, no escapement way provided for men; otherwise mine in first class condition. Ordered outlet begun at once. June 7th, conditions of mine good. Work on second outlet commenced and has since been completed.

Pratt.

Located at Mingo Junction, O. Formerly employed 12 miners and 1 day man. Drift opening; domestic mine, and was abandoned the first of the year.

United States Mines.

Located at Bradley and Plum Run, O., transportation for Bradley mines, W. & L. E. and L. E. A. & W. R. R's., and for the Plum Run mines, C. & P. R. R. Operated by United States Coal Co., Cleveland, O. H. E. Willard, Cleveland, O., general manager. John Newton, Bradley, O., is superintendent of the Bradley mines; H. C. Keim, Rhodesdale, O., superintendent of the Plum Run mines. About October 15th, there was a change in the superintendents at Plum Run, Robert Lane, Rhodesdale, O., accepting place made vacant by Mr. Keim. Drift openings; as a rule all the mines have a very tender top, in many instances there is no roof coal. It requires large quantities of heavy timber and large forces of timbermen to keep haulways in safe condition. However, a large supply is always kept on hand for ready use; as timbers decay and break so easily, Steel "I" beams have been recommended.

Bradley No. 1 District.

Wm. Adamson, Bradley, O., mine boss. July 12th, 116 miners and 36 day men employed. Mine in very poor condition; breakthrough law being overlooked; haulways in bad order, for want of timbering, also drainage and refuge holes in very poor condition. September 1st, very little improvement noted. December 19th, mine was found in very satisfactory condition; haulways and refuge holes cleaned up according to orders and a very large amount of timbering done. O. A. Jacoby, Bradley, Ohio, having succeeded Wm. Adamson, as mine boss. Conditions very satisfactory.

Bradley No. 2. District.

Drift opening. Richard Redfern, Bradley, O., mine boss; 85 miners and 26 day men employed. July 13th, breakthrough law very much violated; ordered [illegible] condition [illegible] September [illegible] [illegible] March [illegible] [illegible] [illegible] October [illegible] conditions [illegible] December [illegible] everything [illegible] conditions [illegible] commendable. [illegible] management.

[illegible] No. [illegible] District.

[illegible] mine boss, [illegible] miners and [illegible] day men employed. [illegible] conditions [illegible] [illegible] September [illegible] October [illegible] [illegible] [illegible] December [illegible] [illegible] conditions [illegible] [illegible] improved.

Bradley No. [illegible] District.

[illegible] J. M. Walker, mine boss, [illegible] miners and [illegible] day men employed. July [illegible], conditions not up to the standard. Conditions [illegible] ordered same improved at once. September [illegible], investigated fatal accident [illegible] E. A. [illegible], motorman, who was killed [illegible] [illegible] falling and breaking through the [illegible] October [illegible] [illegible] in very poor and dangerous condition, as many timbers were broken and [illegible] holes filled up. Ordered this looked after at once. December [illegible] Wm. [illegible], Bradley, O., having succeeded J. M. Walker as mine boss, and conditions improved. A large amount of timbering had been done. [illegible] cleaned out and preparations being made to move [illegible] to more suitable place as advised.

Plum Run No. 1 District.

H. W. Merriman, Rhodesdale, O., mine boss, 110 miners and 11 day men employed. July 22nd, breakthroughs somewhat out of line. Ordered speed of the fan increased to meet requirements of the new law. October [illegible], second fan has been installed at second outlet. Conditions fair, ventilation good. Ordered wiring placed on insulators near face of workings. December [illegible], mine in first class condition. Both the men and company's interests well looked after by Mr. Merriman, as a visit through the mine will disclose the interest shown and the discipline enforced with the men employed. Any advice or orders given are immediately carried out. Taking everything into consideration conditions are [illegible] commendable.

Plum Run No. 3 District.

O. R. Lawmiller, Rhodesdale, O., mine boss, [illegible] miners and [illegible] day men employed. July 21st, condition of mine fair, timbering well kept up. [illegible] 29th, mine had been allowed to get very much out of order and ventilation fail to reach the faces of the workings as it should. Ordered general [illegible] at once. December 29th, condition of mine very much improved. [illegible] conducted, haulways and refuge holes cleaned up and [illegible] [illegible] Jones, Rhodesdale, Ohio, has accepted position as mine boss.

Plum Run No. 4 District.

James Briggs, Rhodesdale, Ohio, mine boss; 89 miners and 24 day men employed. Drift opening; July 20th, mine in poor condition; 11th and 12th right entries affected from a squeeze and in dangerous condition. Ordered man stationed on those entries to look after the safety of drivers. Investigated fatal accident to Julius Felice, who was killed by a fall of stone in No. 25 room on 11th right entry. Contrary to law there were no cap pieces being furnished at this mine. Ordered main haulway cleaned up and timbered its entire length. August 1st, after consulting the Department, appeared before John Whitton, justice of the peace, and swore out warrant for the mine boss, the hearing being set for August 10th. The case was indefinitely postponed by Mr. Briggs paying all costs of the case and the company complying with the law in regard to furnishing timber. October 26th, conditions improved in matter of ventilation and timbering. Have intersected with the No. 5 opening which belongs to this district. No. 5 mine in good order. December 28th, roof bad and very tender. This condition necessitates timbering all haulways shortly after they are driven. David Scourfield, Rhodesdale, O., having just taken charge as mine boss. No. 5 opening belongs to No. 4 district and was found in first-class condition.

LaBelle.

Located at Steubenville, Ohio. Owned and operated by the Labelle Iron Works, which consumes this coal. Shaft opening, 200 ft. deep, No. 6 seam of coal, which at this point is 3½ ft. thick. R. W. McCasland, Supt., Steubenville, O.; Dave Love, same place, mine boss. Machine mining, fan ventilation and motor haulage. All the workings are located on the West Virginia side of the river; 144 miners and 24 day men employed. January 10th, in company with Earl A. Henry, District Inspector of West Virginia, inspection was made. Brattices are built with stone or slate and where they are not cemented there is a great loss of air. This causes a shortage of air at the head of the workings; otherwise conditions fair. March 16th, inspected the portion coming under my jurisdiction. Conditions fair. June 27th, found conditions fair on the Ohio side, but a disaster could occur, as there is no outlet on the West Virginia side. Mine generates some fire damp. The jurisdiction of the Department is limited.

Lagrange.

Located at Brilliant, Ohio. Owned and operated by the Lagrange Coal Co., Brilliant, O. No. 6 seam of coal, 3½ ft. thick. Shaft opening, 265 ft. deep. James Morgan, Brilliant, O., superintendent and mine boss. Machine mining; 8 miners and 8 day men employed. Coal is consumed at the electric power plant. March 2nd, conditions fair. Mine generates fire damp. April 11th air shaft in bad condition, owing to wet weather and timber giving way. May 19th, conditions such that it was found necessary to order mine closed. Force was reduced to ten men, who were employed on repair work. May 21st, met Mr. Laughlin, the owner, and when it was made clear what would be required he stated that it did not seem possible to meet the requirements. June 6th, mine abandoned and all material being removed.

High Shaft.

Located at Steubenville, O. Owned and operated by the Steubenville Coal & Mining Co., Steubenville, O. Shaft opening, 225 ft. deep, No. 6 seam. Machine mining, coal used for domestic trade. Wm. Smurthwaite, Supt., Steubenville, O.; Matthew Cassner, same place, mine boss; 18 miners and 14 day men employed. February 28th, conditions fair, considering the fact that preparations are being made to abandon this section of the mine. August 26th, made inspection of mine in company with Lot Jenkins, as he had supervision of the mine at that time. A few days prior, Mr. Jenkins had ordered the mine to cease operations, owing to some irregularities. The company willingly agreed to comply, and were allowed to resume operations.

Forest City.

Located at Toronto, Ohio. Owned and operated by the American Sewer Pipe Co., Toronto, O. Drift opening, No. 6 seam of coal, 3½ ft. thick. Coal is used at plant for burning sewer pipe; 29 miners and 13 day men employed. W. B. Francy, Supt.; John Ferguson, mine boss, both of Toronto, O. March 18th, mine in first-class condition.

Calumet.

Owned by the same Company as Forest City. Suspended.

American Sewer Pipe.

Owned by same Company as Forest City. Suspended while under my supervision.

Stratton.

Located at Empire, Ohio. Owned and operated by the Stratton Fire Clay Co., Empire, O. Drift opening. Pick mine. H. E. Stratton, Supt., Empire, O.; C. C. Crisman, Port Huron, O., mine boss; 17 miners and 2 day men employed. Coal consumed at sewer pipe plant. March 4th, condition of mine fair. May 4th, advised some other means of ventilation, as the furnace was inadequate to meet the demands of the new law. Conditions of mine fair. The coal averages from 2½ to 6 ft. in thickness. No. 7 seam.

Ohio River Coal.

Located at Empire, Ohio. Owned and operated by the same company as Stratton. L. C. Vance, Empire, Ohio, mine boss. No. 7 seam of coal, 2½ ft. thick, pick mine. Coal consumed at plant; 12 miners and 2 day men employed. Mine had just resumed operations after a long idleness. May 4th, mine in fair condition.

Kaul-Oberkirch.

Located at Toronto, Ohio. Owned and operated by the Kaul-Oberkirch Clay Co., Toronto, O. Drift opening, No. 6 seam of coal, 3 ft. thick; pick mining; natural ventilation; 10 miners and 3 day men employed. Geo. Myers, Toronto, O., Supt.; Geo. Hamilton, same place, mine boss. Coal consumed at clay plant. February 3rd, mine in good condition.

MINES EMPLOYING LESS THAN TEN MEN.

Speakes.

Owned and operated by James Speakes, Steubenville, O. Located two miles southwest of Steubenville, O. No. 8 seam of coal; 8 miners and 1 day man employed. Mine in good condition at working faces, but in danger of being drowned out from old works. March 7th, ordered new outlet made for escapement and safety of men. Mine abandoned in April.

Cox Coal Co., Brilliant, Ohio; 4 miners and 1 day man employed.

H. Niesen, Steubenville, Ohio, R. D. No. 2. Four and one-half miles west of Steubenville, O. Two miners and one day man employed.

E. H. Ekey, Steubenville, Ohio, R. D. No. 2. Five miners and one day man employed. Located four and one-half miles west of Steubenville, O.

Edward Bigerstaff, Mingo Junction, Ohio. Four miners and one day man employed.

Watty Vandine, Steubenville, O. March 23rd, mine in poor condition, and may be abandoned. June 16th, repairing mine; new outlet made and the intention is to work ten or twelve miners.

NOTE: One large mine opened during the year, four domestic mines abandoned and two suspended.

CLAY MINES IN JEFFERSON COUNTY.

Little Giant.

Located at Toronto, Ohio. Owned and operated by the Toronto Fire Brick Co., Toronto, O. Shaft opening, 45 ft. deep. Harry Nicholson, Toronto, O., Supt.; A. S. Peckens, same place, mine boss. February 2nd, condition good; 15 miners and 11 day men employed. May 23rd, mine in its usual good condition. Ordered ruling governing underground stables complied with. June 14th, condition of mine good. Advised Mr. Nicholson as to how the stables should be constructed, with which he willingly agreed to comply.

Nicholson.

Located at Empire, Ohio. Owned and operated by the Toronto Fire Clay Co., Toronto, O. Slope opening; 9 miners and 3 day men employed. Charles Nixon, Empire, O., Supt.; Matthew Friend, Toronto, O., mine boss. March 4th, mine in good condition.

Forest City.

Located at Toronto, O. Owned and operated by the American Sewer Pipe Co., Toronto, O. Slope opening: 11 miners and 8 day men employed. W. B. Francy, Toronto, O., Supt.: James Milne, same place, mine boss. February 2nd, a full force of men employed at repair work retimbering entry. May 23rd, new escapement way added. The mine is always found in first class condition, as all repair work is done in proper time.

Great Western.

Located at Toronto, O. Owned and operated by the American Sewer Pipe Co., Toronto, O. W. B. Francy, Toronto, O., Supt.; Daniel Hinkle, same place, mine boss. February 3rd, mine closed down; 15 men being employed on repair work. Ordered work hastened on escapement way.

Calumet.

Owned by same Company as Great Western, suspended.

American Sewer Pipe Co.

Located at Freeman, [illegible] Owned and operated by the American Sewer Pipe Co., Toronto, O. Suspended.

Kaul-Oberkirch.

(Clay.)

Located at Toronto, O. Owned and operated by the Kaul-Oberkirch Co. of Toronto, O. Frank Hartford, Supt., Toronto, O. [illegible] Evans, Steubenville, O., R. F. D. No. 2, mine boss. February 3rd, conditions good. March [illegible] [illegible] men employed, making new opening preparatory to installing motor haulage. This mine is always found in first class condition.

Minor.

Located at Freeman, Ohio. Owned and operated by the Minor Fire Clay Co., Cleveland, O. L. S. Minor, Empire, O., Supt., Geo. Kneisly, Toronto, O., R. D. No. 2, mine boss. [illegible] miners and 3 day men employed. Mine is always found in good order.

Congo.

Located at Empire, Ohio. Owned and operated by the Standard Fire Brick Co., Empire, O. Suspended.

Stratton, Great Northern and Ohio River, are located near Empire, Ohio. Owned and operated by the Stratton Fire Clay Co., Empire, O. H. F. Stratton is general superintendent of all three mines, Empire, O. Shaft openings, [illegible] to 50 ft. deep. Condition of these mines is always bad.

Ohio River.

D. W. Gray, mine boss, Empire, O. Six miners and 4 day men employed February 14th, conditions poor. May 4th, very little improvement. May 24th, condition of mine and hoisting house such that it was necessary to close the mine May 28th.

Great Northern.

Earnest Thomas, Empire, Ohio, mine boss. February 14th conditions bad. Gave instructions what was necessary to be done. May 24th, conditions [illegible] much improved in way of drainage.

Stratton.

Thomas Drara, contractor and mine boss, Empire, Ohio. Seven miners and 4 day men employed. Mine always found in poor condition. The mining of the clay is given out by contract and every new contractor mines all the clay he [illegible] as cheaply as possible.

MINES VISITED OUTSIDE OF DISTRICT [illegible]

April 22nd and 23rd was [illegible] the [illegible] mine [illegible] O. Coal Co., located at [illegible] Ohio, [illegible] As this time [illegible] a detailed account [illegible] found in [illegible]

[illegible]

June 15th, Jefferson No. 1 mine, located in the Ninth District, investigated fatal accident to Grover Smith.

June 24th, Glen Mine, Eighth District at that time.

OIL WELLS.

From the first of the year up to July 1st, thirteen days were spent in my district looking after the various companies that were drilling new oil wells and abandoning old ones, and in securing maps and seeing that the provisions of the law were being carried out.

Ten days were spent in visiting the various stores in my district, taking samples and seeing that the provisions of the new law were being carried out. October 17th it was necessary to issue a warrant for L. Blou, of Stewartsville, Ohio, for violating law governing the sale of miners oil; October 18th he was taken before J. W. Morrell, a justice of the peace, Bellaire, Ohio, pled guilty and was fined.

ELEVENTH DISTRICT.

JAMES HENNESSY.

Composed of Portions of Belmont, Harrison and Jefferson Counties.

HON. GEORGE HARRISON, *Chief Inspector of Mines, Columbus, Ohio.*

DEAR SIR: — In compliance with the mining laws, I herewith submit to you my first annual report of the Eleventh Mining District, from June 11, 1910, to December 31, 1910, both dates inclusive.

During the time covered by this report seven permanent improvements have been made, 6 in Belmont County, 2 shafts, 3 openings for airways, and 1 set of stairs; Harrison County, 1 new opening; 3 pairs of scales tested, 2 of which were found correct, and 1 incorrect.

I regret to report ten fatal accidents, and two being found dead in the mines and the cause attributed to natural death; one killed on the outside, making 13 in all. Eight of these accidents occurred in Belmont County, and the two found dead are also credited to this county. Two occurred in Jefferson County, and 1 in Harrison County.

Eight arrests were made: 7 for using carbon oil and 1 for propping a mine door open.

I desire to state that my relations with both miners and operators have been pleasant, and with the co-operation of both we were able to secure better conditions.

I wish to thank you and the members of the Department and the office force, for the courtesies shown and the advice given in the discharge of my official duty.

Respectfully,

JAMES HENNESSY,
Barton, Ohio,
Inspector 11th District.

December 31, 1910.

BELMONT COUNTY

Taggart.

Located on a branch of the C. L. & W. R. R. Operated by the Barton Coal Co. George Greene, St. Clairsville, O., Supt. Jabe Goulding, same place, mine foreman. Drift opening, machine mine, employing 11[illegible] loaders, [illegible] pick miners, 1[illegible] machine runners, 3[illegible] day hands. Four visits made. July 8th, ventilation poor; August 5th, ventilation improved, had driven No. 1[illegible] butt entry through the hill and installed a [illegible] ft. Detroit fan in the new opening. October 14th, mine in fair condition. December 13th, on the east side of the mine an air shaft had been sunk, 4[illegible] ft. deep. Mine in fair condition. October [illegible]th arrested two men for burning carbon oil in their lamps.

Victor.

Located near Bannock, O., on the C. L. & W. R. R. Operated by James V. Morris, Cleveland, O. George W. Selway, Bannock, O., Supt. and mine foreman. Shaft, 33 ft. deep. Visited October 28th. 8 men employed cleaning the mine, after an idleness extending over more than a year. This mine has very tender top.

Columbia.

Located at Fairpoint, on C. L. & W. R. R. Operated by the Akron Coal Co., Akron, O. D. W. Selway, Fairpoint, O., Supt.; Ira Watkins, St. Clairsville, O., mine boss. Drift opening; employs 2 pick miners, 1[illegible] machine runners, 139 loaders, 47 day hands. Five visits made. June 23rd, stopped work on the new opening until breakthroughs were made. August 22nd, orders had been complied with. October 6th, investigated fatal accident. October [illegible]th, caused the arrest of two men, one a driver for propping doors open, and a machine man for burning carbon oil in his lamp. December 8th, mine in fair condition.

Tunnell Mine.

Located at Flushing, O., on the C. L. & W. R. R. Operated by the Flushing Coal Co., Elyria, O. Drift opening; J. A. Trimbath, Flushing, O., superintendent and mine boss. Sixteen machine runners, 33 loaders and 10 day hands employed. Compressed air machines are used to cut the coal. Three visits made. July 12th, September 26th, the air on 5 and 6 right entry not sufficient. Ordered new door, and a better one placed on 19 and 20 left entry. November [illegible]th, in company with the mine foreman, examined 5 right where a squeeze had taken place, but very little damage appeared to have been done to the entry. Orders given on previous visit complied with. No. 8 seam, 3[illegible] ft. thick.

Ideal.

Located at Fairpoint, O., on the C. L. & W. R. R. Operated by the Fairpoint Coal & Coke Co., Wheeling, W. Va. Henry Selway, Fairpoint, O., Supt. Thomas Burnot, same place, mine boss. Drift opening, furnace ventilation. This is a new mine; employs 20 loaders, 3 machine runners, [illegible] day hands. [illegible] visits made. September 26th and November [illegible]th, mine in fair condition.

Buckeye.

Located 2½ miles west of Flushing, on the C. L. & W. R. R. Operated by George T. Odbert, Cleveland, O., Supt. [illegible] Randolph, Flushing, O., mine boss.

man. Two visits. October 25th, mine idle, repairing boiler. December 14th, mine idle for want of water for boilers.

Kennon No. 2.

Located one mile west of Flushing, O., on C. L. & W. R. R. Operated by Kennon Coal Mining Co., Cleveland, O. Frank Corey, Flushing, O., Supt.; George Millwood, same place, mine boss. Drift opening; 68 loaders, 9 machine runners, 36 day hands. Three visits made. July 11th, investigated fatal accident. September 19th, ordered intake airway cleaned. November 16th, orders were complied with, and mine in fair condition.

Crescent No. 2, 1-2.

Located at Crescent, O., on C. L. & W. R. R. Operated by the Lorain Coal & Dock Co., Columbus, O. James Birkbeck, St. Clairsville, O., Supt.; S. R. Coats, Maynard, O., mine foreman. Drift opening; 31 pick miners, 10 machine runners, 84 loaders, 27 day hands. Four visits made. July 20th, August 30th, November 3rd, December 30th, investigated death of John Pollock, who was found dead in his working place; also inspected the mine and found it in fair condition.

Crescent No. 3.

Located at Crescent, O., on C. L. & W. R. R. Operated by Lorain Coal & Dock Co., Columbus, O. James Birkbeck, St. Clairsville, O., Supt.; R. Delbridge, Maynard, O., mine foreman. Drift opening; employing 6 machine runners, 5 pick men, 85 loaders, 32 day hands. Four visits made. June 21st, August 12th, October 5th, October 31st, investigated fatal accident. November 22nd, mine in fair condition.

Crescent No. 3, 1-2.

Located at Crescent, O., on C. L. & W. R. R. Operated by Lorain Coal & Dock Co., Columbus, O. James Birkbeck, St. Clairsville, O., Supt.; John Harper, Maynard, O., mine boss. Drift opening; 4 machine runners, 45 loaders, 17 day hands. Three visits made. July 21st, October 3rd, November 25th, mine in fair condition.

Crescent No. 4.

Located at Crescent, O., on C. L. & W. R. R. Operated by Lorain Coal & Dock Co., Columbus, O. James Birkbeck, St. Clairsville, O., Supt.; John Harper, Maynard, O., mine foreman. Drift opening; employing 4 pick miners, 6 machine runners, 63 loaders, 18 day hands. Three visits made. July 22nd, October 4th, November 23rd. Mine in very fair condition.

Lydia.

Located one mile west of Maynard, O., on C. L. & W. R. R. Operated by Purseglove Coal Co., St. Clairsville, O. Samuel Purseglove, St. Clairsville, O., Supt.; W. Reline, same place, mine boss. Drift opening; employs 24 machine runners, 170 loaders, 8 pick miners, 34 day hands. Three visits made. July 5th, scales tested, found correct. July 19th, inspected mine. September 13th, November 7th, new opening completed and mine in fair condition.

Pittsurg-Belmont No. 3.

Located on the Belmont Central R. R., 1½ miles from Lafferty, O. Operated by the Pittsburg-Belmont Coal Co., Cleveland, O. James Prendergast, Lafferty, O., Supt.; John Atkinson, same place, mine boss. Slope opening, 283 ft. long; 14 machine runners, 86 loaders, 42 day hands. Visited July 6th, August 15th. Requested them to pipe the steam off of the traveling road. December 5th, completed stairway in the air shaft. December 15th, investigated fatal accident.

Provident.

Located on W. & L. E. R. R., 1½ miles from St. Clairsville, O. Operated by the Provident Coal Co., St. Clairsville, O. David Thomas St. Clairsville, O., Supt.; Thomas Willis, same place, mine foreman. Shaft 68 ft. deep; 44 machine runners, 326 loaders, 78 day hands. Three inspections made, and three fatal accidents. July 25th, mine in fair condition. August 29th and September 7th, investigated fatal accident. Inspected mine December 6th and 7th. December 19th, visited for the purpose of investigating fatal accident.

Lorena.

Located between St. Clairsville and Maynard, O., on the W. & L. E. R. R. Operated by the Roby-Somers Coal Co., Cleveland, O. W. L. Moke, Adena, O., Supt.; Bruno Ostroski, mine foreman. 110 loaders, 12 machine runners, 29 day hands. June 24th inspected the mine, in company with Inspector Jenkins. August 31st, ordered the men off of 7 and 8 left entries until brattices and doors were repaired. October 27th, mine in fair condition. October 31st, one man arrested for burning carbon oil in the mine.

Black Oak or St. Clair.

Located between Lafferty and Flushing, on the C. L. & W. R. R. Operated by the St. Clair Coal Co., Cleveland, O. John Moon, Flushing, Supt.; Hugh Gaffney, same place, mine foreman. Shaft, 87 ft. deep. Employs 168 loaders, 20 machine runners, 41 day hands, 2 pick miners. July 13th, when inspected, it was necessary to request a considerable amount of work on the intake airway. August 23rd, orders given on former visit complied with. October 10th, November 28th, mine in fair condition. October 15th, 3 men arrested for burning carbon oil in the mine.

Trolls No. 1.

Located near Maynard, O., on W. & L. E. R. R. Operated by Trolls Coal Mining Co., St. Clairsville, O. Jesse Troll, St. Clairsville, O., Supt.; Evan Evans, Maynard, O., bank boss. Drift opening. Employs 245 loaders, 22 machine runners, 47 day hands. Four visits made. July 14th, September 6th, November 10th, found the mine much improved. On the 9th of December 2 men were slightly burned with gas. Investigated mine on December 12th, and could find no indications of gas; new opening has been made on 7 east entry by sinking a 10 ft. shaft. The mine is in fair condition.

Trolls No. 2.

Located near Maynard, O., on the W. & L. E. R. R. Operated by the Troll Coal Mining Co., St. Clairsville, O. Jesse S. Troll, St. Clairsville, O., Supt.; Evan Evans, Maynard, O., mine boss. Drift opening. Employs 164 loaders, 18 machine men, 4 pick men, 42 day hands. Three visits made. July 18th, September 12th, November 11th. Mine in fair condition.

Virginia Hill.

Located at Lafferty, O., on C. L. & W. R. R. Operated by Virginia Hill Coal Co., Cleveland, O. T. J. Jordon, Lafferty, O., Supt.; Wm. Redfern, same place, bank boss. Slope, 95 ft. long. Employs 85 loaders, 6 machine runners, 32 day hands. Six visits made. June 27th, August 8th and August 11th, October 11th, October 12th, took the men off of Ott entries until better ventilation was furnished. November 29th, found conditions somewhat better.

Barton.

Located at Barton, O., on C. L. & W. R. R. Operated by the Y. & O. Coal Co., Cleveland, O. Harry Sharp, Barton, O., Supt.; Wm. Batson, same place, mine foreman. Drift opening. Employs 214 loaders, 24 machine runners, 3 pick miners, 61 day hands. June 20th, tested scales and found them correct. Four inspections made. August 25th and 26th, just completed new opening. December 1st and 2nd, mine in fair condition.

Maple Hill.

Located at Barton, O., on C. L. & W. R. R. Operated by Y. & O. Coal Co., Cleveland, O. Harry Sharp, Barton, O., Supt.; Matthew Anderson, same place, bank boss. Drift opening. Employs 130 loaders, 22 machine runners, 56 day hands. June 20th, scales tested and found incorrect. August 4th, inspected mine, ordered 25 entry timbered. A new opening has been made for a traveling road. August 24th investigated fatal accident. November 17th, inspected mine; orders given on former visit not fully complied with, owing to some labor trouble which closed the mine for the months of September and October. Otherwise, the mine is in fair condition.

Boggs.

Located on a branch of the C. L. & W. R. R., near Barton, O. Operated by the Heatherington Coal Co., Barton, O. Richard Heatherington, Barton, O., Supt.; Patrick Leonard, same place, mine boss. This mine has been idle about 18 months. Visited December 31st; 19 day hands employed, and will soon be shipping coal.

MINES EMPLOYING LESS THAN TEN MEN.

Bethel.

Operated by William Hess, Flushing, O. Drift, employing 4 men.

Humphrey.

Operated by D. R. Humphrey, Flushing, O. Drift, employing 3 men.

Hamilton Glass.

Operated by C. Arnold, Flushing, O. Drift, employing 3 men.

David Applegarth.

Operated by David Applegarth, Maynard, O. Drift, employing 3 men.

William Applegarth.

Operated by Wm. Applegarth, Maynard, O. Drift, employing 6 men.

Watkins.

Operated by Oliver Watkins, Maynard, O. Drift, employing 2 men.

Butler.

Operated by John Butler, Fairpoint, O. Drift, employing 2 men.

H. W. Taylor.

Operated by H. W. Taylor, Fairpoint, O. Drift, employing 3 men.

John Ross.

Operated by John Ross, Flushing, O. Drift, employing 2 men.

White.

Operated by Clarence White, Flushing, O. Drift, employing 2 men.

Smith.

Operated by Albert Smith, Flushing, O. Drift, employing 3 men

Obed Hardesty.

Operated by Obed Hardesty, Barton, O. Drift, employing 2 men.

McAllister.

Operated by John McAllister, Barton, O. Drift, employing 3 men.

S. C. Hardesty.

Operated by John Cunningham, Barton, O. Drift, employing 4 men. Two visits. September 1st, to investigate the death of a man who was found dead December 31st, investigated mine.

HARRISON COUNTY.

Majestic.

Located at Blairmont, on the W. & L. E. R. R. Operated by A. G. Blair Mining Co., Toledo, O. W. L. Moke, Adena, O., Supt.; Patrick Kane, same place, bank boss. Drift opening; employs 100 loaders, 16 machine men, 17 pick miners, 35 day men. Four visits made. August 1st, ventilation poor, main haulway in bad condition for want of timber. September 14th, ventilation improved; mine in fair condition. November 1st. On September 27th, investigated fatal accident.

Adena.

Located one mile west of Adena, O., on W. & L. E. R. R. Operated by the West Mining Co., Adena, O. R. E. West, Adena, O., Supt.; John West, same place, mine foreman. Drift: employs 8 machine men, 30 loaders, 13 day hands. Three visits. July 28th, ventilation poor. September 9th, November 4th, ventilation improved.

Roby No. 1.

Located near Adena, O., on W. & L. E. R. R. Operated by the Roby Coal Co., Cleveland, O. W. L. Moke, Adena, O., Supt.; Thomas Aspinwall, Robyville, O., mine boss. Drift opening; employs 12 machine runners, 2 pick miners, 100 loaders, 32 day men. Three visits made. August 2nd, idle on account of damage done by storm. August 16th, October 17th, mine in fair condition.

Roby No. 2.

Located near Adena, O., on W. & L. E. R. R. Operated by the Roby Coal Co., Cleveland, O. W. L. Moke, Adena, O., Supt.; L. L. Murdock, Robyville, mine foreman. Drift; employs 15 machine men, 1 pick miner, 130 loaders, 40 day hands. Two visits made. August 17th, October 19th. Much credit is due to the management of these mines for the good condition in which they are kept.

Oliver No. 1.

The name of this mine changed from Ginther-Kenwood to Oliver No. 1, located at Kenwood, on W. & L. E. R. R. Operated by the Oliver Coal Co., Pittsburg, Pa. R. C. Simpson, Adena, O., Supt.; Wm. Nixon, Kenwood, O., mine boss. Drift opening; employs 9 machine runners, 69 loaders, 35 day hands. Four visits made. July 29th, conditions of mine, in general, were bad. It was impossible to travel the second opening on account of water and falls; manholes were not made according to law. August 9th, conditions somewhat improved. September 8th, new opening completed, also a change in the management of the mine. Eli Roher, of Kenwood, O., Supt.; Joseph Orell, same place, mine foreman. November 2nd, conditions greatly improved.

Goshen Coal Co.

Located at Tippecanoe, on the C. L. & W. R. R. Operated by John P. Jones, Canton, O. W. C. Kester, Tippecanoe, O., Supt. and mine boss. Drift opening; employs 16 pick miners, 2 day hands. Three visits. July 7th, September 23rd, December 20th. Mine in fair condition.

MINES EMPLOYING LESS THAN TEN MEN IN HARRISON COUNTY.

Wm. Brokaw.

Operated by Wm. Brokaw, Moorefield, O. Drift, employing 1 man.

Johnson.

Operated by John L. Johnson, Moorefield, O. Drift, employing 3 men.

Septer.

Operated by Ross Septer, Moorefield, O. Drift, employing 2 men.

Mills.

Operated by Ellis Mills, Moorefield, O. Drift, employing 3 men.

H. S. Mills.

Operated by H. S. Mills, Moorefield, O. Drift, employing 3 men.

Ford.

Operated by J. W. Ford, Moorefield, O. Drift, employing 2 men.

Komak.

Operated by John Komak, Freeport, O. Slope, employing 7 men.

Moore.

Operated by J. L. Moore, Short Creek, O. Drift, employing 2 men.

Mercer.

Operated by W. E. Mercer, Short Creek, O. Drift, employing 4 men.

Jenkins.

Operated by A. T. Jenkins, Short Creek, O. Drift, employing 8 men.

Burns.

Operated by Add Burns, R. F. D. No. 2, Cadiz, O. Drift, employing 2 men.

Jackson.

Operated by David Jackson, Short Creek, O. Drift, employing 2 men.

Culbertson.

Operated by T. S. Culbertson, New Athens, O. Drift, employing 3 men.

JEFFERSON COUNTY.

Roby No. 3.

Located at Ramsey, O., on the W. & L. E. R. R. Operated by the Roby Coal Co., Cleveland, O. W. L. Moke, Adena, O., Supt.; C. F. Brick, Ramsey, O., mine foreman. Drift opening, employing 12 machine runners, 30 day hands and 118 loaders. Two visits made, August 19th, October 20th. November 21st, investigated what had proven to be a fatal accident.

Roby No. 4.

Located at Ramsey, O., on the W. & L. E. R. R. Operated by the Roby Coal Co., Cleveland, O. W. L. Moke, Adena, O., Supt.; Lewis Moke, Ramsey, O., mine foreman. Drift opening, employing 145 loaders, 18 machine men and 11 day hands. Two visits made. August 18th, October 21st. The coal from Nos. 3, 4 and 5 mines is run over the same tipple. The mine is well cared for.

Roby No. 5.

Suspended.

Dunglen No. 1.

Located at Dunglen, O., on the W. & L. E. R. R. Operated by the Morris Poston Coal Co., Cleveland, O. Chas. Thompson, Dunglen, O., Supt.; H. I. Kirkpatrick, mine foreman, same place. Drift opening, employing 40 pick miners.

12 machine runners, 119 loaders and 33 day hands. Four visits made. July 27th, Sept. 15th, and November 14th. Conditions improved since first visit. December 9th, investigated fatal accident, which occurred near the incline on the outside of the mine. The same tipple is used by both the Number 1 and 2 mines.

Dunglen No. 2.

Located at Dunglen, O., on the W. & L. E. R. R. Operated by the Morris-Poston Coal Co., Cleveland, O. Charles Thompson, Dunglen, O., Supt.; H. E. Cooley, same place, mine foreman. Drift opening, employing 24 pick miners, 12 machine runners, 111 loaders and 27 day hands. Four visits made. August 3rd, ventilation weak. August 10th, volume of air increased. September 16th, requested the men taken out of the mine until fan was repaired and ventilation restored. November 15th, conditions improved.

Dillon No. 4.

Located at Herrick, O., on the W. & L. E. R. R. Operated by Wheeling & Lake Erie Coal Co., Cleveland, O. Joseph Bainbridge, Herrick, O., Supt. and mine foreman. Drift opening, employing 18 machine runners, 142 loaders and 41 day hands. Three visits made. July 26th, September 1st and October 26th. There has been quite a number of brick stoppings put in, increasing the volume of air.

MINES EMPLOYING LESS THAN TEN MEN.

Ainscough.

Operated by Thomas Ainscough, Mt. Pleasant, O. Drift, employs 3 men.

Snyder.

Operated by Frank Snyder, Mt. Pleasant, O. Drift, employs 6 men.

Arnold.

Operated by Fred Kuerrer, Mt. Pleasant, O. Drift, employs 3 men.

Casner.

Operated by Lewis Casner, Adena, O. Drift, employs 4 men.

John Ickes.

Operated by John Ickes, Adena, O. Drift, employs 2 men.

TWELFTH DISTRICT.

ROBERT S. WHEATLEY.

COMPOSED OF THE COUNTIES OF COLUMBIANA, MAHONING, AND A PORTION OF JEFFERSON AND CARROLL.

HON. GEORGE HARRISON, *Chief Inspector of Mines, Columbus, Ohio.*

DEAR SIR: — I herewith submit to you my report of the Twelfth Mining District, consisting of Columbiana, Mahoning, and portions of Carroll and Jefferson Counties, for the six months, from July 1st to December 31st, 1910.

During the period covered by the report, 147 inspections were made and 11 permanent improvements noted, as follows: Five fans, 4 second openings and 2 speaking tubes; 4 new mines were opened and 1 suspended. The list of mines generating fire-damp has been changed by the addition of the Delmore Mine and the elimination of the New Slope and West Pittsburg mines, both of which have been abandoned, a net loss of one.

Five sets of scales were tested, three of which were found correct and two incorrect.

Two fatal accidents occurred in the district during the period covered by the report, both being the result of falls of roof. This most prolific source of accidents merits the serious consideration of all those engaged in the mining industry. In this day of fierce competition and feverish haste the lessons taught by past experience are being disregarded, with the result that hundreds of our fellow craftsmen meet untimely deaths.

Modern mine transportation systems are the source of an increasingly large number of accidents. This is another phase of mining operations that must be taken into account to the end that proper safeguards may be thrown around it and the accidents eliminated.

The condition of the coal trade has been uniformly good throughout this district during the period covered by this report.

I am pleased to report that both miners and mine managements, with but few exceptions, have shown a disposition to comply with the laws embodied in the new Mining Code. A number of important changes in mining practices were inaugurated by the adoption of the new code, and it is pleasing to note that they have been accepted with the proper spirit.

Thanking you for the many courtesies shown me, and for your valuable advice and assistance, I am,

Respectfully,
ROBERT S. WHEATLEY,
Inspector 12th District.

December 31, 1910.

COLUMBIANA COUNTY.

Garside.

Located two miles east of Salineville, on the C. & P. R. R. Owned and operated by the Big Vein Coal Co., Cleveland, O. W. P. Crookston, Supt.; Edward English, mine boss, both of Salineville. Shaft, 200 ft. to No. 7 seam 5¼ ft. thick; fan ventilation; machine mining; mule, motor haulage. Employs 139 miners and 67 day men. This mine generates considerable quantities of light carburetted hydrogen gas; but, as a rule, the ventilation is excellent, and the mine is kept free of standing gas. Visited July 6th, August 8th, August 13th, October 21st and December 2nd. On August 8th, found the safety catches on both shafts out of repair. Ordered that no men be lowered or hoisted until catches were put in good working condition. On August 13th again visited the mine to ascertain whether the catches were working satisfactorily. Those on south shaft were found in good condition and those on north shaft undergoing repairs. On December 2nd found some dust, which was ordered sprinkled. Ordered non-inflammable material used for tamping.

Old Slope.

Located at Salineville, on the C. P. R. R. Owned and operated by the O. & P. Coal Co., Cleveland, O. No. 7 seam, 5¼ ft. thick. J. C. Nelms, Supt.; William Beynon, mine boss, both of Salineville. Fan ventilation, machine mining; mule and motor haulage. Employs 64 miners and 36 day men. Visited July 22nd., September 15th, November 4th and December 23rd. The pillars are being drawn in this mine and considering that fact it was found in good condition. Considerable fine coal is spilled from cars on the roadway. Suggested that cars be repaired to prevent this and ordered accumulated dust removed

Strabley.

Located at Salineville, on the C. & P. R. R. Owned and operated by James S. Strabley, Salineville, O., who is also the superintendent; Thomas Strabley, same place, mine boss. Drift opening to No. 7 seam, 5 ft. thick. Fan ventilation; machine mining; mule and motor haulage. Employs 29 miners and 10 day men. Visited July 5th, September 23rd and October 10th. Found ventilation deficient at face of some of the working places. Ordered ventilation restored. Ordered gasoline engine used for pumping, taken out of the mine. Was called to this mine on December 27th to investigate the death of John Baker, who was killed by a fall of roof.

Strabley No. 2.

Located at Salineville, on the C. & P. R. R. Operated by James S. Strabley, who has full charge. Drift opening to strip vein, 3 ft. thick. This is a mine which was abandoned a number of years ago and which is again being put in condition to operate.

Fairfield No. 3.

Located at New Waterford, on the P. F. W. & C. Ry. Operated by the Fairfield Coal Co., Cleveland, O. W. E. Baysinger, East Palestine, O., Supt.; William Shasteen, New Waterford, mine boss. Drift opening to No. 6 seam, 3 ft. thick. Fan ventilation; pick mining; mule and rope haulage. Employs 85 miners and 20 day men. Visited July 26th and December 6th; on last visit found the ventilation deficient throughout the mine, apparently due, partially at least, to faulty construction of the fan house. Suggested that the fan house be remodeled. This mine has encountered considerable faulty territory.

Big Walnut.

Located two miles west of Washingtonville, on the Y. & O. R. R. Operated by the Card & Prosser Coal Co., Cleveland, O. Thomas Prosser, Lisbon, O., Supt.; J. F. Waters, Washingtonville, O., mine boss. Slope opening to No. 3 seam, 3 ft. 3 in. thick. Fan ventilation; pick mining; mule and rope haulage. Single entry system. Employs 57 miners and 17 day men. Visited July 13th, in company with Inspector Smith, of New Philadelphia. Found in fair condition. November 17th, found that the orders of the mining department, relative to the placing of the shots, were being disregarded. Ordered that not less than half the coal be undercut and that no holes should be drilled beyond the undercutting or shearing. Ordered the shot firers not to fire any shot not placed in accordance with this order.

Klondyke.

Located at Lisbon, O., on the Erie R. R. Operated by the Card & Prosser Coal Co., Cleveland, O. Thomas Prosser, Lisbon, O., Supt.; Thomas Evans, same place, mine boss. Drift opening to No. 6 seam, 2 ft. thick. Fan ventilation, machine mining, mule and motor haulage; employs 21 miners and 7 day men. Visited July 20th and found mine idle. On September 7th found trolley wiring defective in places, ordered repaired; also ordered marker placed on rear of motor trip. December 15th found ventilation deficient in No. 1 right and No. 1 left entries. Ordered brattices built to remedy this and refuge holes made on the traveling way.

West Pittsburg No. 2.

Located 5 miles north of Lisbon, on the Erie R. R. Operated by the Card & Prosser Coal Co., Cleveland, O. Thomas Prosser, Supt.; D. R. Lewis, mine boss, both of Lisbon, O. Drift opening to No. 6 seam, 4½ ft. thick; furnace ventilation, machine mining, mule and motor haulage; double entry system; employs 28 miners and 9 day men. Visited October 11th, found in good condition, except face of No. 1 entry, where ventilation was deficient. This is a new mine, from which shipments commenced on September 8th.

Card & Prosser Clay.

Located at Lisbon, O., on the Erie R. R. Operated by the Card & Prosser Coal Co., Cleveland, O. Thomas Prosser, Supt.; John Suffill, mine boss, both of Lisbon, O. Shaft opening to No. 3 seam of clay, 6 ft. thick. Exhaust steam ventilation, mule haulage. Employs 12 miners and 3 day men. Visited July 20th, September 7th and December 15th. Mine in fair condition, with the exception of main entry, where ventilation was deficient.

McNab.

Located near Salem, O. Operated by the Buck Coal Co., Salem, O. James P. Davis, Supt.; M. J. Flinn, mine boss, both of Salem. Shaft 250 ft. to No. 3 seam, 3 ft. thick, exhaust steam ventilation, pick mining, mule haulage, single entry system; employs 23 miners and 9 day men. Visited July 11th, October 4th and November 28th. On the latter visit found that the orders of the Mining Department, relative to the placing of shots, were being disregarded to some *extent*. Ordered that no shot be fired unless at least one-half of the coal is undermined and that no holes be drilled beyond the undercut. [illegible] ordered that nothing but non-inflammable material be used for tamping.

Delmore.

Located 1½ miles west of Leetonia, O., on the Erie R. R. Operated by the Sterling Coal Co., Ltd., Cleveland, O. Daniel McGrath, Supt.; Andrew Boggs, mine boss, both of Leetonia. Slope opening to No. 3 seam, 3 ft. thick. Fan ventilation, machine mining, motor and rope haulage; employs [illegible] miners and 10 day men. Visited on July 15th, in company with Inspector Smith, of Philadelphia. Found trace of gas oozing from bottom near face of No. [illegible] entry. Visited again September 12th and November 16th. Conditions good. The introduction of mining machines has immeasurably lessened the danger from blown out shots at this mine by rendering unnecessary the excessively large charges of blasting powder in former use, and which have been attended with such disastrous results.

Salem.

Located three miles east of Salem, on the Y. & O. R. R. Operated by the Salem Co., Salem, O. William Dunn, Supt.; R. J. Borden, mine boss, both of Salem, O. Drift opening to No. 3 vein, 3½ ft. thick; fan ventilation, machine mining, mule and motor haulage; single entry system; employs 62 miners and 18 day hands. Visited July 12th and October 5th. Suggested that shaft be sunk at head of workings to improve ventilation and provide an additional escapement way.

Prospect Hill No. 1.

Located at East Palestine, O., transportation P. F. W. & C. R. W. Operated by the Prospect Hill Coal Co., East Palestine, O. Grant Hill, Supt.; Thomas Stackhouse, mine boss, both of East Palestine, O. Slope opening to the No. 6 seam, 3½ ft. thick; fan ventilation, machine and pick mining, mule and rope haulage, and employs [illegible] miners and 15 day men. Visited July 2[illegible]th and December 8th. Ventilation deficient in Lindsay and Clark entries. Found rope haulage trip running without headlight. Ordered this practice discontinued. Also ordered that suitable timber be supplied to working places.

Prospect Hill No. 2.

Located two miles west of East Palestine, O., transportation P. F. W. & C. R. W. Grant Hill, Supt.; Jacob [illegible], mine boss, both of East Palestine, O. Drift opening to the No. [illegible] seam, [illegible] ft. thick; single entry system; furnace ventilation, pick mining, mule haulage and employs [illegible] miners and [illegible] day men. Visited July 28th and December 2[illegible]. [illegible] the mine was found in [illegible] condition.

Francis or West Point

Located at West Point, [illegible] Operated by [illegible] Coal & Coke Co., East Liverpool, O. [illegible] Supt.; William Lewis [illegible] Drift opening to [illegible] fan ventilation [illegible] Visited July 2[illegible] [illegible] substituted for the [illegible] 30 days [illegible] 25th and found that [illegible] had not been complied with. Ordered the mine closed until [illegible] September [illegible] installed and ventilation [illegible] balance. December 5th, ventilation deficient at face of No. 1 right entry; ordered brattices built to overcome this. A small fire burning in a single pillar in the outcrop 400 ft. from mine mouth; fire isolated and under control.

State Line No. 3.

Located one mile east of East Palestine on the P. F. W. & C. Ry. Operated by the National Fireproofing Co., Canton, O. William Weaver, Supt.; Charles Jones, mine boss, both of East Palestine. Drift opening to No. 7 vein of coal, 2½ ft. thick, underlaid with clay 4 ft. thick, which is worked in connection with coal. Fan ventilation; pick mining; mule and rope haulage; employs 17 miners and 7 day men. Visited September 22nd and December 30th; found in good condition. A new opening has been made at the head of the workings, greatly improving the ventilation.

State Line No. 1.

Located one mile east of East Palestine, O., on the P. F. W. & C. Ry. Operated by the State Line Coal Co., East Palestine, O. Hugh Laughlin, Supt.; George Southerin, mine boss, both of East Palestine. Fan ventilation; pick mining; rope haulage; tipple and 1800 ft. of haulage road in Ohio. Present workings all in Pennsylvania. Visited October 3rd and December 30th. Tested scales and found them incorrect.

Beech Hollow.

Located two miles northeast of Salem, operated by Reese Bros., Salem, O. T. G. Reese, Salem, O., has full charge. Slope opening to No. 3 seam, 3 ft. 2 in. thick; natural ventilation; pick mining; mule haulage. Visited August 9th, at which time three miners and one day man were employed. This company is installing a rope haulage system and another opening is being made when a fan will be installed and the capacity of the mine increased.

Round Knob.

Located five miles south of West Point, on the Y. & O. R. R. Operated by the Round Knob Coal Co., Lisbon, O. F. J. Francis, same place, has full charge. Drift opening to No. 6 seam, 3 ft. thick. Fan ventilation; pick mining; mule haulage; single entry system. Visited July 25th and found mine idle. December 1st, found in good condition.

Oak Hill Slope.

Located at Washingtonville, on the Y. & O. R. R. Operated by the Columbia Fire Clay Co., Cleveland, O. W. C. Simpson, Washingtonville, O., has full charge. Slope opening to No. 3 seam of clay, 5½ ft. thick; fan ventilation; mule and rope haulage; employs 8 miners and 8 day men. Visited July 29th, at which time there was but one opening available for ingress and egress. Ordered fan substituted for furnace and stairway constructed in air shaft. Visited October 18th and found above order carried out.

Pleasant Valley No. 6.

Located at Negley, O., on the P. L. & W. R. R. Operated by the Negley Coal Co., Negley O. P. H. Murphy, Supt.; Harvey Burson, mine boss, both of Negley. Drift opening to No. 6 seam, 3 ft. thick. Furnace ventilation; pick mining; mule haulage; employs 17 miners and 4 day men. September 21st, mine idle. December 7th, found in good condition; gasoline engine used for pumping in this mine. Ordered that it be operated only when men were all out of the mine.

Beech Grove.

Located at New Salisbury, O., on C. & P. R. R. Operated by the Buckeye Clay and Coal Co., Cleveland, O. Drift opening to No. 3 seam, 3 ft. 2 in. thick. E. F. Hart, New Salisbury, has full charge. Fan ventilation; pick mining; mule and rope haulage; employs 7 miners and 4 day men. Visited October 12th and found in good condition.

Walnut Hill.

Located at Washingtonville, on the Y. & O. R. R. Operated by J. B. Smith, Washingtonville, O. J. G. Smith, same place, Supt. and mine boss. Slope opening to No. 4 seam, 28 in. thick; fan ventilation; machine mining; mule and rope haulage; employs 6 miners and 4 day men. October 18th, wiring found defective and ordered repaired.

Reichenbach.

Located at North Georgetown, O. Operated and managed by Edward Reichenbach, North Georgetown, O. Shaft 60 ft. deep to No. 3 seam, 3 ft. thick; exhaust steam ventilation; pick mining; employs 6 miners and 3 day hands. December 13th, found in good condition.

Vasey.

Located at Salineville, Ohio. Operated by Sarah Vasey, Salineville, O. Frank Goddard, same place, has full charge. Drift to strip vein, 3 ft. thick; furnace ventilation; pick mining; mule haulage; employs 8 miners and 2 day men. Visited August 11th, October 7th and December 22nd. Ventilation deficient in No. 1 left entry; ordered brattices built and position of door on entry changed to overcome this.

Vasey No. 2.

Located near the Vasey Mine; same owner; William Wright, Salineville, O., manager; employs 4 miners. Visited December 22nd and found in good condition.

Elk Run.

Located at Newhouse, O., on the P. L. & W. R. R. Operated by the Wilson Coal Co., Pittsburgh, Pa. J. W. Barnes, Signal, O., Supt.; Joseph Biggins, Elkton, O., mine boss. Drift opening to No. 6 vein, 3 ft. thick; furnace ventilation; machine mining; mule and motor haulage; single entry system; employs 30 miners and 9 day men. Visited September 8th and December 20th. Found wiring defective in places and shields on mining machines improperly constructed. Ordered wiring repaired and machines equipped with shields of proper design.

Neiheisel.

Located one mile east of Leetonia, O., on the P. F. W. & C. Ry. Operated by the Neiheisel Coal Co., Leetonia, O. F. J. Neiheisel, Supt.; Henry Walzer, mine boss, both of Leetonia. Slope to No. 3 seam, 3 ft. thick; fan ventilation; pick mining; mule and rope haulage; employs 4 miners and 2 day hands. Visited July 29th and October 17th. Condition fair.

Jones or Hoon.

Located at East Palestine, O. Operated by the Jones Coal Co., East Palestine, O. John Jones, Supt.; Thomas Jones, mine boss, both of East Palestine, O.

Drift opening to No. 7 seam, 3 ft. thick; furnace ventilation; pick mining; mule haulage; single entry system; employs 10 miners and 2 day men. Visited July 27th and December 8th. Found in fair condition each time.

Wheat Hill.

Located at East Palestine, O. Operated by the Wheat Hill Coal Co., East Palestine, O. James Atchinson, Supt.; Henry Patton, mine boss, both of East Palestine. Drift to No. 7 seam, 2½ ft. thick; fan ventilation; pick mining; mule haulage; single entry system; employs 5 miners and 2 day men. July 27th, found in good condition.

Beech Ridge.

Located 2½ miles north of Salem, O. Operated by the Shriver Coal Co., Salem, O. Slope to No. 3 seam; furnace ventilation; pick mining; mule haulage. August 9th found idle.

Colonial.

Located at New Salisbury, O., on the C. & P. R. R. Operated by the McClain Fire Brick Co., Pittsburgh, Pa. H. R. Lloyd, Irondale, O., Supt.; Jacob Ehlenbach, mine boss, New Salisbury. Drift opening to strip vein, 2½ ft. thick; natural ventilation; pick mining; mule haulage; single entry system. Employs 8 miners and 1 day man. Visited August 12th and November 14th.

Colonial Clay.

Located at New Salisbury, O., on the C. & P. R. R. Operated by the McClain Fire Brick Co., Pittsburgh, Pa. H. R. Lloyd, Supt.; Matt. Henry, mine boss, both of Irondale, O. Shaft 90 ft. deep; fan ventilation; employs 9 miners and 1 day man. August 12th, found safety catches defective; ordered them put in good condition, speaking tube installed and hoisting signal code observed Visited November 14th and found closed down.

Crook.

Located near Fairfield No. 3 mine, at New Waterford. G. W. Crook, New Waterford, O., owner and manager. Slope opening to No. 6 seam, 3 ft. thick; furnace ventilation; pick mining; single entry system. Employs 2 miners and 1 day man. July 26th, found in good condition.

Reynolds.

Located at New Waterford, O. Operated by Elijah Reynolds, New Waterford, O., who has full charge. Drift opening to No. 6 seam, 3 ft. 3 in. thick. Natural ventilation; pick mining. Employs 2 miners and 1 day man. December 6th, found in good condition.

Eyster.

Located at New Waterford, O. Operated by J. B. Eyster, same place, who is also manager. Drift opening to No. 6 seam, 3 ft. 3 in. thick. Natural ventilation; pick mining. Employs 3 miners and 1 day man. December 6th, found but one traveling way from the interior to the surface, another being made. Ordered ladder placed in escapement shaft.

Negley Clay.

Located at Negley, O., on the P. L. & W. R. R. Operated by the Negley Clay Co., Negley, O. James Powers, Supt.; James W. Sutherin, mine boss, both of Negley, O. Drift opening to No. 5 seam of coal 18 inches thick, and clay 6 ft. thick. Natural ventilation; mule haulage. Employs 7 miners and 1 day hand. December 7th, found some working places inadequately timbered. Ordered suitable timber furnished in sufficient quantities.

Champion Clay.

Located near Wellsville, on the C. & P. R. R. Operated by the Champion Fire Brick Co., Wellsville, O. C. R. McDaniel, East Liverpool, O., superintendent and mine boss. Drift opening; natural ventilation.* Employs 8 miners and 2 day men. Visited September 14th and December 16th. This mine has but one traveling way from the interior to the surface but another is being made. The map of the mine was found to be incomplete. Ordered map made to comply with the requirements of the law.

American Sewer Pipe No. 36.

Located one mile east of Lisbon, O., on the P. L. & W. R. R. Operated by the American Sewer Pipe Co., Akron, O. J. W. McConnell, Supt.; Charles McCaskey, mine boss, both of Lisbon. Drift opening; furnace ventilation; mule haulage. Employs 5 miners and 2 day men. Visited October 6th, advised that fan be substituted for the furnace.

American Sewer Pipe No. 3.

Located at East Liverpool, O., on the C. & P. R. R. Operated by the American Sewer Pipe Co., Akron, O. George Freeman, Supt.; J. C. Young, mine boss, both of East Liverpool, O. Slope opening; natural ventilation; rope haulage. Employs 5 miners and 5 day hands. October 19th, found in good condition. Ordered stairway built in escapement shaft.

Eastern Ohio.

Clay mine, located at East Liverpool, O. Perry McCalister, East Liverpool, O., has full charge. Drift opening; natural ventilation; mule haulage. October 19th, found in good condition.

Vulcan.

Clay mine, located at Wellsville, O., on the C. & P. R. R. Operated by the Vulcan Clay and Brick Co., Wellsville, O. Julius A. Cohn, manager, Wellsville, O. Drift opening to seam of clay 12 ft. thick. Natural ventilation; mule haulage. Employs 4 miners and 2 day men. August 26th, condition satisfactory.

Buckeye.

Clay mine, located at Wellsville, O., on the C. & P. R. R. Operated by the McClain Fire Brick Co., Pittsburgh, Pa. H. H. Hine, Supt.; Stewart Rolley, mine boss, both of Wellsville, O. Drift opening; natural ventilation; mule haulage. Employs 6 miners and 3 day hands. August 26th, found in good condition.

CARROLL COUNTY.

Kirk.

Located two miles west of Salineville, O. Transportation C. & P. R. R. Operated by the Carroll-Storm Coal Co., Cleveland, O. D. P. Loomis, New

Philadelphia, O., Supt.; M. J. Tolson, Salineville, O., mine boss. Drift opening to the strip vein, 3 ft. thick; fan ventilation; machine mining; mule and motor haulage. Employs 46 miners and 21 day hands. July 8th, ventilation poor, ordered stoppings repaired. August 16th, ventilation still deficient. Driving to proposed new opening to overcome this. Ordered defective wiring repaired. November 23rd, ordered stoppings repaired in No. 16 entry to improve ventilation. Ordered holes bored in advance of working places in No. 16 entry to guard against water in abandoned mine adjoining.

Sterling No. 1.

Located 2 miles west of Salineville. Transportation C. & P. R. R. Operated by the Sterling Coal Co., Cleveland, O. M. Hileman, Beaver Falls, Pa., Supt., Matthew Smith, Salineville, O., succeeded Samuel Madison, as mine boss, on December 31st. Drift opening to strip vein, 3 ft. 3 in. thick; fan ventilation; machine mining, motor and rope haulage. Employs 88 miners and 42 day men. July 7th, found a number of barrels of oil stored in the mine; ordered them removed, which was done. August 1st, ordered laws governing the handling of explosives complied with. Ordered headlight kept on rope haulage trip. October 14th mine in excellent condition. December 12th tested two sets of scales and found both correct.

Strip Vein.

Located 2 miles west of Salineville. Transportation C. & P. R. R. Operated by the Sterling Coal Co., Ltd., Cleveland, O. M. Hileman, Beaver Falls, Pa., Supt.; J. T. Hetherington, Salineville, O., succeeded Matthew Smith, same place, as mine boss, on December 1st. Drift opening to strip vein, 3 ft. thick; fan ventilation; machine mining; motor haulage. Employs 66 miners and 26 day hands. July 8th and October 20th, mine in excellent condition.

JEFFERSON COUNTY.

Diamond.

Located two miles west of Yellow Creek, on the C. & P. R. R. Operated by the Diamond Coal and Clay Co., Wellsville, O. W. E. Smith, Wellsville, O., Supt.; Isaac Thomas, Irondale, O., mine boss. Slope opening to No. 3 vein, 3½ ft. thick; fan ventilation; machine mining; mule haulage; 16 miners and 5 day hands employed. August 22nd found shields on mining machine insecurely fastened. November 1st, ordered machines to cease operation until equipped with proper shields. Mine in good condition.

No. 3 Creek Vein.

Located at Irondale, on the C. & P. R. R. Operated by the East Ohio Sewer Pipe Co., Irondale, O. W. E. Williams, same place, has full charge. Drift opening to No. 3 vein, 3 ft. thick; fan ventilation; pick mining; mule haulage; employs 7 miners and 1 day hand. Visited August 19th and November 10th and found in fair condition.

East Ohio Sewer Pipe.

Clay mine, located at Irondale, O., on the C. & P. R. R. Operated by the East Ohio Sewer Pipe Co., Irondale, O. W. E. Williams, same place, has full charge. Shaft, 67 ft., to No. 1 seam of clay, 17 ft. thick; fan ventilation; mule haulage:

employs 9 miners and 6 day hands. Visited August 19th and November 10th, found in exceedingly good condition each time.

McClain & Dando Strip Vein.

Located at Irondale, on the C. & P. R. R. Operated by the McClain Fire Brick Co., Pittsburg, Pa. Fred Dando, Irondale, O., Supt.; Samuel Parsons, Hammondsville, O., mine boss. Drift opening to strip vein, 2 ft. 4 in. thick; fan ventilation; pick mining; single entry system; employs 10 miners and 1 day hand. August 23rd, mine in good condition. November 22nd, ordered dust sprinkled and non-inflammable material used for tamping.

McClain & Dando No. 1.

Located at Irondale, O., on the C. & P. R. R. Operated by the McClain Fire Brick Co., Pittsburg, Pa. George McCarty, Irondale, O., contractor and mine boss. Slope opening, clay 10 ft. thick; natural ventilation; mule haulage; employs 4 miners and 1 day hand. Was called to this mine November 11th to investigate the death of Joseph Dominick, who was killed by a fall of roof.

McClain & Dando No. 2.

Located at Irondale. Same owner and management as No. 1. Shaft, 135 ft. deep; clay 14 ft. thick; natural ventilation; mule haulage; employs 4 miners and 5 day hands. Visited August 23rd and November 22nd. Ordered loose slate taken down in traveling way.

Middle Works.

Located at Empire, O., on the C. & P. R. R. Operated by the Stratton Fire Clay Co., Empire, O. H. E. Stratton, Empire, O., Supt.; C. C. Crissman, Port Homer, O., mine boss. Drift, opening to No. 6 seam, 4 ft. thick; furnace ventilation; pick mining; mule and rope haulage; employs 14 miners and 3 day hands. August 4th, ordered boiler house removed to not less than 60 ft. from mine mouth. November 2nd, new boiler house being constructed at proper distance. Ordered headlight placed on rope haulage trip.

Stratton.

Located at Empire, O., on the C. & P. R. R. Operated by the Stratton Fire Clay Co., Empire, O. H. E. Stratton, Supt.; T. N. Dras, mine boss, both of Empire, O. Shaft, 50 ft. deep; natural ventilation. Visited August 3rd and November 30th. Ordered safety gate placed at top of shaft, and suggested that better fire protection be provided for the engine house.

Ohio River.

Located at Empire, O., on the C. & P. R. R. Operated by the Ohio River Sewer Pipe Co., Empire, O. H. E. Stratton, Supt.; C. L. Vance, mine boss, both of Empire, O. Drift opening; coal 3 ft. 10 in. thick; furnace ventilation; pick mining; employs 17 miners and 4 day hands. August 2nd, ventilation deficient at face of main entry. December 20th, found in good condition.

Ohio River Clay.

Located at Empire, O., on the C. & P. R. R. Operated by the Ohio River Sewer Pipe Co., Empire, O. H. E. Stratton, Supt.; Hugh Hughes, mine boss, both of Empire, O. Shaft opening, to clay, 10 ft. thick; natural ventilation; employs 6 miners and 3 day hands. Visited August 2nd and October 28th. Found in fair condition.

Great Northern.

Located at Empire, O., on the C. & P. R. R. Operated by the Great Northern Sewer Pipe Co., Empire, O. H. E. Stratton, Supt.; Empire, O.; Ernest Thomas, Toronto, mine boss. Shaft, 50 ft. deep; natural ventilation; employs 8 miners and 4 day men. Visited August 3rd and December 9th. Found in fair condition.

Nicholson.

Located at Empire, O., on the C. & P. R. R. Operated by the Toronto Fire Clay Co., Toronto, O. Wm. McGrady, Supt.; Thomas Gilligan, mine boss, both of Toronto, O. Slope opening; fan ventilation; employs 8 miners and 4 day men. August 4th, found wiring defective in escapement shaft, ordered repaired. November 30th, ordered the use of gasoline engine for pumping in this mine discontinued.

Little Giant.

Located at Toronto, O., on the C. & P. R. R. Operated by the Toronto Fire Clay Co., Toronto, O. Harry Nicholson, Supt.; A. S. Peckins, mine boss, both of Toronto, O. Shaft, 45 ft. deep; fan ventilation; employs 15 miners and 11 day hands. Visited August 18th and November 3rd.

Kaul.

Located at Toronto, O., on the C. & P. R. R. Operated by the Kaul Clay Mfg. Co., Toronto, O. Frank Hartford, Supt.; George Hamilton, mine boss; both of Toronto, O. Drift opening to No. 6 vein, 3 ft. thick. Furnace ventiliation; pick mining; mule haulage. Employs 12 miners and 4 day men. Visited July 21st, and October 27th. Found in good condition.

Kaul Clay.

Located at Toronto, O., on the C. & P. R. R. Operated by the Kaul Clay Mfg. Co., Toronto, O. Frank Hartford, Toronto, O. Supt.; J. O. Evans, R. D. No. 2. Steubenville, O., mine boss. Slope opening to Roger vein 3 ft. thick, underlaid with 7½ ft. of clay. Natural ventilation. Employs 7 miners and 10 day hands. Visited July 21st and October 27th. Found in good condition. This company is installing an electric plant for drilling and haulage.

Forest City.

Located at Toronto, O., on the C. & P. R. R. Operated by the American Sewer Pipe Co, Akron O. W. B. Francy, Supt.; John Ferguson, mine boss; both of Toronto, O. Drift opening to No. 7 seam, 3 ft. 3 in. thick. Fan ventilation; pick mining; mule haulage. Employs 31 miners and 13 day men. Visited August 18th and November 25th. Found in good condition.

Forest City Clay.

Located at Toronto, O., on the C. & P. R. R. Operated by the American Sewer Pipe Co., Akron, O. W. B. Francy, Supt.: James Milne, mine boss; both of Toronto, O. Slope opening: fan ventilation. Employs 11 miners and 8 day hands. Visited August 17th and November 3rd. Found in good condition.

Great Western.

Located at Toronto, O., on the C. & P. R. R. Operated by the American Sewer Pipe Co., Akron, O. W. B. Francy, Supt.; Daniel Hinkle, mine boss, both of Toronto. Shaft opening; fan ventilation; animal haulage. Employs [illegible] miners and 6 day men. August 17th, ordered ladder in escapement way repaired. October 27th, found in good condition.

American Sewer Pipe No. 8.

Located at Freeman, O., on the C. & P. R. R. Operated by the American Sewer Pipe Co., Akron, O. W. J. Baxter, R. D. No. 2, Toronto, O., Supt. James Sines, Empire, O., mine boss. Drift opening. Employs 5 miners and 4 day men. August 5th, mine idle owing to a fall of roof in return air course cutting off the ventilation. Company installing a 12' x 4' Brazil fan. November [illegible], mine idle. Gasoline engine, used for pumping, being taken out of mine and a [illegible] volt D. C. Electric motor substituted.

Minor.

Located at Freemans, on the C. & P. R. R. Operated by the Minor Fire Brick Co., Empire, O. E. S. Minor, Empire, O., Supt.; G. M. Knisely, R. D. No. 1, Toronto, O., mine boss. Drift opening; furnace ventilation. Employs 4 miners and 3 day men. August 5th found ventilation deficient in places; ordered places stopped until ventilation was restored. November 7th, found gasoline engine being operated contrary to law; ordered it made to comply with the law. November 11th, order had not been complied with. Ordered the use of the gasoline engine discontinued in the mine.

Standard.

Located at Irondale, O., on the C. & P. R. R. Operated by the Standard Fire Brick Co., Pittsubrg, Pa. Lewis McDaniel, Irondale, O., has full charge. Drift opening; fan ventilation. Employs 8 miners and 1 day man. September 6th, mine idle. November 21st, ordered use of gasoline engine discontinued.

Congo.

Located at Empire, O., on the C. & P. R. R. Operated by the Standard Fire Brick Co., Pittsburg Pa., Alex Hayes, Empire, O., has full charge. Drift opening; natural ventilation. Visited November 11th. Owing to the destruction by fire of the plant using the product of this mine it has been closed down during the entire period covered by this report.

Sloan Bros.

Located two miles west of Toronto, O. Operated by Sloan Bros., R. D. No. 1, Toronto, O. W. E. Sloan, same address, Supt.; James Spencer, Toronto, O., mine boss. Shaft 65 ft. to Roger Vein, 4 ft. thick. Exhaust steam ventilation; pick mining. Employs 4 miners and 2 day men. November [illegible]th ordered second opening made, safety catches on cage and safety gate at top of shaft

Union.

Located at Empire, O., on the C. & P. R. R. Operated by the Union Clay Mfg. Co., Toronto, O. George Myers, Toronto, O., Supt.; W. J. Lafferty, 524

S. 5th St., Steubenville, O., mine boss. Slope opening. Employs 3 miners. Visited November 7th. This is a new mine and has but one opening, but is being driven to another. Company installing 220 volt D. C. electrical equipment for hoisting and drilling.

MAHONING COUNTY.

Fairview.

Located at Washingtonville, on the Erie R. R. Operated by the Sterling Coal Co., Ltd., Cleveland, O. John Hileman, Leetonia, O., Supt.; Charles Abblett, Washingtonville, O., mine boss. Slope opening to the No. 3 seam, 3½ ft. thick; fan ventilation; machine mining; motor and rope haulage. Employs 40 miners and 18 day men. Visited July 14th, in company with Inspector Smith of New Philadelphia. Main air course in poor condition. Ordered door built in No. 3 entry to assist in properly distributing air on return side of that entry. Ordered ladder placed in escapement shaft, and head-light kept on rope haulage trip. Suggested that a shaft be sunk at the head of the workings to improve the ventilation and provide an additional escapement way. November 29th, ordered trolley wiring repaired and escapement way made more readily available.

The introduction of mining machines has greatly improved conditions in this mine by eliminating the necessity for the heavy charges of blasting powder formerly used.

Fisk.

Located at Marquis, on the Erie R. R. Operated by the Mahoning and Lake Erie Coal Co., Cleveland, O. E. E. McCartney, Calla, O., has full charge. Slope opening to cannel seam, 3½ ft. to 4 ft. thick; fan ventilation; pick mining; mule haulage. Employs 15 miners and 9 day men. Visited July 19th, in company with Inspector W. H. Miller, of Massillon. Found the ventilation, which was produced by exhaust steam, wholly inadequate and ordered a fan installed by August 10th. Visited again on August 10th and found previous order not complied with. Ordered the mine closed until the fan was installed and in operation. September 13th, found the fan installed and the ventilation good. November 18th, tested the scales and found them correct.

Lowellville.

Located at Lowellville, O., on the P. & L. E. R. R. Operated by the Lowell Coal Mining Co., Youngstown, O. Roger Horn, Lowellville, O., has full charge. Shaft 75 ft. deep to No. 1 Block seam, 2½ ft. to 4 ft. thick. Fan ventilation; machine and pick mining; mule haulage. Employs 15 miners and 4 day hands. Visited July 18th, September 19th and December 19th. Mine found in fair condition each time.

Holwick.

Located near Salem, O. Operated by Allison and Zimmerman, Salem, O. John Allison, same place, has full charge. Slope opening to No. 3 seam, 3 ft. thick. Natural ventilation; pick mining; mule haulage. Employs 9 miners and 2 day men. December 20th found in good condition.

McDonald.

Located near North Lima, O. Operated by McDonald Bros, North Lima, O. J. A. McDonald, same place, Supt.; Van Cover, Woodsworth, O., mine boss. Shaft 75 ft. deep to No. 3 A seam, 2½ ft. thick. Exhaust steam ventilation; pick mining. Employs 5 miners and 3 day men. Visited September 20th. Ordered safety catches repaired and side plates placed on cage.

Spait.

Located near North Lima, O. Operated by the Spait Coal Co., R. D. No. 3, Poland, O. A Peacock, Supt.; Harry Wilcox, mine boss; both of R. D. No. 3, Poland, O. Shaft 70 ft. deep to No. 3A seam, 2½ ft. thick. Natural ventilation; pick mining. Employs 3 miners and one day man. September 20th, found in good condition.

Paulin.

Located near North Lima, O. Operated by E. Paulin, Poland, O., who has full charge. Drift opening to No. 3 A seam, 2½ ft. thick. Natural ventilation; pick mining. Employs 4 miners and 1 day man. September 20th, found in fair condition.

COAL LIST.

LIST OF LARGE COAL COMPANIES IN OHIO, WITH ADDRESSES FOR 1910.

Name of Owner or Operator.	P. O. Address.
ATHENS COUNTY.	
Baileys Run Coal Co.	Toledo.
Big Four Coal Co.	Broadwell.
Black Diamond Coal Co.	Columbus.
Canaan Coal Co.	Athens.
Carbondale Coal Co.	Carbondale.
C. &. H. C. & I. Co.	Columbus.
Federal-Hocking Coal Co.	Columbus.
Hisylvania Coal Co.	Columbus.
Hocking Mining Co.	Athens.
Imperial Coal Mining Co.	Columbus.
Lama, J. M.	Nelsonville.
Luhrig Coal Washing & Mining Co.	Charleston, W. Va.
L. & H. Coal Co.	Athens.
Maple Mining Co.	Nelsonville.
Northern Fuel Co.	Columbus.
Nelsonville Brick Co.	Nelsonville.
New Pittsburg Coal Co.	Columbus.
New York Coal Co.	Columbus.
Peoples Portland Cement Co.	Sandusky
Poston, C. L.	Athens
Poston Consolidated Coal Co.	Athens.
Schuler, J. F.	Sharpsburg.
Silcott Coal Co., G. C.	Nelsonville.
Sunday Creek Co.	Columbus.
York Clay & Mining Co.	Nelsonville.
BELMONT COUNTY.	
American Sheet & Tin Plate Co.	Pittsburg, Pa.
Akron Coal Co.	Akron.
Barton Coal Co.	Cleveland.
Bakewell Coal Co.	Bellaire.
Big Five Coal Co.	Stewartsville.
Belmont Coal Mining Co.	Pittsburg, Pa.
Cambria Mining Co.	Toledo.
Captina Coal Co.	Armstrongs Mills.
Carnegie Steel Co.	Pittsburg, Pa., and Moundsville, W. Va.
Colburg Coal Co.	Columbus.
Franklin Coal Co.	Stewartsville.
Ft. Pitt Coal Co.	Pittsburg, Pa.,
Flushing Coal Co.	Elyria
Fairpoint Coal & Coke Co.	Wheeling, W. Va.
Gorrell Coal Co., J. W.	Alliance.

LIST OF LARGE COAL COMPANIES IN OHIO—Continued.

Name of Owner or Operator.	P. O. Address.
CARROLL COUNTY—Concluded.	
Robinson Clay Product Co.	Akron.
Somers Mining Co.	Cleveland.
Sterling Coal Co., Limited	Cleveland.
COLUMBIANA COUNTY.	
American Sewer Pipe Co.	Akron.
Buckeye Clay & Coal Co.	Cleveland.
Buck Coal Co.	Salem.
Big Vein Coal Co.	Cleveland.
Columbia Fire Clay Co.	Cleveland.
Champion Brick Co.	Wellsville.
Card & Prosser Coal Co.	Cleveland.
Fairfield Coal Co.	Cleveland.
Hodgekiss Coal Co., The	Lisbon.
Jones Coal Co.	East Palestine.
McLain Fire Brick Co.	Pittsburg, Pa.
Negley Coal Co.	Negley.
Neiheisel Coal Co.	Leetonia.
National Fireproofing Co.	Canton.
Ohio & Pennsylvania Coal Co.	Cleveland.
Prospect Hill Coal Co.	East Palestine.
Round Knob Coal Co.	Lisbon.
Salem Coal Co.	Salem.
Sterling Coal Co., Limited	Cleveland & Leetonia.
Strabley, James S.	Salineville.
Smith, J. D.	Washingtonville.
Vasey, Sarah	Salineville.
Wheat Hill Coal Co.	East Palestine.
West Point Coal & Coke Co.	East Liverpool.
COSHOCTON COUNTY.	
Barnes Coal Mining Co.	Coshocton.
Columbus Coal Mining Co.	Coshocton.
Davis, David	Conesville.
Davis, James G.	Conesville.
Furnell & Son, Thomas	Coshocton.
Locust Grove Coal Co.	Coshocton.
Morgan Run Coal Mining Co.	Cleveland.
Oden Valley Coal Co.	Coshocton.
Powers Coal Co.	Coshocton.
Warwick Coal Co.	Cleveland.
Wade Coal Co.	Cleveland.
Wolford, M. S.	Coshocton.

LIST OF LARGE COAL COMPANIES IN OHIO—Continued.

Name of Owner or Operator.	P. O. Address.
GALLIA COUNTY.	
Carbon Hill Coal Co	Columbus.
Black Diamond Coal Co	Gallia.
Indian Guyan Coal Co	Gallipolis.
Swan Creek Coal Co	Gallipolis
GUERNSEY COUNTY.	
Akron Coal Co	Akron
Byesville Coal Co	Byesville.
Clinton Coal & Mining Co	Cambridge.
Cambridge Coal Mining Co	Parkersburg. W Va.
Cambridge Valley Coal Co	Cambridge.
Cambridge Collieries Co	Cleveland.
Consolidated Ohio Coal Co	Toledo.
Domestic Coal Co	Cambridge.
Forsythe Coal Co	Cambridge.
Leatherwood Consolidated Coal Co	Cambridge.
Loomis-Moss Coal Co	Akron.
Morris Coal Co	Cleveland
National Coal Co	Cleveland.
O'Gara Coal Co	Chicago.
Puritan Coal Co	Cambridge.
Vivian Collieries Co	Chicago, Ill.
Vigo Clay Co	Cambridge.
HARRISON COUNTY.	
Blair Mining Co., A. G	Toledo.
Goshen Coal Co	Canton.
Newton Coal & Mining Co	Dennison.
Oliver Coal Co	Pittsburg, Pa.
Roby Coal Co	Cleveland.
West Mining Co	Adena.
HOCKING COUNTY.	
Carbon Hill Coal Co	Nelsonville.
Carbon Coal Co	Carbon Hill.
Cable, R.	Nelsonville.
Central Hocking Fuel Co	Columbus
Columbus Brick & Terra Cotta Co	Columbus.
C. & H. C. & I. Co	Columbus.
Gem Coal Co	Nelsonville.
Green Coal Co	Nelsonville.
Essex Coal Co., The	New Straitsville.
Edgell Coal Co	Nelsonville.

LIST OF LARGE COAL COMPANIES IN OHIO—Continued.

Name of Owner or Operator.	P. O. Address.
HOCKING COUNTY—Concluded.	
Hocking-Domestic Coal Co.	Murray City.
Keeney, David & Son	Buchtel.
Kennedy Coal Co.	Carbon Hill.
New Pittsburg Coal Co.	Columbus.
National Fireproofing Co.	Pittsburg.
Price, George	New Straitsville.
Royal Coal Co.	Nelsonville.
Starr-Hocking Coal Co.	Starr.
Sunday Creek Co.	Columbus.
JACKSON COUNTY.	
Advance Coal Co.	Dayton.
Armstrong Coal Co.	Jackson.
Brown Coal Co.	Wellston.
Chapman Coal Co.	Jackson.
Crescent Coal Co.	Jackson.
Cochran Coal Co.	Jackson.
Dayton Coal & Iron Co.	Wellston.
Domestic Coal Co.	Wellston.
Davis Fire Brick Co.	Oak Hill.
Elk Fork Coal Co.	Wellston.
Evans Coal Co.	Coalton.
Elkhorn Coal Co.	Jackson.
Emma Coal Co.	Jackson.
Globe Iron Co.	Jackson.
Glen Roy Coal Co.	Jackson.
Gosline & Co., W. A.	Toledo.
Hall Coal Co.	Dayton.
Harper Coal Co.	Coalton.
Jones & Morgan	Jackson.
Jackson Mining Co.	Wellston.
Jackson Iron & Steel Co.	Jackson.
Jackson & Decatur Coal Co.	Jackson.
Leach, Oscar J.	Wellston.
Northern Coal Mining Co.	Jackson.
Ohio Fire Brick Co.	Oak Hill.
Pastor Coal Co.	Wellston.
Rhodes & Sell	Coalton.
Rhodes Coal Co.	Coalton.
Rowe, Wm.	Coalton.
Sun Coal Co.	Jackson.
Star Furnace Co.	Jackson.
Southern Ohio Portland Cement Co.	Remple.
Superior Coal Co.	Wellston.
Tom Corwin Coal Co.	Dayton.

LIST OF LARGE COAL COMPANIES IN OHIO—Continued.

Name of Owner or Operator.	Address.
JACKSON COUNTY—Concluded.	
Ward Coal Co.	Oak Hill.
Webster Colliery Co.	Coalton.
[illegible] Coal Co.	Coalton.
Jackson County Coal Co.	Jackson.
JEFFERSON COUNTY.	
American Sewer Pipe Co.	Akron.
Amsterdam Coal Co.	Parkersburg, W. Va.
Bergholz Coal Co.	Bergholz.
[illegible] Coal Co.	Pittsburg, Pa.
Brilliant [illegible] Coal Co.	Mingo Junction.
Dexter Coal Co.	Pittsburg, Pa.
Diamond Coal & Land Co.	Wellsville.
East Ohio Sewer Pipe Co.	Irondale.
[illegible] Coal Co.	Cleveland.
Jefferson Coal Co.	Cleveland.
[illegible] Coal Co.	Pittsburg.
[illegible] Coal Mining Co.	Toronto.
LaBelle Iron Works	Steubenville.
LaGrange Coal Co.	Wheeling, W. Va.
[illegible] Coal Co.	Cleveland.
[illegible] Fire Clay Co.	Cleveland.
Ohio & Pennsylvania Coal Co.	Cleveland.
Ohio River Sewer Pipe Co.	Empire.
[illegible] Coal Co.	Cleveland.
[illegible] Coal Co.	Pittsburg, Pa.
[illegible] Coal Co.	Cleveland.
Russel Coal Mining Co.	Cleveland.
Sugar Hill Coal Co.	Steubenville.
Standard Fire Brick Co.	Pittsburg, Pa.
Steubenville Coal Mining Co.	Steubenville.
Stratton Fire Clay Co.	Empire.
Toronto Fire Clay Co.	Toronto.
United States Coal Co.	Cleveland.
Union Clay Mfg. Co.	Empire.
[illegible] E. V.	Steubenville.
Wayne Coal Co.	Pittsburg, Pa.
[illegible] Coal Co.	[illegible]
Wolf Run Coal Co.	Cleveland.
W. & L. E. Coal Mining Co.	Cleveland.
Wabash Coal Co.	Cleveland.
Y. & O. Coal Co.	Cleveland.

LIST OF LARGE COAL COMPANIES IN OHIO—Continued.

Name of Owner or Operator.	P. O. Address.
LAWRENCE COUNTY.	
Buckhorn Coal Co	Buckhorn.
Black Fork Coal Co	Black Fork.
Ginn Company, The	Ironton.
Hall Coal Co., John F	Dayton.
Halley Coal Co	Pedro.
Hanging Rock Iron Co	Hanging Rock.
Ironton Portland Cement Co	Ironton.
Johnson Bros.	Strobel.
Kelley Nail & Iron Co	Ironton.
Maxey, W. R	Pedro.
McGugin, R. H	Olive Furnace.
Portsmouth Refractories Co	Portsmouth.
Riley, Michael	Ort.
Superior Portland Cement Co	Superior.
Willard, E. B	Ironton.
York Portland Cement Co	Portsmouth.
MAHONING COUNTY.	
Allison, Zimmerman & Allen	Salem, R. D. No. 6.
Lowell Mining Co	Youngstown.
Mahoning & Lake Erie Coal Co	Cleveland.
McKinley Coal Co	Salem.
Sterling Coal Co., Limited	Cleveland.
MEDINA COUNTY.	
Gertenslager & Son Coal Co	Wadsworth.
Hambleton Bros	Wadsworth.
James Coal Co	Wadsworth.
Williams Coal Co	Wadsworth.
MEIGS COUNTY.	
Ebersbach, Martin	Pomeroy.
Halley Coal Co	Middleport.
Hennessy & Sauer	Pomeroy.
Maynard Coal Co	Columbus.
Monkey Run Coal Co	Middleport.
Noble-Summit Coal Co	Middleport.
Ohio River Coal Co	Columbus.
Pittsburg Mining Co	Minersville.
Pomeroy Fuel Co	Columbus.

LIST OF LARGE COAL COMPANIES IN OHIO—Continued.

Name of Owner or Operator.	P. O. Address.
MEIGS COUNTY—Concluded.	
Pomeroy Coal Co.	Little Washington, Pa.
Peacock Coal Co.	Pomeroy.
Silver Run Coal Co.	Middleport.
Thomas Coal Co.	Racine.
MORGAN COUNTY.	
Carding Coal Co.	Columbus.
The Geo. M. Jones Co.	Toledo.
MUSKINGUM COUNTY.	
Blue Rock Coal Co.	Gaysport.
Danhauer Bros	Philo.
Duncan Run Coal Mining Co.	Detroit, Mich.
Elk Coal Co.	Columbus.
Fair Oaks Coal Mining Co.	Columbus.
Fisher, F	Zanesville.
Grenier, H. L.	Zanesville.
Jonathan Creek Coal Co.	Pittsburg, Pa.
Kramer Coal Co.	New Straitsville
Monitor Coal Co.	Zanesville.
Maynard Coal Co.	Columbus.
McGarvey Coal Co.	Cannelville.
Pan American Coal Co.	Newark.
Rose Hill Coal Co.	Newark.
Redbud Coal Co.	Cannelville.
Victoria Coal Co.	Cleveland.
Weller, W. H.	Zanesville.
Werner, Wm	Zanesville.
NOBLE COUNTY.	
Belle Valley Coal Mining Co.	Cambridge.
Figgin's G. W.	Cumberland.
Guernsey Coal & Mining Co.	Newark.
Marion Coal Co.	Whigville.
O'Gara Coal Co.	Chicago. Ill.
OTTAWA COUNTY.	
American Gypsum Co.	Cleveland.
Consumers Gypsum Co.	Port Clinton.
United States Gypsum Co.	Chicago. Ill.

LIST OF LARGE COAL COMPANIES IN OHIO—Continued.

Name of Owner or Operator.	P. O. Address.
PERRY COUNTY.	
Corning Mining Co.	Corning.
Crooksville Coal Co.	Crooksville.
Cambridge Collieries Co.	Cleveland.
C. & H. C. & I. Co.	Columbus.
Chapman Mining Co.	Moxahala.
Call Company, John	New Straitsville.
Davis Bros	Shawnee.
Essex Coal Co.	New Straitsville.
Gibbs, George	New Straitsville.
Gosline & Co., W. A.	Toledo.
Indian Run Mining Co.	Glouster.
Iron Point Low Vein Co.	Shawnee.
Iron Clay Brick Co.	Columbus.
Jones Coal Co.	New Straitsville.
Lilly Hocking Coal Co.	Columbus.
Santoy Coal Co.	Columbus.
New Perry Coal Co.	Somerset.
Peabody Coal Co.	Chicago, Ill.
Peerless Coal Co.	Saltillo.
Pennsylvania & Ohio Mining Co.	New Lexington.
Simons, A. & Son	Redfield.
Sines Bros. & Co.	New Straitsville.
Shawnee Coal Mining Co.	Shawnee.
Standard Hocking Coal Co.	Chicago, Ill.
Sunday Creek Co.	Columbus.
Twentieth Century Coal Co.	Columbus.
Union Coal Mining Co.	Columbus.
Upson Coal & Mining Co.	Newark.
Zanesville Coal Co.	Crooksville.
PORTAGE COUNTY.	
Hutson Coal Co.	Cleveland.
South Palmyra Coal Co.	Cleveland.
Strong Bros. Coal Co.	Atwater, R. D. No. 14
Wilson, W. L.	Atwater.
SCIOTO COUNTY.	
Buckeye Fire Brick & Clay Co.	Scioto Furnace.
Harbison-Walker Refractories Co.	Pittsburg, Pa.
Hanging Rock Iron Co.	Hanging Rock.
Morgan & Horton	Eifort.
South Webster Face Brick Co.	South Webster.

LIST OF LARGE COAL COMPANIES IN OHIO—Continued.

Name of Owner or Operator.	P. O. Address.
STARK COUNTY.	
Arntz, Charles	North Industry.
Booth Coal Co	Navarre.
Blaugh, E. O	North Industry.
Blank & Bliler Coal Co	Canal Fulton.
Canton Lime & Fertilizer Co	Canton.
Canton Sparta Clay Co	Mineral City.
Canton Mining Co	Cleveland.
Camp, H. B	Aultman.
Evansdale Lime Clay Product Co	Canton.
Eberhart Co	Massillon.
Farmers Lime and Fertilizer Co	Canton.
Keim Brick & Tile Co	Louisville.
Louisville Brick & Tile Co	Louisville.
Lahmiller, J. G	Canton.
Massillon Stone & Fire Brick Co	Massillon.
Massillon Crystal Coal Co	Massillon.
Massillon City Coal Co	Massillon.
Massillon Elm Run Coal Co	Cleveland.
Massillon Coal Mining Co	Cleveland.
National Fireproofing Co	Canton.
Pocock Coal Co	Massillon.
Steiner Coal Co	Canton.
Sonnhalter Coal Co	Canton.
Smith, L. E. (Mrs.)	Greentown.
Smith Coal Co., G. F	New Berlin.
Swire & Llewellyn	Massillon.
Tippecanoe & Goshen Coal Co	Canton.
Taggart Coal Co	Massillon.
Willow Grove Coal Co	Massillon.
The Whitacre Fireproofing Co	Waynesburg.
Wynn & Sons, John	Canton.
SUMMIT COUNTY.	
Beechwood-Massillon Coal Co	Cleveland.
Barberton Coal Mining Co	Barberton.
Cottage Grove Coal Co	S. Akron.
Clinton Coal Co	Clinton.
Robinson Clay Product Co	Akron.
Turkey Foot Mining Co	Akron.
TUSCARAWAS COUNTY.	
Rothacher Bros	Canal Dover.
Bowling, H. E	New Philadelphia.
American Sewer Pipe Co	Akron.

LIST OF LARGE COAL COMPANIES IN OHIO—Continued.

Name of Owner or Operator.	P. O. Address.
TUSCARAWAS COUNTY—Concluded.	
American Sheet & Tin Plate Co.	Pittsburg, Pa.
Buckeye Fire Clay Co.	Uhrichsville.
Cheape, C. R.	Newcomerstown.
Dennison Coal & Fuel Co.	Dennison.
Dover Fire Brick Co.	Strasburg.
Davis & Mathias	New Philadelphia.
Federal Clay Product Co.	Mineral City.
Goshen Valley Coal Co.	Massillon.
Goshen Coal Co.	Cleveland.
Goshen Central Coal Co.	Massillon.
Holden, C. E.	Mineral City.
Howell, Williams & Son	Dennison.
Hibbs, Enos & Sons	Uhrichsville.
Kline, C. R.	New Philadelphia.
Markley, George	Mineral City.
Massillon Tuscarawas Coal Co.	Massillon.
Midvale-Goshen Coal Co.	Cleveland.
Mullins Coal Co., James	Cleveland.
Minnich, Banner	Tuscarawas.
Novelty Brick & Coal Co.	Newcomerstown.
Ohio Coal & Coke Co.	Cleveland.
Peacock Coal Mining Co.	Mineral City.
Ridgeway Burton Co.	Cleveland.
Robinson-Graves Sewer Pipe Co.	Uhrichsville.
Royal Goshen Coal Co.	New Philadelphia.
Rufenacht, Fred	New Philadelphia.
Reeves Coal Co.	Canal Dover.
Somerdale Coal Co.	Cleveland.
Robinson Clay Product Co.	Akron.
VINTON COUNTY.	
Bolar & Irwin	McArthur.
Cardiff Coal Co.	Columbus.
Clarion Coal & Limestone Co.	Columbus.
DeWitt Coal Co.	Wellston.
Elk Fork Coal Co.	Wellston.
Lawler, John L.	Columbus.
McDonald, S. S.	Columbus.
Mohr-Minton Coal Co.	Columbus.
Puritan Brick Co.	Hamden.
Steinmetz Coal Co., John	Coalton.
Starr Supply & Mining Co.	Logan.
Valley Coal Co.	Dayton.
Quinn Coal Co.	Minerton.

LIST OF LARGE COAL COMPANIES IN OHIO—Concluded.

Name of Owner or Operator.	P. O. Address.
WAYNE COUNTY.	
Hametown Coal Co.	Barberton
Kentucky Fire Brick Co.	Portsmouth
Massillon Elm Run Coal Co.	Cleveland.
Massillon-Navarre Coal Co.	Cleveland.
Massillon Coal Mining Co.	Cleveland
Minglewood-Massillon Coal Co.	Cleveland

LIMESTONE OPERATORS.

LIST OF LIMESTONE OPERATORS, WITH ADDRESSES, FOR YEAR 1910.

Name of Owner or Operator.	P. O. Address.
ADAMS COUNTY.	
J. H. Ellison	Manchester.
ALLEN COUNTY.	
Hiner Stone Co	Lima.
E. J. Ford	Delphos.
Kimmel Bros. & Son	Bluffton.
Watt Bros.	Lafayette.
The Lima Stone Company	Lima.
The Goetschius Stone Co	Lima
The Bluffton Stone Co	Lima.
Rockport Stone Co	Beaverdam.
D. P. Schumacher & Sons	Blufftor
BUTLER COUNTY.	
Nelson Good	Hamilton.
Chas. Wrigele, Sta. A	E. Hamilton.
Daniel Pabst, Venice Road	Hamilton.
J H. Killough	College Corners.
Joe Maier, R. R. 4	Hamilton.
Sidney L. Dodsworth, R. D. 2	Hamilton.
CLARK COUNTY.	
Geo. F. Newcomb, R. F. D. No. 8	Springfield.
The H. H. Moores Co., Box 585	Springfield.
W. A. Rubsam	Springfield.
J. W. Jenkins	Springfield.
The Moores Lime Co., Box 467	Springfield.
Mills Bros	Springfield.
The Casparis Stone Co	Columbus.
The Strunk-Meyer Lime Co	Cold Springs.
Ira Roach, R. D. No. 8	Springfield.
The Springfield Coal & Ice Co	Springfield.
S. S. Taylor, 515 Sherman Ave	Springfield.
CLINTON COUNTY.	
A. C. Brant	Blanchester.
G. M. Oglesbee	New Burlington.
G. H. Benlehr	Clinton.
Bloom & Conner	Wilmington.

LIMESTONE OPERATORS — Continued.

Name of Owner or Operator.	P. O. Address.
CLINTON COUNTY—Concluded.	
J. M. Foster	Blanchester.
Jno. Ballard	Blanchester.
CRAWFORD COUNTY.	
Sousley Bros	Ada.
Guss V. Harer Co.	Lykens.
The Brokensword Stone Company	Bucyrus.
Jno. Snavely, R. D. 7	Bucyrus.
DELAWARE COUNTY.	
Scioto Lime & Stone Co	Delaware
M. Meredith & Son	Radnor.
The White Sulphur Stone Co	Marion.
ERIE COUNTY.	
Henry H. Barnes, R. R. 2	Sandusky
The Kelley Island Lime & Transport Co	Cleveland
The Wagner Stone Company	Sandusky
France Co.	Toledo.
FRANKLIN COUNTY.	
Woodruff & Pausch Stone Co	Columbus
Harry Walcutt, Station "A"	Columbus
Scioto Stone Co., 423 Cham. of Com. Bldg	Columbus
Franklin Stone Co	Columbus
S. Casparis	Columbus
Wm. Miller, No. 1422 West Broad St	Columbus
[illegible] Stone Co., Carnegie Bldg	Pittsburg, Pa.
Wm. Lamb	[illegible]
GREENE COUNTY.	
J. M. Fudge	Xenia
[illegible] C. [illegible]	Jamestown
D. S. Ervin	Cedarville
Bros. Conklin & Fudge	Xenia
[illegible]	[illegible]
HANCOCK COUNTY.	
[illegible]	Findlay
[illegible] & M[illegible]	Findlay

LIMESTONE OPERATORS — Continued.

Name of Owner or Operator.	P. O. Address.
HANCOCK COUNTY—Concluded.	
Wm. A. Bible	Arlington.
C. E. Edington	McComb.
HARDIN COUNTY.	
Jas. G. Tressel	Ada.
The France Company	Toledo.
Jno. Herzog & Son	Patterson.
W. H. Kroft	Ada.
HAMILTON COUNTY.	
J. J. Schmitz, No. 3344 Observatory Ave	Cincinnati.
Theo. Connelle, No. 6506 Center St	Madisonville.
Grant Bros., Hyde Park Sta	Cincinnati.
Floyd Campbell, No. 1036 Florence Ave	Cincinnati.
Benj. Cooney, No. 718 Whittier St., Avondale	Cincinnati.
W. Ruebel, Station "L"	Bridgetown.
Henry Stagge, No. 2058 Mills Ave	Norwood.
G. W. Rucker	Greenfield.
C. S. Boone	Milford.
HIGHLAND COUNTY.	
Frank Sharp	Lynchburg.
N. W. Hixson	Highland.
W. E. Alexander	Lynchburg.
W. H. McClelland	Lynchburg.
LOGAN COUNTY.	
Jno. Spencer	New Richland.
East Liberty Stone Co	Bellefontaine.
H. M. Brown & Son	Belle Center.
G. W. Cochran	Middleburg.
Mrs. Jacob Piatt	W. Liberty.
MARION COUNTY.	
D. M. Hinman	Marion.
John D. Owens & Son	Owens.
Ohio & Western Lime Co	Huntington, Ind.
John Evans Lime & Stone Co	Marion.
J. M. Hamilton	Marion.

LIMESTONE OPERATORS — Continued.

Name of Owner or Operator.	P. O. Address.
MERCER COUNTY.	
E. Wagner	Ft. Recovery.
C. E. Edington	McComb.
MIAMI COUNTY.	
R. H. Studebaker	Rex.
C. B. Fletcher	Covington.
Peter R. Shuman	Covington.
Jackson Stone Co	Covington.
J. W. Ruhl	Covington.
Ohio Marble Co	Piqua.
The Statler Stone Co	Piqua.
J. N. Hodges	Troy.
C. P. Hoover, R. R. 4	Covington.
MONTGOMERY COUNTY.	
Samuel Miller	Trotwood.
A. J. Shaffer	Brookville.
H. B. Shoup, R. D. No. 3	Dayton.
E. B. Kimmel, R. D. No. 14	Dayton.
Dayton Limestone Co	Dayton.
Jno. Griffen	Dayton.
OTTAWA COUNTY.	
Kelley Island Lime & Transport Co	Cleveland.
Ohio & Western Lime Co	Huntington, Ind.
PAULDING COUNTY.	
Bobbenmyer, Sherrard & Randolph	Oakwood.
J. B. Carey & Son	Scotts.
PREBLE COUNTY.	
Chas. Pierce, R. 6, Box 7	Camden.
T. A. McCabe, 18 Davis Bldg	Dayton.
Reinheimer Stone Co	New Paris.
Richard Danily	New Paris.
Phillip Deem	Lewisburg.
G. W. Homsher	Camden.
Peter Fouts	Camden.
J. A. Kautz	Eaton.
O. M. Wright	College Corners.
The Lewisburg Stone Co	Lima.

LIMESTONE OPERATORS — Continued.

Name of Owner or Operator.	P. O. Address.
PREBLE COUNTY—Concluded.	
J. Q. Wilson	College Corners.
E. A. Ridenour	College Corners.
PUTNAM COUNTY.	
J. W. McDowell	Ottawa.
Columbus Grove Stone Co	Columbus Grove.
L. A. Rower	Vaughnsville.
Nick Lauer	Ottoville.
Ft. Jennings Stone Co	Ft. Jennings.
J. S. Blosser	Cloverdale.
Rockport Stone Co	Columbus Grove.
SANDUSKY COUNTY.	
Geo. W. Shreffler & Son	Fremont.
Ohio & Western Lime Co	Huntington, Ind.
G. Zeller, Box 110	Maumee.
Bellevue Stone Co	Bellevue.
Swint Bros	Fremont.
Gottrone Bros.	Fremont.
John Welsh & Bro	Helena.
Grape Island Stone Co, Box 110	Maumee.
SENECA COUNTY.	
Thompson Twp. Quarry	Flat Rock.
J. F. Wolf	Scipio Siding.
D. L. Fisher	Bloomville.
P. C. Kline	Bellevue.
S. A. Saul	Bloomville.
J. F. Harpster	Flat Rock.
Ohio & Western Lime Co.	Huntington, Ind.
Weot Lime & Stone	Tiffin.
The France Co	Toledo.
G. F. Sievert, Box 212	Bloomville.
Spence Bros, No. 409 Euclid Ave	Cleveland.
STARK COUNTY.	
Diamond Portland Cement Co	Middle Branch.
Frank Heims	Waco.
Canton Grey Lime Co	Canton.

LIMESTONE OPERATORS—Concluded

Name of Owner or Operator.	P. O. Address.
VAN WERT COUNTY.	
J. L. Bowersock & Crawford	Middlepoint
The Erie Stone Co	Van Wert.
J. B. Carey, R. No. 1	Convoy.
The France Co	Toledo.
WOOD COUNTY.	
North Baltimore Stone Co	North Baltimore.
E. T. Reed	Elmore.
Stony Ridge Stone Co., 309 Chamber of Commerce	Toledo.
Geo. E. Mercer	Bowling Green.
Ohio & Western Lime Co	Huntington, Ind.
Stony Ridge Stone Co	Stony Ridge
Doherty & Co, 103 S. St Clair St	Toledo
The France Co	Toledo
C. E. Edington	McComb
Toledo Stone & Glass Co., 250 Ohio Bldg	Toledo

INDEX.

1900

INDEX.

A.

Coal Companies.

B

Coal Companies

C.

Coal Companies.

Coal Companies.

E.

Coal Companies.

F.

Coal Companies.

G.

Coal Companies.

H.

Coal Companies.

COAL COMPANIES.

J.

COAL COMPANIES.

K.

COAL COMPANIES.

L

Coal Companies.

M.

COAL COMPANIES.

N.

P.

Coal Companies.

COAL COMPANIES.

R.

COAL COMPANIES.

COAL COMPANIES.

T.

COAL COMPANIES.

COAL COMPANIES.

[illegible]

[illegible]

COAL COMPANIES.

COAL COMPANIES.

NOTICE.

Copies of the Mining Laws can be obtained in pamphlet form upon application to this office.

Owing to the fact that since the number of Inspectors has increased, and the State redistricted, some of the coal producing Counties will be found in charge of several Inspectors. Consequently as a matter for ready reference and convenience, all of the coal companies owning and operating mines in the State will be found indexed alphabetically giving the number and page on which a description of their mines will be found.

G. H.

Lightning Source UK Ltd.
Milton Keynes UK
UKHW010119181218
334172UK00014B/862/P

9 781528 500548